Nāgārjuna
on
The Six Perfections

The publication of this book has been enabled by
a generous donation from Chenping and Luther Liu.

A NOTE ON THE PROPER CARE OF DHARMA MATERIALS

Traditional Buddhist cultures treat books on Dharma as sacred. Hence it
is considered disrespectful to place them in a low position, to read them
when lying down, or to place them where they might be damaged by food
or drink.

NĀGĀRJUNA
on
THE SIX PERFECTIONS

An Ārya Bodhisattva Explains
The Heart of the Bodhisattva Path

Exegesis on the Great Perfection of Wisdom Sutra
Chapters 17-30

By the Great Indian Buddhist Patriarch, Ārya Nāgārjuna

Translation by Bhikshu Dharmamitra

KALAVINKA PRESS
Seattle, Washington
WWW.KALAVINKAPRESS.ORG

KALAVINKA PRESS
8603 39th Ave SW
Seattle, WA 98136 USA

WWW.KALAVINKAPRESS.ORG / WWW.KALAVINKA.ORG

Kalavinka Press is associated with the Kalavinka Dharma Association, a non-profit organized exclusively for religious educational purposes as allowed within the meaning of section 501(c)3 of the Internal Revenue Code. Kalavinka Dharma Association was founded in 1990 and gained formal approval in 2004 by the United States Internal Revenue Service as a 501(c)3 non-profit organization to which all donations are tax deductible.

Donations to KDA are accepted by mail and on the Kalavinka website where numerous free Dharma translations and excerpts from Kalavinka publications are available in digital format.

Edition: N6P-SA-1008-1.0
ISBN: 978-1-935413-04-2
Library of Congress Control Number: 2009920872

PUBLISHER'S CATALOGING-IN-PUBLICATION DATA

Nagarjuna, 2nd c.

[Da zhi du lun. English translation.]
Nagarjuna on the Six Perfections. An Arya Bodhisattva Explains the Heart of the Bodhisattva Path. Chapters 17-30 of Arya Nagarjuna's Mahāprajñapāramitā Upadeśa. Translated by Bhikshu Dharmamitra. – 1st ed.
– Seattle, WA: Kalavinka Press, 2009.

p. ; cm.
ISBN: 978-1-935413-04-2
Includes: Text outline; facing-page Chinese source text in both traditional and simplified scripts; notes.

1. Mādhyamika (Buddhism)—Early works to 1800. 2. Bodhisattvas. 3. Spiritual life—Mahayana Buddhism. I. Title

2009920872
0902

Cover and interior designed and composed by Bhikshu Dharmamitra.

Dedicated to the memory of the selfless and marvelous life of the Venerable Dhyāna Master Hsuan Hua, the Weiyang Ch'an Patriarch and the very personification of the Bodhisattva Path.

Dhyāna Master Hsuan Hua

宣化禪師

1918–1995

ABOUT THE CHINESE TEXT

This translation is supplemented by inclusion of Chinese source text on verso pages in both traditional and simplified scripts. Taisho-supplied variant readings from other editions are presented as Chinese endnotes.

This Chinese text and its variant readings are from the April, 2004 version of the Chinese Buddhist Electronic Text Association's digital edition of the Taisho compilation of the Buddhist canon.

Those following the translation in the Chinese should be aware that Taisho scripture punctuation is not traceable to original editions, is often erroneous and misleading, and is probably best ignored altogether. (In any case, accurate reading of Classical Chinese does not require any punctuation at all.)

OUTLINING IN THIS WORK:

Nearly all of the outline headings in this translation originate with the translator. Nāgārjuna's writings are so metaphysically profound and structurally dense that they are best attended by detailed outline headings to facilitate understanding of the text.

CITATION AND ROMANIZATION PROTOCOLS

Kalavinka Press *Taisho* citation style adds text numbers after volume numbers and before page numbers to assist rapid digital searches.

Romanization, where used, is Pinyin with the exception of names and terms already well-recognized in Wade-Giles.

General Table of Contents

Acknowledgments

The accuracy and readability of these first ten books of translations have been significantly improved with the aid of extensive corrections, preview comments, and editorial suggestions generously contributed by Bhikkhu Bodhi, Jon Babcock, Upāsaka Feng Ling, Upāsaka Guo Ke, and Richard Robinson. Additional valuable editorial suggestions and corrections were offered by Bhikshu Huifeng, Timothy J. Lenz, Upāsikā Min Li, and Bruce Munson.

The publication of the initial set of ten translation volumes has been assisted by substantial donations to the Kalavinka Dharma Association by Bill and Peggy Brevoort, Freda Chen, David Fox, Upāsaka Guo Ke, Chenping and Luther Liu, Sunny Lou, Jimi Neal, and "Leo L." (a.k.a. *Camellia sinensis folium*). Additional helpful donations were offered by Doug Adams, Diane Hodgman, Joel and Amy Lupro, Richard Robinson, Ching Smith, and Sally and Ian Timm.

Were it not for the ongoing material support provided by my late guru's Dharma Realm Buddhist Association and the serene translation studio provided by Seattle's Bodhi Dhamma Center, creation of this translation would have been immensely more difficult.

Most importantly, it would have been impossible for me to produce this translation without the Dharma teachings provided by my late guru, the Weiyang Ch'an Patriarch, Dharma teacher, and exegete, the Venerable Master Hsuan Hua.

The Translator's Introduction

The Text

The "six perfections" refers to the perfectly realized practice of giving, moral virtue, patience, vigor, meditative discipline, and world-transcending wisdom. The treatment of the six perfections constituting this text is a fourteen-chapter section from Ārya Nāgārjuna's long and detailed commentary on the 25,000-line *Mahāprajñāpāramitā Sutra*, the title of which I translate as *Exegesis on the Great Perfection of Wisdom Sutra* (*Mahāprajñāpāramitā Upadeśa* / T25, No. 1509).

The fact that Ārya Nāgārjuna chose to present his explanation of the six perfections as a contiguous and highly-detailed discussion within his commentary has allowed us to easily draw forth the entire discussion as an independent title. It is my belief that Nāgārjuna's treatment of the six perfections herein is so subtle and expansive that, at least in breadth and depth of analysis, it likely has no peer anywhere in the extant Buddhist canonical literature.

Although there are other extensive Indian Buddhist treatments of the six perfections in the immense Chinese Buddhist canon (for instance, Śāntideva's *Bodhicaryāvatara*, known in the West as *Guide to the Bodhisattva's Way of Life*), they did not seem to gain a similar level of acclaim in Chinese Buddhist circles. This may be due to the fact that these other admirable Indian six-perfections expositions were translated later than Nāgārjuna's or in less accessible translations. Alternatively, this could be due to the fact that Nāgārjuna's text had already revealed such a highly refined treatment of the six perfections, one which is both metaphysically deep and immensely pleasing in its power to inspire heart-felt and dedicated bodhisattva practice. Yet another factor figuring in the popularity of the *Exegesis* text doubtless lies in Nāgārjuna's rich interweaving of fascinating moral tales and compelling analogies to illustrate these primary practices fundamental to the bodhisattva's life.

On Kumārajīva's Sanskrit-to-Chinese Edition of the *Exegesis*

We owe our opportunity to explore Nāgārjuna's exposition of the six perfections to the translation efforts of Tripiṭaka Master Kumārajīva, that brilliant and prolific fourth-century Serindian bhikshu born to an Indian noble and a princess from Kuchā. Kumārajīva left the home life at the age of seven when his mother became a nun and, with the assistance of monastic tutors, immediately immersed himself in the study of sutras and treatises. At the age of nine, Kumārajīva was taken for continued study to Northern India by his mother and, even at that very young age, began vanquishing learned opponents in debate.

Kumārajīva had apparently already converted to Mahāyāna well before receiving the higher ordination at the age of twenty. He later converted his original guru to the Mahāyāna and then himself became a leader in spreading Mahāyāna teachings in the predominantly Small-Vehicle domain of Serindian Buddhist culture.

When Kumārajīva came to China's Chang'an in 401 CE, it was as a monk whose earlier monastic career was still in close proximity— probably within about 200 years—to the life of Ārya Nāgārjuna. Arriving along with him, perhaps as part of the spoils of the Chinese army's invasion of his native Kuchā, was a copy of Nāgārjuna's *Exegesis on the Great Perfection of Wisdom Sutra* (*Mahāprajñāpāramitā-upadeśa*). Thanks to Kumārajīva's translation efforts, this expansive and beautiful commentary served as a beacon of Mādhyamika wisdom for ensuing generations of Chinese Buddhists.

Kumārajīva directed a highly-organized imperially-sponsored translation bureau consisting of five hundred monastic editors and scribes. The leading figures in the hands-on translation efforts included Sengrui, Kumārajīva's Sanskrit-literate amanuensis, and Yao Xing, the emperor. Kumārajīva's translation corpus quickly grew to dozens of major sutras and treatises and included the most important shastraic works of Nāgārjuna.

For the Chinese Buddhist literati, this massive exegesis devoted to explaining perfect wisdom was one of the most universally enjoyed of Kumārajīva's translation efforts, not least because it explores so deeply such a broad range of important doctrinal subjects in such a sublime fashion, offering a rich array of fine analogies and stories to buttress its doctrinal discussions. Thus it is perhaps not an exaggeration to suggest that Nāgarjunā's *Exegesis on the Great Perfection of Wisdom Sutra* has been one of the most influential texts in all of Chinese Buddhist history in inspiring reverence for the Bodhisattva Path as presented in Mahāyāna emptiness teachings.

The Doctrinal Significance of the Six Perfections

The utter perfection of giving, moral virtue, patience, vigor, meditative discipline, and world-transcending wisdom is a goal exclusive to practitioners coursing along the Bodhisattva Path and resolved on the realization of buddhahood. As such, it is a distinguishing factor defining Mahāyāna Buddhism and differentiating it from the individual-liberation path to arhatship celebrated in Southern Tradition Buddhism's Pali scriptures.

Although these six perfections are rightfully identified most closely with bodhisattvas and buddhas, Mahāyāna doctrine holds that they also collectively constitute the most crucially important set of spiritual practices for all paths to liberation taught by any buddha. How could this be so? This is because the preservation from one world-cycle to the next of all practice modes and paths of Buddhism is held to depend entirely upon an endless series of fully-realized buddhas making their appearance in the world to reveal anew the entire array of Buddhist teachings.

Realization of buddhahood is based on the six perfections. Hence, because all paths of liberation described in all schools of Buddhism depend on the appearance of fully-enlightened buddhas in successive world cycles, the very survival of Buddhism throughout the endless course of time relies totally on the six perfections. The teaching of all paths of Buddhist liberation originates in each successive world cycle with the appearance of a new Buddha. Without the periodic reappearance of buddhas, there could be no arhats, nor could there be any pratyekabuddhas. (Although pratyekabuddhas gain realizations in the absence of a buddha, it is only through instruction under previous buddhas that they are eventually able to realize enlightenment on their own.) Finally, the doctrine taught by arhats (pratyekabuddhas do not teach) is inadequate to educate bodhisattvas and can never serve as the basis for bringing about the development of bodhisattvas into fully-enlightened buddhas.

Other Canonical Formulations of the Perfections

Those familiar with the various schools of Buddhism will be aware that the "perfections" are discussed in lists of varying ennumeration in different Buddhist traditions. For example, a list of "ten perfections" is mentioned in one of the texts of Southern Tradition Buddhism which describes the past-life practices of Shākyamuni Buddha when he was a bodhisattva progressing towards his eventual buddhahood in Northern India a half millennium before Christ. A different list of ten perfections is described in the texts of Northern School Buddhism.

In fact, one may encounter lists of perfections which number as few as four (when identified with the four stations of mindfulness), or two (when identified with compassion and wisdom), or as many as thirty (when the ten perfections are seen as being practiced on three levels). All of these various lists of perfections are simply different condensing or proliferating ennumerations of the same six concepts contained within this most common six-fold formulation of the perfections. Hence those other lists of perfections should not be seen as genuinely different from these six perfections describing the primary practices of the bodhisattva coursing on toward the realization of buddhahood.

Nāgārjuna's *Exegesis* in Academic Buddhology

In contrast to the universal praise which it has enjoyed throughout Chinese Buddhist history, Nāgārjuna's *Exegesis* has drawn only a moderate amount of serious interest among western secular scholars. There is one exception to this: Étienne Lamotte's extensively-annotated French translation of the first third of the *Upadeśa*.

Lamotte proved conclusively that (contrary to the previous opinion of some other scholars) Kumārajīva could not possibly have authored the text. However, Lamotte did eventually convince himself that Nāgārjuna was not the author, either. Exploring the matter more deeply, one finds that Lamotte based his doubts about Nāgārjunian authorship primarily on questionable dating suppositions and on mere theorizations about the degree to which Nāgārjuna would be familiar with Sarvastivadin doctrine and inclined to refute it. Additionally, Lamotte acceded to other scholars' dubious identifications of stanza lines in the text as originating with Middle Way School patriarchs who are traditionally thought to have lived after Nāgārjuna.

In fact, all arguments presented against Nāgārjunian authorship by Lamotte and by others are not solidly grounded in reliable historical evidence. Unfortunately, detailed treatment of each of those issues would require more pages than are available here. Suffice it to say that arguments against Nāgārjunian authorship have relied primarily on the silence of documentation in the meagre surviving historical records of Indian Buddhism. This ignores the principle that "absence of evidence is not evidence of absence." Other scholars have admitted that there really is no objective evidence at all which can conclusively disqualify Kumārajīva's attribution of the *Exegesis* to the same Nāgārjuna who authored the *Middle Treatise*.

In considering the issue of authorship, one really should give due consideration to the fact that Kumārajīva was certainly much more deeply familiar with the texts and traditions of Nāgārjuna's lineage than any modern secular or religious scholar, not least because he lived at a time so close to the life of Nāgārjuna himself, studied the Dharma in North India, and lived his early life in the same Central and South Asian religious cultural milieu through which Nāgārjuna's works were spreading. One should notice as well that there are no genuine contradictions in doctrinal content of the *Exegesis* when compared with other known writings of Nāgārjuna.

Translation-Related Issues

Those familiar with Sanskrit antecedents for terms originally rendered into Chinese as two-character compounds will notice that I often default to translating the literal sense of the two component characters in preference to attempting to reconstruct the sense of a putative antecedent Sanskrit term. This stems from a wish to render the text into English in a manner more-or-less accurately reflecting how a Tang Dynasty Chinese Buddhist literatus might have understood it. I believe this is justified in cases such as this where we have no antecedent Sanskrit text serving as an anchor for well-intended but nonetheless conjectural reconstructions of the Sanskrit.

I have made an exception to this translation approach when rendering standard technical terms. In such cases, I have attempted to anchor the translation to Indian Buddhist conceptions of the meaning of the original terms. In an attempt to assist the reader, I have deliberately included many parenthetically-enclosed Sanskrit equivalencies, sometimes from Hirakawa, sometimes from Lamotte, and sometimes from my own reconstruction. This approach has been taken in order to encourage readers to home in on Sanskrit as the *lingua franca* of the Mahāyāna Buddhist technical terminology.

I have generally avoided reading Lamotte's French translation at all so as to avoid accidentally duplicating his not-so-rare translation errors. A notable exception to this stratagem is with regard to a long, highly compressed, and cryptic technical passage in the latter part of Nāgārjuna's treatment of the perfection of dhyāna meditation wherein Lamotte's translation was crucially helpful in untangling text so condensed and so grammatically idiosyncratic as to be unintelligible unless one already knew full well what the author intended. Especially in the case of this important section, I readily acknowledge a debt of gratitude for Étienne Lamotte's encyclopedic erudition and often superior interpretive skills.

On Outlining, Facing-Page Chinese Text, and Annotation

The outline headings do not originate with the Chinese text. I include in each major doctrinal unit an extensive outline consisting of my own outline headings. These same headings are interwoven into the translation as well. In creating this outline, I cannot pretend to have produced the most perfect reflection of Nāgārjuna's underlying doctrinal architecture. Nonetheless, I felt that it was necessary to add this imperfect interpretive apparatus to facilitate more rapid understanding of Nāgārjuna's immensely complex text.

I have included on *verso* page the *CBETA* Taisho text in traditional and short-form scripts to assist translation-quality assessment and to facilitate others' study of Buddhist Classical Chinese. Bilingual native readers unfamiliar with technical terms and Sanskrit transliterations may find this apparatus helpful to expeditious reading.

Taisho's variant readings from other Chinese editions are included at the end of each section, correlated with the bracketed endnote-numbering embedded in the *verso*-page Chinese text.

My apologies to those who rightfully would have expected more thorough annotation of this translation. I regret that the printer's single-volume page count limitations and my own failing health have limited annotation in this edition to the spur-of-the-moment endnotes composed in the earliest drafts of this translation. Fortunately, extensive helpful annotation is available in Lamotte's French edition: *Le Traité de la Grande Vertu de Sagesse de Nāgārjuna*.

In Summation

Translations of these complex and abstruse texts are vulnerable to translation errors arising from misunderstanding or oversight. Where readers encounter mistakes, I would certainly be grateful for any corrective suggestions potentially improving the quality of later editions. (See the Kalavinka website for email contact address.)

In setting forth this translation, it is my hope that western students of Dharma may be deeply inspired by Nāgārjuna's expansive and lovely exposition of the very heart of the Bodhisattva Path.

Bhikshu Dharmamitra
Autumn, 2008

Part One:

THE PERFECTION OF GIVING

(Chapters 17–20)

Part One Contents

Nāgārjuna on the Perfection of Giving

[2]大智度论释初品中檀波罗蜜[3]义[4]第十七。

[139a24]　[*]【经】[5]佛告舍利弗。菩萨摩诃萨以不住法住般若波罗蜜中。以无所舍[6]法具足檀波罗蜜。施者受者及财物不可得故。

[139a26]　[*]【论】问曰。般若波罗蜜是何等法。答曰。有人言。无漏慧根。是般若波罗蜜相。何以故。一切慧中第一慧。是名般若波罗蜜。无漏慧根是第一。以是故无[139b]漏慧根。名般若波罗蜜。问曰。若菩萨未断结。云何得行无漏慧。答曰。菩萨虽未断结。行相似无漏般若波罗蜜。是故得名行无漏般若波罗蜜。譬如声闻人。行暖法顶法忍法世间第一法。先行相似无漏法。后易得生苦法智忍。

简体字

[2]大智度論釋初品中檀波羅蜜[3]義[4]第十七。

[139a24]　[*]【經】[5]佛告舍利弗。菩薩摩訶薩以不住法住般若波羅蜜中。以無所捨[6]法具足檀波羅蜜。施者受者及財物不可得故。

[139a26]　[*]【論】問曰。般若波羅蜜是何等法。答曰。有人言。無漏慧根。是般若波羅蜜相。何以故。一切慧中第一慧。是名般若波羅蜜。無漏慧根是第一。以是故無[139b]漏慧根。名般若波羅蜜。問曰。若菩薩未斷結。云何得行無漏慧。答曰。菩薩雖未斷結。行相似無漏般若波羅蜜。是故得名行無漏般若波羅蜜。譬如聲聞人。行暖法頂法忍法世間第一法。先行相似無漏法。後易得生苦法智忍。

正體字

THE PERFECTION OF GIVING
By Ārya Nāgārjuna

Chapter 17: On the Meaning of *Dāna Pāramitā*

I.   CHAPTER 17: ON THE MEANING OF *DĀNA PĀRAMITĀ*

Sutra: The Buddha told Śāriputra, "It is by resort to the dharma of non-abiding that the bodhisattva, *mahāsattva* abides in the *prajñā-pāramitā*. It is by means of the dharma of having nothing whatsoever which is relinquished that he perfects *dāna pāramitā* (the perfection of giving).[1] This is because benefactor, recipient, and material object cannot be found."[2]

Exegesis:
   Question: What sort of dharma is the *prajñāpāramitā*?

A.   INTRODUCTORY DISCUSSION OF *PRAJÑĀPĀRAMITĀ*
1.   VARIOUS DEFINITIONS OF *PRAJÑĀPĀRAMITĀ*
a.   ABSENCE OF OUTFLOW IMPURITIES AS *PRAJÑĀPĀRAMITĀ*

Response: There are those who explain that the faculty of possessing wisdom free of outflow impurities (*anāsrava-prajñā*)[3] is what constitutes the mark of *prajñāpāramitā*. Why is this? Among all the types of wisdom, the foremost type of wisdom is the *prajñāpāramitā*. The faculty of non-outflow wisdom is foremost. It is for this reason that the faculty of non-outflow wisdom is known as the *prajñā-pāramitā*.

   Question: If it is the case that the bodhisattva has not yet cut off the fetters (*saṃyojana*),[4] how can he succeed in practicing wisdom free of outflow impurities?

   Response: Although the bodhisattva has not yet cut off the fetters he is still able to practice a semblance of non-outflow *prajñā-pāramitā*. It is for this reason that it can be referred to as practicing the non-outflow *prajñāpāramitā*. This is just as with the Śrāvaka disciples who in their cultivation of the dharma of heat, the dharma of summits, the dharma of patience, and the foremost worldly dharma, first practice a semblance of non-outflow dharma and then later easily gain the dharma-knowledge-of-suffering patience (*duḥkhe dharma-jñāna-kṣānti*).

[7]复有人言菩萨有二种。有断结使清净。有未断结[8]使不清净。断结[*]使清净。菩萨能行无漏般若波罗蜜。问曰。若菩萨断结清净。复何以行般若波罗蜜。答曰。虽断结使。十地未满未庄严佛土未教化众生。是故行般若波罗蜜。复次断结有二种。一者断三毒。心不着人天中五欲。二者虽不着人天中五欲。于菩萨功德果报五欲。未能舍离。如是菩萨应行般若波罗蜜。譬如长老阿泥卢豆。在林中坐禅时。净爱天女等。以净妙之身来试阿泥卢豆。阿泥卢豆言。诸姊作青色来不用杂色。欲观不净不能得观。黄赤白色亦复如是。时阿泥卢豆。闭目不视。语言。诸姊远去。是时天女即灭不现。天[9]福报形犹尚如是。何况菩萨无量功德果报五欲。

简体字

[7]復有人言菩薩有二種。有斷結使清淨。有未斷結[8]使不清淨。斷結[*]使清淨。菩薩能行無漏般若波羅蜜。問曰。若菩薩斷結清淨。復何以行般若波羅蜜。答曰。雖斷結使。十地未滿未莊嚴佛土未教化眾生。是故行般若波羅蜜。復次斷結有二種。一者斷三毒。心不著人天中五欲。二者雖不著人天中五欲。於菩薩功德果報五欲。未能捨離。如是菩薩應行般若波羅蜜。譬如長老阿泥盧豆。在林中坐禪時。淨愛天女等。以淨妙之身來試阿泥盧豆。阿泥盧豆言。諸姊作青色來不用雜色。欲觀不淨不能得觀。黃赤白色亦復如是。時阿泥盧豆。閉目不視。語言。諸姊遠去。是時天女即滅不現。天[9]福報形猶尚如是。何況菩薩無量功德果報五欲。

正體字

b. Severance of Fetters As *Prajñāpāramitā*

Then again there are others who state that bodhisattvas are of two kinds, those who are pure by virtue of having cut off the fetters and those who are not pure on account of not yet having cut off the fetters. Those bodhisattvas who are pure by virtue of having cut off the fetters are able to practice *prajñāpāramitā* free of outflow impurities.

Question: If it is the case that the bodhisattva is pure by virtue of having cut off the fetters, why does he then still practice the *prajñāpāramitā*?

Response: Although he may have cut off the fetters, he has still not yet perfected the ten grounds (*daśa-bhūmi*), he has not yet adorned the buddhalands (*buddha-kṣetra*), and he has not yet taught and transformed beings. It is for these reasons that he practices the *prajñāpāramitā*.

1) Severance of Two Types of Fetters

Furthermore, "cutting off the fetters" is of two types. In the case of the first, one cuts off the three poisons. One's mind does not attach to the objects of the five desires among men and gods. In the case of the second, although one does not attach to the objects of the five desires among men and gods, one has still not yet been able to transcend the objects of the five desires which manifest as a consequence of the bodhisattva's merit. A bodhisattva of this sort should practice the *prajñāpāramitā*.

2) On Fetters Arising Through Others' Merit

a) Aniruddha and the Heavenly Maidens (Story)

This was exemplified by the venerable Aniruddha. When he was dwelling in the forest sitting in dhyāna meditation, the heavenly maidens "Pure Love" and others manifest in their pure and marvelous bodies and came to test Aniruddha. Aniruddha said, "Sisters, make yourselves blue when you come here. Don't appear in a variety of colors. I wish to contemplate impurity and am not otherwise able to carry out the contemplation." They then turned yellow, then red, and then white. Aniruddha then closed his eyes and would not look, saying, "Sisters, go away from here." The heavenly maidens then disappeared. If even the physical forms gained as meritorious reward by the gods are so of this sort, then how much the more [marvelous] are the objects of the five desires which manifest as a consequence of the bodhisattva's immeasurable merit.

又如甄陀罗王。与八万四千
甄陀罗。来到佛所弹琴歌颂
以供养佛。尔时须弥山王及
诸山树木。人民禽兽一切皆
舞。佛边大众乃至大迦叶。
皆于座上不能自安。是时天
[10]须菩萨。问长老大迦叶。
耆年旧宿行十二头陀法之第
一。何以在座不能自安。大
迦叶言。三界五欲不能动
我。是菩萨神通功德果报力
故。令我如是。非我有心不
能自安也。譬如须弥山四
[139c]边风起不能令动。至大
劫尽时毘蓝风起如吹烂草。
以是事故知。二种结中一种
未断。如是菩萨等应行般若
波罗蜜。[11]是阿毘昙中。[12]
如是说。复有人言。般若波
罗蜜是有漏慧。何以故。菩
萨至道树下乃断结。先虽有
大智慧有无量功德。而诸烦
恼未断。是故言菩萨般若波
罗蜜是有漏智慧。复有人
言。从初发意乃至道树下。
于其中间所有智慧。是名般
若波罗蜜。成佛时是般若波
罗蜜。转名萨婆若。

又如甄陀羅王。與八萬四千
甄陀羅。來到佛所彈琴歌頌
以供養佛。爾時須彌山王及
諸山樹木。人民禽獸一切皆
舞。佛邊大眾乃至大迦葉。
皆於座上不能自安。是時天
[10]須菩薩。問長老大迦葉。
耆年舊宿行十二頭陀法之第
一。何以在座不能自安。大
迦葉言。三界五欲不能動
我。是菩薩神通功德果報力
故。令我如是。非我有心不
能自安也。譬如須彌山四
[139c]邊風起不能令動。至大
劫盡時毘藍風起如吹爛草。
以是事故知。二種結中一種
未斷。如是菩薩等應行般若
波羅蜜。[11]是阿毘曇中。[12]
如是說。復有人言。般若波
羅蜜是有漏慧。何以故。菩
薩至道樹下乃斷結。先雖有
大智慧有無量功德。而諸煩
惱未斷。是故言菩薩般若波
羅蜜是有漏智慧。復有人
言。從初發意乃至道樹下。
於其中間所有智慧。是名般
若波羅蜜。成佛時是般若波
羅蜜。轉名薩婆若。

简体字   正體字

b) Mahākāśyapa and the Kinnara King (Story)

This is also illustrated by the instance when the *kinnara* king came together with eighty-four thousand other *kinnaras* to where the Buddha dwelt. They strummed their lutes and sang verses as an offering to the Buddha. At that time, Sumeru, the king among mountains, as well as the other mountains, the trees, the people, the birds, and the beasts all danced. The members of the great assembly which surrounded the Buddha, including even Mahākāśyapa, were all unable to make themselves remain still. Divyamauli Bodhisattva then asked the venerable Mahākāśyapa, "You are of senior years and have long abided as foremost in the cultivation of the dharma of twelve *dhūta* (ascetic) practices. How is it that you are unable to remain still in your seat?"

Mahākāśyapa replied, "The five desires within the sphere of the three realms are unable to move me. It is on account of the power of this *kinnara* bodhisattva's superknowledges manifesting as a consequence of his merit that I am caused to be in this state. It is not that I have any thoughts which might prevent me from remaining still."

This is just as with Mount Sumeru which, when the four directions' winds arise, cannot be shaken, but which, when the *vairambhaka* winds arise at the end of a great kalpa, is blown flat like a blade of dead grass. We can know from these cases that one of the two kinds of fetters has not yet been cut off. A bodhisattva of this sort should practice the *prajñāpāramitā*. The Abhidharma explains the matter in this fashion.

c. Bodhisattva *Prajñāpāramitā* As Involving Outflow Impurities

Then again there are those who explain that the *prajñāpāramitā* is a type of wisdom characterized by the presence of outflow impurities. Why? Because it is only when the bodhisattva reaches the point where he is sitting beneath the bodhi tree that he finally cuts off the fetters. Prior to that, although he possesses great wisdom and possesses immeasurable merit, the afflictions have still not all been cut off. Therefore it is explained that the *prajñāpāramitā* of the bodhisattva is "outflow" wisdom.

d. Bodhisattva Wisdom As *Prajñāpāramitā*

Then again, there are also those who explain that, from the point of first generating the aspiration [to attain buddhahood] on up to reaching the bodhi tree, all wisdom employed during that time is referred to as *prajñāpāramitā*. When one achieves buddhahood, "*prajñāpāramitā*" changes in name to "*sarvajñā*" (omniscience).

复有人言。菩萨有漏无漏智慧。总名般若波罗蜜。何以故。菩萨观涅盘行佛道。以是事故。菩萨智慧应是无漏。以未断结使事未成办故。应名有漏。复有人言。菩萨般若波罗蜜。无漏无为不可见无对。复有人言。是般若波罗蜜不可得相。若有若无若常若无常若空若实。是般若波罗蜜。非[13]阴界入所摄。非有为非无为非法非非法。无取无舍不生不灭。出有无四句。适无所着。譬如火焰四边不可触以烧手故。般若波罗蜜相亦如是。不可触以邪见[14]火烧故。问曰。上种种人说般若波罗蜜。何者为实。答曰。有人言各各有理皆是实。如经说。五百比丘各各说二边及中道义。佛言。皆有道理。有人言。末后答者为实。所以者何。不可破不可坏故。若有法[15]如毫[16]氂许[17]有者。皆有

简体字

復有人言。菩薩有漏無漏智慧。總名般若波羅蜜。何以故。菩薩觀涅槃行佛道。以是事故。菩薩智慧應是無漏。以未斷結使事未成辦故。應名有漏。復有人言。菩薩般若波羅蜜。無漏無為不可見無對。復有人言。是般若波羅蜜不可得相。若有若無若常若無常若空若實。是般若波羅蜜。非[13]陰界入所攝。非有為非無為非法非非法。無取無捨不生不滅。出有無四句。適無所著。譬如火焰四邊不可觸以燒手故。般若波羅蜜相亦如是。不可觸以邪見[14]火燒故。問曰。上種種人說般若波羅蜜。何者為實。答曰。有人言各各有理皆是實。如經說。五百比丘各各說二邊及中道義。佛言。皆有道理。有人言。末後答者為實。所以者何。不可破不可壞故。若有法[15]如毫[16]氂許[17]有者。皆有

正體字

There are also those who say that the bodhisattva's outflow-influenced and outflow-free wisdoms both generally qualify as constituting *prajñāpāramitā*. How is this so? The bodhisattva contemplates nirvāṇa and practices the Buddha Path. On this account the bodhisattva's wisdom is appropriately referred to as "outflow-free." When on account of not yet having severed the fetters, he has still not brought the task to completion, that circumstance is appropriately referred to as "outflow-influenced" in nature.

e. Prajñāpāramitā As Transcendent and Ungraspable

There are also those who explain that the *prajñāpāramitā* of the bodhisattva is free of outflow impurities, unconditioned, imperceptible, and beyond opposites.

There are also those who state that this *prajñāpāramitā* is characterized by [the realization of the] "inapprehensibility" [of such concepts concepts as] existence, nonexistence, permanence, impermanence, emptiness, or substantiality, that this *prajñāpāramitā* is not subsumable within the sphere of the aggregates, sense realms, or sense bases, that it is neither conditioned nor unconditioned, that it is neither Dharma nor a non-Dharma, that it is neither graspable nor relinquishable, and that it is not subject to either production or destruction. It transcends the tetralemma's treatment of existence and nonexistence.[5] When coursing in it, one is free of attachments.

f. Seizing Prajñāpāramitā Like Grasping Flames

This is analogous to flames which cannot be touched from any of the four directions because they burn the hands. It is the characteristic of the *prajñāpāramitā* that it, too, is like this. One cannot touch it because erroneous views are burned up by it.

2. Reconciliation of the Various Definitions

Question: Of the various people's explanations of *prajñāpāramitā* offered above, which of them corresponds to reality?

Response: There are those who say that each of them are principled. They all reflect reality. This is as stated in a sutra which says, "Five hundred bhikshus each explained the two extremes and the meaning of the Middle Way. The Buddha said, 'Each of these explanations is reasonable.'"

There are those who say that the last answer is the one which corresponds to reality. Why? Because it cannot be refuted and cannot be destroyed. If one posits that any dharma possesses even the slightest degree of "existence," any such a position is inherently

过失可破。若言无亦可破。此般若中有亦无无亦无非有非无亦无。如是言说亦无。是名寂灭无量无戏论法。是故不可破不可坏。是名真实般若波罗蜜。最[140a]胜无过者。如转轮圣王降伏诸敌而不自高。般若波罗蜜亦如是。能破一切语言戏论。亦不有所破。复次从此已后品品中种种义门。说般若波罗蜜。皆是实相。[1]以不住法住般若波罗蜜中。能具足六波罗蜜。问曰。云何名不住法住般若波罗蜜中能具足六波罗蜜。答曰。如是菩萨观一切法非常非无常。非苦非乐非空非实。非我非无我。非生灭非不生灭。如是住甚深般若波罗蜜中。于般若波罗蜜相亦不取。是名不住法住。若取般若波罗蜜相。是为住法住。

[140a13]　问曰。若不取般若波罗蜜相。心无所着。如

過失可破。若言無亦可破。此般若中有亦無無亦無非有非無亦無。如是言說亦無。是名寂滅無量無戲論法。是故不可破不可壞。是名真實般若波羅蜜。最[140a]勝無過者。如轉輪聖王降伏諸敵而不自高。般若波羅蜜亦如是。能破一切語言戲論。亦不有所破。復次從此已後品品中種種義門。說般若波羅蜜。皆是實相。[1]以不住法住般若波羅蜜中。能具足六波羅蜜。問曰。云何名不住法住般若波羅蜜中能具足六波羅蜜。答曰。如是菩薩觀一切法非常非無常。非苦非樂非空非實。非我非無我。非生滅非不生滅。如是住甚深般若波羅蜜中。於般若波羅蜜相亦不取。是名不住法住。若取般若波羅蜜相。是為住法住。

[140a13]　問曰。若不取般若波羅蜜相。心無所著。如

简体字   正體字

faulty and open to refutation. If one posits the validity of "nonexistence," that too can be refuted. Within this *prajñā*, "existence" is nonexistent, "nonexistence" is nonexistent, and "neither existence nor nonexistence" is nonexistent. And discussion of this sort is nonexistent as well. This is a dharma of quiescent cessation which is immeasurable and free of frivolous doctrinal discussion. Therefore it cannot be refuted and cannot be destroyed. This is what qualifies as the true and actual *prajñāpāramitā*. It is the most supreme and unsurpassed.

3. *Prajñāpāramitā* Compared to the Universal Monarch

Just as when the wheel-turning sage-king defeats his adversaries but still does not elevate himself above them, so too it is with the *prajñāpāramitā*. It is able to refute any assertion or frivolous doctrinal discussion and yet it still maintains nothing itself which could be the object of refutation.

Finally, from this point onward, many sorts of gateways to the meaning are employed in each chapter in the setting forth of the *prajñāpāramitā*. They all characterized by their accordance with reality. It is by resort to the dharma of non-abiding that one abides in the *prajñāpāramitā* and is able to completely perfect the six *pāramitās*.

B. The Relevance of Non-Abiding to *Prajñāpāramitā*

Question: What is meant when the text states that it is by resort to the dharma of non-abiding that one abides in the *prajñāpāramitā* and thus one is able to completely perfect the six *pāramitās*?

Response: It is in this manner that the bodhisattva contemplates all dharmas as neither eternal nor non-eternal, as characterized neither by suffering nor by bliss, as neither empty [of inherent existence] nor real, as neither possessed of selfhood nor devoid of selfhood, and as neither produced and destroyed nor unproduced and undestroyed. It is in this manner that one abides within the extremely profound *prajñāpāramitā* and yet still does not seize upon any characteristic of the *prajñāpāramitā*.

This is an abiding wherein one refrains from abiding in dharmas. If one were to seize upon any characteristic of the *prajñāpāramitā*, that would be a case of an abiding wherein one abides in dharmas.

C. Reconciliation of Non-grasping and Success in the Path

Question: If one refrains from seizing upon any mark of the *prajñāpāramitā*, the mind has nothing to which it may attach. As the

佛所言一切诸法欲为其本。若不取者。云何得具足六波罗蜜。答曰。菩萨怜愍众生故。先立誓愿我必当度脱一切众生。以精进波罗蜜力故。虽知诸法不生不灭如涅盘相。复行诸功德。具足六波罗蜜。所以者何。[2]以不住法住般若波罗蜜中故。是名不住法住般若波罗蜜[3]中。	佛所言一切諸法欲為其本。若不取者。云何得具足六波羅蜜。答曰。菩薩憐愍眾生故。先立誓願我必當度脫一切眾生。以精進波羅蜜力故。雖知諸法不生不滅如涅槃相。復行諸功德。具足六波羅蜜。所以者何。[2]以不住法住般若波羅蜜中故。是名不住法住般若波羅蜜[3]中。
简体字	正體字

Buddha said, "Zeal is the origin of all dharmas." If it is the case that one does not grasp at anything, how can one succeed in completely perfecting the six *pāramitās*?

Response: Because the bodhisattva takes pity on beings, he first makes a vow: "I must certainly bring all beings to liberation." On account of the power of the *pāramitā* of vigor, even though he realizes that all dharmas are neither produced nor destroyed and characterized by being comparable to nirvāṇa, he nonetheless still cultivates all manner of merit and still strives towards the complete perfection of the six *pāramitās*. Why? It is on account of the dharma of non-abiding that he abides in the *prajñāpāramitā*. This is what is meant [when the above passage of Sutra text states]: "It is by resort to the dharma of non-abiding that [the bodhisattva, *mahāsattva*] abides in the *prajñāpāramitā*."

[4]大智度论[5]释初[6]品中赞檀波罗蜜[7]义[8]第十八。

[140a23]　　问曰。檀有何等利[9]益故。菩萨住般若波罗蜜中。檀波罗蜜具足满。答曰。檀有种种利益。檀为宝藏常随逐人。檀为破苦能与人乐。檀为善御开示天道。檀为善[10]府摄诸善人。（施摄善人与为因缘故言摄）檀为安隐临命终时心不怖畏。檀为慈相能济一切。檀为集乐能破苦贼。檀为大将能伏悭敌。檀为妙果[140b]天人所爱。檀为净道贤圣所游。檀为积善福德之门。檀为立事聚众之缘。檀为善行[11]爱果之种。檀为福业善人之相。檀破贫穷断三恶道。檀能[12]全[13]护福乐之果。

简体字

[4]大智度論[5]釋初[6]品中讚檀波羅蜜[7]義[8]第十八。

[140a23]　　問曰。檀有何等利[9]益故。菩薩住般若波羅蜜中。檀波羅蜜具足滿。答曰。檀有種種利益。檀為寶藏常隨逐人。檀為破苦能與人樂。檀為善御開示天道。檀為善[10]府攝諸善人。（施攝善人與為因緣故言攝）檀為安隱臨命終時心不怖畏。檀為慈相能濟一切。檀為集樂能破苦賊。檀為大將能伏悭敵。檀為妙果[140b]天人所愛。檀為淨道賢聖所遊。檀為積善福德之門。檀為立事聚眾之緣。檀為善行[11]愛果之種。檀為福業善人之相。檀破貧窮斷三惡道。檀能[12]全[13]護福樂之果。

正體字

Chapter 18: In Praise of *"Dāna Pāramitā"*

II. CHAPTER 18: IN PRAISE OF *DĀNA PĀRAMITĀ*

  A. THE BENEFITS OF *DĀNA*

Question: What benefits does *dāna* bestow that lead the bodhisattva abiding in the *prajñāpāramitā* to completely perfect it?

   1. TWENTY-SEVEN SALUTARY ASPECTS OF *DĀNA*

Response:

Dāna brings all manner of benefits:

Dāna serves as a treasure trove which constantly follows along with a person.

Dāna destroys suffering and bestows bliss on people.

Dāna is a good guide showing the way to the heavens.

Dāna is a house of goodness for it draws in good people. (Chinese textual note: Giving draws in good people as a result of one's setting up karmic causes and conditions with them. Hence the text reads "draws in.")[6]

Dāna is a source of peace and security. When one reaches the end of one's life, one's mind remains free of fear.

Dāna itself is itself marked by kindness, for it is able to bring about the rescue of everyone.

Dāna engenders happiness and is able to rout the insurgents of suffering.

Dāna is a great general able to defeat its enemy, miserliness.

Dāna is a marvelous fruit loved by both gods and men.

Dāna is a path of purity traveled by both worthies and āryas.

Dāna is the gateway to the accumulation of goodness and meritorious qualities.

Dāna is a condition for the accomplishment of works and the gathering of a multitude.

Dāna is the seed of the cherished fruits of good actions.

Dāna is the mark of the good person endowed with blessings-generating karma.

Dāna destroys poverty and cuts one off from the three wretched destinies.[7]

Dāna is able to preserve and protect the fruit of karmic blessings and bliss.

檀为涅盘之初缘。入善人聚
中之要法。称誉赞叹之渊
府。入众无难之功德。心不
悔恨之窟宅。善法道行之根
本。种种欢乐之林薮。富贵
安隐之福田。得道涅盘之津
梁。圣人大士智者之所行。
馀人俭德寡识之所效。复次
譬如失火之家。黠慧之人明
识形势。及火未至急出财
物。舍虽烧尽财物悉在。更
修室宅。好施之人亦复如
是。知身危脆财物无常修福
及时。如火中出物后世受
乐。亦如彼人更修宅业福庆
自慰。愚惑之人但知惜屋忽
忽营救。狂愚失智不量火势
猛风绝焰土石为焦。翕[14]响
之间荡然夷灭。屋既不救

檀為涅槃之初緣。入善人聚
中之要法。稱譽讚歎之淵
府。入眾無難之功德。心不
悔恨之窟宅。善法道行之根
本。種種歡樂之林藪。富貴
安隱之福田。得道涅槃之津
梁。聖人大士智者之所行。
餘人儉德寡識之所效。復次
譬如失火之家。黠慧之人明
識形勢。及火未至急出財
物。舍雖燒盡財物悉在。更
修室宅。好施之人亦復如
是。知身危脆財物無常修福
及時。如火中出物後世受
樂。亦如彼人更修宅業福慶
自慰。愚惑之人但知惜屋忽
忽營救。狂愚失智不量火勢
猛風絕焰土石為焦。翕[14]響
之間蕩然夷滅。屋既不救

简体字   正體字

Dāna is the primary condition for the realization of nirvāṇa.

It is the essential dharma for entry into the multitude of good people.

It is the vast repository of good repute and laudatory commendation.

It provides the quality of freedom from difficulties in the midst of any multitude.

It is the den in which the mind remains free of regret.

It is the origin of good dharmas and of one's cultivation of the Path.

It is the dense forest of every manner of delightful bliss.

It is the field of blessings for the reaping of wealth, nobility, and peaceful security.

It is the bridge across to the realization of the Path and to entry into nirvāṇa. It is traversed by the Āryas, the great masters, and those possessed of wisdom.

It is that which everyone else, including those of minor virtue and lesser intelligence, should strive to emulate.

2. *Dāna* Compared to Wisdom in a House Fire

Then again, it can be compared to appropriate actions taken when a house has caught fire. An intelligent person would clearly recognize the gravity of the situation and would then hastily extricate his valuables before the fire reached him. Then, although the house might be burned to the ground, still, his valuables would be preserved so that he might rebuild his residence.

A person who enjoys giving is just like this. Because he is aware of the fragility of the body and of the impermanence of material wealth, he takes advantage of the opportunity to cultivate blessings. Just like that man who, having extricated his possessions from a house fire, is able to rebuild home and livelihood, so too, [one who practices giving] thereby becomes able to experience next-life bliss, consequently enjoying karmic blessings and personal comfort.

3. Miserliness Compared to Poor Judgment in a House Fire

The stupid and deluded person is concerned only with cherishing his house and so rushes about trying to save it. He proceeds madly and foolishly and, losing touch with common sense, fails to recognize the intensity of the blaze. In the fierce wind and towering flames, even the earth and rocks are scorched. In a brief interval, everything is utterly destroyed. Not only is the house not saved,

財物亦尽。饥寒冻饿忧苦毕世。悭惜之人亦复如是。不知身命无常须臾[15]叵保。而更聚[16]歛守护爱惜。死至无期忽焉逝没。形与土木同流。财与委物俱弃。亦如愚人忧苦失计。复次大慧之人有心之士。乃能觉悟知身如幻财不可保。万物无常唯福可恃。将人出苦津通大道。复次大人大心能大布施。能自利己。小人小心不能益他。亦不自厚。复次譬如勇士见敌必期吞灭。智人慧心深得悟理。悭贼虽强亦能挫之必令如意。遇良福田值好时节(时应施之时也遇而不[17]施是名失时)觉事应心能大布施。复次好施之人为人所敬。如月初出无不爱者。好名善誉周闻天下人[140c]所归仰一切皆信。好施之人贵人所念贱人所敬。命欲

简体字

財物亦盡。飢寒凍餓憂苦畢世。慳惜之人亦復如是。不知身命無常須臾[15]叵保。而更聚[16]歛守護愛惜。死至無期忽焉逝沒。形與土木同流。財與委物俱棄。亦如愚人憂苦失計。復次大慧之人有心之士。乃能覺悟知身如幻財不可保。萬物無常唯福可恃。將人出苦津通大道。復次大人大心能大布施。能自利己。小人小心不能益他。亦不自厚。復次譬如勇士見敵必期吞滅。智人慧心深得悟理。慳賊雖強亦能挫之必令如意。遇良福田值好時節(時應施之時也遇而不[17]施是名失時)覺事應心能大布施。復次好施之人為人所敬。如月初出無不愛者。好名善譽周聞天下人[140c]所歸仰一切皆信。好施之人貴人所念賤人所敬。命欲

正體字

but the wealth and valuables are all lost as well. To the very end of his life, he is bound to be tormented by hunger, cold, anguish, and suffering.

Miserly people are just like this. They do not realize that one's physical existence is impermanent and that one cannot guarantee even another moment of life. Nonetheless, they dedicate themselves to accumulating possessions which they protect and treasure. Death arrives unexpectedly and they suddenly pass away.

One's physical form is of the same class with dirt and timbers. One's wealth and worn-out possessions are all bound to be cast aside. [Miserly people] are just like the foolish man compelled to experience anguish and suffering as a result of errors in judgment.

B. Extended Discussion of the Benefits of *Dāna*

Then again, if one is a person of great wisdom or is a gentleman of fine mind, one will be able to awaken and realize that the body is like an illusion, that wealth can never be secure, that the myriad things are all impermanent, and that one can rely only upon one's merit. It is this which has the capacity to pull a person forth from the river of suffering and to open up the great Path.

Additionally, the great man of great mind is able to give greatly. Thus he becomes able to naturally benefit himself as well. The petty man of petty mind is not only unable to benefit others, but he is also unable even to bestow liberal generosity upon himself.

Then again, just as when a brave soldier spies an enemy, he definitely seizes the opportunity and straightaway vanquishes him utterly, so also, when an intelligent man of wise mind gains a deep realization of this principle, even though the insurgents of miserliness may be powerful, he is nonetheless able to fell them and resolutely fulfill his determination. When he meets up with a good field of blessings, encounters an opportune time, and realizes that the situation corresponds to his intentions, he is able to give greatly. (Ch. text note: "Opportune time" means when one ought to give. If one encounters it and yet does not give, this is "missing the time.")

Again, a person who takes pleasure in giving is respected by others. He is just like the moon when first risen above the horizon in that there are none who fail to look on him with fondness. His fine name and good reputation become well-known throughout the world. He is one relied upon and looked up to by others. Everyone trusts him. A person delighting in giving is borne in mind by the noble and respected by those of humble station. As his life draws to

终时其心不怖。如是果报今世所得。譬如树华大果无量。后世福也。生死轮转往来五道无亲可恃。唯有布施若生天上人中得清净果皆由布施。象马畜生得好[18]枥养。亦是布施之所得也。布施之德富贵欢乐。持戒之人得生天上。禅智心净无所染着得涅盘道。布施之福是涅盘道之资粮也。念施故欢喜。欢喜故一心。[19]一心观生灭无常[20]观生灭无常故得道。如人求荫故种树。或求华或求果故种树。布施求报亦复如是。今世后世乐如求荫。声闻辟支佛道如华。成佛如果。是为檀种种功德。

終時其心不怖。如是果報今世所得。譬如樹華大果無量。後世福也。生死輪轉往來五道無親可恃。唯有布施若生天上人中得清淨果皆由布施。象馬畜生得好[18]櫪養。亦是布施之所得也。布施之德富貴歡樂。持戒之人得生天上。禪智心淨無所染著得涅槃道。布施之福是涅槃道之資糧也。念施故歡喜。歡喜故一心。[19]一心觀生滅無常[20]觀生滅無常故得道。如人求蔭故種樹。或求華或求果故種樹。布施求報亦復如是。今世後世樂如求蔭。聲聞辟支佛道如華。成佛如果。是為檀種種功德。

简体字　　　　　　　　　　　　正體字

an end, his mind remains free of any fear.

Such reward-bearing fruits are obtained even in this very life. An analogy can be made with fruit trees where, when the production of blossoms is great, countless fruits are then produced. This speaks to the blessings bound to be received in future lives.

As one turns about in the wheel of cyclic births and deaths, going and coming within the five rebirth destinies, there are no family relatives upon whom one can rely. There is only giving. Whether one is born in the heavens or among men, whenever one gains a pure result, it comes forth as a result of giving. Even among elephants, horses and other animals, their being provided fine shelter and nourishment is also something they have gained as a result of [previous-life] giving.

The qualities gained on account of giving are wealth, nobility, and bliss. Those who uphold the moral precepts succeed in being reborn in the heavens. Through dhyāna and wisdom, one's mind becomes pure and free of defiling attachment. Thus one is bound to gain the path to nirvāṇa. The blessings gained as a result of giving serve as one's provisions as one travels along that road to nirvāṇa.

When one brings giving to mind, one experiences delight. On account of delight, one develops unity of mind. With unity of mind, one proceeds to contemplate birth, death, and impermanence. Because one contemplates birth, death, and impermanence, one becomes able to gain realization of the Path.

This is comparable to when a person plants trees out of a desire to have shade or else plants trees because he seeks their blossoms or seeks their fruit. The aspiration for a reward in the practice of giving is just like this. The bliss acquired in this and future lives is comparable to that shade sought [from planting trees]. The paths of the Śrāvakas and the Pratyekabuddhas are akin to their blossoms. The realization of buddhahood is analogous to their fruits. These are the various sorts of meritorious qualities associated with *dāna*.

[*]大智度论[21]释初品中檀相[22]义[23]第十九。

[140c16] 问曰。云何名檀。答曰。檀名布施心相应善思。是名为檀。有人言。从善思起身口业。亦名为檀。有人言。有信有福田有财物三事和合时。心生舍法能破悭贪。是名为檀。譬如慈法观众生[24]乐而心生慈。布施心数法亦复如是。三事和合心生舍法能破悭贪。檀有三种。或欲界系或色界系或不系。[25]（丹本注云圣人行施故名不系）心相应法随心行共心生。非色法能作缘。非业业相应随业行共业生。非先世业报生。二[26]种修行修得修。二种证身证慧证。若思惟断。若不断。二见断[27]欲界色界尽[28]见断。有觉有观法凡夫圣人共行。如是等阿毗昙中广分别说。复次施有二种。有净有不净。不净施者[29]直施无所[30]为。

简体字

[*]大智度論[21]釋初品中檀相[22]義[23]第十九。

[140c16] 問曰。云何名檀。答曰。檀名布施心相應善思。是名為檀。有人言。從善思起身口業。亦名為檀。有人言。有信有福田有財物三事和合時。心生捨法能破慳貪。是名為檀。譬如慈法觀眾生[24]樂而心生慈。布施心數法亦復如是。三事和合心生捨法能破慳貪。檀有三種。或欲界繫或色界繫或不繫。[25]（丹本注云聖人行施故名不繫）心相應法隨心行共心生。非色法能作緣。非業業相應隨業行共業生。非先世業報生。二[26]種修行修得修。二種證身證慧證。若思惟斷。若不斷。二見斷[27]欲界色界盡[28]見斷。有覺有觀法凡夫聖人共行。如是等阿毗曇中廣分別說。復次施有二種。有淨有不淨。不淨施者[29]直施無所[30]為。

正體字

Chapter 19: On the Characteristics and Import of *Dāna*

III. CHAPTER 19: THE CHARACTERISTICS AND IMPORT OF *DĀNA*

  A. THREE DEFINITIONS OF *DĀNA*

Question: What is meant by *dāna* (giving)?

Response: *Dāna* refers to an instance of giving wherein there is a corresponding instance of wholesome intentionality (*cetanā*). This is what is meant by *dāna*.

There are those who say that the arising of physical and verbal actions following from wholesome intentionality may also qualify as *dāna*.

There are others who say that *dāna* refers to the coming together of three factors: faith, a field of blessings,[8] and a material object, all simultaneous with the mind's generating a dharma of relinquishing capable of destroying miserliness. Just as with the dharma of kindness (*maitrī*) wherein, on contemplating what brings happiness to beings, one's mind then generates kindness, so too it is with *dāna*, another of the dharmas associated with the mind. These three factors come together and the mind then generates a dharma of relinquishing capable of destroying miserliness.

  B. THREE TYPES OF *DĀNA*

Dāna is of three kinds: that attached to the desire realm; that attached to the form realm; and that which is not attached at all.

    (Chinese textual note: "The notes in red record that this refers to giving as practiced by āryas. Hence it is referred to as 'not attached.'")

  C. ADDITIONAL ABHIDHARMIC ANALYTIC DATA

[Giving] is a dharma associated with the mind, occurring in accordance with the mind, and arising in conjunction with the mind....[9] Considerations of this sort are extensively analyzed and discussed in the Abhidharma.

  D. TWO TYPES OF GIVING

Additionally, giving is of two types. There is that which is "pure" and that which is "impure."

    1. IMPURE GIVING (EIGHTEEN EXAMPLES)

As for "impure" giving:

  It may involve superficial giving in which one takes no interest.

或有为求[141a]财故施。或愧人故施。或为嫌责故施。或畏惧故施。或欲[1]取他意故施。或畏死故施。或[2]狂人令喜故施。或自以富贵故应施。或诤胜故施。或妒瞋故施。或憍慢自高故施。或为名誉故施。或为呪愿故施。或解除衰求吉故施。或为聚众故施。或轻贱不敬施。如是等种种名为不净施。净施者。与上相违[3]名为净施。复次为道故施。清净心生无诸结使。不求今世后世报。恭敬怜愍故。是[4]为净施。净施是趣涅盘道之资粮。是故言为道故施。若未得涅盘[5]时施。是人天报乐之因。

简体字

或有為求[141a]財故施。或愧人故施。或為嫌責故施。或畏懼故施。或欲[1]取他意故施。或畏死故施。或[2]狂人令喜故施。或自以富貴故應施。或諍勝故施。或妒瞋故施。或憍慢自高故施。或為名譽故施。或為呪願故施。或解除衰求吉故施。或為聚眾故施。或輕賤不敬施。如是等種種名為不淨施。淨施者。與上相違[3]名為淨施。復次為道故施。清淨心生無諸結使。不求今世後世報。恭敬憐愍故。是[4]為淨施。淨施是趣涅槃道之資糧。是故言為道故施。若未得涅槃[5]時施。是人天報樂之因。

正體字

Or it may perhaps be done for the sake of obtaining wealth.

Or perhaps one gives because one feels shamed.

Or perhaps one gives as a means of reproving others.

Or perhaps one gives out of terror.

Or perhaps one gives to draw favorable attention to oneself.

Or perhaps one gives out of a fear of being killed.

Or perhaps one gives with the intention of manipulating someone into feeling pleased.

Or perhaps one gives out of a feeling of obligation, this because one happens to be rich and of noble birth.

Or perhaps one gives as a means of struggling for dominance.

Or perhaps one gives out of jealousy.

Or perhaps one gives out of hatred.

Or perhaps one gives out of arrogance, desiring to elevate oneself above others.

Or perhaps one gives for the sake of fame or reputation.

Or perhaps one gives out of an attempt to lend efficacy to ritual incantations and prayers.

Or perhaps one gives in an attempt to do away with misfortune and gain good fortune.

Or perhaps one gives in order to gain a following.

Or perhaps one gives in a disrespectful fashion in order to slight someone and make them feel humbled.

All of the various sorts of giving such as these are classified as "impure giving."

2. PURE GIVING

As for "pure" giving, any giving which stands in opposition to the above examples qualifies as pure giving. Then again, giving for the sake of the Path is pure giving. When a pure mind arises which is devoid of any of the fetters, or when one is not seeking for any reward in this or future lives, or when one does so out of reverence or sympathy, these circumstances all qualify as pure giving.

a. SALUTARY EFFECTS OF PURE GIVING

Pure giving creates the provisions for moving on along the path to nirvāṇa. Hence we speak of "giving for the sake of the Path." If one performs acts of giving prior to that time when one might be inclined to strive for realization of nirvāṇa, it creates a cause for the enjoyment of blissful future retribution among gods and men.

[6]净施者如华璎珞初成未坏香洁鲜明。为涅盘净施[7]得果报香亦复如是。如佛说。世有二人为难得。一者出家中非时解脱比丘。二者在家白衣能清净布施。是净施相乃至无量世。世世不失。譬如券要终无失时。是布施果因缘和合时便有。譬如树得时节会。便有华叶果实若时节未至有因而无果。是布施法。若以求道能与人道。何以故结使灭名涅盘。当布施时。诸烦恼薄故。能助涅盘。于所施物中不惜故。除悭敬念受者故。除嫉妒直心布施故。除谄曲。一心[8]布施故。除[9]调[10]深思惟施故。除悔。观受者功德故。除不恭敬。自摄心故。除不惭。知人好功德故。除不愧。

简体字

[6]淨施者如華瓔珞初成未壞香潔鮮明。為涅槃淨施[7]得果報香亦復如是。如佛說。世有二人為難得。一者出家中非時解脫比丘。二者在家白衣能清淨布施。是淨施相乃至無量世。世世不失。譬如券要終無失時。是布施果因緣和合時便有。譬如樹得時節會。便有華葉果實若時節未至有因而無果。是布施法。若以求道能與人道。何以故結使滅名涅槃。當布施時。諸煩惱薄故。能助涅槃。於所施物中不惜故。除慳敬念受者故。除嫉妒直心布施故。除諂曲。一心[8]布施故。除[9]調[10]深思惟施故。除悔。觀受者功德故。除不恭敬。自攝心故。除不慚。知人好功德故。除不愧。

正體字

Pure giving is like a floral wreath when first made and not yet withered, which is fragrant, pure, fresh and radiant. Similarly, when one performs acts of pure giving for the sake of nirvāṇa, one consequently becomes able to enjoy [as an incidental benefit] the fragrance of karmic rewards [even prior to reaching nirvāṇa].

As the Buddha said, "There are two types of people who are rarely encountered in the world: The first, among those who have left the home life, is a bhikshu who eats at the improper time and yet succeeds in gaining liberation. The second, among the white-robed householders, is one who is able to perform an act of pure giving." In life after life, the mark of this pure giving is never lost even after countless lifetimes. It is like a title deed which never loses its validity even to the very end.

This fruit of giving comes forth when the appropriate causes and conditions all come together. This is analogous to the fruit tree which, when it encounters the right season, then has flowers, leaves, fruit and seeds. If the season has not yet arrived, even though the causes may be present, no corresponding fruit will yet come forth.

1) How Giving Gets Rid of the Afflictions

As for this dharma of giving, if it is done in order to seek the Path, one is able to achieve success even in the path of humans. How is this so? The destruction of the fetters is what qualifies as [the basis of] nirvāṇa. When one is giving, because one's afflictions become but slight, one is thereby able to progress towards nirvāṇa.

By not clinging to the object which is given, one gets rid of miserliness (*mātsarya*).

By being respectfully mindful of the recipient, one gets rid of jealousy (*īrṣyā*).

By giving with a straight mind, one gets rid of deviousness (*śāṭhya*).

By giving with a unified mind, one gets rid of agitation (*auddhatya*).

By giving with deep thoughts, one gets rid of regretfulness (*kaukṛtya*).

By contemplating the meritorious qualities of the recipient, one gets rid of irreverence (*anarcana*).

By focusing one's own mind, one gets rid of an absence of a sense of shame (*āhrīkya*).

By becoming aware of another's fine meritorious qualities, one gets rid of an absence of a dread of blame (*anapatrāpya*).

不着财物故。除爱。慈愍受者故。除瞋。恭敬受者故。除憍慢。知行善法故。除无明。信有果报故。除邪见。知决定有报故除疑。如是等种种不善诸烦恼。布施时悉皆薄。种种善法悉皆得。[141b]布施时六根清净善欲心生。善欲心生故。内心清净。观果报功德故。信心生。身心柔软故。喜乐生。喜乐生故。得一心。得一心故。实智慧生。如是等诸善法悉皆得。复次布施时。[11]心生相似八正道。信布施果故。得正见。正见中思惟不乱故。得正思[12]惟。清净说故得正语。净身行故。得正业。不求报故。得正命。

不著財物故。除愛。慈愍受者故。除瞋。恭敬受者故。除憍慢。知行善法故。除無明。信有果報故。除邪見。知決定有報故除疑。如是等種種不善諸煩惱。布施時悉皆薄。種種善法悉皆得。[141b]布施時六根清淨善欲心生。善欲心生故。內心清淨。觀果報功德故。信心生。身心柔軟故。喜樂生。喜樂生故。得一心。得一心故。實智慧生。如是等諸善法悉皆得。復次布施時。[11]心生相似八正道。信布施果故。得正見。正見中思惟不亂故。得正思[12]惟。清淨說故得正語。淨身行故。得正業。不求報故。得正命。

简体字   正體字

By not being attached to objects of material wealth, one gets rid of covetousness (*rāga*).

By feeling kindness and sympathy for the recipient, one gets rid of hatefulness (*pratigha*).

By being respectful to the recipient, one gets rid of arrogance (*māna*).

By learning to cultivate a wholesome dharma, one gets rid of ignorance (*avidya*).

By believing that there are resultant rewards, one gets rid of erroneous views (*mithyā-dṛṣṭi*).

On account of knowing that there will definitely be a retribution, one gets rid of doubtfulness (*vicikitsā*).

All sorts of unwholesome afflictions such as these become scant when one cultivates the practice of giving.[10]

2) How Giving Generates Good Dharmas

All manner of good dharmas are gained:

When one gives, the six faculties (*indriya*)[11] are pure and a thought imbued with wholesome zeal arises.

On account of the arising of a thought imbued with wholesome zeal, one's mind becomes inwardly pure.

On account of contemplating the meritorious qualities of the resultant retribution, thoughts of faith arise.

On account of pliancy developing in the body and mind, delight arises.

Because delight arises, one achieves single-mindedness.

Because one achieves single-mindedness, genuine wisdom develops.

[As a result], all such sorts of good dharmas are realized.

3) How Giving Generates Path Practices

Moreover, when one gives, the mind develops a semblance of the eight-fold right path, as follows:

Because one believes in the effects of giving, one gains right views.

Because when one maintains right views, one's thoughts are not confused, one thereby achieves right thought.

Because one's speech is pure, one achieves right speech.

Because one purifies physical actions, one achieves right action.

Because one does not seek to gain a reward in return, one achieves right livelihood.

勲心施故。得正方便。念施不[13]废故。得正念。心住不散故。得正定。如是等相似三十七品善法心中生。复次有人[14]言。布施是[15]得三十二相因缘。所以者何。施时与心坚固。得足下安立相。布施时。五事围绕受者。是眷属业因缘故。得足下轮相。大勇猛力施故。得足跟广平相。施摄人故。得手足缦网相。美味饮食施故。得手足柔软七处满相。施以益命故。得长指身不曲大直相。施时言我当相与。施心转增故。得足跌高毛上向相。施时受者求之一心好听。慇懃约勅令必疾得故。得伊泥延[16]〔跳-兆+专〕相。不瞋不轻求者故。得臂长过膝相。

勲心施故。得正方便。念施不[13]廢故。得正念。心住不散故。得正定。如是等相似三十七品善法心中生。復次有人[14]言。布施是[15]得三十二相因緣。所以者何。施時與心堅固。得足下安立相。布施時。五事圍繞受者。是眷屬業因緣故。得足下輪相。大勇猛力施故。得足跟廣平相。施攝人故。得手足縵網相。美味飲食施故。得手足柔軟七處滿相。施以益命故。得長指身不曲大直相。施時言我當相與。施心轉增故。得足跌高毛上向相。施時受者求之一心好聽。慇懃約勅令必疾得故。得伊泥延[16]〔跳-兆+專〕相。不瞋不輕求者故。得臂長過膝相。

简体字   正體字

Because one gives with a diligent mind, one gains right skillful effort.[12]

Because one does not neglect being mindful of giving, one gains right mindfulness.

Because one's mind dwells in one place and is not scattered, one gains right meditative absorption.

In this same manner a semblance of the good dharmas of the thirty-seven wings of enlightenment develops within the mind.

4) How Giving Generates the Thirty-Two Marks of a Buddha's Body

Moreover, there are those who say that giving generates the causes and conditions for the development of the thirty-two marks.[13] How is this so?

Because one remains solid in one's resolve as one gives, one gains the mark of the feet being solidly planted on the ground.

When one gives, five factors come to surround the recipient of one's giving.[14] Because this thereby acts as the karmic cause and condition for coming to have a retinue, one gains the mark of the wheel on the bottoms of the feet.

On account of the power of being greatly intrepid in one's giving, one gains the mark of having the heels broad and flat.

Because giving attracts others, one gains the mark of webbed fingers and toes.

Because one gives marvelously flavored drink and food, one gains the mark of softness of the hands and feet as well as the mark of fullness in seven physical locations.

Because one's giving lengthens the life [of others], one gains the mark of long fingers as well as the mark of the body's being markedly erect and not stooped over.

When giving, one says, "It is only fitting that I should offer this." Because one's mind of giving thus increases in strength, one gains as a result the mark of having heels which are tall as well as the mark of having bodily hairs which grow in a superior direction.

Because when giving, one listens well and single-mindedly to the recipient's requests and then diligently accords with such instructions by certainly and hastily getting what is requested, one gains the mark of having legs like the *aiṇeya* antelope.

Because one does not express anger or slighting behavior towards the person making the request, one gains the mark of having long arms extending beyond the knees.

如求者意施不待言故。得阴
藏相。好衣服卧具金银珍宝
施故。得金色身相薄皮相。
布施[17]令受者独得自在[18]
用。故。得一一孔一毛生眉
间白毫相。[19]求者求之即
言。当与以是业故。得上身
如师子肩圆相。病者施药饥
渴者与饮[20]食故。得两腋
下[21]满最上味相。施时劝
人行施而安慰之。开布施道
故。得肉髻相。身圆如尼拘
卢相。有乞求者意欲与时。
柔软实语必与不虚故。得广
长舌相梵音声相如迦陵毗伽
鸟声[141c]相。施时如实语利
益语故。得师子颊相。施时
[22]恭敬受者心清净故。得牙
白齿齐相。施时实语和合语
故。得齿密相四十齿相。施
时不瞋不着等心视彼故。得
青眼相眼睫如牛王相。

简体字

如求者意施不待言故。得陰
藏相。好衣服臥具金銀珍寶
施故。得金色身相薄皮相。
布施[17]令受者獨得自在[18]
用。故。得一一孔一毛生眉
間白毫相。[19]求者求之即
言。當與以是業故。得上身
如師子肩圓相。病者施藥飢
渴者與飲[20]食故。得兩腋
下[21]滿最上味相。施時勸
人行施而安慰之。開布施道
故。得肉髻相。身圓如尼拘
盧相。有乞求者意欲與時。
柔軟實語必與不虛故。得廣
長舌相梵音聲相如迦陵毗伽
鳥聲[141c]相。施時如實語利
益語故。得師子頰相。施時
[22]恭敬受者心清淨故。得牙
白齒齊相。施時實語和合語
故。得齒密相四十齒相。施
時不瞋不著等心視彼故。得
青眼相眼睫如牛王相。

正體字

Because one gives in accordance with the mind of the solicitor, not waiting for him to ask, one gains the mark of well-retracted genitals.[15]

Because one gives fine clothing, bedding, gold, silver, and precious jewels, one gains the mark of having a gold-colored body as well as the mark of having fine skin.

On account of giving in a fashion that allows the recipient the ability to gain exclusive and independent use of the gift, one gains the mark of having a single hair in each and every pore as well as the mark of having the white hair mark between the brows.

On account of responding to the request of the solicitor by saying, "It is only fitting that I perform this act of giving," one gains the mark of having the upper body similar to that of a lion as well as the mark of having rounded shoulders.

On account of giving medication to the sick and giving drink and food to those who are hungry and thirsty, one gains the mark of having the area beneath the two armpits full and also gains the mark of experiencing the most superior of all flavors.

By providing comfort to others through encouraging them to practice giving while one is oneself engaged in giving, one opens up the way to giving. On account of this, one gains the mark of the bulge on the crown of one's head as well as the mark of having the body be as round as a *nyagrodha* tree.

When someone makes a request and one forms the intention to present a gift, because one employs gentle and true words which confirm the definite intention to give and which contain no falsehood, one gains the mark of the broad and long tongue, gains the mark of a voice possessed of the sound of Brahmā, and also gains the mark of a voice like the *kalaviṅka* bird.[16]

On account of speaking the truth and employing beneficial speech as one gives, one gains the mark of having jaws like a lion.

On account of respecting the recipient and maintaining a pure mind as one gives, one gains the mark of white and straight teeth.

On account of speaking true words and using harmonious speech as one gives, one gains the mark of having tightly fitting teeth and also gains the mark of having forty teeth.

Because, when one gives, one remains free of hatefulness and free of attachment while maintaining a mind mind regarding them all as equal, one gains the mark of having blue eyes and also gains the mark of having eyelashes like the king of the bulls.

是为种三十二相因缘。复次
以七宝人民车乘金银灯烛房
舍香华布施故。得作转轮王
七宝具足。复次施得时故。
报亦增多。如佛说。施远行
人远来人。病人看病人。风
寒众难时施。是为时施。复
次布施时随土地所须施故。
得报增多。复次旷路中施
故。得福增多。常施不废
故。得报增多。如求者所欲
施故。得福增多。施物重
故。得福增多。如以精舍园
林浴池等若施善人故。得
报增多。若施僧故。得报
增多。若施者受者俱有德
故。[23](丹注云如菩萨及佛
慈心布施是为施者若施佛及
菩萨阿罗汉辟支佛是为受者
故) 得报增多。种种将迎恭
敬受者故。得福增多。

是為種三十二相因緣。復次
以七寶人民車乘金銀燈燭房
舍香華布施故。得作轉輪王
七寶具足。復次施得時故。
報亦增多。如佛說。施遠行
人遠來人。病人看病人。風
寒眾難時施。是為時施。復
次布施時隨土地所須施故。
得報增多。復次曠路中施
故。得報增多。常施不廢
故。得報增多。如求者所欲
施故。得福增多。施物重
故。得福增多。如以精舍園
林浴池等若施善人故。得
報增多。若施僧故。得報
增多。若施者受者俱有德
故。[23](丹注云如菩薩及佛慈
心布施是為施者若施佛及菩
薩阿羅漢辟支佛是為受者故)
得報增多。種種將迎恭敬受
者故。得福增多。

简体字   正體字

This is how one plants the causes and conditions for the thirty-two marks.

b. Enhanced Effects from Superior Forms of Giving

Furthermore, on account of making gifts of the seven precious things, of workers, of carriages, gold, silver, lamps, candles, buildings, or incense and flowers, one is able to become a wheel-turning monarch possessing the abundance of his seven types of treasures.

Additionally, through making gifts with timely appropriateness, one's resulting karmic reward is increased. This is as explained by the Buddha when he said, "If one gives to a person about to travel far, to a person come from afar, to a sick person, to a person caring for the sick, or if one gives to assist with manifold difficulties arising from winds or cold, this is what is meant by timely giving."

Again, if when one gives in a way which accords with what is most needed in a particular place, one reaps an increased karmic reward from that.

Also, if one performs an act of giving on the road in a wilderness area, one thereby gains an increased measure of merit.

If one continues giving constantly and without neglecting that practice, one gains from that an increased karmic reward.

If one gives a gift which accords with the solicitor's desires, one gains on that account an increased measure of merit.

If one gives gifts which are valuable, one gains an increased measure of merit.

If one gives monastic dwellings, parks, forests, bathing ponds, and so forth—provided that those gifts are bestowed upon people who are good—one gains an increased karmic reward on that account.

If one gives gifts to the Sangha, one thereby gains an increased karmic reward.

If both the benefactor and the recipient are possessed of virtue, an increased karmic reward is gained as a result of that.

(Chinese textual note: "The notes in red read, 'Take for example bodhisattvas and buddhas who give with a mind of compassion. This is what is intended with respect to the benefactor. Giving for example to buddhas, bodhisattvas, arhats, or pratyekabuddhas—this is what is intended in regard to the recipient.'")

When one extends all manner of welcoming courtesies out of respect for the recipient, one gains from this an increased measure of merit.

难得物施故。得福增多。随所有物尽能布施故。得福增多。譬如大月氏弗迦罗城中有一画师。名千那。到东方多[24]刹[25]陀罗国。客画十二年得三十两金。持还本国于弗迦罗城中。闻打鼓作大会声。往见众僧。信心清净即问维那。此众中几许物。得作一日食。维那答曰。三十两金足得一日食。即以所有三十两金付维那。为我作一日食。我明日当来。空手而归。其妇问曰。十二年作得何等物。答言。我得三十两金。即问三十两金今在何所。答言。已在福田中种。妇言。何等福田。答言施与众僧。妇便缚[26]其夫送官治罪断事。大官问。以何事故。妇言我夫[142a]狂痴。十二年[1]客作得三十两金。不怜愍妇儿尽以与他人。依如官制辄缚送来。

難得物施故。得福增多。隨所有物盡能布施故。得福增多。譬如大月氏弗迦羅城中有一畫師。名千那。到東方多[24]刹[25]陀羅國。客畫十二年得三十兩金。持還本國於弗迦羅城中。聞打鼓作大會聲。往見眾僧。信心清淨即問維那。此眾中幾許物。得作一日食。維那答曰。三十兩金足得一日食。即以所有三十兩金付維那。為我作一日食。我明日當來。空手而歸。其婦問曰。十二年作得何等物。答言。我得三十兩金。即問三十兩金今在何所。答言。已在福田中種。婦言。何等福田。答言施與眾僧。婦便縛[26]其夫送官治罪斷事。大官問。以何事故。婦言我夫[142a]狂癡。十二年[1]客作得三十兩金。不憐愍婦兒盡以與他人。依如官制輒縛送來。

简体字　　　　　　　　正體字

If one gives what has been difficult to come by, one gains an increased amount of merit.

If one is able to give all that one has, one gains from that an increased amount of merit.

c. THE PAINTER WHO GAVE AWAY HIS SAVINGS (STORY)

This principle is illustrated by the case of a painter named Karṇa from the city of Puṣkarāvatī in the state of Greater Tokharestan. He had traveled to the east to the state of Takṣaśilā where he served as a painter to that court for a period of twelve years.

He received payment of thirty two-ounce pieces of gold for his work and took it back with him when he journeyed back to the city of Puṣkarāvatī in his home state. He chanced to hear the sound of a drum beating to convene a great assembly. He went there and saw an assembly of the Sangha. With a mind of pure faith he asked the Karmadāna, "How much would be required to provide a day's feast for this assembly?"

The Karmadāna replied, "Thirty two-ounce pieces of gold would be adequate to supply food for one day." At this point, he immediately brought forth the entire sum of thirty two-ounce pieces of gold and entrusted it to the Karmadāna saying, "Prepare on my behalf a day's feast [for this entire assembly]. I will return here tomorrow." He then went back to his home empty-handed.

His wife asked him, "Well, what did you earn for your twelve years of work?"

He replied, "I earned thirty two-ounce pieces of gold."

She immediately asked, "Where are the thirty two-ounce pieces of gold now?"

He replied, "They have already been planted in the merit field."

The wife asked, "What merit field?"

He replied, "I gave them to the assembly of the Sangha." His wife then had him detained and sent before a judge that his crime could be dealt with and the matter properly adjudicated. The Grand Judge asked, "Why is it that we are convened here?"

The wife replied, "My husband has become crazy and deluded. He worked in royal service in a foreign country for twelve years and earned thirty two-ounce pieces of gold. He had no compassionate regard for his wife or child and so gave away the entire sum to other people. Thus, wishing him to be dealt with by judicial decree, I quickly moved to have him detained and brought forth."

大官问其夫。汝何以不供给
妇儿。乃以与他。答言。我
先世不行功德。今世贫穷受
诸辛苦。今世遭遇福田。若
不种福后世复贫。贫贫相续
无得脱时。我今欲顿舍贫
穷。以是故尽以金施众僧。
大官是优婆塞信佛清净。闻
是语已赞言。是为甚难。懃
苦得此少物尽以施僧。汝是
善人。即脱身璎珞及所乘马
并一聚落以施贫人。而语之
言。汝始施众僧。众僧未
食是为谷子未种。[2]牙已得
生。大果方在后[3]身以是故
言。难得之物尽用布施其福
最多。复次有世间檀。有出
世间檀。有圣人所称誉檀。
有圣人所不称誉檀。有佛菩
萨檀。有声闻檀。何等世间
檀。凡夫人布施。亦圣人作
有漏心布施。是名世间檀。
复次有人言。凡夫人布施。
是为世间檀。圣人虽

简体字

大官問其夫。汝何以不供給
婦兒。乃以與他。答言。我
先世不行功德。今世貧窮受
諸辛苦。今世遭遇福田。若
不種福後世復貧。貧貧相續
無得脫時。我今欲頓捨貧
窮。以是故盡以金施眾僧。
大官是優婆塞信佛清淨。聞
是語已讚言。是為甚難。懃
苦得此少物盡以施僧。汝是
善人。即脫身瓔珞及所乘馬
并一聚落以施貧人。而語之
言。汝始施眾僧。眾僧未
食是為穀子未種。[2]牙已得
生。大果方在後[3]身以是故
言。難得之物盡用布施其福
最多。復次有世間檀。有出
世間檀。有聖人所稱譽檀。
有聖人所不稱譽檀。有佛菩
薩檀。有聲聞檀。何等世間
檀。凡夫人布施。亦聖人作
有漏心布施。是名世間檀。
復次有人言。凡夫人布施。
是為世間檀。聖人雖

正體字

The Grand Judge then asked her husband, "Why did you not share it with your wife and child, preferring instead to give the gold away to others?

He replied, "I did not cultivate any merit in previous lives. As a consequence, I am poor in this present life and so have undergone all manner of intense hardship. I have now finally encountered a field of merit in this present life. If I do not plant merit, I will continue to be poor in future lives. As a result, poverty will follow upon poverty continuously with the result that there will never be a time when I become able to escape it. I now wish to immediately relinquish this state of poverty. It is for this reason that I took all of the gold and gave it to the Sangha community."

The Grand Judge happened to be an *upāsaka*[17] who maintained a pure faith in the Buddha. When he heard these words, he praised him, saying, "This is an extremely difficult thing to have done. You applied yourself diligently and underwent hardship in order to obtain such a small material reward. Then you were able to take the entire sum and give it to the Sangha. You are a good man."

He then took off the strand of jewels around his neck and gave it to the poor man along with his horse and the income which he received from the taxes on an entire village. He then declared to him, "At the beginning, when you had made the gift to an assembly of the Sangha, but that assembly of Sangha members had still not partaken of that food, it was a case of the seed still not really having been planted. But now a sprout has already come forth from it. The great fruit of this will come forth in the next life."

It is for reasons such as this that it is said that one gains the most merit if one is able to give all of what has been hard to come by.

E. More Categories of *Dāna*

Moreover, there is worldly *dāna* and there is supramundane *dāna*. There is *dāna* which is praised by the Āryas and there is *dāna* which is not praised by the Āryas. There is the *dāna* performed by the Buddhas and the Bodhisattvas and there is the *dāna* practiced by the Śrāvaka-disciples.

1. Worldly *Dāna* versus Supramundane *Dāna*

What is meant by "worldly *dāna*"? Worldly *dāna* refers to giving as practiced by common people and giving engaged in by āryas when done with a mind still subject to outflow impurities.

Then again, there are those who say that worldly *dāna* refers to giving carried out by common people whereas, although an ārya

有漏心布施。以結使斷故。
名出世间檀。何以故。是圣
人得无作三昧故。复次世间
檀者不净。出世间檀者清
净。二种结使。一种属爱一
种属见。为二种结使所使。
是为世间檀。无此二种结
使。是为出世间檀。若三碍
系心是为世间檀。何以故。
因缘诸法实无吾我。而言我
与彼取。是故名世间檀。复
次我无定处。我以为[4]我彼
以为非。彼以为我我以为
非。以是不定故无实我也。
所施财者从因缘[5]和合有。
无有一法独可得者。如绢如
布。众缘合故成。除丝除缕
则无绢布。诸法亦如是。一
相无相相常自[142b]空。人作
想念计以为有。颠倒不实是
为世间檀。心无三碍实知法
相心不颠倒。是为出世间
檀。出世间檀为圣人所称
誉。世间檀圣人所不称誉。

有漏心布施。以結使斷故。
名出世間檀。何以故。是聖
人得無作三昧故。復次世間
檀者不淨。出世間檀者清
淨。二種結使。一種屬愛一
種屬見。為二種結使所使。
是為世間檀。無此二種結
使。是為出世間檀。若三礙
繫心是為世間檀。何以故。
因緣諸法實無吾我。而言我
與彼取。是故名世間檀。復
次我無定處。我以為[4]我彼
以為非。彼以為我我以為
非。以是不定故無實我也。
所施財者從因緣[5]和合有。
無有一法獨可得者。如絹如
布。眾緣合故成。除絲除縷
則無絹布。諸法亦如是。一
相無相相常自[142b]空。人作
想念計以為有。顛倒不實是
為世間檀。心無三礙實知法
相心不顛倒。是為出世間
檀。出世間檀為聖人所稱
譽。世間檀聖人所不稱譽。

简体字　　　　　　正體字

may give with a mind subject to outflow impurities, because his fetters have been cut off, this action is referred to as supramundane *dāna*. How is this the case? Because this ārya has realized the wishlessness samādhi (*apraṇihita-samādhi*).[18]

Then again, whereas worldly *dāna* is "impure," supramundane *dāna* is "pure."

There are two categories of fetters. One is subsumed under the category of craving and the other under the category of views. When one is under the influence of these two kinds of fetters, this is worldly *dāna*. When these two kinds of fetters are absent, this is supramundane *dāna*.

When the three obstructions[19] tie up the mind, this is worldly *dāna*. How is this so? Dharmas which are the products of causes and conditions are actually devoid of a self. Thus if one says, "It is I who give and he who receives," then that is therefore "worldly" *dāna*.

Additionally, "self" has no fixed location. That which I take to be "self," another person takes to be not so. That which another person takes to be "self," I take to be not so. On account of its being unfixed, there is no actual "self." That valuable object which is given exists through the coming together of causes and conditions. There is no single dharma which, in and of itself, can be found.

This is as exemplified by silk cloth or the other types of fabric. They are composed through the coming together of manifold conditions. Apart from the silk filaments on the one hand and aside from the fibers on the other, there is neither silk cloth nor any other kind of fabric. All dharmas are the same in this respect. They possess one characteristic, that of being devoid of any [inherently existent] characteristics. Their characteristics are themselves eternally empty of any [inherent] existence. People conceptualize and reckon them to be "existent." This is a result of inverted views, for [their existence] is not actually real. [Giving based on such conceptions] is worldly *dāna*.

Where the mind is free of the three obstacles, where one knows the characteristics of dharmas in accordance with reality, and where one's mind remains unaffected by inverted views—this is supramundane *dāna*.

2. *Dāna* Praised and Not Praised by the Āryas

Supramundane *dāna* is that praised by the Āryas. Worldly *dāna* is that not praised by the Āryas.

复次清净檀。不杂[6]结垢如
诸法实相。是圣人所称誉。
不清净杂结使颠倒心着。是
圣人所不称誉。复次实相智
慧和合布施。是圣人所称
誉。若不尔者圣人所不称
誉。复次不为众生。亦不为
知诸法实相故施。但求脱生
老病死。是为声闻檀。为一
切众生故施。亦为知诸法实
相故施。是为诸佛菩萨檀。
于诸功德不能具足。[7]但欲
得少许分。是为声闻檀。一
切诸功德欲具足满。是为诸
佛菩萨檀。畏老病死故施。
是为声闻檀。为助佛道为化
众生不畏老病死。是为诸佛
菩萨檀。是中应说菩萨本生
经。如说阿婆陀那经中。
昔阎浮提中有王。名婆[8]萨
婆。尔时有婆罗门菩萨。名
韦罗摩。是国王师。教王作
转轮圣王法。韦罗摩财富无
量珍宝具足。作是思惟。人
谓我为贵[9]人财富无量。饶
益众生今正是时应当

简体字

復次清淨檀。不雜[6]結垢如
諸法實相。是聖人所稱譽。
不清淨雜結使顛倒心著。是
聖人所不稱譽。復次實相智
慧和合布施。是聖人所稱
譽。若不爾者聖人所不稱
譽。復次不為眾生。亦不為
知諸法實相故施。但求脫生
老病死。是為聲聞檀。為一
切眾生故施。亦為知諸法實
相故施。是為諸佛菩薩檀。
於諸功德不能具足。[7]但欲
得少許分。是為聲聞檀。一
切諸功德欲具足滿。是為諸
佛菩薩檀。畏老病死故施。
是為聲聞檀。為助佛道為化
眾生不畏老病死。是為諸佛
菩薩檀。是中應說菩薩本生
經。如說阿婆陀那經中。
昔閻浮提中有王。名婆[8]薩
婆。爾時有婆羅門菩薩。名
韋羅摩。是國王師。教王作
轉輪聖王法。韋羅摩財富無
量珍寶具足。作是思惟。人
謂我為貴[9]人財富無量。饒
益眾生今正是時應當

正體字

Moreover, pure *dāna* involves no intermixing with the defilement of the fetters and is of a suchness with the true character[20] of dharmas. It is that which is praised by the Āryas. That which is not pure is intermixed with the fetters. It involves attachment by a mind affected by inverted views. It is that which is not praised by the Āryas.

Additionally, that sort ofgiving which occurs in conjunction with the wisdom cognizing the character of reality is that which is praised by the Āryas. If it is not of this sort, then it is not such as is praised by the Āryas.

3. ŚRĀVAKA *DĀNA* VERSUS THAT OF BODHISATTVAS AND BUDDHAS

Moreover, if it is not done for the sake of beings, if it is not done for the sake of realizing the true character of dharmas, and if it is done solely for the sake of gaining liberation from birth, old age, sickness, and death, this is the *dāna* of the Śrāvakas. If one gives for the sake of all beings and if one does so for the sake of realizing the true character of dharmas, this is the *dāna* of the Buddhas and the Bodhisattvas.

If one is unable to make one's giving replete with every manner of meritorious quality, but rather desires only to gain a minor measure thereof, this is the *dāna* of the Śrāvakas. If one wishes to make it entirely replete with every manner of meritorious quality, this is the *dāna* of the Buddhas and the Bodhisattvas.

If one gives out of a fear of old age, sickness, and death, this is the *dāna* of the Śrāvakas. If it is done to assist the realization of the Buddha Path, if it is done for the sake of transforming beings, and if it is not done out of fear of old age, sickness, and death, this is the *dāna* of the Buddhas and the Bodhisattvas.

4. OUTWARD GIVING ILLUSTRATED BY THE STORY OF VELĀMA BODHISATTVA

In this connection, one ought to draw upon the *Sutra of the Past Lives of the Bodhisattva*. As discussed in the *Avadāna Sutra*, in the past, in Jambudvīpa, there was a king named Vāsava. There was at that time a brahman bodhisattva named Velāma who served as the teacher of the King. He taught the King the method for becoming a wheel-turning sage king.[21]

Velāma's own wealth was immeasurable. He possessed an abundance of precious jewels. He had these thoughts: "People look upon me as a noble man possessed of immeasurable wealth. If I am to be of benefit to beings, now is precisely the right time. I should perform

大施。富贵虽乐一切无常。
五家所共令人心散轻[10]泆不
定。譬如猕猴不能暂住。人
命逝速疾于电灭。人身无常
众苦之薮。以是之故应行布
施。如是思惟已自作手疏。
普告阎浮提诸婆罗门及一切
出家人。愿各屈德来集我
舍。欲设大施满十二岁。饭
汁行船以酪为池。米面为山
[11]苏油为渠。衣服饮食卧具
汤药。皆令极妙过十二岁。
欲以布施。八万四千白象犀
甲金饰珞。以名宝[142c]建大
金幢。四宝庄严。八万四千
马。亦以犀甲金饰。四宝[12]
交络。八万四千车。皆以金
银琉璃颇梨宝饰。覆以师子
虎豹之皮。若白剑婆罗宝[13]
[车*宪]杂饰以为庄严。八
万四千四宝床。杂色綩綖种
种茵蓐柔软细滑以为挍饰。
丹枕锦被置床两头。妙衣盛
服皆亦备有。八万四千金钵
盛满银粟。银钵盛金粟。琉
璃钵盛[14]颇梨粟。颇梨钵盛
琉璃粟。八万四千乳牛。牛
出乳一斛。金饰其[15][跳-兆
+甲]角衣以白[16]叠。八万四

大施。富貴雖樂一切無常。
五家所共令人心散輕[10]泆不
定。譬如獼猴不能暫住。人
命逝速疾於電滅。人身無常
眾苦之藪。以是之故應行布
施。如是思惟已自作手疏。
普告閻浮提諸婆羅門及一切
出家人。願各屈德來集我
舍。欲設大施滿十二歲。飯
汁行船以酪為池。米麵為山
[11]蘇油為渠。衣服飲食臥具
湯藥。皆令極妙過十二歲。
欲以布施。八萬四千白象犀
甲金飾珞。以名寶[142c]建大
金幢。四寶莊嚴。八萬四千
馬。亦以犀甲金飾。四寶[12]
交絡。八萬四千車。皆以金
銀琉璃頗梨寶飾。覆以師子
虎豹之皮。若白劍婆羅寶[13]
[車*憲]雜飾以為莊嚴。八萬
四千四寶床。雜色綩綖種種
茵蓐柔軟細滑以為挍飾。丹
枕錦被置床兩頭。妙衣盛服
皆亦備有。八萬四千金鉢盛
滿銀粟。銀鉢盛金粟。琉璃
鉢盛[14]頗梨粟。頗梨鉢盛琉
璃粟。八萬四千乳牛。牛出
乳一斛。金飾其[15][跳-兆＋
甲]角衣以白[16]疊。八萬四

简体字　　　　　　　　　　　　　　　　正體字

a great act of giving. Although being wealthy and noble is blissful, everything is impermanent. This wealth, vulnerable to loss from five destructive agents (the King, thieves, fire, flood, or bad sons), causes a man's mind to be so scattered, agitated and unfocused as to make it like a monkey which is unable to remain still. A person's life passes more quickly than the fading of a lightning bolt. A person's body is impermanent and is a thicket of the manifold sufferings. On account of these things, one ought to practice giving."

After thinking in this way, he wrote out a personal declaration in which he announced to all of the brahmans and monastics throughout Jambudvīpa, "We pray that each shall condescend to come and gather at our estate as we desire to present a great offering lasting for a period of twelve years during which boats will cruise on streams of rice consommé and there will be ponds filled with curds. There will be mountains made of rice and noodles and canals created of *perilla* oil. There will be robes, food, drink, bedding, and medicines. We wish to use such things to make offerings of the most supremely marvelous quality for over a dozen years."

There were eighty-four thousand[22] white elephants girded in gold-adorned rhinoceros-hide armor. Rare gems were strung together to create a huge gold pavilion ornamented with four kinds of precious things. There were eighty-four thousand horses also clad in gold-adorned rhinoceros-hide armor and caparisoned with strands of the four kinds of precious things.

There were eighty-four thousand carriages, each adorned with gold, silver, beryl, and crystal, shaded with the skins of lions, tigers, and leopards, draped with curtains of *pāṇḍukambala* gems, and ornamented with various embellishments.

There were eighty-four thousand precious thrones fitted and adorned with multicolored cushions which were soft and smooth. Arranged at each end of the thrones were crimson pillows and embroidered blankets. Marvelous garments and flowing robes were supplied in abundance. There were eighty-four thousand gold bowls filled with silver nuggets, silver bowls filled with gold nuggets, beryl bowls filled with crystals, and crystal bowls filled with beryl gems.

There were eighty-four thousand dairy cattle. The cows each produced an abundant measure of milk. The horns of the bulls were adorned with gold. They were each dressed in white blankets.

There were eighty-four thousand beautiful women of refined

千美女端正福德。皆以白珠
名宝璎珞其身。略举其要如
是。种种不可胜记。尔时婆
罗婆王及八万四千[17]诸小国
王。并诸臣民豪杰长者。各
以十万旧金钱赠遗劝助。设
此法祠具足施已。释提婆那
民来语韦罗摩菩萨。说此偈
言。
天地难得物。能喜悦一切。
汝今皆[18]以得。为佛道布施。

[142c18] 尔时净居诸天现身而
赞。说此偈言。
开门大布施。汝所为者是。
怜愍众生故。为之求佛道。

[142c21] 是时诸天作是思惟。
我当闭其金瓶令水不下。所
以者何。有施者无福田故。
是时魔王语净居天。此诸婆
罗门。皆出家持戒清净入
道。何以[19]故乃言无有福
田。净居天言。是菩萨为佛
道故布施。今此诸人皆是邪
见。是故我言无有福田。魔
王语天言。云何知是人为佛
道故布施。是时净居天化作
婆罗门身。持金瓶执金杖。
至韦罗摩菩萨所语言。

简体字

appearance and endowed with meritorious qualities. Their bodies were draped in strands of white pearls and precious gems.

This represents only a summary recital of the main features. There were all manner of other arrangements which one could never succeed in detailing.

At that time, King Vāsava and eighty-four thousand kings of lesser states, together with their ministers, national heroes, and those who served as elders each offered a contribution in encouragement and support consisting of ten thousand ancient pieces of gold.

After this Dharma offering had been arranged and completely set forth, the god Śakra Devānām Indra came forth and addressed the Bodhisattva Velāma by uttering this verse:

Those things rarely found in heaven or on earth
Which are able to bring delight to everyone—
You have now already obtained them
And made gifts of them for the sake of the Buddha Path.

The gods of the Pure Dwelling Heaven then appeared there and offered praises through setting forth this verse:

You have thrown open the gate of great giving.
It is on account of feeling pity for all beings
And out of a desire to seek the Buddha Path for their sakes
That you now act here in this manner.

The gods then all thought, "We should stop up his gold vase to prevent the water from flowing forth. Why? Because, although there is a benefactor, there is no one suitable to serve as a field of merit."[23]

The Demon King then said to the gods of the Pure Dwelling Heaven, "All of these brahmans have left behind the home life. They uphold the moral precepts purely and they have entered upon the Path. Why is it that you now say there is no one to serve as a field of merit?"

The gods of the Pure Dwelling Heaven said, "This bodhisattva is giving for the sake of the Buddha Path. All of those now here are possessed of erroneous views. It is for this reason that we claim there is no one to serve as a field of merit."

The Demon King said to the gods, "How do you know that this man is giving for the sake of the Buddha Path?"

One of the Pure Dwelling gods then appeared in the body of a brahman. Holding a gold vase and a staff made of gold, he went

汝大布施难舍能舍欲求何
等。欲作转[143a]轮圣王七宝
千子王四天下耶。菩萨答
言。不求此事。汝求释提婆
那民。为八[1]千那由他天女
主耶。答言不。汝求六欲天
主耶。答言不。汝求梵天王
主三千大千世界为众生祖父
耶。答言不。汝欲何所求。
是时菩萨。说此偈言。
我求无欲处。离生老病死。
[2]欲度诸众生。求如是佛道。

[143a09]　　化婆罗[3]门言。布施
主。佛道难得当大辛苦。汝
心软串乐。必不能求成办此
道。如我先语。转轮圣王释
提婆那民六欲天王梵天王是
易可得。不如求此。菩萨答
言。汝听我一心誓。
假令热铁轮。在我头上转。
一心求佛道。终不怀悔恨。
若使三恶道。人中无量苦。
一心求佛道。终不为此转。

[143a18]　　　化婆罗门言。布施
主。

简体字

汝大布施難捨能捨欲求何
等。欲作轉[143a]輪聖王七寶
千子王四天下耶。菩薩答
言。不求此事。汝求釋提婆
那民。為八[1]千那由他天女
主耶。答言不。汝求六欲天
主耶。答言不。汝求梵天王
主三千大千世界為眾生祖父
耶。答言不。汝欲何所求。
是時菩薩。說此偈言。
我求無欲處。離生老病死。
[2]欲度諸眾生。求如是佛道。

[143a09]　　化婆羅[3]門言。布施
主。佛道難得當大辛苦。汝
心軟串樂。必不能求成辦此
道。如我先語。轉輪聖王釋
提婆那民六欲天王梵天王是
易可得。不如求此。菩薩答
言。汝聽我一心誓。
假令熱鐵輪。在我頭上轉。
一心求佛道。終不懷悔恨。
若使三惡道。人中無量苦。
一心求佛道。終不為此轉。

[143a18]　　　化婆羅門言。布施
主。

正體字

up to the Bodhisattva Velāma and said to him, "What is it that you seek to gain through this act of great giving where you relinquishing what is so hard to give up? Is it that you desire to become a wheel-turning sage king who owns the seven precious things, has a thousand sons, and enjoys dominion over the entire world?"

The Bodhisattva replied, "I do not seek any such circumstance."

"Is it that you seek to become Śakra Devānām Indra so that you might then be lord to eight thousand *nayutas* of heavenly nymphs?"

He replied, "No."

"Are you seeking to become the Lord of the Six Desire Heavens?"

He replied, "No."

"Are you seeking to become the Brahma Heaven God who serves as lord over the great trichiliocosm and who is looked on as the patriarchal father of all beings?"

He replied, "No."

"What is it that you seek?"

The Bodhisattva then uttered a verse, saying:

I seek that place which is free of desire
And which transcends birth, aging, sickness, and death.
I yearn to bring deliverance to all beings.
I seek the Buddha Path which is just so.

That transformationally-produced brahman declared, "Benefactor, the Buddha Path is difficult to achieve. It is beset with great bitterness and suffering. Your mind is soft and accustomed to pleasures. It is certainly the case that you will be unable to seek out and accomplish realization of this path. As I suggested before: to become a wheel-turning sage king, or Śakra Devānām Indra, or King of the Six Desire Heavens, or the King of the Brahma Heaven gods—these would be easily achievable. There would be nothing so good as to seek these."

The Bodhisattva replied, "Listen to my single-minded vow:"

Even were one to cause a wheel of burning-hot steel
To be set spinning right on top of my head,
I would still single-mindedly seek out the Buddha Path
And never cherish any regrets over doing so.

Even were I subjected to the three wretched destinies
And to the countless sufferings of the human realm,
I would still single-mindedly seek the Buddha Path
And would never be turned aside by these things.

善哉善哉求佛如是。便赞偈
言。

汝精进力大。慈愍于一切。
智慧无罣碍。成佛在不久。

[143a22] 是时天雨众华供养菩
萨。诸净居天闭瓶水者即隐
不现。菩萨是时至婆罗门上
座前。以金瓶行水。水闭不
下众人疑怪。此种种[4]大施
一切具足。布施主人功德亦
大。今何以故瓶水不下。菩
萨自念。此非他事。将无我
心不清净耶。得无施物不具
足乎。何以致此。自观祠经
十六种书清净无瑕。是时诸
天语菩萨言。汝莫疑悔。汝
无不办。是诸[143b]婆罗门恶
邪不净故也。即说偈言。

是人邪见网。烦恼破正智。
离诸清净戒。唐苦堕[5]异道。

[143b04] 以是故水闭不下。如
是语已忽然不现。尔时六欲
天放种种光明

善哉善哉求佛如是。便讚偈
言。

汝精進力大。慈愍於一切。
智慧無罣礙。成佛在不久。

[143a22] 是時天雨眾華供養菩
薩。諸淨居天閉瓶水者即隱
不現。菩薩是時至婆羅門上
座前。以金瓶行水。水閉不
下眾人疑怪。此種種[4]大施
一切具足。布施主人功德亦
大。今何以故瓶水不下。菩
薩自念。此非他事。將無我
心不清淨耶。得無施物不具
足乎。何以致此。自觀祠經
十六種書清淨無瑕。是時諸
天語菩薩言。汝莫疑悔。汝
無不辦。是諸[143b]婆羅門惡
邪不淨故也。即說偈言。

是人邪見網。煩惱破正智。
離諸清淨戒。唐苦墮[5]異道。

[143b04] 以是故水閉不下。如
是語已忽然不現。爾時六欲
天放種種光明

简体字

正體字

The transformationally-produced brahman said, "Oh Benefactor, it is good indeed, good indeed that you seek buddhahood in this manner." He then uttered a praise, saying,

> The power arising from your vigor is immense.
> You manifest kindness and pity extending to everyone.
> Your wisdom has become detached and unobstructed.
> Your realization of buddhahood cannot be far off.

The gods then rained down a profusion of blossoms as an offering to the Bodhisattva. The gods of the Pure Dwelling Heaven who had stopped up the water from the vase then disappeared from sight.

The Bodhisattva then went before the most senior ranked among the brahmans and attempted to pour forth the water from the gold vase [and thus formally endow them as recipients of his offerings]. However, the water remained stopped up and would not flow out. The members of the assembly were then overcome with doubt and consternation and wondered, "All of these various kinds of great giving are replete in every way and the benefactor's meritorious qualities are also immense. Why then does the water now fail to flow forth from the vase?"

The Bodhisattva thought to himself, "This circumstance could be due to nothing other than one of these factors: Have I freed my mind of all impurity? Have I achieved a situation where there are no deficiencies in the gifts? What could have brought this about?" He then personally reflected upon the sixteen parts of the *Classic on Giving* and found that all preparations were pure and free of defects.

The gods then spoke to the Bodhisattva, saying, "Do not become overcome by doubt and regret. There is nothing which you have failed to accomplish. Rather, it is because these brahmans themselves are marked by unwholesomeness, error, and impurity." They then set forth a verse:

> These men are caught in the net of erroneous views.
> Their afflictions have brought on destruction of right wisdom.
> They abandon purity in the observance of moral precepts.
> They indulge useless asceticism and fall into unorthodox paths.

"It is for these reasons that the water has become stopped up and so refuses to pour on forth."

Having said this, they suddenly disappeared. The gods of the Six Desire Heavens then emitted many different kinds of light which

照诸众会。语菩萨而说偈言。

[6]邪恶海中行。不顺汝正道。
诸受施人中。无有如汝者。

[143b09] 说是语已忽然不现。是时菩萨闻说此偈自念。会中实自无有与我等者。水闭不下其将为此[7]乎。即说偈言。

若有十方天地中。
诸有好人清净者。
我今归命稽首礼。
右手执瓶灌左手。
而自立愿我一人。
应受如是大布施。

[143b15] 是时瓶水[8]踊在虚空从上来下而灌其左手。是时[9]婆[10]萨婆王。见是感应心生恭敬。而说偈言。

大婆罗门主。清琉璃色水。
从上流注下。来堕汝手中。

[143b20] 是时大婆罗门众恭敬心生。合手作礼归命菩萨。菩萨是时说此偈言。

今我所布施。不求三界福。
为诸众生故。以用求佛道。

[143b24] 说此偈已。一切大地山川树木皆六[11]返震动。韦罗摩

简体字

照諸眾會。語菩薩而說偈言。

[6]邪惡海中行。不順汝正道。
諸受施人中。無有如汝者。

[143b09] 說是語已忽然不現。是時菩薩聞說此偈自念。會中實自無有與我等者。水閉不下其將為此[7]乎。即說偈言。

若有十方天地中。
諸有好人清淨者。
我今歸命稽首禮。
右手執瓶灌左手。
而自立願我一人。
應受如是大布施。

[143b15] 是時瓶水[8]踊在虛空從上來下而灌其左手。是時[9]婆[10]薩婆王。見是感應心生恭敬。而說偈言。

大婆羅門主。清琉璃色水。
從上流注下。來墮汝手中。

[143b20] 是時大婆羅門眾恭敬心生。合手作禮歸命菩薩。菩薩是時說此偈言。

今我所布施。不求三界福。
為諸眾生故。以用求佛道。

[143b24] 說此偈已。一切大地山川樹木皆六[11]返震動。韋羅摩

正體字

illuminated the entire assembly and then spoke to the Bodhisattva, proclaiming in a verse:

> Practices from within the sea of error and unwholesomeness
> Do not accord with your orthodox path.
> Among the recipients of your gifts,
> There are none who can compare with you.

After speaking in this way, they suddenly disappeared. After the Bodhisattva had listened to this verse, he then thought to himself, "If it were actually the case that there was no one in the assembly who could serve as my equal, the water would indeed be stopped up and so would not flow forth. Could it actually be then that it is on account of this?" He then uttered a verse:

> Throughout the ten directions, in the heavens or on earth,
> Wherever there are good and pure people—
> I now take refuge in them and, in reverence, make obeisance.
> With a vase in the right hand, I pour an ablution on the left hand.
>
> Having done so, I pray that I, this one man,
> Should should be able to take on such a great offering.[24]

The water from the vase then straightaway spouted forth into the air, descended from above, and came down as an ablution upon his left hand. Then, when King Vāsava had witnessed this marvelous response, his mind became filled with reverence and he uttered a verse, saying:

> Great Lord of the Brahmans,
> This clear beryl-hued water
> Has flowed on down from above
> And, falling, has come to rest in your hand.

At that time, there arose thoughts of reverence in the minds of those brahmans in the great assembly. They placed their palms together, made obeisance, and took refuge in the Bodhisattva. At this time, the Bodhisattva uttered this verse, saying:

> That which I have now given
> Is not in quest of any blessings within the three realms.[25]
> It is for the sake of all beings,
> And is to be employed in seeking the Buddha Path.

After he had spoken this verse, the entire earth with its mountains, rivers, and trees quaked and moved in six ways. Velāma had

本谓此众应受供养故与。既知[12]此众无堪受者。今以怜愍故。以所受物施之。如是种种檀本生因缘。是中应广说。是为外布施。云何名内布施。不惜身命施诸众生。如本生因缘说。释迦文佛本为菩[143c]萨为大国王时。世无佛无法无比丘僧。是王四出求索佛法。了不能得。时有一婆罗门言。我知佛偈。供养我者当以与汝。王即问言。索何等供养。答[13]言。汝能就汝身上。破肉为灯炷供养我者。当以与汝。王心念言。今我此身危脆不净。世世受苦不可复数。未曾为法今始得用甚不惜也。如是念已唤旃陀罗。遍割身上以作灯炷。而以白[*]叠缠肉酥油灌之。一时遍烧举身。火燃。乃与一偈。又复释迦文佛本作一鸽在雪山中。时大雨雪。有一人失道穷厄辛苦。饥寒

简体字

本謂此眾應受供養故與。既知[12]此眾無堪受者。今以憐愍故。以所受物施之。如是種種檀本生因緣。是中應廣說。是為外布施。云何名內布施。不惜身命施諸眾生。如本生因緣說。釋迦文佛本為菩[143c]薩為大國王時。世無佛無法無比丘僧。是王四出求索佛法。了不能得。時有一婆羅門言。我知佛偈。供養我者當以與汝。王即問言。索何等供養。答[13]言。汝能就汝身上。破肉為燈炷供養我者。當以與汝。王心念言。今我此身危脆不淨。世世受苦不可復數。未曾為法今始得用甚不惜也。如是念已喚旃陀羅。遍割身上以作燈炷。而以白[*]疊纏肉酥油灌之。一時遍燒舉身。火燃。乃與一偈。又復釋迦文佛本作一鴿在雪山中。時大雨雪。有一人失道窮厄辛苦。飢寒

正體字

originally been of the opinion that this assembly should be the recipient of the offering and so he had planned to bestow it upon them. Now, even having realized there was no one present in the assembly worthy to accept the offerings, out of pity, he nonetheless gave to them all those things which he had himself just accepted.

Ideally, one would proceed at this point into an extensive discussion of all sorts of similar past-life causes and conditions associated with *dāna*. The foregoing was an example of "outward giving."

5. INWARD GIVING

What is meant by "inward giving"? It refers to not stinting even in sacrificing one's own life as one gives for the sake of beings.

a. THE BODHISATTVA WHO SACRIFICED HIS BODY FOR DHARMA (STORY)

This idea is as discussed in the [stories of the Buddha's] past-life causes and conditions, in a tale relating a time when, as a bodhisattva, Shākyamuni Buddha was serving as the king of a great country. The world had no buddha, no Dharma, and no sangha of bhikshus. This king searched in the four directions for the Dharma of the Buddha, but was finally unable to find it.

There happened to be at that time a brahman who said, "I know a verse uttered by the Buddha. If an offering is made to me, I will give it to you."

The King then asked, "What sort of offering are you seeking?"

He replied, "If you are able to break open your flesh and turn it into a torch as an offering to me, then I shall give it to you."

The King then thought to himself, "This body of mine is fragile and impure. The amount of suffering which I have undergone on its behalf in life after life is incalculable. It has never been for the sake of Dharma. Only now does it begin to be truly useful. It is certainly not to be spared now."

After reflecting thus, he called forth a *caṇḍāla* and ordered him to scrape the surface of his entire body so that it might serve as a torch. Then the *caṇḍāla* wrapped the King's flesh in white cloth, drenched it in ghee, and set fire to his entire body. Only once the fire had been lit did the brahman bestow on him that single verse.

b. THE BUDDHA'S PAST LIFE AS A PIGEON (STORY)

Additionally, in a previous life, Shakyamuni Buddha was a pigeon in the snowy mountains. On one occasion, there was a great blizzard. There was a man who had lost his way. He was poor and in miserable straits, undergoing bitter suffering. Hunger and cold

并至命在须臾。鸽见此人即
飞求火。为其聚薪然之。又
复以身投火施此饥人。如是
等头目髓脑给施众生。种种
本生因缘经此中应广说。如
是等种种是名内布施。如是
内外布施无量。是名檀相。

并至命在须臾。鴒見此人即
飛求火。為其聚薪然之。又
復以身投火施此飢人。如是
等頭目髓腦給施眾生。種種
本生因緣經此中應廣說。如
是等種種是名內布施。如是
內外布施無量。是名檀相。

简体字

正體字

were both upon him, so much so that his life hung in the balance at that very moment. The pigeon saw this man and immediately flew in search of fire, piling up twigs and then lighting them. He additionally then cast his own body upon the fire as a gift to this starving man.

In just such a manner, he gave up his head, eyes, marrow, and brains for beings. Ideally, one would cite here many comparable instances from the *Sutra on the Causes and Conditions of Previous Lives*. All sorts of similar cases show what is meant by "inward" giving. There are innumerable cases of inward and outward giving such as considered above. These illustrate the defining features of *dāna*.

[*]大智度论[14]释初品中檀波罗蜜法施[15]义第二十。

[143c19] 问曰。云何名法布施。答曰。有人言。常以好语有所利益。是为法施。复次有人言。以诸佛语妙善之法。为人演说。是为法施。复次有人言。以三种法教人。一修妬路二毘尼三阿毘昙。是为法施。复次有人言。以四种法藏教人。一修妬路藏二毘尼藏三阿毘昙藏四杂藏。是为法施。复次有人言。略说以二种法教人。一声闻法二摩诃衍法。是为法施。问曰。如提婆达呵多等。亦以三藏四藏声闻法摩诃衍法教人。而身入地狱是事云何。答曰。提婆达邪见罪多。呵多妄语罪多。[144a]非是为道清净法施。[1]但

[*]大智度論[14]釋初品中檀波羅蜜法施[15]義第二十。

[143c19] 問曰。云何名法布施。答曰。有人言。常以好語有所利益。是為法施。復次有人言。以諸佛語妙善之法。為人演說。是為法施。復次有人言。以三種法教人。一修妬路二毘尼三阿毘曇。是為法施。復次有人言。以四種法藏教人。一修妬路藏二毘尼藏三阿毘曇藏四雜藏。是為法施。復次有人言。略說以二種法教人。一聲聞法二摩訶衍法。是為法施。問曰。如提婆達呵多等。亦以三藏四藏聲聞法摩訶衍法教人。而身入地獄是事云何。答曰。提婆達邪見罪多。呵多妄語罪多。[144a]非是為道清淨法施。[1]但

简体字　　　　　　　　　正體字

Chapter 20: On Dharma Giving & Other Important Topics

IV. CHAPTER 20: ON DHARMA GIVING & OTHER IMPORTANT TOPICS

  A. FIVE DEFINITIONS OF DHARMA GIVING

Question: What is meant by the giving of Dharma?

Response: There are those who say that the giving of Dharma consists of being of benefit to others through the constant use of fine words.

Then again there are those people who explain that the giving of Dharma is an activity which consists of the proclamation to other people of the marvelously fine dharmas contained within the discourses of the Buddhas.

Yet again, there are those people who say that the giving of Dharma consists of using three kinds of Dharma to provide instruction to other people: first, the Sutras; second, the Vinaya; and third, the Abhidharma.

Then again, there are those people who say that the giving of Dharma consists of employing four kinds of Dharma treasuries [within the Buddhist canon] to teach people: first, the Sutra collection; second, the Vinaya collection; third, the Abhidharma collection; and fourth, the "Various Topics" collection.

Additionally, there are people who say that, generally speaking, the giving of Dharma consists of employing two kinds of Dharma to teach people: first, the Dharma of the Śrāvaka-disciples; and second, the Dharma of the Mahāyāna.

  B. WHY SOME DHARMA BENEFACTORS FALL INTO THE HELLS

Question: Individuals such as Devadatta, Hatthaka and others also employed the three collections, the four collections, the Dharma of the Śrāvaka-disciples, and the Dharma of the Mahāyāna to teach people and yet they themselves nonetheless fell into the hells. How did this circumstance develop?

    1. THE ESSENTIAL FACTORS IN GENUINE DHARMA GIVING

Response: Devadatta had incurred many offenses arising from erroneous views. Hatthaka incurred many offenses arising from false speech. It is not the case that their actions qualified as pure giving done for the sake of the Path. It was done solely for the sake

求名利恭敬供养。恶心罪故
提婆达生入地狱。呵多死堕
恶道。复次非但言说名为法
施。常以净心善[2]思。以教
一切是名法施。譬如财施不
以善心不名福德法施亦尔。
不以净心善思则非法施。复
次说法者。能以净心善思赞
叹三宝。开罪福门示四真
谛。教化众生令入佛道。是
为真净法施。复次略说法有
二种。一者不恼众生善心慈
愍。是为佛道因缘。二者观
知诸法真空。是为涅盘道因
缘。在大众中兴愍哀心说此
二法。不为名闻利养恭敬。
是为清净佛道法施。如说。
阿输伽王一日作八万佛图。
虽未见道于佛法中少有信
乐。日日请诸比丘入宫供
养。日日次第留法师说法。

求名利恭敬供養。惡心罪故
提婆達生入地獄。呵多死墮
惡道。復次非但言說名為法
施。常以淨心善[2]思。以教
一切是名法施。譬如財施不
以善心不名福德法施亦爾。
不以淨心善思則非法施。復
次說法者。能以淨心善思讚
歎三寶。開罪福門示四真
諦。教化眾生令入佛道。是
為真淨法施。復次略說法有
二種。一者不惱眾生善心慈
愍。是為佛道因緣。二者觀
知諸法真空。是為涅槃道因
緣。在大眾中興愍哀心說此
二法。不為名聞利養恭敬。
是為清淨佛道法施。如說。
阿輸伽王一日作八萬佛圖。
雖未見道於佛法中少有信
樂。日日請諸比丘入宮供
養。日日次第留法師說法。

简体字　　　　　　　正體字

of seeking fame, self-benefit, reverence, and offerings. On account of the offenses created by his unwholesome mind, Devadatta entered the hells even while still alive. When Hatthaka died, he too fell into the wretched destinies.

Moreover, the giving of Dharma does not consist solely of words and speech. The giving of Dharma consists of constantly employing a pure mind and wholesome thoughts in the offering of instruction to everyone. Just as it is with the giving of material gifts wherein there is no measure of blessings or virtue associated with it if one fails to maintain a wholesome mind, so too it is with the giving of Dharma: If one fails to maintain a pure mind and wholesome thoughts, then it is not the case that this actually qualifies as the giving of Dharma.

Then again, if the speaker of Dharma is able to maintain a pure mind and wholesome thought as he praises the Three Jewels, opens the door to understanding offenses and blessings, explains the four truths, and thus goes about teaching and transforming beings so that they are caused to enter the Buddha Path, this does qualify as true and pure Dharma giving.

Looked at another way, generally speaking, the Dharma [to be given] is of two types: The first consists of refraining from afflicting beings while also maintaining a wholesome mind, kindness, and sympathy. This constitutes the causal basis for the path to buddhahood. The second consists of contemplating and realizing that all dharmas are truly empty. This constitutes the causal basis for the path to nirvāṇa.

If, while in the midst of the Great Assembly, one lets flourish a deeply compassionate mind as one sets forth these two types of Dharma, and if in doing so it is not done for the sake of garnering fame, offerings, or expressions of reverence, this constitutes pure Dharma giving rooted in the Buddha Path.

2. The Monk with the Fragrant Breath (Story)

This concept is illustrated in a story told in connection with King Aśoka who in a single day was responsible for the creation of eighty-thousand buddha stupas. Although he had not yet gained "the path of seeing,"[26] still, he did find a measure of faith and bliss in the Dharma of the Buddha. Every single day, he invited bhikshus to enter the palace to receive offerings. And every single day, he retained one Dharma Master, by order of seniority, to speak the Dharma.

有一三藏年少法师。聪明端
正次应说法。在王边坐。口
有异香。王甚疑怪谓为不
端。欲以香气动王宫人。语
比丘言。口中何等开口看
之。即为开口了无所有。与
水令漱香气如故。王问。大
德新有此香旧有之耶。比丘
答言。如此久有非适今也。
又问有此久如。[3]比丘以偈
答[*]言。
迦叶佛时。集此香法。
如是久久。常若新出。

[144a25] 王言。大德略说未
解。为我广演。答[*]言。王
当一心善听我说。我昔于迦
叶佛法中作说法比丘。常在
大众之中欢喜演说。迦叶世
尊无量功德诸法实相。无量
法门慇懃赞[4]叹教[144b]诲一
切。自是以来常有妙香从口
中出。世世不绝恒如今日。
而说此偈。
草木诸华香。此香气超绝。
能悦一切心。世世常不灭。

简体字

有一三藏年少法師。聰明端
正次應說法。在王邊坐。口
有異香。王甚疑怪謂為不
端。欲以香氣動王宮人。語
比丘言。口中何等開口看
之。即為開口了無所有。與
水令漱香氣如故。王問。大
德新有此香舊有之耶。比丘
答言。如此久有非適今也。
又問有此久如。[3]比丘以偈
答[*]言。
迦葉佛時。集此香法。
如是久久。常若新出。

[144a25] 王言。大德略說未
解。為我廣演。答[*]言。王
當一心善聽我說。我昔於迦
葉佛法中作說法比丘。常在
大眾之中歡喜演說。迦葉世
尊無量功德諸法實相。無量
法門慇懃讚[4]歎教[144b]誨一
切。自是以來常有妙香從口
中出。世世不絕恒如今日。
而說此偈。
草木諸華香。此香氣超絕。
能悅一切心。世世常不滅。

正體字

On one of these days, there was a young Dharma Master, a master of the Tripiṭaka, who was intelligent and handsome and next in order to speak the Dharma. He sat down next to the King. His mouth exuded an exotic fragrance. The King was filled with extreme doubt and suspicion. He was of the opinion that this constituted a deliberate impropriety arising from a desire to employ a fragrant scent to influence the retinue in the royal palace.

The King asked the bhikshu, "What do you have in your mouth? Open your mouth so I can see into it." [The bhikshu] then opened his mouth for [the King] and it turned out that there was nothing whatsoever therein. He was ordered to rinse out his mouth with water after which the fragrance remained just as before. The King asked, "Venerable One, is this fragrance newly manifest or has it been with you for a long time?"

The bhikshu replied, "It has been like this for a long time. It is not the case that it is just appearing now."

He continued, inquiring, "How long has it been this way?"

The bhikshu replied in verse:

It was at the time of Kāśyapa Buddha
That I gathered the Dharma underlying this fragrance.
It has remained so like this for a very long time,
And has always been fresh as if newly arisen.

The King said, "Venerable One, I do not yet understand this brief explanation. Pray, expound on it more extensively for me."

He replied, "The King should listen well and single-mindedly to my explanation. In the past, during the time of Kāśyapa Buddha's Dharma, I was a Dharma-proclaiming bhikshu who, in the midst of the Great Assembly, constantly took pleasure in expounding on the immeasurable qualities of Kāśyapa, the Bhagavān, on the true character of dharmas, and on an incalculable number of methods to access the Dharma.

I conscientiously and earnestly set forth praises and offered instruction to everyone. From that time to the present day, I have always had a marvelous fragrance coming forth from my mouth. This has been the case in life after life without cease. It has constantly been just as it is on this very day." He then set forth a verse:

The fragrance from flowers on shrubs and on trees
Is utterly surpassed by this incense-like fragrance.
It is able to please the minds of all people.
In life after life it abides without ceasing.

[144b04] [5]于时国王愧喜交
集。白比丘言。未曾有也。
说法功德大果乃尔。比丘
言。此名为华。未是果也。
王言其果云何愿为演说。答
言。果略说有十。王谛听
之。即为说偈[6]言。
大名闻端[7]政。得乐及恭敬。
威光如日[8]月。为一切所爱。
辩才有大智。能尽一切结。
苦灭得涅盘。如是名为十。

[144b12] 王言。大德。赞佛功
德云何而得如是果报。尔时
比丘以偈答曰。
赞佛诸功德。令一切普闻。
以此果报故。而得大名誉。
赞佛实功德。令一切欢喜。
以此功德故。世世常端正。
为人说罪福。令得安乐所。
以此之功德。受乐常欢豫。
赞佛功德力。令一切心伏。
以此功德故。常获恭敬报。
显现说法灯。照悟诸众生。
以此之功德。威光如日曜。

简体字

[144b04] [5]于時國王愧喜交
集。白比丘言。未曾有也。
說法功德大果乃爾。比丘
言。此名為華。未是果也。
王言其果云何願為演說。答
言。果略說有十。王諦聽
之。即為說偈[6]言。
大名聞端[7]政。得樂及恭敬。
威光如日[8]月。為一切所愛。
辯才有大智。能盡一切結。
苦滅得涅槃。如是名為十。

[144b12] 王言。大德。讚佛功
德云何而得如是果報。爾時
比丘以偈答曰。
讚佛諸功德。令一切普聞。
以此果報故。而得大名譽。
讚佛實功德。令一切歡喜。
以此功德故。世世常端正。
為人說罪福。令得安樂所。
以此之功德。受樂常歡豫。
讚佛功德力。令一切心伏。
以此功德故。常獲恭敬報。
顯現說法燈。照悟諸眾生。
以此之功德。威光如日曜。

正體字

The King was filled with a mixture of shame and delight. He said to the bhikshu, "This is such as has never been before. The merit of speaking the Dharma brings such a great fruition as this."

The bhikshu said, "This may be thought of as merely the blossom. It is not yet the fruit."

The King asked, "What is its fruit? Pray, explain this for me."

He replied, "Briefly speaking, the fruits are tenfold. May the King listen earnestly." He then uttered a verse for his sake:

There is a grand reputation and finely-formed features.
One experiences bliss and is the object of reverence.
There shines awesome brilliance like sunshine and moonlight.
So thus one becomes a man loved by all people.

There is eloquence and also there is prodigious wisdom.
One is able to end then the grip of the fetters.
One ceases all suffering and reaches nirvāṇa.
And so in this manner the count reaches to ten.

The King asked, "Venerable One, How is it that one gains such a reward as a result of praising the qualities of the Buddha?"

The bhikshu then replied in verse, saying:

If one praises the qualities possessed by the Buddha
And causes this to be heard everywhere by all people,
On account of results which come forth as reward,
One comes to be known by a grand reputation.

If one praises the genuine qualities of Buddha
And causes all people to experience delight,
On account of the [force] which is born from this merit,
In life after life features always are fine.

If one explains for people offenses and blessings,
Allowing them to reach a place of peace and delight,
On account of the merit which is thus produced,
One experiences bliss and is always content.

The powers of praising the merits of Buddha
Cause everyone hearing to have minds made humble.
On account of the power produced by this merit,
One eternally garners men's reverence as reward.

Displaying the lamp of the speaking of Dharma
Illumining and wakening all of the people—
On account of the power produced by this merit,
One's awesome bright brilliance shines forth like the sun.

种种赞佛德。能悦于一切。
以此功德故。常为人所爱。
巧言赞佛德。无量无穷已。
以此功德故。辩才不可尽。
赞佛诸妙法。一切无过者。
以此功德故。大智慧清净。

[144c]

赞佛功德时。令人烦恼薄。
以此功德故。结尽诸垢灭。
二种结尽故。涅盘身已[9]证。
譬如澍大雨。火[10]尽无馀热。

[144c05]　　重告王言。若有未悟今是问时。当以智箭破汝疑军。王白法师。我心悦悟无所疑也。大德福人善能赞佛。如是等种种因缘说法度人。名为法施。问曰。财施法施何[11]者为胜。答曰。如佛所言二施之中法施为胜。所以者何。财施果报在欲界中。

簡体字

種種讚佛德。能悅於一切。
以此功德故。常為人所愛。
巧言讚佛德。無量無窮已。
以此功德故。辯才不可盡。
讚佛諸妙法。一切無過者。
以此功德故。大智慧清淨。

[144c]

讚佛功德時。令人煩惱薄。
以此功德故。結盡諸垢滅。
二種結盡故。涅槃身已[9]證。
譬如澍大雨。火[10]盡無餘熱。

[144c05]　　重告王言。若有未悟今是問時。當以智箭破汝疑軍。王白法師。我心悅悟無所疑也。大德福人善能讚佛。如是等種種因緣說法度人。名為法施。問曰。財施法施何[11]者為勝。答曰。如佛所言二施之中法施為勝。所以者何。財施果報在欲界中。

正體字

If in many a fashion one praises Buddha's merits
And delights thus the hearts of all [by those words],
On account of the power produced by this merit,
One is ever the object of people's affection.

If with clever discourse one praises Buddha's merits
Which cannot be measured and cannot be exhausted,
On account of the power produced by this merit,
One's eloquent speech is never brought to an end.

If one praises the marvelous dharmas of Buddha
Which are such as no one can ever surpass,
On account of the power produced by this merit,
One possesses great wisdom which is pure in its nature.

When one praises the qualities possessed by the Buddha,
One causes afflictions of men to be scant.
On account of the power produced by this merit,
Fetters are cut off and defilements destroyed.

Because both kinds of fetters are brought to an end,
Nirvāṇa in this body has already been achieved,
As when torrents of rain pour down from the sky
All fires are extinguished and no embers remain.

Once again, he addressed the King, saying, "If there still remains anything to which you've not awakened, now is the time to bring questions forth. The arrows of wisdom should be used to demolish your army of doubts."

The King replied to the Dharma master, "My mind has been both delighted and awakened such that now there remain no more objects of doubt. The Venerable One is a blessed man well able to speak forth the praises of Buddha."

When one speaks forth the Dharma in accord with the various causes and conditions discussed above and so brings about the deliverance of beings, this qualifies then as the giving of Dharma.

C. Material Giving and Dharma Giving Compared

Question: Which is supreme, the giving of material wealth or the giving of Dharma?

Response: According to the words of the Buddha, among the two kinds of giving, the giving of Dharma is supreme. Why is that? The reward resulting from the giving of material wealth is experienced within the desire realm. The reward resulting from

法施果报或在三界。或出三界。[12]复次口说清净深得理中。心亦得之故出三界。复次财施有量。法施无量。财施有尽。法施无尽。譬如以薪益火其明转多。复次财施之报净少垢多。法施之报垢少净多。复次若作大施必待众力。法施出心不待他[13]也。复次财施能令四大诸根增长。法施能令无漏根力觉道具足。复次财施之法。有佛无佛世间常有。如法施者唯有佛世乃当有耳。是故当知法施甚难。云何为难。乃至有相辟支佛不能说法。直行乞食飞腾变化而以度人。复次从法施中能出生财施。及诸声闻辟支佛菩萨及佛。复次法施能分别诸法。有漏无漏法。色法无色法。有为无为法。善不善无记

法施果報或在三界。或出三界。[12]復次口說清淨深得理中。心亦得之故出三界。復次財施有量。法施無量。財施有盡。法施無盡。譬如以薪益火其明轉多。復次財施之報淨少垢多。法施之報垢少淨多。復次若作大施必待眾力。法施出心不待他[13]也。復次財施能令四大諸根增長。法施能令無漏根力覺道具足。復次財施之法。有佛無佛世間常有。如法施者唯有佛世乃當有耳。是故當知法施甚難。云何為難。乃至有相辟支佛不能說法。直行乞食飛騰變化而以度人。復次從法施中能出生財施。及諸聲聞辟支佛菩薩及佛。復次法施能分別諸法。有漏無漏法。色法無色法。有為無為法。善不善無記

简体字   正體字

the giving of Dharma may be experienced either within the three realms or beyond the three realms.

Moreover, if one's discourse is pure, if it reaches deeply into its principles, and if one's mind also realizes it, then, on that account, one reaches beyond the three realms.

Again, whereas the giving of material wealth is measurable, the giving of Dharma is immeasurable. Material giving is such as can be exhausted. The giving of Dharma, however, is inexhaustible. It is analogous to increasing the intensity of a fire through the addition of more fuel: its brightness becomes yet greater.

Then again, in the reward gained from the giving of material wealth, there is relatively less purity and more defilement. In the reward gained from the giving of Dharma, there is relatively less defilement and more purity.

Also, if one engages in the giving of material wealth, one depends on the power of many others. The giving of Dharma, however, comes forth from the mind. It does not depend upon others.

Additionally, the giving of material wealth is able to cause enhancement of the faculties associated with the four physical elements. The giving of Dharma is able to bring about perfection of the absence of outflow impurities in the [five] faculties, the [five] powers, the [seven limbs of] enlightenment and the [eight-fold] path.

Also, as for the methods of giving material wealth, they remain in the world constantly, whether or not there is a buddha [actually present in the world]. As for the giving of Dharma, it can only exist in an era when there has been a buddha. Therefore one ought to realize that the giving of Dharma is extremely difficult. How is it difficult? Even one who is a pratyekabuddha possessed of the marks [of a great man] is still unable to speak Dharma. It is only when he proceeds along on his alms round and flies up into the sky performing transformations that he is able thereby to convert people.

Then again, from the giving of Dharma, one is able to generate the giving of material wealth while also being able to reach to the position of a *śrāvaka*-disciple, of a pratyekabuddha, of a bodhisattva and finally, of a buddha.

Moreover, in carrying out the giving of Dharma, one becomes able to differentiate between all dharmas: outflow and non-outflow dharmas, form dharmas and formless dharmas, conditioned and unconditioned dharmas, wholesome, unwholesome and neutral

法。常法无常法。有法无法。一切诸法实相清净不可破不可坏。如是等法略说则八万四千法藏。广说则无量。如是等种种。皆从法施分别了知。以是故法施为胜。是二施和合名[14]之为檀。行是二施愿求作佛。则能令人得至[145a]佛道。何况其馀。问曰。四种舍名为檀。所谓财舍法舍无畏舍烦恼舍。此中何以不说二种舍。答曰。无畏舍与尸罗无别故不说。有般若故不说烦恼舍。若不说六波罗蜜。则应具说四舍。

大智度论释初品中檀波罗蜜[1]法施[2]之馀。（卷第十二）

[*]龙树菩萨造。

[*]后秦龟兹国三藏鸠摩罗什[*]奉诏译。

[145a15]　[3]【论】问曰。云何名檀波罗[4]蜜[5]满。答曰。檀义如上说。波罗(6)秦言彼岸)蜜([*]秦言到)是名渡布施河得到彼岸。问曰。云何名不到彼岸。答曰。譬如渡河未到而还。名为不到彼岸。

dharmas, enduring dharmas and impermanent dharmas, existent and non-existent dharmas, and the true character of dharmas (*dharmatā*) which is pure, beyond refutation, and invulnerable to [dialectical] ruination.[27]

All dharmas such as these, if one speaks in brief, constitute a treasury of eighty-four thousand dharmas. Were one to speak of them extensively, they would become countless. All of these various advantageous factors [described above] become completely comprehended through that ability to make distinctions which is associated with Dharma giving. It is on this account that the giving of Dharma is superior [to the giving of material wealth].

These two kinds of giving together constitute what is known as *dāna*. If one carries on these two kinds of giving as one seeks to become a buddha, then one will be able to cause other people to succeed in reaching the Buddha Path. How much the more so will one be able to bring about any other desired result.

Question: The four kinds of relinquishing (*tyāga*) constitute what is known as *dāna*. These are: relinquishing of wealth; relinquishing of Dharma; relinquishing which leads to fearlessness; and the relinquishing of afflictions. Why have you not spoken herein of two of the types of relinquishment?

Response: Because the relinquishing which leads to fearlessness is no different from *śīla*, it is not discussed here. Because of the presence of *prajñā* as a separate topic, we do not discuss the relinquishing of afflictions. If we were not engaged in a discussion of the six *pāramitās*, it would be appropriate here to completely discuss all four kinds of relinquishing.

D. The "Perfection" of *Dāna Pāramitā*

Question: What is meant by the "perfection" of *dāna pāramitā*?

Response: The meaning of *dāna* is as discussed above. As for [the Sanskrit antecedent for "perfection," namely] "*pāramitā*," it refers here to being able to cross on over the river of [imperfect] giving and to succeed in reaching its far shore. (Ch. text notes: As for "*pāra-*," this means "the other shore." As for "*-mi*," this means "to reach.")

1. *Dāna* Practice That Fails to "Reach the Far Shore"

Question: What is meant by failing to reach the far shore?

Response: It is analogous to crossing over a river but returning before having arrived. This is what is meant by failing to reach the far shore.

如舍利弗。于六[7]十劫中行
菩萨道。欲渡布施河。时有
乞人来乞其眼。舍利弗言。
眼无所[8]任。何以索之。若
须我身及财物者当以相与。
答言。不须汝身及以财物。
唯欲得眼。若汝实行檀者以
眼见与。尔时舍利弗。出一
眼与之。乞者得眼。于舍
利弗前[9]嗅之。嫌臭唾而弃
地。又以脚蹋。舍利弗思惟
言。如此弊人等难可度也。
眼实无[10]用而强索之。既
得而弃又以脚蹋。何弊之
甚。如此人辈不可度也。不
如自调早脱生死。思惟是
已。于菩萨道退迴向小乘。
是名不到彼岸。若[145b]能直
进不退。成办佛道。名到彼
岸。复次于事成办亦名到彼
岸。（天竺俗法凡造事成办
皆言到彼岸）复次此岸名悭
贪檀名河中。彼岸名佛道。
复次有无见名此岸。破有无
见智慧名彼岸。慇修布施是
名河中。

如舍利弗。於六[7]十劫中行
菩薩道。欲渡布施河。時有
乞人來乞其眼。舍利弗言。
眼無所[8]任。何以索之。若
須我身及財物者當以相與。
答言。不須汝身及以財物。
唯欲得眼。若汝實行檀者以
眼見與。爾時舍利弗。出一
眼與之。乞者得眼。於舍
利弗前[9]嗅之。嫌臭唾而棄
地。又以腳蹋。舍利弗思惟
言。如此弊人等難可度也。
眼實無[10]用而強索之。既
得而棄又以腳蹋。何弊之
甚。如此人輩不可度也。不
如自調早脫生死。思惟是
已。於菩薩道退迴向小乘。
是名不到彼岸。若[145b]能直
進不退。成辦佛道。名到彼
岸。復次於事成辦亦名到彼
岸。（天竺俗法凡造事成辦
皆言到彼岸）復次此岸名慳
貪檀名河中。彼岸名佛道。
復次有無見名此岸。破有無
見智慧名彼岸。慇修布施是
名河中。

简体字   正體字

2. Śāriputra Retreats (Story)

For example, Śāriputra cultivated the Bodhisattva Path for a period of sixty kalpas, desiring to "cross over the river" of giving. At that time, there was a beggar who came along and demanded that he give him one of his eyes. Śāriputra said, "The eye would then be useless. What do you want it for? If you need to put my body to use or if you want any valuables I own, then I'll give those to you."

The beggar replied, "I've got no use for your body and I don't want any valuables you might own. I just want an eye, that's all. If you were truly a cultivator of the practice of giving, then I would receive an eye from you."

At that time Śāriputra pulled out one of his eyes and gave it to him. The beggar got the eye and then, right there in front of Śāriputra, he sniffed it, cursed, "It stinks," spat, and then threw it down on the ground. Then, in addition, he smashed it beneath his foot.

Śāriputra thought to himself, "It's a difficult task to cross such base people on over to liberation. He actually had no use for the eye at all, and yet he was forceful in demanding it from me. Having gotten it, he not only threw it away, he even smashed it with his foot. How extremely base! People of this sort cannot be crossed over to liberation. Far better that I just concentrate on disciplining myself so as to gain an early liberation from the cycle of births and deaths."

Having thought thus, he turned from the Bodhisattva Path back towards the Small Vehicle. This is what is meant by "failing to reach the other shore." If one were able to advance straight ahead, refrain from retreating, and thus continue on to the completion of the Buddha Path, this would constitute "reaching the far shore."

3. Extended Discussion of "Reaching the Far Shore"

Then again, to succeed in completing any endeavor is also referred to as "reaching to the far shore." (Chinese textual note: In the common parlance of India, whenever one takes up a task and then completes it, it is referred to as "reaching the far shore.")

Additionally, one may say that "this shore" refers to being miserly, *dāna* refers to being in the midst of the river, and "the far shore" refers to the Buddha Path.

One might also state that holding a view positing "existence" or "nonexistence" qualifies as "this shore," whereas the wisdom which refutes views positing "existence" or "nonexistence" constitutes "the far shore." The diligent cultivation of giving would then correspond to being in the middle of the river.

复次檀有二种。一者魔檀二者佛檀。若为结使贼所夺忧恼怖畏。是为魔檀。名曰此岸。若有清净布施。无结使贼无所怖畏得至佛道。是为佛檀。名曰到彼岸。是为波罗蜜。如佛说毒蛇喻经中。有人得罪于王。王令掌护一箧。箧中有四毒蛇。王勅罪人令看视养育。此人思惟。四蛇难近。近则害人。一犹叵养。而况于四。[11]便弃箧而走。王令五人拔刀追之。复有一人口言附顺。心欲中伤而语之言。养之以理此亦无苦。其人觉之驰走逃命。至一空聚有一善人方便语之。此聚虽空是贼所止处。汝今住此必为贼害慎勿住也。于是复去至一大河。河之彼岸即是异国。其国安乐坦然清净无诸患难。于是集众草木缚

復次檀有二種。一者魔檀二者佛檀。若為結使賊所奪憂惱怖畏。是為魔檀。名曰此岸。若有清淨布施。無結使賊無所怖畏得至佛道。是為佛檀。名曰到彼岸。是為波羅蜜。如佛說毒蛇喻經中。有人得罪於王。王令掌護一篋。篋中有四毒蛇。王勅罪人令看視養育。此人思惟。四蛇難近。近則害人。一猶叵養。而況於四。[11]便棄篋而走。王令五人拔刀追之。復有一人口言附順。心欲中傷而語之言。養之以理此亦無苦。其人覺之馳走逃命。至一空聚有一善人方便語之。此聚雖空是賊所止處。汝今住此必為賊害慎勿住也。於是復去至一大河。河之彼岸即是異國。其國安樂坦然清淨無諸患難。於是集眾草木縛

简体字   正體字

a. Demon *Dāna* versus Buddha Dāna

Then again, one may also say that there are two kinds of *dāna*, the first being the *dāna* of demons and the second being the *dāna* of the Buddhas. If in this practice one is being robbed by the thieves of the fetters to the degree that one is afflicted by worries and abides in fearfulness, this constitutes the *dāna* of the demons and exemplifies what is meant by "this shore."

Where there is pure giving in which there is an absence of the thieves of the fetters and in which there is nothing of which one is fearful, one succeeds thereby in arriving at the Buddha Path. This constitutes the *dāna* of the Buddhas and exemplifies what is meant by "reaching to the far shore." This is *"pāramitā."*

b. The Analogy of the Poisonous Snakes (Story)

By way of illustration, in the *Sutra on the Buddha's Describing the Poisonous Snakes Analogy,* [this story is told]: There once was a man who had offended the King. The King ordered that he be required to carry around a basket and look after it. Inside the basket, there were four poisonous snakes. The King ordered the criminal to look after them and raise them.

This man thought to himself, "It's a difficult thing to have to draw close to four snakes. If one grows close to them, they inflict harm on a person. I could not raise even one of them, how much the less could I do that for four of them." And so he cast aside the basket and ran away.

The King ordered five men carrying knives to chase after him. There was yet another man who, though outwardly speaking most agreeably, wished inwardly to bring him harm and thus instructed him thus: "Just go ahead and raise them in a sensible fashion. There will be no suffering arising from that."

But the man became wise to this, and so ran off, fleeing for his life. When he came to an empty village, there was a good man who assisted him by telling him, "Although this village is empty, it is a place frequented by thieves. If you now take up residence here, you will certainly be harmed by the thieves. Be careful. Don't dwell here."

At this point, the man took off again and next arrived at a great river. On the other side of the river there was a different country. That country was a peaceful, blissful, and easeful place. It was a pure place devoid of any form of calamity or adversity. He then gathered together a mass of reeds and branches and bound them

以为[12]枙进。以手足竭力求渡。既到彼岸安乐无患。王者魔王。箧者人身。四毒蛇者四大。[13]五拔刀贼者五[14]众。一人口善心恶者。是[15]染着空聚是六情。贼是六尘。一人愍而语之是为善师。大河是爱。枙是八正道。手足勤渡是精进。此岸是世间。彼岸是涅盘。度者漏尽阿罗汉。菩萨法中亦如是。若施有三碍。我与彼受所施者财。是为堕魔境界未离众难。如菩萨布施三种清净无[16]此三碍[17]得到彼岸。为诸佛所赞。是名[18]檀波罗[145c]蜜。以是故名到彼岸。此六波罗蜜能令人渡悭贪等烦恼染着大海到于彼岸。以是故名波罗蜜。问曰。阿罗汉辟支佛亦能到彼岸。何以不名波罗蜜。答曰。阿罗汉辟支佛渡彼岸。与

以為[12]枙進。以手足竭力求渡。既到彼岸安樂無患。王者魔王。篋者人身。四毒蛇者四大。[13]五拔刀賊者五[14]眾。一人口善心惡者。是[15]染著空聚是六情。賊是六塵。一人愍而語之是為善師。大河是愛。枙是八正道。手足勤渡是精進。此岸是世間。彼岸是涅槃。度者漏盡阿羅漢。菩薩法中亦如是。若施有三礙。我與彼受所施者財。是為墮魔境界未離眾難。如菩薩布施三種清淨無[16]此三礙[17]得到彼岸。為諸佛所讚。是名[18]檀波羅[145c]蜜。以是故名到彼岸。此六波羅蜜能令人渡慳貪等煩惱染著大海到於彼岸。以是故名波羅蜜。問曰。阿羅漢辟支佛亦能到彼岸。何以不名波羅蜜。答曰。阿羅漢辟支佛渡彼岸。與

简体字   正體字

together to make a raft. He moved it along with his hands and feet, exerting all of his strength in seeking to make a crossing. When he had reached the other shore, he was at peace, happy, and free of distress.

The King represents the demon king. The basket represents the human body. The four poisonous snakes represent the four great elements. The five knife-wielding thieves represent the five aggregates. The man of fine speech but evil mind represents defiled attachment. The empty village represents the six sense faculties. The thieves represent the six sense objects. The one man who took pity on him and instructed him represents the good spiritual guide.

The great river represents love. The raft represents the eightfold right path. The hands and feet earnestly applied to making a crossing represent vigor. This shore represents this world. The far shore represents nirvāṇa. The man who crossed over represents the arhat who has put an end to outflow impurities. This is just the same in the dharma of the bodhisattva.

    c. Three Hindrances: Self, Recipient, Gift

If in giving there exist the three hindrances [involving the conception] of an "I" who gives, of an "other" who receives, and of a valuable object which serves as a "gift," then one falls into a demonic mental state wherein one has not yet left behind multiple difficulties.

In the case of giving as performed by the bodhisattva, it is characterized by three kinds of purity through which there is an absence of these three hindrances and through which one has succeeded in reaching to the far shore. It is such as is praised by the Buddhas. This is what is meant by *dānā pāramitā*. It is based on this that it is referred to as "having reached the far shore."

These six *pāramitās* enable a person to cross beyond the great sea of defiled attachments associated with miserliness and the other afflictions, thus allowing him to reach the far shore. It is for this reason that they are referred to as *"pāramitās."*

    d. The Shortcomings of Two-Vehicles' *Dāna* Practice

Question: The arhat and the pratyekabuddha are also able to "reach to the far shore." Why is that not referred to as having achieved *"pāramitā"*?

Response: The crossing over to the far shore achieved by the arhat and pratyekabuddha, when compared to the crossing over

佛渡彼岸。名同而实异。彼以生死为此岸。涅盘为彼岸。而不能渡檀之彼岸。所以者何。不能以一切物一切时一切种布施。设能布施亦无大心。或以无记心或有漏善心。或无漏心施无大悲心。不能为一切众生施。菩萨施者知布施不生不灭无漏无为。如涅盘相。为一切众生故施。是名檀波罗蜜。复次有人言。一切物一切种内外物尽以布施不求果报。如是布施名檀波罗蜜。复次不可尽故名檀波罗蜜。所以者何。知所施物毕竟空如涅盘相。以是心施众生。是故施报不可尽。名檀波罗蜜。如五通仙人。以好宝物藏着石中。欲护此宝磨金刚涂之。令不可破。菩萨布施亦复如是。以涅盘实相智慧磨涂[19]之布施。令不可尽。复次菩萨为一切众生故布施。众生数不可尽故。布施亦不可尽。

佛渡彼岸。名同而實異。彼以生死為此岸。涅槃為彼岸。而不能渡檀之彼岸。所以者何。不能以一切物一切時一切種布施。設能布施亦無大心。或以無記心或有漏善心。或無漏心施無大悲心。不能為一切眾生施。菩薩施者知布施不生不滅無漏無為。如涅槃相。為一切眾生故施。是名檀波羅蜜。復次有人言。一切物一切種內外物盡以布施不求果報。如是布施名檀波羅蜜。復次不可盡故名檀波羅蜜。所以者何。知所施物畢竟空如涅槃相。以是心施眾生。是故施報不可盡。名檀波羅蜜。如五通仙人。以好寶物藏著石中。欲護此寶磨金剛塗之。令不可破。菩薩布施亦復如是。以涅槃實相智慧磨塗[19]之布施。令不可盡。復次菩薩為一切眾生故布施。眾生數不可盡故。布施亦不可盡。

简体字   正體字

to the far shore accomplished by the Buddha, constitutes one of those cases where, although the designation is the same, the reality is different. They take birth and death to constitute "this shore" and nirvāṇa to constitute "the far shore," but, nonetheless, are still unable to cross over to the far shore of *dāna*.

How is this the case? They are unable to perform giving of every thing at every time and in every way. In the event that they are able to engage in giving, they still lack the great mind in doing so. Perhaps they may employ a neutral mind in their giving, or perhaps a wholesome mind still abiding in the realm of outflow impurities, or perhaps even a non-outflow mind. However, they still lack the mind of great compassion. They are unable to engage in giving which is done for the sake of all beings.

e. *DĀNA PĀRAMITĀ* As PRACTICED BY THE BODHISATTVA

As for that giving which is performed by the bodhisattva, it is done with the realization that the act of giving is neither produced nor destroyed. It is conducted in a state which has gone beyond outflow impurities, is unconditioned, and is characterized by being like nirvāṇa. That giving is performed for the sake of all beings. This is what is referred to as *dāna pāramitā*.

Then again, there are those who say that when one gives everything of every sort, giving exhaustively of all inward and outward resources, and also gives without seeking any reward as a result, then it is this kind of giving which qualifies as *dāna pāramitā*.

Moreover, it is because it is inexhaustible that it is referred to as *dāna pāramitā*. How is this so? One knows that the thing which is given is ultimately empty [of inherent existence] and characterized by being like nirvāṇa. Because one employs this kind of mind in giving to beings, the retribution accruing from it is inexhaustible and it is therefore referred to as *dāna pāramitā*.

This is analogous to a rishi with the five superknowledges hiding away a marvelous jewel in the midst of stone. Desiring to protect his jewel, he accomplishes this by grinding up diamond and coating the jewel with it, thus causing it to become indestructible.

The giving performed by the bodhisattva is just like this. He employs a kind of giving which is coated with nirvāṇa-like reality-concordant wisdom through which [that giving] is made to become inexhaustible. Moreover, the bodhisattva gives for the sake of all beings. Because the number of beings is inexhaustible, that giving, too, is inexhaustible.

复次菩萨为佛法布施。佛法无量无边。布施亦无量无边。以是故阿罗汉辟支佛[20]虽到彼岸。不名波罗蜜。问曰。云何名具足满。答曰。如先说。菩萨能一切布施内外大小多少麁细着不着用不用。如是等种种物一切能舍。心无所惜。等与一切众生。不作是观大人应与小人不应与。出家人应与不出家人不应与。人应与禽兽不应与。于一切众[146a]生平等心施。施不求报。又得施实相。是名具足满。亦不观时无昼无夜无冬无夏无吉无衰。一切时常等施心无悔惜。乃至头目髓脑施而无恡。是为具足满。

[146a05]　复次有人言。菩萨从初发心乃至菩提树下三十四心。于是中间名为布施具足满。

简体字

復次菩薩為佛法布施。佛法無量無邊。布施亦無量無邊。以是故阿羅漢辟支佛[20]雖到彼岸。不名波羅蜜。問曰。云何名具足滿。答曰。如先說。菩薩能一切布施內外大小多少麁細著不著用不用。如是等種種物一切能捨。心無所惜。等與一切眾生。不作是觀大人應與小人不應與。出家人應與不出家人不應與。人應與禽獸不應與。於一切眾[146a]生平等心施。施不求報。又得施實相。是名具足滿。亦不觀時無晝無夜無冬無夏無吉無衰。一切時常等施心無悔惜。乃至頭目髓腦施而無恡。是為具足滿。

[146a05]　復次有人言。菩薩從初發心乃至菩提樹下三十四心。於是中間名為布施具足滿。

正體字

Then again, the bodhisattva gives for the sake of the Buddha's Dharma. The Dharma of the Buddha is immeasurable and boundless. So too then is that giving also immeasurable and boundless.

It is for these reasons that, although the arhat and the pratyekabuddha reach to the far shore, those are not circumstances qualifying as *"pāramitā."*

E. "Perfect Fulfillment" of *Dāna Pāramitā*

Question: What is meant by "perfect fulfillment" [of *dāna pāramitā*]?

Response: It is as explained earlier. The bodhisattva is able to give everything: the inward, the outward, that which is major, that which is minor, that which is of greater quantity, that which is of lesser quantity, that which is coarse, that which is refined, that to which he is attached, that to which he is not attached, that which he uses, and also that which he doesn't use. He is able to relinquish every sort of object such as these.

His mind has nothing to which it clings with fondness. He gives equally to all beings. He does not engage in such contemplations as this: "One should only give to great people and one should not give to lesser people. One should only give to those who have left the home life and one should not give to anyone who has not left behind the home life. One should only give to humans and one should not give to birds or beasts."

In his practice of giving, he maintains an evenhanded and equitable mind toward all beings. When he gives, he does not seek to gain any reward as a result. Moreover, he realizes in accordance with reality the true character of the [dharma] of giving. This is what is meant by "perfect fulfillment."

Additionally, he is not constrained by a regard for the time being right. For him, there is no waiting till morning, till evening, till winter, or till summer. There is no time which is auspicious or inauspicious. At all times, he constantly engages in equitable giving, employing a mind free of regrets and free of clinging fondness. He does so even to the point of sacrificing without stint his own head, his eyes, his marrow, and his brain. This is what is meant by "perfect fulfillment" [of *dāna pāramitā*].

Then again, there are those who say that "perfect fulfillment" of giving takes place as the bodhisattva progresses through the thirty-four mental stages between the initial aspiration and his finally sitting beneath the bodhi tree.

复次七住菩萨得一切诸法实
相智慧。是时庄严佛土教
化众生。供养诸佛得[1]大神
通。能分一身作无数身。一
一身皆雨七宝华香幡盖化作
大灯。如须弥山。供养十方
佛及菩萨僧。复以妙音赞
颂佛德。礼拜供养恭敬将[2]
迎。复次是菩萨。于一切十
方无量饿鬼国中雨种种饮食
衣被令其充满。得满足已。
皆发阿耨多罗三藐三菩提
心。复至畜生道中。令其自
善无相害意。除其畏怖随其
所须各令充足。得满足已。
皆发阿耨多罗三藐三菩提
心。于地狱无量苦中。能令
地狱火灭汤冷。罪息心善除
其饥渴。得生天上人中。以
此因缘故皆发阿耨多罗三藐
三菩提心。若十方人贫穷者
给之以财。富贵者施以异味
异色令其欢喜。以此因缘
故。皆发阿耨多罗三藐三菩
提心。若至欲天中令其除却
天上欲乐。施以妙宝法乐令
其

复次七住菩萨得一切诸法实
簡体字

復次七住菩薩得一切諸法實
相智慧。是時莊嚴佛土教
化眾生。供養諸佛得[1]大神
通。能分一身作無數身。一
一身皆雨七寶華香幡蓋化作
大燈。如須彌山。供養十方
佛及菩薩僧。復以妙音讚
頌佛德。禮拜供養恭敬將[2]
迎。復次是菩薩。於一切十
方無量餓鬼國中雨種種飲食
衣被令其充滿。得滿足已。
皆發阿耨多羅三藐三菩提
心。復至畜生道中。令其自
善無相害意。除其畏怖隨其
所須各令充足。得滿足已。
皆發阿耨多羅三藐三菩提
心。於地獄無量苦中。能令
地獄火滅湯冷。罪息心善除
其飢渴。得生天上人中。以
此因緣故皆發阿耨多羅三藐
三菩提心。若十方人貧窮者
給之以財。富貴者施以異味
異色令其歡喜。以此因緣
故。皆發阿耨多羅三藐三菩
提心。若至欲天中令其除却
天上欲樂。施以妙寶法樂令
其

正體字

Also, when the seventh-stage bodhisattva gains the reality-concordant wisdom cognizing the true character of all dharmas, he adorns buddhalands and engages in the teaching and transformation of beings. He makes offerings to the Buddhas and gains such great superknowledges that he becomes able to divide his one body and create innumerable bodies. Each of those bodies rains down the seven jewels, flower blossoms, incenses, banners, and canopies, while also transformationally creating a great lamp comparable in size to Mount Sumeru. He makes offerings to the Buddhas of the ten directions as well as to the Bodhisattva Sangha.

Additionally, he employs a marvelous voice to make praises and verses describing the virtue of the Buddhas. He pays homage to them, makes offerings to them, treats them with respect, and welcomes them. Moreover, this bodhisattva rains down all sorts of food and drink, clothing, and bedding, raining them down into the countlessly many hungry ghost realms throughout the ten directions, thereby allowing them to become full and satisfied. After they have gained complete satisfaction, they all then bring forth the resolve to gain *anuttarasamyaksaṃbodhi*.

He also goes into the path of the animals, causing them to spontaneously become good and have no intentions of mutual harm, causing them to get rid of their fearfulness and, according to whatever they need, causing them each to become completely full and satisfied. After they have become full, they all bring forth the resolve to gain *anuttarasamyaksaṃbodhi*.

Within the immeasurable suffering of the hells, he is able to cause the fires of the hells to go out, the broth [in the cauldrons] to grow cold, the offenses [of the hell-dwellers] to be extinguished, and their minds to turn to goodness. He gets rid of their hunger and thirst and allows them to be reborn in the heavens and among humans. On account of these causes and conditions, they all bring forth the resolve to gain *anuttarasamyaksaṃbodhi*.

Where there are poverty-stricken people throughout the ten directions, he supplies them with wealth. As for those who are wealthy and noble, he gives them exotic flavors and exotic forms which cause them to be delighted. On account of these causes and conditions, they all bring forth the resolve to gain *anuttarasamyaksaṃbodhi*.

When he goes among the desire-realm gods, he causes them to dispense with the desire-based pleasures of the heavens, gives them the marvelous jewel of Dharma bliss, and thus causes them to

欢喜。以此因缘故。皆发阿耨多罗三藐三菩提心。若至色天中除其乐着。以菩萨禅法而娱乐之。以此因缘故。皆发阿耨多罗三藐三菩提心。如是乃至十住是名檀波罗蜜具足满。复次菩萨有二种身。一者结业生身。二者法身。是二种身中檀波罗蜜[146b]满。是名具足檀波罗蜜。问曰。云何名结业生身檀波罗蜜满。答曰。未得法身结使未尽。能以一切宝物头目髓脑国财妻子内外所有。尽以布施心不动转。如须[3]提拏太子[4]（秦言好爱）以其二子布施婆罗门。次以妻施其心不转。又如萨婆达王[5]（秦言一切施）为敌国所灭。身窜穷林。见有远国婆罗门来欲从己乞。自以国破家亡一身藏窜。

简体字

歡喜。以此因緣故。皆發阿耨多羅三藐三菩提心。若至色天中除其樂著。以菩薩禪法而娛樂之。以此因緣故。皆發阿耨多羅三藐三菩提心。如是乃至十住是名檀波羅蜜具足滿。復次菩薩有二種身。一者結業生身。二者法身。是二種身中檀波羅蜜[146b]滿。是名具足檀波羅蜜。問曰。云何名結業生身檀波羅蜜滿。答曰。未得法身結使未盡。能以一切寶物頭目髓腦國財妻子內外所有。盡以布施心不動轉。如須[3]提拏太子[4]（秦言好愛）以其二子布施婆羅門。次以妻施其心不轉。又如薩婆達王[5]（秦言一切施）為敵國所滅。身竄窮林。見有遠國婆羅門來欲從己乞。自以國破家亡一身藏竄。

正體字

be delighted. Based on these causes and conditions, they are all led to bring forth the resolve to gain *anuttarasamyaksaṃbodhi*.

When he goes among the form-realm gods, he causes them to get rid of their blissful attachment and delights them with the dhyāna dharma of the bodhisattvas. Based on these causes and conditions, they are all inspired to bring forth the resolve to gain *anuttarasamyaksaṃbodhi*.

Matters are of this sort all the way on up to the tenth [bodhisattva] ground. This illustrates what is meant by "perfect fulfillment" of *dāna pāramitā*.

1. The Bodhisattva's Perfection of Dāna in Two Body Types

Additionally, the bodhisattva possesses two kinds of bodies. The first is the body produced from the karma of the fetters. The second is the Dharma body. Accomplishing fulfillment of *dāna pāramitā* in both of these bodies is what is intended by "perfect fulfillment" of *dāna pāramitā*.

a. Dāna Pāramitā in the Fetter-Generated Body

Question: What is meant by fulfillment of *dāna pāramitā* within the body produced from the karma generated by the fetters (*saṃyojana*)?

Response: This refers to when one has not yet gained the Dharma body and to when the fetters have not yet been brought to an end. One becomes able to give completely of all that one possesses, both inwardly and outwardly, including all manner of precious objects, and including one's head, eyes, marrow, brain, country, wealth, wives, and sons, doing so without one's mind moving or turning away from it. Take for instance Prince Sudinna[28] who made a gift of his two sons to a brahman. (Chinese textual note: In our language, this [Sudinna] means "fine fondness.") Next, he relinquished his wife, and even then, his mind still did not turn away from continuing on with this practice.

1) King Sarvada Turns Himself In (Story)

This is also exemplified by King Sarvada who was vanquished by an enemy country and who then fled and hid in the furthest reaches of the forests. (Chinese textual note: In our language, this ["Sarvada"] means "giving everything.") He encountered a brahman from a far-away country who sought to receive alms from him. As for himself, his country had been crushed, his family had been wiped out, and he had been forced to flee alone and go into hiding.

愍其辛苦故。从远来而无所得。语婆罗门言。我是萨婆达王。新王募人求我甚重。即时自缚以身施之。送与新王大得财物。亦如月光太子出行游观。癞人见之要车白言。我身重病辛苦懊恼。太子嬉游独自欢耶。大慈愍念愿见救疗。太子闻之以问诸医。医言当须从生长大无瞋之人血髓。涂而饮之。如是可愈。太子念言。设有此人贪生惜寿何可得耶。自除我身无可得处。即命旃陀罗。令除身肉破骨出髓以涂病人以血饮之。如是等种种身。及妻子施而无恪如弃草木。观所施物知从缘有。推求其实都无所得。一切清净如涅盘相。乃至得无生法忍。是为结业生身行檀波罗蜜满。

愍其辛苦故。從遠來而無所得。語婆羅門言。我是薩婆達王。新王募人求我甚重。即時自縛以身施之。送與新王大得財物。亦如月光太子出行遊觀。癩人見之要車白言。我身重病辛苦懊惱。太子嬉遊獨自歡耶。大慈愍念願見救療。太子聞之以問諸醫。醫言當須從生長大無瞋之人血髓。塗而飲之。如是可愈。太子念言。設有此人貪生惜壽何可得耶。自除我身無可得處。即命旃陀羅。令除身肉破骨出髓以塗病人以血飲之。如是等種種身。及妻子施而無恪如棄草木。觀所施物知從緣有。推求其實都無所得。一切清淨如涅槃相。乃至得無生法忍。是為結業生身行檀波羅蜜滿。

简体字

正體字

Because he felt pity for [the brahman's] hardship in having come from afar and yet having gotten nothing, he said to the brahman, "I am King Sarvada. The new king has sent men out to find me, offering a handsome reward for my capture." He then immediately tied himself up and gave himself up [to the brahman]. [The brahman] then turned him over to the new king and received great wealth and valuables [in reward].

2) Prince Candraprabha Sacrifices Himself (Story)

This concept is also illustrated by [the story of] Prince Candraprabha who had gone out sightseeing when a leper noticed him, presented himself at the carriage, and addressed him, saying, "My body has come down with a serious disease which causes intense suffering and causes me to be grievously tormented. The prince is traveling about for pleasure. Will he only bring happiness to himself? May he bring forth great kindness and bring pity to mind. Pray, may I receive a cure that will rescue me?"

When the Prince heard him, he asked the physicians about this matter. The physician replied, "It would be necessary to obtain the blood and marrow of a man who from the time of birth had grownup without any hatred. It would be topically applied and also drunk. If one proceeded in this fashion, then he could be cured."

The Prince thought to himself, "If there is such a person, he would wish to live on and would cherish his own life. How could such a person be found? Aside from myself, there is nowhere to find such a person." He then issued an order for a *caṇḍāla* to come. He then instructed him to strip away flesh from his body, break his bones, extract his marrow, smear it on the body of the sick man, and then take the blood and provide it as a drink for [the leper].

3) Conclusion of Fetter-Generated Body Discussion

In ways such as this, and in all sorts of physical bodies, one gives even one's own wives and sons and yet does not stint at all, treating the practice as if it merely involved the setting aside of grass or trees. One contemplates those things which are given and realizes that they exist merely on the basis of [a conjunction of] conditions. When one pursues this and seeks to find their reality, it can never be found. Everything is finally characterized by being pure and like nirvāṇa. And so this proceeds until one realizes the unproduced-dharmas patience (*anutpattikadharmakṣānti*). This is what is meant by fulfillment of *dāna pāramitā* while abiding in a body produced from the karma of the fetters.

云何法身菩萨行檀波罗蜜满。菩萨末后肉身得无生法忍。舍肉身得法身。于十方六道中。变身应适以化众生。种种珍宝衣服饮食给施一切。又以头目髓脑国财妻子内外所有尽以布施。譬如释迦文佛。曾为六牙白象。猎者[6]伺便以毒箭射之。诸象竞至欲来蹈杀猎者。白象以身捍之。拥护其人愍之如[146c]子。[7]谕遣群象徐问猎人。何故射我。答曰。我须汝牙。即时以六牙内石孔中血肉俱出。以鼻举牙授与猎者。虽曰象身用心如是。当知此象非畜生行报。阿罗汉法中都无此心。当知此为法身菩萨。有时阎浮提人不知礼敬。[8]耆旧有德。以言化之未可得度。是时菩萨自变其身。作迦频阇罗鸟。是鸟有二亲友。一者大象二者猕猴。

简体字

云何法身菩薩行檀波羅蜜滿。菩薩末後肉身得無生法忍。捨肉身得法身。於十方六道中。變身應適以化眾生。種種珍寶衣服飲食給施一切。又以頭目髓腦國財妻子內外所有盡以布施。譬如釋迦文佛。曾為六牙白象。獵者[6]伺便以毒箭射之。諸象競至欲來蹈殺獵者。白象以身捍之。擁護其人愍之如[146c]子。[7]諭遣群象徐問獵人。何故射我。答曰。我須汝牙。即時以六牙內石孔中血肉俱出。以鼻舉牙授與獵者。雖曰象身用心如是。當知此象非畜生行報。阿羅漢法中都無此心。當知此為法身菩薩。有時閻浮提人不知禮敬。[8]耆舊有德。以言化之未可得度。是時菩薩自變其身。作迦頻闍羅鳥。是鳥有二親友。一者大象二者獼猴。

正體字

b. The *Dāna Pāramitā* of the Dharma Body

How does the Dharma-body bodhisattva cultivate *dāna pāramitā* to fulfillment? In his very last fleshly body, the bodhisattva achieves the unproduced-dharmas patience. He relinquishes the fleshly body and gains the Dharma body.[29] In the six destinies and throughout the ten directions, he transformationally creates bodies in response to what is appropriate, and thereby goes about transforming beings. He provides all sorts of precious jewels, clothing, and food and drink as gifts to everyone and then additionally gives exhaustively of everything he possesses, whether inwardly or outwardly, including even his own head, his eyes, his marrow, his brain, his country, his wealth, and his wives and sons.

1) Buddha's Past Life As an Elephant (Story)

A case in point is that of Shākyamuni Buddha when he was once a six-tusked white elephant. A hunter had ambushed him and shot him with poison arrows. The herd of elephants stampeded towards him with the intention of trampling the hunter to death. The white elephant used his own body to defend [the hunter], protecting that man and having pity upon him just the same as if he had been his own son. He ordered the herd of elephants away and then calmly asked the hunter, "Why did you shoot me?"

He replied, "I need your tusks." Immediately, blood and flesh spontaneously pushed forth all six tusks from their sockets. He then used his trunk to pick up the tusks and give them to the hunter.

Although this was described as the [animal] body of an elephant, where the mind is used in this manner, one should realize that this elephant could not have come into existence as retribution for the karmic actions typical of animals. Nowhere among the dharmas of those [on the path of the] arhat are there mental practices of this sort. One should realize that this was a Dharma-body bodhisattva.

2) The Elephant, the Monkey, and the Bird (Story)

There once was a time when people in Jambudvīpa did not know enough to render proper reverence and respect to those who are older and those who are virtuous. At that time they were not yet amenable to being taught the means to liberation through the use of words alone.

At that time, a bodhisattva transformed his body and manifest there in the form of a *kapiñjala* bird. This bird had two close friends. The first was a great elephant and the second was a monkey. They

共在必鉢罗树下住。自相问言。我等不知谁应为[9]长。象言。我昔见此树在我腹下。今大如是以此推之我应为长。[10]猕猴言。我曾蹲地手[11]挽树头以[12]是推之我应为长。鸟言。我于必鉢罗林中食此树果。子随粪出此树得生。以是推之我应最[*]长。[13]鸟复说言先生宿旧礼应供养。即时大象背负猕猴。鸟在猴上。周游而行。一切禽兽见而问之。何以如此。答曰。以此恭敬供养长老。禽兽受化皆行礼敬。不侵民田不害物命。众人疑怪一切禽兽不复为害。猎[14]者入林见象负猕猴[15]猕猴戴鸟。行敬化物物皆修善传告国人。人各庆曰。时将太平鸟兽而仁。人亦效之。皆行礼敬。自古及今化流万世。当知是为法身菩萨。复次法身菩萨一时之顷。化作无央数身。

简体字

共在必鉢羅樹下住。自相問言。我等不知誰應為[9]長。象言。我昔見此樹在我腹下。今大如是以此推之我應為長。[10]獼猴言。我曾蹲地手[11]挽樹頭以[12]是推之我應為長。鳥言。我於必鉢羅林中食此樹果。子隨糞出此樹得生。以是推之我應最[*]長。[13]鳥復說言先生宿舊禮應供養。即時大象背負獼猴。鳥在猴上。周遊而行。一切禽獸見而問之。何以如此。答曰。以此恭敬供養長老。禽獸受化皆行禮敬。不侵民田不害物命。眾人疑怪一切禽獸不復為害。獵[14]者入林見象負獼猴[15]獼猴戴鳥。行敬化物物皆修善傳告國人。人各慶曰。時將太平鳥獸而仁。人亦效之。皆行禮敬。自古及今化流萬世。當知是為法身菩薩。復次法身菩薩一時之頃。化作無央數身。

正體字

all lived together around the base of a pipal tree. They once happened to inquire of one another, wondering, "We don't know who among us ought to be accorded the status of 'elder.'"

The elephant said, "In the past I viewed this tree when it was shorter than the height of my belly. Now it is so huge. From this we can deduce that I ought to be known as the eldest."

The monkey said, "In the past I've squatted down and plucked with my hand at the top of the tree. From this we can deduce that I should be recognized as the eldest."

The bird said, "In the past I fed on the fruit of such trees in the pipal forest. The seed then passed out with my feces and as a result this tree grew forth. It can be deduced from this that it is I who ought to be recognized as the eldest." The bird continued, saying, "As a matter of propriety, the first born, being the eldest, ought to be the recipient of offerings."

The great elephant immediately took the monkey on his back and the bird then rode on the back of the monkey. They traveled all around in this fashion. When all of the birds and beasts observed this, they asked them, "Why are you going about like this?"

They replied, "We mean by this an expression of reverence and offerings to the one who is the eldest." The birds and the beasts all accepted this teaching and all practiced such reverence. They no longer invaded the fields of the people and no longer brought harm to the lives of other animals. The people were all amazed that all of the birds and beasts no longer engaged in harmful activities.

The hunters went into the forest and observed that the elephant bore the monkey on his back, that the monkey carried along the bird, and that they so transformed the creatures through cultivating respectfulness that the creatures all cultivated goodness. They passed this on to the people of the country. The people all celebrated this and remarked, "The times are growing peaceful. Though but birds and beasts, they are nonetheless possessed of humanity."

And so the people as well modeled themselves on this. They all cultivated propriety and respectfulness. From ancient times until the present, this transformative teaching has flowed on down through a myriad generations. One should know that this was brought about by a Dharma-body bodhisattva.

3) Conclusion of Dharma-body *Dāna* Discussion

Additionally, the Dharma-body bodhisattva, in a single moment, can transformationally produce countless bodies with which he

供养十方诸佛。一时能化无量财宝给足众生。能随一切上中下声一时之顷。普为说法。乃至坐佛树下。如是等种种名为法身菩萨行檀波罗蜜满。复次檀有三种一者物施二者供养恭敬施。三者法施。云何物施。珍宝衣食头目髓脑。如是[147a]等一切内外所有尽以布施。是名物施。恭敬施者。信心清净恭敬礼拜。将送迎逆赞遶供养。如是等种种名为恭敬施。法施者为道德故。语言论议诵读讲说除疑问答授人五戒。如是等种种为佛道故施。[1]是名法施。是三种施满。是名檀波罗蜜满。复次三事因缘生檀。一者信心清净。二者财物。三者福田。心有三种。若怜愍。若

简体字

供養十方諸佛。一時能化無量財寶給足眾生。能隨一切上中下聲一時之頃。普為說法。乃至坐佛樹下。如是等種種名為法身菩薩行檀波羅蜜滿。復次檀有三種一者物施二者供養恭敬施。三者法施。云何物施。珍寶衣食頭目髓腦。如是[147a]等一切內外所有盡以布施。是名物施。恭敬施者。信心清淨恭敬禮拜。將送迎逆讚遶供養。如是等種種名為恭敬施。法施者為道德故。語言論議誦讀講說除疑問答授人五戒。如是等種種為佛道故施。[1]是名法施。是三種施滿。是名檀波羅蜜滿。復次三事因緣生檀。一者信心清淨。二者財物。三者福田。心有三種。若憐愍。若

正體字

makes offerings to the Buddhas of the ten directions. He is able in a single moment to transformationally create an immeasurable number of valuable jewels which he supplies in abundance to beings. He is able in a single moment, in accordance with all of the different superior, middling, and lesser languages, to universally speak Dharma for them. And so he proceeds on in this fashion until he comes to sit at the base of the tree of the Buddhas.

All sorts of cases such as these exemplify the Dharma-body bodhisattva's fulfillment of the practice of *dāna pāramitā*.

F. Three Kinds of Dāna

Then again, *dāna* is of three varieties: The first is the giving of material objects. The second is giving which consists of offerings of reverence. The third is the giving of Dharma.

What is meant by "the giving of material objects"? It refers to jewels, precious things, robes, food, one's head, eyes, marrow and brain. One gives exhaustively of such things as these, giving all that one owns, whether they be inward or outward possessions. This is what is meant by the giving of material objects.

As for "the giving of reverence," it refers to having a mind of faith which is pure as one reverently performs acts of obeisance. It refers to offerings which consist of looking after, seeing off, welcoming, making expressions of praise, and circumambulating. All sorts of actions such as these constitute what is referred to as the giving of reverence.

As for "the giving of Dharma," it refers to actions performed for the sake of virtue associated with the Path. This includes such activities as discoursing, dialectical discussion, reciting, reading, lecturing, dispelling doubts, answering questions, transmitting the five precepts to people, and all sorts of other acts of giving such as these which are performed for the sake of the Buddha Path. This is what is meant by the giving of Dharma. When these three kinds of giving are fulfilled, this is what is meant by "fulfilling *dāna pāramitā*."

G. The Three Essential Components of Dāna

Moreover, the causes and conditions associated with three factors are what produce *dāna*: The first is a faithful mind which is pure. The second is a valuable object. The third is a field of merit.

1. The Mind of the Benefactor

As for the mind [associated with giving], there are three types: that which is characterized by sympathy; that which is characterized by

恭敬。若怜愍恭敬。施贫穷下贱及诸畜生。是为怜愍施。施佛及诸法身菩萨等。是为恭敬施。[2]若施诸老病贫乏阿罗汉辟支佛。是为恭敬怜愍施。施物清净非盗非劫以时而施。不求名誉不求利养。或时从心大得福德。或从福田大得功德。或从妙物大得功德。第一从心如四等心念佛三昧。以身施虎如是名[3]为从心大得功德。福田有二种。一者怜愍福田二者恭敬福田。怜愍福田能生怜愍心。恭敬福田能生恭敬心。如阿输[4]伽（[*]秦言无忧)[5]王以土上佛。复次物施中。如一女人酒醉没心[6]误以七宝璎珞布施迦叶佛塔。以福德故生

简体字

恭敬。若憐愍恭敬。施貧窮下賤及諸畜生。是為憐愍施。施佛及諸法身菩薩等。是為恭敬施。[2]若施諸老病貧乏阿羅漢辟支佛。是為恭敬憐愍施。施物清淨非盜非劫以時而施。不求名譽不求利養。或時從心大得福德。或從福田大得功德。或從妙物大得功德。第一從心如四等心念佛三昧。以身施虎如是名[3]為從心大得功德。福田有二種。一者憐愍福田二者恭敬福田。憐愍福田能生憐愍心。恭敬福田能生恭敬心。如阿輸[4]伽（[*]秦言無憂)[5]王以土上佛。復次物施中。如一女人酒醉沒心[6]誤以七寶瓔珞布施迦葉佛塔。以福德故生

正體字

reverence; and that which is characterized by both sympathy and reverence. If one gives to those who are poverty-stricken, to those of low social station, or to those who inhabit the animal world, this is sympathetic giving. If one gives to buddhas, to Dharma-body bodhisattvas, or to others of this sort, this is reverential giving. If one gives to elderly, sick, or destitute arhats, or to pratyekabuddhas, this constitutes giving which is both reverential and sympathetic.

2. THE GIFT

The object which is given must be pure, having neither been stolen nor obtained through forced confiscation. It is to be given at the right time and it is not to be given because one seeks to gain a reputation from it or because one seeks profit or sustenance.

One may at times gain great merit which arises on account of the quality of the mind. Perhaps one may gain great merit which arises on account of the quality of the field of merit. Or perhaps one may gain great merit which arises on account of having given a marvelous object.

As for the first, where it arises on account of the quality of the mind, it is exemplified by the four equitable minds (*samatā-citta*),[30] by the mindfulness of the Buddha samādhi (*buddhānusmṛti-samādhi*), and by [the Buddha's] having given his body to the tigress. Examples such as these indicate what is meant by gaining great merit on account of the quality of the mind.

3. THE FIELD OF MERIT

As for the field of merit (*puṇyakṣetra*), it is of two types: The first is the compassion-based field of merit (*karuṇā-puṇyakṣetra*). The second is the reverence-based field of merit (*satkāra-puṇyakṣetra*). The field of merit associated with compassion is such that it is able to inspire the arising of a sympathetic mind. The field of merit associated with reverence is such that it is able to inspire the arising of a reverential mind. This is illustrated by the case of King Aśoka who [as a child in an earlier life] had made an offering to the Buddha fashioned from mud. (Chinese textual note: In our language, this [Aśoka] means "free of worry.")

Moreover, regarding the giving of material objects, it is illustrated by the case of the woman who, on account of her mind's being immersed in inebriation, spontaneously made a gift to the stupa of Kāśyapa Buddha, bestowing on it a necklace made of the seven precious things. On account of that merit, she was reborn in

三十三天。如是种种名为物施。问曰。檀名舍财。何以言具足无所舍法。答曰。檀有二种。一者出世间。二者不出世间。今说出世间檀无相。无相故无所舍。是故言具足无所舍法。复次财物不可得故。名为无所舍。是物未来过去空。现在分别无一定法。以是故言无所舍。复次[7]以行者舍财时心念。此施大有功德。[8]倚是而生憍慢爱结等。以是故言无所舍。以无所舍故无憍慢。无憍慢故爱[147b]结等不生。复次施者有二种。一者世间人二者出世间人。世间人能舍财不能舍施。出世间人能舍财能舍施。何以故。以财物施心俱不可得故。以是故言具足无所舍法。复次

三十三天。如是種種名為物施。問曰。檀名捨財。何以言具足無所捨法。答曰。檀有二種。一者出世間。二者不出世間。今說出世間檀無相。無相故無所捨。是故言具足無所捨法。復次財物不可得故。名為無所捨。是物未來過去空。現在分別無一定法。以是故言無所捨。復次[7]以行者捨財時心念。此施大有功德。[8]倚是而生憍慢愛結等。以是故言無所捨。以無所捨故無憍慢。無憍慢故愛[147b]結等不生。復次施者有二種。一者世間人二者出世間人。世間人能捨財不能捨施。出世間人能捨財能捨施。何以故。以財物施心俱不可得故。以是故言具足無所捨法。復次

简体字   正體字

the Heaven of the Thirty-three. All sorts of cases such as this indicate what is meant by the giving of material objects.

a. How "Nothing Whatsoever Is Relinquished"

Question: *Dāna* refers to the relinquishing of valuable things. Why does it state in the *Sutra* text that one perfects it through "the dharma of having nothing whatsoever which is relinquished"?

b. Transcendent versus Non-Transcendent *Dāna*

Response: *Dāna* is of two types: The first transcends the world. The second is that which fails to transcend the world. We are now discussing *dāna* which transcends the world and which, [at the realization level at which it is practiced], accords with signlessness. Because it is characterized by [the cognition of] signlessness, nothing whatsoever is relinquished. Hence it speaks of perfecting "the dharma of having nothing whatsoever which is relinquished."

Moreover, it is because valuable things cannot be gotten at that it refers to having nothing whatsoever which is relinquished. In both the future and the past, these things are empty [of intrinsic existence]. And when they are analyzed in the present moment, they are found to be devoid of any definitely fixed dharma. It is for these reasons that [the *Sutra*] states that there is "nothing whatsoever which is relinquished."

Additionally, when the practitioner relinquishes valuable things, he may be liable to think to himself, "This act of giving is greatly meritorious." Then, based on this, he may become prone to bringing forth such fetters as pridefulness and affection. It is for this reason that it states here that there is nothing herein which is relinquished. Because there is nothing which is actually relinquished, there cannot be any pridefulness. Because there is no pridefulness, other fetters such as affection and so forth are not brought forth either.

c. Transcendent versus Non-transcendent Benefactors

Additionally, there are two types of people who give: First, the worldly person. Second, the person who has transcended the world. The worldly person may be able to relinquish valuable things but is nonetheless not able to relinquish his giving. The person who has transcended the world is able to relinquish valuable things and is also able to relinquish his giving. Why? Because neither valuable things nor the mind which gives can finally be found.

It is for this reason that [the *Sutra*] speaks of perfecting the dharma of having nothing relinquished. What's more, in its treatment of

檀波罗蜜中。言财施受者三
事不可得。问曰。三事和合
故名为檀。今言三事不可
得。云何名檀波罗蜜具足
满。今有财有施有受者。
云何三事不可得。如所[9]施
[10]叠实有。何以故。[*]叠有
名则有[*]叠法。若无[*]叠法
亦无[*]叠名。以有名故应实
有[*]叠。复次[*]叠有长有短
麁细白黑黄赤。有因有缘有
作有破有果报随法生心。十
尺为长五尺为短。缕大为麁
缕小为细。随染有色有缕为
因。织具为缘。是因缘和合
故为[*]叠。人[11]功为作人毁
为破。[12]御寒暑[13]弊身体
名果报。人得之大喜失之大
忧。以之施故得福助道。若
盗若劫戮之都市。死入地
狱。如是等种种因缘。故知
有此[*]叠是名[*]叠法。云何
言施物不可得。

檀波羅蜜中。言財施受者三
事不可得。問曰。三事和合
故名為檀。今言三事不可
得。云何名檀波羅蜜具足
滿。今有財有施有受者。
云何三事不可得。如所[9]施
[10]疊實有。何以故。[*]疊有
名則有[*]疊法。若無[*]疊法
亦無[*]疊名。以有名故應實
有[*]疊。復次[*]疊有長有短
麁細白黑黃赤。有因有緣有
作有破有果報隨法生心。十
尺為長五尺為短。縷大為麁
縷小為細。隨染有色有縷為
因。織具為緣。是因緣和合
故為[*]疊。人[11]功為作人毀
為破。[12]御寒暑[13]弊身體
名果報。人得之大喜失之大
憂。以之施故得福助道。若
盜若劫戮之都市。死入地
獄。如是等種種因緣。故知
有此[*]疊是名[*]疊法。云何
言施物不可得。

簡体字　　　　　　　　正體字

dāna pāramitā, it explains that the three factors of the valuable object, benefactor who gives it, and the recipient of the giving cannot ultimately be apprehended at all.

4. OBJECTION: "NOTHING WHATSOEVER" IS CONCEPTUALLY FALLACIOUS

Question: It is the conjunction of the three factors which constitutes *dāna*. Now, it is being explained that those three factors are ultimately unfindable. How then can one even refer to the perfect fulfilment of *dāna pāramitā*?

We do now have something of value [serving as a gift], the act of giving, and the recipient. How is it that these three factors cannot be found? For example when a piece of cloth is given, it does actually exist. How is this so? If the cloth has a name, then there is the dharma of cloth. If there were no dharma of cloth, then there would not be the name "cloth," either. Because the name exists, then it ought to be the case that cloth itself actually *does* exist.

Furthermore, pieces of cloth may be long, short, coarse, fine, white, black, yellow, or red. There are causes, there are conditions, there is a creation, there is a destruction, and there is a result in the realm of effects whereby a thought is produced which corresponds to the given dharma. A piece of cloth which is ten feet in length is long and one which is five feet in length is short. When the thread is thick, it is deemed to be coarse. When the thread is thin, it is said to be fine. In correspondence with the dye used on it, it has a particular color.

The existence of thread serves as the cause for its existence. The loom serves the condition. Because of the conjunction of this cause and condition, it becomes a piece of cloth. A person's effort brings about its actual creation. A person's damaging of it brings about its destruction. Its ability to control cold and heat and its serviceability in covering up of the body are the rewards in the realm of karmic effects. When a person gains it, there is great delight and when he loses it, there is great distress.

As a result of using it to make a gift, one gains karmic blessings which assist the Path. If one steals it from someone or takes it by force, he undergoes public punishment and then, on dying, enters the hells. On account of all sorts of reasons such as these, one knows that this cloth actually does exist. This is what is meant by the dharma of cloth. How then can one claim that the thing which is used as a gift is ultimately unfindable?

答曰。汝言有名故有是事。
不然。何以知之。名有二种
有实有不实。不实名。如有
一草名[14]朱利。（[15]朱[*]利
秦言贼[16]也）草亦不盗不劫
实非贼而名为贼。又如兔角
龟毛。亦但有名而无实[*]叠
虽不如兔角龟毛无。然因缘
会故有。因缘散故无。如林
如军是皆有名而无实。譬如
[17]木人虽有人名不应求其人
法。[*]叠中虽有名亦不应求
[*]叠真实。[*]叠能生人心念
因缘。得之便喜失之便忧。
是为念因缘。心生有二因
缘。有从实而生。有从不实
而生。如梦中所见如[147c]水
中月。如夜见机树谓为人。
如是名从不实中能令心生。
是缘不定。不应言心生有故
便是有。若心生因缘故有。
更不应求

答曰。汝言有名故有是事。
不然。何以知之。名有二種
有實有不實。不實名。如有
一草名[14]朱利。（[15]朱[*]利
秦言賊[16]也）草亦不盜不劫
實非賊而名為賊。又如兔角
龜毛。亦但有名而無實[*]疊
雖不如兔角龜毛無。然因緣
會故有。因緣散故無。如林
如軍是皆有名而無實。譬如
[17]木人雖有人名不應求其人
法。[*]疊中雖有名亦不應求
[*]疊真實。[*]疊能生人心念
因緣。得之便喜失之便憂。
是為念因緣。心生有二因
緣。有從實而生。有從不實
而生。如夢中所見如[147c]水
中月。如夜見机樹謂為人。
如是名從不實中能令心生。
是緣不定。不應言心生有故
便是有。若心生因緣故有。
更不應求

简体字　　　　　　　　　正體字

a. REFUTATION OF CLAIM THAT INTRINSIC EXISTENCE IS VALID

Response: You claim that, because there is a name, this entity exists. However, this is not the case. How does one know this? Names are of two kinds: those which are reality-based and those which are not reality-based. As for those names which are not reality-based, we have for example a type of grass known as *cauri*. (Chinese textual note: In our language, this means "thief.") For its part, the grass does not steal. It does not take things by force. In truth, it is not the case that it is a thief, and yet it is referred to as "thief."

This is just like the cases of the proverbial hare with horns and the turtle with fur. In those cases as well, they merely possess a name but have no corresponding reality.

Although cloth is not nonexistent in the same fashion as the horns of the hare or the fur of the turtle, still, it is by virtue of the coming together of causes and conditions that it is said to "exist" and by virtue of the scattering of causes and conditions that it becomes "nonexistent." In this respect, it is just like a "forest" and like an "army."[31] These each possess a name but are devoid of any reality.

This is also like a wooden man. Although it possesses the name "man," one ought not to seek there for its dharma of humanity. Although cloth possesses a name, still, one ought not to seek there for a cloth's true reality.

Cloth may be able to serve as a cause or condition associated with a person's thoughts. [For instance], when someone obtains it, he may become delighted whereas, when he loses it, he may become distressed. These circumstances serve as causes and conditions associated with thought. Now, when thoughts arise, there may be two types of originating causes and conditions. It may be that they arise based on something which is actually real. But it may also be that they arise based on something which is not actually real.

This is just like what is seen in a dream, like the moon reflected in water, and like seeing a bare tree trunk at night and being of the opinion that it is a person. Designations of these sorts are cases wherein the mind is caused to arise on the basis of something which is not actually real. Conditions of these sorts are not definite [in terms of their reliability].

One should not claim that, because some thought arises, a corresponding phenomenon must therefore exist. If it were the case that something must exist simply because of the arising of a corresponding thought, then one should not need to seek for any additional

实有。如眼见水中月。心生
谓是月。若从心[18]生便是月
者则无复真月。复次有[19]
有三种。一者相待有。二者
假名有。三者法有。相待者
如长短彼此等。实无长短[20]
亦无彼此。以相待故有名。
长因短有短亦因长。彼亦因
此此亦因彼。若在物东则以
为西。在西则以为东。一物
未异而有东西之别。此皆有
名而无实也。如是等名为相
待有。是中无实法。不如色
香味触等。假名有者。如酪
有色香味触四事。因缘合故
假名为酪。虽有不同因缘法
有。虽无亦不如

實有。如眼見水中月。心生
謂是月。若從心[18]生便是月
者則無復真月。復次有[19]
有三種。一者相待有。二者
假名有。三者法有。相待者
如長短彼此等。實無長短[20]
亦無彼此。以相待故有名。
長因短有短亦因長。彼亦因
此此亦因彼。若在物東則以
為西。在西則以為東。一物
未異而有東西之別。此皆有
名而無實也。如是等名為相
待有。是中無實法。不如色
香味觸等。假名有者。如酪
有色香味觸四事。因緣合故
假名為酪。雖有不同因緣法
有。雖無亦不如

简体字   正體字

verification of valid existence beyond that. Take for instance when the eye sees a reflection of the moon in the water and then a thought arises which takes that to be the moon. If it were the case that a moon should actually exist there merely because of the arising of a thought [which deems this to be the case], then there could be no other genuinely existent moon in addition to that one [thought to exist in the reflection atop the water].

1) THREE TYPES OF FALLACIOUS EXISTENCE

Moreover, "existence" is may be of three sorts. The first is relative existence. The second is [conventional] existence based on false names. The third is existence based on [constituent] dharmas.

2) RELATIVE EXISTENCE

As for relative existence, this is a reference to "long" versus "short," "that" versus "this," and so forth. In reality, there is no "long" or "short," nor is there a "that" or a "this." It is on account of an interdependent relationship that these designations come to exist. "Long" exists because of "short" and "short" exists because of "long." "That" exists because of "this" and "this" exists because of "that." If one is to the east of something, then one takes it to be "westerly." If one is to the west of it, then one takes [that same thing] to be "easterly." [In both cases], it is but a single given entity which has not changed at all, and yet it is given these distinctions of "easterly" [in one case] and "westerly" [in another].

These are all cases wher a designation exists, but there is no corresponding reality [on which it is based]. Cases such as these exemplify relative existence. There is no actual dharma herein. It is not the same [order of existence] as pertains to phenomena [perceptible] through their visible forms, smells, tastes, tangibility, and so forth.

3) CONVENTIONAL EXISTENCE BASED ON FALSE NAMES

As for [conventional] existence based on false names, it refers for example to such things as yoghurt which actually *are* perceptible through their visible forms, smells, tastes, and tangibility. [In these cases], it is simply on account of the coming together of particular causes and conditions that the given phenomenon is provided such false designations as "yoghurt."

Although such phenomena do "exist," their existence is an existence based on the presence of different causal and conditional dharmas. Although such phenomena [may be said to be] "nonexistent," still such nonexistence is not of the same order of nonexistence as

兔角龟毛无。但以因缘合故假名有。酪[*]叠亦如是。复次有极微色香味触故。有毛分。毛分因缘故有毛。毛因缘故有毳。毳因缘故有缕。缕因缘故有[*]叠。[*]叠因缘故有衣。若无极微色香味触因缘。亦无毛分。毛分无故亦无毛。毛无故亦无毳。毳无故亦无缕。缕无故亦无[*]叠。[*]叠无故亦无衣。问曰。亦不必一切物皆从因缘和合故有。如微尘至细故无分。无分故无和合。[*]叠毳故可破。微尘中无分。云何可破。答曰。至微无实强为之名。何以故麁细相待。因麁故有细。是细复应有细。复次若有极微色。则有十方分。若有十方分

兔角龜毛無。但以因緣合故假名有。酪[*]疊亦如是。復次有極微色香味觸故。有毛分。毛分因緣故有毛。毛因緣故有毳。毳因緣故有縷。縷因緣故有[*]疊。[*]疊因緣故有衣。若無極微色香味觸因緣。亦無毛分。毛分無故亦無毛。毛無故亦無毳。毳無故亦無縷。縷無故亦無[*]疊。[*]疊無故亦無衣。問曰。亦不必一切物皆從因緣和合故有。如微塵至細故無分。無分故無和合。[*]疊毳故可破。微塵中無分。云何可破。答曰。至微無實強為之名。何以故麁細相待。因麁故有細。是細復應有細。復次若有極微色。則有十方分。若有十方分

that of the horns of the hare and the fur of the turtle. [In these cases], it is only on account of the coming together of particular causes and conditions that there is this [conventional] existence based on false names. Yoghurt and cloth are both the same in this respect.

4) Existence Based on Constituent Dharmas

Moreover, it is based on the most minute constituent elements perceptible through their visible forms, smells, tastes, and tangibility that there exist the components of a fiber. It is based on the causes and conditions inherent in the components of a fiber that a fiber exists. It is based on the causes and conditions of fibers that there exists a mass of fibers. It is based on the causes and conditions of a mass of fibers that there exist threads. It is based on the causes and conditions of threads that there exists cloth. It is based on the causes and conditions of cloth that there exists a robe.

Wherever there there do not actually exist such causes and conditions of the extremely subtle elements perceptible through their visible forms, smells, tastes and tangibility, then the components of a fiber do not exist either. Because the components of a fiber do not actually exist, then a fiber does not exist either. Because a fiber does not exist, then a mass of fibers does not exist either. Because a mass of fibers does not exist, then thread does not exist either.

Because thread does not exist, then cloth does not exist either. Because cloth does not exist, then a robe does not exist either.

b. Objection: But Irreducibly Minute Entities Do Exist

Question: Still, it's not necessarily the case that everything exists on account of the coming together of causes and conditions. For instance, because tiny particles are the most extremely minute, they have no constituent components. Because they have no components they have no combining [from which they are produced]. It is because cloth is coarse that it can be broken down [into constituent components]. But there are no components within tiny particles. How then can *they* be broken down [into constituent components]?

Response: "The most extremely minute" entity has no reality to it. It is itself a forced designation. Why? Because "coarse" and "subtle" are mere relative terms. It is based on "coarseness" that there exists "subtlety." This entity which is subtle should additionally contain that which is comparatively more subtle yet.

Moreover, if this most extremely minute form were to exist, then it would have spatial divisions corresponding to the ten directions. If it had divisions corresponding to the ten directions [based upon

是不名为极微。若无十方分
则不名为色。复次若有极微
则应有虚空分齐。若有分者
则不名极微。[21]复次若有
极微。是[148a]中有色香味触
作分。色香味触作分。是不
名极微。以是推求微尘则不
可得。如经言。色若麁若细
若内若外。总而观之无常无
我。不言有微尘。是名分破
空。复有观空。是[*]叠随心
[1]有。如坐禅人。观[*]叠或
作地或作水或作火或作风。
或青或黄或白或赤或都空。
如十一切入观。如佛在耆阇
崛山中。与比丘僧俱入王
舍城。道中见大[2]水。佛于
[*]水上敷尼师坛坐。告诸比
丘。若比丘入禅心得自在。
能令大[*]水作地即成实地。

简体字

是不名為極微。若無十方分
則不名為色。復次若有極微
則應有虛空分齊。若有分者
則不名極微。[21]復次若有
極微。是[148a]中有色香味觸
作分。色香味觸作分。是不
名極微。以是推求微塵則不
可得。如經言。色若麁若細
若內若外。總而觀之無常無
我。不言有微塵。是名分破
空。復有觀空。是[*]疊隨心
[1]有。如坐禪人。觀[*]疊或
作地或作水或作火或作風。
或青或黃或白或赤或都空。
如十一切入觀。如佛在耆闍
崛山中。與比丘僧俱入王
舍城。道中見大[2]水。佛於
[*]水上敷尼師壇坐。告諸比
丘。若比丘入禪心得自在。
能令大[*]水作地即成實地。

正體字

which one could divide it up], then this could not be designated as "the most extremely minute" entity. If it did not have divisions corresponding to the ten directions, then it could not be [legitimately] referred to as "form."

Moreover, if this most extremely minute entity exists, then it still ought to have [segmentable perimeter] boundaries which divide it off from empty space. If it is divisible, then it cannot be referred to as "the most extremely minute" entity.

Moreover, if this most extremely minute entity exists, there exist within it the constituent parts perceptible through their visible form, smell, taste, and tangibility. If it possesses constituent parts perceptible through their visible form, smell, taste, and tangibility, then it cannot be referred to as "the most extremely minute" entity.

If one pursues analysis in this manner, as one seeks to find a most extremely minute particle, then one remains unable to find it.

This corresponds to a statement in a sutra: "Forms, whether coarse or whether subtle, whether inward or whether outward, are all inclusively contemplated as impermanent and devoid of self." It does not state therein that there exists a most extremely minute entity. [This mode of analysis] constitutes what is known as "emptiness reached by breaking down into component parts."

c. Emptiness Realized Through Contemplation

In addition to this, there is also "emptiness arrived at through contemplation." This cloth comes into existence in accordance with the mind. In the case of the person who sits in dhyāna meditation, as he contemplates a piece of cloth, he may make it into earth, or make it into water, or make it into fire, or make it into wind. Or he may make it blue, or yellow, or white, or red, or entirely empty, entering contemplation thereby in accordance with the ten universal bases (*kṛtsnāyatana*).

1) Example: the Buddha Sits on Water (Story)

Take for example one time when the Buddha was at Mount Gṛdhrakūṭa. He went together with the Bhikshu Sangha into the city of Kings' Abode. They came upon a large pool of water in the road. The Buddha spread out his sitting cloth on the surface of the water and sat down. He told the Bhikshus, "When a bhikshu's entry into dhyāna reaches the point where his mind gains a state of sovereign independence, he becomes able to cause a great body of water to act as earth and immediately become like solid ground.

何以故。是[*]水中有地分
故。如是水火风。金银种种
宝物即皆成实。何以故。是
[*]水中皆有其分。复次如一
美色。婬人见之以为净妙心
生染着。不净观人视之种种
恶露无一净处。等妇见之
妬瞋[3]憎恶目不欲见以为不
净。婬人观之为乐。妬人观
之为苦。[4]行人观之得道。
无豫之人观之无所适莫。如
见土木。若此美色实净。四
种人观皆应见净。若实不
净。四种人观皆应不净。以
是故知。好丑在心。外无定
也。观空亦如是。复次是[*]
叠中有十八空相故观之便
空。空故不可得。如是种种
因缘财物空。决定不可得。
云何施人不可得。如[*]叠因
缘。和合故有。

何以故。是[*]水中有地分
故。如是水火風。金銀種種
寶物即皆成實。何以故。是
[*]水中皆有其分。復次如一
美色。婬人見之以為淨妙心
生染著。不淨觀人視之種種
惡露無一淨處。等婦見之
妬瞋[3]憎惡目不欲見以為不
淨。婬人觀之為樂。妬人觀
之為苦。[4]行人觀之得道。
無豫之人觀之無所適莫。如
見土木。若此美色實淨。四
種人觀皆應見淨。若實不
淨。四種人觀皆應不淨。以
是故知。好醜在心。外無定
也。觀空亦如是。復次是[*]
疊中有十八空相故觀之便
空。空故不可得。如是種種
因緣財物空。決定不可得。
云何施人不可得。如[*]疊因
緣。和合故有。

简体字   正體字

How is this so? It is because this water contains earthen components within it. Thus, within water, fire, and air, the gold, silver, and various other precious things contained therein may all be made to immediately manifest their solidity. How is this possible? This is possible because the water, [fire, and air] all contain a portion of those things within them."

2)   EXAMPLE: HOW QUALITIES HAVE NO OBJECTIVELY REAL EXISTENCE

This is also exemplified by a particular beautiful physical form. When a lustful person looks at it, he takes it to be pure and marvelous and so his mind develops a defiling attachment. When a person who practices the contemplation of impurity looks at it, he perceives all manner of disgusting discharges and finds that there is not a single part of it that is pure. When one who is also a woman looks at it, she may be jealous and hateful to the point where she is filled with disgust, cannot bear to look upon it, and is of the opinion that it is impure.

The lustful person contemplates this same thing and regards it as pleasurable. The jealous person contemplates this and takes it as a cause of bitterness. The yogin contemplates this and gains the Path. A person with no particular interest contemplates this and finds nothing either attractive or repellent in it. It is the same for him as looking at earth or trees.

If this beautiful form was actually pure, when these four types of people contemplated it, they should all perceive purity. If it was actually impure, when the four kinds of people contemplated it, they should all see it as impure. On account of this one knows "fine" and "ugly" abide in the mind. Objectively, there is nothing which is fixed. When one pursues the realization of emptiness through contemplation, the situation is much the same.

d.   CONCLUSION: THE MATERIAL GIFT CANNOT BE FOUND

Moreover, because this cloth is characterized by the eighteen kinds of emptiness, when one contemplates it, one finds it to be empty [of inherent existence].[32] Because it is empty, it cannot be gotten at. On account of all sorts of causal bases such as these, a valuable material object is empty [of inherent existence]. It definitely cannot finally be apprehended.

5.   HOW THE BENEFACTOR CAN'T BE FOUND EITHER

How is it that the "benefactor" cannot be gotten at? It is just as with the piece of cloth which exists on the basis of the coming together

分分推之 [*]叠不可得。施者亦如是。四大围虚空名为身。是身识动作来往坐起。[5]假名为人。分分求之亦不可得。复次一切众界入中我不可得。我不可得故施人不可得。何以故。我有种种名字。人天男女施人受人受苦人受乐人畜生等。是但有名而实法不可得。问曰。[148b]若施者不可得。云何有菩萨行檀波罗蜜。答曰。因缘和合故有名字。如屋如车实法不可得。问曰。云何我不可得。答曰。如上我闻一时中已说。今当更说。佛说六识。眼识及眼识相应法共缘色。不缘屋舍城郭种种诸名。耳鼻舌身识亦如是。意识及意识[6]相应法。知眼知色知眼识。乃至知意知法知意识。

简体字

分分推之 [*]疊不可得。施者亦如是。四大圍虛空名為身。是身識動作來往坐起。[5]假名為人。分分求之亦不可得。復次一切眾界入中我不可得。我不可得故施人不可得。何以故。我有種種名字。人天男女施人受人受苦人受樂人畜生等。是但有名而實法不可得。問曰。[148b]若施者不可得。云何有菩薩行檀波羅蜜。答曰。因緣和合故有名字。如屋如車實法不可得。問曰。云何我不可得。答曰。如上我聞一時中已說。今當更說。佛說六識。眼識及眼識相應法共緣色。不緣屋舍城郭種種諸名。耳鼻舌身識亦如是。意識及意識[6]相應法。知眼知色知眼識。乃至知意知法知意識。

正體字

of causes and conditions, and which cannot be gotten at through analysis of its constituent parts.

It is just the same with the one who gives. It is the four primary elements surrounded by empty space which constitute the body. This body's consciousness, movements, comings and goings, sitting and rising are artificially designated as a "person." However, when, part by part, one seeks to locate [this person], it still cannot be found anywhere.

Additionally, the self cannot be found among any of the aggregates, sense realms, or sense bases. Because the self cannot be gotten at, the benefactor cannot be gotten at. How is this so? The self has all manner of designations: human, god, male, female, person who gives, person who receives, person who experiences suffering, person who experiences bliss, animal, and so forth. These possess only a name. Hence an actual dharma cannot be found there.

a. Objection: If So, Bodhisattvas Couldn't Exist to Practice *Dāna*

Question: If the "benefactor" cannot be gotten at, how can there exist a bodhisattva who practices *dāna pāramitā*?

Response: It is based on the coming together of causes and conditions that a name exists. It is just as with a building or a cart wherein actual dharmas cannot be found.[33]

1) Objection: How Is it That the Self Cannot Be Found?

Question: How is it that the self cannot be found?

Response: This is as discussed above in the explanation of "Thus I have heard at one time…".[34] Now we shall discuss it further.

2) Refutation of Self in Objects of the Consciousnesses

In the Buddha's discussion of the six consciousnesses, he indicated that the eye consciousness as well as dharmas associated with eye consciousness together take visible forms as the objective condition. They do not take as objective conditions all sorts of names such as "building," "house," "city," and "outlying precincts." The consciousnesses of ear, nose, tongue, and body function in the same way in this respect.

The intellectual mind consciousness and the dharmas associated with the intellectual mind consciousness are aware of the eye, aware of form, aware of eye consciousness, and so forth until we come to their being aware of the intellectual mind faculty, aware of dharmas [as objects of mind], and aware of the intellectual mind consciousness itself.

是识所缘法皆空无我生灭
故。不自在故。无为法中亦
不计我。苦乐不受故。是中
若强有我法。应当有第七识
识我。而今不尔。以是故
知无我。问曰。何以[7]识无
我。一切人各[8]于自身中生
计我。不于他身中生我。若
自身中无我。而妄见为我
者。他身[9]中无我亦应于他
身而妄见为我。复次若内无
我。色识念念生灭。云何分
别知是色青黄赤白。复次若
无我今现在人识。[10]渐渐
生灭。身命断时亦尽诸行罪
福。谁随谁受。谁受苦乐谁
解脱者。如是种种内缘故。
知有我。答曰。此俱有难。
若于他身生计我者。复当
言。何以不自身中生计我。

是識所緣法皆空無我生滅
故。不自在故。無為法中亦
不計我。苦樂不受故。是中
若強有我法。應當有第七識
識我。而今不爾。以是故
知無我。問曰。何以[7]識無
我。一切人各[8]於自身中生
計我。不於他身中生我。若
自身中無我。而妄見為我
者。他身[9]中無我亦應於他
身而妄見為我。復次若內無
我。色識念念生滅。云何分
別知是色青黃赤白。復次若
無我今現在人識。[10]漸漸
生滅。身命斷時亦盡諸行罪
福。誰隨誰受。誰受苦樂誰
解脫者。如是種種內緣故。
知有我。答曰。此俱有難。
若於他身生計我者。復當
言。何以不自身中生計我。

简体字   正體字

Those dharmas which are taken as objective conditions by these consciousnesses are all empty and devoid of any "self." This is on account of their being produced and destroyed, and on account of their not being inherently existent.

Nor can one reckon the existence of a self within the sphere of the dharmas which are unconditioned. This is because there is no experiencing therein of either suffering or bliss.

If, in the midst of all of this, one must still insist on the existence of a self, then it would have to involve the existence of a seventh consciousness which is aware of the existence of a self. However, that is not now the case. For this reason we know that there is no self.

b. Objection: A Self Must Exist

Question: How can one know that there is no self? Everyone gives rise to the idea of a self with respect to their own bodies. They do not give rise to such an idea with respect to the bodies of others. If there is no self associated with one's own body and yet one erroneously perceives that it constitutes a self, one ought to also erroneously perceive the existence of a self in other people's bodies where there is no self either.

Furthermore, if it is the case that subjectively there is no self, given that consciousness of forms is newly produced and destroyed in every thought-moment, how could one distinguish and know that these colors are blue, yellow, red or white?[35]

Moreover, if it were the case that there were no self, since the human consciousnesses are now continuously being newly[36] produced and destroyed, when the physical lifespan is cut off, that would also put an end to the offenses and merits associated with one's actions. Who then would there be to follow along with and undergo retributions? Who then would experience subsequent suffering or bliss? Who would obtain liberation? On account of all of these inward conditions [specific to the individual], one knows that a self must exist.

Response: These ideas all have problems:

1) Refutation of Any Self Based on Its Assumed Location

If it were the case that one reckoned the existence of a self in the body of someone else, then we ought to next ask, "Why is it that [in such a hypothetical case], one would not [still continue to] reckon the existence of a self in one's own body?"

复次五众因缘生故空无我。从无明因缘生二十身见。是我见[11]自于五阴相续生。以从此五众缘生故。即计此五众为我。不在他身以其习故。复次若有神者可有彼我。汝神有无未了而问彼我。其犹人问兔角。答[12]似马角。马角若实有可以证兔角。马角犹尚未了。而欲以证兔角。复次自于身生我故便自谓有神。汝言神遍亦应计他身为我以是故不应言自身中生计我心于他身[148c]不生。故知有神。复次有人于他物中我心生。如外道坐禅人。用地一切入观时。见地则是我我则是地。

復次五眾因緣生故空無我。從無明因緣生二十身見。是我見[11]自於五陰相續生。以從此五眾緣生故。即計此五眾為我。不在他身以其習故。復次若有神者可有彼我。汝神有無未了而問彼我。其猶人問兔角。答[12]似馬角。馬角若實有可以證兔角。馬角猶尚未了。而欲以證兔角。復次自於身生我故便自謂有神。汝言神遍亦應計他身為我以是故不應言自身中生計我心於他身[148c]不生。故知有神。復次有人於他物中我心生。如外道坐禪人。用地一切入觀時。見地則是我我則是地。

简体字   正體字

Moreover, because the five aggregates, [which form the supposed bases for imputing a "self"], are themselves produced from causes and conditions, they are empty and devoid of the presence of any self. The twenty views associated with the body are produced from causes and conditions associated with ignorance. This view which perceives a self therein naturally arises through the apparent continuity of the five aggregates. Because it is produced from the conditions associated with these very five aggregates, one straightaway reckons that these five aggregates are what constitute the self. This does not occur with respect to another person's body, this on account of the specificity of individual habituation.

Furthermore, if there did exist a spiritual soul (*ātman*), it could in fact be that one reckoned the existence of one's "self" in the body of another. You have not yet even understood about the existence or nonexistence of your own spiritual soul and yet you inquire about reckoning the existence of one's "self" in the body of some other person.

This is like being asked by someone about the horns of a hare and then replying to him that they are like the horns of a horse, this based on the assumption that, if the horns of a horse actually do exist, then they may be used as a basis for proving the existence of the horns of a hare. And so one proceeds in this manner, not yet having understood about the existence of the horns of a horse, yet still desiring to take them as proof for the existence of the horns of a hare.

Moreover, as for your idea that it is because one naturally generates the idea of a self with respect to one's own body that one then holds the opinion that a spiritual soul exists, since you claim that the spiritual soul is all-pervading, one ought indeed to reckon the existence of a self in the bodies of others. Therefore one should not be asserting that one gives rise to the idea of a self with respect to one's own body but does not give rise to it in relation to another person's body and that therefore one knows that a spiritual soul exists.

Then again, there actually *are* people who *do* have the idea of a self arise in relation to other phenomena. Take for example certain non-Buddhists who sit in dhyāna meditation. When they employ the "earth" universal-basis (*kṛtsnāyatana*) contemplation and thus perceive the [pervasive] existence of the earth element, they may then think, "The earth is me and I am the earth." They may also

水火风空亦如是。颠倒故于
他身中亦计我。复次有时于
他身生我。如有一人受使远
行。独宿空舍。夜中有鬼担
一死人来着其前。复有一鬼
逐来瞋骂前鬼。是死人是我
物。汝何以担来。先鬼言是
我物我自持来。后鬼言是死
人实我担来。二鬼各捉一手
争之。前鬼言[13]此有人可
问。后鬼即问。是死人谁担
来。是人思惟。此二鬼力
大。若实语亦当死。若妄语
亦当死。俱不免死何为妄
语。[14]语言。前鬼担来。后
鬼大瞋。捉人手拔出着地。
前鬼取死人一臂[15]拊之即
着。如是两臂两脚头胁举身
皆易。于是二鬼共食所易人
身拭口而去。其人思惟。我
[16]人母生身眼见二鬼食尽。
今我此身尽是他肉。我今定
有身耶。为

简体字

水火風空亦如是。顛倒故於
他身中亦計我。復次有時於
他身生我。如有一人受使遠
行。獨宿空舍。夜中有鬼擔
一死人來著其前。復有一鬼
逐來瞋罵前鬼。是死人是我
物。汝何以擔來。先鬼言是
我物我自持來。後鬼言是死
人實我擔來。二鬼各捉一手
爭之。前鬼言[13]此有人可
問。後鬼即問。是死人誰擔
來。是人思惟。此二鬼力
大。若實語亦當死。若妄語
亦當死。俱不免死何為妄
語。[14]語言。前鬼擔來。後
鬼大瞋。捉人手拔出著地。
前鬼取死人一臂[15]拊之即
著。如是兩臂兩腳頭脇舉身
皆易。於是二鬼共食所易人
身拭口而去。其人思惟。我
[16]人母生身眼見二鬼食盡。
今我此身盡是他肉。我今定
有身耶。為

正體字

be prone to do this in regard to water, fire, wind or space. Thus, on account of such inverted views, they may then also be prone to reckoning the self as existing within the bodies of others.

2) The Traveler and the Ghost (Story)

Additionally, there are times when someone generates the idea that his "self" inhabits some other person's body. Take for example the case of a man who had been assigned a mission whereby he was compelled to travel a great distance. [While on the road], he spent the night alone in a vacant dwelling. In the middle of the night, a ghost carried in a man's corpse and laid it down in front of him. Then there was another ghost who chased along behind and angrily castigated the first ghost, yelling, "This corpse is mine! Why did you carry it in here?"

The first ghost said, "It belongs to me! I carried it in here myself!"

The second ghost retorted, "The fact of the matter is, *I* am the one who carried this corpse in here!" Then each of the ghosts grabbed one of the hands of the corpse and tried to pull it away from the other. Thereupon the first ghost said, "There's a man here. We can ask *him* to settle this."

The ghost who had come in later then asked the traveler, "Well, who was it that carried this corpse in here?"

The traveler thought to himself, "Both of these ghosts are very strong. If I report the facts, I'm bound to die. If I lie, I'm also bound to die. So, since I can't avoid being killed in either case, what's the point in lying about it?" And so he replied, "It was the first ghost who carried in the corpse."

The second ghost flew into a rage, grabbed one of the [traveling] man's hands, tore that limb off, and then threw it down on the ground. At this, the first ghost pulled off one of the arms from the corpse and attached it as a replacement. They then proceeded in this fashion with both arms, both feet, the head, the two sides, and so forth until the traveler's entire body had been switched. The two ghosts then proceeded to devour the body which they had gotten from the exchange. When they had finished, they wiped their mouths and departed.

At that point the traveler thought to himself, "With my very own eyes I saw those two ghosts entirely devour the body born of my mother! This body which I now have here is composed entirely of someone else's flesh! Do I really still have a body now? Or is it the

无身耶。若以为有尽是他身。若以为无今现有身。如是思惟。其心迷闷。譬如狂人。明朝寻路而去。到前国土见[17]有佛塔众僧。不论[18]馀事但问己身为有为无。诸比丘问。汝是何人。答言。我亦不自知是人非人。即为众僧广说上事。诸比丘言。此人自知无我易可得度。而语之言。汝身从本已来恒自无我。非适今也。但以四大和合故计为我身。如[19]汝本身与今无异。诸比丘度之为道断诸烦恼。即得阿罗汉是为有时他身亦计为我。不可以有彼此故谓有[20]我。复次是[*]我实性决定不可得。若常相非常相自在相不自在相作相不作相[149a]色相非色相。如是等种种皆不可得。若有相则有法。无相则无法。[*]我今无相则知

無身耶。若以為有盡是他身。若以為無今現有身。如是思惟。其心迷悶。譬如狂人。明朝尋路而去。到前國土見[17]有佛塔眾僧。不論[18]餘事但問己身為有為無。諸比丘問。汝是何人。答言。我亦不自知是人非人。即為眾僧廣說上事。諸比丘言。此人自知無我易可得度。而語之言。汝身從本已來恒自無我。非適今也。但以四大和合故計為我身。如[19]汝本身與今無異。諸比丘度之為道斷諸煩惱。即得阿羅漢是為有時他身亦計為我。不可以有彼此故謂有[20]我。復次是[*]我實性決定不可得。若常相非常相自在相不自在相作相不作相[149a]色相非色相。如是等種種皆不可得。若有相則有法。無相則無法。[*]我今無相則知

简体字　　　　　　　　　　正體字

case that I have no body at all? If I hold the view that I *do* indeed have a body—that body is actually somebody else's entirely. If I hold that I *don't* have one—still, there *is* a body here right now! He continued to ponder like this until his mind became so confused and distressed that he became like a man gone mad.

The next morning, he went off down the road. When he reached the neighboring country, he saw that there was a buddha stupa and a group of monks. He couldn't talk about anything else. He could only keep asking whether his body was existent or nonexistent. The bhikshus asked him, "Just who are you, anyway?"

The traveler replied, "Well, as for me, I don't know myself whether I'm a person or a non-person." He then described in detail for the group of Sanghins the events which had transpired.

The bhikshus remarked, "This man has comprehended on his own the nonexistence of a self. He could easily gain deliverance." And so they offered an explanation, saying, "From its origin on up until the present, your body has always naturally been devoid of any self. It's not something that just happened now. It is merely on account of an aggregation of the four primary elements that one conceives of it as *my* body. In this respect, your original body and this one you now have are no different."

Thus the bhikshus succeeded in bring about the traveler's deliverance to the Path, whereupon he cut off all afflictions and immediately realized arhatship. This is a case of there being times when one reckons the existence of oneself in the body of another person.

One cannot posit the existence of a self based on [the concept of] "that versus this."

3) Refutation of Any Valid Characteristics of a Self

Moreover, any actual [inherently existent] nature to this "self" most definitely cannot be gotten at. And whether it be the characteristic of permanency, the characteristic of being impermanent, the characteristic of being inherently existent, the characteristic of not being inherently existent, the characteristic being compounded, the characteristic of not being compounded, the characteristic of being form, or the characteristic of being formless—all such different sorts of characteristics cannot finally be found.

If a particular characteristic exists, then a corresponding dharma must also exist. If there is no such characteristic, then there is no corresponding dharma. Because it is now the case that this "self" is devoid of any characteristics, one knows consequently that there

无[*]我。若[*]我是常不应有
杀罪。何以故身可杀非常
故。[*]我不可杀。常故。问
曰。[*]我虽常故不可杀。但
杀身则有杀罪。答曰。若杀
身有杀罪者。毘[1]尼中言。
自杀无杀罪。罪福从恼他益
他生。非自供养身自杀身故
有罪有福。以是[2]故毘尼中
言。自杀身无杀罪。有愚痴
贪欲瞋恚之咎。若神常者不
应死不应生。何以故汝等法
神常。一切遍满五道中。云
何有死生。死名此处失。生
名彼处出。以是故不得言神
常。若神常者亦应[3]不受苦
乐。何以故苦来则忧乐至则
喜。若为忧喜所变者则非常
也。若常应如虚空雨不能
湿热不能乾。亦无今世后
世。[4]若神常者示不应有后
世生今世死。若神常者则常
有我见。不应

無[*]我。若[*]我是常不應有
殺罪。何以故身可殺非常
故。[*]我不可殺。常故。問
曰。[*]我雖常故不可殺。但
殺身則有殺罪。答曰。若殺
身有殺罪者。毘[1]尼中言。
自殺無殺罪。罪福從惱他益
他生。非自供養身自殺身故
有罪有福。以是[2]故毘尼中
言。自殺身無殺罪。有愚癡
貪欲瞋恚之咎。若神常者不
應死不應生。何以故汝等法
神常。一切遍滿五道中。云
何有死生。死名此處失。生
名彼處出。以是故不得言神
常。若神常者亦應[3]不受苦
樂。何以故苦來則憂樂至則
喜。若為憂喜所變者則非常
也。若常應如虛空雨不能
濕熱不能乾。亦無今世後
世。[4]若神常者示不應有後
世生今世死。若神常者則常
有我見。不應

简体字　　　　　　　　正體字

is no self. And if the "self" were actually permanent, then there should be no such thing as the offense of killing. Why is this so? The body might be able to be killed, this because it is impermanent. However, the self could not be killed, this due to the [supposed fact] of its being permanent.

c.   OBJECTION: OFFENSE LIES IN PHYSICAL KILLING

Question: Although one could not kill the self on account of its being permanent, even if one only killed the body, one would thereby incur the offense of killing.

Response: As for incurring the offense of killing from the killing of the body, it says in the Vinaya that if one commits suicide, there is no killing offense *per se*. Offense on the one hand or merit on the other derives from either afflicting someone else or, alternatively, from benefiting someone else. It is not the case that if one makes offerings to one's own body or kills one's own body one will have either offense or merit. It is for this reason that it says in the Vinaya that in the event that one kills one's own body, there is no offense of killing per se. However, the faults of stupidity, greed, and hatred *are* present in such a case.[37]

1)   REFUTATION OF THE PERMANENCE OF THE ĀTMAN

If the spiritual soul (*ātman*) were eternal, then one should not be born and should not die. Why is this the case? According to the dharma of those such as yourself, the spiritual soul is eternal. It pervades everywhere filling up the five paths of rebirth. How could there be death or birth? Death is defined by disappearing from this place. Birth is defined by coming forth in another place. For this reason one cannot say that the spiritual soul is eternal.

If it were the case that the spiritual soul were eternal, it should also be the case that it does not experience either suffering or bliss. How is this the case? If suffering comes, then one is distressed. If bliss comes, then one is delighted. If it is the case that it is changed by distress or delight, then it is impermanent. If it were permanent, then it should be like empty space which cannot be moistened by rain nor dried by heat.

Nor would there be either present or future lifetimes. If it were the case that the spiritual soul were eternal, then it is manifestly the case that one should not have either birth into a later existence or any dying in the present existence.

If it were the case that the spiritual soul were eternal, then one would constantly have a view of a self and one should not then be

得涅盘。若神常者则无起无
灭。不应有妄失。以其无神
识无常故。有忘有失。是故
神非常也。如是等种种因缘
可知神非常相。若神无常相
者亦无罪无福。若身无常神
亦无常。二事俱灭则堕断灭
边。堕断灭则无到后世受罪
福者。若断灭则得涅盘。不
须断结亦不用后世罪福因
缘。如是等种种因缘可知神
非无常。若神自在相作相
者。则应随所欲得皆得。今
所欲更不得。非所欲更得。
若神自在。亦不应有作恶行
堕畜生恶道中。复次一切众
生皆不乐苦。谁当好乐而更
得苦。以是故

简体字

得涅槃。若神常者則無起無
滅。不應有妄失。以其無神
識無常故。有忘有失。是故
神非常也。如是等種種因緣
可知神非常相。若神無常相
者亦無罪無福。若身無常神
亦無常。二事俱滅則墮斷滅
邊。墮斷滅則無到後世受罪
福者。若斷滅則得涅槃。不
須斷結亦不用後世罪福因
緣。如是等種種因緣可知神
非無常。若神自在相作相
者。則應隨所欲得皆得。今
所欲更不得。非所欲更得。
若神自在。亦不應有作惡行
墮畜生惡道中。復次一切眾
生皆不樂苦。誰當好樂而更
得苦。以是故

正體字

able to realize nirvāṇa. If the spiritual soul were eternal, then there would be no arising and no destruction. There should then be no forgetting and no errors.

On account of there being no consciousness on the part of this "spiritual soul" and on account of its being impermanent, there *is* forgetting and there *is* also error. Therefore it is *not* the case that the spiritual soul is eternal. On account of all sorts of reasons such as these, one can know that this spiritual soul [which you posit] would not actually be characterized by permanence.

2) REFUTATION OF IMPERMANENCE OF THE ĀTMAN

If on the other hand the spiritual soul were characterized by impermanence, there would be neither offenses nor merits. If the body were impermanent, then the spiritual soul would be impermanent as well. If the two phenomena were both destroyed, then one would fall into the extreme view known as annihilationism.

If one falls into this annihilationism, then that carries as a consequence the result that there would be no arriving at a later lifetime wherein one would undergo retribution for karmic offenses or meritorious deeds. If annihilation were the case, then in gaining nirvāṇa, it would not be necessary to cut off the fetters nor would there be any function in later lives for the causes and conditions associated with karmic offenses and meritorious deeds. On account of all sorts of reasons such as these, one can know that the spiritual soul is not impermanent either.

3) REFUTATION OF ĀTMAN FREEDOM, INVOLVEMENT, NON-INVOLVEMENT

If it were the case that the spiritual soul were characterized by being sovereignly independent or characterized by having that which it does, then it ought to be the case that, no matter what it desired, it would gain it in every case. Now, however, there are cases where one desires something, but, on the contrary, one does not gain it, while in other cases where there is something which one does *not* desire and nonetheless, contrary to one's wishes, one gains precisely *that*.

If the spiritual soul were sovereignly independent, then it should not be the case that it could engage in evil conduct and then fall into the wretched destiny of birth among the animals. Moreover, it is the case that all beings are displeased by suffering. Who then would take pleasure in bliss and yet, contrary to those inclinations, deliberately procure suffering? On account of these factors, one

知神不自在。亦[5]不[6]作。又如人畏罪[149b]故自强行善。若自在者。何以畏罪而自强修福。又诸众生不得如意。常为烦恼爱缚所牵。如是等种种因缘。知神不自在不自作。若神不自在不自作者。是为无神相。[7]言我者即是[8]六识更无异事。复次若不作者。云何阎罗王问罪人。谁使汝作此罪者。罪人答言。是我自作。以是故知非不自作。若神色相者是事不然。何以故。一切色无常故。问曰。人云何言色是我相。答曰。有人言。神在心中微细如芥子。清净名为净色身。更有人言如麦。有言如豆。有言半寸。有言一寸。初受身时最在前受。譬如[9]像骨及其成身如[*]像已[10]庄。有言大小随人身。死坏时此亦前出。

知神不自在。亦[5]不[6]作。又如人畏罪[149b]故自強行善。若自在者。何以畏罪而自強修福。又諸眾生不得如意。常為煩惱愛縛所牽。如是等種種因緣。知神不自在不自作。若神不自在不自作者。是為無神相。[7]言我者即是[8]六識更無異事。復次若不作者。云何閻羅王問罪人。誰使汝作此罪者。罪人答言。是我自作。以是故知非不自作。若神色相者是事不然。何以故。一切色無常故。問曰。人云何言色是我相。答曰。有人言。神在心中微細如芥子。清淨名為淨色身。更有人言如麥。有言如豆。有言半寸。有言一寸。初受身時最在前受。譬如[9]像骨及其成身如[*]像已[10]莊。有言大小隨人身。死壞時此亦前出。

简体字   正體字

knows that the spiritual soul is not sovereignly independent. Nor does it involve itself in actions.

Again, take for instance when people force themselves to practice goodness out of fear of punishments. If it were the case that [the spiritual soul] is sovereignly independent, why would they force themselves to cultivate merit out of fear of punishments?

Furthermore, beings do not succeed in having things happen in accordance with their intentions. They are constantly dragged about by the bonds of afflictions and affection. For all sorts of reasons such as these one should realize that the spiritual soul is not sovereignly independent nor does it involve itself in actions. If it is the case that the spiritual soul is not sovereignly independent and does not involve itself in actions, then this constitutes the mark of the nonexistence of any spiritual soul. When one speaks of a "self," this is actually just the six consciousnesses. There are no additional factors beyond that.

Then again, if [the soul] does not involve itself in actions, why is it that when King Yama asks a karmic malefactor—"Who ordered you to commit these offenses?"—the person who committed the offenses replies, "They were committed by myself alone"? One knows from this that it is not the case either that it does *not* involve itself in actions. As for the spiritual soul being characterized by [a basis in] form, this case is not valid, either. Why? Because all manifestations of form are impermanent.

d. Objection: Why Then Do Some Say That Self Is Form?

Question: Why then do people claim that the self is characterized by [a basis in] form?

Response: There are those who say that the spiritual soul resides in the heart, is as tiny as a mustard seed, is pure, and is referred to as the pure form body. There are other people who say that it is the size of a grain of wheat. There are those who say it is in size like a bean. There are those who say that its dimension is one half inch. There are those who say it is an inch in size and that in the beginning, when one takes on a body, it is taken on as the very first thing.

It is supposed to be in shape like the skeleton of an elephant and as one's body matures it becomes in shape like an elephant already well-formed. There are those who say its size corresponds to that of the given person's body and that when one passes away at death, it is the first to go then as well.

如此事皆不尔也。何以故。
一切色四大所造。因缘生故
无常。若神是色色无常神亦
无常。若无常者如上所说。
问曰。身有二种。麁身及细
身。麁身无常细身是神。世
世常去入五道中。答曰。此
细身不可得。若有细身应有
处所可得。如五藏四体。一
一处中求皆不可得。问曰。
此细身微细。初死时已去。
若活时则不可[11]求得汝云
何能见。又此细身非五情能
见能知。唯有神通圣人乃能
得见。答曰。若尔者与无无
异。如人死时。舍此生阴入
中阴中。是时今世身灭受中
阴身。此无前后灭时即生。
譬如蜡印印泥。泥中受印印
即时坏。成坏一时亦无前
后。是时受中阴中有。

如此事皆不爾也。何以故。
一切色四大所造。因緣生故
無常。若神是色色無常神亦
無常。若無常者如上所說。
問曰。身有二種。麁身及細
身。麁身無常細身是神。世
世常去入五道中。答曰。此
細身不可得。若有細身應有
處所可得。如五藏四體。一
一處中求皆不可得。問曰。
此細身微細。初死時已去。
若活時則不可[11]求得汝云
何能見。又此細身非五情能
見能知。唯有神通聖人乃能
得見。答曰。若爾者與無無
異。如人死時。捨此生陰入
中陰中。是時今世身滅受中
陰身。此無前後滅時即生。
譬如蠟印印泥。泥中受印印
即時壞。成壞一時亦無前
後。是時受中陰中有。

简体字   正體字

All cases such as these do not correspond to the truth. Why not? All forms are created from the four primary elements. On account of their being produced from causes and conditions, they are impermanent. If it were the case that the spiritual soul were [based in] form, because form is impermanent, the spiritual soul would be impermanent as well. If it is the case that it is impermanent, then the inherent fallacies are such as have already been discussed previously.

e. Objection: The Spiritual Soul Is a Minute Entity

Question: There are two kinds of bodies, the gross body and the minute body. The gross body is impermanent. The minute body is the spiritual soul. In life after life, it constantly goes along and enters into the five paths of rebirth.

Response: This "minute body" cannot be found. If a minute body does exist, then there ought to be a location in which it can be found such as, for instance, in the five organs or in the four limbs. However, one can look for it in every single place, but it still cannot be found.

f. Objection: Only an Ārya Can See It

Question: This minute body is extremely minute. When one first dies, it has already gone. When one is alive, one cannot search for and find it. How could you be able to view it? Additionally, this minute body is not such as the five sense faculties would be able to perceive or would be able to be aware of. Only if one were an ārya possessed of the superknowledges would one then be able to succeed in seeing it.

1) Refutation of a Form-Based Ātman

Response: If that were the case, then it would be no different from being entirely nonexistent. And as for when a person dies, thereby relinquishing the aggregates of this life and entering the intermediary aggregates, at that moment when the body of the present life dies and one receives the intermediary-aggregates body, this process has no earlier and later stages. When one dies, one is immediately born [into the intermediary-aggregates body].

This is analogous to using a seal made of wax to stamp an impression in the mud. When the impression is received in the mud, the seal is immediately ruined. The creation and destruction occur at a single moment in which there is no prior and later. At that very time, one takes on the intermediary existence in the intermediary

舍此中阴受生阴有。汝言细身即此中阴。中阴身无出无入。譬如然灯生灭相续不常不断。佛言一切色众。若 [149c]过去未来现在。若内若外若麁若细皆悉无常。汝神微细色者。亦应无常断灭。如是等种种因缘可知非色相。神非无色相。无色者四众及无为。四众无常故。不自在故。属因缘故。不应是神。三无为中不计有神。无所[12]受故。如是等种种因缘。知神非无色相。如是天地间若内若外。三世十方求[*]我不可得。但十二入和合生六识。三事和合名触。触生受想思等心数法。是法中无明力故身见生。

捨此中陰受生陰有。汝言細身即此中陰。中陰身無出無入。譬如然燈生滅相續不常不斷。佛言一切色眾。若 [149c]過去未來現在。若內若外若麁若細皆悉無常。汝神微細色者。亦應無常斷滅。如是等種種因緣可知非色相。神非無色相。無色者四眾及無為。四眾無常故。不自在故。屬因緣故。不應是神。三無為中不計有神。無所[12]受故。如是等種種因緣。知神非無色相。如是天地間若內若外。三世十方求[*]我不可得。但十二入和合生六識。三事和合名觸。觸生受想思等心數法。是法中無明力故身見生。

简体字   正體字

aggregates. Then, when one relinquishes these intermediary aggregates, one takes on existence in the aggregates of the next life.

As for your saying that the minute body is just these intermediary aggregates, the body of the intermediary aggregates has no going on forth and it has no entering [the next incarnation]. This process is analogous to the lighting of a lamp wherein production and extinction occur continuously and wherein there is neither permanence nor complete interruption [of the appearance of that lamp flame].

The Buddha said that every constituent of the form aggregate, whether past, future, or present, whether inward, whether outward, whether gross or whether minute—all are utterly impermanent. Consequently this "extremely minute form" supposedly adopted by this spiritual soul of yours ought also to be impermanent and bound to utter destruction. Based on all sorts of reasons such as these, one can know that it is not the case that [this "spiritual soul"] is characterized by [a basis in] form.

2) Refutation of Formless Ātman

Nor is it characterized by being formless. As for that which is formless, it consists of the four [non-form] aggregates and the unconditioned. Because those four aggregates are impermanent, because they are not inherently existent, and because they are subsumed within the sphere of causes and conditions, it should not be the case that they qualify as constituting a "spiritual soul." Among the three unconditioned dharmas, there can be no reckoning of the existence of a spiritual soul. This is because there is nothing therein which may be experienced. Based on all sorts of reasons such as these, one realizes that it is not the case that this "spiritual soul" is characterized by formlessness.

3) Summary Statement on Non-Existence of Ātman

In this manner, one looks for a self throughout heaven and earth, and, no matter whether one looks among that which is inward or that which is outward, or whether one looks throughout the three periods of time or the ten directions, it cannot be found. There is only a coming together of the twelve sense bases which in turn generate the six consciousnesses. Where these three factors[38] coincide, it is referred to as "contact." "Contact" generates feeling, perception, consideration and other dharmas associated with the mind.

In the midst of these dharmas, on account of the power of ignorance, a view of the body as constituting a self (*satkāyadṛṣṭi*) arises.

身见生故谓有神。是身见见
苦谛苦法智及苦比智则断。
断时则不见有神。汝先言若
内无神色。识念念生灭。云
何分别知色青黄赤白。汝若
有神亦不能独知。要依眼识
故能知。若尔者神无用也。
眼识知色色生灭。相似生相
似灭。然后心中有法生名为
念。是念相有为法。虽灭过
去[13]是念能知。如圣人智慧
力。能知未来世事。念念亦
如是。能知过去法。若前眼
识灭生后眼识。后眼识转[14]
利有力。色虽暂有不住。以
念力利故能知。以是事故虽
念念生灭无常。

身見生故謂有神。是身見見
苦諦苦法智及苦比智則斷。
斷時則不見有神。汝先言若
內無神色。識念念生滅。云
何分別知色青黃赤白。汝若
有神亦不能獨知。要依眼識
故能知。若爾者神無用也。
眼識知色色生滅。相似生相
似滅。然後心中有法生名為
念。是念相有為法。雖滅過
去[13]是念能知。如聖人智慧
力。能知未來世事。念念亦
如是。能知過去法。若前眼
識滅生後眼識。後眼識轉[14]
利有力。色雖暫有不住。以
念力利故能知。以是事故雖
念念生滅無常。

简体字   正體字

On account of the arising of the view of the body as constituting a self, one is led to the opinion that a spiritual soul must somehow exist. As for this "view of a body constituting a self," it is cut off at the point when one experiences the seeing of the truth of suffering (*duḥkhasatyadarśana*) and consequently gains the suffering-related dharma knowledge (*duḥkhe dharmajñāna*) and the suffering-related inferential knowledge (*duḥkhe 'nvayajñāna*). Once [the view of the body as constituting the self] is thereby cut off, one then no longer reckons the existence of any spiritual soul.

4) Refutation of Relevance of Ātman to Ongoing Awareness

As for your earlier question which asked, "If there was no inward spiritual soul or related form, since consciousness is newly produced and destroyed in every instant, how could one distinguish and know the colors of blue, yellow, red and white?"—If it were the case that you in fact possessed such a spiritual soul, it would be equally unable to be aware of such data on its own. It would necessarily rely upon eye consciousness in order to be aware of them. This being the case, the spiritual soul would have no relevant function in this regard.

The eye consciousness is aware of visible forms and of the production and extinction of visual forms [by way of] a facsimile of production and a facsimile of extinction. Subsequently, a dharma arises in the mind referred to as "mindfulness." This conditioned dharma characterized by mindfulness is such that, even though [a given objective condition] has already become extinguished and hence has already entered the past, this instance of mindfulness is nonetheless still able to maintain an awareness of it.

In the case of an ārya, by resort to the power of wisdom, he is able to know matters having to do with future time and is also able in each successive thought-moment to retain in much the same way an awareness of dharmas associated with the past.

When an earlier instance of eye consciousness is extinguished, there follows the production of a subsequent instance of eye consciousness. As for the later instances of eye consciousness, they become more acute [in their intensity] and become possessed with an attendant power. Thus, although the visual forms exist only temporarily and so do not continue to abide, due the acuity of the power of mindfulness, one is nonetheless able to remain aware of them. It is on account of these factors that, although there is impermanence by virtue of the production and extinction which takes

能分別知色。又汝言今現在
人识新新生灭。身命断时亦
尽。诸行罪福谁随谁受。谁
受苦乐谁解脱者。 今当答
汝。[15]今未得实道。是人诸
烦恼覆心。作生因缘业。死
时[16]从此五阴相续生[17]五
阴。譬如一灯更然一灯。又
如[18]谷生。有三因缘地水种
子。后世身生[19]亦如是。
有身有[20]有漏业有结使。三
事故后身生。是中身业因缘
不可断不可破。但诸结使可
断。结使断时虽有残身残业
可得解脱。如有谷[150a]子有
地无水故不生。如是虽有身
有业。无爱结水润则不生。
是名虽无神亦名得解脱。无
明故缚。智慧故解。则[*]我
无[1]所用。复次是名色和合
假名为

能分別知色。又汝言今現在
人識新新生滅。身命斷時亦
盡。諸行罪福誰隨誰受。誰
受苦樂誰解脫者。 今當答
汝。[15]今未得實道。是人諸
煩惱覆心。作生因緣業。死
時[16]從此五陰相續生[17]五
陰。譬如一燈更然一燈。又
如[18]穀生。有三因緣地水種
子。 後世身生[19]亦如是。
有身有[20]有漏業有結使。三
事故後身生。是中身業因緣
不可斷不可破。但諸結使可
斷。結使斷時雖有殘身殘業
可得解脫。如有穀[150a]子有
地無水故不生。如是雖有身
有業。無愛結水潤則不生。
是名雖無神亦名得解脫。無
明故縛。智慧故解。則[*]我
無[1]所用。復次是名色和合
假名為

简体字　　　　　　　　　正體字

place in each successive thought-moment, one is nonetheless able to distinguish and be aware of visual forms.

5)　Refutation of Remaining Continuity-Severance Objections

Next, I shall now reply to your claim that, since a person's present-life consciousness is continuously being newly produced and destroyed, it must therefore come to an end when the lifespan is cut off, [and shall also reply to your subsidiary questions about] who would then be bound to accord with and undergo retribution for offenses and merits accruing from actions, who would then experience suffering or bliss, and who would then gain liberation.

Now, when a person has not yet gained the genuine path, afflictions cover over his mind. He engages in karmic actions which serve as the causes and conditions for being reborn. When he dies, following upon these five aggregates [of this present life], there is a subsequent production of five aggregates.

a)　Lamp and Seed-Growth Analogies

This is analogous to one particular lamp being used to ignite the flame in another lamp. It is also comparable to the production of grain. There are three causes and conditions: earth, water, and seed. The birth of the body in the later life is just like this: there is the body, there is karmic activity characterized by outflow impurities, and there are the fetters. It is on account of these three factors that the subsequent body is produced. During this process, the causes and conditions associated with the karma of the body are such that they cannot be cut off and cannot be destroyed. Only the fetters can be cut off. When the fetters are cut off, although there still exists a residual body and residual karma, one nonetheless then becomes able to succeed in gaining liberation.

Just as when one has a seed and soil, but the seed is unable to grow for lack of water, so too, although one may have the body and have the karma, if there is no moistening by the water of affection-related fetters, one is not bound to be reborn. This is how one is still able to gain liberation even though there is no "spiritual soul" (*ātman*). It is on account of ignorance that one is bound up. It is on account of wisdom that one is released. This being the case, then the "self" [whose existence you assert] would serve no function.

b)　Fetter-Rope and Wisdom-Claw Analogies

Then again, it is the coming together of this "name-and-form" (*nāmarūpa*, i.e. the five aggregates)[39] that is artificially referred to as

人。是人为诸结所系。得无
漏智慧[2]爪解此诸结。是时
名人得解脱。如绳结绳解。
绳即是结。结无异法。世界
中说结绳解绳。名色亦如
是。名色二法和合假名为
人。是结使与名色不异。但
名为名色结。名色解受罪
福亦如是。虽无一法为人[3]
实。名色故受罪福果。而人
得名。譬如车载物。一一推
之竟无车实。然车受载物之
名。人受罪福亦如是。名色
受罪福而人受其名。受苦乐
亦如是。如是种种因缘神不
可得。神即是施者。受者
亦如是。汝以神为人。以
是故施人不可得。受人不
可得。[4]亦如是如是种种因
缘。是名财物施人受人不可
得。

人。是人為諸結所繫。得無
漏智慧[2]爪解此諸結。是時
名人得解脫。如繩結繩解。
繩即是結。結無異法。世界
中說結繩解繩。名色亦如
是。名色二法和合假名為
人。是結使與名色不異。但
名為名色結。名色解受罪
福亦如是。雖無一法為人[3]
實。名色故受罪福果。而
人得名。譬如車載物。一
一推之竟無車實。然車受載
物之名。人受罪福亦如是。
名色受罪福而人受其名。受
苦樂亦如是。如是種種因緣
神不可得。神即是施者。受
者亦如是。汝以神為人。
以是故施人不可得。受人不
可得。[4]亦如是如是種種因
緣。是名財物施人受人不可
得。

简体字   正體字

a "person." This "person" is tied up by the fetters. When one gains the "claw" of that wisdom which is free of outflow impurities, then one [uses that claw to] untie all of these fetters. It is at this time that we have what is referred to as "a person who has succeeded in gaining liberation."

This process is analogous to the tying up and untying of a rope. [The "tying up" of] the rope is just [an analogy for] the fetters. There are no other dharmas involved in being tied up. In worldly parlance, one speaks of the tying up done with a rope and the untying of a rope. Name-and-form are just like this. The two dharmas of "name" and "form" are together referred to by artificial convention as "a person." These fetters are no different from name-and-form. There is only that which might be referred to as name-and-form when "tied up" [by the fetters, or alternatively as] name-and-form when "untied," [and hence "freed" from being bound up by the fetters].

Being constrained to undergo retribution for offenses and merits is just like this. Although there is no single dharma by which a "person" might be deemed "real," it is based on "name-and-form" that there is the process of undergoing the karmic fruition resulting from either karmic offenses or meritorious deeds. Thus it is that a "person" becomes so named.

c) ANALOGY: AS CARTS HOLD GOODS, NAME-AND-FORM CARRY KARMA

This is analogous to a cart's carrying of goods. If one examines it in terms of each and every component part, then one finds that there is finally no reality inhering in the term "cart." Rather "cart" is simply a name reflecting the ability to hold a load of goods.

The taking on of karmic offenses or meritorious deeds on the part of a "person" is just the same. Name-and-form take on offenses and merit and so the corresponding designation "person" is derived. The undergoing of suffering or bliss are also just the same.

Based on all sorts of causal bases such as these, a "spiritual soul" can never be found. This "spiritual soul" is really simply [a designation applied to] that which serves as the "benefactor" [in any act of giving]. That which acts as the "recipient" is just the same. You take it that it is a "spiritual soul" which constitutes this "person." However, for all of these reasons, a person who performs the giving cannot finally be found. A recipient cannot be found, either. It is on account of all sorts of causes and conditions such as these that it is said that the "valuable object," the "benefactor," and the "recipient" all finally cannot be found.

问曰。若[5]施于诸法[6]是如
实相无所破无所灭无所生无
所作。何以故。言三事破[7]
析不可得。答曰。如凡夫
人。见施[8]者见受[*]者见财
物。是为颠倒妄见。生世间
受乐福尽转还。是故佛欲令
菩萨行实道得实果报。实果
报则是佛道。[9]佛为破妄见
故。言三事不可得。实无所
破。何以故。诸法从本[10]已
来毕竟空故。如是等种种无
量因缘不可得。故名为檀波
罗蜜具足满。复次若菩萨行
檀波罗蜜。能生六波罗蜜。
是时名为檀波罗蜜具足满。
云何布施生檀波罗蜜。檀有
[11]下中上。从下生中从中
生上。若以饮食麁物[*]软心
布施。是名为下。习施转增
[150b]能以衣服宝物布施。是
为从下生中。

简体字

問曰。若[5]施於諸法[6]是如
實相無所破無所滅無所生無
所作。何以故。言三事破[7]
析不可得。答曰。如凡夫
人。見施[8]者見受[*]者見財
物。是為顛倒妄見。生世間
受樂福盡轉還。是故佛欲令
菩薩行實道得實果報。實果
報則是佛道。[9]佛為破妄見
故。言三事不可得。實無所
破。何以故。諸法從本[10]已
來畢竟空故。如是等種種無
量因緣不可得。故名為檀波
羅蜜具足滿。復次若菩薩行
檀波羅蜜。能生六波羅蜜。
是時名為檀波羅蜜具足滿。
云何布施生檀波羅蜜。檀有
[11]下中上。從下生中從中
生上。若以飲食麁物[*]軟心
布施。是名為下。習施轉增
[150b]能以衣服寶物布施。是
為從下生中。

正體字

g. Objection: Unfindability Contradicts Reality

Question: If the act of giving as well as its other associated dharmas actually correspond to the true character of reality wherein there is nothing demolished through reductive analysis, nothing extinguished, nothing produced, and no actions engaged in, why then is it claimed that, when subjected to reductive analysis, those three factors [involved in giving] cannot be found?

Response: In cases such as that of the common person who *does* perceive the existence of a benefactor, a recipient and a valuable object, this constitutes an inverted and false view. When one is born into the world, one may experience bliss. When the merit is exhausted, one then reverts to the circumstance of being bound to compensate [for whatsoever ease one thenceforth enjoys]. It is on account of this that the Buddha wished to cause the bodhisattva to practice the genuine path and gain the genuine resultant reward. The genuine resultant reward is just the Buddha Path.

It was in order to demolish false views by resorting to reductive analysis that the Buddha said that the three factors are ultimately unfindable. In actuality, there is nothing which is demolished through reductive analysis. How is this the case? It is because all dharmas, from their origin on forward to the present always have been ultimately empty [of any inherent existence]. The incalculable number of other such causes and conditions cannot be gotten at, either. It is based on [realizing] this that one speaks of the perfect fulfillment of *dāna pāramitā*.

Then again, if the bodhisattva practices *dāna pāramitā*, he is able on that account to generate all six of the *pāramitās*. It is at this time that it is properly referred to as "perfect fulfillment of *dāna pāramitā*."

H. *Dāna's* Generation of the Six *Pāramitās*

1. How *Dāna Pāramitā* Generates *Dāna Pāramitā*

a. Three Levels of the Practice of Giving

How can giving bring forth *dāna pāramitā*? *Dāna* may be of lesser, middling or superior quality. From the lesser is born the middling. From the middling is born the superior. If one draws upon drink, food, or coarse things and employs a weak mind in giving, this is what is known as lesser giving. If one practices giving so that it transforms and increases resulting in one's becoming able to draw upon clothing or precious things and use them in one's giving, this amounts to bringing forth the middling from the lesser. When the

施心转增无所爱惜。能以头
目血肉国财妻子尽用布施。
是为从中生上。如释迦牟尼
佛初发心时。作大国王名曰
光明。求索佛道少多布施。
转受后身作陶师。能以澡浴
之具及石蜜浆。布施异释迦
牟尼佛及比丘僧。其后转身
作大长者女。以灯供养憍陈
若佛。如是等种种名为菩萨
下布施。如释迦文尼佛。本
身作长者子。以衣布[12]施
大音声佛。佛灭度后起九十
塔。后更转身作大国王。以
七宝盖供养师子佛。后复受
身作大长者。供养妙[13]目佛
上好房舍及七宝妙华。如是
等种种名为菩萨中布施。如
释迦牟尼佛本身。作仙人见
憍陈若佛端[14]政殊妙便从
高山上自投佛前。其身安隐
在一面立。又如众生喜见菩
萨。以身为灯

施心轉增無所愛惜。能以頭
目血肉國財妻子盡用布施。
是為從中生上。如釋迦牟尼
佛初發心時。作大國王名曰
光明。求索佛道少多布施。
轉受後身作陶師。能以澡浴
之具及石蜜漿。布施異釋迦
牟尼佛及比丘僧。其後轉身
作大長者女。以燈供養憍陳
若佛。如是等種種名為菩薩
下布施。如釋迦文尼佛。本
身作長者子。以衣布[12]施
大音聲佛。佛滅度後起九十
塔。後更轉身作大國王。以
七寶蓋供養師子佛。後復受
身作大長者。供養妙[13]目佛
上好房舍及七寶妙華。如是
等種種名為菩薩中布施。如
釋迦牟尼佛本身。作仙人見
憍陳若佛端[14]政殊妙便從
高山上自投佛前。其身安隱
在一面立。又如眾生喜見菩
薩。以身為燈

简体字   正體字

mind of giving transforms and increases such that there is nothing whatsoever which one cherishes as too dear with the result that one becomes able to employ one's head, eyes, blood, flesh, country, wealth, wives, and sons, exhaustively using them all in one's giving, this amounts to bringing forth the superior from the middling.

1) The Buddha's Past-Life Practice of Lesser-Level Giving

Take for example when Shakyamuni Buddha first brought forth the aspiration [to achieve buddhahood]. At that time he was the king of a great country who was named "Brilliance." In seeking after the Buddha Path, he performed a lesser or greater amount of giving. When he passed on and took on his next body, he next became a potter who was able to make gifts of bathing implements and rock honey condiments to a previous Buddha named Shakyamuni and the members of that sangha of bhikshus. Subsequently, he passed on, changed bodies again, and next became the daughter of a great elder who adopted the practice of making offerings of lamps to Kauṇḍinya Buddha. All sorts of instances such as these illustrate what is meant by the bodhisattva's practice of lesser-level giving.

2) The Buddha's Past Life Practice of Middling-Level Giving

Next, we have the example of when Shakyamuni Buddha in a former life was the son of an elder. In that instance, he made offerings of robes to Great Voice Buddha. After that buddha had crossed on over into extinction, he erected ninety stupas [in commemoration]. He subsequently changed bodies again and became the king of a great country who made an offering to Lion Buddha of a canopy which had been made from the seven precious things.

He afterwards took on a body wherein he became a greater elder who made offerings to Marvelous Eyes Buddha of supremely fine buildings together with marvelous flowers created from the seven precious things. All sorts of instances such as these illustrate what is meant by the bodhisattva's practice of middling-level giving.

3) The Buddha's Past-Life Practice of Superior-Level Giving

Now, take for example when Shakyamuni Buddha in a former life was a rishi. On seeing Kauṇḍinya Buddha who was so handsome, upright, and exceptionally marvelous, he threw himself down off of a mountain in front of that buddha. His body remained unharmed and he then stood off to one side.

Again, take for example the bodhisattva named "He Who Beings Delight in Seeing" who used his own body as a lamp in making

供养日月光德佛。如是等种
种不惜身命供养诸佛。是为
菩萨上布施。是名菩萨三种
布施。若有初发佛心布施众
生亦复如是。初以饮食布
施。施心转增能以身肉与
之。先以种种好浆布施。后
心转增能以身血与之。先以
纸墨经书布施。及以衣服饮
食四种供养供养法师。后得
法身为无量众生。说种种法
而为法施。如是等种种从檀
波罗蜜中。生檀波罗蜜。云
何菩萨布施生尸[15]罗波罗
蜜。菩萨思惟众生不[16]布
施故。后世贫穷。以贫穷故
劫盗心生。以劫盗故而有杀
害。以贫穷故不足于色。色
不足故而行邪婬。又以贫[17]
穷故为人下贱。下贱畏怖而
[18]生[150c]妄语。如是等贫穷
因缘故。行

供養日月光德佛。如是等種
種不惜身命供養諸佛。是為
菩薩上布施。是名菩薩三種
布施。若有初發佛心布施眾
生亦復如是。初以飲食布
施。施心轉增能以身肉與
之。先以種種好漿布施。後
心轉增能以身血與之。先以
紙墨經書布施。及以衣服飲
食四種供養供養法師。後得
法身為無量眾生。說種種法
而為法施。如是等種種從檀
波羅蜜中。生檀波羅蜜。云
何菩薩布施生尸[15]羅波羅
蜜。菩薩思惟眾生不[16]布
施故。後世貧窮。以貧窮故
劫盜心生。以劫盜故而有殺
害。以貧窮故不足於色。色
不足故而行邪婬。又以貧[17]
窮故為人下賤。下賤畏怖而
[18]生[150c]妄語。如是等貧窮
因緣故。行

简体字   正體字

offerings to Sun and Moonlight Virtue Buddha. All sorts of examples such as these of not cherishing even one's own body and life in making offerings to the Buddhas illustrate the bodhisattva's practice of superior-level giving.

b. How New Bodhisattvas Generate the Levels of Giving

This is what is meant by the bodhisattva's three kinds of giving. If there is a being who has just brought forth the aspiration to achieve buddhahood who takes up the practice of giving, he too may act in just such ways. He may first draw upon food and drink in his practice of giving. When that mind of giving transforms and increases, he will eventually be able to take even the flesh of his own body and use it as an offering.[40]

He may initially use all manner of fine condiments in his giving. Later, when the mind transforms and increases in its strength, he may be able to give even the blood from his own body. He may first employ paper, ink, and scriptures in his giving while also making offerings to Dharma masters of robes, drink, food, and the four kinds of offerings.

Finally, once he has gained the Dharma body, for the sake of an incalculable number of beings, he may speak many varieties of Dharma and so carry forth the giving of Dharma. All sorts of cases such as these illustrate the development of *dāna pāramitā* from within the practice of *dāna pāramitā*.

2. How *Dāna Pāramitā* Generates *Śīla Pāramitā*

a. Failing to Give Generates Ten Bad Karmas

How is it that the bodhisattva's practice of giving can generate *śīla pāramitā*? The bodhisattva reflects, "Beings become poor and destitute in later lives through failing to practice giving. Then, on account of having become poor and destitute, the thought of stealing arises in them. From engaging in stealing, the harm of killing then occurs.

"Due to being poor and destitute, one may encounter circumstances wherein one is sexually unsatisfied. On account of being sexually unsatisfied, one might then engage in sexual misconduct.

"Additionally, through being poor and destitute, one may be regarded by others as of low social station. On account of the fearfulness associated with being of low social station, one might then engage in false speech.

"Thus, based on such causes and conditions linked to being poor and destitute, one may consequently course along on the path

十不善道。若行布施生有财物。有财物故不为非法。何以故五[19]尘充足无所乏短故。如提婆达。本生曾为一蛇。与一虾蟇一龟在一池中共结亲友。其后池水竭尽。饥穷困乏无所控告。时蛇遣龟以呼虾蟇。虾蟇说偈[20]以遣龟言。

若遭贫穷失本心。
不惟本义食为先。
汝持我声以语蛇。
虾蟇终不到汝边。

[150c10]　若修布施后生有福无所短乏。则能持戒无此众恶。是为布施能生尸罗波罗蜜。复次布施时能令破戒诸结使薄。益持戒心令得坚固。是为布施因缘增益于戒。复次菩萨布施。常于受者生慈悲心。不着于财自物不惜。何况劫盗。慈悲受者何有杀意。如是等能遮破戒。是为[21]施生戒。

of the ten unwholesome deeds. However, if one practices giving, then one will be reborn into circumstances wherein one possesses things of value. Because one will then already own valuable possessions, one will tend to refrain from engaging in endeavors contrary to Dharma. Why is this the case? It is because the five sense objects will already exist in abundance and thus there will never be a shortage of anything."

b. The Snake, the Turtle, and the Frog (Story)

This principle is illustrated by the case of Devadatta in a previous life when he was a snake who dwelt together with a frog and a turtle in a pond. They had all become close friends. Later, the water of the pond dried up. They all became hungry, poor, in desperate straits, and lacking in any other resources. The snake then dispatched the turtle to call forth the frog. The frog then sent back the turtle through uttering this verse:

> "On encountering poverty, one may stray from his original intent.
> Ignoring one's fundamental principles, eating becomes foremost.
> You should take my words and pass them on to that snake:
> "This frog will never come over to show up at your side."

If one cultivates the practice of giving, then in later lives one will possess such merit that there will be nothing which one lacks. If this is the case, then one will be able to uphold the moral precepts and will remain free of these many types of bad deeds. This is how the practice of giving is able to bring forth *śīla* pāramita.

Additionally, when one gives, one is able to bring about a scarcity of all of the fetters associated with breaking precepts while also bolstering the mind's devotion to upholding moral precepts, thus causing it to become solidly established. These are the causal bases through which giving brings about an increase in the cultivation of the moral precepts.

Moreover, when the bodhisattva practices giving, he constantly brings forth thoughts of kindness and compassion for the recipient. He is not attached to valuables and does not cherish his own goods. How much the less would he engage in stealing. When one feels kindness and compassion for the recipient, how could one maintain any ideation intent on killing? Through means such as these, he becomes able to block off any tendency to transgress against the moral precepts. This is how the practice of giving brings forth observance of the moral precepts.

若能布施以破悭心。然后持
戒忍辱等易可得行。如文殊
师利。在昔过去久远劫时。
曾为比丘入城乞食。得满鉢
百味欢喜丸。城中一小儿追
而从乞不即与之。乃至佛图
手捉二丸而要之言。汝若能
自食一丸。以一丸施僧者当
以施汝。即相然可。以一欢
喜丸布施众僧。然后于文殊
师利许受戒发心作佛。如是
布施能令受戒发心作佛。是
为布施生尸罗波罗蜜。复次
布施之报得四事供养好国善
师无所乏少。故能持戒。又
布施之报其心调柔。心调柔
故能生持戒。能生持戒故从
不善法中能自制心。如是种
种因缘。从布施生尸罗波罗
蜜。云何布施生羼提[151a]波
罗蜜。菩萨布施时受者逆
骂。若大求索若不时索。

简体字

If one is able to engage in giving while employing a mind intent on destroying miserliness, then he will subsequently find easy success in the practice moral virtue, patience, and so forth.

c. Mañjuśrī Teaches a Beggar Child (Story)

This principle is illustrated by the case of Mañjuśrī when he was a bhikshu long ago in the past in a far distant kalpa. Having gone into the city to seek alms, he received a bowl full of "hundred-flavored delightful dumplings." There was a small child in that city who followed along after him, begging. [Mañjuśrī] did not immediately give anything to him.

Then, when they had reached a Buddha stupa, [the monk] picked up two of the dumplings in his hand and required of the child, "If you are able to eat only one of the dumplings yourself, while taking one of the dumplings and giving it to the Sangha, I will give these to you."

The child immediately agreed and so then took one of the delightful dumplings and presented it to the Sangha community. Later, he obtained Mañjuśrī's consent to receive the precepts and then subsequently brought forth the aspiration to become a buddha.

In just such a fashion, the practice of giving may be able to cause one to take on the moral precepts and to bring forth the aspiration to become a buddha. This illustrates how the practice of giving brings forth *śīla pāramitā*.

Furthermore, it is as a reward for giving that one subsequently receives offerings of the four requisites, lives in a fine country, finds a good spiritual master, and has nothing in which he is lacking. One thereby becomes able to uphold the moral precepts.

Additionally, it is as a karmic reward for giving that one's mind becomes well-regulated and supple. Because one's mind becomes well-regulated and supple, one becomes able to observe the moral precepts. Because one is able to observe the moral precepts, one becomes able to control one's own mind even in the midst of circumstances involving unwholesome dharmas. All sorts of causes and conditions such as these demonstrate the bringing forth of *śīla pāramitā* on the basis of the practice of giving.

3. How *Dāna Pāramitā* Generates *Kṣānti Pāramitā*

How is it that giving is able to bring forth *kṣānti pāramitā*? When the bodhisattva performs an act of giving and then the recipient subjects him to verbal abuse, or makes unreasonably great demands, or presses his demands at an inopportune time, or seeks to obtain

或不应索而索。是时菩萨自
思惟言。我今布施欲求佛
道。亦无有人使我布施。我
自为故云何生瞋。如是思惟
已而行忍辱。是名布施生羼
提波罗蜜。复次菩萨布施
时。若受者瞋恼。便自思
惟。我今布施内外财物。难
舍能舍。何况空声而不能
忍。若我不忍所可布施则为
不净。譬如白象入池澡浴。
出已还复以土坌身。布施不
忍亦复如是。如是思惟已行
于忍辱。如是等种种布施因
缘生羼提波罗蜜。云何布施
生毘梨耶波罗蜜。菩萨布施
时常行精进。何以故。菩萨
初发心时功德未大。尔时欲
行二施充满一切众生之愿。
以物不足故。懃求财法以给
足之。如释迦文尼佛本身。
作大医王疗一切病不求名
利。为怜愍众生故。病者甚
多力不周救。忧念一切而不
从心。懊恼而死即生忉利天
上。自思惟言。我今生天。
但食福报无所长

或不應索而索。是時菩薩自
思惟言。我今布施欲求佛
道。亦無有人使我布施。我
自為故云何生瞋。如是思惟
已而行忍辱。是名布施生羼
提波羅蜜。復次菩薩布施
時。若受者瞋惱。便自思
惟。我今布施內外財物。難
捨能捨。何況空聲而不能
忍。若我不忍所可布施則為
不淨。譬如白象入池澡浴。
出已還復以土坌身。布施不
忍亦復如是。如是思惟已行
於忍辱。如是等種種布施因
緣生羼提波羅蜜。云何布施
生毘梨耶波羅蜜。菩薩布施
時常行精進。何以故。菩薩
初發心時功德未大。爾時欲
行二施充滿一切眾生之願。
以物不足故。懃求財法以給
足之。如釋迦文尼佛本身。
作大醫王療一切病不求名
利。為憐愍眾生故。病者甚
多力不周救。憂念一切而不
從心。懊惱而死即生忉利天
上。自思惟言。我今生天。
但食福報無所長

what he should not seek, the bodhisattva thinks to himself, "Now, as I am giving, I am wishing to search out the Buddha Path. It is not the case that anyone ordered me to do this giving. As I am doing it at my own behest, why should I allow myself to become angry?" After he reflected in this manner, he proceeds with the cultivation of patience. This is a case in which giving generates *kṣānti pāramitā*.

Then again, when the bodhisattva gives, if the recipient is hateful and abusive, he then thinks to himself, "As I now cultivate giving both inward and outward things, I am able to relinquish even what is difficult to relinquish, how much the less should I be unable to have patience with what is merely an empty sound? If I am not patient with it, then what I am able to give will thereby become impure. It would be just as when a white elephant enters into a pool, bathes, and then having gotten out, goes back and covers himself with dirt again. To give and yet be impatient would be just like this." Having reflected in this manner, he then carries on with the practice of patience.

All sorts of such causes and conditions associated with giving result in the bringing forth of *kṣānti pāramitā*.

4. How *DĀNA PĀRAMITĀ* Generates *VĪRYA PĀRAMITĀ*

How is it that giving brings forth *vīrya pāramitā*? When the bodhisattva engages in the practice of giving, he constantly cultivates vigor. Why is this? When the bodhisattva first brings forth the aspiration [to achieve buddhahood], his merit is not yet vast. He then desires to cultivate the two kinds of giving in order to fulfill the aspirations of all beings. Because of a shortage of things to give, he seeks earnestly for valuables and Dharma with which to be able to provide for them adequately.

5. THE BUDDHA'S PERFECTION OF VIGOR (STORY)

This is illustrated by the case of Shākyamuni Buddha when, in a previous lifetime, he was a great physician king who worked to cure every manner of disease without any concern for fame or profit. It was done out of pity for all beings. The sick were extremely numerous and so his powers were inadequate to rescue everyone. He was concerned about and mindful of everyone and yet matters did not correspond in their outcome to his aspirations. He became so distressed and agitated that he died.

He was then reborn in the Trāyastriṃśa Heaven. He thought to himself, "Now, I've been reborn in the heavens. All I'm doing here is consuming my reward of blessings without any sort of progress

益。即自方便自取灭身。舍此天寿生[1]婆[2]迦陀龙王宫中为龙太子。其身长大父母爱重。欲自取死就金翅鸟王。鸟即取此龙子。于舍摩利树上吞之。父母[3]嘑啕啼哭懊恼。龙子既死生阎浮提中。为大国王太子。名曰能施。生而能言。问诸左右。今此国中有何等物。尽皆持来以用布施。众人[4]怪畏皆舍之走。其母怜爱独自守之。语其母言。我非罗刹众人何以故走。我本宿命常好布施。我为一切人之檀越。母闻其言以语众人。众人即还母好养育。及[151b]年长大自身所有尽以施尽。至父王所索物布施。父与其分复以施尽。见阎浮提人贫穷辛苦。思[5]欲给施而财物不足。便自啼泣问诸人言。作何方便当令一切满足于财。诸宿人言。我等曾闻有如意宝珠。若得此珠则能随心所索无不必得。菩萨闻是语已白其父母。欲入大海求龙王头上如意宝珠。

益。即自方便自取滅身。捨此天壽生[1]婆[2]迦陀龍王宮中為龍太子。其身長大父母愛重。欲自取死就金翅鳥王。鳥即取此龍子。於舍摩利樹上吞之。父母[3]嘑咷啼哭懊惱。龍子既死生閻浮提中。為大國王太子。名曰能施。生而能言。問諸左右。今此國中有何等物。盡皆持來以用布施。眾人[4]怪畏皆捨之走。其母憐愛獨自守之。語其母言。我非羅刹眾人何以故走。我本宿命常好布施。我為一切人之檀越。母聞其言以語眾人。眾人即還母好養育。及[151b]年長大自身所有盡以施盡。至父王所索物布施。父與其分復以施盡。見閻浮提人貧窮辛苦。思[5]欲給施而財物不足。便自啼泣問諸人言。作何方便當令一切滿足於財。諸宿人言。我等曾聞有如意寶珠。若得此珠則能隨心所索無不必得。菩薩聞是語已白其父母。欲入大海求龍王頭上如意寶珠。

简体字　　　　　　　　　　　正體字

arising from it." He then used a skillful means to bring that personal existence to an end.

Having relinquished this rebirth into the long life of the heavens, he was next reborn as a dragon prince in the palace of Sāgara, the Dragon King. His body grew to full maturity. His parents were extremely attached in their love for him. But he desired to die, and so he went to the king of the golden-winged [*garuḍa*] birds. The bird immediately seized this young dragon and devoured him in the top of a *śālmalī* tree. His father and mother then wailed and cried in grief-stricken distress.

Having died, the young dragon was then reborn in Jambudvīpa as a prince in the house of the king of a great country. He was named "Able to Give." From the moment he was born, he was able to speak. He asked all of the retainers, "Now, what all does this country contain? Bring it all forth so that it can be used to make gifts."

Everyone was struck with amazement and became fearful. They all withdrew from him and ran off. His mother, however, felt kindness and love for him and so looked after him by herself. He said to his mother, "I am not a *rākṣasa* ghost. Why has everyone run off? In my previous lives, I have always taken pleasure in giving and thus have been a benefactor to everyone."

When his mother heard his words, she reported them to everyone else. The others then all returned. The mother thenceforth delighted in raising him. By the time he had grown older, he had given away everything he owned. He then went to his father, the King, and requested things to give. His father responded by giving him his share. Again, he gave it all away.

He observed that the people of Jambudvīpa were all poverty-stricken and lived lives of intense hardship. He thought to supply them all with gifts, but the valuables were inadequate. He then began to weep and inquired of everyone, "How will I be able to cause everyone to become completely supplied with wealth?"

The wise elders said, "We have heard of the existence of a precious wish-fulfilling pearl. If you were able to obtain this pearl then, no matter what your heart desired, there would be nothing which would not be certainly be obtained."

When the Bodhisattva had heard these words, he spoke to his mother and father, saying, "I desire to go out upon the great sea and seek the precious wish-fulfilling pearl worn on the head of the Dragon King."

父母报言。我唯有汝一儿
耳。若入大海众难难度。一
旦失汝我等亦当何用活为。
不须去也。我今藏中犹亦有
物当以给汝。儿言。藏中有
限。我意无量。我欲以财充
满一切令无乏短。愿见听
许。得遂本心使阎浮提人一
切充足。父母知其志大。不
敢制之。遂放令去。是时五
百贾客。以其福德大。人皆
乐随从。知其行日集海道
口。菩萨先闻婆伽陀龙王头
上有如意宝珠。问众人言。
谁知水道至彼龙宫。有一盲
人名陀舍。曾以七反入大
海中具知海道。菩萨即命
共行。答[6]曰。我年既老两
目失明。曾虽数入今不能
去。菩萨[7]语言。我今此行
不自为身。普为一切求如意
宝珠。欲给足众生令身无
乏。[8]次以道法因缘而教化
之。汝是智人何得辞耶。我
愿得成岂非汝力。陀舍闻其
要言。欣然同怀语菩萨言。
我今共汝俱入大海我必不[9]
全。汝当安我尸骸着大海之
中金沙洲上。

父母報言。我唯有汝一兒
耳。若入大海眾難難度。一
旦失汝我等亦當何用活為。
不須去也。我今藏中猶亦有
物當以給汝。兒言。藏中有
限。我意無量。我欲以財充
滿一切令無乏短。願見聽
許。得遂本心使閻浮提人一
切充足。父母知其志大。不
敢制之。遂放令去。是時五
百賈客。以其福德大。人皆
樂隨從。知其行日集海道
口。菩薩先聞婆伽陀龍王頭
上有如意寶珠。問眾人言。
誰知水道至彼龍宮。有一盲
人名陀舍。曾以七反入大
海中具知海道。菩薩即命
共行。答[6]曰。我年既老兩
目失明。曾雖數入今不能
去。菩薩[7]語言。我今此行
不自為身。普為一切求如意
寶珠。欲給足眾生令身無
乏。[8]次以道法因緣而教化
之。汝是智人何得辭耶。我
願得成豈非汝力。陀舍聞其
要言。欣然同懷語菩薩言。
我今共汝俱入大海我必不[9]
全。汝當安我尸骸著大海之
中金沙洲上。

简体字   正體字

His father and mother replied, "We have only you, our one son. If you go out upon the great sea the many difficulties will be difficult to overcome. If ever we were to lose you, what use would we have for going on living? It is not necessary for you to go. We do still have other things in our treasury with which we will be able to supply you."

The son said, "There is a limit to the contents of the treasury. My intentions are boundless. I wish to bestow enough wealth to satisfy everyone so that they will never again be found wanting. I pray that you will give your permission so that I may succeed in my original aspiration to cause everyone in Jambudvīpa to be completely provided for."

His parents knew that his determination was immense. They did not dare to restrain him and so subsequently relented and allowed him to go. There were five hundred merchants at that time who, because his special qualities were so extraordinary, took pleasure in following him wherever he went. They happened to know the day when he was due to depart and so gathered at the port.

The Bodhisattva had heard earlier that Sāgara, the Dragon King, had a precious wish-fulfilling pearl. He inquired of everyone, "Who knows the route across the sea to his dragon palace?" There was a blind man named Dāsa who had been to sea seven times and who knew all of the sea routes. The Bodhisattva instructed him to travel along with him.

He replied, "As I have grown old, both of my eyes have lost their acuity. Although I have been to sea many times, I cannot go this time."

The Bodhisattva said, "In going forth this time, I do not do it for my own sake. I seek the precious wish-fulfilling pearl for the universal benefit of everyone. I desire to completely supply all beings so that they are caused to never again be found wanting. Then I wish to instruct them in the causes and conditions relating to the Dharma of the Path. You are a wise man. How can you withdraw? Without the power of your assistance, how could my vow possibly succeed?"

When Dāsa heard his entreaty, he happily shared the Bodhisattva's aspiration and said to him, "I'll now go out with you onto the great sea. However, I most certainly will not survive. You should lay my body to rest on the island of gold sands out in the middle of the ocean."

行事都集断第七绳。船去如
驼到众宝渚。众贾竞取七宝
各各已足。语菩萨言。何以
不取。菩萨报言。我所求者
如意宝珠。此有尽物我不须
[151c]也。汝等各当知足知量
无令船重不自[10]免也。是时
众贾白菩萨言。大德。为我
呪愿令得安隐。于是辞去。
陀舍是时语菩萨言。别留艇
舟当随是别道而去。待风七
日。[11]博海南岸至一险处。
当有绝崖枣林枝皆覆水。大
风吹船[12]船当摧覆。汝当仰
[13]板枣枝可以自济。我身
无目于此当死。过此隘岸当
有金沙洲。可以我身置此沙
中。金沙清净是我愿也。即
如其言。风至而去。既到绝
[14]崖。如陀舍语。菩萨仰[*]
板枣枝得以自[15]免。置陀舍
尸安厝金地。于是独去如其
先教。深水中浮七日。[16]至
[17]坐咽水中行七日。坐腰
水中行七日。坐膝水中行七
日。[18]泥中行七日。见好莲
华鲜洁柔软。自思惟言。此
华软脆当入虚空三昧。自轻
其身行莲华上七日。

简体字

行事都集斷第七繩。船去如
駞到眾寶渚。眾賈競取七寶
各各已足。語菩薩言。何以
不取。菩薩報言。我所求者
如意寶珠。此有盡物我不須
[151c]也。汝等各當知足知量
無令船重不自[10]免也。是時
眾賈白菩薩言。大德。為我
呪願令得安隱。於是辭去。
陀舍是時語菩薩言。別留艇
舟當隨是別道而去。待風七
日。[11]博海南岸至一險處。
當有絕崖棗林枝皆覆水。大
風吹船[12]船當摧覆。汝當
仰[13]板棗枝可以自濟。我
身無目於此當死。過此隘岸
當有金沙洲。可以我身置此
沙中。金沙清淨是我願也。
即如其言。風至而去。既到
絕[14]崖。如陀舍語。菩薩仰
[*]板棗枝得以自[15]免。置陀
舍屍安厝金地。於是獨去如
其先教。深水中浮七日。[16]
至[17]坐咽水中行七日。坐腰
水中行七日。坐膝水中行七
日。[18]泥中行七日。見好蓮
華鮮潔柔軟。自思惟言。此
華軟脆當入虛空三昧。自輕
其身行蓮華上七日。

正體字

When the provisions for the journey had all been loaded, they set loose the last of the seven lines. The ship went forth like a camel until it arrived at the Isle of Many Gems. The host of merchants all tried to outdo each other in gathering up the seven precious jewels. When they had all satisfied themselves, they asked the Bodhisattva, "Why do you refrain from gathering them yourself?"

The Bodhisattva replied, "It is the precious wish-fulfilling pearl which I seek. I have no use for things of this sort which will inevitably be used up. You all should know when enough is enough and should realize the limits so as to avoid overloading the ship. We must not fail to prevent our own self-destruction."

The group of merchants then said to the Bodhisattva, "Virtuous One, please invoke a spell for us to insure our safety." They then withdrew.

At this point Dāsa instructed the Bodhisattva, "Hold alongside the landing dinghy. We will want to use it to go off on this other route. After we have been driven by the wind for seven days, we will arrive at a treacherous place on the southern shore of the vast sea. There should be a steep cliff with a date tree forest's branches overhanging the water. If a strong wind blows, the ship could be overturned and capsized. By reaching up and clinging to the date branches, you may be able to save yourself. As I am sightless, I will likely die then. Beyond this precipitous shoreline there will be the isle of gold sand. You can take my body and lay it to rest in the midst of those sands. Those gold sands are pure. This is what I desire."

And so it was just as foretold. The wind came and they set off. Having come to the steep cliffs, it was just as Dāsa had described. The Bodhisattva reached up, grabbed onto the date branches, and so avoided disaster. He interred Dāsa's body in the ground of gold. From this point, he went on alone, following his earlier instructions. He floated in deep water for seven days. He then walked for seven days in water the depth of his throat. Then he moved for seven days through water up to his waist. After that, he walked for seven days through water up to his knees. Then he walked through mud for seven days.

Next, he came upon marvelous lotus flowers which were fresh and pure and soft. He thought to himself, "These blossoms are so soft and fragile. I should enter into the empty space samādhi." And so he made his body light and then walked upon the lotus blossoms for another seven days.

简体字	正體字
见诸毒蛇念言。含毒之虫甚可畏也。即入慈心三昧。行毒蛇头上七日。蛇皆擎头授与菩萨令蹈上而过。过此难已见有七重宝城。有七重堑。堑中皆满毒蛇有[19]三大龙守门。龙见菩萨形容端[*]政相好严仪。能度众难得来至此念言。此非凡夫必是菩萨大功德人。即听令前迳得入宫。龙王夫妇丧儿未久犹故哀泣。见菩萨来龙[20]王妇有神通。知是其子。两乳[21]汁流出。命之令坐。而问之言。汝是我子。舍我命终生在何处。菩萨亦自识宿命。知是父母而答母言。我生阎浮提上。为大国王太子。怜愍贫人饥寒勤苦不得自在故。来至此欲求如意宝珠。母言。汝父头上有此宝[152a]珠以为首饰。难可得也。必当将汝入[1]诸宝藏。随汝所欲必欲与汝。汝当报言。其馀杂宝我不须也。唯欲大王头上宝珠。若见怜愍愿以与我。如此可得。	見諸毒蛇念言。含毒之虫甚可畏也。即入慈心三昧。行毒蛇頭上七日。蛇皆擎頭授與菩薩令蹈上而過。過此難已見有七重寶城。有七重塹。塹中皆滿毒蛇有[19]三大龍守門。龍見菩薩形容端[*]政相好嚴儀。能度眾難得來至此念言。此非凡夫必是菩薩大功德人。即聽令前逕得入宮。龍王夫婦喪兒未久猶故哀泣。見菩薩來龍[20]王婦有神通。知是其子。兩乳[21]汁流出。命之令坐。而問之言。汝是我子。捨我命終生在何處。菩薩亦自識宿命。知是父母而答母言。我生閻浮提上。為大國王太子。憐愍貧人飢寒勤苦不得自在故。來至此欲求如意寶珠。母言。汝父頭上有此寶[152a]珠以為首飾。難可得也。必當將汝入[1]諸寶藏。隨汝所欲必欲與汝。汝當報言。其餘雜寶我不須也。唯欲大王頭上寶珠。若見憐愍願以與我。如此可得。

Next, he came upon poisonous snakes and thought to himself, "These poisonous serpents are extremely fearsome." He then entered the samādhi of loving kindness and proceeded to walk upon the heads of the poisonous snakes for seven days. As he did this, the snakes all extended their heads up to receive the Bodhisattva, thus allowing him to tread upon them as he passed.

After he had traversed these difficulties, he saw there was a jeweled city up ahead protected by seven sets of city walls. There were seven successive moats. Each of the moats was filled with poisonous snakes and there were three huge dragons guarding the gates.

The dragons saw that the Bodhisattva was possessed of a handsome and fine appearance, that he was a bearer of refined features and solemn deportment, and that he had been able to successfully pass through numerous difficulties in arriving at this place. They thought to themselves, "It is not the case that this is any ordinary man. It must certainly be that he is a bodhisattva, a man possessed of much merit." They then immediately allowed him to advance and directly enter the palace.

It was not so long ago that the mate of the Dragon King had lost her son and so she continued as before to grieve and weep. She had observed the arrival of the Bodhisattva. The Dragon King's mate possessed superknowledges and so, realizing that this was her son, milk spontaneously flowed forth from her two breasts. She gave the order allowing him to sit down and then spoke to him, "You are my son. After you left me and then died, where were you reborn?"

The Bodhisattva was also able to know his own previous lives. He knew that these were his parents and so replied, "I was reborn on the continent of Jambudvīpa as a prince to the king of a great country. I felt pity for the poverty-stricken people afflicted by the intense sufferings of hunger and cold who thus are unable to enjoy their own freedom. It is because of this that I have come here seeking to obtain the precious wish-fulfilling pearl."

His mother replied, "Your father wears this precious pearl as an adornment on his head. It is a difficult thing to acquire. Surely he will take you into the treasury of jewels where he certainly will wish to give you whatever you desire. You should reply by saying, 'I have no need of the various other jewels. I only desire the precious pearl atop the head of the Great King. If I may receive such kindness, I pray that you will bestow it upon me.' It may be that you can acquire it in this way."

即往见父。父大悲喜[2]欢庆无量。愍[3]念其子远涉艰难乃来至此。指示妙宝随意与汝须者取之。菩萨言。我从远来愿见大王。求王头上如意宝珠。若见怜愍当以与我。若不见与不须馀物。龙王报言。我唯有[4]此一珠常为首饰。阎浮提人薄福下贱不应见也。菩萨白言。我以此故。远涉艰难冒死远来。为阎浮提人薄福贫贱。欲以如意宝珠济其所愿。然后以佛道因缘而教化之。龙王与珠而要之言。今以此珠与汝。汝既去世当以还我。答曰。敬如王言。菩萨得珠飞腾虚空。如屈伸臂顷到阎浮提。人王父母见儿吉还。欢悦踊跃[5]抱而问言。汝得何物。答[6]言。得如意宝珠。问言。今在何许。白言。在此衣角里中。父母言。何其[7]泰小。白言。在其神德不在大也。白父母言。当勅城中内外扫灑烧香。悬缯

简体字

He then went to see his father. His father was overcome with nostalgia and delight and experienced boundless rejoicing. He thought with pity on his son's coming from afar, having to undergo extreme difficulties, and now arriving at this place. He showed him his marvelous jewels and said, "I will give you whatever you want. Take whatever you need."

The Bodhisattva said, "I came from afar wishing to see the Great King. I am seeking to obtain the precious wish-fulfilling pearl on the King's head. If I may receive such kindness, may it be that you will bestow it upon me. If I am not given that, then I have no need of any other thing."

The Dragon King replied, saying, "I have only this single pearl which I always wear as crown. The people of Jambudvīpa possess only scant merit and are of such base character that they should not even be allowed to catch a glimpse of it."

The Bodhisattva replied, "It is on this account that I have come from afar, experiencing extreme difficulties and risking death. It is for the sake of the people of Jambudvīpa who have only scant merit, who are poverty-stricken, and who are possessed of base character. I wish to use the precious wish-fulfilling pearl to provide for them everything they desire so that I may then use aspects of the Buddha Path to teach and transform them."

The Dragon King gave him the pearl and placed a condition on it by saying, "I will now give you this pearl. But when you are about to depart from the world, you must first return it to me."

He replied, "With all respect, it shall be as the King instructs." When the Bodhisattva had acquired the pearl, he flew up into space and, with the ease of extending and withdrawing his arm, he instantly arrived back in Jambudvīpa.

When his human royal parents observed his auspicious return, they were delighted and danced about with joy. They hugged him and then asked, "Well, what did you acquire?"

He replied, "I have obtained the precious wish-fulfilling pearl."

They asked, "Where is it now?"

He told them, "It's in the corner of my robe."

His parents said, "How could it be so small?"

He explained, "Its power resides in its supernatural qualities. It is not a function of its size." He told his parents, "It should be ordered that, both inside and outside of the city, the grounds are to be swept clean and incense is to be burned. Banners should be

幡盖持斋受戒。明日清旦以
长木为表以珠着上。菩萨是
时自立誓愿。若我当成佛道
度脱一切者。珠当如我意愿
出一切宝物。随人所[8]须尽
皆备有。是时阴云普遍雨种
种宝物。衣服饮食卧具汤
药。人之所须一切具足。至
其命尽常尔不绝。如是等名
为菩萨布施生精进波罗蜜。
云何菩萨布施生禅波罗蜜。
菩萨布施时能除悭贪。除悭
贪已因此布施而行一心渐除
五盖。[152b]能除五盖是名为
禅。复次心依布施入于初
禅。乃至灭定禅。云何为
依。若施行禅人时心自念
言。我以此人行禅定故。净
心供养。我今何为自替于
禅。即自[9]歘心思惟行禅。
若施贫人念此宿命。作诸不
善不求一心不修福业今世贫
穷。以是自勉修善一心以入
禅定。

幡蓋持齋受戒。明日清旦以
長木為表以珠著上。菩薩是
時自立誓願。若我當成佛道
度脫一切者。珠當如我意願
出一切寶物。隨人所[8]須盡
皆備有。是時陰雲普遍雨種
種寶物。衣服飲食臥具湯
藥。人之所須一切具足。至
其命盡常爾不絕。如是等名
為菩薩布施生精進波羅蜜。
云何菩薩布施生禪波羅蜜。
菩薩布施時能除慳貪。除慳
貪已因此布施而行一心漸除
五蓋。[152b]能除五蓋是名為
禪。復次心依布施入於初
禪。乃至滅定禪。云何為
依。若施行禪人時心自念
言。我以此人行禪定故。淨
心供養。我今何為自替於
禪。即自[9]歘心思惟行禪。
若施貧人念此宿命。作諸不
善不求一心不修福業今世貧
窮。以是自勉修善一心以入
禪定。

简体字　　　　　　　正體字

hung and canopies set up. Everyone should observe the standards of pure diet and take on the moral precepts."

The next morning at dawn he set up a tall wooden pillar as a display pedestal and attached the pearl up on the very top of it. The Bodhisattva then swore an oath, "If it is the case that I am to be able to complete the Buddha Path and bring everyone to deliverance, then this pearl should, in accordance with my vow, bring forth all kinds of precious things so that whatever anyone needs, it will manifest in utter repletion."

Dark clouds then covered the entire sky and rained down every type of precious thing, including clothes, drink, food, bedding, and medicines. Whatever people needed became abundantly available. This remained ever so, never ceasing until the very end of his life.

Instances such as this illustrate what is meant by a bodhisattva's practice of giving coincidentally serving as the means to bring forth the *pāramitā* of vigor.

6.   How *Dāna Pāramitā* Generates Dhyāna *Pāramitā*

How is it that the bodhisattva's practice of giving generates the *pāramitā* of dhyāna? When the bodhisattva gives, he is able to eliminate stinginess. Having gotten rid of stinginess, he is further enabled by this giving to devote himself single-mindedly to the gradual elimination of the five hindrances (*nīvaraṇa*). It is the ability to eliminate the five hindrances which in itself constitutes [the basis for realizing success in] dhyāna meditation.[41]

Then again, it is on account of giving that the mind enters into the first dhyāna and so forth on up to the dhyāna of the extinction-samādhi. How is it that this is supposedly is "on account of" giving? It may be, for instance, that on giving to a practitioner of dhyāna, one reflects, "It is because of this person's cultivation of dhyāna absorption that I make an offering with a pure mind. Why do I settle for only a vicarious experience of dhyāna?" And so one may then focus his own mind and thenceforth take up contemplation and the practice of dhyāna meditation.

Then again, it could be that, on giving to a poverty-stricken person, one reflects on that person's previous lives in which he engaged in all sorts of unwholesomeness, failed to seek single-mindedness, failed to cultivate works generating karmic blessings, and then consequently became poverty-stricken in this life. On account of this, one may provoke himself to cultivate skillful single-mindedness, thus enabling himself to enter the dhyāna absorptions.

如说。喜见转轮圣王八万四千小王来朝。皆持七宝妙物来献。王言我不须也。汝等各可自以修福。诸王自念。大王虽不肯取。我等亦复不宜自用。即共造工立七宝殿。[10]殖七宝行树作七宝浴池。于大殿中造八万四千七宝[11]楼。楼中皆有七宝床座。杂色被枕置床两头。悬缯幡盖香熏涂地。众事备已。白大王言。愿受法殿宝树浴池。王默然受之。而自念言。我今不应先处新殿以自娱乐。当求善人诸沙门婆罗门等先入供养。然后我当处之。即集善人先入宝殿。种种供养微妙具足。诸人出已王入宝殿登金楼坐银床。念布施除五盖摄六情却六尘受喜乐入初禅。次登银楼坐金床入二禅。次登毘琉璃楼坐[12]颇梨宝床入三禅。次登颇梨宝楼坐毘琉璃床入四禅。独坐思惟终竟三月。

简体字

如說。喜見轉輪聖王八萬四千小王來朝。皆持七寶妙物來獻。王言我不須也。汝等各可自以修福。諸王自念。大王雖不肯取。我等亦復不宜自用。即共造工立七寶殿。[10]殖七寶行樹作七寶浴池。於大殿中造八萬四千七寶[11]樓。樓中皆有七寶床座。雜色被枕置床兩頭。懸繒幡蓋香熏塗地。眾事備已。白大王言。願受法殿寶樹浴池。王默然受之。而自念言。我今不應先處新殿以自娛樂。當求善人諸沙門婆羅門等先入供養。然後我當處之。即集善人先入寶殿。種種供養微妙具足。諸人出已王入寶殿登金樓坐銀床。念布施除五蓋攝六情却六塵受喜樂入初禪。次登銀樓坐金床入二禪。次登毘琉璃樓坐[12]頗梨寶床入三禪。次登頗梨寶樓坐毘琉璃床入四禪。獨坐思惟終竟三月。

正體字

7. Sudarśana, the Wheel-Turning Sage-King (Story)

According to the story about Sudarśana, a wheel-turning sage-king, eighty-four thousand of the lesser kings came to his court, all bringing marvelous things made of the seven treasures which they presented as offerings. The King declared, "I do not need them. You may each use them yourselves to cultivate karmic blessings."

Those kings thought to themselves, "Although the great King cannot bring himself to accept them, it still wouldn't be appropriate for us to take them for our own use." And so they collectively saw to the construction of a seven-jeweled pavilion. They planted rows of seven-jeweled trees and created bathing pools made of the seven jewels. Within the great pavilion, they built eighty-four thousand halls, each made from the seven precious things.

Within each of the halls, there was a seven-jeweled throne with multi-colored cushions at each end of the throne. Decorated canopies were suspended above and the ground below was sprinkled with fragrances. After all of these preparations had been made, they addressed the King, saying, "We pray that his majesty will accept this Dharma pavilion with its bejeweled trees and bathing pools."

The King indicated his acceptance by remaining silent and then thought to himself, "I ought not to indulge myself with the pleasure of being the first to dwell within this new pavilion. I should invite good people such as the Śramaṇas and the Brahmans to first enter here to receive offerings. After that, I may go ahead and dwell in it." He then gathered together those good personages and had them be the first to enter the jeweled pavilion. There they were provided an abundance of all manner of fine and marvelous offerings.

After those people had all left, the King entered the jeweled pavilion, ascended into the hall of gold, and then sat down upon the silver throne. There he reflected upon giving, dispensed with the five hindrances, withdrew the six sense faculties, did away with the six sense objects, and, experiencing joy and bliss, entered into the first dhyāna.

Next, he ascended into the hall of silver, sat down upon the throne of gold, and then entered into the second dhyāna. Next he ascended into the hall of beryl, sat down upon the crystal throne, and then entered into the third dhyāna. And then, finally, he ascended into the jeweled hall of crystal, sat down upon the beryl throne, and entered into the fourth dhyāna. He sat there alone in contemplation for a total of three months.

玉女宝后与八万四千诸侍女
俱。皆以白珠名宝璎珞其
身。来白[13]大王。久违亲
觐。敢来问讯。王告诸妹。
汝等各当端心。当[14]为知识
勿为我怨。玉女宝后垂泪而
言。[*]大王何为谓我为妹。
必有异心愿闻其意。云何见
勅当为知识勿为我怨。王告
之言。汝若以我为[152c]世因
缘。共行欲事以为欢乐。是
为我怨。若能觉悟非常知身
如幻。修福行善绝去欲情。
是为知识。诸玉女言敬如王
勅。说此语已各遣令还。诸
女出已王登金楼坐银床行慈
三昧。登银楼坐金床行悲三
昧。登毘琉璃楼坐颇梨床行
喜三昧。登颇梨宝楼坐毘琉
璃床行舍三昧。是为菩萨布
施生禅波罗蜜。云何菩萨布
施生般若波罗蜜。菩萨布施
时。知此布施必有果报而不
疑惑。能破邪见无明。是为
布施生般若[15]波罗蜜。

玉女寶后與八萬四千諸侍女
俱。皆以白珠名寶瓔珞其
身。來白[13]大王。久違親
覲。敢來問訊。王告諸妹。
汝等各當端心。當[14]為知識
勿為我怨。玉女寶后垂淚而
言。[*]大王何為謂我為妹。
必有異心願聞其意。云何見
勅當為知識勿為我怨。王告
之言。汝若以我為[152c]世因
緣。共行欲事以為歡樂。是
為我怨。若能覺悟非常知身
如幻。修福行善絕去欲情。
是為知識。諸玉女言敬如王
勅。說此語已各遣令還。諸
女出已王登金樓坐銀床行慈
三昧。登銀樓坐金床行悲三
昧。登毘琉璃樓坐頗梨床行
喜三昧。登頗梨寶樓坐毘琉
璃床行捨三昧。是為菩薩布
施生禪波羅蜜。云何菩薩布
施生般若波羅蜜。菩薩布施
時。知此布施必有果報而不
疑惑。能破邪見無明。是為
布施生般若[15]波羅蜜。

简体字   正體字

The jade ladies, the precious queen, and eighty-four thousand female retainers all draped their bodies in strands of pearls and rare jewels and then came to see the King, saying, "As His Majesty has for so long now withdrawn from intimate audiences, we have dared to come and offer our greetings."

The King announced to them, "Sisters, each of you should maintain a mind imbued with correctness. You should serve me as friends. Don't act as my adversaries."

The jade ladies and the precious queen then began to weep and, as their tears streamed down, they inquired, "Why does the Great King now refer to us as 'sisters'? Surely, he must be thinking of us in a different way now. Pray, may we hear his intent? Why do we now receive the remonstrance: 'You should serve me as friends. Don't act as my adversaries'?"

The King instructed them, saying, "If you look upon me as a mere worldly entity with whom to indulge desires and thus abide in bliss, this amounts to acting as my adversary. If, however, you are able to awaken to the fact of impermanence, realize that the body is like an illusion, cultivate karmic blessings, practice goodness, and cut away desire-laden affections—it is this which amounts to serving me as a friend."

The jade ladies responded, "We shall adhere respectfully to the dictates of the King." After they had spoken thus, they were sent back to their quarters.

After the women had gone, the King ascended into the hall of gold and sat upon the silver throne where he immersed himself in the samādhi of kindness. He then ascended into the hall of silver, sat upon the throne of gold, and immersed himself in the samādhi of compassion. Next, he ascended into the hall of beryl, sat down upon the crystal throne, and immersed himself in the samādhi of sympathetic joy. Finally, he ascended into the jeweled hall of crystal and sat down upon the throne of beryl where he immersed himself in the samādhi of evenmindedness. This is an instance of the bodhisattva's practice of giving generating the *pāramitā* of dhyāna.

8. How *Dāna Pāramitā* Generates *Prajñāpāramitā*

How does the bodhisattva's giving bring about *prajñāpāramitā*? When the bodhisattva gives, he knows that this giving will definitely have a resulting karmic reward and so he is not beset by the delusions of doubt. Thus he is able to shatter erroneous views and ignorance. This is a case of giving bringing forth *prajñāpāramitā*.

复次菩萨布施时能分别知。不持戒人若鞭打拷掠闭系。枉法得财而作布施。生象马牛中。虽受畜生形负重鞭策[16]羁鞿乘骑。而常得好屋好食。为人所重以人供给。又[17]知恶人多怀瞋恚。心曲不端而行布施当堕龙中。得[18]七宝宫殿妙食好色。又[19]知憍人多慢瞋心布施。堕金翅鸟中。常得自在。有如意宝珠以为璎珞。种种所须皆得自恣无不如意。变化万端无事不办。又[20]知宰官之人。枉[21]滥人民不顺治法而取财物。以用布施堕鬼神中。作[22]鸠盘荼鬼。能种种变化五尘自娱。

復次菩薩布施時能分別知。不持戒人若鞭打拷掠閉繫。枉法得財而作布施。生象馬牛中。雖受畜生形負重鞭策[16]羈鞿乘騎。而常得好屋好食。為人所重以人供給。又[17]知惡人多懷瞋恚。心曲不端而行布施當墮龍中。得[18]七寶宮殿妙食好色。又[19]知憍人多慢瞋心布施。墮金翅鳥中。常得自在。有如意寶珠以為瓔珞。種種所須皆得自恣無不如意。變化萬端無事不辦。又[20]知宰官之人。枉[21]濫人民不順治法而取財物。以用布施墮鬼神中。作[22]鳩槃荼鬼。能種種變化五塵自娛。

简体字　　　　　　　　　　正體字

I. The Bodhisattva's Causality Realizations

Furthermore, when the bodhisattva engages in giving, he is able to distinguish and know the circumstances of the person who fails to observe the moral precepts.

1. Benefactors Who Beat or Tie Up Others

If someone whips, strikes, beats up, flogs, confines, or ties up others, or if he circumvents the law and so comes by valuables, and then proceeds to perform acts of giving [with such wealth], he is reborn among elephants, horses, or cattle. Although he takes on the form of an animal which must carry heavy burdens, which is whipped and prodded, which is restrained by halters and fetters, and which is ridden, still, he always obtains good living quarters and fine food, is prized by people, and is provided for by people.

2. Benefactors Who Are Hateful

Additionally, he knows about the circumstances of evil people who are much obsessed with hatefulness and anger, whose minds are devious and not upright, and yet who practice giving. He knows that they will fall into rebirths among the dragons where they will obtain a palace composed of the seven precious things and will have fine food and marvelous sensual pleasures.

3. Benefactors Who Are Arrogant

He also knows that people who are arrogant and who engage in giving with a mind beset with conceit and hatefulness will fall into births among the golden-winged [*garuḍa*] birds where they will always experience sovereign independence and will have a necklace made of precious "as-you-wish-it" pearls. All sorts of things which they require will all be obtained without need for restraint in indulging in them and there will be nothing which will not follow in accordance with their wishes. They will be able to perform magical transformations of a myriad sorts and there will be no matter which they will be unable to bring to completion.

4. Benefactors Who Are Corrupt Officials

He also knows of the circumstances of high government officials who circumvent the law, indulge in unscrupulous excesses at the expense of the people, do not follow regulatory laws, and appropriate valuable goods. If they use them to perform acts of giving, they then fall into births among ghosts and spirits. There they become *kumbhāṇḍa* ghosts who are able to perform all sorts of transformations while pleasing themselves with the five objects of the senses.

又[*]知多瞋[23]恨戾嗜好酒肉之人。而行布施[24]墮[25]地夜叉鬼中。常得种种欢乐音乐饮食。又[*]知有人刚[26]愎强梁。而能布施车马代步。墮虚空夜叉中。而有大力所至如风。又知有人妬心好静。而能以好房舍卧具衣服饮食布施故。生宫观飞行夜叉中。有种种娱乐便身之物。如是种种当布施时能分别知。是为菩萨布施生般[153a]若。复次布施饮食得力色命乐瞻。若布施衣服得生知惭愧。威德端正身心安乐。若施房舍则[1]得种种七宝宫观。自然而有五欲自娱。若施井池泉水种种好浆。所生则得无饥无渴五欲备有。

又[*]知多瞋[23]恨戾嗜好酒肉之人。而行布施[24]墮[25]地夜叉鬼中。常得種種歡樂音樂飲食。又[*]知有人剛[26]愎強梁。而能布施車馬代步。墮虚空夜叉中。而有大力所至如風。又知有人妬心好静。而能以好房舍臥具衣服飲食布施故。生宫觀飛行夜叉中。有種種娛樂便身之物。如是種種當布施時能分別知。是為菩薩布施生般[153a]若。復次布施飲食得力色命樂瞻。若布施衣服得生知慚愧。威德端正身心安樂。若施房舍則[1]得種種七寶宫觀。自然而有五欲自娱。若施井池泉水種種好漿。所生則得無飢無渴五欲備有。

简体字　　　　　　　　　正體字

5. TYRANNICAL BENEFACTORS FOND OF MEAT AND DRINK

He also knows of the circumstances of people who are beset with much hatred, who are tyrannical, who are much obsessed in their fondness for liquor and meat, and who then perform acts of giving. They fall into births among the earth-coursing *yakṣa* ghosts. There they always obtain all sorts of pleasures, music, drink, and food.

6. OBSTINATE BENEFACTORS WHO GIVE CARRIAGES AND HORSES

He also knows of the existence of those people who are obstinate and stubborn and who are unruly and defiant, and yet who are able to perform acts whereby they make gifts of carriages and horses as substitutes for foot travel. They fall into births among the space-coursing *yakṣas* who are possessed of great strength and who arrive at their destinations with wind-like speed.

7. JEALOUS AND ARGUMENTATIVE BENEFACTORS

He also knows of the existence of those people who have jealous minds and who enjoy disputation, but who, on account of making gifts of fine dwellings, bedding, clothing, drink and food, are able to be reborn among the flying *yakṣas* abiding in palaces and temples. They possess all sorts of pleasurable things which provide them with personal convenience.

In all sorts of cases such as these, when giving is performed, he is able to make distinctions and know their import. This illustrates what is meant by the bodhisattva's practice of giving being able to produce prajñā.

8. HUMAN REALM REWARDS FROM GIVING

Furthermore, when one makes offerings of drink and food, one gains strength, physical attractiveness, long life, and admiration.

If one makes gifts of clothes, even from one's very birth, one gains an awareness of a sense of shame and a dread of blame. One possesses the quality of awesome deportment, is physically handsome, and enjoys peace and bliss in both body and mind.

If one makes gifts of dwellings, then one obtains all manner of palaces and towers composed of the seven precious things. One naturally comes to have the five objects of desire with which to afford oneself pleasure.

If one makes gifts of the waters of wells, ponds and springs, and makes gifts of all sorts of fine condiments, then, wherever one is born, one will succeed in being free of hunger or thirst and will possess an abundant repletion of the five objects of desire.

若施桥船及诸履屣。生有种
种车马具足。若施园林则得
豪尊。为一切依止。受身
端[*]政心乐无忧。如是等种
种。人中因缘布施所得。若
人布施修作福德。不好有为
作业生活。则得生四天王
处。若人布施。加以供养父
母及诸伯叔[2]兄弟姊妹。无
瞋无恨不好静讼。又不喜见
静讼之人。得生忉利天上
焰[3]摩兜[4]术化自在他化自
在。如是种种分别布施。是
为菩萨布施生般若。若人布
施心不染着。厌患世间求涅
盘乐。是为阿罗汉辟支佛布
施。若人布施为佛道为众生
故。是为菩萨布施。如是等
种种布施中分别[*]知。是为
布施生般若波罗蜜。复次菩
萨布施时。思惟三事实相。
如上说。如是能知是为布施
生般若波罗蜜。复次一切智
慧功德因缘。皆由布施。如

簡体字

若施橋船及諸履屣。生有種
種車馬具足。若施園林則得
豪尊。為一切依止。受身
端[*]政心樂無憂。如是等種
種。人中因緣布施所得。若
人布施修作福德。不好有為
作業生活。則得生四天王
處。若人布施。加以供養父
母及諸伯叔[2]兄弟姊妹。無
瞋無恨不好靜訟。又不喜見
靜訟之人。得生忉利天上
焰[3]摩兜[4]術化自在他化自
在。如是種種分別布施。是
為菩薩布施生般若。若人布
施心不染著。厭患世間求涅
槃樂。是為阿羅漢辟支佛布
施。若人布施為佛道為眾生
故。是為菩薩布施。如是等
種種布施中分別[*]知。是為
布施生般若波羅蜜。復次菩
薩布施時。思惟三事實相。
如上說。如是能知是為布施
生般若波羅蜜。復次一切智
慧功德因緣。皆由布施。如

正體字

If one gives bridges, boats, or shoes, then, even from birth, one will have an abundance of all sorts of carriages and horses. If one gives parks and forests, then one will achieve the honor of aristocratic social station and will become one to whom everyone looks in reliance. One will take on a body which is handsome and one's mind will be blissful and free of worries.

All sorts of causes and conditions such as these within the realm of people constitute what is gained through the practice of giving.

9. CELESTIAL REALM REWARDS FROM GIVING

If a person gives as a way of cultivating meritorious qualities associated with karmic blessings and does not find the life of conditioned karmic activity to be agreeable, then he succeeds in being reborn in the dwelling place of the four heavenly kings.

If in his practice of giving a person supplements it by making offerings to his father, mother, uncles, brothers, and sisters, if he gives without hatefulness or enmity, and if he is not fond of disputation and also does not delight in seeing disputatious people, he then succeeds in being born in the Trāyastriṃśa heaven or in the Yāma, Tuṣita, Nirmāṇarati, or Paranirmita-vaśavartin heavens.

In all sorts of ways such as these he makes distinctions regarding giving. These examples illustrate how the bodhisattva's practice of giving brings forth *prajñā*.

10. GIVING PERFORMED BY ARHATS AND PRATYEKABUDDHAS

If when one is giving, his mind remains free of any defiling attachment and if one tends to be disgusted with and distressed by the world and thus consequently seeks to realize nirvāṇa, this qualifies as the sort of giving performed by arhats and pratyekabuddhas.

11. GIVING PERFORMED BY BODHISATTVAS

If one gives for the sake of the Buddha Path and for the sake of beings, this constitutes the giving of the bodhisattva.

Among all the different sorts of giving such as these, he makes distinctions and derives understanding. This constitutes the practice of giving bringing forth *prajñāpāramitā*.

Again, when the bodhisattva gives, he contemplates in accordance with reality the true character of the three factors as discussed above. When he is able to know these things in this manner, this constitutes the practice of giving bringing forth *prajñāpāramitā*.

Moreover, all of the causes and conditions associated with wisdom and merit come forth from giving. This is exemplified by

千佛始发意时。种种财物布
施诸佛。或以华香或以衣
服。或以杨枝布施而以发
意。如是等种种布施。是为
菩萨布施生般若波罗蜜

大智度论卷第十[5]二

千佛始發意時。種種財物布
施諸佛。或以華香或以衣
服。或以楊枝布施而以發
意。如是等種種布施。是為
菩薩布施生般若波羅蜜

大智度論卷第十[5]二

简体字

正體字

the Thousand Buddhas who, on first bringing forth the intention [to achieve buddhahood], each used all kinds of valuable things to make gifts to the Buddhas. In some cases, they used flowers and incense as gifts while in other cases they used robes as gifts. In other instances, they took up willow branches as gifts and so brought forth the resolve [intent on buddhahood] in that way.

All sorts of giving of these sorts demonstrate how the bodhisattva's practice of giving brings forth the *prajñāpāramitā*.

The Exegesis on the Great Perfection of Wisdom Sutra
The End of Fascicle Number Twelve.

Part One Endnotes

1. In this brief section of sutra text that it becomes clear that *prajñā-pāramitā*, the perfection of transcendental wisdom, is the very foundation of perfect giving. It is for this reason that Nāgārjuna launches into an extended discussion here of the nature of the perfection of wisdom.

2. The three entities of donor, recipient, and gift are defined as the three essential components involved in any act of giving. The degree of transcendental realization possessed by the donor in regarding these three is held to be key to whether or not genuine "perfection" of giving can be realized.

3. Wisdom free of "outflow impurities" is the wisdom of the spiritually liberated, the Āryas. It is that wisdom which is free of any of the spiritually corrupting and defiling afflictions. This metaphoric designation of "outflow" and "non-outflow" is explained by Vasubandhu as finding its origin in the fact that these defilements "flow" from the six sense faculties (eye, ear, nose, tongue, body, intellectual mind) as if from open wounds, doing so in all spiritually unliberated beings, from the celestial beings in the highest heavens all the way on down to the tortured residents of the Avīci Hells. Examples of the "outflow impurities" include not only the "three poisons" of desire, hatred, and delusive ignorance, but also arrogance, jealousy, miserliness, deception, injuriousness, absence of a sense of shame, absence of a dread of blame, absence of faith, etc. Extensive treatment of this entire topic may be found in the fifth chapter of Vasubandhu's *Abhidharmakośa-bhāṣyam*. See the Pruden translation.

4. The "fetters" are a subset of the spiritually-corrupting afflictions and wrong views which "tie" one to continued suffering in cyclic existence. They vary somewhat in their articulations, but typically refer to a standard list which includes: desire, hatred, arrogance, delusive ignorance, doubtfulness, clinging to wrong views, miserliness, and jealousy.

5. "Unattainability" is a reference to the fact that one possessed of prajñā is unable to locate any genuinely real "inherent existence" in any conditioned phenomenon or dharma.

    As for the "tetralemma," it is a standard set of four alternatives in Buddhist dialectics of the form: 1 – affirmation; 2 – negation; 3 – both affirmed and negated; 4 – neither affirmed nor negated. Intellectual formulations are held in Buddhism to be entirely inadequate to arrive at the truth of ultimate reality reflected in the perfection of wisdom. Hence it is said that it is like a great blaze which will burn the hands when approached from any of these four directions.

6. These reduced-font parenthetical notes are all integral to the received Chinese text preserved in the *Taisho* Tripiṭaka. They may or may not originate with Kumārajīva's oral explanations to his scribes.

7. "Three wretched destinies" refers to the three realms of rebirth wherein suffering is most extreme and intractable and from which it is exceedingly difficult to escape: the hells, the hungry ghosts, and the animals.

8. The "field of blessings" (*puṇyakṣetra*) is the recipient in any act of giving and is so named because, figuratively speaking, giving plants a seed whereby one reaps in the future the fruit of one's act of generosity. Proof of the earliest origins of this concept is found in the patchwork design of a Buddhist monk's robes. Very early on, the Buddha ordered Ānanda to incorporate just such a design into the monk's outer robe. He did so in order to illustrate this concept and also did so because lay devotees had been having trouble distinguishing the Buddha's monastic disciples from mendicants of other traditions.

9. Not translated in this first edition. This is a brief barely-decipherable formulaic and cryptic recitation of only marginally-relevant *abhidharma* data which Nāgārjuna passes over without comment. Since the passage is clearly intended only to make oblique reference to standard abhidharmic categories, I am preferring non-translation to possible mistranslation. Abhidharma specialists are invited to offer suggested translations of this passage for gratefully-attributed inclusion in the next edition.

10. The above fourteen categories comprise, in the case of the first eight, an abbreviated list of subsidiary afflictions (*upakleśa*), and in the case of the final six, a complete listing of the root afflictions (*mūlakleśa*).

11. The "six faculties" refers to eye, ear, nose, tongue, body and intellectual mind.

12. This component of the eight-fold Path is also known as "right effort," or "right vigor."

13. "Thirty-two marks" is a reference to the primary set of special physical features possessed by a fully-enlightened buddha's body. There are another eighty subsidiary characteristics as well.

14. This refers to benefits to the recipient of a donor's gift of food: life, color, strength, bliss and quick-witted intelligence. (This list is mentioned earlier in N's exegesis at T25.1509.82b.)

15. For those confused by the term, "Well-retracted genitals" may be understood by comparing the anatomy of a stallion.

16. Though earlier in the *Exegesis* (90a–91a), the mark of the ten-foot radius aura of light is included, it is not found in this discussion. Here, in its stead, we have one of Buddha's voice attributes elevated in status.

17. An *upāsaka* (feminine: *upāsikā*) is a Buddhist layman, the minimum qualification for which is having formally received from duly-ordained clergy (usually a bhikshu with at least five years full ordination) the Three Refuges: refuge in the Buddha; refuge in the Dharma; and refuge in the Ārya (enlightened) Sangha. Although not a strict requirement to obtain the Refuges and become formally "Buddhist," the universal ethical standard for the Buddhist layperson consists in the five precepts which prohibit: killing; stealing; sexual misconduct; false speech; intoxicants.

18. The "wishlessness samādhi" is one of "the three samādhis," also known as "the three gates to liberation." They are: emptiness, signlessness, and wishlessness.

19. "Three obstructions" refers in this instance to the seizing on the inherent existence of the three essential components involved in an act of giving: the benefactor, the recipient, and the gift.

20. "True character of dharmas" (諸法實相) is Kumārajīva's translation for *dharmatā*. It is simply a reference to the "genuine character" or "actual nature" of dharmas (i.e. "phenomena") in their very essence as seen in accordance with ultimate truth (*paramārtha-satya*). It is simply a reference to dharmas as they really are. In the dialectic of the *Exegesis*, this is repeatedly identified both implicitly and explicitly with nondual emptiness, nirvāṇa, and an utter absence of inherent existence, all non-nihilistic and non-affirming emblematic Mādhyamika expressions of the highest truth.

21. This refers to a *cakravartin*, a universal monarch possessed of personal qualities, powers, reign duration, and dominion vastly beyond those possessed by any royalty who have ever held sway in recorded human history.

22. "Eighty-four thousand" is, in Indian Buddhist literature, similar to the American vernacular use of "millions" which actually just means "lots," or, in more formal terms: "numerous."

23. Just as a fertile field planted with good seed yields abundant crops, so, too, a "field of merit" (*puṇya-kṣetra*) in the form of an adequately virtuous recipient yields karmic fruits for the benefactor. The problem about which these celestial beings were so concerned was the possibility of planting a marvelously potent karmic seed (in the form of this extravagant generosity) in a barren field. In short, they were worried that the karmic seed would be wasted.

24. Although the text does not specifically say so, the implication of the verse is that the Bodhisattva is agreeing to receive the offering on behalf of all of those "good and pure persons" in whom he has just declared refuge and offered reverence and obeisance.

25. "The three realms" is synonymous with all of existence and refers to the three progressively more refined zones of reincarnation coursed through by beings stranded in cyclic birth-and-death: the desire realm (home of hell-dwellers, animals, hungry ghosts, humans, demi-gods, and the lesser gods); the form realm; and the formless realm.

    Both of these latter zones may be entered in the deeper levels of meditative absorption, but also comprise the abodes of the higher and highest classes of god realms, each of which is itself comprised of a number of different subsidiary levels of celestial existence. Even though they involve immensely long lifetimes and freedom from suffering, because these celestial existences are impermanent and bound to eventual deterioration, even the gods are seen in Buddhism to be tragically-enmeshed in karma-bound suffering, no less so in fact than the hell-dwellers.

26. "The path of seeing" is synonymous with leaving behind the predicament of a foolish common person and becoming an ārya whose ultimate spiritual liberation is an absolute certainty.

27. One should not suppose that the last part of this sentence implies the existence of some eternal "essence" or "nature" at the core of any phenomenon. Rather, this is a reference to the inconceivable and ineffable ultimate truth as directly experienced by the Āryas, those who directly cognize the true character of any and all phenomena.

28. Although Mochizuki offers a reconstruction of "Sudāna" for this 須提拏 (2483c), it seems questionable. Hence I'm preferring Lamotte's suggestion about which he himself seemed not entirely certain.

29. Generally speaking, a "Dharma-body bodhisattva" refers to a bodhisattva who has at least reached the first bodhisattva ground, a level which may sound rather elementary but which, on the contrary, is already the culmination of countless lifetimes of preparatory practice on the Bodhisattva Path.

30. Of the two primary categories of equitable minds, equitability with respect to beings (*sattvasamatā*) and equitability with respect to dharmas (*dharmasamatā*), these four refer to the former: maintaining a uniformly equitable mental stance towards all beings in one's thoughts about them (*citta*), in one's mindfulness of them (*smṛti*), in one's affections for them (*anunaya*), and in one's beneficial actions for their sakes (*arthakriyā*).

31. The basis of identity is that these are all conceptual umbrella terms imputing mere nominal unity on aggregations of separate entities.

32. Nāgārjuna discusses the 18 emptinesses at length inthe subject of a long exposition by Nāgārjuna comprising Fascicle 31 of the *Exegesis*. Paramārtha translates another Nāgārjunian treatment of the 18

emptinesses (十八空論 / T31.1616.861-7).

33. "Cart" is just a collection of wheels, axles, frame, etc. "House" is just an aggregation of foundation, framing, sheathing, roofing, etc.

34. "Thus I have heard, at one time..." is the opening line of each scripture attributed to the Buddha. This was discussed in the first fascicle of the *Exegesis*.

35. The questioner is pointing out a problem in the apparent absence of any continuous consciousness faculty lasting longer than a *kṣaṇa*. (A *kṣaṇa* is a micro-moment held to equal one ninetieth the duration of a finger snap.)

36. Emending an obvious scribal error: I have preferred the alternate reading shared by four editions of "newly" for *Taisho's* "gradually."

37. This should not be interpreted as an indication that suicide is somehow devoid of seriously negative karmic consequences. On the contrary, suicide typically makes one prone to falling into extremely unfortunate circumstances in the immediately ensuing rebirth, not least because the nature of one's ensuing incarnation relies to a great extent on the nature of one's thoughts at the moment of death.

38. "Three factors" refers to the six sense faculties, to the six sense objects, and to the six corresponding consciousnesses.

39. It is because all four of the non-form aggregates (feeling, perception, karmic formative factors, and consciousness) depend upon "naming" that one uses "name" as a collective shorthand reference for all of them. Consequently all five of the aggregates are subsumed under the simple binomial term: "name-and-form."

40. Beginning-level practitioners should understand that instances of "superior-level" giving involving any form of physical "self-sacrifice" are best not undertaken by neophytes tempted to indulge a high tide of impetuous religiosity. Offerings of this sort depend on perfectly pure motivation and perfectly stable realization of rarified meditative states. Once one has reached the fourth dhyāna, for instance, one becomes immune to being moved by either pain or pleasure with the result that one can then treat his body as if it is a mere object such as a stone or a log. This level of development allows one to avoid performing some sort of well-meant self-sacrifice in one moment, only to be seized with unbearable pain, grief, and bitter regret in the next, psychic events which tend to destroy all of the merit of the act while also propelling one towards less fortunate rebirth circumstances.

41. The five hindrances are: desire; ill-will; lethargy-and-sleepiness; excitedness-and-regretfulness; and doubt. Nāgārjuna explains them in Fascicle Seventeen of the *Exegesis* early on in his discussion of the perfection of dhyāna meditation.

Part One Variant Readings from Other Chinese Editions

[139n02] (大智度論) - [明]

[139n03] 義 = = 上 [宮]

[139n04] 第十七 = 第十五 [宋] [宮],(第十七) - [元] [明]

[139n05] (佛告舍利弗) - [宮]

[139n06] 法 +(應) [元] [明]

[139n07] (復) - [宋] [元] [明] [宮]

[139n08] (使) - [宋] [元] [明] [宮]* [* 1]

[139n09] (福) - [宮]

[139n10] 須 = 鬚 [宋] [元] [明], = 冠 [宮]

[139n11] (是阿毘曇中如是說) - [宮]

[139n12] (如是) - [宋] [元] [明]

[139n13] 陰界 = 眾界陰 [宮]

[139n14] (火) - [宋]

[139n15] 如 = 無 [元] [明]

[139n16] 氂 = 釐 [宮]

[139n17] (有) - [宋] [元] [明] [宮]

[140n01] 以 = 如是 [宋] [元] [明] [宮]

[140n02] (以) - [宋] [元] [明] [宮]

[140n03] (中) - [宋] [元] [明] [宮]

[140n04] (大智度論) - [明] [宮]* [* 1 2]

[140n05] (釋初…十八)十三字 - [宮]

[140n06] (品) - [宋]

[140n07] (義第十八) - [元],義 = 品 [宋]

[140n08] 第十八 = 第十九 [宋],(第十八) - [明]

[140n09] (益) - [宋] [宮]

[140n10] 府 = 符 [元] [明]

[140n11] 愛 = 受 [宋] [元] [明]

[140n12] 全 = 令 [宮]

[140n13] 護 = 獲 [宋] [元] [明] [宮]

[140n14] 響 = 𩏩 [宋] [宮]

[140n15] 叵 = 詎 [宮]

[140n16] 欻 = 敘 [宋] [宮]

[140n17] 施 = 作 [宋] [元] [明] [宮]

[140n18] 櫪 = 歷 [宋] [宮]

[140n19] (一心) - [宋] [元] [明] [宮]

[140n20] (觀生滅無常) - [宋] [元] [明] [宮]

[140n21] (釋初…十九)十字 - [宮]

[140n22] 義 +(品) [宋]

[140n23] 第十九 = 第二十 [宋],(第十九) - [元] [明]

[140n24] 樂而 = 樂 [宋] [元], = 無樂 [明]

[宮]

[140n25] (丹本注云聖人行施故名不繫)十二字 - [宋] [宮], (丹本注云) - [元] [明]

[140n26] 種 +(修應) [宋] [元] [明] [宮]

[140n27] (欲界…斷)七字 - [宮]

[140n28] (見) - [元] [明]

[140n29] 直 = 愚癡 [宋] [元] [明]

[140n30] 為 = 分別 [宋] [元] [明]

[141n01] 取 = 求 [宋] [元] [明] [宮]

[141n02] 狂 = 誑 [宋] [元] [明] [宮]

[141n03] (名為淨施) - [宋] [宮]

[141n04] 為 = 名 [宋] [元] [明] [宮]

[141n05] 時 = 是 [宋] [宮]

[141n06] (淨施者) - [宋] [元] [明] [宮]

[141n07] (得果報香) - [宋] [宮]

[141n08] (布) - [宋] [元] [明] [宮]

[141n09] 調 = 掉 [元] [明]

[141n10] 深 = 染 [宮]

[141n11] 心 +(中) [元] [明]

[141n12] (惟) - [宮]

[141n13] 廢 = 癈 [宮]

[141n14] (言) - [宋] [元] [明] [宮]

[141n15] (得) - [宋] [元] [明] [宮]

[141n16] [跳-兆 + 專] = 膊 [元] [明]

[141n17] 令受者獨得 = 時適可前人意起 [元] [明]

[141n18] 用 = 業因緣 [元] [明]

[141n19] 求 = 乞 [宋] [元] [明] [宮]

[141n20] 食 +(起少病業因緣) [元] [明]

[141n21] 滿 +(相) [元] [明]

[141n22] 恭敬 = 供養 [宋] [元] [明] [宮]

[141n23] (丹注…故)三十三字 - [宋] [元] [明] [宮]

[141n24] 刹 = 利 [宋] [元] [明] [宮]

[141n25] 陀 = 施 [宮]

[141n26] (其) - [宋] [元] [明] [宮]

[142n01] (客) - [宋] [元] [明] [宮]

[142n02] 牙 = 芽 [宋] [元] [明] [宮]

[142n03] 身 = 耳 [宋] [元] [明] [宮]

[142n04] 我 = 彼 [宋] [元] [明] [宮]

[142n05] (和) - [宋] [元] [明] [宮]

[142n06] 結 = 諸 [宋] [元] [明] [宮]

[142n07] 但 = 相 [元]

[142n08] 薩 = 羅 [明]

[142n09] (人) - [宋] [元] [明] [宮]

[142n10] 洙 = 躁 [宋] [元] [明] [宮]

[142n11] 蘇 = 酥 [宋] [元] [明] [宮]

[142n12] 交 = 校 [宋] [元] [明] [宮]

[142n13] [車*憲] = 幰 [宋] [元] [明] [宮]

[142n14] 頗梨 = 玻璃 [宋] [元] [宮]下同, = 玻瓈 [明]下同

[142n15] [跳-兆 + 甲] = 甲 [元] [明]

[142n16] 疊 = [疊*毛] [宋] [元] [明] [宮]* [* 1]

[142n17] (諸) - [宋] [元] [明] [宮]

[142n18] 以 = 已 [宋] [元] [明] [宮]

[142n19] (故) - [宋] [元] [明] [宮]

[143n01] 千 = 十 [宋] [元] [明] [宮]

[143n02] 欲 = 能 [宋] [元] [明] [宮]

[143n03] 門 + (問) [宋] [元] [明] [宮]

[143n04] 明註曰大南藏作布

[143n05] 明註曰異南藏作惡

[143n06] 邪惡 = 惡邪 [宋] [元] [明] [宮]

[143n07] (乎) - [宋] [元] [明] [宮]

[143n08] 踊 = 涌 [宋] [元] [明] [宮]

[143n09] (婆) - [宮]

[143n10] 薩 = 羅 [宋] [元] [明] [宮]

[143n11] 返 = 反 [宋] [元] [明] [宮]

[143n12] (此眾) - [宋] [元] [明] [宮]

[143n13] 言 = 曰 [宋] [元] [明] [宮]* [* 1 2]

[143n14] (釋初…二十)十四字 - [宮]

[143n15] 義第二十 = 第二十一 [宋],(義第二十) - [元] [明]

[144n01] 但求乃至譬如五十一字斷缺 [宮]

[144n02] 思 = 心 [宋] [元] [明] [宮]

[144n03] (比丘) - [宋] [元] [明] [宮]

[144n04] 歎 = 講 [宋] [元] [明] [宮]

[144n05] 于 = 於 [明]

[144n06] (言) - [宋] [元] [明] [宮]

[144n07] 政 = 正 [宋] [元] [明] [宮]

[144n08] 月 = 明 [宋] [元] [明] [宮]

[144n09] 證 = 畢 [宋] [元] [明] [宮]

[144n10] 盡 = 滅 [宋] [元] [明] [宮]

[144n11] 者 = 等 [宋] [元] [明] [宮]

[144n12] (復次…界)十八字 - [宋] [元] [明] [宮]

[144n13] 也 = 心 [宋] [元] [明] [宮]

[144n14] (之) - [宋] [元] [明] [宮]

[145n01] 法施之餘 = 下第十六 [宮]

[145n02] (之餘卷第) - [石]

[145n03] ([論]) - [宋] [元] [明] [宮]

[145n04] (蜜) - [宋]

[145n05] (滿) - [元] [明] [宮] [石]

[145n06] 秦言 = 此言 [明]*, = 秦云 [石] [* 1 2]

[145n07] 十 = 中 [石]

[145n08] 任 = 住 [元] [明] [石]

[145n09] 嗅之嫌臭唾而棄地 = 嫌惡便棄 [宮]

[145n10] 用 + (無用) [石]

[145n11] 便 = 使 [石]

[145n12] 柀 = [禾*我] [宮]

[145n13] 五 + (人) [宮]

[145n14] 眾 = 蔭 [宋], = 陰 [元] [明]

[145n15] 染 = 深 [石]

[145n16] (此三) - [宋] [元] [明] [宮] [石]

[145n17] (得到彼岸) - [宋] [元] [明] [宮] [石]

[145n18] (檀波…名)八字 - [宋] [元] [明] [宮] [石]

[145n19] (之) - [宋] [元] [明] [宮] [石]

[145n20] 雖 + (俱) [宋] [元] [明] [宮] [石]

[146n01] (大) - [石]

[146n02] 迎 = 匜 [宮]

[146n03] 提 + (犁) [宋] [元] [明] [宮] [石]

[146n04] 明註曰北藏無秦言好愛四字

[146n05] 明註曰北藏無秦言一切施五字

[146n06] 伺 = 向 [石]

[146n07] 諭 = 喻 [宋] [元] [明] [宮]

[146n08] 耆 = 宿 [宮] [石]

[146n09] 長 = 大 [宋] [元] [明] [宮] [石]* [* 1]

[146n10] (獼) - [宋] [元] [明] [宮] [石]

[146n11] 挽 = 捉 [宮]

[146n12] 是 = 此 [宋] [元] [明] [宮]

[146n13] 鳥 = 象 [元] [明]

[146n14] 者 = 師 [宋] [元] [明] [宮] [石]

[146n15] 獼猴 = 復 [宋] [元] [明] [宮] [石]

[147n01] 是 = 者 [石]

[147n02] (若) - [宋] [元] [明] [宮] [石]

[147n03] (為) - [宋] [元] [明] [宮] [石]

[147n04] 伽 + (王) [宋] [元] [明] [宮]

[147n05] (王) - [宋] [元] [明] [宮]

[147n06] (誤) - [宋] [元] [明] [宮] [石]
[147n07] (以) - [宋] [元] [明] [宮]
[147n08] 倚 = 猗 [宋] [宮]
[147n09] (施) - [石]
[147n10] 疊 = [疊*毛] [宋]* [元]* [明]* [* 1 2 3 4 5 6 7 8 9 10 11 12 13 14 15 16 17 18 19 20 21 22 23 24]
[147n11] 功 = 成 [明] [宮] [石]
[147n12] 御 = 禦 [元] [明]
[147n13] 弊 = 蔽 [宋] [元] [明] [宮]
[147n14] 朱 = 株 [明]*
[147n15] 朱利作本文 [宋] [元] [明] [宮]
[147n16] (也) - [元] [明]
[147n17] 木 = 不 [明]
[147n18] (生) - [宋] [元] [明] [宮] [石]
[147n19] (有) - [宋] [元] [明] [宮]
[147n20] (亦無) - [宮] [石]
[147n21] (復) - [石]
[148n01] (有) - [宋] [元] [明] [宮]
[148n02] 水 = 木 [元] [明] [宮] [石]* [* 1 2 3 4]
[148n03] 憎 = 增 [宋] [元] [明] [宮]
[148n04] (淨) + 行 [元] [明]
[148n05] (假) - [宮] [石]
[148n06] (相) - [石]
[148n07] 識 = 說 [宋] [元] [明] [宮]
[148n08] 於 = 各 [宋] [元] [明] [宮] [石]
[148n09] (中) - [宋] [元] [明] [宮] [石]
[148n10] 漸漸 = 新新 [宋] [元] [明] [宮], = 新 [石]
[148n11] 自 = 身 [宮]
[148n12] 似 = 以 [石]
[148n13] 此 + (中) [宋] [元] [明] [宮]
[148n14] (語) - [宋] [元] [明] [宮]
[148n15] 拊 = 附 [宋] [元] [明] [宮]
[148n16] 人 = 父 [宋] [元] [明] [宮] [石]
[148n17] (有) - [宮] [石]
[148n18] 餘 = 使 [石]
[148n19] 汝 = 法 [石]
[148n20] 我 = 神 [宋] [元] [明] [宮] [石]* [* 1 2 3 4 5 6 7 8]
[149n01] (尼) - [石]
[149n02] 故 + (故) [宋] [元] [明] [宮]
[149n03] 不 = 名 [石]

[149n04] (若神常者示) - [宋] [元] [明] [宮] [石]
[149n05] 不 + (自) [宋] [元] [明]
[149n06] 作 + (樂) [宮] [石]
[149n07] (汝) + 言 [宋] [元] [明] [宮]
[149n08] (六) - [宋] [元] [明] [宮] [石]
[149n09] 像 = 象 [宋] [宮]* [* 1]
[149n10] 莊 = 壯 [宮]
[149n11] 求得 = 得求 [宋] [元] [明] [宮]
[149n12] 受 = 愛 [宮]
[149n13] 是念 = 而 [宋] [元] [明] [宮] [石]
[149n14] 利 + (能) [石]
[149n15] 今 = 人 [石]
[149n16] 從此五陰相續 = 次第相續五陰 [宋] [元] [明] [宮] [石]
[149n17] (五陰) - [宋] [元] [明] [宮] [石]
[149n18] 穀 + (子) [宋] [元] [明]
[149n19] 亦 + (復) [宋] [元] [明] [宮]
[149n20] (有) - [宋] [元] [明] [宮] [石]
[150n01] (所) - [宋] [元] [明] [宮] [石]
[150n02] 爪 = 抓 [宮]
[150n03] 實 = 空 [宋] [元] [明] [宮] [石]
[150n04] (亦如是) - [宋] [元] [明] [宮] [石]
[150n05] 施 = 諸佛 [宋] [宮] [石], = 諸佛但說如實法相 [元] [明]
[150n06] (是如實相) - [宋] [元] [明] [宮] [石]
[150n07] 析 = 折 [宋]
[150n08] 者 = 人 [宋] [元] [明] [宮] [石]* [* 1]
[150n09] (佛) - [宋] [宮]
[150n10] 已 = 以 [石]
[150n11] 下中上 = 上中下 [宋] [元] [明] [宮]
[150n12] 施 + (布施) [宋] [元] [明] [宮]
[150n13] 目 = 因 [宋] [元] [明] [宮]
[150n14] 政 = 正 [宋] [元] [明] [宮]* [* 1 2]
[150n15] (羅) - [宋] [元] [明] [宮]
[150n16] 布施故 = 知布施 [宋] [元] [明] [宮] [石]
[150n17] (窮) - [宋] [元] [明] [宮] [石]
[150n18] 生 = 行 [宮]
[150n19] 塵 = 欲 [宋] [元] [明] [宮] [石]
[150n20] (以) - [宋] [元] [明] [宮]
[150n21] (布) + 施 [宋] [元] [明] [宮]

[151n01] 婆 = 娑 [元] [明]

[151n02] 迦 = 伽 [宋] [元] [明] [宮]

[151n03] 嘷 = 號 [宋] [元] [明] [宮]

[151n04] 怪 = 怖 [宋] [元] [明] [宮]

[151n05] 欲 = 惟 [宋] [元] [明] [宮]

[151n06] 曰 = 言 [宋] [元] [明] [宮]*

[151n07] (語) - [宋] [元] [明] [宮] [石]

[151n08] 次 = 欲 [宋]

[151n09] 全 = 令 [石]

[151n10] 免 = 勉 [石]*

[151n11] 博 = 搏 [元] [明], = 轉 [宮]

[151n12] (船) - [石]

[151n13] 板 = 攀 [宋] [元] [明] [宮]* [* 1]

[151n14] 崖 = 岸 [宋] [元] [明] [宮]

[151n15] 免 = 勉 [宋] [宮] [石]

[151n16] (至) - [宋] [石] [明] [宮]

[151n17] 坌 = 齊 [宋] [元] [明] [宮]下同

[151n18] (塗) + 泥 [宋] [元] [明],泥 = 塗 [宮]

[151n19] 三 = 二 [元] [明] [宮] [石]

[151n20] (王婦) - [宋] [宮]

[151n21] (汁) - [宋] [元] [明] [宮] [石]

[152n01] 諸 = 珠 [宋] [元] [明] [宮] [石]

[152n02] 歡 = 欣 [宋] [元] [明] [宮] [石]

[152n03] 念 = 令 [宋] [元], = 憐 [明]

[152n04] (此) - [宋] [元] [明] [宮] [石]

[152n05] 抱 = 挹 [宮]

[152n06] (言) - [石]

[152n07] 泰 = 太 [宋] [元] [明] [宮]

[152n08] 須 = 願 [石]

[152n09] 歛 = 檢 [宋] [元] [明] [宮]

[152n10] 殖 = 植 [元] [明]

[152n11] 樓 = 樹 [宮]

[152n12] 頗梨 = 玻璃 [宋] [元] [宮]下同, = 玻瓈 [明]下同

[152n13] 大 = 天 [宮] [石]* [* 1]

[152n14] 為 + (我) [宋] [元] [明] [宮]

[152n15] (波羅蜜) - [宋] [元] [明] [宮] [石]

[152n16] 羈 = 羇 [宋] [元] [明] [宮]

[152n17] 知 = 如 [宋]* [* 1 2 3]

[152n18] 七 = 十 [宮]

[152n19] 知 = 如 [宋] [宮]

[152n20] 知 = 如 [宋] [宮] [石]

[152n21] 濫 = 攬 [宋], = 欖 [宮]

[152n22] 鳩 = 究 [宋] [宮] [石]

[152n23] 很 = 狠 [明]

[152n24] 墮 = 隨 [石]

[152n25] 地 + (行) [宋] [元] [明] [宮]

[152n26] 愎 = 烈 [宮] [石]

[153n01] (得) - [宋] [元] [明] [宮]

[153n02] 兄弟姊妹 = 兄姊 [宋] [元] [明] [宮] [石]

[153n03] 摩兜術 = 天兜率 [宮], = 天兜師 [石]

[153n04] 術 = 率 [宋] [元] [明]

[153n05] 二 = 三 [石]

Part Two:

THE PERFECTION OF MORAL VIRTUE

(Chapters 21–23)

Part Two Contents

Nāgārjuna on the Perfection of Moral Virtue

大智度论释初品[6]中尸罗波罗蜜[7]义第二十一（卷第十三）。

[*]龙树菩萨造。

[*]后秦龟兹国三藏鸠摩罗什[*]奉诏译。

[153b08]　[8]【经】罪不罪不可得故。应具足尸罗波罗蜜。

[153b09]　　[9]【论】尸罗（[10]秦言性善）好行善道不自放逸。是名尸罗。或受戒行善或不受戒行善。皆名尸罗。尸罗者。略说身口律仪有八种。不恼害不劫盗不邪婬不妄语不两舌不恶口不绮语不饮酒及净命。是名戒[11]相。若不护放舍。是名破戒。破此戒者堕三恶道中。若下持戒生人中。中持戒生六欲[12]天中。

简体字

The Perfection of Moral Virtue

By Ārya Nāgārjuna

Chapter 21: Introductory Discussion of Moral Virtue[1]

I. Introductory Discussion of the Perfection of Moral Virtue

  A. The Sutra Text

Sutra: It is based on the unfindability of offense and non-offense that one should pursue the perfection of moral virtue (*śīla pāramitā*).

  B. Nāgārjuna's Commentary

Exegesis:

    1. General Definition of Moral Virtue (*Śīla*)

Śīla refers to being fond of coursing along in the way of goodness while not allowing oneself to be negligent (*pramāda*). This is what is meant by *śīla*. Perhaps one takes on the moral precepts and practices goodness or perhaps one refrains from taking on the moral precepts and yet still practices goodness. Both of these cases qualify as "*śīla*." (Chinese textual note: In our language, ["*śīla*"] means "to be good by nature.")[2]

    2. Proscribed Behavior Categories

As for *śīla*, generally described, the regulation behaviors specific to the body and mouth are of eight kinds. They include refraining from taking life (*prāṇātipāta*), refraining from taking what is not given (*adattādāna*), refraining from engaging in sexual misconduct (*kāmamithyācāra*), refraining from engaging in false speech (*mṛṣā-vāda*), refraining from engaging in divisive speech (*paiśunyavāda*),[3] refraining from engaging in harsh speech (*pāruṣyavāda*), refraining from engaging in frivolous speech (*saṃbhinnapralāpa*),[4] and refraining from partaking of intoxicants (*madyapāna*). This includes pure livelihood (*pariśuddhājīva*) as well. These are the specific characteristics of the moral precepts.

If one fails to guard them and so lets go of and relinquishes them, this amounts to "breaking" the moral precepts. One who breaks these moral precepts is bound to fall into the three wretched destinies.

    3. Levels of Precept Observance and the Consequences

If one upholds the moral precepts at an inferior level, then one is born among humans. If one upholds the precepts at a middling level, one is born among the six desire heavens. If one upholds the

上持戒又行四禅四空定。生
色无色界清净天中。上持戒
有三种。下清净持戒得阿罗
汉。中清净持戒得辟支佛。
上清净持戒得佛道。不着不
[13]猗不破不缺圣所赞爱。如
是名为上清净[14]持戒。若慈
愍众生故。为度众生故。亦
知戒实相故心不猗着。如此
持戒[15]将来[16]令人至佛道。
如是名为得无上佛道戒。若
人求大善利。当坚持戒如惜
重宝。如护身命。何以故譬
如大地一切万物有形之类。
皆依地而住。戒亦如是戒为
一切善法住处。复次譬如无
足欲行无翅欲飞无船[17]欲
渡。是不可得。若无戒欲[18]
得好果亦复如是。若人弃舍
此戒。虽山居[19]苦行食果服
药。与禽兽无异。或有人但
服水为戒。

简体字

上持戒又行四禪四空定。生
色無色界清淨天中。上持戒
有三種。下清淨持戒得阿羅
漢。中清淨持戒得辟支佛。
上清淨持戒得佛道。不著不
[13]猗不破不缺聖所讚愛。如
是名為上清淨[14]持戒。若慈
愍眾生故。為度眾生故。亦
知戒實相故心不猗著。如此
持戒[15]將來[16]令人至佛道。
如是名為得無上佛道戒。若
人求大善利。當堅持戒如惜
重寶。如護身命。何以故譬
如大地一切萬物有形之類。
皆依地而住。戒亦如是戒為
一切善法住處。復次譬如無
足欲行無翅欲飛無船[17]欲
渡。是不可得。若無戒欲[18]
得好果亦復如是。若人棄捨
此戒。雖山居[19]苦行食果服
藥。與禽獸無異。或有人但
服水為戒。

正體字

precepts at a superior level and also cultivates the four dhyānas and the four emptiness absorptions, one is born in the pure heavens of the form or formless realms.

The superior observance of the moral precepts is of three types: If one adheres to the lesser level of pure observance of the precepts, one achieves arhatship. If one adheres to the middle level of pure observance of the precepts, one attains pratyekabuddhahood. If one adheres to the superior level of pure observance of the precepts, one gains the Buddha Path.

If one neither attaches to them nor leans upon them and if one neither breaks them nor has deficiencies with respect to them, he is one who is praised and cherished by the Āryas. Instances such as these illustrate what is meant by superior purity in the observance of the moral precepts.

If one acts out of kindness and sympathy for beings, if one is motivated by the intention to bring beings across to liberation, and if one knows in accordance with reality the true character of the moral precepts, then one's mind does not lean upon or attach to them. If one upholds the precepts in this way, in the future one will influence people to arrive at the Buddha Path. This is what is meant by gaining the moral precepts of the unsurpassed Buddha Path.

4. The Necessity of Scrupulous Observance

If one wishes to obtain great wholesome benefit, then one should uphold the moral precepts solidly, just as if one were cherishing a valuable treasure and as if one were guarding one's own physical life. Why? Just as the myriad beings possessed of physical form all rely upon the earth and abide there, so too it is with the moral precepts. The moral precepts are the dwelling place of all wholesome dharmas.

Moreover, [dispensing with moral precepts] is like wishing to walk without legs, like wishing to fly without wings and like wishing to cross over a body of water without a boat. This cannot be done. If one is lacking in the moral precepts and yet one wishes to obtain a fine result, it is just the same. If a person casts off and relinquishes these moral precepts, although he may abide in the mountains, practicing ascetic practices and eating fruits and taking herbs, he is still no different from the birds or the animals.

5. Uselessness of Unprecepted Asceticism

There may be people who take on the observance of ascetic practices and thus who adopt the discipline of drinking only water, of

或服乳或服气或剃发或长发。或顶上留少许发。或着袈裟或着白衣或着草衣或木皮衣。或冬入水或夏火炙。若自坠高岩若于恒河中洗。若日三浴再供养火。种种祠[20]祀种种呪愿受行苦行。以无此戒空无所得。若有人虽处高堂大殿好衣美食。而能行此戒者得生好处。及得道果。若贵若贱若小若大。[21]能行此净戒皆得大利。若破此戒无贵无贱无大无小。皆不得随意生善处。复次破戒之人。譬如清凉池而有毒蛇不中澡浴。亦如好华果树而多逆刺。若人虽在贵家生身体端[22]政广学多闻。而不乐持戒无慈愍心。亦复如是如偈说。

贵而无智则为衰。
智而憍慢亦为衰。

持戒之人而毁戒。
今世后世一切衰。

或服乳或服氣或剃髮或長髮。或頂上留少許髮。或著袈裟或著白衣或著草衣或木皮衣。或冬入水或夏火炙。若自墜高巖若於恒河中洗。若日三浴再供養火。種種祠[20]祀種種呪願受行苦行。以無此戒空無所得。若有人雖處高堂大殿好衣美食。而能行此戒者得生好處。及得道果。若貴若賤若小若大。[21]能行此淨戒皆得大利。若破此戒無貴無賤無大無小。皆不得隨意生善處。復次破戒之人。譬如清涼池而有毒蛇不中澡浴。亦如好華果樹而多逆刺。若人雖在貴家生身體端[22]政廣學多聞。而不樂持戒無慈愍心。亦復如是如偈說。

貴而無智則為衰。
智而憍慢亦為衰。

持戒之人而毀戒。
今世後世一切衰。

简体字　　　　　　　　　正體字

drinking only milk, of consuming only vital energy, of shaving off the hair, of letting the hair grow long, of reserving a only a small patch of hair atop the head, of wearing a *kāṣāya* robe, of wearing a white robe, of wearing clothes made of grass, of wearing clothes made of tree bark, of plunging into water in winter, of burning themselves with fire in the summer, of throwing themselves off of a high cliff, of washing themselves in the Ganges River, of taking three baths each day, of repeatedly making offerings to fire, of carrying out all kinds of sacrificial offerings, or of resorting to all sorts of spells and prayers. However, insofar as they may not have taken on these moral precepts, those practices are useless and thus there is nothing to be gained through pursuing them.

6. THE IRRELEVANCE OF SOCIAL STATION

Although a person may abide in an exalted position, living in a grand palace, wearing fine clothes, and consuming exquisite cuisine, if he is nonetheless able to cultivate these moral precepts, he will be able to be reborn into a fine place and eventually will achieve the fruits of cultivating the Path. No matter whether one is of noble or humble social station and no matter whether one has little status or great status, if one is able to cultivate these precepts of purity, he will gain from it a great resulting benefit.

However, if one breaks these moral precepts, there are no considerations reserved for noble or humble class or greater or lesser status. In every case, one will remain unable to succeed in being born in a good place which accords with one's aspirations.

7. THE BREAKER OF PRECEPTS

Moreover, the circumstance of a person who breaks the precepts is comparable to a clear and cool pool containing a poisonous snake. One refrains from bathing in such a place. It is also like a tree bearing fine flowers and fruit but an abundance of thorns. Although a person may abide in a family of the nobility, may possess a body which is handsome and fine, and may have accumulated an abundance of learning, if he finds no pleasure in upholding the moral precepts and his mind is devoid of kindness and pity, he is just like this. His situation is as described in this verse:

If one is of noble birth, but has no wisdom, this is ruination.
If one is intelligent, but is arrogant, this too is ruination.
If one is an upholder of precepts, but then violates the precepts,
In this life and in later lives, all is ruination.

[153c16]　人虽贫贱。而能持戒胜于富贵。而破戒者华香木香不能远闻。持戒之香周遍十方。持戒之人具足安乐。名声远闻天人敬爱。现世常得种种快乐。若欲天上人中富贵长寿。取之不难。持戒清净所愿皆得。复次持戒之人。见破戒人刑狱[23]考掠种种苦恼。自知永离此事以为欣庆。若持戒之人。见善人得誉名闻快乐。心自念言。如彼得誉。我亦有分。持戒之人寿终之时刀风解身筋脉断绝。自知持戒清净心不怖畏。如偈说。

　大恶病中　　戒为良药。
　大恐怖中　　戒为守护。

　死暗冥中　　戒为明灯。
　于恶道中　　戒为桥梁。

　死海水中　　戒为大船。

[154a01]　复次持戒之人。常得今世人所敬养

[153c16]　人雖貧賤。而能持戒勝於富貴。而破戒者華香木香不能遠聞。持戒之香周遍十方。持戒之人具足安樂。名聲遠聞天人敬愛。現世常得種種快樂。若欲天上人中富貴長壽。取之不難。持戒清淨所願皆得。復次持戒之人。見破戒人刑獄[23]考掠種種苦惱。自知永離此事以為欣慶。若持戒之人。見善人得譽名聞快樂。心自念言。如彼得譽。我亦有分。持戒之人壽終之時刀風解身筋脈斷絕。自知持戒清淨心不怖畏。如偈說。

　大惡病中　　戒為良藥。
　大恐怖中　　戒為守護。

　死闇冥中　　戒為明燈。
　於惡道中　　戒為橋樑。

　死海水中　　戒為大船。

[154a01]　復次持戒之人。常得今世人所敬養

简体字　　　　　　　　　　　　正體字

8. THE OBSERVER OF THE PRECEPTS

Although one may be poor and of low social station, if one is able to uphold the moral precepts, this is superior to being wealthy or of noble birth while yet being a breaker of the precepts.

The fragrance of flowers and the fragrance of the trees is such that one is unable to smell them from afar. However, the fragrance from upholding the precepts universally pervades throughout the ten directions. The person who upholds the moral precepts perfects the realization of peacefulness and happiness. His name is heard in faraway quarters and he is revered and cherished by both men and gods. In this present life, he always achieves all manner of happiness. If he desires wealth, nobility, and long life in the heavens or among people, it is not difficult for him to obtain it. If one is pure in upholding the moral precepts, he gains whatever he wishes.

Moreover, a person who upholds the moral precepts observes the precept breaker's suffering and affliction encountered through punishments, confinements, beatings, and floggings, knows with respect to himself that he has eternally transcended such vulnerabilities, and is overjoyed on that account.

If a person who upholds the precepts sees a good person gaining a good name, fame, and happiness, and thinks to himself, "In just the same fashion as he has come by a good reputation, I too have a measure of that." When the life of a person who upholds the moral precepts comes to an end, when the knife-like wind cuts loose the body, and when the sinews and blood vessels are severed, he knows that he has upheld the precepts purely. His mind remains free of fearfulness. This situation is as described in a verse:

In an epidemic of great evil,
The moral precepts serve as fine medicine.
In a circumstance of great fearfulness,
The precepts are a guardian protector.

In the midst of the darkness of death,
The precepts serve as a bright lamp.
Where one might fall into the wretched destinies,
The precepts act as a bridge.

Within the waters of the sea of mortality,
The precepts are a great ship.

Furthermore, the person who upholds the precepts always finds that he is revered and supported by people of his time. His mind

心乐不悔。衣食无乏。死得生天后得佛道。持戒之人无事不得。破戒之人一切皆失。譬如有人常供养天。其人贫穷一心供养满十二岁求索富贵。天愍此人自现其身而问之曰。汝求何等。答言。我求富贵。欲令心之所愿一切皆得。天与一器名曰德瓶。而语之言。所须之物从此瓶出。其人得已应意所欲无所不得。得如意已具作好舍象马车乘。七宝具足。供给宾客事事无乏。客问之言。汝先贫穷。今日[1]所由得如此富。答言。我得天瓶。瓶能出此种种众物故富如是。客言。出瓶见示并所出物。即为出瓶。瓶中引出种种众物。其人憍泆立瓶上舞。瓶即破坏。一切众物亦一时灭。持戒之人亦复如是。种种妙乐无愿不得。若人破戒憍泆[2]自恣

简体字

心樂不悔。衣食無乏。死得生天後得佛道。持戒之人無事不得。破戒之人一切皆失。譬如有人常供養天。其人貧窮一心供養滿十二歲求索富貴。天愍此人自現其身而問之曰。汝求何等。答言。我求富貴。欲令心之所願一切皆得。天與一器名曰德瓶。而語之言。所須之物從此瓶出。其人得已應意所欲無所不得。得如意已具作好舍象馬車乘。七寶具足。供給賓客事事無乏。客問之言。汝先貧窮。今日[1]所由得如此富。答言。我得天瓶。瓶能出此種種眾物故富如是。客言。出瓶見示并所出物。即為出瓶。瓶中引出種種眾物。其人憍泆立瓶上舞。瓶即破壞。一切眾物亦一時滅。持戒之人亦復如是。種種妙樂無願不得。若人破戒憍泆[2]自恣

正體字

remains blissful and free of regrets. He has no shortage of either clothing or food. When he dies, he is born in the heavens and then subsequently gains realization of the Buddha Path. For the person who upholds the precepts, there is no matter in which he is not successful. For a person who breaks the precepts, everything is lost.

9. THE MAN WITH THE MARVELOUS VASE (STORY)

This situation is analogous to that of the man who constantly devoted himself to making offerings to a particular deity. As this man was poverty-stricken, for twelve full years he single-mindedly made offerings out of a desire to gain wealth and nobility. The god was moved to feel pity for this man, manifest himself before him, and asked, "What is it that you seek?"

The man replied, "I'm seeking to gain wealth and nobility. I desire to have it occur that I may obtain everything I wish for."

The god then gave him a vessel known as "the vase of virtue" and told the man, "Everything you need will come forth from this vase."

After the man got it, there was nothing which he wished for that he did not succeed in obtaining. After he had acquired the ability to get anything he wished for, he built himself a fine house complete with elephants, horses, and carriages, and also came to possess an abundance of the seven kinds of jewels. He gave generously to all of his guests so that they were never wanting in any respect.

One of his guests inquired of him, "You used to be poverty-stricken. How is it that now you have come by such wealth?"

The man replied, "I received this celestial vase. The vase is able to put forth all of these different kinds of things. It's on account of this that I have gained such wealth."

The guest asked, "Would you show me the vase and something which it has put forth?"

He immediately brought out the vase. From within the vase, he drew forth all manner of objects. Then, in prideful carelessness, he began to dance about on the top rim of the vase, whereupon the vase was immediately shattered. At the very same time, all of the different sorts of things which it had produced all simultaneously disappeared.

One who upholds the moral precepts is just like this. He receives all manner of marvelous bliss and there is no wish which he does not realize. However, if a person breaks the precepts—if he becomes pridefully careless and gives free rein to willfulness—he will

亦如彼人破瓶失[3]物。复次持戒之人名称之香。今世后世[4]周满天上及在人中。复次持戒之人。人所乐施不惜财物。不修世利而无所乏得生天上。十方佛前入三乘道而得解脱。唯种种邪见。持戒后无所得。复次若人虽不出家。但能修行戒法。亦得生天。若人持戒清净[5]行禅智慧。欲求度脱老病死苦此愿必得。持戒之人虽无兵仗众恶不加。持戒之财无能夺者。持戒亲亲虽死不离。持戒庄严胜于七宝。以是之故。当护于戒如护身命如爱宝物。破戒之人受苦万端。如向贫人破瓶失物。[6]以是之故应持净戒。复次持戒之人。观破戒人罪应自勉励一心持戒。

简体字

亦如彼人破瓶失[3]物。復次持戒之人名稱之香。今世後世[4]周滿天上及在人中。復次持戒之人。人所樂施不惜財物。不修世利而無所乏得生天上。十方佛前入三乘道而得解脫。唯種種邪見。持戒後無所得。復次若人雖不出家。但能修行戒法。亦得生天。若人持戒清淨[5]行禪智慧。欲求度脫老病死苦此願必得。持戒之人雖無兵仗眾惡不加。持戒之財無能奪者。持戒親親雖死不離。持戒莊嚴勝於七寶。以是之故。當護於戒如護身命如愛寶物。破戒之人受苦萬端。如向貧人破瓶失物。[6]以是之故應持淨戒。復次持戒之人。觀破戒人罪應自勉勵一心持戒。

正體字

become just like this man who broke his vase and consequently lost everything.

10. The Good Fortune of the Observer of Precepts

Furthermore, the reputation of the person who upholds the precepts spreads like a fragrance and pervades both the heavens and the human realm in both current and later lives. Additionally, the person who upholds the precepts is one to whom people enjoy making gifts, not stinting in giving even their valuable possessions. He does not cultivate worldly profit and yet there is nothing for which he is wanting. He succeeds in being born in the heavens. He enters the way of the Three Vehicles in the presence of the Buddhas of the ten directions and then succeeds in achieving liberation. It is only in a case where all manner of erroneous views figure in one's upholding of precepts that there might be nothing gained later.

Then again, even though a person may not have left behind the home life, if he is only able to cultivate the dharma of the precepts, he too will succeed in being reborn in the heavens. If a person is pure in his upholding of the precepts while also cultivating dhyāna and wisdom, and if he seeks thereby to cross himself over to liberation from the suffering of aging, sickness, and death, this wish will certainly be realized. Even though a person who upholds the precepts may not be under the protection of the military's weaponry, awful events will not befall him.

The wealth of upholding precepts is such that none can steal it away. The upholding of precepts is the most intimate of intimates. Even when one dies, one still does not become estranged from it. The adornment furnished by the upholding of precepts is superior to that of the seven precious things. It is for these sorts of reasons that one should remain just as protective of the moral precepts as one is protective of one's own physical life and just as cherishing of them as one is in cherishing precious possessions.

The person who breaks the precepts undergoes a myriad forms of suffering. He is like that man who used to be poor, subsequently became rich, but then broke the vase, and lost everything as a consequence. It is for these reasons that one should uphold the precepts of purity.

Moreover, when the person who upholds the precepts observes the karmic punishments of those who have broken the precepts, he should encourage himself on that account to devote himself to single-minded observance of the moral precepts.

云何名为破戒人罪。破戒之人人所不敬。其家如冢人所不到。破戒之人失诸功德。譬如枯树人不爱乐。破戒之人如霜莲花人不喜见。破戒之人恶心可畏譬如罗刹。破戒之人人不归向。譬如渴人不向枯井。破戒之人心常疑悔。譬如犯事之人常畏罪至。破戒之人如田被雹不可依仰。破戒之人譬如苦[7]苽。虽形似甘种而不可食。破戒之人如贼聚落不可依止。破戒之人譬如大病人不欲近。破戒之人不得免苦。譬如恶道难可得过。破戒之人不可共止。譬如恶贼难可亲近。破戒之人譬如[8]大坑行者避之。破戒之人难可共住譬如毒蛇。破戒之人不可近触譬如大火。破戒之人譬如破船不可乘渡。破戒之人譬如吐食不可更噉。

云何名為破戒人罪。破戒之人人所不敬。其家如塚人所不到。破戒之人失諸功德。譬如枯樹人不愛樂。破戒之人如霜蓮花人不喜見。破戒之人惡心可畏譬如羅刹。破戒之人人不歸向。譬如渴人不向枯井。破戒之人心常疑悔。譬如犯事之人常畏罪至。破戒之人如田被雹不可依仰。破戒之人譬如苦[7]苽。雖形似甘種而不可食。破戒之人如賊聚落不可依止。破戒之人譬如大病人不欲近。破戒之人不得免苦。譬如惡道難可得過。破戒之人不可共止。譬如惡賊難可親近。破戒之人譬如[8]大坑行者避之。破戒之人難可共住譬如毒蛇。破戒之人不可近觸譬如大火。破戒之人譬如破船不可乘渡。破戒之人譬如吐食不可更噉。

简体字　　　　　　　　　　　　　正體字

11. THE WRETCHED STATE OF THE PRECEPT BREAKER: 32 ANALOGIES

What is meant by "the karmic punishments of those who have broken the moral precepts"?

A person who breaks the precepts is not respected by others. His house becomes like a tomb in that people do not choose to go there.

The person who breaks the moral precepts loses all of his meritorious qualities. He becomes like a dead and leafless tree in which people take no pleasure.

A person who breaks the precepts becomes like a frost-damaged lotus which people take no delight in viewing.

The person who breaks the precepts possesses an evil and fearsome mind like that of a *rākṣasa* ghost.

Just as thirsty people avoid a dried-up well, so too do people avoid returning into the presence of a precept-breaker.

The mind of the person who breaks the precepts is constantly beset with doubts and regrets. He is comparable to a criminal in that he is always fearful that punishment may come his way.

The person who breaks the precepts becomes like farmland struck by a hail storm which people cannot rely on for sustenance.

A person who breaks the precepts is like a bitter melon which, though resembling the sweet varieties, is inedible.

A person who breaks the precepts is like a village populated by thieves wherein one cannot remain.

A person who breaks the precepts is like a person afflicted with a serious disease in that one does not wish to grow close to him.

The breaker of the precepts is unable to avoid suffering. It is just as with a wretchedly bad path on which it is difficult to travel.

One cannot remain together with a person who breaks the precepts. Just as with an evil thief, it is difficult to grow close to him.

A person who breaks the precepts is like a great abyss. Those who travel by avoid it.

A person who breaks the precepts is difficult to dwell together with. In this he is comparable to a poisonous snake.

A person who breaks the precepts cannot be approached or touched. Thus he is comparable to a huge conflagration.

A person who breaks the precepts is like a wrecked boat in which one cannot ride to ferry on across the waters.

A person who breaks the precepts is like food which has been vomited up and which cannot be feasted on again.

破戒之人在好众中。譬如恶马在善马[9]群。破戒之人与善人异。如驴在牛群。破戒之人在精进众。譬如[10]儜儿在健人中。破戒之人虽似比丘。譬如死尸在眠人中。破戒之人譬如伪珠在真珠中。破戒之人譬如伊兰在栴檀[11]林。破戒之人虽形似善人内无善法。虽复剃头染衣次第捉筹名为比丘。实非比丘。破戒之人若着法衣。则是热铜铁[12]鍱以缠其身。若持鉢盂则是盛洋铜器。若所噉食则是吞烧铁丸。饮热洋铜。若受人供养供给。则是地狱狱[13]鬼守之。若入精舍则是入大地狱。若坐众僧床榻。是为坐热铁床上。复次破戒之人。常怀怖懅如重病人常畏死至。亦如五逆罪人。心常自念我为佛贼。藏覆避隈如贼畏人。岁月日过常不安隐。

简体字

破戒之人在好眾中。譬如惡馬在善馬[9]群。破戒之人與善人異。如驢在牛群。破戒之人在精進眾。譬如[10]儜兒在健人中。破戒之人雖似比丘。譬如死屍在眠人中。破戒之人譬如偽珠在真珠中。破戒之人譬如伊蘭在栴檀[11]林。破戒之人雖形似善人內無善法。雖復剃頭染衣次第捉籌名為比丘。實非比丘。破戒之人若著法衣。則是熱銅鐵[12]鍱以纏其身。若持鉢盂則是盛洋銅器。若所噉食則是吞燒鐵丸。飲熱洋銅。若受人供養供給。則是地獄獄[13]鬼守之。若入精舍則是入大地獄。若坐眾僧床榻。是為坐熱鐵床上。復次破戒之人。常懷怖懅如重病人常畏死至。亦如五逆罪人。心常自念我為佛賊。藏覆避隈如賊畏人。歲月日過常不安隱。

正體字

When a person who breaks the precepts is present within a group of good people, it is like when a bad horse is present in a herd of good horses.

A person who breaks the precepts is different from good people. It is just as when a donkey is present within a herd of cattle.

When a person who breaks the precepts is present within the vigorous assembly, it is like when a weakling child is present among strong men.

Although a person who breaks the precepts may look like a bhikshu, he is like a corpse in the midst of a group of sleeping men.

A person who breaks the precepts is like a counterfeit pearl in the midst of true pearls.

A person who breaks the precepts is like an *eraṇḍa* tree[5] in the midst of a forest of sandalwood.

Although the person who breaks the precepts resembles a good person in appearance, he contains no good dharmas within. Although he may shave his head, dye the robes, take up vouchers according to seniority, and be referred to as a bhikshu, he is not really a bhikshu.

If a person who breaks the precepts dons the Dharma robes, [it is as if] he were to encase his body in sheets of hot brass.

If he takes up the bowl, then it is [as if it were] a vessel filled with molten brass.

If he consumes food, this amounts to swallowing burning iron pellets and drinking molten brass.

If he accepts offerings or support from people, [it is as if] they are just the minion ghosts of hell who imprison him.

If he enters a monastic dwelling, [then it is as if] he is entering a great hell.

If he sits on a seat belonging to the members of the Sangha, [it is as if] he is sitting down on a bed of hot iron.[6]

Additionally, a person who breaks the precepts constantly experiences a feeling of fearfulness. Like a person with a serious illness, he is always afraid that death is about to come.

He is also just like a person who has committed the five relentless (*ānantarya*) transgressions.[7] He constantly thinks to himself, "I am a thief who steals from the Buddha. He stays in hiding and avoids contact by staying in less-frequented places. He is just like a thief who is fearful of others. As the months and days of each year go by, he always feels ill-at-ease and insecure.

破戒之人虽得供养利乐是乐不净。譬如愚人供养庄严死尸。智者闻之[14]恶不欲见。如是种种无量。破戒之罪不可称说。行者应当一心持戒。	破戒之人雖得供養利樂是樂不淨。譬如愚人供養莊嚴死屍。智者聞之[14]惡不欲見。如是種種無量。破戒之罪不可稱說。行者應當一心持戒。
简体字	正體字

Although a person who breaks the precepts may gain the benefit and pleasure of offerings, this pleasure is not pure. This circumstance is comparable to when a fool makes offerings to and adorns a corpse. When the wise hear of such a thing, they do not even wish to lay eyes on it.

There are innumerably many different sorts of examples such as these. The punishments endured by those who break the precepts are such as cannot be described. Thus it is that the cultivator should be single-minded in upholding the moral precepts.

简体字

[15]大智度论释初品中戒相义[16]第二十二之一。

[154c08] 问曰。已知如是种种功德果报。云何[17]名为戒[18]相。答曰。恶止不更[19]作。若心生若口言若从他受。息身口恶是为戒[*]相。云何名为恶。若实是众生。知是众生发心欲杀而夺其命。生身业有作色。是名杀生罪。其馀系闭鞭打等。是助杀法。复次杀他得杀罪。非自杀身心知众生而杀。是[20]名杀罪。不如夜中见人谓为杌树而杀者。故杀生得杀罪。非不[21]故也。快心杀生得杀罪非狂痴。命根断是杀罪。

正體字

[15]大智度論釋初品中戒相義[16]第二十二之一。

[154c08] 問曰。已知如是種種功德果報。云何[17]名為戒[18]相。答曰。惡止不更[19]作。若心生若口言若從他受。息身口惡是為戒[*]相。云何名為惡。若實是眾生。知是眾生發心欲殺而奪其命。生身業有作色。是名殺生罪。其餘繫閉鞭打等。是助殺法。復次殺他得殺罪。非自殺身心知眾生而殺。是[20]名殺罪。不如夜中見人謂為杌樹而殺者。故殺生得殺罪。非不[21]故也。快心殺生得殺罪非狂癡。命根斷是殺罪。

Chapter 22: Details and Import of the Moral Precepts

II. DETAILS AND IMPORT OF THE MORAL PRECEPTS

  A. PRECEPTS DEFINED: CESSATON OF AND RESTRAINT FROM EVIL

Question: We are already aware of the many sorts of meritorious qualities and resultant rewards [associated with the precepts]. What are the characteristic features of the moral precepts?

Response: They consist of the stopping of evil and the refraining from any further commission of it. This is the case whether it comes forth from the mind, whether it involves utterances by the mouth, or whether it involves external influences. It includes the putting to rest of evil on the part of the body and the mouth. These are what constitute the characteristic features of the precepts.

  1. THE LAYPERSON'S PRECEPTS

  a. THE FIVE PRECEPTS

  1) THE PRECEPT AGAINST KILLING

  a) KILLING DEFINED

What constitutes evil? In this case, it is where there actually is a being, one knows it is a being, and one brings forth the thought desirous of killing and thus takes its life. One then does generate the physical action. It is a case where there does exist a created physical form. This constitutes the offense of killing a being. The other factors: the tying up, the confining, the whipping, the beating, and so forth—these are dharmas which are auxiliary to killing.

Additionally, it is when one kills another being that one incurs the offense of killing. In a circumstance where one kills one's own body—even if one knows it to be a being and then performs the act of killing, it is still not the case that this constitutes the offense of killing.

It does not qualify as an offense when one sees a person at night, thinks him to be a leafless tree trunk, and then kills him. It is when one deliberately kills a being that one incurs the killing offense. It is not the case [that an offense is incurred] when the act is not intentional. When one kills a being and does so with a pleased mind, one incurs the offense of killing. This is not the case where one is in a state of crazed delusion. It is at that very point in time when the root of life is cut off that it constitutes the offense of killing.

非作疮身业是杀罪。非但口
教勅口教是杀罪。非但心[22]
生如是等名杀[23]罪。不作
是罪名为戒。若人受戒心生
口言。我从今日不复杀生。
若身不动口不言。而独心生
自誓。我从今日不复杀生。
是名不杀生戒。有人言。是
不杀生戒或善或无记。问
曰。如阿毘昙中说。一切戒
律仪皆善。今何以言无记。
答曰。如迦栴延子阿毘昙中
言一切善。如馀阿毘昙中
言。不杀戒或善或无记。何
以故。若不杀戒常善者。持
此戒人应如得道人常不堕恶
道。以是故或时应无记。无
记无[24]果报故。不生天上
人中。问曰。不以戒无记故
堕地狱。更有恶心生故堕地
狱。答曰。不杀生得无量善
法。作无作福

简体字

It is not the case that the physical action of creating a wound in itself constitutes the offense of killing. It is not the case that when one has only given the verbal instructions as an order [to kill] that those verbal instructions in and of themselves constitute the offense of killing. Nor is it the case that the generation of the thought alone [constitutes the killing offense]. Cases which accord with the indications of these criteria are what constitute the offense of killing. So long as one refrains from creating these offenses, it still amounts to remaining in compliance with the precepts.

In a case where a person takes the precept, the thought arises and the mouth speaks, saying, "From this day on, I will not again kill beings." If it happens that the body does not actually move and the mouth does not actually speak, but the mind alone is nonetheless active and thus one mentally vows to oneself, "From this very day onward, I will refrain from ever killing beings again," this *does* constitute the taking on of the non-killing precept.

There are those who say that this "not killing" precept may be categorized as "good" or it may be "neutral."

Question: According to the testimony of the Abhidharma, all moral regulations associated with the precepts are good. Why then do you now say that they may be "neutral"?

b) Abhidharmic Analysis of Killing Precept

Response: According to the Abhidharma of Kātyāyanīputra they are all categorized as "good."[8] According to the statements contained in other *abhidharmas*, the precept of not killing may be good or it may be neutral. Why? If it were the case that the not killing precept were always good, then it ought to be the case that those who uphold this precept should never fall into the wretched destinies just as in the case of those who have already gained realization of the Path. Using this rationale as a basis, there may be times when it should be neutral. Because that which is neutral has no resulting retribution, it may be the case that one has no resulting rebirth in the heavens or in the human realm [solely traceable to having adhered to this particular moral precept].

Question: It is not the case that one would fall into the hells based solely on the neutrality of a precept. It is because of the additional factors associated with the generation of evil thoughts that one falls into the hells.

Response: By not killing beings, one develops an immeasurable number of good dharmas. This is because the creating of merit

常日夜生故。若作少罪有限有量。何以故。随有量而不[1]随无量。以是故知。不杀戒中或有无记。复次有人不从师受戒。而但心生自誓。我从今日不复杀生。如是不杀或时[2]无记。问曰。是不杀戒何界系。答曰。如迦栴延子阿毘昙中言一切受戒律仪。皆欲界系。馀阿毘昙中言。或欲界系或不系。以实言之应有三种。或欲界系或色界系或[3]无漏。杀生法虽欲界。不杀戒应随杀在欲界。但色界不杀。无漏不杀远遮故。是真不杀戒。复次有人不受戒。而从生已来不好杀生。或善或无记是名无记。是不杀生[4]法非心非心数法亦非心相应。或共心生或不共心生。迦栴延子阿毘昙中言。不杀生是身口业。

常日夜生故。若作少罪有限有量。何以故。隨有量而不[1]隨無量。以是故知。不殺戒中或有無記。復次有人不從師受戒。而但心生自誓。我從今日不復殺生。如是不殺或時[2]無記。問曰。是不殺戒何界繫。答曰。如迦栴延子阿毘曇中言一切受戒律儀。皆欲界繫。餘阿毘曇中言。或欲界繫或不繫。以實言之應有三種。或欲界繫或色界繫或[3]無漏。殺生法雖欲界。不殺戒應隨殺在欲界。但色界不殺。無漏不殺遠遮故。是真不殺戒。復次有人不受戒。而從生已來不好殺生。或善或無記是名無記。是不殺生[4]法非心非心數法亦非心相應。或共心生或不共心生。迦栴延子阿毘曇中言。不殺生是身口業。

简体字   正體字

through non-commission of the offense is accumulating constantly day and night. However, if one is simultaneously committing a few karmic offenses, one's merit then becomes limited and measurable. How is this so? The relative balance gravitates towards that which is measurable and does not go the way of the immeasurable. It is on this basis that one can realize that within the sphere of the not killing precept, there may be instances in which it becomes "neutral."

Moreover, there are those people who do not receive the precepts from a Master but who only bring forth in their minds a vow to themselves, "From this day on, I shall no longer kill any beings." The refraining from killing under this sort of circumstance may have times when it is only neutral.

Question: To which of the realms is this precept requiring abstention from killing connected?

Response: According to the statements in the Abhidharma of Kātyāyanīputra, all moral regulations associated with received precepts are connected to the desire realm. According to statements in other *abhidharmas*, it may be connected to the desire realm or may not be connected to any realm at all. To speak of it in a manner corresponding to reality, there are three ways of classifying it: It may be connected to the desire realm; it may be connected to the form realm; or it may be connected to states beyond outflow impurities. Although it would seem that the not-killing precept should be most properly associated with the desire realm where killing is actually carried out, because in the form realm and realms free of outflow impurities one is far removed from actually engaging in killing, it is those spheres which best exemplify the true implementation of the not-killing precept.

Additionally, there are those people who do not actually take the killing precept but who, from birth onwards, nonetheless find no pleasure in killing beings. [Abstention from killing] may be either "good" or "neutral." This is one of those circumstances qualifying as "neutral."

c) ADDITIONAL ABHIDHARMA ANALYTIC DATA

This dharma of abstention from killing is not mind, is not a mind dharma, and is not a dharma associated with the mind. It may arise in association with the mind or it may be that it does not arise in association with the mind.

It is stated in the abhidharma of Kātyāyanīputra that abstention from killing beings is either body karma or mouth karma, that it may

或作色或无作色。或[5]时随心行或不随心行。[6](丹注云随心行定共戒不随心意五戒)非先世业报。二种修应修。二种证应证。[7](丹注云身证慧证)思惟断一切欲界最后得见断时断。凡夫圣人所得是色法。或可见或不可见法。或有对法或无对法。有报法有果法。有漏法有为法有上法。[8](丹注云非极故有上)非相应因。如是等分别是名不杀戒。问曰。八直道中戒亦不杀生。何以独言不杀生戒有报有漏。答曰。此中但说受戒律仪[9]法。不说无漏[10]戒律仪。复次馀阿毘昙中言。不杀法常不逐心行。非身口业。不随心业行。或有报或无报[11]非心相应法或有漏或无漏。是为异法。馀者[12]皆同。

简体字

或作色或無作色。或[5]時隨心行或不隨心行。[6](丹注云隨心行定共戒不隨心意五戒)非先世業報。二種修應修。二種證應證。[7](丹注云身證慧證)思惟斷一切欲界最後得見斷時斷。凡夫聖人所得是色法。或可見或不可見法。或有對法或無對法。有報法有果法。有漏法有為法有上法。[8](丹注云非極故有上)非相應因。如是等分別是名不殺戒。問曰。八直道中戒亦不殺生。何以獨言不殺生戒有報有漏。答曰。此中但說受戒律儀[9]法。不說無漏[10]戒律儀。復次餘阿毘曇中言。不殺法常不逐心行。非身口業。不隨心業行。或有報或無報[11]非心相應法或有漏或無漏。是為異法。餘者[12]皆同。

正體字

involve visible or invisible form, that it may conform with actions of the mind or may not conform with the actions of the mind. It is not the case that it constitutes karmic retribution from earlier lives. (Chinese textual note: The notes in red state that "conforming with the mind" refers to "precepts linked to meditative absorption" whereas "not conforming with the mind" refers to the five precepts.)

There are two types of cultivation which should be cultivated and two types of realization which should be realized. (Chinese textual note: The notes in red state that this refers to "physical realization" and "wisdom realization.") There is severance through thought. In all desire realms, it is the last to be achieved. This may involve severance through cognition or severance linked to a particular temporal circumstance.

That which is gained by both the common person and an ārya is a form dharma. It may be visible or it may be invisible. It may involve a dharma which is opposable or it may involve a dharma which is not opposable. It is a dharma which has a reward. It is a dharma which has a fruition. It is a dharma within the sphere of outflow impurities. It is a conditioned dharma. It is a surpassable dharma. (Chinese textual note: The notes in red state that it is surpassable because it is not ultimate.) It is a non-corresponding cause. Analyses such as these are employed [in *abhidharma* writings] to describe the precept proscribing killing.

Question: The killing of beings is also proscribed by the moral-precept standard included in the eightfold right path. Why do you merely note here that the precept of abstention from killing beings has a retribution and is in the realm of outflow impurities?

Response: We discuss herein only the regulatory dharmas associated with taking the precepts. We do not discuss here the regulations associated with beings who have become free of outflow impurities. Moreover, in other *abhidharmas*, it is stated that the dharma of abstention from killing is practiced through the mind's constantly avoiding pursuit [of ideation tending towards killing], that it is not the case that it constitutes karma of the body or mouth, that it is practiced through refraining from following along with the karma associated with one's mind, that it may or may not involve karmic retribution, that it is not a dharma associated with the mind, and that it may or may not involve outflow impurities. These are dharmas which vary [in their analysis from author to author]. They are in agreement on the other issues.[9]

复有言。诸佛贤圣不戏论诸法。[13]（丹注云种种异说名为戏也）现前众生各各惜命。是故佛言。莫夺他命。夺他命世世受诸苦痛。众生有无后当说。问曰。人能以力胜人并国杀怨。或田猎皮肉所济处大。[14]令不杀生得何等利。答曰。得无所畏安乐无怖。我以无害于彼故。彼亦无害于我。以是故无怖无畏。好杀之人虽复位极人王。亦不自安。如持戒之人。单[15]行独游无所畏难。复次好杀之人。有命之属皆不喜见。若不好杀。一切众生皆乐依附。复次持戒之人。命欲终时其心安乐无疑无悔。若生天上若在人中常得长寿。是为得道因缘。乃至得佛住寿无量。复次杀生之人。今世后世受种种身心苦痛。不杀之人无此众难。是为大利。

復有言。諸佛賢聖不戲論諸法。[13]（丹注云種種異說名為戲也）現前眾生各各惜命。是故佛言。莫奪他命。奪他命世世受諸苦痛。眾生有無後當說。問曰。人能以力勝人并國殺怨。或田獵皮肉所濟處大。[14]令不殺生得何等利。答曰。得無所畏安樂無怖。我以無害於彼故。彼亦無害於我。以是故無怖無畏。好殺之人雖復位極人王。亦不自安。如持戒之人。單[15]行獨遊無所畏難。復次好殺之人。有命之屬皆不喜見。若不好殺。一切眾生皆樂依附。復次持戒之人。命欲終時其心安樂無疑無悔。若生天上若在人中常得長壽。是為得道因緣。乃至得佛住壽無量。復次殺生之人。今世後世受種種身心苦痛。不殺之人無此眾難。是為大利。

简体字　　　　　　　　　　　　正體字

d) Resumption of Expository Killing-Precept Discussion

There are yet others who make the point that the Buddhas, the Worthies, and the Āryas are not inclined towards frivolous debate about dharmas and that, no matter which being one may encounter, in all cases it is inclined to cherish its own life. Therefore the Buddha said, "Do not take another's life. If one takes another's life, one will be bound to undergo all manner of bitter pain in life after life." The issue of whether or not beings actually exist shall be discussed later on. (Chinese textual note: The notes in red state that "frivolous" refers to all sorts of variant discussions.)

i) Objection: Killing is Justified. Why Abstain?

Question: People are able to use their strength to be victorious over others, annex adjacent countries, and demolish enemies. Sometimes the skins and meat hunted in the field provide great benefits in rescuing [people from hunger]. What then is the value of preventing one from killing beings?

ii) Refutation of Arguments for Killing

Response: One gains from this a state of fearlessness. One becomes peaceful, happy and free of dread. Because there has been no harm on my part towards others, they harbor no harmful intentions towards me, either. On account of this, one is never terrified and abides in fearlessness. Although a man who likes to kill may rise to the highest position wherein he becomes a king among men, he is still not at peace with himself. However, if one is a man who upholds the precepts, he may travel by himself and roam about alone, fearing nothing, and encountering no calamities.

Moreover, any being who possesses a life span does not enjoy encountering a person who takes pleasure in killing. If one dislikes killing, all beings happily rely on him. Again, when the life of a person who upholds the precepts is about to come to its end, his mind is at peace, happy, free of doubts, and free of regrets. Then, whether he is reborn in the heavens or among men, he always gains a long life span. This behavior constitutes a cause and condition for realizing the Path. When such a person finally achieves buddhahood, his lifespan in the world is incalculably long.

Additionally, in both present and future lives, a person who kills beings experiences all kinds of physical and mental bitterness and pain. A person who refrains from killing remains free of such manifold difficulties. This amounts to a great benefit.

复次行者思惟。我自惜命爱身。彼亦如是与我何异。以是之故不应杀生。复次若[16]人杀生者。为善人所诃怨家所嫉。负他命故常有怖畏为彼所憎。死时心悔当堕地狱若畜生中。若出为人常当短命。复次假令后世无罪。不为善人所诃怨家所嫉。尚不应故夺他命。何以故。善相之人所不应行。何况[17]两世有罪弊恶果报。复次杀为罪中之重。何以故人有死急不惜重宝。但以活命为先。譬如贾客[18]入海采宝。垂出大海其船卒坏珍宝失尽。而自喜庆举手而言。几失大宝。众人怪言。汝失财物裸形得脱。云何喜言几失大宝。答言。一切宝中人命第一。人为命故求财。不为财故求命。以是故。佛说十不善道中杀[19]罪最在初。五戒中亦最在初。若人种种修诸福德。而无不杀生戒

復次行者思惟。我自惜命愛身。彼亦如是與我何異。以是之故不應殺生。復次若[16]人殺生者。為善人所訶怨家所嫉。負他命故常有怖畏為彼所憎。死時心悔當墮地獄若畜生中。若出為人常當短命。復次假令後世無罪。不為善人所訶怨家所嫉。尚不應故奪他命。何以故。善相之人所不應行。何況[17]兩世有罪弊惡果報。復次殺為罪中之重。何以故人有死急不惜重寶。但以活命為先。譬如賈客[18]入海採寶。垂出大海其船卒壞珍寶失盡。而自喜慶舉手而言。幾失大寶。眾人怪言。汝失財物裸形得脫。云何喜言幾失大寶。答言。一切寶中人命第一。人為命故求財。不為財故求命。以是故。佛說十不善道中殺[19]罪最在初。五戒中亦最在初。若人種種修諸福德。而無不殺生戒

简体字   正體字

Furthermore, the practitioner reflects to himself, "I cherish my own life and am fond of this body. Others are the same in this respect. How are they any different from me? I should therefore refrain from killing any being."

Moreover, if one is a killer of beings, he is denounced by good people and is hated by his enemies. Because he is responsible for taking the lives of others, he is constantly afflicted with fearfulness and is detested by those beings.[10] When he dies, his mind is full of regrets and he is bound to fall into the hells or into the realm of animals. When he emerges from those realms, his lifespan is bound to always be brief.

Then again, even if one were able to cause there to be no karmic retributions in later lives, no denunciation by good people, and no detestation by enemies, one should still refrain from deliberately taking another's life. Why? This is a thing which should not be done by those who are good. How much the more so is this the case where one encounters in both eras[11] the resulting retribution arising from the baseness and evil of one's own offenses.

Furthermore, killing amounts to the most serious of all offenses. How is this so? When a person encounters a life-threatening situation, he will not spare even the most valuable treasures [in the quest to save his own life]. He takes simply being able to survive as what is of primary importance.

e) THE MERCHANT WHO LOST HIS JEWELS (STORY)

This principle is illustrated by the case of the merchant who went to sea to gather jewels. When he had just about gotten back from the great sea, his boat suddenly broke apart and the precious jewels were all lost. He was nonetheless overjoyed and exultant, throwing up his hands and exclaiming, "I almost lost a great jewel!"

Everyone thought this strange and said, "You lost all your valuable possessions and escaped without even any clothes on your back. How can you joyfully exclaim, "I almost lost a great jewel!"

He replied, "Among all the jewels, a person's life is foremost. It is for the sake of their lives that people seek wealth. It is not that they seek to live for the sake of wealth."

f) KILLING AS THE WORST AND NOT KILLING AS THE FINEST OF ACTIONS

It is for this reason that the Buddha said that, among the ten bad karmic actions, the offense of killing is foremost. It is also the first among the five precepts. Even if a person cultivates all sorts of merit, so long as he fails to uphold the precept against taking life,

则无所益。何以故。虽在富贵处生势力豪强。而无寿命谁受此乐。以是故知。诸馀罪中杀罪最重。诸功德中不杀第一。世间中惜命为第一。何以知之。一切世人甘受刑罚[20]刑残[*]考掠以护寿命。复次若有人受戒心[21]生。从今日不杀一切众生。是于无量众生中。[22]已以所爱重物施与。所得功德亦复无量。如佛说有五大施。何等五。一者不杀生是为最大施。不盗不邪婬不妄语不饮酒亦复如是。复次行慈三昧其福无量。水火不害刀兵不伤。一切恶毒所不能[23]中。以五大施故所得如是。复次三世十方中尊佛为第一。如佛语难提迦优婆塞。杀生有十罪。何等为十。一者心常怀毒世世不绝。二者众生憎恶眼不喜见。三者常怀恶念思惟恶事。四者众生畏之如见蛇虎。

则無所益。何以故。雖在富貴處生勢力豪強。而無壽命誰受此樂。以是故知。諸餘罪中殺罪最重。諸功德中不殺第一。世間中惜命為第一。何以知之。一切世人甘受刑罰[20]刑殘[*]考掠以護壽命。復次若有人受戒心[21]生。從今日不殺一切眾生。是於無量眾生中。[22]已以所愛重物施與。所得功德亦復無量。如佛說有五大施。何等五。一者不殺生是為最大施。不盜不邪婬不妄語不飲酒亦復如是。復次行慈三昧其福無量。水火不害刀兵不傷。一切惡毒所不能[23]中。以五大施故所得如是。復次三世十方中尊佛為第一。如佛語難提迦優婆塞。殺生有十罪。何等為十。一者心常懷毒世世不絕。二者眾生憎惡眼不喜見。三者常懷惡念思惟惡事。四者眾生畏之如見蛇虎。

简体字　　　　　　　　　　正體字

there is nothing to be gained from it. Why? Even though one might be born into a circumstance wherein one enjoys karmic blessings and noble birth attended by the power of aristocratic connections, if he still does not have a long lifespan, who would be able to survive to experience such bliss?[12]

For these reasons, one knows that, among all of the offenses, the offense of killing is the most serious and, among all of the meritorious practices, refraining from killing is foremost. In the world, it is the preserving of one's own life which is the primary concern. How do we know this? Everyone in the world would agree to undergo the physical cruelty of corporeal punishment, including even beating and flogging, in order to spare their own lives.

Then again, if the thought to take on the moral precepts arises in a person in such a way that he thinks, "From this very day onward, I shall not kill any beings," by doing this he has already given a gift to an incalculable number of beings of something which they prize as valuable. The merit which he gains thereby is also incalculable.

According to what the Buddha said, there are five great gifts. What are the five? The first is not killing beings. This is the greatest gift. Not stealing, not engaging in sexual misconduct, not lying, and not drinking intoxicants are the others which are the similar in this respect.

Additionally, the merit of practicing the samādhi of kindness (*maitrī-samādhi*) is incalculable. Water and fire will not harm one. Knives and military weapons will not injure one. No matter what the evil poison, one is unable to be poisoned by it. These are the sorts of things which one gains from giving the five great gifts.

g) Ten Karmic Effects from Killing

Moreover, the Buddha, foremost among all revered throughout the three periods of time and ten directions, told the *upāsaka* Nandika, "There are ten punishments which accrue from killing beings. What are the ten?

1. In life after life without cease, one's mind constantly nurtures a poisonous disposition.
2. Beings detest, regard as evil, and find no joy in seeing such a person.
3. One constantly cherishes malicious thoughts and contemplates evil endeavors.
4. Beings fear one just as if they had encountered a snake or tiger.

五者睡时心怖觉亦不安。六
者常有恶梦。七者命终之时
狂怖恶死。八者种短命业因
缘。九者身坏命终堕[24]泥
梨中。十者若出为人常当短
命。复次行者心念。一切有
命乃至[25]昆虫皆自惜身。云
何以衣服饮食。自为身故而
杀众生。复次行者当学大人
法。一切大人中佛为最大。
何以故。一切智慧成就十力
具足。能度众生常行慈愍。
持不杀戒自致得佛。亦教弟
子行此慈愍。行者欲学大人
行故亦当不杀。问曰。不侵
我者杀心可息。若为侵害强
夺逼迫。是当云何。答曰。
应当量其轻重。若人杀己先
自思惟。[26]全戒利重[*]全身
为重。破戒为失丧身为失。
如是思惟已。知持戒为重[*]
全身

简体字

五者睡時心怖覺亦不安。六
者常有惡夢。七者命終之時
狂怖惡死。八者種短命業因
緣。九者身壞命終墮[24]泥
梨中。十者若出為人常當短
命。復次行者心念。一切有
命乃至[25]昆虫皆自惜身。云
何以衣服飲食。自為身故而
殺眾生。復次行者當學大人
法。一切大人中佛為最大。
何以故。一切智慧成就十力
具足。能度眾生常行慈愍。
持不殺戒自致得佛。亦教弟
子行此慈愍。行者欲學大人
行故亦當不殺。問曰。不侵
我者殺心可息。若為侵害強
奪逼迫。是當云何。答曰。
應當量其輕重。若人殺己先
自思惟。[26]全戒利重[*]全身
為重。破戒為失喪身為失。
如是思惟已。知持戒為重[*]
全身

正體字

5. One becomes terrified when asleep and unable to be at peace when awake.

6. One always has bad dreams.

7. As one's life draws to an end, one descends into madness and terror of dying.

8. One plants the karmic causes and conditions for having only a brief life.

9. When the body deteriorates and one's life ends, one falls into *niraya* (the hells).

10. When one emerges and finally regains human rebirth, one is bound to always have only a short life.

h) CONTEMPLATIONS TO REINFORCE NOT KILLING

Additionally, the practitioner thinks to himself, "All things possessed of life, including even the insects, cherish their own physical bodies. How could one kill beings for clothing, food and drink, or for the sake of one's own body?"

Moreover, the practitioner should study the dharmas of the great men. Among all of the great men, the Buddha is the greatest. Why? He has perfected every wisdom and has brought the ten powers to complete fulfillment. He is able to cross beings over to liberation and he constantly implement kindness and pity. It was through upholding the precept against killing that he arrived at the achievement of buddhahood. He then also instructed his disciples to course in this kindness and pity. Because the practitioner wishes to emulate the practices of the great men, he too ought to refrain from killing.

i) OBJECTION: WHAT IF MY LIFE IS THREATENED?

Question: If it is not a case of my being attacked, then the thought of killing may be put to rest. However, if one has been attacked, overcome by force, and is then being coerced by imminent peril, what should one do then?

Reply: One should weigh the relative gravity of the alternatives. If someone is about to take one's life, one should first consider whether the benefit from preserving the precept is more important or whether the benefit from preserving one's physical life is more important, considering also whether it is precept breakage which determines loss or whether it is physical demise which determines what amounts to a loss.

After having reflected in this manner, one realizes that maintaining the precept is momentous and that preserving one's physical life

为轻。若苟免[*]全身身何所
得。是身名为老病死薮。必
当坏败。若为持戒失身其利
甚重。又复思惟。我前后失
身世世无数。或作恶贼禽兽
之身。但为财利诸不善事。
今乃得为持净戒故。不惜
此身舍命持戒。胜于毁禁[*]
全身。百千万[1]倍不[2]可为
喻。如是定心应当舍身。以
护净戒。如一须陀洹人。生
屠杀家年向成人。应当修其
家业而不肯杀生。父母与刀
并一口羊闭着屋中。而语之
言。若不杀羊。不令汝出得
见日月生活饮食。儿自思惟
言。我若杀此一羊。便当终
为此业。岂以身故为此大
罪。便以刀自杀。父母开户
见。羊在一面立儿已命绝。
当自杀时即生天上。若如
此者是为不惜寿命[*]全护净
戒。如是等义是名不杀生
戒。

| |
| 简体字 |

為輕。若苟免[*]全身身何所
得。是身名為老病死藪。必
當壞敗。若為持戒失身其利
甚重。又復思惟。我前後失
身世世無數。或作惡賊禽獸
之身。但為財利諸不善事。
今乃得為持淨戒故。不惜
此身捨命持戒。勝於毀禁[*]
全身。百千萬[1]倍不[2]可為
喻。如是定心應當捨身。以
護淨戒。如一須陀洹人。生
屠殺家年向成人。應當修其
家業而不肯殺生。父母與刀
并一口羊閉著屋中。而語之
言。若不殺羊。不令汝出得
見日月生活飲食。兒自思惟
言。我若殺此一羊。便當終
為此業。豈以身故為此大
罪。便以刀自殺。父母開戶
見。羊在一面立兒已命絕。
當自殺時即生天上。若如
此者是為不惜壽命[*]全護淨
戒。如是等義是名不殺生
戒。

| |
| 正體字 |

is a minor matter. If in avoiding peril one is able only to succeed in preserving one's body, then what advantage is gained with having preserved the body? This body is the swamp of senescence, disease and death. It will inevitably deteriorate and decay. However, if it is for the sake of upholding the precept that one loses one's body, the benefit of it is extremely consequential.

Furthermore, one should consider thus: "From the past on up to the present, I have lost my life an innumerable number of times. At turns, I have taken birth as a malevolent brigand or as a bird or beast where I have lived solely for profit or all manner of other unworthy pursuits.

"I have now encountered a situation where [loss of life] might be for the sake of preserving the purity of the moral precepts. To not be stinting of this body and to sacrifice my life to uphold the precepts would be a billion times better than, and in fact incomparable, to merely safeguarding my body at the expense of violating the prohibitions." Thus one may decide in this manner that one should forsake the body in order to protect the integrity of the pure precepts.

j) THE BUTCHER'S SON REFUSES TO KILL (STORY)

For example, there once was a man who, having reached the rank of *srota-āpanna*,[13] had taken rebirth into the family of a butcher and then grown up to the threshold of adulthood. Although he was expected to pursue his household occupation, he was unable to kill animals. His father and mother gave him a knife and a sheep and shut him up in a room, telling him, "If you do not kill the sheep, we will not allow you to come out and see the sun or the moon, or to have the food and drink necessary for your survival."

The son thought to himself, "If I kill this sheep, then I will be compelled to pursue this occupation my entire life. How could I commit such a great crime solely for the sake of this body?" He then took up the knife and killed himself. The father and mother eventually opened the door to take a look only to discover that the sheep was standing off to one side whilst the son was laying there, already deceased.[14]

Having killed himself, he then took rebirth in the heavens. If one were to act in this manner, this would amount to not sparing even one's own life in safeguarding the integrity of the pure precepts.

Concepts such as we have treated here form the bases for the precept against killing.

不与取者。知他物生盗心。取物去离本处物属我。是名盗。若不作是名不盗。其馀方便[3]计挍。乃至手捉未离地[4]者名助盗法。财物有二种。有属他有不属他。取属他物是[5]为盗罪。属他物亦有二种。一者聚落中二者空地。此二处物。盗心取得盗罪若物在空地当捡挍。知是物近谁国。是物应当[6]有属不应取。如毘尼中说种种不盗。是名不盗相。问曰。不盗有何等利。答曰。人命有二种。一者内。二者外。若夺财物是为夺外命。何以故。命依饮食衣[7]被[8]等故活。若劫若夺是名夺外命。如[9]偈说。

一切诸众生　衣食以自活。
若夺若劫取　是名劫夺命。

[156b01] 以是事故有智之人不应劫夺。

简体字

不與取者。知他物生盗心。取物去離本處物屬我。是名盗。若不作是名不盗。其餘方便[3]計挍。乃至手捉未離地[4]者名助盗法。財物有二種。有屬他有不屬他。取屬他物是[5]為盗罪。屬他物亦有二種。一者聚落中二者空地。此二處物。盗心取得盗罪若物在空地當撿挍。知是物近誰國。是物應當[6]有屬不應取。如毘尼中說種種不盗。是名不盗相。問曰。不盗有何等利。答曰。人命有二種。一者內。二者外。若奪財物是為奪外命。何以故。命依飲食衣[7]被[8]等故活。若劫若奪是名奪外命。如[9]偈說。

一切諸眾生　衣食以自活。
若奪若劫取　是名劫奪命。

[156b01] 以是事故有智之人不應劫奪。

正體字

2) The Precept Against Stealing

a) Stealing Defined

As for taking what is not given, if one knows it is something belonging to another, if one brings forth a thought intent on stealing it, if one takes that thing away from its original location, and if the thing is then considered to be "mine," this is what is meant by stealing. If one does not do this, then this amounts to refraining from stealing. The other associated factors, from the planning of the act on up to and including grasping it with the hand when it has not yet left the ground—these constitute dharmas auxiliary to stealing.

Valuable objects are of two types: those which belong to someone else and those which do not belong to someone else. If one takes a thing which belongs to someone else, this constitutes an offense of stealing.

Things which belong to someone else are also of two kinds: those which are within the boundaries of a village and those which are in the wilderness. If one's taking of things from either of these places is accompanied by a mind intent on stealing, then one incurs the offense of stealing. If the object is in the wilderness, then one should consider critically and come to an understanding as to whose kingdom this object might be in close proximity to, and as to whether or not it has an owner and thus should not be taken. Accordance with the Vinaya[15] discussions of the various circumstances not constituting stealing defines the character of what does not qualify as stealing.

b) The Benefits of Not Stealing

Question: What are the benefits of refraining from stealing?

Response: There are two parts to a person's life, that which is personal (lit. "inward") and that which is beyond the personal (lit. "outward"). If one steals valuable objects, this amounts to stealing the bases of someone else's life. How is this so? Life depends upon drink, food, clothing, bedding, and other such things for its survival. If one robs or if one steals, this amounts to the stealing of someone else's life. This is as described in a verse:

Each and every one of all the beings
Depends on clothes and food for his survival.
Whether one takes by stealing or by robbing,
This amounts to the robbing or stealing of a life.

On account of this fact, a wise person should refrain from robbing or stealing.

复次当自思惟。劫夺得物以自供养。虽身充足会亦当死。死入地狱。家室亲属虽共受乐。独自受罪。亦不能救。已得此观应当不盗。复次是不与取有二种。一者偷。二者劫。此二共名不与取。于不与取中盗为最重。何以故。一切人以财自活。而或[10]穿逾盗取是最不净。何以[11]故。无力胜人畏死。盗取故。劫夺之中盗为[12]罪重。如偈说。

饥饿身羸瘦 受罪大苦[13]剧。
他物不可触 譬如大火聚。

若盗取他物 其主泣[14]懊恼。
假使天王等 犹亦以为苦。

[156b14] 杀生人罪虽重。然于所杀者是贼。偷盗人于一切有物人中贼。若犯馀戒。于异国中有不以为罪者。[15]若偷盗人。一切诸国无不治罪。

復次當自思惟。劫奪得物以自供養。雖身充足會亦當死。死入地獄。家室親屬雖共受樂。獨自受罪。亦不能救。已得此觀應當不盜。復次是不與取有二種。一者偷。二者劫。此二共名不與取。於不與取中盜為最重。何以故。一切人以財自活。而或[10]穿踰盜取是最不淨。何以[11]故。無力勝人畏死。盜取故。劫奪之中盜為[12]罪重。如偈說。

飢餓身羸瘦 受罪大苦[13]劇。
他物不可觸 譬如大火聚。

若盜取他物 其主泣[14]懊惱。
假使天王等 猶亦以為苦。

[156b14] 殺生人罪雖重。然於所殺者是賊。偷盜人於一切有物人中賊。若犯餘戒。於異國中有不以為罪者。[15]若偷盜人。一切諸國無不治罪。

简体字   正體字

Moreover, one ought to reflect, "If it is by robbing or stealing that one comes by the possessions he bestows on himself, even though he may be personally well provided for, he will nonetheless come to that time when he too must die. On dying, he will enter the hells. Then, even though his family might still be experiencing bliss, he will be compelled to undergo punishment all by himself and will then be ensconced in a situation from which he cannot be rescued." Having contemplated in this fashion, one should then refrain from stealing.

c) Two Main Categories of Stealing

Additionally, this [offense of] "taking what is not given" falls into two categories: The first is stealing. The second is robbery. They are both generally referred to as "taking what is not given."

d) The Reprehensibility of Robbery in Particular

Within the sphere of taking what is not given, robbery is the most serious form of the offense. How is this so? All people rely upon their wealth to keep themselves alive. If one nonetheless breaks in and commits robbery, this constitutes the most defiled sort of conduct. Why? It is because one has no power in such circumstances to allay the victim's fear of being murdered. It is because, in the course of committing robbery, one [forcefully] seizes possessions that robbery is the most serious class of stealing offense. This is as described in a verse:

Hungry and starving, one's body emaciated and thin,
One undergoes punishment amidst intensely great suffering.[16]
The belongings of others are such as cannot even be touched.
In this they are comparable to a great flaming bonfire.

If one seizes through robbery the possessions of others,
Their owners start weeping in anguished affliction.
Even were one a god king or one of that sort,
One would still look on this as freighted with suffering.

e) The Gravity and Universal Condemnation of Theft

Although one does commit a serious offense by killing, still, from the standpoint of the victim of the killing, he is seen as having acted as a thief [of a life]. A person who steals is a thief to all people who own material possessions. If one transgresses against other precepts, it may be that in other countries there are those who do not take that to constitute an offense. However, if one is a person who steals, there is no country which does not punish it as an offense.

问曰。劫夺之人。今世有人赞美其健。于此劫夺何以[16]不作。答曰。不与[17]而盗是不善相。劫盗之中虽有差降俱为不善。譬如美食杂毒恶食杂毒。美恶虽殊杂毒不异。亦如明暗蹈火昼夜虽异烧足一也。今世愚人不识罪福二世果报。无仁慈心。见人能以力相侵强夺他财。赞以为[18]强。诸佛贤圣慈愍一切。了达三世殃[19]祸不朽。所不称誉。以是故知劫盗之罪俱为不善。善人行者之所不为。如佛说。不与取有十罪。何等为十。

一者物主常瞋。

二者重疑[20]。

（丹注云重罪人疑）

三者非[21]行时不筹量。

简体字

f) OBJECTION: BUT ISN'T THE VERY BOLDNESS ADMIRABLE?

Question: As for people who engage in robbery by force, there are people in the present era who praise them and see their boldness as admirable. Why then should one refrain from engaging in this sort of thievery?

g) CONDEMNATION OF THEFT OF ANY SORT

Response: If one takes something which has not been given, this is an act characterized by unwholesomeness. Although there are lesser infractions within the realm of stealing, all of them are inherently bad. This is comparable to mixing poison into fine food or mixing poison into bad food. Although there may be distinctions between fine and poor cuisine, still, in the sense that they have both been mixed with poison, they do not differ at all.

This is also comparable to stepping into fire when it is light out and when it is dark. Although there is the difference of day as opposed to night, they are the same as regards the burning of one's feet. The foolish people of the present age are not aware of the resultant retribution from offenses and merit as it occurs in the two periods of time. Devoid of thoughts of humanity and kindness, they observe that a man is able to use his strength to invade and take another's wealth by force and then praise it as being a measure of his power.

The Buddhas, the Worthies, and the Āryas maintain kindness and pity for all. They have completely understood that there is no fading away of the [inevitability of] encountering disasters and misfortunes [as karmic retributions for such acts] as one moves through the three periods of time. Hence they do not praise such acts. One should therefore realize that all stealing offenses are inherently bad. Any practitioner who is a good person will refrain from engaging in these actions.

h) TEN KARMIC EFFECTS OF STEALING

As described by the Buddha, taking what is not given has ten associated punishments.

1. The owner always nourishes hatred.
2. One is repeatedly called into doubt. (Chinese textual note: The notes in red state, "With repeated offenses, people harbor doubts".)
3. Even when not engaged in the act, one is liable to encounter unforeseen events.[17]

四者[22]朋党恶人远离贤善。

五者破善相。

六者得罪于官。

七者财物没入。

八者种贫穷业因缘。

九者死入地狱。

十者若出为人勤苦求财。五家所共若王若贼若火若水若不爱子用。乃至藏埋亦失。邪婬者。[23]若女人为父母兄弟姊妹夫主儿子世间法王法守护。若犯者是名邪婬。若有虽不守护以法为守。云何法守。一切出家女人在家。受一日戒。是名法守。若以力若以财若[24]诳诱若自有妻受戒有[25]娠乳儿非道。[26]如是犯者名为邪婬。如是种种乃至以华鬘与婬女为要。如是犯者名为邪婬。如是种种不作。名为不邪婬。问曰。人守人瞋

四者[22]朋黨惡人遠離賢善。

五者破善相。

六者得罪於官。

七者財物沒入。

八者種貧窮業因緣。

九者死入地獄。

十者若出為人勤苦求財。五家所共若王若賊若火若水若不愛子用。乃至藏埋亦失。邪婬者。[23]若女人為父母兄弟姊妹夫主兒子世間法王法守護。若犯者是名邪婬。若有雖不守護以法為守。云何法守。一切出家女人在家。受一日戒。是名法守。若以力若以財若[24]誑誘若自有妻受戒有[25]娠乳兒非道。[26]如是犯者名為邪婬。如是種種乃至以華鬘與婬女為要。如是犯者名為邪婬。如是種種不作。名為不邪婬。問曰。人守人瞋

简体字　　　　　　　　　　　　正體字

4.　One associates with evil men and departs far from those who are worthy and good.

5.　One destroys one's wholesome qualities.

6.　One becomes known as a criminal by the authorities.

7.　One's valuables are bound to be lost.

8.　One plants the karmic causes and conditions for being poor and destitute.

9.　When one dies, he enters the hells.

10.　When one emerges and takes a human rebirth again, he undergoes intense bitterness in the quest for wealth. Then, even so, that wealth ends up being shared with five different groups consisting of the King, thieves, fire, water, and unloving sons. Even if one hides it away or buries it, it is still bound to be lost.

3)　The Precept Against Sexual Misconduct
a)　Sexual Misconduct Defined

As for the precept against sexual misconduct, if one violates [the "protected" status] of a female under the protection of the father, the mother, the elder or younger brother, the elder or younger sister, the husband as head of family, a son, the law of the world, or the law of a king, this constitutes sexual misconduct.

Sometimes there are those who, although they are not "under protection" in this sense, are nonetheless under the protection of the Dharma. How is it that one is under the protection of the Dharma? This refers to all women who have left the home life and to those who are householders but who have taken the "one day" precept. This is referred to as being under the protection of the Dharma.

If one uses force, or if one uses money, or if one engages in deceptive seduction, or if one has a wife who has taken the precept, who is pregnant or who is nursing an infant, or if one engages in sexual activity involving an inappropriate orifice—if one transgresses in such ways, this constitutes sexual misconduct.

All sorts of situations like these even extending to the giving of a flower garland to a courtesan as an indication of intent—if one transgresses in such ways, this constitutes sexual misconduct. If in all sorts of situations such as this one refrains from taking such actions, this qualifies as not engaging in sexual misconduct.

b)　Objection: How Could This Apply to One's Wife?

Question: When the woman is under the protection of a man, one engenders the man's hatred. When she is under the protection of the

法守破法应名邪婬。人自有妻何以为邪。答曰。既听受一日戒。堕于法中。本虽是妇今不自在。过受戒时则非法守。有[*]娠妇人以其身重。厌本所习。又为伤[*]娠。乳儿时婬其母乳则竭。又以心着婬欲不复护儿。非道之处则非女根女心不乐。强以非理故名邪婬。是事不作名为不邪婬。问曰。若夫主不知不见不恼。他有何罪。答曰。以其邪故既名为邪。是为不正。是故有罪。复次此有种种罪过。夫妻之情异身同体。夺他所爱破其本心。是名为

简体字

法守破法應名邪婬。人自有妻何以為邪。答曰。既聽受一日戒。墮於法中。本雖是婦今不自在。過受戒時則非法守。有[*]娠婦人以其身重。厭本所習。又為傷[*]娠。乳兒時婬其母乳則竭。又以心著婬欲不復護兒。非道之處則非女根女心不樂。強以非理故名邪婬。是事不作名為不邪婬。問曰。若夫主不知不見不惱。他有何罪。答曰。以其邪故既名為邪。是為不正。是故有罪。復次此有種種罪過。夫妻之情異身同體。奪他所愛破其本心。是名為

正體字

Dharma, one violates the Dharma. In these cases, it should qualify as sexual misconduct. However, when it involves a man's own wife, how can it constitute misconduct?

i) In Instances of the One-day Precept

Response: When one has agreed to the taking of the one day precept, one falls under the jurisdiction of the Dharma. Although originally, she may indeed be one's spouse, now one no longer exercises sovereign independence in the matter. Once the time has passed when that precept is in force, then that situation no longer qualifies as one of being "under the protection of the Dharma."

ii) In Instances of Pregnancy or Nursing

There are cases where the wife is pregnant and, because the body is heavy, there is aversion for what was originally practiced. Moreover, it can be injurious to the pregnancy. If one engages in sexual relations with the mother during the time she is nursing an infant, the milk may dry up. Moreover, if the mind becomes attached to sexual desire, then there may not be continued protective regard for the infant.

iii) In Instances Involving Inappropriate Orifice or Force

If one resorts to a place which is not the [genital] orifice, then that is not the female organ and the mind of the woman is not pleased. [Also,], if one resorts to force, because that is unprincipled, that would qualify as sexual misconduct. If one does not engage in such things, this constitutes refraining from sexual misconduct.

c) Objection: If Her Husband Doesn't Know, What's the Problem?

Question: If the husband does not know, does not observe it, and is not afflicted by it, what offense do others incur?

i) Offense Is Based on the Act Itself

Response: It is on account of the action's inherent erroneousness that it is consequently referred to as "misconduct." This is a case of doing what is not right. It is on this basis that this qualifies as an offense.

ii) Alienation of Affections Entails Theft

Moreover, there are all sorts of transgressions inherent in this. The feelings existing between husband and wife are such that, although they are of different bodies, they are substantially the same [unified entity]. If one steals the object of another person's love and destroys her original thoughts [of affection for him], one qualifies thereby

贼。复有重罪。恶名丑声为人所憎少乐多畏。或畏刑戮又畏夫主傍人所知多怀妄语。圣人所呵罪中之罪[27] (丹注云婬罪邪婬破戒故名罪中之罪) 复次婬[28]妷之人当自思惟。我妇他妻同为女人。骨肉情[29]态彼此无异。而我何为横生惑心随逐邪意邪婬之人。破失今世后世之乐。(好名善誉身心安乐今世得也。生天得道涅盘之利后世得也) 复次迴己易处以自制心。若彼侵我妻我则忿[1]恚。我若侵彼彼亦何异。恕己自制故应不作。复次如佛[2]所说。邪婬之人后堕剑树地狱众苦备受。得出为人。家道不穆。常值婬妇邪僻残[3]贼

贼。復有重罪。惡名醜聲為人所憎少樂多畏。或畏刑戮又畏夫主傍人所知多懷妄語。聖人所呵罪中之罪[27] (丹注云婬罪邪婬破戒故名罪中之罪) 復次婬[28]妷之人當自思惟。我婦他妻同為女人。骨肉情[29]態彼此無異。而我何為橫生惑心隨逐邪意邪婬之人。破失今世後世之樂。(好名善譽身心安樂今世得也。生天得道涅槃之利後世得也) 復次迴己易處以自制心。若彼侵我妻我則忿[1]恚。我若侵彼彼亦何異。恕己自制故應不作。復次如佛[2]所說。邪婬之人後墮劍樹地獄眾苦備受。得出為人。家道不穆。常值婬婦邪僻殘[3]賊

| 简体字 | 正體字 |

as a thief. Thus one simultaneously commits yet another serious offense.

iii) DISREPUTE, HATRED, UNHAPPINESS, FEAR, DANGER, LIES, CENSURE

One gains a bad name and an ugly reputation. One is detested by others and thus experiences diminished happiness and increased fearfulness. One may live in fear of brutal punishment. Additionally, one is fearful that the husband and other people will find out about it. Hence one is much involved in maintaining lies. It is an activity which is denounced by the Āryas. It involves offenses within offenses. (Chinese textual note: The notes in red say, "Regarding this lust-related offense, it is because one breaks [yet other] precepts in the course of committing sexual misconduct that it refers to 'offenses within offenses.'")

iv) IDENTITY OF LOVERS MAKES IT POINTLESS

Furthermore, the sexually dissolute person ought to consider to himself, "My wife and his wife are both women. In terms of bone and flesh, feelings and demeanor, that one and this one are no different. So why do I perversely bring forth these deluded thoughts and pursue such incorrect intentions?"

v) PRESENT AND FUTURE HAPPINESS IS LOST

A person who engages in sexual misconduct destroys and loses any happiness in both this life and later lives. (Chinese textual note: A fine name, a reputation for goodness, and peace and happiness of body and mind are gained in the present life. The benefits of rebirth in the heavens, gaining the Path, and reaching nirvāṇa are realized in later lives.)

vi) ONE SHOULD HAVE SYMPATHY FOR THE PROSPECTIVE CUCKOLD

Then again, one should turn one's situation around and change places as a means of controlling one's mind, considering, "If he were to violate my wife, I would be enraged. Hence, if I were to violate his wife, how is it that he would feel any differently?" Through the natural self-control arising realizing one's own circumstance, one should be motivated to refrain from such acts.

vii) THE KARMIC RETRIBUTION IS HORRIBLE

What's more, as the Buddha said, a person who engages in sexual misconduct later falls into the hell of sword trees where he undergoes an abundance of many sorts of sufferings. When one succeeds in emerging and becoming a human, one's family life is not harmonious. One always meets up with a licentious wife who is devious, remote, and ruthlessly cruel.

简体字

邪婬为患。譬如蝮蛇亦如大火。不急避之祸害将及。如佛所说。邪婬有十罪。

一者常为所婬夫主欲危害之。

二者夫妇不穆常共鬭諍。

三者诸不善法日日增长。于诸善法日日损减。

四者不守护身妻子孤寡。

五者财产日耗。

六者有诸恶事常为人所疑。

七者亲属知识所不爱憙。

八者种怨家业因缘。

九者身坏命终死入地狱。

十者若出为女人多人共夫。

若为男子妇不贞洁。如是等种种因缘不作。是名不邪婬。妄语者。不净心欲诳他。覆隐实出异语生口业。是名妄语。妄语之罪从言声相[4]解生。若不相解虽不实语。无妄语罪。是妄语。知言不知不知言知。见言不见

正體字

邪婬為患。譬如蝮蛇亦如大火。不急避之禍害將及。如佛所說。邪婬有十罪。

一者常為所婬夫主欲危害之。

二者夫婦不穆常共鬭諍。

三者諸不善法日日增長。於諸善法日日損減。

四者不守護身妻子孤寡。

五者財產日耗。

六者有諸惡事常為人所疑。

七者親屬知識所不愛憙。

八者種怨家業因緣。

九者身壞命終死入地獄。

十者若出為女人多人共夫。

若為男子婦不貞潔。如是等種種因緣不作。是名不邪婬。妄語者。不淨心欲誆他。覆隱實出異語生口業。是名妄語。妄語之罪從言聲相[4]解生。若不相解雖不實語。無妄語罪。是妄語。知言不知不知言知。見言不見

d) Ten Karmic Effects of Sexual Misconduct

Sexual misconduct is a calamity analogous to a venomous snake or a great fire which, should one fail to immediately avoid it, entails the encroachment of disastrous harm. As stated by the Buddha, sexual misconduct has ten resulting karmic punishments:

1. The husband of [the offender's] sexual conquest is constantly bent on destroying him.

2. The husband and wife are not harmonious and are constantly engaged in mutual strife.

3. Bad dharmas proliferate with each passing day, whereas good dharmas diminish with each passing day.

4. One does not protect one's own physical health while one simultaneously widows one's wife and orphans one's children.

5. One's wealth and business deteriorate daily.

6. All manner of unfortunate situations develop while one is also constantly doubted by others.

7. One's relatives and friends no longer feel affection or fondness for him.

8. One plants the karmic causes and conditions for having enemies.

9. At the break-up of the body when the life comes to an end, one dies and enters the hells.

10. If when one emerges, one takes birth as a woman, many men simultaneously engage in the acts of a husband. If one takes birth as a man, one's wife is not chaste.

If one refrains from all such causes and conditions as these, then this qualifies as refraining from sexual misconduct.

4) The Precept Against False Speech

a) False Speech Defined

As for false speech, if there is a thought which is not pure, if one wishes to deceive someone else, if one hides the truth, and if one speaks forth words which differ from the truth, thus generating karma of the mouth, this is what constitutes "false speech." The offense of false speech arises from the sound of the words and mutual understanding. If there is no understanding, then although they are untrue words, there is no offense of false speech.

As for this false speech: if one actually does know, yet nonetheless claims that he does not know; if one does not know, yet claims that he does know; if one has seen, yet claims that he has not seen;

不见言见。闻言不闻不闻言
闻。是名妄语。若不作是名
不妄语。问曰。妄语有何等
罪。答曰。妄语之人。先自
诳身然后诳人。以实为虚以
虚为实。虚实颠倒不受善
法。譬如覆瓶水不得入。妄
语之人心无惭愧。闭塞天道
涅盘之门。观知此罪。是故
不作。复次观知实语其利甚
广。实语之利自从己出甚
为易得。是为一切出家[5]人
[6]力。如是功德居家出家人
共有此利。善人之相。复次
实语之人其心端直。其心端
直易得免苦。譬如稠林曳木
直者易出。问曰。若妄语有
如是罪。人何以故妄语。答
曰。有人愚痴少智。遭事苦
厄妄语求脱不知事发。今世
得罪不知后世有大罪报。复
有人虽知妄语罪。悭贪瞋恚
愚痴多故而作妄语。

简体字

不見言見。聞言不聞不聞言
聞。是名妄語。若不作是名
不妄語。問曰。妄語有何等
罪。答曰。妄語之人。先自
誑身然後誑人。以實為虛以
虛為實。虛實顛倒不受善
法。譬如覆瓶水不得入。妄
語之人心無慚愧。閉塞天道
涅槃之門。觀知此罪。是故
不作。復次觀知實語其利甚
廣。實語之利自從己出甚
為易得。是為一切出家[5]人
[6]力。如是功德居家出家人
共有此利。善人之相。復次
實語之人其心端直。其心端
直易得免苦。譬如稠林曳木
直者易出。問曰。若妄語有
如是罪。人何以故妄語。答
曰。有人愚癡少智。遭事苦
厄妄語求脫不知事發。今世
得罪不知後世有大罪報。復
有人雖知妄語罪。慳貪瞋恚
愚癡多故而作妄語。

正體字

if one has not seen, yet claims that he has seen; if one has heard, yet claims that he has not heard; or if one has not heard, yet claims that he has heard—these all constitute instances of false speech. If one has not acted in such a manner, then this qualifies as refraining from committing false speech.

b) The Inherent Faults in False Speech

Question: What faults are there in false speech?

Response: The person who commits false speech first of all cheats himself, and then proceeds to deceive others. He takes what is real as false and what is false as real. He turns false and real upside down and refuses to accept good dharmas. He is comparable to an inverted vase into which water cannot be poured.

The mind of a person who commits false speech is devoid of a sense of shame or a dread of blame. He blocks off both the way to the heavens and the gate to nirvāṇa. One contemplates this matter, realizes the existence of these disadvantages, and therefore refrains from coursing in it.

Additionally, one contemplates this matter and realizes that the benefits of true speech are extremely vast. The benefits of true speech naturally come forth from one's self and are extremely easily gained. This is the power of all who have left the home life. Both householders and those who have left the home life possess the benefits of this sort of merit. It is the mark of a good person.

Moreover, the mind of a person whose words are true is correct and straight. Because his mind is correct and straight, it is easy for him to succeed in avoiding suffering. It is just as when pulling forth logs from a dense forest. The straight ones come forth easily.

c) Why Then Do People Engage in False Speech?

Question: If false speech entails disadvantages such as these, why then do people engage in false speech?

Response: There are those who are foolish and deficient in wisdom who, when they encounter anguishing difficulties, tell lies as a stratagem to escape them. They fail to recognize the manner in which matters are bound to unfold. When they commit a transgression in this present life, they do not realize that there will be an immense retribution in a later life which is brought on as a result of that transgression.

Then again, there are people who, although they are aware of the fact that false speech entails a transgression, nonetheless course in lies due to an abundance of greed, hatred, or delusion.

复有人虽不贪恚。而妄证人罪心谓实尔。死堕地狱如提婆达多弟子俱伽离。常求舍利弗目揵连过失。是时二人夏安居竟。游行诸国值天大雨。到陶作家宿盛陶器舍。此舍中先有一女人在暗中宿。二人不知。此女人其夜梦失不净。晨朝趣水澡[7]洗。是时俱伽离偶行见之。俱伽离能相知人交会情状。而不知梦与不梦。是时俱伽离顾语弟子。此女人昨夜与人情通。即问女人汝在何处卧。答言。我在陶师屋中寄宿。又问共谁。答言。二比丘。是时二人从屋中出。俱伽离见已。又以相验之。意谓二人必为不净。先怀嫉妒既见此事。遍诸城邑聚落告之。次到[8]只洹唱此恶声。于是中间梵天王来欲见佛。佛入静室寂然三昧。诸比丘众亦各闭房三昧。皆不可觉。即自思惟。我[9]故来见佛。佛入三昧

復有人雖不貪恚。而妄證人罪心謂實爾。死墮地獄如提婆達多弟子俱伽離。常求舍利弗目揵連過失。是時二人夏安居竟。遊行諸國值天大雨。到陶作家宿盛陶器舍。此舍中先有一女人在闇中宿。二人不知。此女人其夜夢失不淨。晨朝趣水澡[7]洗。是時俱伽離偶行見之。俱伽離能相知人交會情狀。而不知夢與不夢。是時俱伽離顧語弟子。此女人昨夜與人情通。即問女人汝在何處臥。答言。我在陶師屋中寄宿。又問共誰。答言。二比丘。是時二人從屋中出。俱伽離見已。又以相驗之。意謂二人必為不淨。先懷嫉妒既見此事。遍諸城邑聚落告之。次到[8]祇洹唱此惡聲。於是中間梵天王來欲見佛。佛入靜室寂然三昧。諸比丘眾亦各閉房三昧。皆不可覺。即自思惟。我[9]故來見佛。佛入三昧

简体字   正體字

d) Kokālika's Slanderous Offense (Story)

Additionally, there are people who, although not afflicted with greed or hatred, nonetheless falsely testify to another man's transgression because, in their own minds, they are of the opinion that their testimony is true. When they die, they plummet into the hells just as did Kokālika, a disciple of Devadatta. He constantly sought to find fault with Śāriputra and Maudgalyāyana.

At that time, those two men had just reached the end of the summer retreat and so they proceeded to travel about, journeying through the various states. Having encountered a great rain storm, upon arriving at the home of a potter, they spent the night in a pottery storage building.

Before they had arrived, unbeknownst to these two, a woman had already gone in and fallen asleep in a darkened part of the building. That night, this woman had an orgasm in her dreams. In the early morning, she went to get water with which to bathe. Kokālika happened to be walking by at the time and took notice of her. Kokālika possessed the ability to know about a person's sex life simply by observing one's countenance. Even so, he couldn't deduce whether the activity had happened in a dream state or while awake.

Kokālika then mentioned to a disciple, "This woman had sex with someone last night," whereupon he asked the woman, "So, where did you spend the night last night?"

She replied, "I spent the night over in the pottery building."

Next, he asked, "Who else was there?"

She replied, "There were a couple of bhikshus there." At just that time, those very two men happened to emerge from inside that building. Having noticed them, Kokālika examined their countenances and convinced himself that the two men were definitely not pure. It so happened that he had formerly nurtured jealousy towards them. Having observed this situation, he proceeded to spread it all about in the various cities, villages and hamlets. Next, he went to the Jeta Grove where he openly proclaimed this evil rumor.

At this time, it so happened that Brahmā, the King of the Gods, had come wishing to have an audience with the Buddha. However, the Buddha had entered into a silent room where he remained very still, immersed in samādhi. All of the bhikshus too had shut their doors and entered samādhi. None of them could be roused. Then he thought to himself, "I originally came to see the Buddha, but, as it happens, the Buddha has gone into samādhi."

简体字

且欲还去。即复念言。佛从
定起亦将不久。于是小住。
到俱伽离房前。扣其户而
言。俱伽离俱伽离。舍利弗
目揵连心净柔软。汝莫谤之
而长夜受苦。俱伽离问言。
汝是何人。答言。我是梵天
王。问言。佛说汝得阿那含
道。汝何以故来。梵王心念
而说偈言。

无量法欲量　不应以相取。
无量法欲量　是[10]野人覆没。

[157b29] 说[11]此偈已。到佛所
具说其[12]事。佛言。善哉善
哉。快说此偈。尔时世尊复
说此偈。

无量法欲量　不应以相取。
无量法欲量　是[*]野人覆没。

[157c04]　　梵天王听佛说已。
忽然不现即还天上。尔时俱
迦离到佛所。头面礼佛足却
住一面。佛告俱伽离。舍利
弗目揵连心净柔软。汝莫谤
之而长夜受苦。俱伽离白佛
言。我于佛语不敢不信。但
自目见了了。定知二人实行
不净。

简体字

正體字

且欲還去。即復念言。佛從
定起亦將不久。於是小住。
到俱伽離房前。扣其戶而
言。俱伽離俱伽離。舍利弗
目揵連心淨柔軟。汝莫謗之
而長夜受苦。俱伽離問言。
汝是何人。答言。我是梵天
王。問言。佛說汝得阿那含
道。汝何以故來。梵王心念
而說偈言。

無量法欲量　不應以相取。
無量法欲量　是[10]野人覆沒。

[157b29] 說[11]此偈已。到佛所
具說其[12]事。佛言。善哉善
哉。快說此偈。爾時世尊復
說此偈。

無量法欲量　不應以相取。
無量法欲量　是[*]野人覆沒。

[157c04]　　梵天王聽佛說已。
忽然不現即還天上。爾時俱
迦離到佛所。頭面禮佛足却
住一面。佛告俱伽離。舍利
弗目揵連心淨柔軟。汝莫謗
之而長夜受苦。俱伽離白佛
言。我於佛語不敢不信。但
自目見了了。定知二人實行
不淨。

正體字

He was about to return [to his celestial abode] when he had another thought, "It won't be long before the Buddha arises from meditative absorption. I'll just wait here a for a little while longer." He then went over to the entrance to Kokālika's room, knocked on the door, and called out, "Kokālika! Kokālika! The minds of Śāriputra and Maudgalyāyana are pure and pliant. Do not slander them or you will be bound to spend the long night [of your future lifetimes] enduring sufferings."

Kokālika asked, "Who are you?"

He replied, "I am Brahmā, the King of the Gods."

He asked, "The Buddha has said that you have realized the path of the *anāgāmin* (lit. "never-returner").[18] Why then have you returned here?"

Brahmā, King of the Gods, thought for a moment and then uttered this verse:

In wishing to fathom immeasurable dharmas,
One should not seize on what is mere appearance.
In wishing to fathom immeasurable dharmas,
A boor of this sort is bound to capsize and drown.

After he had spoken this verse, he went to where the Buddha was and set forth the entire matter. The Buddha said, "Good indeed. Good indeed. This verse should be proclaimed straightaway." The Bhagavān himself then repeated the verse:

In wishing to fathom immeasurable dharmas,
One should not seize on what is mere appearance.
In wishing to fathom immeasurable dharmas,
A boor of this sort is bound to capsize and drown.

After Brahmā, King of the Gods, had heard the Buddha proclaim this, he suddenly disappeared and immediately returned to the heavens.

Kokālika then went to where the Buddha was, prostrated in reverence before the Buddha, and then stood off to one side. The Buddha told Kokālika, "The minds of Śāriputra and Maudgalyāyana are pure and pliant. Do not slander them or you will spend the long night [of future lifetimes] undergoing sufferings."

Kokālika addressed the Buddha, saying, "I don't dare disbelieve the words of the Buddha. However, I saw this clearly with my own eyes. I know definitely that these two men have actually committed impure acts."

佛如是三呵。俱伽离亦三不
受。即从坐起而去。还其房中
举身生疮。始如芥子渐大如豆
如枣如[13]奈。转大如苽。翕然
烂坏如大火烧。叫唤[14]嗥哭其
夜即死。入大莲华地[15]狱。有
一梵[16]天夜来白佛。俱伽离已
死复有一梵天言。堕大莲华地
狱。其夜过已佛命僧集而告之
言。汝等欲知俱伽离所堕地狱
寿命长短不。诸比丘言。愿乐
欲闻。佛言。有六十斛胡麻。
有人过百岁取一胡麻。如是至
尽。阿浮陀地狱中寿故未尽。
二十阿浮陀地狱中寿。为一尼
罗浮陀地狱中寿。如二十尼罗
浮陀地狱中寿为一[17]阿罗逻地
狱中寿。二十[*]阿罗逻地狱中
寿。为一[*]阿婆婆地狱中寿。
二十[*]阿婆婆地狱中寿。为一
休休地狱中寿。二十休休地狱
中寿。为一沤波罗地狱中寿。
二十沤波罗地狱中寿。为一分
陀梨迦地狱中寿。二十分陀梨
迦地狱中寿。为一摩呵波头摩
地狱中寿。俱伽离堕是摩呵波
头摩地狱中。出其大舌以[18]百
钉钉之。五百具犁耕之。尔时
世尊说此偈言。

[1]夫士之生　斧在口中。
所以斩身　由其恶言。
应呵而赞　应赞而呵。
口集诸恶　终不见乐。

简体字

佛如是三呵。俱伽離亦三不
受。即從坐起而去。還其房中
舉身生瘡。始如芥子漸大如豆
如棗如[13]奈。轉大如苽。翕然
爛壞如大火燒。叫喚[14]嗥哭其
夜即死。入大蓮華地[15]獄。有
一梵[16]天夜來白佛。俱伽離已
死復有一梵天言。墮大蓮華地
獄。其夜過已佛命僧集而告之
言。汝等欲知俱伽離所墮地獄
壽命長短不。諸比丘言。願樂
欲聞。佛言。有六十斛胡麻。
有人過百歲取一胡麻。如是至
盡。阿浮陀地獄中壽故未盡。
二十阿浮陀地獄中壽。為一尼
羅浮陀地獄中壽。如二十尼羅
浮陀地獄中壽為一[17]阿羅邏地
獄中壽。二十[*]阿羅邏地獄中
壽。為一[*]阿婆婆地獄中壽。
二十[*]阿婆婆地獄中壽。為一
休休地獄中壽。二十休休地獄
中壽。為一漚波羅地獄中壽。
二十漚波羅地獄中壽。為一分
陀梨迦地獄中壽。二十分陀梨
迦地獄中壽。為一摩呵波頭摩
地獄中壽。俱伽離墮是摩呵波
頭摩地獄中。出其大舌以[18]百
釘釘之。五百具犁耕之。爾時
世尊說此偈言。

[1]夫士之生　斧在口中。
所以斬身　由其惡言。
應呵而讚　應讚而呵。
口集諸惡　終不見樂。

正體字

The Buddha rebuked him in this manner three times and Kokālika three times still refused to accept it. He then got up from his place, left, and returned to his room. His entire body then broke out in sores. At first, they were the size of sesame seeds. They gradually became as big as beans, as big as dates, as big as mangoes, and finally, as big as melons. Then, they all simultaneously broke open, leaving him looking as if he had been burned by a great fire. He wailed and wept. Then, that very night, he died and entered the Great Lotus Blossom Hell. A Brahma Heaven god came and informed the Buddha, "Kokālika has already died."

Then yet another Brahma Heaven god declared, "He has fallen into the Great Lotus Blossom Hell." After that night had passed, the Buddha ordered the Sangha to assemble, and then asked, "Do you all wish to know the length of the life in that hell into which Kokālika has fallen?"

The Bhikṣus replied, "Pray, please tell us. We wish to hear it."

The Buddha said, "It is as if there were sixty bushels of sesame seeds and then a man came along only once every hundred years and took away but a single sesame seed. If this went on until all of the sesame seeds were gone, the lifespan endured in the Arbuda Hells would still not have come to an end. Twenty Arbuda Hell lifespans equal the lifespan in the Nirarbuda Hells. Twenty Nirarbuda Hell lifespans equal the lifespan in the Aṭaṭa Hells. Twenty Aṭaṭa Hell lifespans equal the lifespan in the Hahava Hells. Twenty Hahava Hell lifespans equal the lifespan in the Huhuva Hells. Twenty Huhuva Hell lifespans equal the lifespan in the Utpala Hells. Twenty Utpala Hell lifespans equal the lifespan in the Puṇḍarīka Hells. Twenty Puṇḍarīka Hell lifespans equal the lifespan in the Mahāpadma Hells. Kokālika has fallen into these Mahāpadma Hells.[19] His tongue is drawn forth and nailed down with a hundred nails where it is plowed by five hundred plows." The Bhagavān then spoke forth this verse:

When a person takes rebirth there,
Hatchets are plunged into his mouth.
The reason for the body's being hacked
Is found in his utterance of evil words.

What should be criticized, he nonetheless has praised.
What should be praised, he nonetheless has criticized.
The mouth thus piles up all manner of evil deeds,
With the result that one is never able to experience any bliss.

心口业生恶　堕尼罗浮狱。
具满百千世　受诸[2]毒苦痛。

若生阿浮陀　具满三[3]十六。
别更有[4]五世　皆受诸苦毒。

心依邪见　破贤圣语。
如竹生实　自毁其[5]形。

[158a10]　　　如是等心生疑谤。
遂至决定亦是妄语。妄语人
乃至佛语而不信受。受罪如
是。以是故不应妄语。复次
如佛子罗睺罗。其年幼稚未
知慎口。人来问之。世尊在
不。诡言不在。若不在时。
人问罗睺罗。世尊在不。诡
言佛在。有人语佛。佛语
罗睺罗。澡[6]盘取水与吾洗
足。洗足已。语罗睺罗。
覆此澡[*]盘。如勅即覆。佛
言。以水注之。注已问言。
水入中不。答言。不入。佛
告罗睺罗。无惭愧人妄语覆
心道法不入。亦复如是。

简体字

心口業生惡　墮尼羅浮獄。
具滿百千世　受諸[2]毒苦痛。

若生阿浮陀　具滿三[3]十六。
別更有[4]五世　皆受諸苦毒。

心依邪見　破賢聖語。
如竹生實　自毀其[5]形。

[158a10]　　　如是等心生疑謗。
遂至決定亦是妄語。妄語人
乃至佛語而不信受。受罪如
是。以是故不應妄語。復次
如佛子羅睺羅。其年幼稚未
知慎口。人來問之。世尊在
不。詭言不在。若不在時。
人問羅睺羅。世尊在不。詭
言佛在。有人語佛。佛語
羅睺羅。澡[6]槃取水與吾洗
足。洗足已。語羅睺羅。
覆此澡[*]槃。如勅即覆。佛
言。以水注之。注已問言。
水入中不。答言。不入。佛
告羅睺羅。無慚愧人妄語覆
心道法不入。亦復如是。

正體字

The actions of mind and mouth generate evil.
One plummets then into the Nirarbuda Hells.
For a term of fully a hundred thousand lifetimes,
He endures there all manner of excruciating pain.

When one takes rebirth into the Arbuda Hells,
He is bound to endure it for a full thirty-six lives,
And then suffer for yet another additional five lives,
Where in all of them he suffers all manner of suffering anguish.

The mind comes to rely upon erroneous views,
And speaks then in a way destroying the Worthies and Āryas.
In this, it's like that bamboo which, in putting forth its fruit,
Thereby brings on the destruction of its very own physical form.

In just such a manner, the mind generates doubts and slanders. Once they have become rigidly established, they also become manifest in false speech. Thus a person who courses in false speech refuses to believe in or accept even the words of the Buddha. He becomes bound then to undergo punishments just such as these. It is for these reasons that one must refrain from engaging in false speech.

e) RĀHULA'S LESSON ABOUT FALSE SPEECH (STORY)

Then again, a case in point is that of the Buddha's son Rāhula who, being in years but a child, had still not yet understood the importance of taking care with his words. When people would come and ask him, "Is the Bhagavān here, or not?" he would deceive them by saying, "He's not here."

If in fact he was not present, when others would ask Rāhula, "Is the Bhagavān here or not?" he would deceive them by saying, "The Buddha is here."

Someone informed the Buddha about this. The Buddha then told Rāhula, "Get a wash basin, fill it with water, and then wash my feet for me." After his feet had been washed, he instructed Rāhula, "Now put the lid on this wash basin."

Then, obeying the command, he immediately covered it. The Buddha then said, "Take water and pour it in." After it had been poured, he asked, "Did the water go in or not?"

He replied, "No, it didn't go in."

The Buddha told Rāhula, "The lies of a person devoid of a sense of shame or dread of blame cover over his mind so that, in just this same manner, the Dharma of the Path is unable to enter into it."

如佛说。妄语有十罪。何等为十。

一者口气臭。

二者善神远之非人得便。

三者虽有实语人不信受。

四者智人[7]语议常不参豫。

五者常被诽谤。丑恶之声周闻天下。

六者人所不敬。虽有教勅人不承用。

七者常多忧愁。

八者种诽谤业因缘。

九者身坏命终当堕地狱。

十者若出为人常被诽谤。

如是种种不作。是为不妄语。名口善律仪。不饮酒者。酒有三种。一者谷酒。二者果酒。三者药草酒。果酒者。[8]蒲桃阿梨咤树果。如是等种种名为果酒。药草酒者。种种药草。合和米[9]麴甘蔗汁中。能变成酒。同[10]蹄畜乳酒。一切乳热者可中作酒。略说。若乾若湿若清若浊。如是等能令人心动放逸。是名为酒。

简体字

如佛說。妄語有十罪。何等為十。

一者口氣臭。

二者善神遠之非人得便。

三者雖有實語人不信受。

四者智人[7]語議常不參豫。

五者常被誹謗。醜惡之聲周聞天下。

六者人所不敬。雖有教勅人不承用。

七者常多憂愁。

八者種誹謗業因緣。

九者身壞命終當墮地獄。

十者若出為人常被誹謗。

如是種種不作。是為不妄語。名口善律儀。不飲酒者。酒有三種。一者穀酒。二者果酒。三者藥草酒。果酒者。[8]蒲桃阿梨咤樹果。如是等種種名為果酒。藥草酒者。種種藥草。合和米[9]麴甘蔗汁中。能變成酒。同[10]蹄畜乳酒。一切乳熱者可中作酒。略說。若乾若濕若清若濁。如是等能令人心動放逸。是名為酒。

正體字

f) Ten Karmic Effects of False Speech

As stated by the Buddha, false speech has ten karmic retributions. What are the ten? They are as follows:

1. The breath always smells bad.
2. The good spirits depart far from him and the non-humans are then free to have their way with him.
3. Even though there may be instances when he does speak the truth, people nonetheless do not believe or accept it.
4. He can never participate in discussions with the wise.
5. He is always slandered and his ugly and foul reputation is heard throughout the land.
6. He is not respected by others. Thus, although he may issue instructions and orders, people do not accept or follow them.
7. He is constantly afflicted with many worries.
8. He plants the karmic causes and conditions resulting in his being slandered.
9. When his body deteriorates and his life comes to an end, he is bound to fall into the hells.
10. When he emerges and becomes a person, he is always the object of slander.

If one does not engage in actions such as described here, this qualifies as refraining from committing false speech. This is a moral regulation defining goodness in the sphere of mouth karma.

5) The Precept Against Intoxicants

a) Alcoholic Beverages Defined

As for abstention from alcoholic beverages, alcoholic beverages are of three kinds, the first being alcohol made from grain, the second being alcohol made from fruit, and the third being alcohol made from botanical herbs.

As for alcohol made from fruit, it includes grapes and the fruit of the *ariṣṭaka* tree. All other such varieties also qualify as alcohol from fruit. As for alcohol from botanical herbs, all sorts of botanical herbs, when mixed into rice or wheat, and sugar cane juice are capable then of being transformed into alcoholic beverages. This is also true of milk from hooved animals, for any sort of fermented milk may be used in the same fashion to make alcoholic beverages.

To summarize, whether they be dry, wet, clear, or turbid, any such things possessing the capacity to influence a person's mind to move or backslide are collectively referred to as alcoholic beverages.

一切不应饮。是名不饮酒。
问曰。酒能破冷益身令心欢
喜。何[11]以不饮。答曰。益
身甚少所损甚多。是故不应
饮。譬如美饮其中杂毒。是
何等毒。如佛语难提迦优婆
塞。酒有三十五失。何等三
十五。

一者[12]现世财物虚竭。何以
故。人饮酒醉心无节限。用
费无度故。

二者众[13]病之门。

三者斗诤之本。

四者裸露无耻。

五者丑名恶声人所不敬。

六者覆没智慧。

七者应所得物而不得。已所
得物而散失。

八者伏匿之事尽向人说。

九者种种事业废不成办。

十者醉为愁本。何以故。醉
中多失。醒已惭愧忧愁。

十一者身力转少。

十二者身色坏。

十三者不知敬父。

十四者不知敬母。

一切不應飲。是名不飲酒。
問曰。酒能破冷益身令心歡
喜。何[11]以不飲。答曰。益
身甚少所損甚多。是故不應
飲。譬如美飲其中雜毒。是
何等毒。如佛語難提迦優婆
塞。酒有三十五失。何等三
十五。

一者[12]現世財物虛竭。何以
故。人飲酒醉心無節限。用
費無度故。

二者眾[13]病之門。

三者鬥諍之本。

四者裸露無恥。

五者醜名惡聲人所不敬。

六者覆沒智慧。

七者應所得物而不得。已所
得物而散失。

八者伏匿之事盡向人說。

九者種種事業廢不成辦。

十者醉為愁本。何以故。醉
中多失。醒已慚愧憂愁。

十一者身力轉少。

十二者身色壞。

十三者不知敬父。

十四者不知敬母。

One must not drink any of them. This is what is meant by abstention from alcoholic beverages.

b) OBJECTION: WITH SO MANY BENEFITS, WHY ABSTAIN?

Question: Alcohol is able to dispel coldness, benefit the body, and cause the mind to be delighted. Why then should one refrain from drinking it?

Response: The benefits to the body are extremely minor. The harmful aspects are extremely numerous. Therefore, one should not drink it. It is analogous to a marvelous beverage into which one has mixed poison. What sorts of "poison" are being referred to here? As told by the Buddha to the *upāsaka*, Nandika, alcohol has thirty-five faults. What are the thirty-five? They are:

c) THIRTY-FIVE KARMIC EFFECTS OF CONSUMING INTOXICANTS

1. Valuables owned in the present life are squandered. Why? When people consume intoxicants, their minds know no limits. Consequently they indulge in unconstrained wastefulness.
2. It is the entry point for affliction with the many sorts of diseases.
3. It is the basis for generating strife.
4. One's nakedness is allowed to become shamelessly exposed.
5. One develops an ugly name and terrible reputation leading to not being respected by others.
6. It obscures and submerges one's wisdom.
7. Those things which ought to obtained are nonetheless not obtained, whilst whatever has already been obtained becomes scattered and lost.
8. Matters which should remain confidential are told in their entirety to others.
9. All sorts of endeavors deteriorate and are not brought to completion.
10. Intoxication is the root of worry. How so? When one is inebriated, much is lost. After one returns to a condition of mental clarity, one feels shame and blame, and abides in a state of worry.
11. The strength of the body decreases.
12. The appearance of the body deteriorates.
13. One does not know to respect one's father.
14. One does not know to respect one's mother.

简体字	正體字
十五者不敬沙门。	十五者不敬沙門。
十六者不敬婆罗门。	十六者不敬婆羅門。
十七者不敬伯叔及尊长。何以故。醉闷[14]忱惚无所别故。	十七者不敬伯叔及尊長。何以故。醉悶[14]忱惚無所別故。
十八者不尊敬佛。	十八者不尊敬佛。
十九者不敬法。	十九者不敬法。
二十者不敬僧。	二十者不敬僧。
二十一者朋党恶人。	二十一者朋黨惡人。
二十二者疎远贤善。	二十二者疎遠賢善。
二十三者作破戒人。	二十三者作破戒人。
二十四者无惭无愧。	二十四者無慚無愧。
二十五者不守六情。	二十五者不守六情。
二十六者纵[15]色放逸。	二十六者縱[15]色放逸。
二十七者人所憎恶不喜见之。	二十七者人所憎惡不喜見之。
二十八者贵重亲属及诸知识所共摈弃。	二十八者貴重親屬及諸知識所共擯棄。
二十九者行不善法。	二十九者行不善法。
三十者弃舍善法。	三十者棄捨善法。
三十一者明人智士所不信用。何以故。酒放逸故。	三十一者明人智士所不信用。何以故。酒放逸故。
三十二者远离涅盘。	三十二者遠離涅槃。
三十三者种狂痴因缘。	三十三者種狂癡因緣。
三十四者身坏命终堕恶道泥梨中。	三十四者身壞命終墮惡道泥梨中。
三十五者若得为人所生之处常当狂騃。如是等种种过失。是故不饮。如偈说。	三十五者若得為人所生之處常當狂騃。如是等種種過失。是故不飲。如偈說。
酒失觉知相　身色浊而恶。 智心动而乱　惭愧已被劫。	酒失覺知相　身色濁而惡。 智心動而亂　慚愧已被劫。

15. One does not respect the Śramaṇas.
16. One does not respect the Brahmans.
17. One does not respect one's uncles or venerable elders. Why is this? One is so stupefied by drunkenness as to fail to make any such distinctions.
18. One does not honor or respect the Buddha.
19. One does not respect the Dharma.
20. One does not respect the Sangha.
21. One associates with bad people.
22. One remains distant from the worthy and the good.
23. One becomes a breaker of the precepts.
24. One becomes devoid of a sense of shame or dread of blame.
25. One fails to guard the six sense faculties [through appropriate restraint].
26. One falls away into sexual profligacy.
27. One becomes so detested and abhorred by others that they find no delight in laying eyes on him.
28. One becomes abandoned and rejected by those who are esteemed, by one's relatives, and by one's friends.
29. One courses in those dharmas which are not good.
30. One relinquishes good dharmas.
31. One is neither trusted nor employed by intelligent people or wise personages. Why? Because, through intoxication, one has fallen into neglectful ways.
32. One departs far from nirvāṇa.
33. One plants the causes and conditions for becoming crazy and stupid.
34. When the body deteriorates and the life comes to an end, one is bound to fall into the wretched destinies and, in particular, into *niraya* (the hells).
35. When one finally succeeds in taking human rebirth gain, wherever one is reborn, one is crazy and stupid.

It is on account of all manner of such faults that one should abstain from drinking. This is as described in the following verse:

Intoxicants are marked by a loss of awareness in judgment.
One's physical appearance becomes murky and detestable.
While one's intelligence becomes agitated and confused,
And one is robbed of both sense of shame and dread of blame.

失念增瞋心　失欢毁宗族。
如是虽名饮　实为饮死毒。
不应瞋而瞋　不应笑而笑。
不应哭而哭　不应打而打。
不应语而语　与狂人无异。
夺诸善功德　知愧者不饮。

[158c11]　如是四罪不作。是身善律仪。妄[16]语不作是口善律仪。名为优婆塞五戒律仪。问曰。若八种律仪。及净命是名为戒。何以故。

优婆塞。于口律仪中。无三律仪及净命。答曰。白衣居家。受世间乐兼修福德。不能尽行戒法。是故佛令持五戒。复次四种口业中妄语最重。复次妄语心生故作。馀者或故作或不故作。复次但说妄语已摄三事。复次诸善法中实为

失念增瞋心　失歡毁宗族。
如是雖名飲　實為飲死毒。
不應瞋而瞋　不應笑而笑。
不應哭而哭　不應打而打。
不應語而語　與狂人無異。
奪諸善功德　知愧者不飲。

[158c11]　如是四罪不作。是身善律儀。妄[16]語不作是口善律儀。名為優婆塞五戒律儀。問曰。若八種律儀。及淨命是名為戒。何以故。

優婆塞。於口律儀中。無三律儀及淨命。答曰。白衣居家。受世間樂兼修福德。不能盡行戒法。是故佛令持五戒。復次四種口業中妄語最重。復次妄語心生故作。餘者或故作或不故作。復次但說妄語已攝三事。復次諸善法中實為

简体字　　　　　　　　　　正體字

One loses one's mindfulness, multiplies hate-ridden thoughts,
Forfeits one's happiness, and does damage to the clan.
Thus, although it may be referred to as "drinking,"
In truth, it is synonymous with consuming deadly poison.

Where one should not be hateful, one is nonetheless hateful.
Where one should not laugh, one nonetheless laughs.
Where one should not cry, one nonetheless cries.
Where one should not inflict blows, one nonetheless inflicts blows.

What one should not say, one nonetheless says.
One becomes indistinguishable from a crazy person.
All of one's good qualities are stolen away.
Whoever knows a sense of shame abstains from drink.

6) ADDITIONAL FIVE-PRECEPT TOPICS
a) SUMMATION OF THE PRIMARY BASIS OF LAY MORALITY

In this manner, abstention from four offenses constitutes accordance with the moral regulations governing goodness in physical actions whereas abstention from false speech constitutes accordance with the moral regulations governing goodness in verbal actions. These collectively constitute the moral regulations comprising the *upāsaka's* five precepts (*upāsakapañcaśīla*).

b) EIGHT PRECEPTS, OTHER MOUTH KARMAS, PURE LIVELIHOOD

Question: If it is the case that eight moral regulations and pure livelihood collectively constitute the precepts, why is there no mention here for the *upāsaka* of either the other three moral regulations associated with the mouth[20] or of pure livelihood?

i) LIMITED CAPACITIES OF LAY BUDDHISTS

Response: The laity (lit. "the white-robed ones") dwell in the midst of the home life where they accept the pleasures of the world while also concurrently cultivating merit. Hence they are unable to fully practice the Dharma as prescribed by the moral precepts. Therefore the Buddha decreed that they uphold the five precepts.

ii) HOW THE FALSE SPEECH PRECEPT SUBSUMES THE OTHERS

Moreover, within the four moral regulations associated with mouth karma, false speech is the most serious. Additionally, with false speech, the thought arises and then one deliberately engages in it. As for the others, one may deliberately engages in them or may do so without any particular deliberate intention.

Then again, when one mentions only false speech, one thereby already subsumes within it the other three related endeavors. Moreover, among all good dharmas, truthfulness is the one of

最大。若说实语四种正语皆已摄得。复次白衣处世。当官理务家业作使。是故难持不恶口法。妄语故作[17]事重故不应作。是五戒有五种受。名五种优婆塞。一者一分行优婆塞。二者少分行优婆塞。三者多分行优婆塞。四者满行优婆塞。五者断婬优婆塞。一分行者。于五戒中受一戒。不能受持四戒。少分行者。若受二戒若受三戒。多分行者。受四戒。满行者。尽持五戒。断婬者。受五戒已师前更作[18]自誓言。我于自妇不复行婬。是名五戒。如佛偈说。

不杀亦不盗　亦不有邪婬。
实语不饮酒　正命以净心。

若能行此者　二世忧畏除。
戒福恒随身　常与天人俱。

世间六时华　荣曜色相发。
以此一岁华　天上一日具。

最大。若說實語四種正語皆已攝得。復次白衣處世。當官理務家業作使。是故難持不惡口法。妄語故作[17]事重故不應作。是五戒有五種受。名五種優婆塞。一者一分行優婆塞。二者少分行優婆塞。三者多分行優婆塞。四者滿行優婆塞。五者斷婬優婆塞。一分行者。於五戒中受一戒。不能受持四戒。少分行者。若受二戒若受三戒。多分行者。受四戒。滿行者。盡持五戒。斷婬者。受五戒已師前更作[18]自誓言。我於自婦不復行婬。是名五戒。如佛偈說。

不殺亦不盜　亦不有邪婬。
實語不飲酒　正命以淨心。

若能行此者　二世憂畏除。
戒福恒隨身　常與天人俱。

世間六時華　榮曜色相發。
以此一歲華　天上一日具。

简体字   正體字

greatest importance. If one speaks true words, all four types of right speech are completely subsumed and realized.

iii) Lay Life's Inherent Connection to Harsh Speech

Additionally, the layperson abides in the world where he becomes responsible for oversight and management. He takes responsibility for the family business and issues orders. Hence it is difficult to uphold the dharma which requires abstention from harsh speech. False speech, however, is a thing which is intentionally done. Because it is a serious matter, one must not engage in it.

iv) Five Degrees of Five-Precept Acceptance

There are five degrees of acceptance of the five precepts which determine the five kinds of *upāsaka*. The first is the single-practice *upāsaka*. The second is the lesser-practice *upāsaka*. The third is the greater-practice *upāsaka*. The fourth is the full-practice *upāsaka*. The fifth is the celibate *upāsaka*.

As for the first, the single-practice *upāsaka*, it refers to taking on one precept from among the five moral precepts while being unable to take on and uphold the other four precepts. As for the lesser-practice *upāsaka*, it refers to taking on two or three precepts. The greater-practice *upāsaka* is one who takes on four precepts. The full-practice *upāsaka* completely upholds all five precepts. As for the celibate *upāsaka*, after taking on the five precepts, in the presence of his spiritual teacher, he additionally makes a vow for himself, saying, "I will no longer engage in sexual activity even with my own wife. This is what is meant by the five precepts. They are as described by the Buddha in verse:

v) Buddha's Verse on Five-Precept Karmic Rewards

One does not kill, does not steal,
Nor does one engage in sexual misconduct.
One maintains true speech, abstains from alcohol,
And upholds right livelihood. One thereby purifies his mind.

For whoever is able to put this into practice,
During the two eras,[21] worry and fear will be dispensed with,
Precept merit will constantly follow along with him,
And he will always enjoy the company of gods and men.

In the six-seasoned flower of the worldly existence,
Glory and physical appearance bloom together.
This single flower of all of our years,
Is contained in a single day of heavenly existence.[22]

天树自然生　花鬘及璎珞。
丹葩如灯照　众色相间错。

天衣无央数　其色若干种。
鲜白映天日　轻密无间[1]叠。

金色[2]映绣文　斐亹如云气。
如是上妙服　悉从天树出。

明珠天耳珰　宝碟曜手足。
随心所好[3]爱　亦从天树出。

金华琉璃茎　金刚为华[4]须。
柔软香芬熏　悉从宝池出。

琴瑟筝箜篌　七宝为挍饰。
器妙故音清　皆亦从树出。

波［(匕/示)*(入/米)］质姤树。
天上树中王。

在彼欢喜园　一切无有比。

持戒为耕田　天树从中出。
天厨甘露味　饮食除饥渴。

天女无监碍　亦无[5]妊身难。
[6]嬉怡纵逸乐　食无便利患。

持戒常摄心　得生自恣地。

简体字	正體字

天樹自然生　花鬘及璎珞。
丹葩如燈照　眾色相間錯。

天衣無央數　其色若干種。
鮮白映天日　輕密無間[1]疊。

金色[2]映繡文　斐亹如雲氣。
如是上妙服　悉從天樹出。

明珠天耳璫　寶碟曜手足。
隨心所好[3]愛　亦從天樹出。

金華琉璃莖　金剛為華[4]鬚。
柔軟香芬熏　悉從寶池出。

琴瑟箏箜篌　七寶為挍飾。
器妙故音清　皆亦從樹出。

波［(匕/示)*(入/米)］質姤樹。
天上樹中王。

在彼歡喜園　一切無有比。

持戒為耕田　天樹從中出。
天廚甘露味　飲食除飢渴。

天女無監礙　亦無[5]妊身難。
[6]嬉怡縱逸樂　食無便利患。

持戒常攝心　得生自恣地。

The celestial trees spontaneously produce
Flower garlands and necklaces.
The crimson flowers bloom as luminously as lamps.
The many colors there are displayed each among the others.

The celestial apparel of countless varieties,
In hues of so many sorts,
Is fresh and pure, reflects the heavenly sun,
And is light, tightly-woven, and free of any wrinkle.

The golden light is reflected in embroidered motifs.
The graceful color patterns appear like formations of airy clouds.
Such supremely marvelous apparel
All comes forth from the trees in the heavens.

Bright jewels, celestial earrings,
And precious bracelets brighten the hands and feet.
Whatever the mind finds delightful
Comes forth as well from the heavenly trees.

There are flowers of gold with stems of *vaiḍūrya*,
With floral stamens and pistils created from *vajra*.
Soft and pliant, exuding a pervasive fragrance,
They all grow forth from pools of jewels.

The guitar, bass, harp, and lute[23]
Are inlaid with ornaments of seven precious things.
The instruments are marvelous, the ancient sounds clear.
All of these also come forth from the trees.

The Pārijātaka tree[24]
Is the king of the trees in the heavens.
It grows there within the "Garden of Delight" (Nandanavana)
Where it remains unmatched by any other.

Upholding the precepts amounts to the tilling of the fields.
From which these heavenly trees all grow forth.
The celestial kitchens issue flavors of sweet-dew ambrosia.
Its drink and food dispel both hunger and thirst.

The heavenly maidens have no interference from guardians,
Nor do they have the hindrance of a pregnancy-prone body.
One may enjoy oneself, relax, and be unrestrained in pleasures,
Whilst eating remains free of the troubles of elimination.

If one upholds the precepts and constantly controls the mind,
One succeeds in being born in a land where one may indulge.

无事亦无难　常得肆乐志。

诸天得自在　忧苦不复生。
所欲应念至　身光照幽冥。

如是种种乐　皆由施与戒。
若欲得此报　当勤自勉励　。

[159b02] 　问曰。今说尸罗波罗蜜当以成佛。何以[7]故乃赞天福。答曰。佛言。三事必得报果不虚。布施得大[8]富。持戒生好处。修定得解脱。若单行尸罗得生好处。若修定智慧慈悲和合得三乘道。今但赞持戒。现世功德名闻安乐。后世得报。如偈所赞。譬如小儿蜜涂苦药然后能服。今先赞戒福然后人能持戒。[9]能持戒已立大誓愿得至佛道。是为尸罗生尸罗波罗蜜。又以一切人皆着乐世间之乐天上为最。若闻天上种种快乐。便能受行尸罗。

简体字

無事亦無難　常得肆樂志。

諸天得自在　憂苦不復生。
所欲應念至　身光照幽冥。

如是種種樂　皆由施與戒。
若欲得此報　當勤自勉勵　。

[159b02] 　問曰。今說尸羅波羅蜜當以成佛。何以[7]故乃讚天福。答曰。佛言。三事必得報果不虚。布施得大[8]富。持戒生好處。修定得解脱。若單行尸羅得生好處。若修定智慧慈悲和合得三乘道。今但讚持戒。現世功德名聞安樂。後世得報。如偈所讚。譬如小兒蜜塗苦藥然後能服。今先讚戒福然後人能持戒。[9]能持戒已立大誓願得至佛道。是為尸羅生尸羅波羅蜜。又以一切人皆著樂世間之樂天上為最。若聞天上種種快樂。便能受行尸羅。

正體字

There are no tasks to be done and there are no difficulties.
And one is ever able to fulfil aspirations for bliss.

All of the gods achieve sovereign freedom.
Distress and suffering no longer arise.
Whatever one desires comes in response to one's thoughts,
While the light from one's body illuminates all darkness.

All sorts of such pleasures as these
All come from giving and the observance of precepts.
If one wishes to gain this reward,
One ought to be diligent and exhort oneself in this.

(1) Buddhahood is the Goal; Why Praise Heavens?

Question: Now we are discussing the *śīla* pāramitā. It should be for the purpose of realizing buddhahood. Why is there now this praising of the merits of the heavens?

(2) Three Endeavors Entailing Certain Rewards

Response: The Buddha said that there are three endeavors which certainly entail rewards and for which the gaining of results is not a false matter: If one gives, one gains great fortune. If one upholds the precepts, one will be reborn in a fine place. If one cultivates the meditative absorptions, one will gain liberation.

If one practices *śīla* alone, one will succeed in being born in a fine place. If one additionally implements the combined practice of the absorptions, wisdom, kindness and compassion, one will succeed in gaining the path of the Three Vehicles.

(3) Attraction to Karmic Rewards Conducing to the Path

We are just now praising the upholding of precepts in particular. This brings meritorious qualities, fame, peace, and bliss in the present life while gaining in later lives rewards such as were praised in the verse. This is analogous to smearing honey on bitter medicine for a small child so that he then becomes able to swallow it. We now initially praise the merit from the precepts so that a person then becomes able to uphold the precepts. After one has been able to uphold the precepts, he makes the great vow to succeed in arriving at the Buddha Path. This amounts to the practice of *śīla* finally producing *śīla* pāramitā.

Also, because all people are attached to bliss and because, among all of the world's blisses, those in the heavens are the most supreme, if people hear of all of the various sorts of pleasure and happiness in the heavens, they will then be able to take on the practice of *śīla*.

后闻天上无常。厌患心生能
求解脱。更闻佛无量功德。
若慈悲心生。依尸罗波罗
蜜。得至佛道。以是故虽说
尸罗报无咎。问曰。白衣居
家唯此五戒。更有馀法耶。
答曰。有一日戒六斋日持功
德无量。若十二月一日至十
五日。受持此戒其福[10]甚
多。问曰。云何受一日戒。
答曰。受一日戒法长跪合掌
应如是言。我某甲今一日一
夜。归依佛归依法归依僧。
如是二如是三归依。我某甲
归依佛竟。归依法竟。归依
僧竟。如是二如是三归依
竟。我某甲若身业不善。若
口业不善。若意业不善。贪
欲瞋恚愚痴故。若今世若[11]
过世有如是罪。今日诚心忏
悔。身清净口清净心清净。
受行八戒是则布萨。[12]秦言
[13]共住。

後聞天上無常。厭患心生能
求解脫。更聞佛無量功德。
若慈悲心生。依尸羅波羅
蜜。得至佛道。以是故雖說
尸羅報無咎。問曰。白衣居
家唯此五戒。更有餘法耶。
答曰。有一日戒六齋日持功
德無量。若十二月一日至十
五日。受持此戒其福[10]甚
多。問曰。云何受一日戒。
答曰。受一日戒法長跪合掌
應如是言。我某甲今一日一
夜。歸依佛歸依法歸依僧。
如是二如是三歸依。我某甲
歸依佛竟。歸依法竟。歸依
僧竟。如是二如是三歸依
竟。我某甲若身業不善。若
口業不善。若意業不善。貪
欲瞋恚愚癡故。若今世若[11]
過世有如是罪。今日誠心懺
悔。身清淨口清淨心清淨。
受行八戒是則布薩。[12]秦言
[13]共住。

简体字   正體字

Later, when they have heard of the impermanence of the heavens, thoughts of aversion and abhorrence will develop, and they will finally be able to take up the quest for liberation.

When people additionally hear of the incalculable meritorious qualities of the Buddha, it may be then that thoughts of kindness and compassion will arise in them. As a result, they may then become able to rely upon *śīla* pāramitā as the means to succeed in arriving at the Buddha Path. It is on account of these factors that, although we do discuss the rewards associated with *śīla*, there is no fault inherent in it.[25]

b. The Specific-Term Practice of Eight Precepts

Question: Is it that the householder has only these these five precepts, or are there other relevant dharmas in addition to these?

Response: There are also the one-day precepts and the six days of abstinence. The merit gained from upholding those is incalculable. If one is able to observe these precepts from the first through the fifteenth of the twelfth month, his merit will become extremely abundant.

1) The Ceremony for Specific-Term Eight-Precept Practice

Question: How does one go about taking the one-day precepts?

Response: The dharma for accepting the one-day precepts entails kneeling on both knees with the palms joined while making a statement such as this: "I, so-and-so, now, for one day and one night, take refuge in the Buddha, take refuge in the Dharma, and take refuge in the Sangha." One proceeds in this manner, proclaiming the taking of the refuges for a second and a third time.

Next, one proclaims, "I, so-and-so, have now taken refuge in the Buddha. I have now taken refuge in the Dharma. I have now taken refuge in the Sangha." One proceeds in this manner, declaring the completion of the refuges for a second and a third time.

Next, one proclaims, "I, so-and-so, whether it be bad karma of the body, bad karma of the mouth, or bad karma of the mind, whether it be on account of greed, on account of hatred, or on account of stupidity, and whether it be that I have offenses such as these in the present life or in former lives, today, with a sincere mind, I repent of them all in order to achieve purity of the body, purity of the mouth and purity of the mind."

If one then takes on the practice of the eight precepts this constitutes the *upavāsa*. (Chinese textual note: In our language, this means "dwelling together.")

如诸佛尽寿不杀生。我某甲一日一夜。不杀生亦如是。如诸佛尽寿不盗。我某甲一日一夜。不盗亦如是。[14]如诸佛尽寿不婬。我某甲一日一夜不婬亦如是。如诸佛尽寿不妄语。我某甲一日一夜不妄语亦如是。如诸佛尽寿不饮酒。我某甲一日一夜不饮酒亦如是。如诸佛尽寿不坐高大床上。我某甲一日一夜。不坐高大床上亦如是。如诸佛尽寿不着花璎珞。不香涂身不着香熏衣。我某甲一日一夜。不着花璎珞不香涂身不着香熏衣亦如是。如诸佛尽寿不自歌舞作乐[15]亦不往观听。我某甲一日一夜。不自歌舞作乐不往观听亦如是。已受八戒。如诸佛尽寿不过中食。我某甲一日一夜。不过中食亦如是。我某甲受行八戒随学诸佛法。名为布萨。愿持是布萨福报。[16]愿生生不堕三恶八难。我亦不求转轮圣王梵释天王世界之乐。

简体字

如諸佛盡壽不殺生。我某甲一日一夜。不殺生亦如是。如諸佛盡壽不盜。我某甲一日一夜。不盜亦如是。[14]如諸佛盡壽不婬。我某甲一日一夜不婬亦如是。如諸佛盡壽不妄語。我某甲一日一夜不妄語亦如是。如諸佛盡壽不飲酒。我某甲一日一夜不飲酒亦如是。如諸佛盡壽不坐高大床上。我某甲一日一夜。不坐高大床上亦如是。如諸佛盡壽不著花璎珞。不香塗身不著香熏衣。我某甲一日一夜。不著花璎珞不香塗身不著香熏衣亦如是。如諸佛盡壽不自歌舞作樂[15]亦不往觀聽。我某甲一日一夜。不自歌舞作樂不往觀聽亦如是。已受八戒。如諸佛盡壽不過中食。我某甲一日一夜。不過中食亦如是。我某甲受行八戒隨學諸佛法。名為布薩。願持是布薩福報。[16]願生生不墮三惡八難。我亦不求轉輪聖王梵釋天王世界之樂。

正體字

Next, one proclaims, "Just as the Buddhas, for the remainder of their entire lives did not kill beings, in the same manner, I, so-and-so, for one day and one night, will not kill beings.

"Just as the Buddhas for the remainder of their entire lives did not steal, in the same manner, I, so-and-so, for one day and one night, will not steal.

"Just as the Buddhas for the remainder of their entire lives did not engage in sexual activity, in the same manner, I, so-and-so, for one day and one night, will not engage in sexual activity.

"Just as the Buddhas for the remainder of their entire lives did not commit false speech, in the same manner, I, so-and-so, for one day and one night, will not commit false speech.

"Just as the Buddhas for the remainder of their entire lives did not drink intoxicants, in the same manner, I, so-and-so, for one day and one night, will not drink intoxicants.

"Just as the Buddhas for the remainder of their entire lives did not sit on a high or grand couch, in the same manner, I, so-and-so, for one day and one night, will not sit on a high or grand couch.

"Just as the Buddhas for the rest of their entire lives did not wear flowers or necklaces and did not perfume their bodies and did not perfume their robes, in the same manner, I, so-and-so, for one day and one night, will not wear flowers or necklaces and will not perfume my body or my robes.

"Just as the Buddhas for the remainder of their entire lives did not themselves sing or dance or make music and did not go to watch or listen to it, in the same manner, I, so-and-so, for one day and one night, will not myself sing or dance or make music or go and observe or listen to it."

At this point, one completes the taking of the eight precepts.

One then continues by proclaiming, "Just as the Buddhas for the remainder of their entire lives did not eat past midday, in the same manner, I, so-and-so, for one day and one night, will not eat past midday.

"I, so-and-so, accept and practice the eight precepts and pursue the study of the Dharma of the Buddhas. This constitutes the *upavāsa*. I pray I will be able to sustain the meritorious retribution of this *upavāsa* and so pray that in life after life I will not fall into the three wretched destinies or experience the eight difficulties.

"I do not seek the pleasures of a wheel-turning sage king, of Brahmā or Śakradevendra, the kings of the gods, or of worldly

愿诸烦恼尽逮[17]得萨婆若成就佛道。问曰。云何受五戒。答曰。受五戒法。长跪合[18]掌言。我某甲归依佛归依法归依僧。如是[19]二如是三。我某甲归依佛竟。归依法竟。归依僧竟。如是二如是三。我是释迦牟尼佛优婆塞证知我。[20]我某甲从今日尽寿归依。戒师应言。汝优婆塞听。是多陀阿伽度阿罗呵三藐三佛陀知人见人。为优婆塞说五戒如是。[21]是汝尽寿持。何等五。尽寿不杀生是优婆塞戒。是中尽寿不应故杀生。是事若能当言诺。尽寿不盗。是优婆塞戒。是中尽寿不应盗。是事若能当言诺。尽寿不邪婬。是优婆塞戒。是中尽寿不应邪婬。是事若能当言诺。尽寿不妄语。是优婆塞戒。是中尽寿不应妄语。是事若能当言诺。尽寿不饮酒。是优婆塞戒。是中尽寿不应饮酒。是事若能当言诺。

简体字

願諸煩惱盡逮[17]得薩婆若成就佛道。問曰。云何受五戒。答曰。受五戒法。長跪合[18]掌言。我某甲歸依佛歸依法歸依僧。如是[19]二如是三。我某甲歸依佛竟。歸依法竟。歸依僧竟。如是二如是三。我是釋迦牟尼佛優婆塞證知我。[20]我某甲從今日盡壽歸依。戒師應言。汝優婆塞聽。是多陀阿伽度阿羅呵三藐三佛陀知人見人。為優婆塞說五戒如是。[21]是汝盡壽持。何等五。盡壽不殺生是優婆塞戒。是中盡壽不應故殺生。是事若能當言諾。盡壽不盜。是優婆塞戒。是中盡壽不應盜。是事若能當言諾。盡壽不邪婬。是優婆塞戒。是中盡壽不應邪婬。是事若能當言諾。盡壽不妄語。是優婆塞戒。是中盡壽不應妄語。是事若能當言諾。盡壽不飲酒。是優婆塞戒。是中盡壽不應飲酒。是事若能當言諾。

正體字

existence. I pray that I will be able to bring an end to all afflictions, will be able to succeed in gaining *sarvajñāna* (omniscience), and will be able to succeed in perfect realization of the Buddha Path."

2) THE CEREMONY FOR LIFE-LONG FIVE-PRECEPT PRACTICE

Question: How does one go about taking the five precepts?

Response: The dharma for accepting the five precepts is as follows: One kneeling on both knees with the palms joined, and then proclaiming, "I, so-and-so, take refuge in the Buddha, take refuge in the Dharma, and take refuge in the Sangha." One proceeds in this fashion for a second and a third time.

Next, one proclaims, "I, so-and-so, have now taken refuge in the Buddha. I have now taken refuge in the Dharma. I have now taken refuge in the Sangha." One proceeds thus a second and third time.

Next, one states, "I am an *upāsaka* disciple of Shakyamuni Buddha. Pray, certify and be aware that I, so-and-so, take these refuges from this day onward, for the rest of my life."

The Precept Master then says, "You, Upāsaka, hear me: The Tathāgatha, the Arhan and Samyāksambuddha, is a man of knowledge and a man of vision. He proclaimed the five precepts for the *upāsaka* in just this way. They are to be upheld by you for the rest of your life.

"What are the five? They are: To not kill beings for the rest of one's life is an *upāsaka* precept. Herein, for the rest of one's life, one must not deliberately kill beings. If you are able to carry out this matter, then you should say, 'I do so swear.'

"To not steal for the rest of one's life is an *upāsaka* precept. Herein, for the rest of one's life, one must not steal. If you are able to carry out this matter, then you should say, 'I do so swear.'

"To not engage in sexual misconduct for the rest of your life is an *upāsaka* precept. Herein, for the rest of your life, you must not engage in sexual misconduct. If you are able to carry out this matter, then you should say, 'I do so swear.'

"To not engage in false speech for the rest of one's life is an *upāsaka* precept. Herein, for the rest of one's life, one must not engage in false speech. If you are able to carry out this matter, then you should say, 'I do so swear.'

"To not drink intoxicants for the rest of one's life is an *upāsaka* precept. Herein, for the rest of one's life, one must not drink intoxicants. If you are able to carry out this matter, then you should say, 'I do so swear.'

是优婆塞五戒尽寿受持。当
供养三宝佛宝法宝比丘僧
宝勤修福[1]业以来佛道。问
曰。何以故。六斋日受八戒
修福德。答曰。是日恶鬼逐
人欲夺人命。疾病凶衰令人
不吉。是故劫初圣人。教人
持斋修善作福以避凶衰。是
时斋法不受八戒。直以一日
不食为斋。后佛出世教语之
言。汝当一日[2]一夜如诸佛
持八戒过中不食。是功德将
人至涅盘。如四天王经中佛
说。月六斋日使者太子及四
天王。自下观察众生布施持
戒孝顺父母。少者便上忉利
以启帝释。帝释诸天心皆不
[3]悦言。阿修罗种多诸天种
少。若布施持戒孝顺父母
多者。诸天帝释心皆欢喜
说言。增益[4]天众减损阿修
罗。是时释提婆那民[5]见诸
天欢喜。说此偈言。

六日神足月　受持清净戒。
是人寿终后　功德必如我。

是優婆塞五戒盡壽受持。當
供養三寶佛寶法寶比丘僧
寶勤修福[1]業以來佛道。問
曰。何以故。六齋日受八戒
修福德。答曰。是日惡鬼逐
人欲奪人命。疾病凶衰令人
不吉。是故劫初聖人。教人
持齋修善作福以避凶衰。是
時齋法不受八戒。直以一日
不食為齋。後佛出世教語之
言。汝當一日[2]一夜如諸佛
持八戒過中不食。是功德將
人至涅槃。如四天王經中佛
說。月六齋日使者太子及四
天王。自下觀察眾生布施持
戒孝順父母。少者便上忉利
以啟帝釋。帝釋諸天心皆不
[3]悅言。阿修羅種多諸天種
少。若布施持戒孝順父母
多者。諸天帝釋心皆歡喜
說言。增益[4]天眾減損阿修
羅。是時釋提婆那民[5]見諸
天歡喜。說此偈言。

六日神足月　受持清淨戒。
是人壽終後　功德必如我。

简体字　　　　　　　　　　正體字

"These five precepts of the *upāsaka* are to be accepted and upheld for the remainder of one's life. One should make offerings to the Triple Jewel: the Buddha Jewel, the Dharma Jewel, and the Bhikshu Sangha Jewel. One should diligently cultivate meritorious karma and thereby come forth into the Buddha Path."

3) WHY EIGHT PRECEPTS ARE OBSERVED ON SIX DAYS

Question: Why is it that, on the six days of abstinence, one takes the eight precepts and cultivates merit?

Response: It is on these days that evil ghosts pursue people desiring to steal their lives. They bring acute illnesses and calamitous ruination and thus cause people misfortune. Therefore the sages at the beginning of the kalpa instructed people to observe days of abstinence, cultivate good, and do meritorious deeds to thereby avoid calamity and ruination.

At that time, the abstinence dharma did not involve taking these eight precepts. It only took going one day without food as constituting abstinence. Later, when the Buddha came forth into the world, he instructed people, saying, "In the manner of the Buddha, you should uphold the eight precepts for one day and one night while also refraining from eating after midday. This merit will take a person forth to nirvāṇa."

According to what the Buddha said in the *Sutra of the Four Heavenly Kings*, on these six monthly abstinence days the retainers, princes, and the four heavenly kings themselves descend, observe, and investigate the status of beings' giving, maintenance of the precepts, and filial piety towards their fathers and mothers. In an instance where it is deficient, they then ascend to the Trāyastriṃśa heaven and inform Śakra of this. In such a case, Śakra and the other gods are all disappointed and proclaim, "The clan of the *asuras*[26] is on the increase and the clan of the gods is diminishing."

If, however, it is the case that the giving, maintenance of precepts, and filial piety towards fathers and mothers is greater, then the gods and Śakra are all delighted and thus proclaim, "There is increase in the company of the gods and a decrease among the *asuras*. At one such time, Śakradevendra observed the delight among the gods and uttered a verse, saying:

If, on six days and [on fifteen] in "spiritual" months,[27]
Someone is able to uphold the pure precepts—
After this person's life has come to an end,
His merit will certainly be comparable to mine.

[160a20]　　佛告诸比丘。释提桓因不应说如是偈。所以者何。释提桓因[6]三衰三毒未除。云何妄言持一日戒功德福报必得如我。若受持此戒心应如佛。是则实说。诸大尊天欢喜因缘故。得福增多。复次此六斋日。恶鬼害人恼乱一切。若所在丘聚郡县国邑。有持斋受戒[7]行善人者。以此因缘恶鬼远去。住处安隐。以是故六日持斋受戒得福增多。问曰。何以故诸恶鬼[8]神辈。以此六日恼害于人。答曰。天地本起经说。劫初成时有异梵天王子。诸鬼神父。修梵志苦行。满天上十二岁。于此六日。割肉出血以着火中。以是故诸恶鬼神。于此六日辄有势力。问曰。诸鬼神父。何以于此六日割身肉血以着火中。答曰。诸神中摩醯首罗神最大第一。诸神皆有日分。摩醯首罗。一月有四日分。八日二十三日十四日二十九日。馀神一月有二日分。月一日十六日

[160a20]　　佛告諸比丘。釋提桓因不應說如是偈。所以者何。釋提桓因[6]三衰三毒未除。云何妄言持一日戒功德福報必得如我。若受持此戒心應如佛。是則實說。諸大尊天歡喜因緣故。得福增多。復次此六齋日。惡鬼害人惱亂一切。若所在丘聚郡縣國邑。有持齋受戒[7]行善人者。以此因緣惡鬼遠去。住處安隱。以是故六日持齋受戒得福增多。問曰。何以故諸惡鬼[8]神輩。以此六日惱害於人。答曰。天地本起經說。劫初成時有異梵天王子。諸鬼神父。修梵志苦行。滿天上十二歲。於此六日。割肉出血以著火中。以是故諸惡鬼神。於此六日輒有勢力。問曰。諸鬼神父。何以於此六日割身肉血以著火中。答曰。諸神中摩醯首羅神最大第一。諸神皆有日分。摩醯首羅。一月有四日分。八日二十三日十四日二十九日。餘神一月有二日分。月一日十六日

简体字　　　　　　　　　　　正體字

The Buddha told the Bhikshus, "Śakradevendra should not have uttered a verse such as this. Why? Śakradevendra has not yet gotten rid of the five signs of deterioration[28] or the three poisons. How could he falsely state, 'If there is one who upholds the one-day precepts, he will certainly gain a meritorious reward comparable to mine.'? If one upholds these precepts, he ought as a result to become similar in mind to the Buddha. If he had said this, then it would have qualified as true speech."

Because the great and revered gods are delighted, one gains an increased amount of merit. Additionally, on these six abstinence days, evil ghosts bring harm to people and strive to visit affliction and confusion upon everyone. If, in the open country, village, prefecture, province, country, or city-state where one abides, there is a person who observes the days of abstinence, takes the precepts, and practices goodness, because of this, the evil ghosts depart far away and the place in which one dwells becomes peaceful and secure. For this reason, if one observes the abstinences and takes the precepts on these six days, one thereby gains increased merit.

4) WHY GHOSTS ACT UP SIX DAYS EACH MONTH (STORY)

Question: Why do the evil ghosts and spirits take advantage of these six days to visit affliction and harm on people?

Response: In the *Sutra on the Origins of Heaven and Earth*, it states that when this kalpa first began, there was a different "Brahmā" diety's son who was the father of the ghosts and spirits. He cultivated a form of *brahmacārin* ascetic practice whereby, for a full twelve heavenly years, on the occasion of these six days, he cut away portions of his own flesh, drew off a measure of his own blood, and then placed them in a fire. It was on account of this that the evil ghosts and spirits would suddenly come into possession of particularly strong powers on these six days.

Question: Why on these six days did the father of the ghosts and spirits cut away the flesh and blood of his body, placing them into a fire?

Response: Among all of the ghosts and spirits, the Maheśvara spirit is the biggest and the most primary in status. All of the spirits have an allotted number of days. Maheśvara has an allotment of four days out of each month: the eighth, the twenty-third, the fourteenth, and the twenty-ninth.

The other spirits have an allotment of two days out of each month: their first day out of the month is the sixteenth and their

月二日十七日。其十五日三十日属一切神。摩醯首罗为诸神主。又得日多故数其四日为斋。二日是一切诸神日。亦数以为斋。是故诸鬼神。于此六日辄有力势

[160b13]　　　复次诸鬼[9]神父于此六日割肉出血以着火中。过十二岁已。天王来下语其子言。汝求何愿。答言。我求有子。天王言。仙人供养法。以烧香甘果诸清净事。汝云何以肉血着火中。如罪恶法。汝破善法乐为恶事。令汝生恶子噉肉饮血。当说。是时火中有八大鬼出。身黑如墨发黄眼赤有大光明。一切鬼神皆从此八鬼生。以是故。于此六日割身肉血以着火中而得势力。如佛法中日无好恶。随世恶日因缘故。教持斋受[10]八戒。问曰。五戒一日戒何者为胜。答曰。有因缘故二戒俱等。但五戒

月二日十七日。其十五日三十日屬一切神。摩醯首羅為諸神主。又得日多故數其四日為齋。二日是一切諸神日。亦數以為齋。是故諸鬼神。於此六日輒有力勢

[160b13]　　　復次諸鬼[9]神父於此六日割肉出血以著火中。過十二歲已。天王來下語其子言。汝求何願。答言。我求有子。天王言。仙人供養法。以燒香甘果諸清淨事。汝云何以肉血著火中。如罪惡法。汝破善法樂為惡事。令汝生惡子噉肉飲血。當說。是時火中有八大鬼出。身黑如墨髮黃眼赤有大光明。一切鬼神皆從此八鬼生。以是故。於此六日割身肉血以著火中而得勢力。如佛法中日無好惡。隨世惡日因緣故。教持齋受[10]八戒。問曰。五戒一日戒何者為勝。答曰。有因緣故二戒俱等。但五戒

简体字　　　　　　　　正體字

second day out of the month is the seventeenth. The fifteenth and the thirtieth belong collectively to all spirits.

Because Maheśvara is the lord of all of the spirits and because he has been allotted the most days, his four days came to be counted as abstinence days. The other two days also counted as abstinence days are the days belonging collectively to all of the spirits. Hence, all of the ghosts and spirits suddenly possess strong powers on these six days.

Furthermore, after the father of ghosts and spirits had continued for twelve years his practice of cutting away his flesh, drawing off his blood, and placing them in fire, the king of the gods descended and asked his son, "What prayer do you seek to fulfill by doing this?"

He replied, "I seek to have sons."

The king of the gods said, "It is the offering method of the rishis to employ the burning of incense, the offering up of sweet fruits, and the carrying out of all manner of pure endeavors. Why do you employ this method of placing flesh and blood into fire, a method associated with offensive and evil dharmas? Your destruction of the dharma of goodness and your taking pleasure in carrying out evil endeavors will cause you to give birth to evil sons who feast on flesh and drink blood."

Then, in accordance with his proclamation, eight huge ghosts came forth at that very moment from within the fire. Their bodies were as black as ink. Their hair was yellow, their eyes were red, and they shone with abundant light. Then, all manner of ghosts and spirits were subsequently born from these eight ghosts. Thus it was that this practice of carving off his own flesh, drawing his own blood, and then placing them into fire resulted in the generation of such power.

As for the Dharma of the Buddha, though, these days are devoid of any particular auspiciousness or adversity. But nonetheless, as an adaptation to the world's treatment of these as inauspicious days, one is instructed to observe the abstinences and take the eight precepts on these days.

c. Comparison of Five and Eight Precepts

Question: Which is superior, the five precepts or the one-day precepts?

Response: There may be causal bases whereby the two precept categories can be considered equal. However, the five precepts are

终身持。八戒一日持。又五
戒常持时多而戒少。一日戒
时少而戒多。复次若无大心
虽复终身持戒。不如有大心
人一日持戒也。譬如软夫为
将。虽复[11]将兵终身。智
勇不足卒无功名。若如英雄
奋发祸乱立定。一日之勋功
盖天下。是二种戒。名居家
优婆塞法。居家持戒凡有四
种。有下中上。有上上。下
人持戒为今世乐故。或为怖
畏称誉名闻故。或为家法曲
随他意故。或避苦[12]役求离
[13]危难故。如是种种是下
人持戒。中人持戒。为人中
富贵欢娱适意。或期后世福
乐。[14]克己自勉为苦。日少
所得甚多。

終身持。八戒一日持。又五
戒常持時多而戒少。一日戒
時少而戒多。復次若無大心
雖復終身持戒。不如有大心
人一日持戒也。譬如軟夫為
將。雖復[11]將兵終身。智
勇不足卒無功名。若如英雄
奮發禍亂立定。一日之勳功
蓋天下。是二種戒。名居家
優婆塞法。居家持戒凡有四
種。有下中上。有上上。下
人持戒為今世樂故。或為怖
畏稱譽名聞故。或為家法曲
隨他意故。或避苦[12]役求離
[13]危難故。如是種種是下
人持戒。中人持戒。為人中
富貴歡娛適意。或期後世福
樂。[14]剋己自勉為苦。日少
所得甚多。

简体字   正體字

taken for the rest of one's life, whereas the eight precepts are upheld for only a single day at a time. But then again, although the five precepts are constantly upheld over a longer period of time, the precepts observed are fewer in number. With the one-day precepts, the time is less, but the number of precepts observed is greater.

As another consideration, if one is not possessed of a great mind, although one may uphold the precepts for one's entire life, the goodness involved does not measure up to that of a person of the great mind upholding the precepts for but a single day.[29]

This is analogous to a weak man serving as a general. Although he may serve as a general of the troops for the rest of his life, because of his inadequacies in wisdom and bravery, the shock troops will have no reputation for meritorious service. But if a greatly heroic man brings forth high resolve to immediately stabilize a disastrous and chaotic situation, through just a single day of devoted service, his meritorious reputation may spread throughout the world.

1) Four Grades of Lay Precept Observance

These two categories of precepts are dharmas intended for the householder, the *upāsaka*. The upholding of precepts on the part of the householder is commonly of four degrees. There are the lesser, the middling, the superior, and the superior among the superior.

2) The Lesser Grade of Lay Precept Observance

When a lesser person upholds the precepts, it may be for the sake of gaining pleasures in the present life, or perhaps it may be out of fearfulness, out of a desire to be praised, or out of a motivation to gain a prestigious reputation. Or it may be that for the sake of adhering to family standards, he will constrain himself to go along with someone else's ideas. It may also be done out of a desire to avoid a misery-ridden period of conscription or may be done because one seeks to avoid dangerous circumstances. All sorts of factors such as these may characterize the lesser person's observance of moral precepts.

3) The Middling Grade of Lay Precept Observance

When the middling person upholds the precepts, it is for the sake of wealth and noble status in the human realm and for the sake of gaining delights and pleasures which accord with his aspirations. Or perhaps, hoping for good fortune and bliss in later lives, one will endure self-denial and encourage himself, thinking, "The days one must suffer this are but few, whereas the gains to be achieved are extremely great."

如是思惟堅固持戒。譬如商人遠出深入得利必多。持戒之福令人受后世福樂亦復如是。上人持戒為涅盤故。知諸法一切無常故。欲求離苦常樂無為故。復次持戒之人其心不悔。心不悔故得喜樂。[15]得喜樂故得一心。得一心故得實智。得實智故得厭心。得厭心故得離欲。得離欲故得解脫。得解脫故得涅盤。如是持戒為諸善法根本。復次持戒為八正道初門入道初門必至涅盤

简体字

如是思惟堅固持戒。譬如商人遠出深入得利必多。持戒之福令人受後世福樂亦復如是。上人持戒為涅槃故。知諸法一切無常故。欲求離苦常樂無為故。復次持戒之人其心不悔。心不悔故得喜樂。[15]得喜樂故得一心。得一心故得實智。得實智故得厭心。得厭心故得離欲。得離欲故得解脫。得解脫故得涅槃。如是持戒為諸善法根本。復次持戒為八正道初門入道初門必至涅槃

正體字

Through making such considerations, one may come to uphold the precepts solidly. This is comparable to a merchant's traveling far and investing heavily. The profit to be gained is bound to be great. The merit from upholding the precepts causes people to receive good fortune and bliss in later lives in just this fashion.

4) The Superior Grade of Lay Precept Observance

When the superior person observes the moral precepts, it is for the sake of nirvāṇa and because he knows that all dharmas are impermanent. It is because he wishes to transcend suffering and gain eternal enjoyment of the unconditioned.

a) How These Precepts Are the Causes for Nirvāṇa

Furthermore, the mind of the person who observes the moral precepts remains free of regrets. Because his mind remains free of regrets, he gains delight and enjoyment. Because he gains delight and enjoyment from it, he achieves single-mindedness. Because he achieves single-mindedness, he gains real wisdom. Because he gains real wisdom, he develops the mind of renunciation. Because he develops the mind of renunciation, he succeeds in transcending desire. Because he succeeds in transcending desire, he gains liberation. Because he gains liberation, he gains nirvāṇa. In this manner, upholding the precepts constitutes the foundation for all of the good dharmas.

Moreover, the upholding of precepts constitutes the initial entryway into to the eightfold right Path. This initial entryway onto the Path certainly extends all the way to nirvāṇa.

[16]大智度论释初品中赞尸**[17]**罗波罗蜜义

[18]第二十**[19]**三

[160c19]　　　问曰。如八正道。正语正业在中。正见正行在初。今何以言戒为八正道初门。答曰。以数言之大者为始。正见最大。是故在初。复次行道故以见为先。诸法次第故戒在前。譬如作屋栋梁虽大以地为先。上上人持戒怜愍众生。为佛道故。以知诸法求实相故。不畏恶道不求乐故。如是种种。是上上人持戒。是四总名优婆塞戒。出家戒亦有四种。一者沙弥沙弥尼戒。二者式叉摩那戒。三者比丘尼戒。四者比丘僧戒。问曰。若居家戒得生天上。得

[16]大智度論釋初品中讚尸**[17]**羅波羅蜜義

[18]第二十**[19]**三

[160c19]　　　問曰。如八正道。正語正業在中。正見正行在初。今何以言戒為八正道初門。答曰。以數言之大者為始。正見最大。是故在初。復次行道故以見為先。諸法次第故戒在前。譬如作屋棟梁雖大以地為先。上上人持戒憐愍眾生。為佛道故。以知諸法求實相故。不畏惡道不求樂故。如是種種。是上上人持戒。是四總名優婆塞戒。出家戒亦有四種。一者沙彌沙彌尼戒。二者式叉摩那戒。三者比丘尼戒。四者比丘僧戒。問曰。若居家戒得生天上。得

簡体字　　　　　　　正體字

Chapter 23: Aspects of *Śīla Pāramitā*
Part One: Additional Precept Specifics[30]

b) How Can Precepts Be Foremost in the Eightfold Path?

Question: According to the sequence in the eightfold right path, right speech and right livelihood are in the middle whereas right views and right action are at the beginning. Why then do you now state that the precepts serve as the initial entryway into the eightfold right path?

Response: When we speak of numerical priorities, those of greatest significance are listed first. Right views is the one which is of greatest significance. Therefore it is placed at the beginning. Moreover, because one is coursing along a path, one takes seeing clearly as the foremost priority. Because all dharmas involve a particular sequence, it is the moral precepts which come first. This is analogous to the construction of a building wherein, although the beams and rafters may be huge, one nonetheless must take the ground itself as the first priority.

5) The Superior-Superior Grade of Lay Precept observance

In the case of a person who is the most superior among the superior in the upholding of precepts, it is done out of pity for beings and for the sake of the Buddha Path. It is in order to understand all dharmas and fathom their true character in accordance with reality. It is not done on account of fear of the wretched destinies and it is not done because one seeks to gain pleasures.

All sorts of motives such as these characterize the practice of one who is the most superior among the superior in the upholding of the precepts. These four categories generally constitute an *upāsaka's* practice of the precepts.

2. The Monastic Precepts

The precepts of those who have left the home life involve four categories: The first consists of the precepts of a *śrāmaṇera* and *śrāmaṇerikā*. The second consists of the precepts of a *śikṣamāṇā*. The third consists of the precepts of a bhikshuni. The fourth consists of the precepts of the Bhikshu Sangha.

Question: If by relying on the householder's precepts, one succeeds in being reborn in the heavens, succeeds in gaining the

菩萨道亦得至涅盘。复何用出家戒。答曰。虽俱得度然有难易。居家生[1]业种种事务。若欲专心道法家业则废。若欲专修家业道事则废。不取不舍乃应行法。是名为难。若出家离俗绝诸[2]纷乱。一向专心行道为易。

[161a06] 复次居家愦闹多事多务。结使之根众恶之府。是为甚难。若出家者。譬如有人出在空野无人之处而一其心。无思无虑内想既除。外事亦去。如偈说。

闲坐林树间	寂然灭众恶。
恬澹得一心	斯乐非天乐。
人求富贵利	名衣好床褥。
斯乐非安隐	求利无厌足。
纳衣行乞食	动止心常一。

简体字

菩薩道亦得至涅槃。復何用出家戒。答曰。雖俱得度然有難易。居家生[1]業種種事務。若欲專心道法家業則廢。若欲專修家業道事則廢。不取不捨乃應行法。是名為難。若出家離俗絕諸[2]紛亂。一向專心行道為易。

[161a06] 復次居家慣鬧多事多務。結使之根眾惡之府。是為甚難。若出家者。譬如有人出在空野無人之處而一其心。無思無慮內想既除。外事亦去。如偈說。

閑坐林樹間	寂然滅眾惡。
恬澹得一心	斯樂非天樂。
人求富貴利	名衣好床褥。
斯樂非安隱	求利無厭足。
納衣行乞食	動止心常一。

正體字

Bodhisattva Path, and also succeeds in reaching nirvāṇa, of what further use are the monastic precepts?

a. The Value of the Monastic Precepts

1) Inherent Path-Defeating Difficulties in Lay Life

Response: Although one may gain liberation through both approaches, still, there are ways which are difficult and ways which are easier.

The actions involved in the life of a householder involve all manner of endeavors and responsibilities. If one desires to focus one's mind especially on the dharmas of the Path, then the business of the family deteriorates. If one desires to focus one's mind especially on cultivating the business of the family, then the matters associated with the Path deteriorate.

2) Comparison of Lay and Monastic Situations

Neither seizing on nor forsaking anything—it is in this manner that one should cultivate the Dharma. This is renowned for its difficulty. However, if one leaves the home life, separates from the circumstances of the laity, cuts off all complexity and chaos, and maintains a focused mind, then cultivating the Path becomes easy.

Moreover, the befuddlement and boisterousness of the householder's life involves many endeavors and much responsibility. It is the root of the fetters and the repository of the manifold ills. This is an extremely difficult situation.

When one leaves the home life, it is analogous to a person being able to go forth into the unpopulated and empty wilderness to unify his mind. He is then able under those circumstances to become free of immersion in ideation and mental discursion. Once the inward thoughts have been gotten rid of, the outward matters depart as well. This is as described in a verse:

> When sitting undisturbed within the forest,
> In a state of stillness, one extinguishes the manifold ills.
> Calmly and contentedly, one gains unity of mind.
> This sort of bliss is unequaled even by the bliss of the heavens.

> People seek after the benefit of wealth and noble status,
> For famous fashions and for fine furnishings.
> This sort of pleasure affords no peace or security.
> One thus pursues one's own benefit, but finds no satiation.

> The one with the patchwork robes practices reliance on alms,
> And, whether moving or still, his mind is thus always unified.

自以智慧眼　　观知诸法实。
种种法门中　　皆以等观入。
解慧心寂然　　三界无能及。

[161a18]　以是故知出家修戒行道为易。复次出家修戒。得无量善律仪。一切具足满。以是故白衣等应[3]当出家受[4]具足戒。复次佛法中出家法第一难修。如阎浮呿提梵志问舍利弗。于佛法中何者最难。舍利弗答曰。出家为难。又问。出家[5]有何等难。答曰。出家乐法为难。既得乐法复何者为难。修诸善法难。以是故应出家。复次若人出家时。魔王惊[6]愁言。此人诸结使欲薄。必得涅盘堕僧宝数中。复次佛法中出家人。虽破[7]戒堕罪。罪毕得解脱。如[8]优钵罗华比丘尼本生经中说。

简体字

自以智慧眼　　觀知諸法實。
種種法門中　　皆以等觀入。
解慧心寂然　　三界無能及。

[161a18]　以是故知出家修戒行道為易。復次出家修戒。得無量善律儀。一切具足滿。以是故白衣等應[3]當出家受[4]具足戒。復次佛法中出家法第一難修。如閻浮呿提梵志問舍利弗。於佛法中何者最難。舍利弗答曰。出家為難。又問。出家[5]有何等難。答曰。出家樂法為難。既得樂法復何者為難。修諸善法難。以是故應出家。復次若人出家時。魔王驚[6]愁言。此人諸結使欲薄。必得涅槃墮僧寶數中。復次佛法中出家人。雖破[7]戒墮罪。罪畢得解脫。如[8]優鉢羅華比丘尼本生經中說。

正體字

He spontaneously employs the eye of wisdom,
And so contemplates and knows the reality of all dharmas.

Among all the different entryways into the Dharma,
All are entered through equanimous contemplation.
When the understanding and wise mind abides in stillness,
Nothing anywhere in the three realms is able to equal this.

For these reasons, one should realize that it is easiest to practice the Path through leaving behind the home life and cultivating the precepts under those circumstances.

Additionally, if one leaves the home life and cultivates the monastic precepts, one becomes able to achieve the complete perfection of an incalculable number of aspects of good moral conduct. It is for these reasons that members of the lay community should leave the home life and take on the complete precepts.

3) Difficulties Specific to the Monastic Life

Then again, it is also the case that, within the Dharma of the Buddha, the particular dharma of leaving the home life is the one which is the most difficult to cultivate. This is as alluded to in the questions of the *brahmacārin* Jambukhādaka to Śāriputra, wherein he asked, "What is most difficult within the Buddha's Dharma?"

Śāriputra replied, "Leaving behind the home life is difficult."

He also asked, "What are the difficulties involved in leaving the home life?"

He replied, "Having left the home life, it is finding bliss in the Dharma which is difficult."

"If one succeeds in finding bliss in the Dharma, then what beyond this is difficult?"

"To cultivate all good dharmas is difficult."

For the above reasons, one should leave behind the home life. Moreover, when one leaves behind the home life, the king of the demons becomes frightened and worried, saying, "The fetters of this man are about to become scant. He will certainly gain nirvāṇa and thus fall in among the members of the Sangha Jewel."

4) Utpalavarṇā Promotes Monasticism (Story)

Also, although among those who have left the home life in the Dharma of the Buddha there are those who break the precepts and fall into offenses, when the corresponding karmic retribution has come to an end, they then succeed in gaining liberation. This is as described in the *Bhikshuni Utpalavarṇā Jātaka Sutra*.

佛在世时。此比丘尼得六神
通阿罗汉。入贵人舍常赞出
家法。语诸贵人妇女言。姊
妹可出家。诸贵妇女言。我
等少壮容色盛美持戒为难。
或当破戒。比丘尼言。但出
家破戒便破。问言。破戒当
堕地狱。云何可破。答言。
堕地狱便堕。诸贵妇[9]女笑
之言。地狱受罪云何可堕。
比丘尼言。我自忆念本宿
命。时作戏女着种种衣服而
说旧语。或时着比丘尼衣以
为戏笑。以是因缘故。迦叶
佛时作比丘尼。自恃贵姓端
[*]政。心生憍慢而破禁戒。
破戒罪故堕地狱受种种罪。
受罪毕竟值释迦牟尼佛。出
家得六神通阿罗汉道。以是
故知。出家受戒。虽复破戒
以戒因缘故。得阿罗汉道。

佛在世時。此比丘尼得六神
通阿羅漢。入貴人舍常讚出
家法。語諸貴人婦女言。姊
妹可出家。諸貴婦女言。我
等少壯容色盛美持戒為難。
或當破戒。比丘尼言。但出
家破戒便破。問言。破戒當
墮地獄。云何可破。答言。
墮地獄便墮。諸貴婦[9]女笑
之言。地獄受罪云何可墮。
比丘尼言。我自憶念本宿
命。時作戲女著種種衣服而
說舊語。或時著比丘尼衣以
為戲笑。以是因緣故。迦葉
佛時作比丘尼。自恃貴姓端
[*]政。心生憍慢而破禁戒。
破戒罪故墮地獄受種種罪。
受罪畢竟值釋迦牟尼佛。出
家得六神通阿羅漢道。以是
故知。出家受戒。雖復破戒
以戒因緣故。得阿羅漢道。

简体字　　　　　　　　　　　正體字

When the Buddha was still abiding in the world, this bhikshuni gained the six superknowledges and arhatship. She made a practice of going into the households of the nobility where she constantly praised the tradition of leaving the home life. In doing so, she spoke to the wives and daughters of the nobility, saying, "Sisters, you could leave behind the home life."

The wives and daughters among the nobility replied, "But we are young and strong. Our countenances and physical forms are full and beautiful. It would be difficult to uphold the precepts. It might happen that we would break the precepts."

The Bhikshuni then replied, "Just go ahead and leave the home life, anyway. If it does happen that you end up breaking the precepts, then so it is: You break them."

They responded, "If we break the precepts, we'll fall into the hells. How could it be conceivable that they might be broken?"

She replied, "If it happens that you end up falling into the hells, then you fall."

The wives and daughters of the nobility all laughed at this, saying, "When one falls into the hells, one is compelled to undergo punishments. How then could one even contemplate a situation where one might fall?"

The Bhikshuni replied, "I recall that in a previous life I was an actress who put on all sorts of costumes in which I would play traditional parts. There were times when I would put on the robes of a bhikshuni and then act in that guise as a comedienne. It was due to this causal circumstance that, at the time of Kāśyapa Buddha, I was actually able to become a bhikshuni. However, on account of my noble birth and beauty, I was overcome with arrogance and then broke the restrictive prohibitions. On account of the karmic offenses associated with breaking the precepts, I fell into the hells where I underwent all manner of punishment as retribution.

"When I had finished undergoing retribution for those offenses, I was able to encounter Shakyamuni Buddha and leave the home life again, whereupon I then succeeded in gaining the six superknowledges and the path of arhatship. Based on this, one should realize that, if one leaves the home life and takes those precepts, even though one may happen to break the precepts, one is nonetheless bound to succeed in gaining the path of arhatship as a result of the causal circumstances associated with having taken those precepts in the first place.

若但作恶无戒因缘不得道
也。我乃昔时世世堕地狱。
地狱出为恶人。恶人死还入
地狱都无所得。今以此证知
出家受戒。虽复破戒以是因
缘可得道果。复次如佛在[10]
只洹。有一醉婆罗门。来到
佛所求作比丘。佛勅阿难与
剃头着法衣。醉酒既醒惊怪
己身忽为比丘即便走去。诸
比丘问佛。何以听此醉婆罗
门作比丘。佛言。此婆罗门
无量劫中初无出家心。今因
醉故暂发微心。以是因缘故
[11]后当出家得道。如是种种
因缘。出家之利功德无量。
以是故白衣虽有五戒不如出
家。是出家律仪有四种。沙
弥沙弥尼式叉摩[12]那比丘尼
比丘。

若但作惡無戒因緣不得道
也。我乃昔時世世墮地獄。
地獄出為惡人。惡人死還入
地獄都無所得。今以此證知
出家受戒。雖復破戒以是因
緣可得道果。復次如佛在[10]
祇洹。有一醉婆羅門。來到
佛所求作比丘。佛勅阿難與
剃頭著法衣。醉酒既醒驚怪
己身忽為比丘即便走去。諸
比丘問佛。何以聽此醉婆羅
門作比丘。佛言。此婆羅門
無量劫中初無出家心。今因
醉故暫發微心。以是因緣故
[11]後當出家得道。如是種種
因緣。出家之利功德無量。
以是故白衣雖有五戒不如出
家。是出家律儀有四種。沙
彌沙彌尼式叉摩[12]那比丘尼
比丘。

简体字   正體字

"However, if one merely commits evil deeds, but yet does so in the absence of that causal circumstance of having taken the precepts, then one will not succeed in gaining the Path. And so it was that I fell into the hells in many previous lifetimes, only to emerge from the hells and become an evil person again, whereupon I would fall right back down into the hells. As a consequence, I failed in those instances to gain anything worthwhile as a result."

Now, based on this, we can verify that, if one simply leaves behind the home life and takes the precepts, even though one might eventually break the precepts, one will nonetheless finally succeed in gaining the fruition of the Path through the force of those causal circumstances."

5) An Inebriated Brahman Becomes a Monk (Story)

Then again, this point is also illustrated by that time when the Buddha dwelt in the Jeta Grove and a drunken brahman came before the Buddha requesting to become a bhikshu. The Buddha ordered Ānanda to administer tonsure and outfit the man in the Dharma robes. When that brahman awoke from his inebriation, he was startled and amazed that he had suddenly become a bhikshu, whereupon he immediately ran off.

The other bhikshus then inquired of the Buddha, "Why did the Buddha permit this drunken brahman to become a bhikshu?"

The Buddha replied, "Even in innumerable eons, this brahman has never thought to leave the home life. Now, due to his inebriation, he briefly generated a feeble intention to do so. On account of this causal circumstance, he will later become able to leave the home life and gain the Path."

6) Concluding Statement on Lay Life versus Monasticism

Based on all sorts of causal circumstances such as these, one can see that the benefits and merit of leaving the home life are incalculable. Hence, although the members of the lay community do possess the five precepts, they cannot be compared to those associated with leaving the home life.

b. The Four Categories of Monastic Precepts

The moral regulations of those who have left the home life consist of four categories: those of the *śrāmaṇera* and *śrāmaṇerikā* (male and female novices); those of the *śikṣamāṇā* (a female postulant nun); those of the bhikshuni (fully-ordained nun); and those of the bhikshu (a fully ordained monk).

云何沙弥沙弥尼。出家受戒法。白衣来欲求出家。应求二师。一[13]和上。一[14]阿阇梨。和上如父阿阇梨如母。以弃本生父母。当求出家父母。着袈[15]裟[16]剃除须发。应两[17]手捉和上两足。何以捉足。天竺法以捉足。为第一恭敬供养。阿阇梨应教十戒。如受戒法。沙弥尼亦如是。唯以比丘尼为和上。式叉摩那受六法二岁。问曰。沙弥十戒便受具足戒。比丘尼法中。[18]何以有式叉摩那。然后得受具足戒。答曰。佛在世时。有一长者妇。不觉怀妊出家受具足戒。其后身大转现。诸长者讥嫌比丘。因此制。有二[19]岁学戒受六法。然后受具足戒。问曰。若为讥嫌。式叉摩那岂不致讥。答曰。式叉摩那未受具足[20]戒。譬如小儿亦如给使。虽有罪秽人不讥嫌。[21]是[22]名式叉摩那[23]受六法。

云何沙彌沙彌尼。出家受戒法。白衣來欲求出家。應求二師。一[13]和上。一[14]阿闍梨。和上如父阿闍梨如母。以棄本生父母。當求出家父母。著袈[15]裟[16]剃除鬚髮。應兩[17]手捉和上兩足。何以捉足。天竺法以捉足。為第一恭敬供養。阿闍梨應教十戒。如受戒法。沙彌尼亦如是。唯以比丘尼為和上。式叉摩那受六法二歲。問曰。沙彌十戒便受具足戒。比丘尼法中。[18]何以有式叉摩那。然後得受具足戒。答曰。佛在世時。有一長者婦。不覺懷妊出家受具足戒。其後身大轉現。諸長者譏嫌比丘。因此制。有二[19]歲學戒受六法。然後受具足戒。問曰。若為譏嫌。式叉摩那豈不致譏。答曰。式叉摩那未受具足[20]戒。譬如小兒亦如給使。雖有罪穢人不譏嫌。[21]是[22]名式叉摩那[23]受六法。

简体字　　　　　正體字

What are the means by which a *śrāmaṇera* and *śrāmaṇerikā* leave the home life and take on those precepts? The lay follower who comes seeking to leave the home life should request two masters: one *upādhyāya* and one *ācārya*. The *upādhyāya* is comparable to one's father whereas the *ācārya* is comparable to one's mother. Having set aside one's original parents, one should thus seek out among the monastics those capable of serving in those roles.

One next dons the *kāṣāya* robe while also cutting off the hair and beard. [In bowing down in respect], one should then grasp the feet of the *upādhyāya* with his two hands. Why does one grasp his feet? It is the custom of India that to grasp the feet demonstrates the most superior form of reverential offering. The *ācārya* should then provide instruction in the ten precepts. This is done in accordance with the protocols for receiving those precepts. For the *śrāmaṇerikā* it is just the same, the difference being that she takes a bhikshuni to serve as her *upādhyāya*. As for the *śikṣamāṇā*, she takes on six dharmas for a [pre-novitiate probationary] period of two years.

1) The Origin of the Śikṣamāṇā Postulant Nun Category

Question: The *śrāmaṇera* first takes the ten precepts and then takes the complete precepts. Why, within the dharma of the bhikshuni, does there exist the *śikṣamāṇā* stage, and only afterwards, the receiving of the complete precepts?

Response: When the Buddha was in the world, there once was the wife of an elder who, unaware that she had already become pregnant, nonetheless left the home life and received the complete precepts. Afterwards, her body swelled and her pregnancy began to show. On account of this, the elders ridiculed and criticized the bhikshus. It was on account of this that it was laid down that there would be a two-year period of studying the precepts and accepting six dharmas after which one would progress towards taking the complete precepts.

a) Why Wouldn't a Pregnant Śikṣamāṇā Be as much a Liability?

Question: If the community had been ridiculed and criticized in the former circumstance, how is it that a *śikṣamāṇā* would not bring about ridicule in a similar situation?

Response: The *śikṣamāṇā* has not yet taken the complete precepts. That status is analogous to that of a small child or a servant whom people still do not ridicule or criticize even though they may incur the defilement of an offense. This refers to the *śikṣamāṇā's* taking on the discipline of six dharmas.

是式叉摩那有二种。一者十八岁童女受六法。二者夫家十岁得受六法。若[24]欲受具足戒应二部僧中。[25]用五衣鉢[26]盂。比丘尼。为和上及教师。比丘为戒师。馀如受戒法。略说则五[27]百戒。广说则八万戒。第三[28]羯磨讫。即得无量律仪。成就比丘尼。比丘则有三衣鉢[*]盂。三师十僧如受戒法。略说二百五十。广说则八万。第三羯磨[29]讫。即得无量律仪法。是总名为戒。是为尸罗。

大智度论卷第十三。

简体字

是式叉摩那有二種。一者十八歲童女受六法。二者夫家十歲得受六法。若[24]欲受具足戒應二部僧中。[25]用五衣鉢[26]盂。比丘尼。為和上及教師。比丘為戒師。餘如受戒法。略說則五[27]百戒。廣說則八萬戒。第三[28]羯磨訖。即得無量律儀。成就比丘尼。比丘則有三衣鉢[*]盂。三師十僧如受戒法。略說二百五十。廣說則八萬。第三羯磨[29]訖。即得無量律儀法。是總名為戒。是為尸羅。

大智度論卷第十三。

正體字

b) Two Subcategories of Śikṣamāṇā

This *śikṣamāṇā* category is of two types: The first is the eighteen-year-old virgin girl who has taken on six dharmas. The second is a woman who has been with the husband's family for a period of ten years but who is then able to take on the discipline of six dharmas.

2) The Bhikshuni Ordination

When she wishes to take the complete precepts, she should do so in the midst of the two divisions of the Sangha, wearing the five-stripe robe and carrying the bowl. Bhikshunis serve as the *upādhyāya* and as the teacher providing instruction. A bhikshu serves as the precept master.

The rest corresponds to the standard protocol for receiving the precepts. Generally speaking, this involves five hundred precepts. Extensively speaking, there are eighty thousand precepts. At the conclusion of the third *karmavācanā*, one then accesses an incalculable number of moral regulations in becoming a bhikshuni.

3) The Bhikshu Ordination

In the case of the bhikshu, there are three robes and a bowl. There are three masters along with an additional ten members of the Sangha, this in accordance with the standard protocol for receiving the precepts. [For the bhikshu], generally speaking, there are two hundred and fifty precepts. To speak of it in extensive terms, there are eighty thousand. At the conclusion of the third *karmavācanā*, one then accesses an incalculable number of moral regulation dharmas.

B. Conclusion of Precept Details Discussion

This has been a general presentation of what constitutes the moral precepts. These comprise [the bases] of what is intended by "*śīla*" (moral virtue).

大智度论释初品中尸罗波罗蜜[1]义之馀（卷第十四）。

[*]龙树菩萨造。

[*]后秦龟兹国三藏鸠摩罗什[*]奉诏译。

[162a08] 问曰。已知尸罗相。云何为尸罗波罗蜜。答曰。有人言。菩萨持戒宁自失身不毁小戒。是为尸罗波罗蜜。如[2]上苏陀苏摩王经中说。不惜身命以[3]全禁戒。如菩萨本身曾作大力毒龙。若众生在前。身力弱者眼视便死。身力强者气[4]往而死。是龙受一日戒。出家求静入林树间。思惟坐久疲懈而睡。龙法睡时形状如蛇。身有文章七宝杂色。猎者见之惊喜言曰。以此希有难得之皮。献上国王以为[5]服饰不亦宜乎。便以杖[6]按其头以刀剥其皮。龙自念言。我力如意。倾覆此国其如反掌。此人小物岂能困我。我今以持戒故不计

简体字

Chapter 23, Part 2: The Perfection of Moral Virtue[31]

III. An Extended Discussion of the Perfection of Moral Virtue
  A. Definition of the Perfection of Moral Virtue

Question: Now that we have already become aware of the specific aspects involved in "*śīla*" itself, what is it then that constitutes "*śīla pāramitā*" (the perfection of moral virtue)?

  1. Indifference to Sacrificing One's Life in Upholding Precepts

Response: There are those who say that when the bodhisattva upholds the precepts and would rather lose his physical life than damage minor precepts, it is this which constitutes *śīla* pāramitā. As described in the previously-cited *Sutra of King Sutasoma*, one does not spare even one's own physical life in order to preserve the integrity of the restrictive precepts.

  2. Buddha's Past Life as a Dragon (Illustrative Story)

For example, in a former life, the Bodhisattva was a greatly powerful poisonous dragon. Whenever any being came to stand before him, in the case of those who were physically weak, if he so much as gazed upon them, they would die on the spot. As for those who were physically strong, if he breathed on them, they would die.

This dragon had taken the one-day precepts. He left his dwelling seeking quietude and had gone into the forest. He had been sitting in contemplation for a long time, became tired and lax, and then had fallen asleep. It is the way of dragons that when they fall asleep their bodies become in appearance like a snake. His body had patterns on it which were composed of the various colors of the seven precious things.

It so happened that some hunters noticed him and, both startled and delighted, said, "Wouldn't it be appropriate to take this skin, so rare and difficult to come by, and offer it up to the King as an adornment for his robes?" They then held its head down with a staff and used a knife to strip away its skin.

The dragon thought to himself, "My strength is such that, were I only to wish it, turning this entire country upside down would be as easy as turning over one's hand. These people are but little creatures. How could they be able to put me in difficult straits? Because I am now upholding the precepts, I shall relinquish all regard for

此身当从佛语。于是自忍[7]眠目不视。闭气不息怜愍此人。为持戒故一心受剥不生悔意。既以失皮赤肉在地。时日大热宛转土中欲趣大水。见诸小虫来食其身。为持戒故不复敢动。自思惟言。今我此身以施诸虫。为佛道故今以肉施以充其身。后成佛时当以法施以益其心。如是誓已身乾命[8]绝。即生第二忉利天上。尔时毒龙释迦文佛是。[9]是时猎者提婆达等六师是也。诸小虫辈。释迦文佛初转法轮八万诸天得道者是。菩萨护戒不惜身命。决定不悔。其事如是。是名尸罗波罗蜜。复次菩萨持戒。为佛道故作大要誓。必度众生不求今世后世之乐。不为名闻[10]虚誉法故。亦不自为早求涅盘。但为众生没在长流。恩爱所欺愚惑所误。我当度之令到彼岸。

简体字

此身當從佛語。於是自忍[7]眠目不視。閉氣不息憐愍此人。為持戒故一心受剝不生悔意。既以失皮赤肉在地。時日大熱宛轉土中欲趣大水。見諸小蟲來食其身。為持戒故不復敢動。自思惟言。今我此身以施諸蟲。為佛道故今以肉施以充其身。後成佛時當以法施以益其心。如是誓已身乾命[8]絕。即生第二忉利天上。爾時毒龍釋迦文佛是。[9]是時獵者提婆達等六師是也。諸小蟲輩。釋迦文佛初轉法輪八萬諸天得道者是。菩薩護戒不惜身命。決定不悔。其事如是。是名尸羅波羅蜜。復次菩薩持戒。為佛道故作大要誓。必度眾生不求今世後世之樂。不為名聞[10]虛譽法故。亦不自為早求涅槃。但為眾生沒在長流。恩愛所欺愚惑所誤。我當度之令到彼岸。

正體字

this body. I should just follow along with the instructions of the Buddha."

And so he remained patient while this was going on, kept his eyes closed, and refrained from gazing upon them. He held his breath and, out of pity for these men, kept himself from breathing on them. For the sake of upholding the precepts, he single-mindedly endured the peeling away of his skin, and did not develop any thoughts of regret.

Then, having lost his skin, his bare flesh rested directly on the ground. It was in a season where the sun was very hot. He slithered along through the dirt desiring to make his way to a large body of water. He then observed all of the little insects which came to eat his body. At that point, for the sake of upholding the precepts, he did not dare to move any more.

He thought to himself, "Now I'll just donate my body to the insects. For the sake of the Buddha Path, I will now make a gift of this flesh so that their bodies may become full. Later, when I have achieved buddhahood, I will resort to the giving of Dharma to benefit their minds."

Having made this vow, his body dried up and his life was cut off. He was then born in the second level of the Trāyastriṃśa heavens. That poisonous dragon was a former incarnation of Shakyamuni Buddha. In the present era, those hunters manifest as Devadatta and the six [non-buddhist] masters. The little insects were the eighty-thousand gods who gained the Path when Shakyamuni Buddha first turned the wheel of Dharma.

B. More Defining Characteristics of Śīla Pāramitā

The bodhisattva guards the precepts not sparing even his own physical life in doing so. He is decisive in this and has no regrets. When his endeavors are of this sort, this constitutes śīla pāramitā.

Then again, as he observes the precepts, the bodhisattva makes a great vow for the sake of the Buddha Path: "I will certainly bring beings across to liberation, will not seek the pleasures of this or later lives, will not do it for the sake of fame or the dharmas of an empty reputation, and will not do it for the sake of seeking an early nirvāṇa for myself. I will do it solely for the sake of beings who are submerged in the long-continuing flow [of the river of cyclic existence], who are cheated by their affections, and who are deceived by their own delusion. I will bring them across to liberation, causing them to reach the other shore."

一心持戒为生善处。生善处故见善人。见善人故生[11]智慧。生[*]智慧故得行六波罗蜜。[12]得行六波罗蜜故得佛道。如是持戒名为尸罗波罗蜜。复次菩萨持戒心乐善清净。不为畏恶道。亦不为生天。但求善[13]净以戒[14]熏心令心乐善。是为尸罗波罗蜜。复次菩萨以大悲心持戒得[15]至佛道。是名尸罗波罗蜜。复次菩萨持戒。能生六波罗蜜。是则名为尸罗波罗蜜。云何持戒能生戒。因五戒得沙弥戒。因沙弥戒得[16]律仪戒。因[*]律仪戒得禅定戒因禅定戒得无漏戒。是为戒生戒。云何持戒能生于檀。檀有三种。一者财施。二者法施。三者无畏施。

简体字

一心持戒為生善處。生善處故見善人。見善人故生[11]智慧。生[*]智慧故得行六波羅蜜。[12]得行六波羅蜜故得佛道。如是持戒名為尸羅波羅蜜。復次菩薩持戒心樂善清淨。不為畏惡道。亦不為生天。但求善[13]淨以戒[14]熏心令心樂善。是為尸羅波羅蜜。復次菩薩以大悲心持戒得[15]至佛道。是名尸羅波羅蜜。復次菩薩持戒。能生六波羅蜜。是則名為尸羅波羅蜜。云何持戒能生戒。因五戒得沙彌戒。因沙彌戒得[16]律儀戒。因[*]律儀戒得禪定戒因禪定戒得無漏戒。是為戒生戒。云何持戒能生於檀。檀有三種。一者財施。二者法施。三者無畏施。

正體字

He is single-mindedly in observance of the moral precepts and is consequently reborn in a good place. Through rebirth in a good place, he meets good people. Through meeting good people, he develops wisdom. By developing wisdom, he succeeds in practicing the six pāramitās. Because he succeeds in practicing the six pāramitās, he gains realization of the Buddha Path. When one upholds the moral precepts in this manner, it is this which constitutes *śīla* pāramitā.

Moreover, in the bodhisattva's observance of the moral precepts, it is done with a mind which finds happiness in goodness and purity. It is not motivated by fear of the wretched destinies nor is it motivated by a desire to be reborn in the heavens. He seeks only to embody goodness and purity. It is through the mind's being imbued with the moral precepts that it is caused to take pleasure in goodness. It is this which constitutes *śīla* pāramitā.

Moreover, in the bodhisattva's observance of the moral precepts, he employs the mind of great compassion and thus succeeds in arriving at the Buddha Path. It is this which constitutes *śīla* pāramitā.

1. How Śīla Generates All Six Perfections

Furthermore, in his upholding of the precepts, the bodhisattva is able to generate all six of the pāramitās. It is this then which qualifies as "*śīla* pāramitā."

2. Śīla's Generation of Śīla Pāramitā

How is it that observing the moral precepts is itself able to generate [perfection in] the practice of the moral precepts? It is on account of the five precepts that one gets the *śrāmaṇera* (novice) precepts. It is on account of the *śrāmaṇera* precepts that one accesses the [complete] moral regulation precepts. It is on account of those moral regulation precepts that one gains the moral precept observance associated with dhyāna absorption. It is on account of the moral precept observance associated with dhyāna absorption that one brings about that level of moral precept observance which is entirely free of outflow impurities. This is the process by which the moral precepts themselves generate [perfection in] the practice of the moral precepts.

3. Śīla's Generation of Dāna Pāramitā
a. The Three Types of Giving

How does upholding the precepts engender *dāna*? There are three kinds of *dāna*: The first kind involves the giving of material wealth. The second kind is the giving of Dharma. The third kind is the giving of fearlessness.

持戒自捡不侵一切众生财物。是[17]名财施。众生见者慕其所行。又为说法令其开悟。又自思惟。我当坚持净戒。与一切众生作供养福田。令诸众生得无量福。如是种种名为法施。一切众生皆畏于死。持戒不害。是则无畏施。复次菩萨自念。我当持戒以此戒报。为诸众生作转轮圣王。或作阎浮提王。若作天王令诸众生。满足于财无所乏短。然后坐佛树下。降伏魔王破诸魔军。成无上道。为诸众生说清净法。令无量众生度老病死海。是为持戒因缘生檀波罗蜜。云何持戒生忍辱。持戒之人心自念言。我今持戒为[18]持心故。若持戒无忍当堕地狱。虽不破戒以无忍故不免恶道。

持戒自撿不侵一切眾生財物。是[17]名財施。眾生見者慕其所行。又為說法令其開悟。又自思惟。我當堅持淨戒。與一切眾生作供養福田。令諸眾生得無量福。如是種種名為法施。一切眾生皆畏於死。持戒不害。是則無畏施。復次菩薩自念。我當持戒以此戒報。為諸眾生作轉輪聖王。或作閻浮提王。若作天王令諸眾生。滿足於財無所乏短。然後坐佛樹下。降伏魔王破諸魔軍。成無上道。為諸眾生說清淨法。令無量眾生度老病死海。是為持戒因緣生檀波羅蜜。云何持戒生忍辱。持戒之人心自念言。我今持戒為[18]持心故。若持戒無忍當墮地獄。雖不破戒以無忍故不免惡道。

1) THE GIVING OF WEALTH

When one observes the moral precepts, one is frugal oneself while also refraining from encroaching on the material wealth of any other being. This itself amounts to the giving of wealth.

2) THE GIVING OF DHARMA

When beings witness this [practice of observing the moral precepts], they respond with an admiring emulation of his actions. He then additionally speaks Dharma for them, thus causing them to awaken. He then reflects: "I should be firm in adhering to the precepts of moral purity, thereby providing for all beings a field of karmic blessings for the offerings they make." He consequently causes beings to gain countless karmic blessings. All sorts of instances such as these qualify as the giving of Dharma.

3) THE GIVING OF FEARLESSNESS

All beings fear death. When one upholds the precepts, one refrains from bringing any harm to them. This in itself amounts to the giving of fearlessness.

b. THE ALTRUISTIC VOW OF THE BODHISATTVA

Moreover, the bodhisattva thinks to himself, "I shall uphold the precepts and, for the sake of all beings, shall employ the karmic reward from these precepts to become a wheel-turning sage king or perhaps a king of Jambudvīpa. In the event that I become a king among the the gods, then I will cause all beings to be amply supplied with wealth and to have nothing in which they are wanting.

"Later on, I will sit beneath the bodhi tree, vanquish the demon king, destroy the demon armies, perfect the unsurpassed Path, and speak the pure Dharma for the sake of all beings, thus causing an incalculable number of beings to cross beyond the sea of aging, sickness, and death."

These instances demonstrate how the causal factors associated with upholding the precepts bring forth *dāna* pāramitā.

4. ŚĪLA'S GENERATION OF KṢĀNTI PĀRAMITĀ
a. THE PRECEPTS' DEPENDENCE ON ESTABLISHING PATIENCE

How is it that observing the moral precepts engenders patience? A person who upholds the precepts reflects to himself: "I now uphold the precepts for the sake of maintaining my own mind. If I fail to maintain patience in my observance of the precepts, then I am bound to fall into the hells. Although I may not have actually broken any of the moral precepts, due to failing to maintain patience, I will still have failed to avoid the wretched destinies.

何可纵恣不自制心。但以心
故入三恶趣。是故应当好自
勉强懃修忍辱。复次行者欲
令戒德坚强。当修忍辱。所
以者何。忍为大力。能牢固
戒令不动摇。复自思惟。我
今出家形与俗别。岂可纵心
如世人法。宜自勉励以忍调
心以身口忍心亦得忍。若心
不忍身口亦尔。是故行者当
令身口心忍绝诸忿恨。复次
是戒略说则有八万。广说则
无量。我当云何能具持此无
量戒法。唯当忍辱众戒自
得。譬如有人得罪于王。王
以罪人载之刀车。六边利刃
[19]间不容间。奔逸驰[20]走
行不择路。若能持身不为刀
伤。是则杀而不死。持戒之
人亦复如是。戒为利刀忍为
持身。若忍心不固戒亦伤
人。

何可縱恣不自制心。但以心
故入三惡趣。是故應當好自
勉強懃修忍辱。復次行者欲
令戒德堅強。當修忍辱。所
以者何。忍為大力。能牢固
戒令不動搖。復自思惟。我
今出家形與俗別。豈可縱心
如世人法。宜自勉勵以忍調
心以身口忍心亦得忍。若心
不忍身口亦爾。是故行者當
令身口心忍絕諸忿恨。復次
是戒略說則有八萬。廣說則
無量。我當云何能具持此無
量戒法。唯當忍辱眾戒自
得。譬如有人得罪於王。王
以罪人載之刀車。六邊利刃
[19]間不容間。奔逸馳[20]走
行不擇路。若能持身不為刀
傷。是則殺而不死。持戒之
人亦復如是。戒為利刀忍為
持身。若忍心不固戒亦傷
人。

简体字   正體字

"This being the case, how could I give free rein to anger and thus fail to control my own mind? It is solely on account of the mind that one enters into the three wretched destinies. I should therefore be skillful in strictly restraining myself while diligently cultivating patience."

Moreover, the practitioner who desires the virtue of his precept practice to be solid and strong should cultivate patience. Why? Patience constitutes a great power which is able to strengthen the precepts and cause one to remain unmoved and unshaken.

One additionally reflects to himself: "Now that I have left the home life, I have taken on a different mode from that of the common person. How then could I give free rein to the mind after the manner typical of worldly people?"

It is appropriate that one encourage oneself to employ patience to train the mind. It is through patience of body and mouth that the mind also succeeds in becoming patient. Again, if the mind itself fails to maintain patience, the body and mouth become just the same. Therefore, the practitioner should influence his body, mouth, and mind to maintain patience, thus severing all instances of anger and enmity.

Furthermore, briefly described, these moral precepts number eighty thousand. If one discusses them extensively, then they are found to be incalculably numerous. One might think: "How could I possibly succeed in perfectly observing these innumerable precept dharmas?" One need only exercise patience. As a consequence, all of the many precepts are naturally brought to realization.

b.   THE EXECUTION WAGON ANALOGY

This is analogous to a circumstance where a man has committed an offense in his relations with the King and the King has consequently ordered that miscreant placed in a wagon of knives where in he is surrounded on all six sides by sharp blades with no intervening space between himself and the blades. The wagon is then turned loose at a fast gallop, racing along aimlessly through the streets. If he is able to control his body and thus avoid being harmed by the knives, this would be a case of being slain yet still not dying. A person who upholds the precepts is just like this. The precepts are like the sharp knives. Patience is analogous to the controlling of the body. If one's mind of patience fails in its solidity, then the precepts themselves may injure a person.

又复譬如老人夜行无杖则[21]
蹶。忍为戒杖扶人至道。福
乐因缘不能动摇。如是种
种。名为持戒生羼提波罗
蜜。云何持戒而生精进。持
戒之人除去放逸。自力懃修
习无上法。舍世间乐入于善
道。志求涅盘以度一切。大
心不懈以求佛为本。是为持
戒能生精进。复次持戒之人
疲厌世苦老病死患。心生精
进必[22]求自脱。亦以度人。
譬如野干在林树间。依随师
子及诸虎豹。求其残肉以自
存活。[23]有时空乏夜半逾城
深入人舍。求肉不得[24]屏
处睡息不觉夜竟惶怖无计。
走则虑不自免。住则惧畏死
痛。便

简体字

又復譬如老人夜行無杖則[21]
蹶。忍為戒杖扶人至道。
福樂因緣不能動搖。如是
種種。名為持戒生羼提波羅
蜜。云何持戒而生精進。持
戒之人除去放逸。自力懃修
習無上法。捨世間樂入於善
道。志求涅槃以度一切。大
心不懈以求佛為本。是為持
戒能生精進。復次持戒之人
疲厭世苦老病死患。心生精
進必[22]求自脫。亦以度人。
譬如野干在林樹間。依隨師
子及諸虎豹。求其殘肉以自
存活。[23]有時空乏夜半踰城
深入人舍。求肉不得[24]屏
處睡息不覺夜竟惶怖無計。
走則慮不自免。住則懼畏死
痛。便

正體字

c. THE WALKING STICK ANALOGY

This is also analogous to an elderly person who might be prone to fall down if he walks along at night without the aid of a walking stick. Patience serves as a "walking stick" for in one's practice of observing the moral precepts. It supports a person in successfully arriving at realization of the Path. It insures that circumstances produced by merit-generated bliss remain unable to shake him [from his observance of the precepts].

All sorts of instances such as these demonstrate how upholding the moral precepts generates *kṣānti* pāramitā.

5. ŚĪLA'S GENERATION OF VĪRYA PĀRAMITĀ

a. ŚĪLA'S EXPULSION OF NEGLIGENCE

How is it that one may engender vigor through observing the moral precepts? The person who upholds the precepts gets rid of negligence (*pramāda*). Through one's own power, one earnestly cultivates the unsurpassed Dharma. One relinquishes the pleasures of the world and enters into the path of goodness. One resolves to seek nirvāṇa for the sake of all. One possesses a great mind, refrains from laziness, and takes striving for buddhahood as one's fundamental priority. This is how observing the moral precepts is able to bring forth vigor.

b. ŚĪLA'S ENGENDERING OF RENUNCIATION

Moreover, the person who observes the moral precepts becomes weary and abhorrent of the sufferings of the world and the calamities of aging, sickness, and death. His mind generates vigor and the resolve that he will certainly seek his own liberation while also bringing about the deliverance of others.

c. A COYOTE MAKES HIS ESCAPE (ILLUSTRATIVE STORY)

This is analogous to the case of the coyote who lived in the forest depending for his survival on following along after lions, tigers and leopards, scavenging the leftover carcasses of their prey. There happened to be a period of time when there was a shortage of available food for him. This led him to slip into the city in the middle of the night, making his way deep into a man's household. He was seeking for some meat but failed to find any.

He happened to fall asleep in a screened-off spot and, unaware that the night had already ended, awoke, startled, frightened, and at a loss for what to do. If he tried to run out, he figured he would be unable to save himself, but if he remained, he feared he would fall victim to the pain of being killed. Consequently, he then just

自定心诈死在地众人来见有
一人言。我须野干耳即便截
取。野干自念。截耳虽痛但
令身在。次有一人言。我须
野干尾便复截去。野干复
念。截尾虽痛犹是小事。次
有一人言。我须野[1]干牙。
野干心念。取者转多傥取我
头则无活路。即从地起奋
其智力。绝踊[2]间關径得自
济。行者之心求脱苦难亦复
如是。若老至时犹故自宽。
不能慇懃决断精进。病亦如
是。以有[3]差期未能决计。
死欲至时自知无冀。便能自
勉果敢慇懃大修精进。从死
地中[4]毕至涅盘。复次持戒
之法。譬如人射。先得平地
地平然后心安。心安然后挽
满。挽满然后陷深。戒为平
地定意为弓。挽满为精进箭
为智慧。贼是无明。

自定心詐死在地眾人來見有
一人言。我須野干耳即便截
取。野干自念。截耳雖痛但
令身在。次有一人言。我須
野干尾便復截去。野干復
念。截尾雖痛猶是小事。次
有一人言。我須野[1]干牙。
野干心念。取者轉多儻取我
頭則無活路。即從地起奮
其智力。絕踊[2]間關徑得自
濟。行者之心求脫苦難亦復
如是。若老至時猶故自寬。
不能慇懃決斷精進。病亦如
是。以有[3]差期未能決計。
死欲至時自知無冀。便能自
勉果敢慇懃大修精進。從死
地中[4]畢至涅槃。復次持戒
之法。譬如人射。先得平地
地平然後心安。心安然後挽
滿。挽滿然後陷深。戒為平
地定意為弓。挽滿為精進箭
為智慧。賊是無明。

简体字   正體字

fixed his mind on just laying there on the ground, pretending that he was dead.

Many people came to see this. There was one man who said, "I have need of the ears of a coyote." He then cut them off and took them away.

The coyote thought to himself, "Although it hurts to have one's ears cut off, still, the body is allowed to survive."

Next, there was a man who said, "I have need of the tail of a coyote." He then cut that off as well and departed.

The coyote next thought, "Although it hurts to have one's tail cut off, still, it's a relatively minor matter."

Next, there was a man who said, "I need a coyote's teeth."

The coyote thought, "The scavengers are becoming more numerous. Suppose they were to take my head. Were they to do that, I would have no way to survive." He then sprang up from the ground and, arousing the strength of his own intelligence, suddenly bolted for a narrow exit, thus immediately saving himself.

d. The Mind's Self-Exhortation to Action

In seeking liberation from the trials of suffering, the mind of the practitioner is just like this. When old age arrives, he may still find reason to forgive himself and may still be unable to be diligent, earnest, and decisive in the application of vigor. It may be just the same when encountering sickness. Because there is still hope for a cure, he may still be unable to be resolute in carrying out his strategy.

But when death is about to arrive, he realizes that there is no further hope. He is able to dare to be decisive and diligent in devoting himself mightily to the cultivation of vigor. Then, escaping from the spot where death is upon him, he finally succeeds in reaching nirvāṇa.

e. The Archery Analogy

Moreover, the dharma of observing the moral precepts is analogous to archery wherein a person first finds a level spot of ground. Having found level ground, one then stabilizes the mind. After the mind has become stable, one draws back the bow completely. When one has drawn it back completely, the arrow then plunges deeply into the target. The precepts are analogous to level ground. The decisive mind is comparable to the bow. Drawing it back completely corresponds to vigor. The arrow is comparable to wisdom and the insurgent adversaries are analogous to ignorance.

If one is able to bring forth one's strength and be vigorous in this

若能如是展力精进。必至大
道以度众生。复次持戒之人
能以精进自制五情不受五
欲。若心已去能摄令还。是
为[5]持戒能护诸根。护诸根
则生禅定。生禅定则生智
慧。生智慧得至佛道。是为
持戒生毘梨耶波罗蜜。云何
持戒生禅。人有三业作[6]诸
善。若身口业善。意业自然
入善。譬如曲草生于麻中不
扶自直。持戒之力能赢诸结
使。云何能赢。若不持戒。
瞋恚事来杀心即生。若欲事
至婬心即成。若持戒者虽有
微瞋不生杀心。虽有婬念婬
事不成。是为持戒能令诸结
使赢。诸结使赢禅定易得。

若能如是展力精進。必至大
道以度眾生。復次持戒之人
能以精進自制五情不受五
欲。若心已去能攝令還。是
為[5]持戒能護諸根。護諸根
則生禪定。生禪定則生智
慧。生智慧得至佛道。是為
持戒生毘梨耶波羅蜜。云何
持戒生禪。人有三業作[6]諸
善。若身口業善。意業自然
入善。譬如曲草生於麻中不
扶自直。持戒之力能贏諸結
使。云何能贏。若不持戒。
瞋恚事來殺心即生。若欲事
至婬心即成。若持戒者雖有
微瞋不生殺心。雖有婬念婬
事不成。是為持戒能令諸結
使贏。諸結使贏禪定易得。

简体字　　　　　　　　　　　　　　　正體字

fashion, he will certainly arrive at realization of the great Path and will thereby bring beings across to liberation.

f. Śīla's Natural Promotion of Diligent Self-control

Then again, the person who upholds the precepts is able to employ vigor to self-regulate his own five sense faculties. He does not indulge in pursuit of the five types of desire. If his mind has already gone off course, he is able to draw it back and cause it to return. This is a case of observing the moral precepts being able to bring about a guarding of the sense faculties. If one guards the sense faculties, then one develops dhyāna absorption. If one develops dhyāna absorption, then one develops wisdom. If one develops wisdom, then one succeeds in arriving at realization of the Buddha Path.

These are circumstances wherein upholding the moral precepts brings forth *vīrya* pāramitā.

6. Śīla's Generation of Dhyāna Pāramitā

a. Rectification of Mind Through Physical and Verbal Goodness

How is it that upholding the precepts brings forth dhyāna? People possess the three karmic actions whereby they may do what is good. If the actions of the body and mouth are good, then the actions of the mind naturally enter into goodness.

b. The Grass-in-Sesame Analogy

This is analogous to normally crooked grasses which are caused to grow vertically when in the midst of sesame plants. Thus, even without being propped up, they naturally grow straight in such circumstances.

c. The Fetter-Diminishing Effect of the Precepts

The power of observing the moral precepts is able to cause the fetters to waste away. How is this able to cause such wasting away? If one fails to observe the moral precepts, when a matter comes along which provokes rage, the intention to kill may immediately arise. If a situation arrives which conduces to lust, sensual thoughts are immediately conceived.

However, in the case of one who observes the moral precepts, although there may be slight anger, one refrains from bringing forth the intention to kill. Although there may be sensual thoughts, lustful activity is not indulged. This is how observing the moral precepts is able to cause the fetters to waste away. As the fetters waste away, dhyāna absorption is easily achieved.

d. The Invalid's-Fragility Analogy

譬如老病失力死事易得。[7]
结使羸故禅定易得。复次人
心未息常求[8]逸乐。行者持
戒弃舍世福心不放逸。是故
易得禅定。复次持戒之[9]人
得生人中。次生六欲天[10]
上。次至色界。[11]若破色相
生无色界。持戒清净。断诸
结使得阿罗汉道。大心持戒
愍念众生是为菩萨。复次戒
为捡麤禅为摄细。复次戒摄
身口。禅止乱心。如人上屋
非梯不升。不得戒梯禅亦不
立。复次破戒之人。结使风
强散乱其心。其心散乱则禅
不可得。持戒之人。烦恼风
软心不大散。禅定易得。如
是等种种因缘。是为持戒生
禅波罗蜜。

譬如老病失力死事易得。[7]
結使羸故禪定易得。復次人
心未息常求[8]逸樂。行者持
戒棄捨世福心不放逸。是故
易得禪定。復次持戒之[9]人
得生人中。次生六欲天[10]
上。次至色界。[11]若破色相
生無色界。持戒清淨。斷諸
結使得阿羅漢道。大心持戒
愍念眾生是為菩薩。復次戒
為撿麤禪為攝細。復次戒攝
身口。禪止亂心。如人上屋
非梯不昇。不得戒梯禪亦不
立。復次破戒之人。結使風
強散亂其心。其心散亂則禪
不可得。持戒之人。煩惱風
軟心不大散。禪定易得。如
是等種種因緣。是為持戒生
禪波羅蜜。

简体字   正體字

This is analogous to when someone has become aged and sick to the point where he has lost his typical vitality. In such a case, complete demise comes easily. Similarly, in a case where the fetters have wasted away, dhyāna absorption is easily established.

e.   THE CLARITY-PROMOTING EFFECTS OF MORAL RESTRAINT

Moreover, when a person's thoughts have not yet been put to rest, he tends to constantly seek unrestrained indulgence in pleasures. However, when the practitioner observes the moral precepts, he renounces worldly karmic blessings. His mind refrains from falling into negligence. As a consequence, it becomes easy for him to succeed in developing dhyāna absorption.

f.   ŚĪLA'S PRODUCTION OF HIGHER REBIRTH AND PATH ACQUISITION

Also, the person who observes the moral precepts succeeds thereby in being reborn among humans. Next, he is reborn in the six desire heavens. Thereafter, he reaches the form realm. If he is then able to break through the characteristic aspects of form, he is able to be reborn in the formless realm. If he remains pure in his observance of the moral precepts, he cuts off the fetters and gains the path of arhatship. If he upholds the precepts with the great mind while maintaining sympathetic regard for beings, this is a bodhisattva.

g.   THE COOPERATIVE LINK BETWEEN PRECEPTS AND DHYĀNA

Additionally, the precepts involve restraint with regard to what is coarse. Dhyāna involves focusing on the subtle. Also, the moral precepts restrain the body and the mouth. Dhyāna brings stillness to the scattered mind.

1)   THE PRECEPTS-AS-STAIRS ANALOGY

This process is analogous to moving higher in a building. If there were no stairs, one would be unable to ascend. If one fails to gain the stairs of the precepts, dhyāna absorption cannot be established either.

2)   THE FETTER-INDUCED MENTAL WIND ANALOGY

Then again, in a person who breaks the precepts, the wind of the fetters is strong and so it scatters and confuses his mind. If his mind is scattered and confused, then dhyāna cannot be realized. In the case of a person who upholds the moral precepts, the wind of the fetters is weak and so his mind is not much scattered by it. Thus, for him, dhyāna absorption is easily gained.

All sorts of causal circumstances such as these illustrate how observing the moral precepts generates dhyāna pāramitā.

云何持戒能生智慧。持戒之人观此戒相从何而有。知从众罪而生。若无[12]众罪。则亦无戒。戒相如是。从因缘有。何故生着。譬如莲华出自[13]污泥。色虽鲜好出处不净。以是悟心不令生着。是为持戒生般若波罗蜜。复次持戒之人心自思惟。若我以持戒贵而可取。破戒贱而可舍[14]者。若有此心不应般若。以智[15]慧筹量心不着戒无取无舍。是为持戒生般若波罗蜜。复次不持戒人虽有利智以营世务。种种欲求生业之事。慧根渐钝。譬如利刀以割泥土遂成钝器。若出家持戒不营世业。常观诸法实相无

云何持戒能生智慧。持戒之人觀此戒相從何而有。知從眾罪而生。若無[12]眾罪。則亦無戒。戒相如是。從因緣有。何故生著。譬如蓮華出自[13]污泥。色雖鮮好出處不淨。以是悟心不令生著。是為持戒生般若波羅蜜。復次持戒之人心自思惟。若我以持戒貴而可取。破戒賤而可捨[14]者。若有此心不應般若。以智[15]慧籌量心不著戒無取無捨。是為持戒生般若波羅蜜。復次不持戒人雖有利智以營世務。種種欲求生業之事。慧根漸鈍。譬如利刀以割泥土遂成鈍器。若出家持戒不營世業。常觀諸法實相無

简体字

正體字

7. Śīla's Generation of *Prajñāpāramitā*

a. A Wisdom Generating Contemplation of Precepts

How is it that upholding the moral precepts is able to bring forth wisdom? The person who observes the precepts contemplates the origins of the specific aspects of the moral precepts. He realizes that they originate with the numerous sorts of karmic offenses which have been committed. If none of those numerous karmic offenses been committed in the first place, then there would not be any moral precepts, either. Since the specific aspects of the moral precepts exist in this manner—on the basis of causes and conditions—how could one generate any attachment them?

b. The Lotus-from-Mud Analogy

In this sense, the moral precepts are comparable to lotus blossoms growing forth from grime-ridden mud. Although their form is fresh and fine, the place from which they arise is impure. If one awakens one's mind in this fashion, then one does not allow it to develop attachments. This is an instance of the upholding of precepts bringing forth *prajñāpāramitā*.

c. Making Precept Practice Reflect Prajñā

Additionally, one who observes the moral precepts should reflect, "Were I to regard upholding precepts as noble and therefore a justification for grasping while regarding breaking precepts as base and therefore as a justification for rejection, such thought would not correspond to prajñā. This is because, when one relies on wisdom as the basis of one's analyses, one's mind refrains from seizing on the moral precepts and one remains free of either grasping or rejection." This [reflection] is an instance wherein upholding the precepts serves as the basis for generating *prajñāpāramitā*.

d. The Keen Mind, Lacking Precepts, Becomes Dull

What's more, even though one who fails to uphold the precepts may possess keen intelligence, because all manner of endeavors associated with managing worldly responsibilities involve creating karma through one's striving, the faculty of intelligence gradually grows dull. This is analogous to using a sharp blade to cut mud. As a consequence, it eventually becomes a dull instrument.

e. The Dull Mind, Imbued with Precepts, Becomes Keen

If one leaves behind the home life, upholds the precepts, desists from engaging in worldly endeavors, and constantly contemplates in accordance with reality the true character of dharmas as devoid

相。先虽钝根以渐转利。如是等种种因缘。名为持戒生般若波罗蜜。[16]如是名为尸罗波罗蜜生六波罗蜜。复次菩萨持戒不以畏故。亦非愚痴非疑非[17]惑。亦不自为涅盘故。持戒但为一切众生故。为得佛道故。为得一切佛法故。如是相名为尸罗波罗蜜。复次若菩萨[18]于罪不罪不可得[19]故。是时名为尸罗波罗蜜。问曰。[20]若舍恶行善是为持戒。云何言罪不罪不可得。答曰。非[21]谓邪见麁心言不可得[22]也。若深入诸法相。行空三昧。慧眼观故罪不可得。罪无故不罪亦不可得。复次众生不可得故。杀罪亦不可得。罪不可得故戒亦不可得。何以故。以有杀罪故则有戒。若无杀罪则亦[23]无戒。

简体字

相。先雖鈍根以漸轉利。如是等種種因緣。名為持戒生般若波羅蜜。[16]如是名為尸羅波羅蜜生六波羅蜜。復次菩薩持戒不以畏故。亦非愚癡非疑非[17]惑。亦不自為涅槃故。持戒但為一切眾生故。為得佛道故。為得一切佛法故。如是相名為尸羅波羅蜜。復次若菩薩[18]於罪不罪不可得[19]故。是時名為尸羅波羅蜜。問曰。[20]若捨惡行善是為持戒。云何言罪不罪不可得。答曰。非[21]謂邪見麁心言不可得[22]也。若深入諸法相。行空三昧。慧眼觀故罪不可得。罪無故不罪亦不可得。復次眾生不可得故。殺罪亦不可得。罪不可得故戒亦不可得。何以故。以有殺罪故則有戒。若無殺罪則亦[23]無戒。

正體字

of any [inherently existent] characteristic, although one may have formerly had dull faculties, they gradually become ever sharper.

All sorts of causal circumstances similar to the above illustrate how upholding moral precepts engenders *prajñāpāramitā*. Causal circumstances of the sort cited previously illustrate how *śīla* pāramitā brings forth all six pāramitās.

8. CONCLUDING STATEMENT ON THE NATURE OF ŚĪLA PĀRAMITĀ

Additionally, the bodhisattva's upholding of the moral precepts is not done on account of fear, nor is it the case that it is done out of stupidity, or doubt, or delusion, or out of a private quest for his own nirvāṇa. The upholding of the moral precepts is carried out solely for the sake of all beings, for the sake of success in the Buddha Path, and for the sake of gaining all of the dharmas of buddhahood. Characteristic features of this sort demonstrate what is meant by *śīla* pāramitā.

C. UNFINDABILITY OF OFFENSE AND NON-OFFENSE

Then again, if the bodhisattva's practice is based in the unfindability of either offense or non-offense, it is at this time that it qualifies as *śīla* pāramitā.

1. OBJECTION: OFFENSE AND NON-OFFENSE DO EXIST

Question: If one is able to relinquish evil and practice goodness, it is this which constitutes the upholding of the precepts. How then can it be said that offense and non-offense cannot be found?

2. THE MEANING OF UNFINDABILITY OF OFFENSE AND NON-OFFENSE

Response: This is not referring to the concept of "unfindability" described by those of erroneous views and coarse minds. If one enters deeply into the characteristic aspects of all dharmas and courses in the samādhi of emptiness, because one employs the wisdom eye in one's contemplation, one discovers that offenses are not apprehensible. Because offenses themselves are [ultimately] nonexistent, non-offense cannot be found, either.[32]

a. THE LINK TO UNFINDABILITY OF BEINGS AND UNFINDABILITY OF PRECEPTS

Moreover, because beings themselves cannot be gotten at, the offense of killing cannot be gotten at, either. Because the offense itself cannot be gotten at, the corresponding moral precept cannot be gotten at, either. How is this? It is on account of the existence of the offense of killing that the corresponding moral precept exists. If there were [ultimately] no offense of killing, then there would [finally] be no corresponding moral precept, either.

问曰。今众生现有。云何言
众生不可得。答曰。肉眼所
见是为非见。若以慧眼观则
不得众生。如上檀中说。无
施者无受者。无财物此亦如
是。复次若有众生是五众耶
离五众耶。若是五众五众有
五众生为一。如是者五[24]
可为一一可为五。譬如市易
物。直五匹以一匹取之则不
可得。何以故。一[25]不得
作五故。以是故知五众[*]不
得作一众生。复次五众生灭
无常相众生法从先世来至后
世。受罪福于三界。若五众
是众生。譬如草木自生自
灭。如是则无罪缚亦无解
脱。以是故知非五众是众
生。若离五众有众生。如先
说神常遍中已破。

問曰。今眾生現有。云何言
眾生不可得。答曰。肉眼所
見是為非見。若以慧眼觀則
不得眾生。如上檀中說。無
施者無受者。無財物此亦如
是。復次若有眾生是五眾耶
離五眾耶。若是五眾五眾有
五眾生為一。如是者五[24]
可為一一可為五。譬如市易
物。直五匹以一匹取之則不
可得。何以故。一[25]不得
作五故。以是故知五眾[*]不
得作一眾生。復次五眾生滅
無常相眾生法從先世來至後
世。受罪福於三界。若五眾
是眾生。譬如草木自生自
滅。如是則無罪縛亦無解
脫。以是故知非五眾是眾
生。若離五眾有眾生。如先
說神常遍中已破。

简体字　　　　　　　正體字

b. OBJECTION: HOW CAN ONE CLAIM BEINGS DON'T EXIST?

Question: It is manifestly the case that "beings" *do* now exist. How can you claim that "beings" cannot be gotten at?

c. CLARIFICATION OF UNFINDABILITY OF BEINGS

Response: As for what is seen by the fleshly eye, this amounts to non-seeing. However, if one contemplates with the wisdom eye, then one does not find any "being." This is as explained above in the section on *dāna* pāramitā wherein it was stated that there is no donor, no recipient, and no material object offered as a gift.

1) REFUTATION: INCOMPATIBILITY OF SINGULARITY AND MULTIPLICITY

Additionally, if, as you claim, a being *does* exist, is it identical with the five aggregates, or does it exist apart from the five aggregates? If it is supposedly identical with the five aggregates, [one must confront the fact that] the five aggregates are fivefold, whereas a "being" is a singular entity. If what you assert were actually the case, then [this would amount to the absurd and untenable assertion that] "five" would somehow equal "one" and "one" would somehow equal "five."

To use the trading of goods in the market as an analogy, a person is unable to get something worth five currency units in exchange for only a single currency unit. Why? It is because "one" cannot equal "five." As a consequence, one must realize that the five-fold aggregates cannot constitute a singular being.

2) REFUTATION OF BEINGS: IMPOSSIBILITY OF KARMIC RETRIBUTION

Moreover, the five aggregates are characterized by the process of creation, destruction, and impermanence. It is the characteristic dharma of beings that they come forth from a former life and arrive at a later life and undergo karmic punishments and karmic blessings within the three realms. If the five aggregates make up a being, then they would be born naturally and die naturally after the manner of grass or trees. If this were actually the case, then there would be no being bound by offenses nor would there be any liberation to be gained. Based on this, one knows that it is not true that the five aggregates constitute a being.

3) REFUTATION OF NON-AGGREGATE BEINGS: ETERNALIST FALLACY

If one asserts the existence of a being distinct from the five aggregates, this is precisely what was already refuted in the prior discussion addressing the fallacy of a supposedly eternally existent and universally pervasive spiritual soul (*ātman*).

复次离五众则我见心不生。若离五众有众生。是为堕常。若堕常者是则无生无死。何以故。生名先无今[26]有。死名已生便灭。若众生常者。应遍[27]满五道中。先[28]已常有云何今复来生。若不有生则无有死。问曰。定有众生。何以故言无。五众因缘有众生法。譬如五指因缘[29]拳法生。答曰。此言非也。若五众因缘有众生法者。除五众则别有众生法然不可得。眼自见色耳自闻声鼻嗅香舌知味身知触意知法空无我法。离此六事更无众生。诸外道辈倒见故。言眼能见色是为众生。乃至意能知法是为众生。又能忆念能受苦乐是为众生。但作是见不知众生实。

復次離五眾則我見心不生。若離五眾有眾生。是為墮常。若墮常者是則無生無死。何以故。生名先無今[26]有。死名已生便滅。若眾生常者。應遍[27]滿五道中。先[28]已常有云何今復來生。若不有生則無有死。問曰。定有眾生。何以故言無。五眾因緣有眾生法。譬如五指因緣[29]拳法生。答曰。此言非也。若五眾因緣有眾生法者。除五眾則別有眾生法然不可得。眼自見色耳自聞聲鼻嗅香舌知味身知觸意知法空無我法。離此六事更無眾生。諸外道輩倒見故。言眼能見色是為眾生。乃至意能知法是為眾生。又能憶念能受苦樂是為眾生。但作是見不知眾生實。

简体字   正體字

Furthermore, if one asserts there exists such a being distinct from the five aggregates, then the thought imputing existence of a self therein would not even arise. If one asserts existence of a being apart from the five aggregates, one falls into an eternalist view.

If one falls into an eternalist view, then this entails the nonexistence of birth and the nonexistence of death. Why? Birth refers to something formerly nonexistent now coming into existence. Death refers to something already born then being extinguished. If it were the case that beings were eternally existent, then it ought to be the case that they exist everywhere filling up the five paths of rebirth.[33] If something already exists eternally, why would it then now come to birth yet again? And if it does not have a birth, then it has no death, either.

4) OBJECTION: AGGREGATE-BASED BEINGS ARE LIKE A FINGER-BASED FIST

Question: It is definitely the case that beings exist. How can one claim that they are nonexistent? It is based on the causes and conditions of the five aggregates that the dharma of a being exists. This is analogous to the case of the causes and conditions of the five fingers generating the dharma of a fist.

5) REFUTATION: ABSENCE OF ANY APPREHENSIBLE "BEING" DHARMA

Response: This statement is fallacious. If the dharma of a being exists among the causes and conditions associated with the five aggregates, then, aside from the five aggregates themselves, there exists some separate "being" dharma. However, no such thing can be found. The eye itself sees forms. The ear itself hears sounds. The nose smells fragrances. The tongue knows flavors. The body knows tangibles. The intellectual mind faculty knows dharmas as objects-of-mind. They are all empty and devoid of any dharma of a self. Apart from these six [sense-based] phenomena, there is no additional "being."

a) SYNOPSIS OF RELATED NON-BUDDHIST POSITIONS

Based on inverted views, non-Buddhists claim, "When the eye is able to see forms, this involves a being," and so forth until we come to, "When the mind is able to know dharmas, this involves a being." They also claim that, when one remembers and when one is able to undergo suffering and pleasure, these circumstances involve a being. However, they merely create this view. They do not actually possess any direct knowledge of any genuinely-existent entity associated with this "being" they posit.

譬如一长老大德比丘。人谓是阿罗汉多致供养。其后病死。诸弟子惧失供养故。夜盗出之。于其卧处安施被枕。令如师在其[1]状如卧。人来问疾师在何许。诸弟子言。汝不见床上被枕耶。愚者不审察之。谓师病卧大送供养而去。如是非一。复有智人来而问之。诸弟子亦如是答。智人言。我不问被枕床褥。我自求人发被求之竟无人可得。除六事相更无我人。知者见者亦复如是。复次若众生于五众因缘有者。五众无常众生亦[2]应无常。何以故。因果相似故。若众生无常则不[3]至后世。复次若如汝言。众生从本[*]已来常有。若尔者众生应生五众。五众不应生众生。今五众因缘生众生名字。无智之人逐名求实。

譬如一長老大德比丘。人謂是阿羅漢多致供養。其後病死。諸弟子懼失供養故。夜盜出之。於其臥處安施被枕。令如師在其[1]狀如臥。人來問疾師在何許。諸弟子言。汝不見床上被枕耶。愚者不審察之。謂師病臥大送供養而去。如是非一。復有智人來而問之。諸弟子亦如是答。智人言。我不問被枕床褥。我自求人發被求之竟無人可得。除六事相更無我人。知者見者亦復如是。復次若眾生於五眾因緣有者。五眾無常眾生亦[2]應無常。何以故。因果相似故。若眾生無常則不[3]至後世。復次若如汝言。眾生從本[*]已來常有。若爾者眾生應生五眾。五眾不應生眾生。今五眾因緣生眾生名字。無智之人逐名求實。

简体字　　　　　　　　正體字

b) A Deceased Guru Disguised (Illustrative Story)

This is analogous to the case of an old, senior, and very venerable bhikshu. People were of the opinion that he had become an arhat and so brought forth many offerings. Later on, he became ill and died. Because the disciples were alarmed that they would lose the offerings, they surreptitiously removed him during the night and in that place where he had been laying down, they arranged blankets and pillows, causing it to appear as if their master was still present, but merely lying down. People came and asked about his illness, inquiring "Where is the Master?"

The disciples replied, "Don't you see the blankets and pillows on the bed?" The gullible ones did not investigate into it. They believed this master was lying down there stricken with illness, went ahead and presented large offerings, and then left. This happened more than once.

Next, a wise man came along and asked after the Master. The disciples replied in the same way. That wise man then said, "I did not ask about blankets, pillows, beds, or cushions. I'm looking instead for a 'person.'" He then threw back the covers, looking for that master. In the end, there was no 'person' to be found there at all.

Apart from the characteristic features of the six [sense-based] phenomena, there is no additional "self" or "person" at all. As for a "knower" or a "perceiver," they are identical in this respect.

6) Refutation Based on Consequence of Beings' Impermanence

Moreover, if it were the case that a "being" existed somewhere in the causes and conditions of the five aggregates, since the five aggregates are impermanent, beings, too, ought to be impermanent. Why? This is on account of the similitude in the causes and conditions. If beings were impermanent, then it would be impossible for them to extend on to any subsequent lifetime.

7) Refutation Based on Later Arising of Aggregates

Furthermore, if it is as you say, then beings must have existed eternally from the very beginning on forward through time to the present. If that were so, then it should be that beings are what produce the five aggregates. It should not be the case that the five aggregates produce beings. Now, however, it is actually the causes and conditions associated with the five aggregates which give rise to the application of this name: "being." People who have no wisdom then proceed to chase after these names in search of what is real.

以是故众生实无。若无众生
亦无杀罪。无杀罪故亦无持
戒。复次是五众深入观之。
分别知空如梦所见如镜中
像。若杀梦中所见及镜中像
无有杀罪。杀五阴空相众生
亦复如是。复次若人不[4]乐
罪贪着无罪。是人见破戒罪
人则轻慢。见持戒善人则爱
敬。如是持戒则是起罪因
缘。以是故言于罪不罪不可
得故。应具足尸罗波罗蜜。

以是故眾生實無。若無眾生
亦無殺罪。無殺罪故亦無持
戒。復次是五眾深入觀之。
分別知空如夢所見如鏡中
像。若殺夢中所見及鏡中像
無有殺罪。殺五陰空相眾生
亦復如是。復次若人不[4]樂
罪貪著無罪。是人見破戒罪
人則輕慢。見持戒善人則愛
敬。如是持戒則是起罪因
緣。以是故言於罪不罪不可
得故。應具足尸羅波羅蜜。

简体字

正體字

3. Concluding Discussion of Unfindability and Its Import

For all of these reasons, beings are in fact nonexistent. If beings are nonexistent, then the karmic offense of killing is nonexistent as well. Because the karmic offense of killing is nonexistent, then the observance of moral precepts is also nonexistent.

Also, when one enters deeply into the contemplation of these five aggregates, one analyzes them and consequently realizes that they are empty of inherent existence, are like something seen in a dream, and are like images appearing in a mirror. If one kills something only seen in a dream or kills what is only an image in a mirror, then there is no karmic offense of "killing" which is actually committed. One merely engages in killing the empty marks of the five aggregates.[34] Beings, too, are [unfindable] in this same way.

Additionally, if a person is displeased by karmic offenses and thus is covetously attached to being free of karmic offenses, if he observes someone with karmic offenses which have arisen from breaking moral precepts, he will act in a slighting and arrogant manner. If he observes a good, precept-observing person, he will behave towards them in an affectionate and respectful fashion. If one's upholding of moral precepts is carried out in this manner, then this itself generates causal bases for the commission of karmic offenses. It is for this reason that [the *Sutra*] states, "It is based on the unfindability of offense and non-offense that one should engage in perfecting śīla pāramitā."

Part Two Endnotes

1. Because my outline is concerned with correctly tracking the actual structure of Nāgārjuna's discussion, it does not always precisely mirror the chapter titles included in the Chinese text. The title of this chapter as recorded in *Taisho* is "On the Meaning of *Śīla Pāramitā* (the perfecton of moral virtue)." This would perhaps be a fine title for the entire three-chapter discussion, but it is not particularly accurate for the content of *this* chapter which is, after all, simply a general introductory discussion.

   The reader may care to notice that the "chapter titles" supplied by the Chinese translation editors do not originate with Nāgārjuna and are occasionally wrongly placed and/or are incorrectly titled. This becomes particularly obvious later in this section on moral virtue where we notice that the *Taisho* version of the ensuing chapters are both wrongly placed and inaccurately named.

2. These reduced-font parenthetical notes are all integral to the received Chinese text preserved in the *Taisho* Tripiṭaka. They may or may not originate with Kumārajīva's oral explanations to his translation scribes.

3. This "divisive speech" includes not only the milder evils such as mindless rumor-mongering, but also the more clearly evil forms of deceit such as back-stabbing, character assassination, and slander into which the afflicted mind may stray even while still not having the direct intention to impart those deliberately formulated lies which are the primary concern of the "false speech" precept.

4. Frivolous speech" refers primarily to lewd speech, but also secondarily includes all of the forms of useless, time-wasting, and distracting chatter which pull the mind away from focus on the Path, involving it instead in any of a host of sensual and worldly concerns.

5. The *eraṇḍa* tree has red blossoms which, though beautiful in appearance, stink horribly even when miles away.

6. These statements refer to the future retributions due for the respective actions.

7. The five "relentless" (*ānantarya*) transgressions are patricide, matricide, killing an arhat, spilling the blood of a buddha, and causing a schism in the harmoniously-united monastic Sangha. The Sanskrit term connotes immediacy, unavoidability, and relentlessness of hell-bound retribution. These transgressions are discussed in Chapter Four of the *Abhidharma-kośa-bhāṣyam*.

8. Kātyāyanīputra lived about 200 BCE.

9. At the very conclusion of primary expository sections in this work,

Nāgārjuna's text sometimes supplements those expositions with recitation of standard *abhidharma* analytic data, often in very cryptic, highly-condensed, and barely decipherable format. My translation of this and other such brief sections is necessarily only tentative.

10. This may refer not only to those who denounce the killer, but also to the ghosts of the killer's victims.

11. "Both eras" refers to both present and future lives.

12. The rationale of this statement takes for granted that we realize, based on the retributive power of karmic actions, that killing brings about the karmic effect of having a short lifespan.

13. A *srota-āpanna* is a "stream-enterer," or "first-stage arhat."

14. One should understand that taking one's own life is a matter not to be taken lightly. For most of us, it would involve psychically depressed circumstances attended by deeply-afflicted and intensely emotional influences. These are conditions which tend to conduce to less fortunate rebirth circumstances. The situation of the *srota-āpanna* was quite different: Because he was a "stream-enterer," he had already gained the Path at a level where his liberation was guaranteed. He had already moved beyond being affected significantly by the afflictions and he was no longer subject to falling into lower states of rebirth. Because most of us do not enjoy such spiritually-advanced circumstances, it would be better for us to forego taking our own lives while also refusing to kill the sheep.

15. The Vinaya is one of the three primary divisions of the Buddhist canon. It contains all of the authoritative pronouncements on moral ethics in general and in particular articulates the various sets of moral codes for the different categories of Buddhist disciples among the monks, the nuns, and the laity.

16. The reference here is to karmic retribution arising from stealing.

17. "Unforeseen events" probably refers to being recognized as the perpetrator by accidentally encountering a witness after the fact. One may care to note that in alternate editions there is a variant reading involving transposition of characters (substituting 時行 for 行時). That reading would translate as: "Bad timing leads to unforeseen circumstances." This could be interpreted as a reference to the common circumstance wherein the robber ends up committing other crimes to cover up his actions or else ends up being injured or killed by either the victim or authorities who happen on the scene.

18. According to all standard provisional-level dispensations of the Buddha's teachings, an *anāgāmin*, otherwise known as a "never-returner," is not bound to take up future human or lower-realm rebirths. Rather, all remaining births are taken in celestial realms.

Nonetheless, they still retain the option of returning to visit the human realm.

19. Explanations of the Sanskrit names for these and most of the other hells may be found towards the end of Nāgārjuna's extensive explanation of the perfection of vigor. The characteristic sufferings endured in each hell are described in considerable detail there as well.

20. The other three offenses in addition to false speech are duplicitous speech, harsh speech, and frivolous (i.e. lewd or useless) speech).

21. Again, "two eras" is a reference to the present and the future.

22. In this analogy of an entire human life to the life of a single flower, the six seasons most likely refer to the major life-phases such as: birth, youth, the prime of life, old age, sickness, and death. In a story illustrating the shortness of a human life compared to that in the heavens, a heavenly maiden suffered accidental death one morning, subsequently lived a long life among humans during which she constantly made offerings to her former heavenly lord, and then was reborn again in the same heaven, arriving back there even before that single heavenly day had ended.

23. These are approximate Western correlates for Kumārajīva's *qin*, *si*, *zheng*, and *konghou*, four ancient Chinese instruments.

24. The Pārijātaka tree is in the Trāyastriṃśa heaven. It is said to be one hundred *yojanas* tall, fifty *yojanas* wide, to have roots going down fifty *yojanas*, and is supposed to be a place wherein one avails oneself of the most excellent sensual pleasures (Lamotte, 823).

25. Nāgārjuna devotes Chapter Thirty-six of the *Exegesis* to the "eight recollections," among which is "recollection of the heavens," wherein this same question about an apparent contradiction regarding rewards of the Path comes up. We find there supplementary arguments and a fine analogy.

26. *Asuras* are demigods renowned for their lack of merit, their jealousy of the gods, and their combative nature which provokes them to make repeated attacks on the domains of the gods.

27. "Six days" refers to the eighth, fourteenth, fifteenth, twenty-third, twenty-ninth, and thirtieth of each lunar month whereas "spiritual" months refers to the first, fifth and ninth lunar months and most specifically to the first through fifteenth days of those three months.

28. I have preferred the "five" signs of deterioration which accords with four other editions instead of the "three" appearing through scribal error in *Taisho*. The most common version of this list includes dirtiness of the heavenly garments, wilting of the floral chaplet, armpit perspiration, body odor, and unhappiness at remaining in one's seat. For a god, these indicate imminent death.

29. "Great mind" is almost certainly a reference to the bodhisattva vow to defer final nirvāṇa indefinitely in favor of striving endlessly for the spiritual liberation of all beings.

30. The "original" chapter title as recorded in *Taisho* is incorrectly placed and erroneously named. As it stands, it reads, "In Explanation of [Sutra] Chapter One's Praise of *Śīla Pāramitā*," this even though the text is simply continuing on at this point with an ongoing discussion of particular aspects of moral precept observance not directly associated with the treatment of *śīla pāramitā* explored elsewhere in this section. As a consequence, while keeping the text's placement of the chapter break, I have felt compelled to alter the title somewhat while also breaking the chapter itself into two parts, the first of those noting the continued discussion of precept specifics and the second of those two parts marking the commencement of the *śīla pāramitā* discussion.

31. There is no new-chapter break *per se* at this point in the text as preserved in *Taisho*. Rather *Taisho* only records a new-fascicle break titled: "The Remaining Portion of the Explanation of [Sutra] Chapter One's Praise of Śīla Pāramitā," this even though this point in the text is where Nāgārjuna begins his focused discussion of *śīla pāramitā*. As a consequence, I have introduced a "Chapter 23, Part 2" title here reflecting the actual pivot point in the discussion.

32. Lest the reader be mystified by Nāgārjuna's assertion that offenses don't exist, we should hasten to point out that he is referring solely to the ultimate reality of the matter. He in no way means to infer that they do not exist on the level of conventional reality. Nor does he mean to infer that karmic consequences are ever somehow suspended by virtue of cognizing the ultimate reality of which he speaks.

33. This is the *reductio ad absurdum* consequence of eternally-existing beings never dying.

34. Again, the author is speaking in terms of ultimate truth, but does not intend to infer that understanding this truth provides immunity from karmic accountability. In other words, even if one directly perceives the absence of inherent existence in all phenomena and in all beings, if he nonetheless deliberately sets up and carries through the conditions resulting in the death of someone only perceptible as a "being" on the level of conventional reality, he still engenders the offense of killing and still produces the causes for future retribution. He will then be bound to undergo that retribution at some point later in his own karmic continuum—this in spite of the fact that he all-the-while directly perceives the complete absence of inherent existence in all phenomena and in all beings.

A failure to understand this concept may constitute a karmically disastrous misinterpretation of emptiness and may bring on what is referred to in the tradition as "grasping the snake of emptiness by the tail." (One thus becomes subject to the karmically-fatal snake bite inflicted by erroneous interpretation of emptiness.) Those new to the doctrine of emptiness should take heed, realizing that the "unfindability" of offense and non-offense confers no license to ignore cause-and-effect and the inevitable karmic consequences.

Part Two Variant Readings from Other Chinese Editions

[153n06] [中] - [宋][元][宮]
[153n07] 義第二十一 = 上第二十二[宋], = 上[元], = 上第十七[宮], = 上第六[石],[義第二十一] - [明]
[153n08] [[經]] - [宋][宮][石]
[153n09] [[論]] - [宋][宮][石]
[153n10] 秦 = 此[明]
[153n11] [相] - [宋][元][明][宮][石]
[153n12] 天 + （天）[石]
[153n13] 猗 = 倚[元]
[153n14] [持戒] - [宋][宮][石]
[153n15] [將來] - [宋][宮][石]
[153n16] [令人] - [元][明]
[153n17] 欲 = 求[宋][宮][石]
[153n18] 得 = 求[宋][宮][石]
[153n19] 苦 = 共[石]
[153n20] 祀 = 禮[石]
[153n21] [能] - [宋][宮][石]
[153n22] 政 = 正[宋][元][明][宮]* [* 1]
[153n23] 考 = 拷[宋][元][明][宮]* [* 1]
[154n01] 所 = 何[宮]
[154n02] 自 = 亦[宮]
[154n03] 物 = 利[宋][元][明][宮][石]
[154n04] [周滿] - [宋][宮][石]
[154n05] 行禪 = 禪定[宋][元][明][宮][石]
[154n06] [以是...戒]八字 - [宋][元][明][宮][石]
[154n07] 芘 = 瓜[元][明]
[154n08] 大 = 火[宋][元][明][宮]
[154n09] 群 + （中）[宋][元][明][宮][石]
[154n10] 嬞 = [病-丙+(心/皿/丁)][宋][宮]
[154n11] 林 + （中）[宋][元][明][宮]
[154n12] 鰈 = 葉[宮]
[154n13] 鬼 = 卒[宋][元][明][宮][石]
[154n14] 惡 = 便[宮]
[154n15] [大智度論釋初品中戒相義第二十二之一] - [宮][石],[大智度論] - [明]*
[154016] 第二十二之一 = 第二十三[宋], - [元][明]
[154n17] [名] - [宋][宮][石]
[154n18] [相] - [宋][宮][石]* [* 1]
[154n19] 作 + （是名為戒）[元][明]

[154n20] [名] - [宋][元][明][宮][石]
[154n21] 故 = 殺[宮]
[154n22] 生 + （惡）[元][明]
[154n23] 罪 + （相）[元][明]
[154n24] [果] - [宋][元][明][宮]
[155n01] 隨 = 限[宋]
[155n02] 無 + （量）[石]
[155n03] 無漏 = 不繫[宋][元][明][宮][石]
[155n04] [法] - [宋][宮][石]
[155n05] [時] - [宋][元][明][宮][石]
[155n06] [丹注...戒]十五字 - [宋][元][明][宮][石]
[155n07] [丹注...證]七字 - [宋][元][明][宮][石]
[155n08] [丹注...上]八字 - [宋][元][明][宮][石]
[155n09] [法] - [宋][元][明][宮][石]
[155n10] [戒] - [宋][元][明][宮][石]
[155n11] [非心相應法] - [宋][元][明][宮][石]
[155n12] [皆] - [宋][石]
[155n13] [丹注...也]十一字 - [宋][元][明][宮][石]
[155n14] 令 = 今[元][明][石]
[155n15] 行獨遊 = 獨遊行[宋][元][明][宮][石]
[155n16] [人] - [宋][元][明][宮][石]
[155n17] 兩 = 後[宮][石]
[155n18] 入 + （汝）[石]
[155n19] [罪] - [宋][元][明][宮][石]
[155n20] 刑 = 形[石]
[155n21] 生 + （口言）[宋][元][明]
[155n22] [已] - [宋][元][明][宮]
[155n23] 中 = 申[石]
[155n24] 泥梨 = 泥犁[宋][元][明][宮]下同
[155n25] 昆 = 蜫[宋][元][明][宮]
[155n26] 全 = 令[石]* [* 1 2 3 4 5]
[156n01] 倍 = 億[宮]
[156n02] 可 = 以[宋][宮][石]
[156n03] 計挍 = 挍計[宋][元][明][宮][石]
[156n04] 者 + （是）[宋][元][明][宮][石]
[156n05] [為] - [宋][元][明][宮][石]
[156n06] [有] - [宋][宮]

[156n07] 被 = [月*皮][宮]

[156n08] [等] - [宮][石]

[156n09] 偈說 = 說偈[石]

[156n10] 穿踰 = 穿窬[宋][元][明][宮], = [穴/身]踰[石]

[156n11] [故] - [宋][宮]

[156n12] 罪重 = 重罪[元][明], = 罪[宮]

[156n13] 劇 = 處[宋][元][明][宮]

[156n14] 懊 = 淚[石]

[156n15] [若] - [宋][元][明][宮]

[156n16] 不作 = 放捨[宋][元][明][宮][石]

[156n17] 而 + （偷）[宋][元][明][宮],[而] - [石]

[156n18] 強 = 健[宮][石]

[156019] 禍 = 福[石]

[156n20] [丹注云重罪人疑] - [宋][石], [丹注云] - [元][明]

[156n21] 行時 = 時行[宋][元][明][宮][石]

[156n22] 朋 = 多[宮]

[156n23] [若] - [宮]

[156n24] 誑誘 = 誘誑[宋][元][明][宮]

[156n25] 娠 = 身[宋][元][明][宮][石]* [* 1 2]

[156n26] [如是...種]十二字 - [宋][元][明][宮][石]

[156n27] [丹注...罪]十五字 - [宋][元][明][宮][石]

[156n28] 妷 = 泆[宋][元][明][宮]

[156n29] 態 = 能[石]

[157n01] 恚我若 = 毒若我[宋][元][明][宮][石]

[157n02] [所] - [宋][元][明][宮]

[157n03] [賊] - [石]

[157n04] 解生 = 生解[石]

[157n05] 人 + （為）[石]

[157n06] 力 = 為[宮]

[157n07] 洗 = 浴[宋][元][明][宮]

[157n08] 祇洹 = 祇桓[宋][元][宮][石]

[157n09] 故 = 欲[宮]

[157n10] 野人 = 人為[宮]* [* 1]

[157n11] 此 = 是[宋][元][明][宮]

[157n12] 事 = 意[宋][元][明][宮][石]

[157n13] 奈 = 柰[宋][元][明], = 奈[宮]

[157n14] 嘷哭 = 號咷[宋][元][明][宮]

[157n15] 獄 + （地獄）[石]

[157n16] 天 = 王[石]

[157n17] 阿 = 呵[宋][元][明][宮][石]* [* 1 2 3]

[157n18] （五）+ 百[宋][元][明][宮][石]

[158n01] 夫士之生 = 夫世之士[宮]

[158n02] 毒苦 = 苦毒[宋][元][明][宮]

[158n03] 十 = 千[石]

[158n04] 五 = 三[宮]

[158n05] 形 = 刑[石]

[158n06] 樊 = 盤[宋][元][明][宮]* [* 1]

[158n07] 語 = 謀[宋][元][明][宮][石]

[158n08] 蒲桃 = 蒲萄[宋][元][明][宮], = 蒲陶[石]

[158n09] 麪 = 麨[宋][元][明][宮]

[158n10] 蹄 = 跡[宮]

[158n11] 以 + （故）[宋][元][明][宮]

[158n12] 現 + （在）[宋][元][明][宮]

[158n13] 病 = 疾[宋][元][明][宮]

[158n14] 悗 = 恍[宋][元][明][宮]

[158n15] 色 = 已[元][明]

[158n16] 語 = 言[宋][元][明][宮]

[158n17] 事重 = 重事[宋][元][明][宮][石]

[158n18] [自] - [宋][元][明][宮]

[159n01] 壟 = 瓏[宋][宮]

[159002] 映繡 = 照文繡[元][明]

[159n03] 愛 = 服[宋][元][明][宮][石]

[159n04] 鬚 = 飾[宮][石]

[159n05] 妊 = 任[石]

[159n06] 嬉 = 熙[元][明]

[159n07] [故] - [宋][元][明][宮][石]

[159n08] 富 = 福[宋][元][明][宮]

[159n09] [能] - [宋][元][明][宮]

[159n10] 甚 = 最[宋][元][明][宮]

[159n11] 過 = 失[宋][元][明][宮][石]

[159012] 秦 = 此[明]

[159n13] 共住 = 善宿[宋][元][明][宮][石]

[159n14] [如] - [宋][元][明][宮]

[159n15] [亦] - [宋][元][明][宮]

[159n16] [願] - [宋][元][明][宮]

[159n17] [得] - [宋][元][明][宮][石]

[159n18] 掌 = 手[宮][石]

[159n19] 二 = 一[宮]

[159n20] [我] - [宋][元][明][宮][石]

[159n21] [是] - [宋][元][明][宮][石]

[160n01] 業 = 德[宋][元][明][宮][石]

[160n02] [一] - [石]
[160n03] 悅 + （說）[宋][元][明][宮][石]
[160n04] （諸） + 天[宋][元][明][宮][石]
[160n05] [見諸天歡喜] - [宮][石]
[160n06] 三 = 五[宋][元][明][宮]
[160n07] [行] - [宋][元][明][宮]
[160n08] [神] - [宋][元][明][宮]
[160n09] [神父] - [石]
[160n10] [八] - [宋][元][明][宮]
[160n11] 將 = 持[宋][元][明][宮][石]
[160n12] 役 = 伎[宮]
[160n13] 危 = 厄[宋][元][明][宮]
[160n14] 剋 = 克[宋][元][明][宮]
[160n15] [得] - [石]
[160n16] [大智…三]十九字 - [宮][石]
[160n17] [羅] - [宋][元][明][宮]
[160n18] [第二十三] - [元][明]
[160n19] 三 = 四[宋]
[161n01] 業 = 生[石]
[161n02] 紛 = 忿[宋][元][明][宮]
[161n03] [當] - [宋][元][明][宮][石]
[161n04] [具足] - [宋][元][明][宮][石]
[161n05] [有] - [宋][元][明][宮][石]
[161n06] 愁 = 疑[宋][元][明][宮][石]
[161n07] 戒 = 形[元][明]
[161n08] 優 = 欝[宋][元][明][宮][石]
[161n09] 女 + （皆）[宋][元][明][宮]
[161n10] 祇洹 = 祇桓[宋][元][宮][石]
[161n11] [後] - [宋][元][明][宮][石]
[161n12] 那 = 尼[宋][元][宮]
[161n13] 和上 = 和尚[宋][元][明][宮]下同
[161n14] 阿闍梨 = 阿闍黎[明]下同
[161n15] 裟 + （衣）[宋][元][明][宮][石]
[161n16] 剃 = 涕[宮]
[161n17] 手 + （急）[宋][元][明][宮]
[161n18] [何] - [石]
[161n19] 歲 = 年[宋][元][明][宮]
[161n20] [戒] - [宋][元][明][宮][石]
[161n21] [是名…法]九字 - [石]
[161n22] [名] - [宋][元][明][宮]
[161n23] [受六法是式叉摩那]八字 - [宋][元][明][宮], [受六法] - [石]
[161n24] [欲] - [宋][元][明][宮][石]
[161n25] [用] - [宮][石]
[161n26] 盂 = 杅[石]* [* 1]
[161n27] [百] - [石]
[161n28] 羯磨 = 羯摩[宋][元][宮]
[161n29] 訖 = 說[元]
[162n01] 義之餘 = 下第二十三之餘[宋], = 下[元], = 之餘[明], = 下第十八[宮], = 下第十八羼提波羅蜜上[石]
[162n02] 上 = 是[石]
[162n03] 全 = 令[石]
[162n04] 往 = 住[宮]
[162n05] 服 = 莊[宮]
[162n06] 按 = 桉[宮], = 案[石]
[162n07] 眠 = 眼[宋][元][明]
[162n08] 絕 = 終[宋][元][明][宮]
[162n09] 是 = 也[宋][元][明][宮][石]
[162n10] 虛 = 稱[元][明]
[162n11] 智慧 = 善智[宋][元][明][宮][石]* [* 1]
[162n12] [得] - [宋][元][明][宮][石]
[162n13] （清） + 淨[宋][元][明][宮]
[162n14] 熏 = 動[石]
[162n15] 至 = 生[宋][宮][石]
[162n16] 律儀戒 = 戒律儀[宋][元][明][宮]* [* 1]
[162n17] 名 = 則[宋][元][明][宮]
[162n18] 持 = 治[宋][元][明][宮][石]
[162n19] 明註曰間南藏作門
[162n20] 走 = 赴[宋][宮][石]
[162n21] 蹶 = 蹹[宮]
[162n22] 求自 = 自求[宋][元][明][宮]
[162n23] 有時 = 時間[宋][元][明][宮][石]
[162n24] 屏 = 避[宋][宮][石], = 并[元]
[163n01] 干 = 千[宮]
[163n02] 明註曰間闕南藏作門開
[163n03] 差 = 瘥[宋][元][明][宮]
[163n04] 畢 = 得[宋][元][明][宋][石]
[163n05] 持 = 於[宋][元][明][宮][石]
[163n06] 諸 + （不）[宋][宮][石]
[163n07] 結使 = 使結[石]
[163n08] 逸 = 實[宋][元][明][宮][石]
[163n09] 人 = 下[宋][宮][石]
[163n10] 上 = 下[石]
[163n11] [若] - [宋][元][明][宮][石]
[163n12] 眾 + （生）[石]
[163n13] 污 = 淤[元][明]
[163n14] [者] - [宋][元][明][宮][石]

[163n15] [慧] - [宋][元][明][宮]

[163n16] 如是名 = 如是等名[宋][元][明][宮], = 如是等[石]

[163n17] 惑 = 戒盜[宋][元][明], = 戒[宮], = 惑盜[石]

[163n18] 於 = 持[石]

[163n19] [故] - [宋][元][明][宮][石]

[163n20] 若 + （人）[宋][元][明][宮][石]

[163n21] 謂 = 為[宋][元][明][宮]

[163n22] [也若] - [宋][元][明][宮]

[163n23] 無戒 = 戒無[石]

[163n24] （不）+ 可[元][明]*

[163n25] 不 + （可）[元][明]* [* 1]

[163n26] 有 = 出[宋][宮][石]

[163n27] [滿] - [宋][元][明][宮]

[163n28] 已 = 以[石]* [* 1]

[163n29] 拳 = 捲[石]* [* 1]

[164n01] 狀 = 床[宋][宮]

[164n02] [應] - [宋][元][明][宮][石]

[164n03] 至 = 生[石]

[164n04] 樂 + （殺）[元][明]

Part Three:

THE PERFECTION OF PATIENCE

(Chapters 24–25)

Part Three Contents

Nāgārjuna on the Perfection of Patience

[5]大智度论释初品中羼提波罗蜜[6]义第二十四。

[164b01]　[7]【经】心不动故。应具足羼提波罗蜜。

[164b01]　　[8]【论】问曰。云何名羼提。答曰。羼提[9]秦言忍辱。忍辱有二种。生忍法忍。菩萨行生忍得无量福德。行法忍得无量智慧。福德智慧二事具足故。得如所愿。譬如人有目有足随意能到。菩萨若遇恶口骂詈。若刀杖所加。思惟知罪福业因缘。诸法内外毕竟空无我无我所。以三法印。印诸法故。力虽能报不生恶心不起恶口业。尔时心数法生名为忍。得是忍法故忍智牢固。譬如画彩得胶则坚着。

简体字

[5]大智度論釋初品中羼提波羅蜜[6]義第二十四。

[164b01]　[7]【經】心不動故。應具足羼提波羅蜜。

[164b01]　　[8]【論】問曰。云何名羼提。答曰。羼提[9]秦言忍辱。忍辱有二種。生忍法忍。菩薩行生忍得無量福德。行法忍得無量智慧。福德智慧二事具足故。得如所願。譬如人有目有足隨意能到。菩薩若遇惡口罵詈。若刀杖所加。思惟知罪福業因緣。諸法內外畢竟空無我無我所。以三法印。印諸法故。力雖能報不生惡心不起惡口業。爾時心數法生名為忍。得是忍法故忍智牢固。譬如畫彩得膠則堅著。

正體字

The Perfection of Patience

By Ārya Nāgārjuna

Chapter 24: The Meaning of the Perfection of Patience

Sutra Text: It is through non-movement of the mind that one should perfect *kṣānti pāramitā* (the perfection of patience).

Exegesis Text:

Question: What is meant by *"kṣānti"* (patience)?

I. Introductory Discussion of *Kṣānti*
    A. Two Types of Patience

Response: (Chinese textual note: In our language, *kṣānti* means patience.)[1] Patience is of two types: patience with respect to beings (*sattva-kṣānti*) and patience with respect to dharmas (*dharmakṣānti*).

B. The Fruits of the Two Types of Patience Practice

When the bodhisattva practices patience with respect to beings, he gains an incalculable measure of merit. When he practices patience with respect to dharmas, he gains an incalculable measure of wisdom. Because he perfects the two factors of merit and wisdom, his achievements are then able to accord with his aspirations.[2] This is analogous to a person who, because he possesses both eyes and feet, is able to go wherever his mind intends.

C. The Bodhisattva's Basis for Generating Patience

If the bodhisattva encounters harsh speech or cursing, or if he is set upon with knives or clubs, he reflects and realizes that these events result from causes and conditions associated with prior karmic offenses and [a deficiency of] merit, and that all dharmas, whether inward or outward, are ultimately empty, devoid of self, and devoid of anything belonging to a self. This is because the three seals of Dharma (*dharmamudrā*) imprint all dharmas.[3] Thus, although he may have the power to respond in kind, he does not generate evil thoughts and does not bring forth the karma of harsh speech.

D. Patience's Stabilizing Effect

At this time, there arises a mental dharma (*caitasikadharma*) known as "patience." Because he has gained this dharma of patience, the patiences and knowledges are able to become durable and solidly established.[4] This is analogous to painting. If the pigments are mixed with a binder, then they are able to adhere solidly.

有人言。善心有二种有麁有
细。麁名忍辱细名禅定。未
得禅定心乐能遮众恶。是名
忍辱。心得禅定乐不为众
恶。是名禅定。是忍是心数
法与[10]心相应随心行。非业
非业报随业行。有人言。二
界系。有人言。但欲界系。
或不系。色界无外恶可忍
故。亦有漏亦无漏。凡夫圣
人俱得故。障己心他心不善
法故。名为善。善故。或思
惟断或不断。如是等种种阿
毘昙广分别。问曰。云何[11]
名生忍。答曰。有二种众生
来向菩萨。一者恭敬供养。

有人言。善心有二種有麁有
細。麁名忍辱細名禪定。未
得禪定心樂能遮眾惡。是名
忍辱。心得禪定樂不為眾
惡。是名禪定。是忍是心數
法與[10]心相應隨心行。非業
非業報隨業行。有人言。二
界繫。有人言。但欲界繫。
或不繫。色界無外惡可忍
故。亦有漏亦無漏。凡夫聖
人俱得故。障己心他心不善
法故。名為善。善故。或思
惟斷或不斷。如是等種種阿
毘曇廣分別。問曰。云何[11]
名生忍。答曰。有二種眾生
來向菩薩。一者恭敬供養。

简体字　　　　　　　　　　正體字

E. PATIENCE AS THE COARSER OF TWO KINDS OF GOOD MIND

There are those who say that a mind imbued with goodness may be of two sorts: There is that which is coarse and there is that which is subtle. The coarse is characterized by patience whereas the subtle is characterized by dhyāna absorption. When one has not yet gained the mental bliss of dhyāna absorption but is nonetheless able to block himself off from committing the manifold evils, this is [goodness characterized by] patience. When the mind has gained the mental bliss of dhyāna absorption and so does not engage in the manifold evils, this is [goodness characterized by] dhyāna absorption.

F. ABHIDHARMIC CONSIDERATIONS

This patience is a dharma associated with the mind. It is interactive with the mind and follows along with the actions of the mind. It is not the case that it is karma in and of itself and it is not the case that it occurs as a karmic retribution. It occurs in conjunction with karmic actions.

There are those who say that it is connected with two of the [three] realms. There are those who say that it can only be connected with the desire realm or that it has no particular connections. This analysis is based on the fact that are no external evils to be endured in the form realm.

It may either be attended by outflow impurities or character-ized by the absence of outflow impurities. This is because it may be gained either by a common person or by an ārya. Because one blocks off unwholesome dharmas originating in both one's own mind and the minds of others it is referred to as "good." Because it is good, it may be subject to severance through meditation or perhaps one may refrain from severing it. There are all sorts of other issues such as these which are extensively analyzed in the Abhidharma literature.[5]

II. PATIENCE WITH RESPECT TO BEINGS

Question: What is meant by patience with respect to beings?

A. TWO TYPES OF BEINGS REQUIRING PATIENCE

Response: There are two kinds of beings who come and approach the bodhisattva: The first are those who are respectful and who con-tribute offerings. The second are those who are hateful, who scold, and who may even bring injury through blows. At such times, the bodhisattva's mind is able to remain patient. He does not develop affection for the respectful beings who contribute offerings, nor

二者瞋骂打害。尔时菩萨其
心能忍。不爱敬养众生不瞋
加恶众生。是名生忍。问
曰。云何恭敬供养。名之为
忍。答曰。有二种结使。一
者属爱结使。二者属恚结
使。恭敬供养虽不生恚令心
爱着。是名[12]软贼。是故
于此应当自忍不着不爱。云
何能忍。观其无常是结使生
处。如佛所说利养[13]疮深。
譬如断皮至肉断肉至骨断骨
至髓。人着利养则破持戒
皮。断禅定肉。破智慧骨。
失微妙善心[164c]髓。如佛初
游迦毘罗婆国。与千二百五
十比丘俱。悉是梵志之身。
供养火故。形容憔悴。绝食
苦行故。肤体瘦黑。净饭王
心念言。我子侍从虽复心[14]
净清洁竝无容貌。我当择取
累重多子孙者。家出一人为
佛弟子。如是思[165a]惟已。
勅下国中。[15]简择诸释贵[16]
戚子弟。

二者瞋罵打害。爾時菩薩其
心能忍。不愛敬養眾生不瞋
加惡眾生。是名生忍。問
曰。云何恭敬供養。名之為
忍。答曰。有二種結使。一
者屬愛結使。二者屬恚結
使。恭敬供養雖不生恚令心
愛著。是名[12]軟賊。是故
於此應當自忍不著不愛。云
何能忍。觀其無常是結使生
處。如佛所說利養[13]瘡深。
譬如斷皮至肉斷肉至骨斷骨
至髓。人著利養則破持戒
皮。斷禪定肉。破智慧骨。
失微妙善心[164c]髓。如佛初
遊迦毘羅婆國。與千二百五
十比丘俱。悉是梵志之身。
供養火故。形容憔悴。絕食
苦行故。膚體瘦黑。淨飯王
心念言。我子侍從雖復心[14]
淨清潔竝無容貌。我當擇取
累重多子孫者。家出一人為
佛弟子。如是思[165a]惟已。
勅下國中。[15]簡擇諸釋貴[16]
戚子弟。

簡体字　　　　　　　　　　　　　　　　正體字

does he become hateful of those beings who heap evil upon him. This behavior embodies patience with respect to beings.

1. PATIENCE WITH BEARERS OF REVERENCE AND OFFERINGS

Question: How is it that one can even speak of "patience" in regard to respectfulness and the giving of offerings?

Response: There are two kinds of fetters (*saṃyojana*): The first are the fetters which belong to the sphere of affection. The second are those fetters which belong to the sphere of hatefulness. Although respectfulness and the giving of offerings do not inspire the generation of hatefulness, they do cause the mind to become affectionately attached. These are referred to as the soft thieves. Hence one should constrain himself to be patient with these things so that he does not become attached and thus remains unmoved by affection.

a. ANALOGY: ATTACHMENT AS A DEEP WOUND

How is one able to be patient? One contemplates that these situations are impermanent and that they constitute a point for the potential arising of the fetters. As stated by the Buddha, the wounds which occur through offerings go deep. It is as if they cut through the skin and reach the flesh, cut through the flesh and reach the bone, and then break through the bones and reach the marrow. When a person becomes attached to offerings, then they break through the skin of upholding the precepts, cuts into the flesh of dhyāna absorption, breaks through the bones of wisdom, and brings about loss of the marrow of the subtle and marvelous mind of goodness.

b. DEVADATTA'S AFFECTION FOR OFFERINGS (STORY)

This principle is illustrated by a case which began when the Buddha first roamed to the state of Kapilavastu. He went together with twelve hundred and fifty bhikshus, all of whom had the physical appearance of *brahmacārins*. Because they had previously been involved in making offerings to fire, their physical appearance was haggard. Due to their earlier ascetic practice of fasting, their bodies were emaciated and black.

King Śuddhodana thought to himself, "Although my son's present retinue is entirely pure in both mind and conduct, they are utterly lacking as regards their appearance. I should select from among those families with many sons and grandsons and have each send forth one man to become a disciple of the Buddha." After he had this thought, he issued an edict throughout the country so as to be able to select candidates from among the sons of the Śākyan

应书之身皆令出家。是时斛
饭王子提婆达多。出家学道
诵六万法聚。精进修行满十
二年。其后为供养利故来至
佛所。求学神通。佛告憍
[17]昙。[18]汝观五阴无常可
以得道。亦得神通。而不为
说取通之法。出求舍利弗目
揵连乃至五百阿罗汉。皆不
为说言。汝当观五阴无常。
可以得道可以得通。不得所
求涕泣不乐。到阿难所求学
神通。是时阿难未得他心
智。[19]敬其兄故如佛所言以
授提婆达多。[20]受学通法入
山不久便得五神通。得五神
通已自念。谁当与我作檀越
者。如王子阿阇世。有大王
相。欲与为亲厚。到天上取
天食。还到罽[21]旦罗越。取
自然粳米。至阎浮林中取阎
浮果。与王子阿阇世。或时
自变其身。作象宝马宝以惑
其心。或作[22]婴孩坐其膝
上。王子抱之呜[23]唛与唾。

简体字

應書之身皆令出家。是時斛
飯王子提婆達多。出家學道
誦六萬法聚。精進修行滿十
二年。其後為供養利故來至
佛所。求學神通。佛告憍
[17]曇。[18]汝觀五陰無常可
以得道。亦得神通。而不為
說取通之法。出求舍利弗目
揵連乃至五百阿羅漢。皆不
為說言。汝當觀五陰無常。
可以得道可以得通。不得所
求涕泣不樂。到阿難所求學
神通。是時阿難未得他心
智。[19]敬其兄故如佛所言以
授提婆達多。[20]受學通法入
山不久便得五神通。得五神
通已自念。誰當與我作檀越
者。如王子阿闍世。有大王
相。欲與為親厚。到天上取
天食。還到罽[21]旦羅越。取
自然粳米。至閻浮林中取閻
浮果。與王子阿闍世。或時
自變其身。作象寶馬寶以惑
其心。或作[22]嬰孩坐其膝
上。王子抱之嗚[23]唛與唾。

正體字

nobility. Those who came forth in response to the official declaration were all ordered to leave the home life.

It was at this time that Devadatta, son of King Droṇadana, left the home life, studied the Path, and memorized the sixty-thousand verse Dharma collection. He cultivated vigorously for a full twelve years. Afterwards, motivated by a desire to gain the benefit of offerings, he came to where the Buddha dwelt, seeking to study the superknowledges. The Buddha told him, "Gautama, if you contemplate the impermanence of the five aggregates, you can succeed in gaining the Path while also developing the superknowledges." But he did not instruct him in the methods for direct acquisition of superknowledges.

Devadatta left and sought this same thing from Śāriputra, from Maudgalyāyana, and eventually from five hundred arhats. None of them would explain it to him, saying instead, "You should contemplate the impermanence of the five aggregates. You can thereby gain the Path while also acquiring the superknowledges."

He did not get what he was seeking and so wept and felt unhappy. He went to where Ānanda was and sought to study the superknowledges. This was at the time when Ānanda had not yet achieved the knowledge of others' thoughts. Out of respect for his elder brother, he passed these techniques on to Devadatta just as they had been explained to him by the Buddha himself. Having finally obtained the method for studying the superknowledges, he went directly into the mountains and before long gained the five superknowledges.

Having gained the five superknowledges, he thought to himself, "Who should become my *dānapati*?[6] There is, for instance, Prince Ajātaśatru. He possesses the features of a great king." Seeking then to become the Prince's intimate acquaintance, he went up to the heavens and acquired a type of heavenly cuisine. Then, returning by way of Uttaravatī, he also obtained some "spontaneous" rice. Finally, he went to the *jambū* forest, got some *jambū* fruit (*Eugenia jambolana*),[7] and then presented all of these as gifts to Prince Ajātaśatru.

Sometimes he would transform himself into a precious elephant or into a prized horse so as to play tricks on the Prince's mind. At other times he would turn himself into an infant and sit down on the Prince's knee. The Prince would then be moved to cradle him in his arms, whereupon the infant would coo and gurgle and drool.

时时自说己名令太子知之。
种种变态以动其心。王子意
惑。于[24]奈园中[25]大立精
舍。四种供养并种种杂供无
物不备。以给提婆达多。日
日率诸大臣。自为送五百釜
羹饭。提婆达多大得供养而
徒众尟少。自念。我有三十
相减佛未几。直以弟子未
集。若大众围绕与佛何异。
如是思惟已生心破僧得五百
弟子。舍利弗目犍连说法教
化。僧还和合。尔时提婆达
多便生恶心推山压佛。金刚
力士以金刚杵而遥掷之。碎
石迸来伤佛足指。华色比丘
尼呵之。复以[*]拳打尼。尼
即时眼出而死。作三逆罪。
与恶邪师富兰那外道等为亲
厚。断诸善根心无愧悔。复
以恶毒着指[1]爪中。欲因礼
佛以中伤佛。欲去未[2]到王
舍城中。地自然破裂火车来
迎生入地狱。提婆达多身有
三十相。而不能忍伏其心。
为供养利故而作大

時時自說己名令太子知之。
種種變態以動其心。王子意
惑。於[24]奈園中[25]大立精
舍。四種供養并種種雜供無
物不備。以給提婆達多。日
日率諸大臣。自為送五百釜
羹飯。提婆達多大得供養而
徒眾尟少。自念。我有三十
相減佛未幾。直以弟子未
集。若大眾圍繞與佛何異。
如是思惟已生心破僧得五百
弟子。舍利弗目犍連說法教
化。僧還和合。爾時提婆達
多便生惡心推山壓佛。金剛
力士以金剛杵而遙擲之。碎
石迸來傷佛足指。華色比丘
尼呵之。復以[*]拳打尼。尼
即時眼出而死。作三逆罪。
與惡邪師富蘭那外道等為親
厚。斷諸善根心無愧悔。復
以惡毒著指[1]爪中。欲因禮
佛以中傷佛。欲去未[2]到王
舍城中。地自然破裂火車來
迎生入地獄。提婆達多身有
三十相。而不能忍伏其心。
為供養利故而作大

简体字   正體字

Whenever he did this, he would repeatedly utter his own name, thus causing the Prince to become aware of it. He manifested all sorts of unusual appearances in order to affect the Prince's thoughts.

The Prince's mind was tricked by this. He built an immense *vihāra*[8] in Ambavana Park and prepared the four kinds of offerings together with all sorts of other assorted gifts so that nothing was not present in abundance. He then provided all of them to Devadatta. Every day, he brought along all of the great officials and personally offered up five hundred dishes of fine foods with rice.

Devadatta received offerings in great measure and yet his following of disciples was still very small in number. He thought to himself, "I possess thirty of the marks of a great man, only slightly less than the Buddha. It is only that I have not yet had disciples gathering around me. If I was surrounded by a great assembly, how would I be any different from the Buddha?" Having reflected in this manner, he conceived the idea to break up the Sangha and thereby succeeded in taking on five hundred disciples. Śāriputra and Maudgalyāyana responded to this circumstance by speaking Dharma and provided instruction to them. As a consequence, the Sangha became harmonious and united once again.

Devadatta then had the evil idea to push a boulder down from the mountain to crush the Buddha. A *vajra*-bearing stalwart intervened from a distance by throwing his *vajra* cudgel to deflect it. A broken piece of the boulder rolled up, injuring the Buddha's toe.

Floral Appearance Bhikshuni[9] rebuked Devadatta who responded by striking the bhikshuni with his fist. The bhikshuni's eyes popped out from the force of the blow and she immediately died.

Devadatta committed three of the "relentless" (*ānantarya*) transgressions[10] and drew close to such evil and fallacy-promoting non-Buddhist masters as Pūraṇa. He severed all roots of goodness and his mind became devoid of a sense of shame or regret. Additionally, he imbedded a noxious poison under his fingernails, wishing to take the occasion of bowing to the Buddha to injure the Buddha through poisoning. He was about to proceed, but had not yet followed through when the earth in the city of Kings' Abode (Rājagṛha) spontaneously split open and a fiery carriage came forth. It took him on board and transported him, still alive, down into the hells.

Devadatta's body possessed thirty of the marks of a great man and yet he was unable to resist and overcome his own mind. Motivated by the benefits accruing from offerings, he created great

罪。生入地獄。以是故言利養[*]疮深破皮至髓[3]应当除却爱供养人心。是为菩萨忍心不爱着供养恭敬人。复次供养有三种。一者先世因缘福德故。二者今世功德修戒禅定智慧故[4]为人敬养。三者虚妄欺惑内无实德外如清白。以诳时人而得供养。于此三种供养中。心自思惟。若先世因缘懃修福德今得供养。是为懃身作之而自得耳。何为于此而生贡高。譬如春种秋获。自以力得何足自憍。如是思惟已。忍伏其心不着不憍。若今世故功德而得供养当自思[5]惟。我以智慧。若知诸法实相。若能断结。以此功德故。是人供养于我无事。如是思惟已。自伏其心不自憍高。此实

简体字

罪。生入地獄。以是故言利養[*]瘡深破皮至髓[3]應當除却愛供養人心。是為菩薩忍心不愛著供養恭敬人。復次供養有三種。一者先世因緣福德故。二者今世功德修戒禪定智慧故[4]為人敬養。三者虛妄欺惑內無實德外如清白。以誑時人而得供養。於此三種供養中。心自思惟。若先世因緣懃修福德今得供養。是為懃身作之而自得耳。何為於此而生貢高。譬如春種秋穫。自以力得何足自憍。如是思惟已。忍伏其心不著不憍。若今世故功德而得供養當自思[5]惟。我以智慧。若知諸法實相。若能斷結。以此功德故。是人供養於我無事。如是思惟已。自伏其心不自憍高。此實

正體字

offenses and fell into the hells even while still alive. It is for this reason that it is said that the wounds inflicted by offerings go deep, breaking through the skin and reaching even to the marrow.

One should cast out any thoughts of affection which might arise specifically towards whoever presents offerings. This is what is intended when it is said that the bodhisattva's mind of patience refrains from becoming affectionately attached to those who present offerings or demonstrate respect.

c. THREE KINDS OF OFFERINGS

As an additional point, there are three kinds of offerings: The first are those resulting from the causes and conditions associated with past-life merit. The second are those wherein one receives respect and offerings on account of present-life merit associated with cultivating the moral precepts, dhyāna absorption, and wisdom. The third are those wherein one gains offerings through falseness and pretense. Although one is inwardly devoid of actual meritorious qualities, one makes it appear outwardly as if one is utterly pure. One thereby deceives whoever is present at the time and thus succeeds in obtaining offerings as a result.

With respect to these three kinds of offerings, one should reflect, "If one now obtains offerings through previous-life causal circumstances involving diligent cultivation of merit, this is just something created through personal diligence and thus is obtained in the natural course of things. What would be the point in becoming haughty over something like this? This is just like planting in the spring and reaping in the fall. This is something gained individually through the application of one's own efforts. What in it is sufficient cause for arrogance?" After one has reflected in this manner, he is able to endure and overcome his own mind so that he is able to refrain from becoming attached or prideful.

Where, due to present-life efforts, one generates merit and consequently obtains offerings, one should reflect, "This comes to me perhaps on account of my having some measure of wisdom, perhaps through awareness of the true character of dharmas, or perhaps through being able to cut off the fetters. It is on account of these meritorious factors that this person makes such offerings. It does not actually have anything specifically to do with me."

Having reflected in this fashion, one is able to overcome his own thoughts and refrain from falling into arrogance or condescension. He realizes, "Truly, this is just a case of people having a fondness

爱乐功德不爱我也。譬如罽
宾三藏比丘。行阿兰若法至
一王寺。寺设大会。守门人
见其衣服尨弊遮门不前。如
是数数以衣服弊故每不得
前。便作方便假借好衣而
来。门家见之听前不禁。既
至会坐得种种好食。[165b]先
以与衣。众人问言。何以尔
也。答言。我比数来每不得
入。今以衣故得在此坐得种
种好食。实是衣故得之。故
以与衣。行者以修行功德持
戒智慧故而得供养。自念此
为功德非为我也。如是思惟
能自伏心是名为忍。若虚妄
欺伪而得供养。是为自害不
可近也。当自思惟。若我以
此虚妄而得供养。与恶贼劫
盗得食无异。是为堕欺妄
罪。如是于三种供养

简体字

愛樂功德不愛我也。譬如罽
賓三藏比丘。行阿蘭若法至
一王寺。寺設大會。守門人
見其衣服尨弊遮門不前。如
是數數以衣服弊故每不得
前。便作方便假借好衣而
來。門家見之聽前不禁。既
至會坐得種種好食。[165b]先
以與衣。眾人問言。何以爾
也。答言。我比數來每不得
入。今以衣故得在此坐得種
種好食。實是衣故得之。故
以與衣。行者以修行功德持
戒智慧故而得供養。自念此
為功德非為我也。如是思惟
能自伏心是名為忍。若虛妄
欺偽而得供養。是為自害不
可近也。當自思惟。若我以
此虛妄而得供養。與惡賊劫
盜得食無異。是為墮欺妄
罪。如是於三種供養

正體字

for certain meritorious qualities. It is not that they have any specific fondness for me as such."

d. THE KASHMIRI TRIPIṬAKA MASTER (STORY)

This is well illustrated by the case of the Kashmiri tripiṭaka master bhikshu who cultivated the dharma of the *araṇya*.[11] He happened to go one day to one of the King's temples where that temple had arranged a great convocation. When the door guard observed the coarse weave and low-quality of his robes, he blocked the door and refused to permit the monk to proceed. This same thing happened to him time and time again. Due to the poor quality of his robes, he was never allowed to go forth.

He then availed himself of a skillful means whereby he simply borrowed a fine robe before coming. The doorman observed this and permitted him to go right on in without even being detained. Having arrived at a seat in the convocation, he obtained all manner of fine foods. Before eating, he first made an offering of the food to his robes. Everyone around him would be moved to inquire of him, "Why is it that you do that?"

He replied, "I have been coming here repeatedly of late, but on every occasion have been unable to gain entry. Now, because I have taken to wearing these robes, I have been allowed to sit in this seat and obtain all kinds of fine foods. It is actually on account of the robes that I have been able to obtain it. This is why I make an offering of it to these robes."

When one obtains offerings on account of the merit of cultivation, on account of upholding the moral precepts, and on account of wisdom, the practitioner should think to himself, "This occurrence is a consequence of karmic merit. It is not the case that it arises directly from me." When one contemplates in this fashion and thus becomes able to overcome his own thoughts, this qualifies as "patience."

If one were to gain offerings through falseness and deception, this would be tantamount to self-destruction and thus it is a behavior to which one cannot draw near. One should reflect, "If I were to employ such falseness and then obtain offerings as a result, it would be no different from an evil thief committing a robbery to obtain his sustenance." This would be a case of falling into the karmic offense of deliberate deception.

When one's mind restrains itself in this manner from becoming affectionately attached to these three types of offering-bearing

简体字	正體字
人中心不爱着亦不自高。是名生忍。问曰。人未得道衣[6]食为急。云何方便能得忍。心不着不爱给施之人。答曰。以智慧力观无常相苦相无我相心常厌患。譬如罪人临当受戮。虽复美味在前家至[7]劝喻。以忧死故。[8]虽饮食肴膳不觉[9]滋味。行者亦尔。常观无常相苦相。虽得供养心亦不着。又如麞鹿为虎搏逐追之不舍。虽得好草美水饮食心无染着。行者亦尔。常为无常虎逐不舍须臾思惟厌[10]患。虽得美味亦不染着。是故行者于供养人中心得自忍。	人中心不愛著亦不自高。是名生忍。問曰。人未得道衣[6]食為急。云何方便能得忍。心不著不愛給施之人。答曰。以智慧力觀無常相苦相無我相心常厭患。譬如罪人臨當受戮。雖復美味在前家至[7]勸喻。以憂死故。[8]雖飲食餚膳不覺[9]滋味。行者亦爾。常觀無常相苦相。雖得供養心亦不著。又如麞鹿為虎搏逐追之不捨。雖得好草美水飲食心無染著。行者亦爾。常為無常虎逐不捨須臾思惟厭[10]患。雖得美味亦不染著。是故行者於供養人中心得自忍。

persons while also refraining from developing an arrogant attitude, this qualifies as "patience with respect to beings."

e. How to Avoid Attachment to Benefactors

Question: When a person has not yet achieved realization of the Path, clothing and food remain as urgent issues for him. How then does such a person adopt a skillful means to gain that patience which prevents the mind from developing attachment and affection for benefactors?

Response: One resorts to the power of wisdom to contemplate the mark of impermanence, to contemplate the mark of suffering, and to contemplate the mark of the absence of an inherently-existent self so that the mind is influenced to abide in a state of constant renunciation and vigilant concern.

1) Death-Row Inmate Analogy

This circumstance is comparable to that of the criminal who is drawing close to the time when he must undergo capital punishment. Even though he may have fine flavors set before him, even though his family may have come to offer him encouragement, and even though the refreshments and meals may consist of the most exquisite cuisine, because of his distress over the thought of being put to death, he remains undistracted by their distinctive flavors.

The practitioner behaves in just the same way. He constantly contemplates the mark of impermanence and the mark of suffering. Then, although he may obtain offerings, his mind nonetheless still remains free of any attachment to them.

2) The Antelope and Tiger Analogy

This situation is also analogous to that of the antelope (*jang*, a.k.a. *Moschus chinloo*) which is hotly pursued by the tiger and remains unable to lose him completely. As a consequence, even though he may be able to feed on fine grasses and drink from the best waters, even while drinking and eating, the antelope's mind remains free of any taint of attachment to these things.

The practitioner acts in much the same way. He is constantly pursued by the tiger of impermanence and remains unable to escape it for even a moment. His mental reflections are characterized by renunciation and vigilant concern. Even though he may be able to consume finely flavored foods, he nonetheless refrains from indulging any corrupting attachment to it. Therefore, even when in the midst of people who present offerings, the practitioner's mind naturally abides in patience.

复次若有女人来欲娱乐诳惑菩萨。菩萨是时当自伏心忍不令起。如释迦文尼佛在菩提树下。魔王忧愁遣三[11]玉女。一名乐见。二名悦彼。三名渴爱。来现其身作种种姿态欲坏菩萨。菩萨是时心不倾动目不暂视。三女念言。人心不同好爱[12]各异。或有好少或爱中年或好长好短[13]好黑好白。如是众好各有所爱。是时三女各各化作五百美女。[14]一一化女作无量变态从林中出。譬如黑云[165c]电光暂现。或扬眉顿[15]睫娈娱细视。作众伎乐种种姿媚。来[16]近菩萨欲以态身触[17]逼菩萨。尔时密迹金刚力士瞋目叱之。此是何人而汝妖媚敢来触娆。尔时密迹说偈呵之。

汝不知天[18]命　失好而黄髯。
大海水清美　今日尽苦醎。

復次若有女人來欲娛樂誑惑菩薩。菩薩是時當自伏心忍不令起。如釋迦文尼佛在菩提樹下。魔王憂愁遣三[11]玉女。一名樂見。二名悅彼。三名渴愛。來現其身作種種姿態欲壞菩薩。菩薩是時心不傾動目不暫視。三女念言。人心不同好愛[12]各異。或有好少或愛中年或好長好短[13]好黑好白。如是眾好各有所愛。是時三女各各化作五百美女。[14]一一化女作無量變態從林中出。譬如黑雲[165c]電光暫現。或揚眉頓[15]睫娈娛細視。作眾伎樂種種姿媚。來[16]近菩薩欲以態身觸[17]逼菩薩。爾時密迹金剛力士瞋目叱之。此是何人而汝妖媚敢來觸嬈。爾時密迹說偈呵之。

汝不知天[18]命　失好而黄髯。
大海水清美　今日盡苦醎。

简体字　　　　　　　　　　正體字

3) DESIRE-RELATED CHALLENGES TO CULTIVATING THE PATH

Furthermore, if it happens that women desirous of sensual pleasures come and seek to seduce the bodhisattva, the bodhisattva should then subdue his own thoughts, have patience, and not allow them to arise.

a) BUDDHA AT THE BODHI TREE (STORY)

This circumstance is comparable to that of Shakyamuni Buddha beneath the Bodhi Tree. The king of the demons was distressed and so sent forth three of his "jade" daughters. The first was named "Blissful to Behold." The second was named "Pleasurable to Others." The third was named "Lust." They came, revealed their bodies, and assumed various poses, desiring to destroy the Bodhisattva. At this time, the mind of the Bodhisattva did not move for even a moment, nor did he even lay eyes on them for even a moment.

The three maidens thought to themselves, "The minds of men are not all the same. That of which they are enamored is different in each case. Some are fond of the young, some are fond of the middle-aged. Some are fond of those who are tall and some are fond of those who are short. Some are fond of those who are black and some are fond of those who are white. There are many preferences like these. Everyone has that which they love."

At this time the three maidens each transformed themselves into five hundred beautiful maidens. Each of those transformationally produced maidens assumed countless unusual poses upon emerging from the forest, like flashes of lightning appearing momentarily from the midst of black clouds. Some displayed their eyebrows and fluttered their eyelids, or posed alluringly, or offered subtle gazes. They made many sorts of music and showed all kinds of seductive mannerisms. They drew close to the Bodhisattva, desiring with posed bodies to touch and pressure the Bodhisattva.

The secret *vajra*-bearing stalwarts then bellowed and glowered hatefully at them, "Who do you think this is that you dare to approach him seductively, attempting to touch and bother him?" At that time those secret stalwarts uttered a verse in which they scolded them:

> You are unaware of the fate of the gods.
> They lose what is fine and their beards turn yellow.
> The waters of the great sea which were clear and beautiful,
> Today have become entirely bitter and salty.

简体字	正體字
汝不知[19]日減　婆薮诸天堕。 火本为天口　而今一切噉。	汝不知[19]日減　婆藪諸天墮。 火本為天口　而今一切噉。
[165c09] 汝不知此事　敢轻此圣人。	**[165c09]** 汝不知此事　敢輕此聖人。
是时众女逡巡小退。语菩萨言。今此众女端严无比可自娱意。端坐何为。菩萨言。汝等不净臭秽可恶去勿妄谈。菩萨是时即说偈言。	是時眾女逡巡小退。語菩薩言。今此眾女端嚴無比可自娛意。端坐何為。菩薩言。汝等不淨臭穢可惡去勿妄談。菩薩是時即說偈言。
是身为秽薮　不净物腐积。 是实为行厕　何足以乐意。	是身為穢藪　不淨物腐積。 是實為行廁　何足以樂意。
[165c15]　　女闻此偈自念。此人不知我等清净天身而说此偈。即自变身还复本形。光曜[20]昱烁照林树间作天伎乐。语菩萨言。我身如是有何可呵。菩萨答言。时至自知。问曰。此言何谓。以偈答言。	**[165c15]**　　女聞此偈自念。此人不知我等清淨天身而說此偈。即自變身還復本形。光曜[20]昱爍照林樹間作天伎樂。語菩薩言。我身如是有何可呵。菩薩答言。時至自知。問曰。此言何謂。以偈答言。
诸天园林中　七宝莲华池。 天人相娱乐　失时汝自知。	諸天園林中　七寶蓮華池。 天人相娛樂　失時汝自知。
是时见无常　天人乐皆苦。 汝当厌欲乐　爱乐正真道。	是時見無常　天人樂皆苦。 汝當厭欲樂　愛樂正真道。
[165c24]　女闻偈已心念。此人大智无量。	**[165c24]**　女聞偈已心念。此人大智無量。

You are unaware that your days are diminishing.
All of the Vasu gods are bound to fall away.[12]
Fire ultimately acts as a mouth consuming the heavens.
So that everything now therein is finally bound to be devoured.[13]

You remain unaware of all these matters.
And so it is that you dare to slight this ārya.

The crowd of maidens then suddenly retreated a little and spoke to the Bodhisattva, saying, "Now, these gathered maidens are beautiful and adorned beyond compare. They could serve to delight your mind. Why then do you just sit there in such an upright fashion?"

The Bodhisattva said, "You all are impure, foul-smelling, filthy and detestable. Depart from here and cease this deceptive discourse." The Bodhisattva then set forth a verse, saying,

This body is a thicket of filthiness.
It is but a collection of decaying matter.
This truly is a walking toilet.
What in it is sufficient to please the mind?

When the maidens heard this verse, they thought to themselves, "It is because this man is unaware of our pure heavenly bodies that he speaks such a verse." They then immediately transformed their bodies again, returning to their original forms. They radiated light which shimmered and illuminated the forest and proceeded to make heavenly music. They then spoke to the Bodhisattva, saying, "Since our bodies are actually of this sort, what could there be to criticize?"

The Bodhisattva replied, "When the time comes, you will naturally understand."

They asked, "What do you mean by these words?"

He then replied with a verse:

In the parks and forests of the heavens,
And in the seven-jeweled lotus blossom pools,
The gods enjoy with one another the pleasures of the senses,
When that is lost, you will naturally understand.

At this time, you will observe impermanence
And realize the pleasures of the gods are all wedded to suffering.
You should renounce the pleasures of desire
And cherish the Path that's right and true.

When the maidens had heard this verse, they thought to themselves, "This man is possessed of a great wisdom which is boundless in its

天乐清净犹知其恶不可当也。即时灭去。菩萨如是观婬欲乐。能自制心忍不[21]倾动。复次菩萨观欲种种不净。于诸衰中女衰[22]最重。刀火雷电霹雳怨家毒蛇之属犹可暂近。女人悭妬瞋谄妖秽鬪諍贪嫉不可亲近。何以故。女子[166a]小人心浅智薄唯欲是[1]视。不观富贵智[2]德名闻。专行欲恶破人善根。桎梏枷锁闭系囹圄。虽曰难解是犹易开。女锁系人[3]染固根深。无智没之难可得脱。众病之中女病最重。如佛偈言。

宁以赤铁　宛转眼中。
不以散心　邪视女色。

含笑作姿　憍慢羞[4]耻。
迴面摄眼　美言妬瞋。

行步妖秽　以惑于人。

简体字

天樂清淨猶知其惡不可當也。即時滅去。菩薩如是觀婬欲樂。能自制心忍不[21]傾動。復次菩薩觀欲種種不淨。於諸衰中女衰[22]最重。刀火雷電霹靂怨家毒蛇之屬猶可暫近。女人慳妬瞋諂妖穢鬪諍貪嫉不可親近。何以故。女子[166a]小人心淺智薄唯欲是[1]視。不觀富貴智[2]德名聞。專行欲惡破人善根。桎梏枷鎖閉繫囹圄。雖曰難解是猶易開。女鎖繫人[3]染固根深。無智沒之難可得脫。眾病之中女病最重。如佛偈言。

寧以赤鐵　宛轉眼中。
不以散心　邪視女色。

含笑作姿　憍慢羞[4]恥。
迴面攝眼　美言妬瞋。

行步妖穢　以惑於人。

正體字

scope. He realizes the ills inherent even in the pure pleasures of the gods. He is not of the sort who are amenable to obstruction." They then immediately disappeared.

It is in this fashion that the bodhisattva contemplates the pleasures associated with sexual desire. Thus he is able to control his own mind and abide in a patience wherein he is not the least bit moved by such matters.

b) For Monks: The Hazards of Involvement with Women[14]

Then again, the bodhisattva contemplates all sorts of impurity in desire. Of all the kinds of ruination, ruination by women is the most severe. One may still remain briefly close to such phenomena as knives, fire, lightning storms, enemies, and poisonous snakes. But one cannot grow close to the miserliness, jealousy, hatred, flattery, seductive defilement, disputatiousness, avarice, and anger of women. Why not? Women are prone to be petty people. Their minds are shallow and their wisdom is scant. Their eyes are only directed towards desire. They have no particular regard for whether one is wealthy, of noble birth, wise, virtuous, or famous. They focus on carrying through with the unwholesome endeavors associated with desire and thus bring about the destruction of a man's roots of goodness.

Although one may say that it is difficult to escape fetters, shackles, the cangue, being confined and tied up, or being imprisoned, these are still comparatively easy to break out of. When the lock of womanhood restrains a man, the defilement grows solid and its roots go deep. One who has no wisdom becomes immersed in it and finds it a difficult thing to escape. Of all of the many kinds of illness, the "female affliction" is most severe. This is illustrated by a verse once spoken by the Buddha:

> One should rather use a red-hot iron rod
> And twist it around in the eyes:
> One must not allow the scattered mind
> To gaze with improper intent at the body of a woman.

> The subtle smile, the artful pose,
> The arrogance, the shamelessness,
> The turn of the head, the inviting gaze,
> The lovely words, the jealousy and hate,

> The walking along with defiling seductiveness—
> These are all used to trick a man

婬罗弥[5]网　人皆没身。

坐卧行立　迴[6]眄巧媚。
薄智愚人　为之心醉。

执剑向敌　是犹可胜。
女贼害人　是不可禁。

蚖蛇含毒　犹可手捉。
女情惑人　是不可触。

有智之人　所[7]应不视。
若欲观之　当如母姊。

谛视观之　不净填积。
婬火不除　为之烧灭。

[166a17]　复次女人相者。若得敬待则令夫心高。若敬待情舍则令夫心怖。女[8]人如是恒以烦恼忧怖与人。云何可近。亲好乖离女人之罪。巧察人[9]要女人之智。大火烧人是犹可近。清风无形是亦可捉。蚖蛇含毒犹亦可触。女[10]人之心不可得实。何以故女人之相。不观富贵端[11]政名闻智德族姓

婬羅彌[5]網　人皆沒身。

坐臥行立　迴[6]眄巧媚。
薄智愚人　為之心醉。

執劍向敵　是猶可勝。
女賊害人　是不可禁。

蚖蛇含毒　猶可手捉。
女情惑人　是不可觸。

有智之人　所[7]應不視。
若欲觀之　當如母姊。

諦視觀之　不淨填積。
婬火不除　為之燒滅。

[166a17]　復次女人相者。若得敬待則令夫心高。若敬待情捨則令夫心怖。女[8]人如是恒以煩惱憂怖與人。云何可近。親好乖離女人之罪。巧察人[9]要女人之智。大火燒人是猶可近。清風無形是亦可捉。蚖蛇含毒猶亦可觸。女[10]人之心不可得實。何以故女人之相。不觀富貴端[11]政名聞智德族姓

简体字　　　　　　　　　　正體字

Into the net of lustfulness
Where men are all bound to become entrapped.

Whether sitting, lying down, walking, or standing,
The sidelong glance in return, and clever flattery—
With a foolish man of only scant wisdom,
His mind is prone to be intoxicated by this.

When taking up a sword against an enemy,
In this, one can still be victorious.
But when the feminine insurgent visits harm on a man,
This is such as cannot be restrained.

Even with venomous insects and snakes,
One might still be able to grasp them in hand.
But feelings for women so delude a man
That they are such as cannot be touched.

For a man who is possessed of wisdom,
They are such as should not be looked upon.
If one wishes to observe them,
It should be as one would one's mother or sister.

If one trains upon them a gaze anchored in reality,
Their bodies are just collections of impurities.
If one fails to do away with the fire of lust,
One is bound to be utterly burned up by it.

Moreover, as for the characteristic nature of women, if they encounter a situation where they are treated with veneration, then they allow the husband's mind to be buoyant. If the worshipful emotions slip away, then they cause the husband's mind to become beset with dread. In this fashion, women constantly deliver emotional afflictions, distress, and fearfulness to men. How then can one even draw close to them? The subversion of intimacy and good feeling through contrariness and estrangement is an offense committed by women. The clever assessment of the vulnerabilities of men is a strain of intelligence possessed by women.

A great conflagration which incinerates people might nonetheless still be approachable. A light breeze devoid of form might nonetheless still be laid hold of. Poisonous insects and venomous snakes might nonetheless still be touched. But in the mind of a woman one can find nothing substantial. Why is this? It is the characteristic nature of women that they have no regard for wealth, nobility, uprightness and correctness, fame, wisdom, virtue, family

技艺辩言亲厚爱重。都不在心唯欲是[*]视。譬如蛟龙不择好丑唯欲杀人。又复[12]女人不瞻视忧苦憔悴。给养敬待憍奢叵制。复次若在善人之中。则自畜心高。无智人中视之如怨。富贵人中追之敬爱。贫贱人中视之如狗。常随欲心不随功德。如说国王有女[166b]名曰拘牟头。有捕鱼师名[13]述婆伽。随道而行。遥见王女在高楼上窻中见面。想像染着心不暂舍。弥历日月不能饮食。母问其故以情答母。我见王女心不能忘。母谕儿言。汝是小人。王女尊贵不可得也。儿言。我心愿乐不能暂忘。若不如意不能活也。母为子故入王宫中。常送肥鱼[14]美肉以遗王女而不取价。王女怪而问之欲求何愿。

技藝辯言親厚愛重。都不在心唯欲是[*]視。譬如蛟龍不擇好醜唯欲殺人。又復[12]女人不瞻視憂苦憔悴。給養敬待憍奢叵制。復次若在善人之中。則自畜心高。無智人中視之如怨。富貴人中追之敬愛。貧賤人中視之如狗。常隨欲心不隨功德。如說國王有女[166b]名曰拘牟頭。有捕魚師名[13]述婆伽。隨道而行。遙見王女在高樓上窻中見面。想像染著心不暫捨。彌歷日月不能飲食。母問其故以情答母。我見王女心不能忘。母諭兒言。汝是小人。王女尊貴不可得也。兒言。我心願樂不能暫忘。若不如意不能活也。母為子故入王宮中。常送肥魚[14]美肉以遺王女而不取價。王女怪而問之欲求何願。

简体字　　　　　　　　　　　　　　　正體字

background, artistic ability, eloquence, intimacy, or deep love. None of these have priority in their minds. Their vision esteems only whatsoever they desire. They act like poisonous dragons which do not discriminate between those who are fine and those who are detestable, but rather seek only to kill people.

Moreover, women will not even lay eyes upon anyone who is in distress, suffering, or haggard. Their interest lies in being provided with material support and worshipful admiration. Their vanity and extravagance are uncontrollable.

Additionally, when in the company of the good, then they tend to appropriate to themselves a lofty attitude. When among those who are unintelligent, they tend to look upon them as if they were enemies. When in the company of the wealthy and those of noble birth, they pursue them with admiring affection. When among those who are poor or of humble station, they look upon them as if they were dogs. They constantly follow the mind of desire and do not tend to pursue meritorious qualities.

c) The Fisherman and the King's Daughter (Story)

In this connection, there once was a king with a daughter named Kumuda. A fisherman named Śubhakara was walking along the road when he looked from afar and observed the princess's countenance in an upper-story window. He then fantasized with thoughts of defiling attachment which he remained unable to relinquish for even a moment. He then passed through days and months of being incapable of drinking or eating normally. His mother eventually inquired why this was happening, whereupon he revealed his feelings to her: "Ever since I laid eyes on the daughter of the King, my mind has been helpless to forget her."

The mother explained to her son, "Whereas you are a man of lesser social station, the King's daughter is a highly esteemed member of the nobility. You would not be able to pursue a relationship with her."

The son replied, "But my mind prays for this bliss and remains unable to forget it for even a moment. If I cannot have it as I will it, then I will be unable to go on living."

For the sake of her son, the mother entered the palace of the King, constantly providing gifts of fat fish and fine meats which she left for the King's daughter without requesting any remuneration. The Princess thought this strange and so inquired as to what wish she was seeking to fulfill.

母白王女。愿却左右当以情
告。我唯有一子敬慕王女情
结成病。命不云远。愿垂愍
念赐其生命。王女言。汝去
月十五日于某甲天祠中住天
像后。母还语子。汝愿已得
告之如上。沐浴新衣在天像
后住。王女至时白其父王。
我有不吉须至天祠以求吉
福。王言大善。即严车五百
乘出至天祠。既到勅诸从
者。齐门而止独入天祠。天
神思惟。此不应尔。王为
[15]世主不可令此小人毁辱
王女。即厌此人令睡不觉。
王女既入见其睡。重推之不
悟。即以璎珞直十万两金遗
之而去。去后此人得觉见有
璎珞。又问众人知王女来。
情愿不遂忧恨懊恼。婬火内
发自烧而死。以是证故知。
女人之心不择

母白王女。願却左右當以情
告。我唯有一子敬慕王女情
結成病。命不云遠。願垂愍
念賜其生命。王女言。汝去
月十五日於某甲天祠中住天
像後。母還語子。汝願已得
告之如上。沐浴新衣在天像
後住。王女至時白其父王。
我有不吉須至天祠以求吉
福。王言大善。即嚴車五百
乘出至天祠。既到勅諸從
者。齊門而止獨入天祠。天
神思惟。此不應爾。王為
[15]世主不可令此小人毀辱
王女。即厭此人令睡不覺。
王女既入見其睡。重推之不
悟。即以瓔珞直十萬兩金遺
之而去。去後此人得覺見有
瓔珞。又問眾人知王女來。
情願不遂憂恨懊惱。婬火內
發自燒而死。以是證故知。
女人之心不擇

简体字   正體字

The mother addressed the Princess, "Pray, dismiss the retainers. I must relate a personal matter." She then continued: "I have only one son. He cherishes a respectful admiration for the daughter of the King. His feelings have taken hold so strongly that it has caused him to be taken with illness. He is not likely to survive much longer. I pray that you will take pity on him and give him back his life."

The Princess replied, "On the fifteenth of the month have him go into such-and-such a deity's shrine and then remain back behind the image of that deity."

The mother returned and told her son, "Your wish has already been fulfilled." She then described what had transpired. When the time came, he bathed, put on new clothes, and stood back behind the image of the deity.

When the appointed day arrived, the Princess told her father, the King, "I have something inauspicious which has come up. I must go to the shrine of the deity and seek for auspiciousness and blessings."

The King replied, "That is very good." He then immediately ordered forth five hundred nicely adorned carriages and had them escort her to that deity's shrine. Once she arrived at her destination, she ordered her retainers to close the doors and wait as she entered the shrine alone.

The shrine's celestial spirit thought, "This should not be occurring. The King is the lord of the land. I simply cannot allow this man of lesser station to corrupt and dishonor the Princess." He then caused the fisherman to become so tired that he fell into a sleep from which he could not awaken.

Having entered, the Princess saw that he had fallen asleep and so shook him very hard. Even so, he did not awaken. She then left him a necklace worth a hundred thousand double-ounces of gold and went upon her way.

After she had left, this man was finally able to wake up again, only to notice that the necklace was there. Next, he inquired of people in the surrounding crowd. He then realize that the King's daughter had in fact come to him. But because he was unable to follow up on his infatuation, he became distressed, full of regret, and overcome with grief-ridden torment. The fire of lust broke loose within him, so much so that he was burned up by it and died.

With this as corroboration, one may consequently realize that a woman's mind may be such that she might be unable to distinguish

贵贱唯欲是从。复次昔有国
王女。逐游陀罗共为不净。
又有仙人女随逐师子。如是
等种种女人之心无所选择。
以是种种因缘。于女人中除
去情欲忍不爱着。云何瞋恼
人中而得忍辱。当自思惟。
一切众生有罪因缘更相侵
害。我今受恼亦本行因缘。
虽非今世所作。是我先世恶
报。我[166c]今偿之。应当甘
受何可逆也。譬如负债。债
主索之应当欢喜偿债不可瞋
也。复次行者常行慈心。虽
有恼乱逼身必能[16]忍受。
譬如羼提仙人。在大林中修
忍行慈。时迦利王将诸婇女
入林游戏。饮食既讫王小睡
息。诸婇女辈[17]游花林间。
见此仙人加敬礼拜在一面
立。仙人尔时为诸婇女赞说
慈忍。其言美妙听者

貴賤唯欲是從。復次昔有國
王女。逐游陀羅共為不淨。
又有仙人女隨逐師子。如是
等種種女人之心無所選擇。
以是種種因緣。於女人中除
去情欲忍不愛著。云何瞋惱
人中而得忍辱。當自思惟。
一切眾生有罪因緣更相侵
害。我今受惱亦本行因緣。
雖非今世所作。是我先世惡
報。我[166c]今償之。應當甘
受何可逆也。譬如負債。債
主索之應當歡喜償債不可瞋
也。復次行者常行慈心。雖
有惱亂逼身必能[16]忍受。
譬如羼提仙人。在大林中修
忍行慈。時迦利王將諸婇女
入林遊戲。飲食既訖王小睡
息。諸婇女輩[17]遊花林間。
見此仙人加敬禮拜在一面
立。仙人爾時為諸婇女讚說
慈忍。其言美妙聽者

简体字   正體字

between the noble and the base, with the result that she may only be concerned with pursuing desires.

Again, there once was the daughter of a king who pursued a *caṇḍāla* and went so far as to consummate impure acts with him. Also, there once was the daughter of a rishi who followed after and pursued a lion. All sorts of examples such as these demonstrate that a woman's mind may be unable to be selective in these matters.

For reasons as these, one should get rid of emotional desires towards women and patiently refrain from indulging affectionate attachments to them.

2. PATIENCE WITH THOSE WHO ARE HATEFUL

How does one succeed in being patient even in the midst of people who are hateful and tormenting? One should reflect thus: "All beings are freighted with causes and conditions linked to transgressions and thus alternate in attacking and wreaking harm on one another. That I am now compelled to undergo such torment is also a consequence of such causes and conditions arising from my own past-life deeds.

"Although this is not something I have committed in this present life, it is the retribution for evil committed in a previous life. I am now having to pay for it. Hence I should just accept it agreeably. How could I go against it?" This is analogous to the circumstances surrounding indebtedness. When the lender asks for it, one ought to repay it happily. One can't legitimately get angry over it.

Moreover, the practitioner constantly resorts to thoughts of loving-kindness. Although there may be torment and chaos inflicted on his own person, he must certainly nonetheless be able to have patience and undergo it.

a. THE PATIENCE-CULTIVATING RISHI (STORY)

This is illustrated by the rishi who devoted himself to the practice of *kṣānti* (patience). He dwelt in a great forest where he cultivated patience and practiced loving-kindness. It was at this time that King Kali once brought his courtesans along with him as he entered the forest to wander around and sport about. Having finished his refreshments and a meal, the King then took a short nap.

Meanwhile, the courtesans wandered off amongst the flowers and trees and happened to encounter this rishi. They offered their reverential respects and stood off to one side. The rishi then spoke in praise of loving-kindness and patience for the benefit of the courtesans. His words were so fine and so marvelous that the listeners

无厌。久而不去。迦利王觉不见婇女拔剑追踪。见在仙人前立。憍妬隆盛。瞋目奋剑而问仙人。汝作何物。仙人答言。我今在此修忍行慈。王言。我今试汝。当以利剑截汝耳鼻斩汝手足。若不瞋者知汝修忍。仙人言任意。王即拔剑截其耳鼻斩其手足。而问之言。汝心动不。答言。我修慈忍心不动也。王言。汝一身在此无有势力。虽口言不动谁当信者。是时仙人即作誓言。若我实修慈忍血当为乳。即时血变为乳。王大惊喜。将诸婇女而去。是时林中龙神为此仙人雷电霹雳。王被毒害没不还宫。以是故言于恼[18]乱中能行忍辱。复次菩萨修行[19]悲心。一切众生常有众苦。处胎[20]迫隘受诸苦痛。生时迫迮骨肉如

简体字

無厭。久而不去。迦利王覺不見婇女拔劍追蹤。見在仙人前立。憍妬隆盛。瞋目奮劍而問仙人。汝作何物。仙人答言。我今在此修忍行慈。王言。我今試汝。當以利劍截汝耳鼻斬汝手足。若不瞋者知汝修忍。仙人言任意。王即拔劍截其耳鼻斬其手足。而問之言。汝心動不。答言。我修慈忍心不動也。王言。汝一身在此無有勢力。雖口言不動誰當信者。是時仙人即作誓言。若我實修慈忍血當為乳。即時血變為乳。王大驚喜。將諸婇女而去。是時林中龍神為此仙人雷電霹靂。王被毒害沒不還宮。以是故言於惱[18]亂中能行忍辱。復次菩薩修行[19]悲心。一切眾生常有眾苦。處胎[20]迫隘受諸苦痛。生時迫迮骨肉如

正體字

were transfixed by them and could not get enough. They remained there for quite a long time and could not bring themselves to leave.

By this time, King Kali had awoken from his nap and, failing to see his courtesans, picked up his sword and followed along behind so as to catch up with them. He came upon them standing before that rishi and consequently became full of arrogance and jealousy. With hate-filled glowering, he brandished his sword and demanded of the rishi, "Just what is it you think you're doing?!"

The rishi replied, saying, "I'm just abiding here in the cultivation of patience and the practice of loving-kindness."

The King said, "I'm now going to put you to the test. I'm going to take a sharp sword and slice off your ears and nose. I'm going to chop off your hands and feet. If you don't get angry, then we'll know that you really *do* cultivate patience."

The rishi replied, "Well, just do what you will."

The King immediately drew forth his sword and sliced off the rishi's ears and nose. After that, he chopped off his hands and feet as well. He then inquired, "Well, has your mind moved yet, or not?"

The rishi replied, "I cultivate loving-kindness and compassion. My mind has not moved at all."

The King said, "You are just a single isolated person here. You have no power in this situation. Although you can claim that you have not been moved, who could really believe that?"

The rishi then straightaway made a vow, "If I truly *do* cultivate loving-kindness and patience, all of this flowing blood ought to turn into milk." The blood then immediately transformed into milk.

At this, the King became both greatly frightened and delighted. He then departed, leading the courtesans away with him. Because of the actions he had taken against this rishi, the dragons and spirits of the forest then set loose a furious storm of thunder and lightning bolts. The King was grievously injured by it and died there, unable even to make it back to his palace.

It is on this sort of basis that it is said one should be able to practice patience even in the midst of the chaos of being tormented.

b. EMPLOYING COMPASSION

Additionally, the bodhisattva cultivates the mind of compassion. All beings are constantly undergoing manifold sufferings. They dwell in the womb where they are forced to abide in a tight space and undergo all manner of intense pain. When born, they are subjected to such forceful pressure, it is as if their bones and flesh are

破。冷风触身甚于剑戟。是
故佛言。一切苦中生苦最
重。如是老病死苦种种困
厄。云何行人复加其苦。是
为疮中复[21]加刀破。复次菩
萨自念。我不应如诸馀人常
随生死水流。我当逆流以求
尽源入泥洹道。一切凡人侵
至则瞋。益至则喜。怖处则
畏。我为菩萨不可如彼。虽
未断结当自抑制[167a]修行忍
辱恼害不瞋敬养不喜。众苦
艰难不应怖畏。当为众生[1]
兴大悲心。复次菩萨若见众
生来为恼乱。当自念言。是
为我之亲厚亦是我师。益加
亲爱敬心待之。何以故。彼
若不加众恼[2]恼我则[3]我不
成忍[4]辱。以是故言。是我
亲厚亦是我师。复次菩萨心
知如佛所说。众生无始世界
无际。往来五道轮转无量。

破。冷風觸身甚於劍戟。是
故佛言。一切苦中生苦最
重。如是老病死苦種種困
厄。云何行人復加其苦。是
為瘡中復[21]加刀破。復次菩
薩自念。我不應如諸餘人常
隨生死水流。我當逆流以求
盡源入泥洹道。一切凡人侵
至則瞋。益至則喜。怖處則
畏。我為菩薩不可如彼。雖
未斷結當自抑制[167a]修行忍
辱惱害不瞋敬養不喜。眾苦
艱難不應怖畏。當為眾生[1]
興大悲心。復次菩薩若見眾
生來為惱亂。當自念言。是
為我之親厚亦是我師。益加
親愛敬心待之。何以故。彼
若不加眾惱[2]惱我則[3]我不
成忍[4]辱。以是故言。是我
親厚亦是我師。復次菩薩心
知如佛所說。眾生無始世界
無際。往來五道輪轉無量。

简体字   正體字

being crushed. The cold air strikes their bodies more severely than a sword or halberd.

It was on account of this circumstance that the Buddha stated that, among all of the types of suffering, the suffering of being born is most intense. In much the same fashion, the suffering of aging, sickness, and death are fraught with difficulty and misery. How then could a practitioner allow himself to increase their sufferings even more? This would be like plunging a knife into the center of an open wound.

c. Going Against the Current

Additionally, the bodhisattva reminds himself, "I should not be like everyone else who constantly follows along in the flowing current of cyclic births and deaths. I should move up against the current in order to seek out the very source and enter the path to nirvāṇa.

"All common people, when met with attack, are hateful, when met with benefit, are delighted, and when in a frightening place, become fearful. In becoming a bodhisattva, I cannot act in the way that they do. Even though I have not yet succeeded in cutting off the fetters, I should nonetheless still exert self-restraint as I pursue the cultivation of patience.

"When tormented and injured, I will not become hateful, and when encountering respect and offerings, I will not be moved to delight. I should not be fearful of the intense difficulties involved in the manifold forms of suffering. And, for the sake of beings, I should let flourish the mind of great compassion."

d. Seeing Tormenters as Friends and Gurus

Moreover, if the bodhisattva sees a being coming to afflict him with torment and aggravation, he should think to himself, "This is my close friend and he is also my guru. I must enhance my treatment of him with familial affection and respectful thoughts. Why? Because if he does not afflict me with manifold forms of torment, then I will be unable to perfect the practice of patience." It is for this reason that he says, "He is my close friend and he is also my guru."

e. Seeing Tormenters as Close Relatives

Also, the bodhisattva's awareness accords with the Buddha's explanation that, "Throughout beginningless time and in a boundless number of world systems, beings have been going and coming, circulating an incalculable number of times through the five destinies of rebirth."[15]

我亦曾为众生父母兄弟。众
生亦皆曾为我父母兄弟。当
来亦尔。以是推之不应恶心
而怀瞋害。复次思惟。众生
之中佛种甚多。若我瞋意向
之则为瞋佛。若我瞋佛则为
已了。如说鸽鸟当得作佛。
今虽是鸟不可轻也。复次诸
烦恼中瞋为最重。不善报中
瞋报最大。馀结无此重罪。
如释提婆那民问 [5] 佛。偈
言。

何物杀安隐　何物杀不悔。
何物毒之根　吞灭一切善。
何物杀而赞　何物杀无忧。

[167a19] 佛答 [6] 偈言。

杀瞋心安隐　杀瞋心不悔。
瞋为毒之根　瞋灭一切善。
杀瞋诸佛赞　杀瞋则无忧。

[167a23]　　菩萨思惟。我今行
悲。欲令众生得乐。瞋为吞
灭诸善毒害一切。我当云何
行此重罪。若有瞋恚

我亦曾為眾生父母兄弟。眾
生亦皆曾為我父母兄弟。當
來亦爾。以是推之不應惡心
而懷瞋害。復次思惟。眾生
之中佛種甚多。若我瞋意向
之則為瞋佛。若我瞋佛則為
已了。如說鴿鳥當得作佛。
今雖是鳥不可輕也。復次諸
煩惱中瞋為最重。不善報中
瞋報最大。餘結無此重罪。
如釋提婆那民問 [5] 佛。偈
言。

何物殺安隱　何物殺不悔。
何物毒之根　吞滅一切善。
何物殺而讚　何物殺無憂。

[167a19] 佛答 [6] 偈言。

殺瞋心安隱　殺瞋心不悔。
瞋為毒之根　瞋滅一切善。
殺瞋諸佛讚　殺瞋則無憂。

[167a23]　　菩薩思惟。我今行
悲。欲令眾生得樂。瞋為吞
滅諸善毒害一切。我當云何
行此重罪。若有瞋恚

简体字　　　　　　　　　　　　正體字

Thus he reflects, "I myself have been the father, mother and elder and younger brother of these beings. These beings have also all served as my father, as my mother, and as my elder and younger brother. It will be just the same in the future as well." Extrapolating in this manner, he realizes that he should not nurture an evil mind cherishing hatefulness and harmful intent.

f.   SEEING TORMENTERS AS BUDDHAS

He additionally considers: "Among all these beings, those belonging to the lineage of the Buddhas are extremely many. If I harbor hateful intentions towards them, then this is just the same as acting hatefully towards the Buddhas themselves. If I behave hatefully towards the Buddhas, then I am surely done for."

This point is nicely illustrated by the earlier discussion about the pigeon. Even it will eventually succeed in achieving buddhahood. Although it may be only a pigeon just now, one must nonetheless refrain from even from slighting it in the present.[16]

g.   REALIZING THE DISASTROUSNESS OF HATRED

Additionally, among all of the sorts of affliction, hatefulness is the most serious. Among all of the retributions for committing bad acts, the retribution for hatred is the greatest. The other fetters do not have such severe punishments. This is demonstrated in Śakra Devānām Indra's verse in which he queried the Buddha:

> What thing is it which, murdered, brings peace and security?
> What thing is it which, slain, one has no regrets?
> What thing is it which is the root of venomousness?
> And which devours and destroys all forms of goodness?
>
> What thing is it which one slays and then one is praised?
> What thing is it which, slain, brings on no more distress?

The Buddha replied with a verse in which he said:

> If one murders anger, the mind will be peaceful and secure.
> If one slays anger, the mind will have no regrets.
> It is anger which is the root of venomousness.
> It is anger which destroys all forms of goodness.
>
> When one slays anger, all buddhas offer praise.
> If one slays anger, one has no more distress.

The bodhisattva considers, "As I now practice compassion, I wish to cause beings to gain happiness. Hatred devours all forms of goodness and visits poisonous injury on everyone. How then could I commit such a severe karmic offense? If one cherishes hatefulness,

自失乐[7]利。云何能令众生
得乐。复次诸佛菩萨以大悲
为本。从悲而出瞋为灭悲之
毒。特不相宜。若坏悲本何
名菩萨。菩萨从何而出。以
是[8]之故应修忍辱。若众生
加诸瞋恼当念其功德。今此
[167b]众生虽有一罪。更自别
有诸妙功德。以其功德故不
应[9]瞋。复次此人若骂若打
是为治我。譬如金师[10]炼
金垢随火去真金独在。此亦
如是。若我有罪是从先世因
缘。今当偿之不应瞋也。当
修忍辱。复次菩萨慈念众生
[11]犹如赤子。阎浮提人多诸
忧愁少有欢日。若来骂詈或
加谗贼。心得欢乐此乐难得
恣汝骂之。何以故。我本发
心欲令众生得欢喜故。

自失樂[7]利。云何能令眾生
得樂。復次諸佛菩薩以大悲
為本。從悲而出瞋為滅悲之
毒。特不相宜。若壞悲本何
名菩薩。菩薩從何而出。以
是[8]之故應修忍辱。若眾生
加諸瞋惱當念其功德。今此
[167b]眾生雖有一罪。更自別
有諸妙功德。以其功德故不
應[9]瞋。復次此人若罵若打
是為治我。譬如金師[10]煉
金垢隨火去真金獨在。此亦
如是。若我有罪是從先世因
緣。今當償之不應瞋也。當
修忍辱。復次菩薩慈念眾生
[11]猶如赤子。閻浮提人多諸
憂愁少有歡日。若來罵詈或
加讒賊。心得歡樂此樂難得
恣汝罵之。何以故。我本發
心欲令眾生得歡喜故。

简体字　　　　　　　　　　正體字

one loses even one's own happiness and benefit. How then could one be able to bring about happiness in others?

"Moreover, all buddhas and bodhisattvas take the great compassion as their foundation. They come forth from compassion. Hatred is the poison which destroys compassion. Given that connection, hatefulness is especially inappropriate. If one destroys the very foundation of compassion, how can he qualify as a bodhisattva at all? From what then could bodhisattvahood be supposed to emerge?"

For reasons such as these, one should persevere in the cultivation of patience.

h. Mindfulness of a Tormentor's Other Fine Qualities

If a beings visits all manner of hatred and torment upon one, then one should remain mindful of his other meritorious qualities, thinking, "Now, although this being has committed this one offense, still, aside from this, he possesses all sorts of other marvelous meritorious qualities." Based on his possession of these other meritorious qualities, one should refrain from becoming hateful.

i. Reflection on a Tormenter's Helpfulness

One should also reflect: "Additionally, if this person curses me or strikes me, he is helping to refine me. This is analogous to a goldsmith's refining of gold where the impurities are gotten rid of with fire so that only true gold remains. This is the very same sort of process.

"If I encounter punishments, then this derives from the causes and conditions of earlier lifetimes. I should now proceed with paying off this debt and so should refrain from becoming hateful. I should exercise patience in this matter."

j. Employing Kindness to Bestow Happiness on Tormenters

Furthermore, the bodhisattva brings loving-kindness to his mindfulness of beings, looking upon them just as he would his own children, thinking, "The people of Jambudvīpa have an abundance of every kind of distress and worry and they experience only a few days of happiness. If they find enjoyment in coming here and cursing and reviling or in inflicting slander and injury, such happiness is a only rarely enjoyed."

He thinks, "Carry on then with the cursing as much as you please. Why? Because when I originally brought forth the resolve, it was done out of a desire to cause beings to be happy."

復次世間眾生常為眾病所
惱。又為死賊。常隨伺之。
譬如怨家恒伺人便。云何善
人而不慈愍。復欲加苦苦未
及彼先自受害。如是思惟不
應瞋彼當修忍辱。復次當觀
瞋恚其咎最深。三毒之中無
重此者。九十八使中此為最
堅。諸心病中第一難治。瞋
恚之人不知善不知非善。不
觀罪福不知利害不自憶念。
當墮惡道善言忘失。不惜名
稱不知他惱。亦不自計身心
疲惱。瞋覆慧眼專行惱他。
如一五通仙人。以瞋恚故雖
修淨行殺害一國如旃陀羅。
復次瞋恚之人。譬如虎狼難
可共止。又如惡瘡易發易
壞。瞋恚之人譬如毒蛇人不
憙見。積瞋之人。惡心漸大

復次世間眾生常為眾病所
惱。又為死賊。常隨伺之。
譬如怨家恒伺人便。云何善
人而不慈愍。復欲加苦苦未
及彼先自受害。如是思惟不
應瞋彼當修忍辱。復次當觀
瞋恚其咎最深。三毒之中無
重此者。九十八使中此為最
堅。諸心病中第一難治。瞋
恚之人不知善不知非善。不
觀罪福不知利害不自憶念。
當墮惡道善言忘失。不惜名
稱不知他惱。亦不自計身心
疲惱。瞋覆慧眼專行惱他。
如一五通仙人。以瞋恚故雖
修淨行殺害一國如旃陀羅。
復次瞋恚之人。譬如虎狼難
可共止。又如惡瘡易發易
壞。瞋恚之人譬如毒蛇人不
憙見。積瞋之人。惡心漸大

簡体字 | 正體字

k. Refraining from Inflicting Yet More Suffering

"Also, the beings of the world are constantly tormented by the many sorts of diseases. Additionally, they are constantly pursued and spied upon by the insurgents of death which stalk them like an enemy always waiting for an opportunity to seize advantage. How then could a good person fail to act out of loving-kindness and pity, wishing instead to inflict additional suffering on them? One should prefer that, before suffering falls on someone else, one would first take the injury on himself."

One should take up reflections of these sorts, thereby refraining from being hateful towards others as one invokes the cultivation of patience.

l. More Reflections on Hatred's Faults

Furthermore, one should contemplate that the faults of hatred run extremely deep. Of the three poisons, nothing is more serious than this. Of the ninety-eight secondary fetters (*saṃyojana*), this one is the most stubborn. Of all of the disorders which afflict the mind, this is the one which is the most difficult to cure.

People affected by hatred fail to distinguish between what is good and what is unwholesome. They lose all regard for whether their actions create karmic offenses or karmic blessings. They retain no awareness of what is beneficial as opposed to what is injurious. They do not even reflect upon the consequences for themselves. They are bound to fall into the wretched destinies. All discourse associated with goodness is lost in them. They do not cherish a good reputation and have no awareness of the torment undergone by others. Nor do they bother to reckon the toll taken on themselves in physical and mental weariness and aggravation.

Hatred so covers over their own eye of wisdom that they focus exclusively on proceeding with the persecution of others. This is analogous to the case of the rishi with the five superknowledges who, even though he cultivated pure practices, slaughtered the inhabitants of an entire country after the manner of a *caṇḍāla* [butcher].[17]

Again, it is difficult to keep company with someone possessed by hatred, just as it would be so with a tiger or a wolf. Such a person is comparable to a purulent sore readily exuding discharges and easily becoming decayed. A person full of hatred is like a venomous snake. People take no delight in encountering him. The evil mind of the person who accumulates hatreds gradually increases in

简体字	正體字
至不可至。杀父杀君恶意向佛。如拘睒弥国比丘。以小因缘瞋心转[12]大分为二部。若欲断当终竟三月犹不可了。佛来在众举相[13]轮手遮而[14]告言。	至不可至。殺父殺君惡意向佛。如拘睒彌國比丘。以小因緣瞋心轉[12]大分為二部。若欲斷當終竟三月猶不可了。佛來在眾舉相[13]輪手遮而[14]告言。
[15]汝诸比丘　勿起闘诤。 恶心相续　苦报甚重。	[15]汝諸比丘　勿起闘诤。 惡心相續　苦報甚重。
汝求涅盘　弃舍世利。 在善法中　[167c]云何瞋诤。	汝求涅槃　棄捨世利。 在善法中　[167c]云何瞋诤。
世人忿诤　是犹可恕。 出家之人　何可诤闘。	世人忿诤　是猶可恕。 出家之人　何可诤闘。
出家心中　怀毒自害。 如冷云中　[16]火出烧身。	出家心中　懷毒自害。 如冷雲中　[16]火出燒身。
[167c04]　　诸比丘白佛言。佛为法王愿小默然。是辈侵我不可不答。佛念是人不可度也。于众僧中凌虚而去。入林树间寂然三昧。瞋罪如是乃至不受佛语。以是之故应当除瞋修行忍辱。	[167c04]　　諸比丘白佛言。佛為法王願小默然。是輩侵我不可不答。佛念是人不可度也。於眾僧中凌虛而去。入林樹間寂然三昧。瞋罪如是乃至不受佛語。以是之故應當除瞋修行忍辱。

简体字　　　　　　　　　　　　　　　　　　正體字

its intensity to the point that he ends up doing what one cannot do, killing even his father, killing even his sovereign, and even conceiving evil intentions towards the Buddha.

m. THE CONTENTIOUS KAUŚĀMBĪ MONKS (STORY)

This idea is well illustrated by the case of the bhikshus in the state of Kauśāmbī. For relatively minor reasons, their hateful thoughts for each other became so severe that they split into two factions. If they had wished to come to a breaking off of relations, they should ordinarily have had to wait to the end of their three-month retreat. But they remained unable to put their differences to rest. The Buddha eventually came and, in the midst of the Assembly, raised up his wheel-marked hand to quiet them. He then told them:

All of you bhikshus—
Don't generate such disputation.
When evil thoughts continue on,
The bitter retribution grows extremely severe.

You are seeking to gain nirvāṇa.
You should cast aside and relinquish worldly benefits.
When abiding in the dharmas of goodness,
How could you be so hateful and full of disputation?

When worldly men become angry and contentious,
This is something one might yet forgive.
But with men who have left the home life,
How can it be that they dispute and struggle?

When in the mind of one who has left the home life,
One cherishes venomousness, this brings harm on oneself.
It is as if from amidst a cool cloud
Lightning struck forth and burned the body.

Those bhikshus then addressed the Buddha, saying, "The Buddha is the Dharma King. He would prefer that we maintain a brief period of silence. However, this group assailed us. We cannot but respond."

The Buddha thought, "These men cannot be crossed over to liberation." He then soared forth from the midst of that group of Sanghins and disappeared, going then into the forest where he remained still in samādhi.

In this way, the offense of hatred becomes such that, at its extreme, one does not accept even the words of the Buddha. For this reason, one should get rid of hatred and cultivate patience.

复次[17]能修忍辱慈悲易得。
得慈悲者则至佛道。问曰。
忍辱法皆好。而有一事不
可。小人[18]轻慢谓为怖畏。
以是之故不应皆忍。答曰。
若以小人轻慢谓为怖畏。而
欲不忍。不忍之罪甚于此
也。何以故。不忍之人贤圣
善人之所轻贱。忍辱之人为
小人所慢。二轻之中。宁为
无智所慢。不为贤圣所贱。
何以故。无[19]智之人轻所不
轻。贤圣之人贱所可贱。以
是之故当修忍辱。复次忍辱
之人。虽不[20]行布施禅定。
而常得微妙功德生天上人
中。后得佛道。何以故。心
柔软故。复次菩萨思惟。若
人今世恼我毁辱夺利。轻骂
系缚且当含忍。若我不忍。
当堕地狱铁垣热地受无量
苦。烧炙[21]燔煮不可具说。
以是故知。小人无智虽轻而
贵。不忍用

復次[17]能修忍辱慈悲易得。
得慈悲者則至佛道。問曰。
忍辱法皆好。而有一事不
可。小人[18]輕慢謂為怖畏。
以是之故不應皆忍。答曰。
若以小人輕慢謂為怖畏。而
欲不忍。不忍之罪甚於此
也。何以故。不忍之人賢聖
善人之所輕賤。忍辱之人為
小人所慢。二輕之中。寧為
無智所慢。不為賢聖所賤。
何以故。無[19]智之人輕所不
輕。賢聖之人賤所可賤。以
是之故當修忍辱。復次忍辱
之人。雖不[20]行布施禪定。
而常得微妙功德生天上人
中。後得佛道。何以故。心
柔軟故。復次菩薩思惟。若
人今世惱我毀辱奪利。輕罵
繫縛且當含忍。若我不忍。
當墮地獄鐵垣熱地受無量
苦。燒炙[21]燔煮不可具說。
以是故知。小人無智雖輕而
貴。不忍用

简体字   正體字

Moreover, when one is able to cultivate patience, it is easy to succeed in developing loving-kindness and compassion. If one has succeeded in developing loving-kindness and compassion, one succeeds thereby in reaching the path to buddhahood.

n. Enduring a Petty Person's Arrogance

Question: The dharma of patience is entirely fine, but there is one situation where it is unacceptable. This is where a petty person acts in a slighting and arrogant manner with the presumption that one will shrink in fearfulness. Thus one should not constrain oneself to be patient under every circumstance.

Response: If one is the victim of slighting and arrogance on the part of a petty person who presumes that one is afraid of him and so one desires to desist from patience, the karmic offense of not being patient in that circumstance represents an even more serious situation. Why? A person who fails to act with patience is looked upon lightly and is seen as base by the Worthies, by the Āryas, and by people who are good. The person who perseveres in patience is looked on with arrogance by petty people.

Of the two cases of being looked upon lightly, one ought rather to be the victim of arrogance on the part of those devoid of wisdom, thus avoiding being seen as base by the Worthies and Āryas. Why? Those devoid of wisdom slight what should not be slighted. People who are Worthies and Āryas treat as base what really should be seen as base. Hence one should persevere in the cultivation of patience.

Moreover, although a person who is patient may not practice giving or dhyāna absorption, still, he constantly earns subtle and marvelous merit whereby he is reborn among gods and men and later gains success in the Buddha Path. Why? It is because his mind is pliant.

Then again, the bodhisattva reflects, "Even if people torment me in this present life, bringing ruinous defamation on me, forcefully seizing wealth, slighting me, scolding me, and putting me in bondage, I should nonetheless still maintain patience. If I fail to be patient, I am bound to fall into the hells and undergo countless forms of suffering on their iron-walled hot grounds, enduring roasting and broiling and punishments such as one cannot completely describe."

For these reasons, one should realize that, although one may be slighted by petty people devoid of wisdom, one may still retain one's nobility. If one fails to exercise patience and thus resorts to the use

威虽快而贱。是故菩萨应当
忍辱。复次菩萨思惟。我初
发心誓为众生治其心病。今
此众生为瞋恚结使所病。我
当治之。云何而复以之自病
应当忍辱。譬如药师疗治众
病。若鬼狂病拔刀骂詈不识
好丑。医知鬼病但为治之而
不瞋恚。菩萨若为众生瞋恼
骂詈。知其为瞋恚[22]者[168a]
烦恼所病狂心所使。方便治
之无所嫌责亦复如是。复次
菩萨育养一切爱之如子。若
众生瞋恼菩萨。菩萨愍之不
瞋不责。譬如慈父抚育子
孙。子孙幼稚未有所识。或
时骂詈打掷不敬不畏。其父
愍其愚小爱之[1]愈至。虽有
过罪不瞋不恚。菩萨忍辱亦
复如是。复次菩萨思惟。若
众生瞋恼加我我当忍辱。若
我不

威雖快而賤。是故菩薩應當
忍辱。復次菩薩思惟。我初
發心誓為眾生治其心病。今
此眾生為瞋恚結使所病。我
當治之。云何而復以之自病
應當忍辱。譬如藥師療治眾
病。若鬼狂病拔刀罵詈不識
好醜。醫知鬼病但為治之而
不瞋恚。菩薩若為眾生瞋惱
罵詈。知其為瞋恚[22]者[168a]
煩惱所病狂心所使。方便治
之無所嫌責亦復如是。復次
菩薩育養一切愛之如子。若
眾生瞋惱菩薩。菩薩愍之不
瞋不責。譬如慈父撫育子
孫。子孫幼稚未有所識。或
時罵詈打擲不敬不畏。其父
愍其愚小愛之[1]愈至。雖有
過罪不瞋不恚。菩薩忍辱亦
復如是。復次菩薩思惟。若
眾生瞋惱加我我當忍辱。若
我不

简体字   正體字

of force, even though he might gain some satisfaction, he thereby debases his own character. Therefore the bodhisattva should maintain patience.

o. SEEING OTHERS' HATEFULNESS AS DISEASE OR AS POSSESSION

Additionally, the bodhisattva considers, "When I first brought forth the resolve [to gain bodhi], I vowed to cure the mental diseases of beings. This being has now fallen ill with the fetter of hatred. I should be engaged in curing him. How then could I instead voluntarily make myself sick on this account? I should persevere in the practice of patience."

This is analogous to the master of medicines who cures the manifold diseases. If he encounters someone so afflicted by the disease of being driven crazy by ghosts that he pulls out a knife, curses, reviles others, and fails to distinguish good and evil, the physician knows that this is the disease of ghost possession. He then simply proceeds with curing it and thus avoids becoming angry himself.

If the bodhisattva is hated, tormented, cursed, and reviled by other beings, he realizes that they have fallen ill with the affliction of hatred and that these actions are brought on by a crazed mind. He employs skillful means to cure them, and in just this same manner, finds no cause for blame or condemnation.

p. SEEING OTHERS AS ONE'S OWN CHILDREN

Furthermore, the bodhisattva engages in the raising and nurturing of everyone, loving everyone as if they were his own children. Even if beings happen to act in a hateful and tormenting fashion towards the bodhisattva, the bodhisattva takes pity on them, refrains from feeling hatred for them, and does not condemn them.

This is analogous to a father who acts out of loving-kindness in raising his sons and grandsons to maturity. Because his sons and grandsons are young and immature, they don't yet understand anything. Thus there may be times when they curse and strike out, being disrespectful and careless of consequences. The children's father feels sympathy for their stupidity and immaturity and so feels even stronger affection for them. Even though they may commit transgressions, he does not hate them and does not allow himself to become angry. The bodhisattva's patience is just like this.

q. BEING WARY OF THE CONSEQUENCES OF RETALIATION

Additionally, the bodhisattva considers, "If beings heap hatred and torment on me, I should nonetheless continue to be patient. If I fail

忍今世心悔。后入地狱受苦
无量。若在畜生。作毒龙恶
蛇师子虎狼。若为饿鬼火从
口出。譬如人被火烧。烧时
痛轻后痛转重。复次菩萨思
惟。我为菩萨欲为众生益
利。若我不能忍辱。不名菩
萨名为恶人。复次菩萨思
惟。世有二种。一者众生
数。二者非众生数。我初发
心誓为一切众生。若有非众
生数山石树木风寒冷热水雨
侵害。但求[2]［冲-重+素］之
初不瞋恚。今此众生是我所
为。加恶于我。我当受之。
云何而瞋。复次菩萨知从久
远已来。因缘和合假名为人
无实人法。谁可瞋者。是中
但有骨血皮肉。譬如[3]累[4]
墼又如木人机关动作有去有
来。

简体字

忍今世心悔。後入地獄受苦
無量。若在畜生。作毒龍惡
蛇師子虎狼。若為餓鬼火從
口出。譬如人被火燒。燒時
痛輕後痛轉重。復次菩薩思
惟。我為菩薩欲為眾生益
利。若我不能忍辱。不名菩
薩名為惡人。復次菩薩思
惟。世有二種。一者眾生
數。二者非眾生數。我初發
心誓為一切眾生。若有非眾
生數山石樹木風寒冷熱水雨
侵害。但求[2]［衝-重+素］之
初不瞋恚。今此眾生是我所
為。加惡於我。我當受之。
云何而瞋。復次菩薩知從久
遠已來。因緣和合假名為人
無實人法。誰可瞋者。是中
但有骨血皮肉。譬如[3]累[4]
墼又如木人機關動作有去有
來。

正體字

to maintain patience, then my thoughts will be full of regret in this present life and what's more, I will fall into the hells in the future life and become bound then to undergo countless forms of suffering. If I should then come to abide among animals, I will become a venomous dragon, an evil snake, a lion, a tiger, or a wolf. In the event that I become a hungry ghost, then I will have flames which pour forth from my mouth.

This is analogous to that circumstance where someone is burned by fire. At the moment when one is burned, the pain may still be relatively mild. It is only afterwards that the pain becomes so extremely severe.

    r.   Reflecting on One's Bodhisattva Vows

Additionally, the bodhisattva reflects, "I am a bodhisattva. I desire to be of benefit to beings. If I become unable to maintain patience, then I can't be called a "bodhisattva" at all, but rather should be known as one who is evil."

    s.   Seeing Others' Hatred as Mere Environmental Events

Further, the bodhisattva considers, "There are two kinds of phenomena in the world. The first are those which are sentient beings. The second are those not belonging to the sphere of sentient beings. When I first brought forth the resolve [to realize bodhi], I made vows for the sake of other beings.

"If I happened to be assailed and harmed by things which don't belong to the sphere of sentient beings, things such as mountain rocks, forest trees, wind, cold, heat, floods or rain, I simply seek a way to control the situation and, from the very outset, do not allow myself to become angry. Now it is these very beings who are the ones on whose behalf I am supposedly acting. Thus, when they happen to heap evil on me, I should endure it. How could I take this occasion as a reason to become hateful?"

    t.   Realizing Absence of Self in Those Who Are Hateful

Moreover, the bodhisattva knows that from long ago on up to the present, it has always been the case that causes and conditions come together and are falsely referred to as a "person" even though in actual fact there is no genuine dharma of a "person" involved at all. Who then is it that could be hated in such circumstances? There exist herein only bones and blood and skin and flesh. This is comparable to something laid up with bricks or to a wooden puppet displaying mechanical movements and manifesting comings and goings.

知其如此不应有瞋。若我瞋者是则愚痴自受罪苦。以是之故应修忍辱。复次菩萨思惟。过去无量恒河沙等诸佛。本行菩萨道时。皆先[5]行生忍然后修行法忍。我今求学佛道。当如诸佛法。不应起瞋恚如魔[6]界法。以是故应当忍辱。如是等种种无量因缘故能忍。是名生忍。

知其如此不應有瞋。若我瞋者是則愚癡自受罪苦。以是之故應修忍辱。復次菩薩思惟。過去無量恒河沙等諸佛。本行菩薩道時。皆先[5]行生忍然後修行法忍。我今求學佛道。當如諸佛法。不應起瞋恚如魔[6]界法。以是故應當忍辱。如是等種種無量因緣故能忍。是名生忍。

简体字   正體字

When one understands that the situation is of just this very sort, then one should be able to refrain from cherishing any hatred and should reflect, "If I become hateful, then this is just stupidity and amounts to a voluntary acceptance of the suffering of the punishments bound to follow as a consequence." For these reasons too, one should persevere in the cultivation of patience.

u. RECALLING THE NECESSITY OF EMULATING THE BUDDHAS

Additionally, the bodhisattva considers, "Throughout the past, during their original practice of the Bodhisattva Path, an incalculable number of Ganges sands of buddhas all first practiced patience with respect to beings and then later cultivated patience with respect to dharmas. I too am now seeking to study the path of the Buddhas. I should therefore accord with the Dharma of the Buddhas. Hence I should not allow myself to generate hatefulness in a manner characteristic of demon-realm dharmas. For this reason too, I should persevere in the practice of patience."

For all sorts of incalculably numerous reasons such as these, one remains able to abide in patience. This is what is meant by "patience with respect to beings."

[168a]大智[7]度论卷第十四。
大智度论释初品中羼提波罗蜜[8]法忍义[9]第二十五（卷第十五）。
龙树菩萨造。
[10]后秦[11]龟兹国三[12]藏鸠摩罗什[13]奉诏译 。
[168b08]　　云何名法忍。忍诸恭敬供养众生及诸瞋恼婬欲之人。是名生忍。忍其供养恭敬法及瞋恼婬欲法。是为法忍。复次法忍者。于内六情不着。于外六尘不受。能于此二不作分别。何以故。内相如外外相如内。二相俱不可得故。一相故。因缘合故。其实空故。一切法相常清净故。如真际法性相故。不二入故。虽无二亦不一。如是观诸法心信不转。是名法忍。如毘摩罗[14]鞊经中。法[15]住菩萨说生灭为二不生不灭是不二入法门。

简体字

[168a]大智[7]度論卷第十四。
大智度論釋初品中羼提波羅蜜[8]法忍義[9]第二十五（卷第十五）。
龍樹菩薩造。
[10]後秦[11]龜茲國三[12]藏鳩摩羅什[13]奉詔譯 。
[168b08]　　云何名法忍。忍諸恭敬供養眾生及諸瞋惱婬欲之人。是名生忍。忍其供養恭敬法及瞋惱婬欲法。是為法忍。復次法忍者。於內六情不著。於外六塵不受。能於此二不作分別。何以故。內相如外外相如內。二相俱不可得故。一相故。因緣合故。其實空故。一切法相常清淨故。如真際法性相故。不二入故。雖無二亦不一。如是觀諸法心信不轉。是名法忍。如毘摩羅[14]鞊經中。法[15]住菩薩說生滅為二不生不滅是不二入法門。

正體字

Chapter 25: Patience with Dharmas

III. Patience with Respect to Dharmas

  A. Patience with Dharmas Defined

Just what is meant by "patience with respect to dharmas"?[18] "Patience with respect to beings" refers to having patience toward all beings who display reverence or who make offerings and refers as well to having patience with all persons who are under the influence of hatred or sexual desire. "Patience with respect to dharmas" refers to maintaining patience towards their dharmas of expressing reverence or presenting offerings as well as to maintaining patience with their dharmas of hatefulness and sexual desire.

Additionally, "patience with respect to dharmas" involves remaining unattached inwardly regarding one's own six sense faculties while one also refrains from taking on the outward six sense objects. One thus remains able to refrain from making any discriminating distinctions with respect to either of these two spheres.

How so? "Inward" characteristics are identical to those which are "outward." "Outward" characteristics are identical to those which are "inward." This is because neither of these two categories of characteristics can finally be gotten at. This is because they are of a single characteristic, because they are only a conjunction of causes and conditions, because, in reality, they are empty [of any inherent existence], because the characteristics of all dharmas constantly abide in a state of purity, because they are characterized by identity with ultimate truth and the nature of dharmas, and because they are subsumed within the non-dual. Although they are not dual, they are not singular, either. When one contemplates all dharmas in this manner and yet one's thoughts of faith remain undeflected, this qualifies one as possessing "patience with respect to dharmas."

  B. Scriptural Citation

This is as set forth in the *Vimalakīrti Sutra* where Dharma Dwelling Bodhisattva said, "Production and extinction are dual phenomena whereas it is that which is neither produced nor destroyed which constitutes the Dharma gateway of non-duality."

乃至文殊尸利说。无闻无见一切[16]心灭[17]无说无语。是不二入法门。毘摩罗[*]鞊默然无言。诸菩萨赞言。善哉善哉。是真不二入法门。复次一切法有二种。一者众生。二者[18]诸法。菩萨于众生中忍如[19]先说。今说法中忍。法有二种。心法非心法。非心法中有内有外。外有寒热风雨等。内有饥渴老病死等。如是等种种名为非心法。心法中有二种。一者瞋恚忧愁疑等。二者婬欲憍慢等。是二名为心法。菩萨于此二法能忍不动。是名法忍。问曰。于众生中若瞋恼害命得罪。怜愍得福。寒热风雨无有增损。云何而忍。

乃至文殊尸利說。無聞無見一切[16]心滅[17]無說無語。是不二入法門。毘摩羅[*]鞊默然無言。諸菩薩讚言。善哉善哉。是真不二入法門。復次一切法有二種。一者眾生。二者[18]諸法。菩薩於眾生中忍如[19]先說。今說法中忍。法有二種。心法非心法。非心法中有內有外。外有寒熱風雨等。內有飢渴老病死等。如是等種種名為非心法。心法中有二種。一者瞋恚憂愁疑等。二者婬欲憍慢等。是二名為心法。菩薩於此二法能忍不動。是名法忍。問曰。於眾生中若瞋惱害命得罪。憐愍得福。寒熱風雨無有增損。云何而忍。

简体字 　　　　　　　　　　 正體字

And so it continued until Mañjuśrī said, "In the absence of hearing and the absence of seeing, where thought is extinguished and there is no utterance and no discourse—this is the Dharma gateway of non-duality."

Then Vimalakirti, [in offering his comment on the matter], remained silent and said nothing. All of the bodhisattvas exclaimed in praise, "Good Indeed! Good Indeed! This is the true non-dual Dharma gateway."

Then again, one may say that "all dharmas" consists of two categories: The first is beings. The second is dharmas. The bodhisattva maintains patience in the midst of beings as explained above. Now we shall explain how it is that one maintains patience in the midst of dharmas.

C. Two Types of Dharmas: Mental and Non-Mental

In this context, "dharmas" may classified into two types: "mental" dharmas and "non-mental" dharmas. Among the "non-mental" dharmas there are those which are inward and those which are outward. Outwardly, there are cold, heat, wind, rain, and so forth. Inwardly, there are hunger, thirst, aging, sickness, death, and so forth. All other sorts of phenomena of this type qualify as "non-mental" dharmas.

"Mental" dharmas themselves consist of two sub-types: The first includes hatred, worry, doubt, and so forth. The second includes sexual desire, arrogance, and so forth.[19] These two sub-types make up the "mental" dharmas.

1. "Patience" Is Towards Both Mental and Non-Mental Dharmas

When the bodhisattva is able to maintain patience and remain unmoved in relation to the two primary types of dharmas (i.e. both the mental and the non-mental), it is this which qualifies as "patience with respect to dharmas."

2. Challenge: Why Have Patience with Non-Mental Dharmas?

Question: If, in relation to other beings, one becomes hateful, engages in torment, and inflicts injury on their lives, one commits a karmic transgression, whereas, if one acts out of sympathy for them, one gains karmic blessings as a result. However, in reacting to cold, heat, wind, and rain, there is no production of any gain or any loss for anyone. Why is it then that one should remain patient with such phenomena?

答曰。虽无[168c]增损[20]而自生恼乱忧苦害菩萨道。以是故应当忍。复次非但杀恼众生故得罪。为恶心作因缘故有罪。所以者何。虽杀众生而无记心是便无罪。慈念众生虽无所与而大得福。[21]以是故寒热风雨虽无增损。然以能生恶意故得罪。以是故应当忍。复次菩萨。自知宿罪因缘生此苦处。此我自作我应自受。如是思惟是故能忍。复次菩萨思惟。国土有二种。有净有不净。菩萨若生不净国中。受此辛苦饥寒众恼。自发净愿。我成佛时国中无此众苦。此虽不净乃是我利。复次菩萨思惟。世间八法贤圣所不能免。何况

简体字

3. Response: Non-patience Generates Karma Even Here

Response: Although one does not thereby bring about any gain or loss for anyone, still, if one brings forth disruptive afflictions and distressful bitterness, one does inflict injury upon one's own practice of the Bodhisattva Path. It is for this reason that one should maintain patience.

Additionally, it is not the case that one commits karmic transgressions solely through the killing and tormenting of beings. Wherever one courses in causes and conditions associated with evil thoughts, one generates karmic transgressions as a consequence.

How might this be the case? For instance, one might happen to cause the death of a being, but if it was done with a neutral mind, this would not necessarily involve any incurring of a offense.[20] On the other hand, if one were to maintain a lovingly-kind mindfulness of beings, although there might be nothing which one actually provides for them, one would thereby still gain a great measure of karmic blessings.

Hence, although there may be no gain or loss for anyone wrought through one's reactions to cold, heat, wind, or rain, still, allowing them to instigate one's own generation of evil thought does indeed involve the commission of associated karmic transgressions. Therefore one should maintain patience with these phenomena.

D. Reflections Inspiring Patience with Non-Mental Dharmas

Moreover, the bodhisattva naturally realizes, "It is on account of the causes and conditions associated with karmic offenses in previous lives that one is reborn in this place so fraught with suffering. This is something I created myself. Hence I ought to be bound to personally endure it." It is through reflecting in this fashion that one remains able to maintain patience.

Additionally, the bodhisattva considers and realizes that there are two kinds of countries: There are those which are pure and there are those which are impure. If the bodhisattva is born into an impure country and experiences these bitter sufferings, hunger, cold, and the manifold torments, he makes a purifying vow to himself: "When I achieve buddhahood, the country will have none of these manifold sufferings. Although this place is impure, it will ultimately work to my benefit."

Furthermore, the bodhisattva reflects, "Not even the Worthies and Āryas are able to avoid encountering circumstances precipitating the eight worldly dharmas.[21] How much the less could this be

于我。以是故应当忍。复次菩萨思惟。知此人身无牢无强。为老病死所逐。虽复天身清净无老无病。耽着天乐。譬如醉人。不得修行道福出家离欲。以是故。于此人身自忍修福利益众生。复次菩萨思惟我受此四大五众身。应有种种苦分。无有受身而不苦者。富贵贫贱出家在家。愚智明暗无得免者。何以故。富贵之人常有[22]畏怖守护财物。譬如肥羊早就屠机。如乌衔肉众[23]乌逐之。贫贱之人有饥寒之苦。出家之人今世虽苦后世受福得道。在家之人今世虽乐。后世受苦。愚人先求今世乐。无常对至后则受苦。智[24]人思惟无常苦。后则受乐[25]得道。如是等受身之人无不有

於我。以是故應當忍。復次菩薩思惟。知此人身無牢無強。為老病死所逐。雖復天身清淨無老無病。耽著天樂。譬如醉人。不得修行道福出家離欲。以是故。於此人身自忍修福利益眾生。復次菩薩思惟我受此四大五眾身。應有種種苦分。無有受身而不苦者。富貴貧賤出家在家。愚智明闇無得免者。何以故。富貴之人常有[22]畏怖守護財物。譬如肥羊早就屠机。如烏銜肉眾[23]烏逐之。貧賤之人有飢寒之苦。出家之人今世雖苦後世受福得道。在家之人今世雖樂。後世受苦。愚人先求今世樂。無常對至後則受苦。智[24]人思惟無常苦。後則受樂[25]得道。如是等受身之人無不有

简体字   正體字

the case for me." On account of this, one should be able to maintain patience.

Moreover, the bodhisattva reflects and realizes that this human body doesn't possess any particular durability or strength. It is pursued by aging, sickness, and death. Although the bodies of the gods are pure, show no aging, and have no illness, they become indulgently attached to the pleasures of the heavens. In this they are comparable to people who have become intoxicated. They are unable to cultivate the karmic blessings associated with the Path and are unable to leave the home life and transcend desire. Because of this, one constrains oneself even while in this human body to maintain patience, cultivate karmic blessings, and benefit to other beings.[22]

Then again, the bodhisattva considers, "I have taken on this body composed of the four great elements and the five aggregates. It ought therefore to be the case that it is freighted with all manner of aspects entailing suffering as a consequence. There is no one who takes on such a body and yet remains invulnerable to suffering."

Whether one is rich and of noble birth or poor and of humble status, whether one is a monastic or a householder, whether one is foolish or wise, and whether one is intelligent or dull, no one is able to avoid it. How is this?

Those persons who are rich and of noble birth are constantly subject to fearfulness and the compulsion to protect their material wealth. They are analogous to the fat sheep taken early to the butcher's chopping block. They are like the crow which holds a piece of meat in its beak and is pursued by a flock of other crows.

Those who are poor and of humble status are subject to the sufferings of hunger and cold. Although monastics are subject to sufferings in the present existence, they receive karmic blessings in their future lives while also achieving success in the Path. Although householders may experience pleasures in the present life, they are bound to endure sufferings in their future lives.

Foolish people take pleasure-seeking in the present life as their primary priority. When they encounter death (lit. "impermanence"), they are bound to undergo subsequent suffering. The wise initially contemplate impermanence and suffering and consequently become able later on to experience happiness and realize success in the Path. Examples of these sorts serve to illustrate that there is no one who takes on a body who does not thereby become subject to

苦。是故菩萨应当行忍。复次菩萨思惟一切世间皆苦我当云何于中而欲求乐。复次菩萨思惟。我于无量劫中常受众苦[169a]无所利益未曾为法。今日为众生求佛道。虽受此苦当得大利。是故外内诸苦悉当忍受。复次菩萨大心誓愿。若阿鼻泥犁苦我当忍之。何况小苦而不能忍。若[1]小不忍何能忍大。如是种种外法中忍名曰法忍。问曰。云何内心法中能忍。答曰。菩萨思惟。我虽未得道诸结未断。若当不忍与凡人不异。非为菩萨。复自思惟。若我得道断诸结使则无法可忍。复次。饥渴寒热。是外魔军。结使烦恼。是内魔贼。[2]我当破此二军。以成佛道。若不尔者。佛道不成。如说。佛苦行六年。

苦。是故菩薩應當行忍。復次菩薩思惟一切世間皆苦我當云何於中而欲求樂。復次菩薩思惟。我於無量劫中常受眾苦[169a]無所利益未曾為法。今日為眾生求佛道。雖受此苦當得大利。是故外內諸苦悉當忍受。復次菩薩大心誓願。若阿鼻泥犁苦我當忍之。何況小苦而不能忍。若[1]小不忍何能忍大。如是種種外法中忍名曰法忍。問曰。云何內心法中能忍。答曰。菩薩思惟。我雖未得道諸結未斷。若當不忍與凡人不異。非為菩薩。復自思惟。若我得道斷諸結使則無法可忍。復次。飢渴寒熱。是外魔軍。結使煩惱。是內魔賊。[2]我當破此二軍。以成佛道。若不爾者。佛道不成。如說。佛苦行六年。

简体字　　　　　　　　　　　正體字

suffering. Therefore the bodhisattva should course in the practice of patience.

Furthermore, the bodhisattva reflects, "The entire world is subject to suffering. How then could I possibly abide within it and yet still expect to enjoy happiness?"

Again, the bodhisattva considers, "I have constantly endured manifold sufferings throughout the course of an incalculable number of kalpas and yet have not derived any benefit from it. So far, it has never been for the sake of the Dharma. Today, for the sake of beings, I strive to realize the Buddha Path. Although I now undergo this suffering, I will gain great benefit from it in the future. Therefore, whether it be outward suffering or inward suffering, I should patiently undergo all of these forms of suffering."

Additionally, the bodhisattva makes vows with the great mind, "I will patiently undergo even the sufferings of the *avīci niraya* (hells). How much the less might it be that I would fail to maintain patience with minor sufferings? If I fail to maintain patience with even minor sufferings, how could I be able to maintain patience with major sufferings?"

When one maintains patience with all sorts of external dharmas such as these, this is what qualifies as "patience with respect to dharmas."

E. PATIENCE WITH RESPECT TO MENTAL DHARMAS

Question: How does one become able to maintain patience with the inward dharmas of one's own mind?

Response: The bodhisattva reflects, "Although I have not yet gained realization of the Path and have not yet cut off the fetters, if I fail to maintain patience, then I become no different from a common person and do not qualify as a bodhisattva."

He also thinks to himself, "If I gain realization of the Path and thus cut off all of the fetters, then there will be no further dharmas requiring the exercise of patience. Additionally, hunger, thirst, cold, and heat are the outward demon armies. The fetters and afflictions are the inward demon insurgents. I should crush both of these armies and thereby gain perfect realization of the Buddha Path. So long as I fail to proceed in this fashion, I will have no success in the Buddha Path."

1. THE DEMON KING CONFRONTS THE BUDDHA (STORY)

This is illustrated by the story told of the Buddha when he was cultivating ascetic practices for a period of six years. The king of the

魔王来言。刹利贵人。汝千
分生中正有一分活耳。速起
还国布施修福。可得今世后
世人中天上之乐道。不可得
汝唐勤苦。汝若不受[*]软言
守迷不起。我当将大军众来
击破汝。菩萨言。我今当破
汝大力内军。何况外军。魔
言。何等是我内军。答曰。

欲是汝初军　忧愁为第二。
饥渴第三军　渴爱为第四。

睡眠第五军　怖畏为第六。
疑[3]悔第七军　瞋恚为第八。

利养虚称九　自高[4]蔑人十。
如是等军众　厌没出家人。

我以禅智力　破汝此诸军。
得成佛道已　度脱一切人。

[169a26]　　菩萨于此诸军虽未
能破。着忍辱铠捉智慧剑执
禅定[5]楯。遮诸烦恼箭。是
名内忍。复次菩萨于诸烦恼
中。应当修忍不应断结。何
以故。若断

魔王來言。刹利貴人。汝千
分生中正有一分活耳。速起
還國布施修福。可得今世後
世人中天上之樂道。不可得
汝唐勤苦。汝若不受[*]軟言
守迷不起。我當將大軍眾來
擊破汝。菩薩言。我今當破
汝大力內軍。何況外軍。魔
言。何等是我內軍。答曰。

欲是汝初軍　憂愁為第二。
飢渴第三軍　渴愛為第四。

睡眠第五軍　怖畏為第六。
疑[3]悔第七軍　瞋恚為第八。

利養虛稱九　自高[4]蔑人十。
如是等軍眾　厭沒出家人。

我以禪智力　破汝此諸軍。
得成佛道已　度脫一切人。

[169a26]　　菩薩於此諸軍雖未
能破。著忍辱鎧捉智慧劍執
禪定[5]楯。遮諸煩惱箭。是
名內忍。復次菩薩於諸煩惱
中。應當修忍不應斷結。何
以故。若斷

简体字　　　　　　　　　　正體字

demons came and said, "Noble man of kṣatriyan lineage. Of a thousand parts of your life, you have only a single part left to live. You should hurry up, rise from this spot, and return to your country to perform acts of giving and cultivate blessings. Then you will still be able to gain the bliss among men and in the heavens in both the present life and later lives.

"Your path is unattainable. It is in vain that you subject yourself to such intense suffering. If you don't yield to these gentle words, but instead persist in this confusion, failing to rise from this spot, I will lead forth a great mass of troops to attack and break you."

The Bodhisattva replied, "I am now going to break even your extremely powerful inwardly-attacking army, how much the more so your outwardly-attacking army."

The demon said, "What is it that composes my 'internal' army?"

The Bodhisattva then replied:

Desire is the first among your armies,
Worry is the second.
Hunger and thirst are the third army.
Craving is the fourth.

Drowsiness is the fifth of the armies.
Fearfulness is number six.
Doubt and regret are the seventh army.
Hatred and anger are the eighth.

Offerings and an empty reputation are the ninth.
Elevating oneself and belittling others is the tenth.
Such a company of armies as these
May vanquish those who have left the home life.

I employ the power of dhyāna and wisdom
To break these armies of yours,
And after perfecting the Buddha Path,
Deliver everyone to liberation.

Although a bodhisattva may not yet be able to break all of these armies, he dons the armor of patience, takes up the sword of wisdom, holds onto the shield of dhyāna absorption, and deflects the arrows of the afflictions. This is what is meant by inward patience.

2. THE NEED TO REFRAIN FROM SEVERING THE FETTERS COMPLETELY

Then again, a bodhisattva ought to cultivate patience with respect to the afflictions but ought not to cut off the fetters. Why? If he cuts off

结者所失甚多。堕阿罗汉[169b]道中。与根败无异。是故遮而不断。以修忍辱不随结使。问曰。云何结使未断而能不随。答曰。正思惟故。虽有烦恼而能不随。复次思惟。观空无常相故。虽有妙好五欲不生诸结。譬如国王。有一大臣。自覆藏罪。人所不知。王言。取无脂肥羊来。汝若不得者当与汝罪。大臣有智。系一大羊以草谷好养。日三以狼而畏怖之。羊虽得养肥而无脂。牵羊与王。王遣人杀之肥而无脂。王问云何得尔。答以上事。菩萨亦如是。见无常苦空狼。令诸结使脂消诸功德肉肥。复次菩萨功德福报无量故。其心柔[*]软诸结使薄易修忍辱。譬如师子王在林中吼。有人见之叩头求[6]哀则放令去。虎豹小物不能尔也。何以故。

简体字

結者所失甚多。墮阿羅漢[169b]道中。與根敗無異。是故遮而不斷。以修忍辱不隨結使。問曰。云何結使未斷而能不隨。答曰。正思惟故。雖有煩惱而能不隨。復次思惟。觀空無常相故。雖有妙好五欲不生諸結。譬如國王。有一大臣。自覆藏罪。人所不知。王言。取無脂肥羊來。汝若不得者當與汝罪。大臣有智。繫一大羊以草穀好養。日三以狼而畏怖之。羊雖得養肥而無脂。牽羊與王。王遣人殺之肥而無脂。王問云何得爾。答以上事。菩薩亦如是。見無常苦空狼。令諸結使脂消諸功德肉肥。復次菩薩功德福報無量故。其心柔[*]軟諸結使薄易修忍辱。譬如師子王在林中吼。有人見之叩頭求[6]哀則放令去。虎豹小物不能爾也。何以故。

正體字

the fetters, that which he loses is extensive indeed. He thus falls into the path of the arhat. This would be indistinguishable from ruining his roots in the Bodhisattva Path]. He therefore merely deflects the fetters while not severing them completely. It is on account of his cultivation of patience that he then refrains from following along with the influence of the fetters.

3. How Bodhisattvas Avoid Influence by Fetters

Question: How is it that when the fetters are not yet cut off, one remains able to refrain from following along with them?

Response: It is on account of right thought that, although one is still subject to afflictions, one is remains able to refrain from following along with them.

Additionally, because one reflects and contemplates the marks of emptiness and impermanence, even though one may possess marvelous and fine objects of the five desires, one still does not respond to them by giving rise to any of the fetters.

This is similar to the case of the king who discovered one of his officials had committed an offense and then kept it hidden so that others wouldn't become aware of it. The King told him, "Bring me a plump sheep free of any fat. If you are unable to find one, you will be subjected to punishment."

That great official was particularly intelligent. He proceeded to tie up a big sheep and feed it liberally with both grass and grain. Three times each day, he frightened it with a wolf. Although the sheep was able to grow plump, it still did not have any fat. He then brought the sheep before the King.

The King ordered someone to slaughter it and found that it was plump but had no fat. The King asked, "How were you able to bring this about?" He replied by relating the above circumstances. The bodhisattva is just like this. He sees the wolf of impermanence, suffering, and emptiness. This causes the fat of the fetters to melt away while the flesh of his merit grows plump.

Then again, because the bodhisattva's merit and resultant karmic blessings are incalculably extensive, his mind remains pliant, the fetters are but scant, and it is easy for him to cultivate patience.

This circumstance [of refraining from completely cutting off the fetters] is also comparable to that of the Lion King who roars in the forest. When a person encounters it, if he bows down before it and prays for mercy, then it may let him go. But the tiger, leopard, and lesser beasts would be unable to act in such a fashion. Why?

师子王贵兽有智分别故。虎
豹贱虫不知分别故。又如坏
军得值大将则活[7]值遇小兵
则死。复次菩萨智慧力。观
瞋恚有种种诸恶。观忍辱有
种种功德。是故能忍结使。
复次菩萨心有智力能断结
使。为众生故。久住世间知
结使是贼。是故忍而不随。
菩萨系此结贼。不令纵逸而
行功德。譬如有贼以因缘故
不杀。坚闭一处而自修事
业。复次菩萨实知诸法相
故。不以诸结使为恶。不以
功德为妙。是故于结不瞋功
德不爱。以此智力故。能修
忍辱。如偈说。

菩萨断除诸不善。
乃至极微灭无馀。
大功德福无有量。
所造事业无不办。

菩萨大智慧力故。
于诸结使不能恼。
是故能知诸法相。
生死涅盘一无二。

師子王貴獸有智分別故。虎
豹賤蟲不知分別故。又如壞
軍得值大將則活[7]值遇小兵
則死。復次菩薩智慧力。觀
瞋恚有種種諸惡。觀忍辱有
種種功德。是故能忍結使。
復次菩薩心有智力能斷結
使。為眾生故。久住世間知
結使是賊。是故忍而不隨。
菩薩繫此結賊。不令縱逸而
行功德。譬如有賊以因緣故
不殺。堅閉一處而自修事
業。復次菩薩實知諸法相
故。不以諸結使為惡。不以
功德為妙。是故於結不瞋功
德不愛。以此智力故。能修
忍辱。如偈說。

菩薩斷除諸不善。
乃至極微滅無餘。
大功德福無有量。
所造事業無不辦。

菩薩大智慧力故。
於諸結使不能惱。
是故能知諸法相。
生死涅槃一無二。

| 简体字 | 正體字 |

Because the Lion King is a noble animal which possesses intelligence and discrimination. The tiger and leopard are base beasts which do not know to make such distinctions.

This situation is also like that of defeated soldiers who, if they are overcome by the forces of a great general, will be allowed to live. If they encounter lesser soldiers, however, they are bound to be put to death.

Moreover, the bodhisattva employs his power of wisdom to contemplate hatred as freighted with all manner of evil and to contemplate patience as possessing all sorts of meritorious qualities. Realizing this, he thereby becomes able to maintain patience with the fetters.

Furthermore, the mind of the bodhisattva possesses a power of wisdom whereby he is capable of cutting off the fetters. But, for the sake of beings, he nonetheless abides for a long time in the world, realizing that the fetters are just like insurgent thieves. He therefore maintains patience towards them while refraining from following along with them. The bodhisattva thereby ties up the thieves of the fetters and so does not allow them to run rampant as he proceeds to engage in the cultivation of merit. This is analogous to those situations wherein there may be insurgents which, for a particular reason, one refrains from executing. One instead confines them securely in a single place and then devotes himself to doing his own work.

Then again, because the bodhisattva possesses a reality-based awareness of the marks of all dharmas, he does not take the fetters to be inherently evil and does not take merit to be inherently marvelous. Therefore he does not nurture any hatred for the fetters nor does he cherish any particular affection for merit. Relying on account of the power of this wisdom, he is able to cultivate patience. This is as described in a verse:

> The bodhisattva cuts off and eliminates all which is not good.
> Even down to the most subtle, he destroys it, leaving no residue.
> The blessings from his greatly meritorious qualities are countless.
> In the works that he carries on, none are not completed.

> On account of the power of the bodhisattva's great wisdom,
> Even in the midst of the fetters, he is invulnerable to torment.
> He is thereby able to be aware of the marks of all dharmas.
> Birth, death, and nirvāṇa are a unity devoid of duality.

[169c02]　　如是种种因缘虽未得道。于诸烦恼法中能忍。是名法忍。复次菩萨。于一切法。知一相无二。一切法可识[8]相故言一。眼识识色。乃至意识识法。是可识相法。故言一。复次一切法可知相故言一。苦法智苦比智。知苦谛。集法智集比智。知集谛。灭法智灭比智。知灭谛。道法智道比智。知道谛。及善世智亦知苦集灭道虚空非智缘灭。是可知相法故言一。复次一切法可缘相故言一。眼识及眼识相应法缘色。耳识鼻识舌识身识亦如是。意识及意识相应法。亦缘眼

简体字

[169c02]　　如是種種因緣雖未得道。於諸煩惱法中能忍。是名法忍。復次菩薩。於一切法。知一相無二。一切法可識[8]相故言一。眼識識色。乃至意識識法。是可識相法。故言一。復次一切法可知相故言一。苦法智苦比智。知苦諦。集法智集比智。知集諦。滅法智滅比智。知滅諦。道法智道比智。知道諦。及善世智亦知苦集滅道虛空非智緣滅。是可知相法故言一。復次一切法可緣相故言一。眼識及眼識相應法緣色。耳識鼻識舌識身識亦如是。意識及意識相應法。亦緣眼

正體字

For all sorts of reasons such as these, although one has not yet gained realization of the Path, one is nonetheless able to maintain patience in the midst of affliction-related dharmas. It is this which constitutes "patience with respect to dharmas."

F. ANALYSIS AND REFUTATION ACCORDING TO NUMERICAL CATEGORIES

Additionally, with respect to all dharmas, the bodhisattva knows them to be characterized by singularity and knows them to be non-dual. Because all dharmas have the character of being perceptible by consciousness, they may be said to be of a singular nature. Where "the eye consciousness is conscious of forms," and so forth [with the ear, nose, tongue, and body consciousnesses being conscious of sounds, smells, tastes, and tangibles] on up to the case of "the mind consciousness is conscious of dharmas," these are all instances of dharmas having the character of being subject to awareness on the part of consciousness. They are all therefore said to be of a singular nature.

Then again, it is because all dharmas have the character of knowability that they may be said to be of a single nature. [For example], the dharma knowledge of suffering (*duḥkhe dharmajñāna*) and the consecutive knowledge of suffering (*duḥkhe 'nvayajñāna*) know the truth of suffering. The dharma knowledge of accumulation (*samudaye dharmajñāna*) and the consecutive knowledge of suffering (*samudaye 'nvayajñāna*) know the truth of accumulation. The dharma knowledge of cessation (*nirodhe dharmajñāna*) and the consecutive knowledge of cessation (*nirodhe 'nvayajñāna*) know the truth of cessation. The dharma knowledge of the Path (*mārge dharmajñāna*) and the consecutive knowledge of the Path (*mārge 'nvayajñāna*) know the truth of the Path.

And so, too, worldly knowledge characterized by goodness may know suffering, accumulation, cessation, the Path, space, and the cessation not based on comprehension (*apratisaṃkhyānirodha*). It is on account of this characteristic of knowability that dharmas are said to be of a singular nature.

Then again, it is on account of the fact that all dharmas are subject to being taken as objective conditions that they are said to be of a singular nature. Eye consciousness as well as dharmas associated with eye consciousness take forms as objective conditions. Ear consciousness, nose consciousness, tongue consciousness and body consciousness are the same in this respect. The mind consciousness and dharmas associated with mind consciousness take the eye

亦缘色亦缘眼识。乃至缘意缘法缘意识。一切法可缘相故言一。复次[9]有人言一切法各皆一。一复有一名为二。三一名为三。如是乃至千万皆是一。而假名为千[10]万。复次一切法中有相故言一。一相故名为一。一切物名为法。法相故名为一。如是等无量一门。破异相不着一。是名法忍

[169c20]　复次菩萨观一[11]切为二。何等二。二名内外相。内外相故内非外相。外非内相。复次一切法有无相故为[12]二。空不空常非常我非我色非色可见不可见有对非有对有漏无漏有为无为心法非心法心数法非心数法心相应法非心相应法。如是无量二门

简体字

亦緣色亦緣眼識。乃至緣意緣法緣意識。一切法可緣相故言一。復次[9]有人言一切法各皆一。一復有一名為二。三一名為三。如是乃至千萬皆是一。而假名為千[10]萬。復次一切法中有相故言一。一相故名為一。一切物名為法。法相故名為一。如是等無量一門。破異相不著一。是名法忍

[169c20]　復次菩薩觀一[11]切為二。何等二。二名內外相。內外相故內非外相。外非內相。復次一切法有無相故為[12]二。空不空常非常我非我色非色可見不可見有對非有對有漏無漏有為無為心法非心法心數法非心數法心相應法非心相應法。如是無量二門

正體字

faculty, take [visual] forms, and take eye consciousness as objective conditions, and so forth until we come to their also taking even the [intellectual] mind faculty, dharmas as objects of mind, and mind consciousness as objective conditions. Thus it is also on account of this characteristic of being subject to being taken as objective conditions that all dharmas are said to be singular entities.

Yet again, there are those who say that each one of all dharmas is singular in nature, and that "duality" is based on there being a second singular entity in addition to the first. [Similarly, they say] that it is three singular entities taken together which constitute a trinity, and so forth like this until we come to [their stating that] a thousand myriads is simply a case of that many singular entities being taken together and artificially referred to as "a thousand myriads."

Then again, [it might be said that], because there exists a particular aspect common to all dharmas [taken as a group], one speaks of them as "one." It is because they are characterized by "oneness" that are referred to as "one." All phenomena may be referred to as "dharmas." Because they are characterized by being dharmas, they are said to be "one."

In this same fashion, there are an incalculable number of approaches to [the comprehension of] singularity. When one thus refutes the concept of a differentiating characteristic while still not becoming attached to the concept of singularity, this qualifies as "patience with respect to dharmas."

Then again, the bodhisattva may contemplate everything as being dual. In what way are they dual? Duality refers to the characteristic of having a subject and an object. Because this circumstance is characterized by the presence of a subject and object, it is not the case that the subject has the character of being the object and it is not the case that the object has the character of being the subject.

Yet again, it is also because all dharmas may be characterized by existence or nonexistence that they may be seen as dual. [Other examples of duality-based conceptions are]: empty and non-empty, eternal and non-eternal, self and non-self, form and non-form, perceptible and non-perceptible, opposable and non-opposable, outflow and non-outflow, conditioned and unconditioned, mind dharma and non-mind dharma, dharmas belonging to the mind and dharmas not belonging to the mind, and dharmas associated with the mind and dharmas not associated with the mind. There are an incalculable number of access points to [the comprehension

破一不着二。是名为法忍。
复次菩萨[13]或观一切法为
三。何等为三。下中上善不
善无记有无非有非无。见谛
断思惟断无断学无学非学非
无学报有报非报非有报。
如是无量三门破[170a]一不着
异。是名为法忍。复次菩萨
虽未得无漏道结使未断。能
信无漏圣法及三种法印。一
者一切有为生法无常等印。
二者一切法无我印。三者涅
盘实法印。得道贤圣人自得
自知。菩萨虽未得道。能信
能受是名法忍。复次于十
四[1]难不答法中。有常无常
等。观察无碍不失中道。是
法能忍是为法忍。

破一不著二。是名為法忍。
復次菩薩[13]或觀一切法為
三。何等為三。下中上善不
善無記有無非有非無。見諦
斷思惟斷無斷學無學非學非
無學報有報非報非有報。
如是無量三門破[170a]一不著
異。是名為法忍。復次菩薩
雖未得無漏道結使未斷。能
信無漏聖法及三種法印。一
者一切有為生法無常等印。
二者一切法無我印。三者涅
槃實法印。得道賢聖人自得
自知。菩薩雖未得道。能信
能受是名法忍。復次於十
四[1]難不答法中。有常無常
等。觀察無礙不失中道。是
法能忍是為法忍。

簡体字   正體字

of] duality. When one refutes the concept of singularity while still not becoming attached to the concept of duality, this qualifies as "patience with respect to dharmas."

Then again, the bodhisattva may contemplate all dharmas as having the nature of triplicity. In what way are they characterized by triplicity? [Examples of triplicity-based conceptions include]: inferior, middling, and superior; good, not good, and neutral; existent, nonexistent, and neither-existent-nor-nonexistent; severance through comprehension of the truths, severance through meditative skill, and non-severance; still being in training, being beyond training, and being neither still in training nor beyond training; and retributional, non-retributional and neither retributional [nor non-retributional]. In this same fashion there are an incalculable number of access points to [the comprehension of] triplicity.

When one refutes the concept of singularity but still does not become attached to the concept of difference, this qualifies as "patience with respect to dharmas."

G. Additional Factors in the Bodhisattva's Dharma Patience

1. The Bodhisattva's Faith in the Three-fold Imprint of Dharmas

Furthermore, although the bodhisattva has not yet gained realization of the path beyond outflow impurities and has not yet cut off the fetters, he is nonetheless able to maintain faith in the non-outflow Dharma of the Āryas and faith in the three-fold imprint of dharmas. The first of these is that all dharmas which are the product of composite conditions are all equally imprinted by the characteristic of being impermanent. The second is that all dharmas are imprinted by the characteristic of being non-self. The third is that they are imprinted by the genuine dharma of nirvāṇa.

These are such as the Worthies and Āryas who have gained the Path naturally realize and naturally know. Although the bodhisattva has not yet gained realization of the Path, he is nonetheless able to relate to these with faith and acceptance. This qualifies as "patience with respect to dharmas."

2. The Bodhisattva's Patience with the Fourteen Difficult Questions

Furthermore, with respect to the unanswered dharmas associated with the fourteen difficult questions such as permanence, impermanence, and so forth, one finds no obstacle to investigating them but still does not lose the Middle Way.[23] When one is able to have patience with these dharmas, this constitutes "patience with respect to dharmas."

如一比丘。于此十四难思惟
观察。不能通达心不能忍。
持衣鉢至佛所白佛言。佛能
为我解[2]此十四难。使我意
了者当作弟子。若不能解我
当更求馀道。佛告痴人汝本
共我要誓。若答十四难汝作
我弟子耶。比丘言不也。佛
言。汝痴人今何以言。若不
答我不作弟子。我为老病死
人说法济度。此十四难是鬭
诤法。于法无益但是戏论。
何用问为。若为[3]汝答汝心
不了。至死不解不能得脱生
老病死。譬如有人身被毒
箭。亲属呼医欲为出箭涂
药。便言未可出箭。我先当
知汝姓字亲里父母年岁。次
欲知箭出在何山何木何羽。
作箭镞者为是何人是何等
铁。复欲知弓何山木何虫
角。复[4]欲知药是何处生是
何种名。如是等事尽了了知
之。然后听汝出箭涂药。

如一比丘。於此十四難思惟
觀察。不能通達心不能忍。
持衣鉢至佛所白佛言。佛能
為我解[2]此十四難。使我意
了者當作弟子。若不能解我
當更求餘道。佛告癡人汝本
共我要誓。若答十四難汝作
我弟子耶。比丘言不也。佛
言。汝癡人今何以言。若不
答我不作弟子。我為老病死
人說法濟度。此十四難是鬭
諍法。於法無益但是戲論。
何用問為。若為[3]汝答汝心
不了。至死不解不能得脱生
老病死。譬如有人身被毒
箭。親屬呼醫欲為出箭塗
藥。便言未可出箭。我先當
知汝姓字親里父母年歲。次
欲知箭出在何山何木何羽。
作箭鏃者為是何人是何等
鐵。復欲知弓何山木何蟲
角。復[4]欲知藥是何處生是
何種名。如是等事盡了了知
之。然後聽汝出箭塗藥。

简体字   正體字

3. The Bhikshu Impatient with the Fourteen Difficult Questions (Story)

A related case is that of the bhikshu who contemplated and investigated these fourteen difficult questions, found that he was so unable to break through them that his mind was unable to endure it. He took up his robe and bowl and went to where the Buddha was and addressed the Buddha, saying, "If the Buddha is able to explain these fourteen difficult questions for me so that my mind is caused to completely understand them, then I will continue to be a disciple. If he is unable to explain them, then I will seek after another path."

The Buddha told him, "You foolish man. Are you not basically presenting me with an ultimatum whereby only if I provide answers to the fourteen difficult questions will you continue to be my disciple?"

The bhikshu replied, "No."

The Buddha said, "You foolish man. Why then do you now say, 'If you don't answer these for me, I will not remain as a disciple? I explain Dharma for the rescue and deliverance of persons who are subject to aging, sickness and death. These fourteen difficult questions are dharmas of disputation. They possess no benefit in relation to the Dharma. They are only frivolous dialectics. What is the point of inquiring into them? If I were to offer an answer for your sake, your mind would not completely comprehend it. You would go to your dying day without being able to understand it and would then be unable to gain liberation from birth, aging, sickness, and death.

"This is analogous to a man who has been shot by a poisoned arrow. His relatives call a physician who is about to extract the arrow for him and then apply medications. But he then says, 'You can't take the arrow out yet. I must first know your first and last name, the village from whence you come as well as the ages of your father and mother. Next, I wish to know from which mountain this arrow came, from which tree it is made, from what sort of feathers it is fletched, who the arrowhead maker is, and from which sort of metal it is cast. I wish also to know from which wood and on what mountain the bow was made as well as what animal's horns were used in its construction. Additionally, I wish to know where the poison was produced and what type it is. After I have completely understood all sorts of other related matters I shall then give my permission for you to extract the arrow and apply medications.'"

佛问比丘此人可得知此众事
然后出箭不。比丘言。不可
得知。若待尽知此则已死。
佛言。汝亦如是。为邪见箭
爱毒涂已入汝心。欲拔此箭
作我弟子。而不欲出箭。方
欲求尽世间常无常边无边
等。求之未得则失慧命。与
畜生同死。自投黑暗。比丘
惭愧深识佛[170b]语。即得阿
罗汉道。复次菩萨。欲作一
切智人。应推求一切法。知
其实相。于十四难中不滞不
碍。知其是心重病。能出能
忍。是名法忍。复次佛法甚
深清净微妙。演畅种种无量
法门。能一心信受不疑不
悔。是名法忍。如佛所言。
诸法虽空。亦不断亦不灭。
诸法因缘相续生亦非常。诸
法虽无神亦不失罪福。

佛問比丘此人可得知此眾事
然後出箭不。比丘言。不可
得知。若待盡知此則已死。
佛言。汝亦如是。為邪見箭
愛毒塗已入汝心。欲拔此箭
作我弟子。而不欲出箭。方
欲求盡世間常無常邊無邊
等。求之未得則失慧命。與
畜生同死。自投黑闇。比丘
慚愧深識佛[170b]語。即得阿
羅漢道。復次菩薩。欲作一
切智人。應推求一切法。知
其實相。於十四難中不滯不
礙。知其是心重病。能出能
忍。是名法忍。復次佛法甚
深清淨微妙。演暢種種無量
法門。能一心信受不疑不
悔。是名法忍。如佛所言。
諸法雖空。亦不斷亦不滅。
諸法因緣相續生亦非常。諸
法雖無神亦不失罪福。

简体字   正體字

The Buddha asked the bhikshu, "Would it or would it not be possible for this man to first come to know these many matters and only later have the arrow extracted?"

The bhikshu said, "He would not be able to succeed in knowing them beforehand. If he waited to completely understand them, then he would already have died by that time."

The Buddha said, "You are just like this. You have been shot by the arrow of erroneous views which has been smeared with the poison of craving. It has now already entered your heart. It was out of a desire to extricate this arrow that you became my disciple, and yet now, you do not wish to pull out the arrow, but instead next wish to find out in its entirety whether the world is eternal or non-eternal, bounded or unbounded, and so forth. Before you have succeeded in finding these things out you will have lost your wisdom life and will have died in a fashion identical with the beasts. You hereby cast yourself into darkness."

The bhikshu felt ashamed, deeply understood the words of the Buddha, and then immediately gained the path of arhatship.

4. The Bodhisattva's Transcendence of Fourteen Difficult Questions

Furthermore, the bodhisattva desires to become a person possessed of omniscience. He should pursue investigations into all dharmas and understand their true character. He should not be bogged down in or obstructed by the fourteen difficult questions and so should know that they are a severe illness of the mind. When he is able to transcend them and is able to endure them, this qualifies as possessing patience with respect to dharmas.

5. The Bodhisattva's Eloquence, Faith, and Freedom from Doubts

Moreover, the Dharma of the Buddha is extremely profound, pure, subtle and marvelous. [The bodhisattva] is able to broadly expound all sorts of accesses to Dharma of incalculable scope. He is able to single-mindedly believe in and accept them without doubts or regrets. This qualifies as having patience with respect to dharmas.

6. The Bodhisattva's Deep Understanding of the Nature of Dharmas

As stated by the Buddha, although all dharmas are empty, they are still not cut off and are not destroyed. Although all dharmas are produced of a continuity of causes and conditions, still, they are not eternal. Although all dharmas are devoid of any spiritual soul, still, there is no diminishment of retribution for either offenses or blessings.

[5]一心念頃。身诸法诸根诸慧转灭不停。[6]不至后念。[7]新新生灭。亦不失无量世中因缘业。诸众界入中皆空无神。而众生轮转五道中受生死。如是等种种甚微妙法。虽未得佛道。能信[8]能受不疑不悔。是为法忍。复次阿罗汉辟支佛。畏恶生死早求入涅盘。菩萨未得成佛。而欲求一切智。[9]欲怜愍众生。欲了了分别知诸法实相。是中能忍是名法忍。问曰。云何观诸[10]法实相。答曰。观知诸法无有瑕隙。不可破不可坏是为实相。问曰。一切语皆可答可破可坏。云何言不可破坏是为实相。答曰。以诸法不可破故。佛法中一切言语道过。心行处灭

簡体字

[5]一心念頃。身諸法諸根諸慧轉滅不停。[6]不至後念。[7]新新生滅。亦不失無量世中因緣業。諸眾界入中皆空無神。而眾生輪轉五道中受生死。如是等種種甚深微妙法。雖未得佛道。能信[8]能受不疑不悔。是為法忍。復次阿羅漢辟支佛。畏惡生死早求入涅槃。菩薩未得成佛。而欲求一切智。[9]欲憐愍眾生。欲了了分別知諸法實相。是中能忍是名法忍。問曰。云何觀諸[10]法實相。答曰。觀知諸法無有瑕隙。不可破不可壞是為實相。問曰。一切語皆可答可破可壞。云何言不可破壞是為實相。答曰。以諸法不可破故。佛法中一切言語道過。心行處滅

正體字

In each single thought moment, all personal dharmas and all of one's faculties and manifestations of intelligence are brought to destruction. This goes on without cease such that they are not carried forward even to the next thought-moment (*kṣaṇa*). They are continually being newly produced and destroyed again and yet there is no loss of the karmic causes and conditions carried forth through an incalculable number of lifetimes.

Among all of the aggregates, sense realms and sense bases, everything is empty of inherent existence and devoid of a spiritual soul and yet beings *do* circulate about throughout the five destinies, undergoing cyclic birth and death. Even though one may not yet have gained the Buddha Path, one is still able to believe and is still able to accept without doubts and without regrets all sorts of such extremely profound, subtle and marvelous dharmas. This qualifies as possessing patience with respect to dharmas.

7. Bodhisattva Motivation's Relationship to Patience

Then again, the arhats and pratyekabuddhas fear and abhor cyclic birth and death and so seek an early entry into nirvāṇa. The bodhisattva has not yet gained buddhahood and so he desires to seek after all-knowledge, desires to act out of pity for beings, and desires to utterly understand, distinguish, and realize the true character of dharmas. When one is able to maintain patience even in the midst of all these endeavors, this qualifies as patience with respect to dharmas.

H. Extended Discussion on the True Nature of Dharmas
1. On the True Character of Dharmas

Question: How does one proceed with contemplating in accordance with reality the true character of dharmas (*dharmatā*)?

Response: One contemplates and knows [the true character of] dharmas as free of any flaw, and as invulnerable to refutation or [dialectical] ruination. This corresponds to their true character.

2. Refutation of the Ultimacy of the Tetralemma

Question: All discourse can be responded to, can be refuted, and can be demolished. How can you claim that whatsoever cannot be refuted or demolished corresponds to the true character of of dharmas?

Response: This is because dharmas cannot be the object of refutation. In the Dharma of the Buddha, one goes beyond the path of all discourse. The very basis of the mind's actions is itself extinguished.

常不生不灭。如涅盘相。何
以故。若诸法相实[11]有不应
无。若诸法先有今无。[12]
则是断灭。复次诸法不应是
常。何以故。若常[*]则无罪
无福无所伤杀。亦无施命亦
无修行利益亦无缚无解。世
间则是涅盘。如是等因缘
故。诸法不应常。若诸法无
常。则是断灭亦无罪无福亦
无增[13]损。功[14]德业因缘
果报亦失。如是等因缘故。
诸法不应无常。问曰。汝
言佛法中常亦不实无常亦
不实。[170c]是事不然。何以
故。佛法中常亦实无常亦
实。常者数缘尽非数缘尽。
虚空不生不住不灭故。是常
相。无[15]常者。五众生住
灭故无常相。汝何以言常无
常皆不实。答曰。圣人有二
种语。一者方便语。二者直
语。方便语者。为人为因缘
故。为人者为众生说。

常不生不滅。如涅槃相。何
以故。若諸法相實[11]有不應
無。若諸法先有今無。[12]
則是斷滅。復次諸法不應是
常。何以故。若常[*]則無罪
無福無所傷殺。亦無施命亦
無修行利益亦無縛無解。世
間則是涅槃。如是等因緣
故。諸法不應常。若諸法
無常。則是斷滅亦無罪無福
亦無增[13]損。功[14]德業因
緣果報亦失。如是等因緣
故。諸法不應無常。問曰。
汝言佛法中常亦不實無常亦
不實。[170c]是事不然。何以
故。佛法中常亦實無常亦
實。常者數緣盡非數緣盡。
虛空不生不住不滅故。是常
相。無[15]常者。五眾生住
滅故無常相。汝何以言常無
常皆不實。答曰。聖人有二
種語。一者方便語。二者直
語。方便語者。為人為因緣
故。為人者為眾生說。

简体字   正體字

[Dharmas] are eternally neither produced nor destroyed and are characterized by being like nirvāṇa.

How is this so? If the marks of dharmas actually existed, then it should not be that they could become nonexistent. If any dharma was formerly existent but now is nonexistent, then this amounts to an extinction through severance (i.e. annihilationism).

Additionally, it should not be the case either that any dharma is eternal. Why? If it were eternal, then there could be no karmic punishments or blessings in reward and nothing therein would be subject to being injured or killed. Neither could one bestow life. There would be no benefit from spiritual cultivation nor would there be either bondage or liberation. If this were the case, then the world would be nirvāṇa. On account of reasons such as these, it should not be the case that any dharma qualifies as eternal either.

Then again, if any dharma was impermanent, then this would be an extinction through severance whereby there could be no karmic punishments, no blessings in reward, and neither increase nor decrease. The causes and conditions of meritorious karma and resultant rewards would also be lost. On account of reasons such as these, it should not be the case that any dharmas qualify as impermanent either.

Question: You claim that, within the Dharma of the Buddha, permanence is not a reality and impermanence is unreal as well. This is not the case. Why? Within the Dharma of the Buddha, permanence is a reality and impermanence is a reality as well. As for that which is permanent, it includes extinction due to comprehension (*pratisaṃkhyā-nirodha*), extinction not due to comprehension (*apratisaṃkhyā-nirodha*), and also empty space. Because they are not produced, do not abide, and are not destroyed, they are characterized by permanence.

As for impermanence, the five aggregates are characterized by impermanence because they are produced, do abide, and are then destroyed. Why then do you claim that both permanence and impermanence are not realities?

Response: The Āryas engage in two types of speech: The first is discourse characterized by skillful means. The second is direct discourse. As for the skillful means, they are set forth for the sake of individual persons and on account of particular causes and conditions. As for that which is set forth for the sake of individual persons, it is explained for the sake of particular beings that this entity

是常是无常。如对治悉檀中
说。若说无常。欲拔众生三
界着乐。佛思惟。以何令众
生得离欲。是故说无常法。
如偈[16]说。

若观无生法　于生法得离。
若观无为法　于有为得离。

[0170c12]　云何生生名因缘
和合。无常不自在属因[17]
缘。[18]有老病死相欺诳相
破坏相。是名生生。则是有
为法。如对治悉檀说。常无
常非实相。二俱过故。若诸
法非有常非无常。是为愚痴
论。所以者何。若非有则破
无。若非无则破有。若破此
二事更有何法可说。问曰。
佛法常空相中。非有非无。
空以除有空。空遮无。是为
非有非无。何以言愚痴论。
答曰。佛法实相不受不着。

是常是無常。如對治悉檀中
說。若說無常。欲拔眾生三
界著樂。佛思惟。以何令眾
生得離欲。是故說無常法。
如偈[16]說。

若觀無生法　於生法得離。
若觀無為法　於有為得離。

[0170c12]　云何生生名因緣
和合。無常不自在屬因[17]
緣。[18]有老病死相欺誑相
破壞相。是名生生。則是有
為法。如對治悉檀說。常無
常非實相。二俱過故。若諸
法非有常非無常。是為愚癡
論。所以者何。若非有則破
無。若非無則破有。若破此
二事更有何法可說。問曰。
佛法常空相中。非有非無。
空以除有空。空遮無。是為
非有非無。何以言愚癡論。
答曰。佛法實相不受不著。

簡体字　　　　　　　　正體字

is permanent, whereas that one is impermanent. This is as was explained in the discussion of the counteractive *siddhānta's* [doctrinal perspective] (*prātipākṣika siddhānta*).[24]

If one speaks of impermanence, it is out of a desire to extricate beings from their attachment to the pleasures of the three realms. The Buddha deliberated, "What might be employed to influence beings to leave behind desire?" Consequently he set forth the dharma of impermanence. This is as explained in a verse:

If one contemplates the dharma of non-production,
One succeeds in transcending dharmas which are produced.
If one contemplates unconditioned dharmas,
One succeeds in transcending whatsoever is conditioned.

Why is it that rebirth in cyclic existence is defined as a mere conjunction of causes and conditions? It is impermanent, possesses no inherent existence of its own, and belongs to the sphere of causes and conditions. It is characterized by being subject to aging, sickness, and death, is characterized by being deceptive, and is characterized by being subject to destruction. This is [the character] of rebirth in cyclic existence. It is therefore a conditioned dharma. This accords with the explanation presented in the counteractive *siddhānta* [doctrinal perspective].

Being "both permanent and impermanent" also fails to correspond to the true character [of dharmas]. This is because both fallacies are inherent therein. If one claims that dharmas are "neither permanent nor impermanent," this is just the dialectics of foolishness. How is this so? If one claims of some quality that it is "neither existent...," then this refutes it by indicating its non-existence. And if one claims of some quality that it is "nor nonexistent...," then this refutes it by pointing out its existence. If one has refuted both of these matters, then what dharmas remain to be discussed?

Question: In the Buddha Dharma's [tenet of everything] being characterized by constantly being empty of inherent existence, there is this concept of being "neither existent nor nonexistent." Emptiness is employed to get rid of [attachment to] existence. The emptiness of emptiness blocks off [attachment to] nonexistence.[25] This amounts to positing [that a dharma is] "neither existent nor nonexistent." Why then do you say that this is just "the dialectics of foolishness"?

Response: The true character [of dharmas as understood] in the Buddha's Dharma involves both non-acceptance [of the ultimate

汝非有非无受着故。是[19]为痴论。若言非有非无。[20]是则可说可破。是心生处是闘静处。佛法则不然。虽因缘故说非有非无。不生着。不生着则不可坏不可破。诸法若有边若无边若有无边若非有无边。若死后有去若死后无去若死后有去无去若死后非有去非无去。是身是神身异神异亦如是皆不实。于六十二见中。观诸法亦皆不实。如是一切除却。信佛法清净不坏相。心不悔不转。是名法忍。复次[171a]有无二边。观诸法生时住时则为有见相。观诸法老时坏时则为无见相。三界众生多着此二见相。是二种法虚

汝非有非無受著故。是[19]為癡論。若言非有非無。[20]是則可說可破。是心生處是闘諍處。佛法則不然。雖因緣故說非有非無。不生著。不生著則不可壞不可破。諸法若有邊若無邊若有無邊若非有無邊。若死後有去若死後無去若死後有去無去若死後非有去非無去。是身是神身異神異亦如是皆不實。於六十二見中。觀諸法亦皆不實。如是一切除却。信佛法清淨不壞相。心不悔不轉。是名法忍。復次[171a]有無二邊。觀諸法生時住時則為有見相。觀諸法老時壞時則為無見相。三界眾生多著此二見相。是二種法虛

简体字　　　　　　正體字

reality of any characteristic] and non-attachment [to the existence of any characteristic]. It is because your "neither-existence-nor-nonexistence" is a position characterized by both acceptance and attachment that it amounts to the dialectics of foolishness.

If one makes a claim in favor of "neither-existence-nor-nonexistence," this posits a view of something which can be described and refuted. It thereby constitutes a basis for the generation of ideation and a basis for disputation. The Dharma of the Buddha is not of this sort. Although it is the case that, on account of certain causes and conditions, one does indeed set forth this concept of "neither-existence-nor-nonexistence," in doing so, one does not become attached thereto. If one does not become attached to it, then it does not become an issue vulnerable to destruction and refutation.

No matter whether in one's treatment of dharmas one speaks [of the world and the self] as being bounded or as being boundless, or as being both bounded and boundless, or as being neither bounded nor boundless, no matter whether one speaks of there being a continuing on after death, of there not being a continuing on after death, of there both being and not being a continuing on after death, or of there being neither a continuing on nor a not continuing on after death, and no matter whether one speaks of the body as identical with a spiritual soul or as different from a spiritual soul, they are all just like this. None of these concepts correspond to reality.

3. Freedom from Views as a Qualification for Dharma Patience

When one contemplates the dharmas of the sixty-two views and recognizes that none of them correspond to reality—when one does away with all of them in this manner while still having such faith in the Buddha Dharma's characteristics of being pure and indestructible that one's mind is not regretful and is not turned away—this qualifies as patience with respect to dharmas.

4. The Erroneousness of Extreme Views

Then again, as for the two extremes of existence and nonexistence, if one's contemplations are focused on the time when dharmas arise and the time when they dwell, these constitute characteristic indicators of a view clinging to the concept of existence. If one's contemplations focus on the time when dharmas grow old or when they undergo destruction, then these constitute the characteristic indicators of a view which clings to the concept of nonexistence.

The beings of the three realms mostly cling to the characteristic features of these two views. These two kinds of dharmas are false

诳不实。[1]若实有相则不应无。何以故。今无[2]先有则堕断中。若断是则不然。复次一切诸法。名字和合故谓之为有。以是故。名字和合所生法不可得。问曰。名字所生法虽不可得。则有名字和合。答曰。若无法。名字为谁而和合。是则无名字。复次若诸法实有。不应以心识故知有。若以心识故[3]知有。是则非有。如地坚相。以身根身识知故有。若无身根身识知则无坚相。问曰。身根身识若知若不知。而地常是坚相。答曰。若先自知有坚相。若从他闻则知有坚相。若先不知不闻则无坚相。

諠不實。[1]若實有相則不應無。何以故。今無[2]先有則墮斷中。若斷是則不然。復次一切諸法。名字和合故謂之為有。以是故。名字和合所生法不可得。問曰。名字所生法雖不可得。則有名字和合。答曰。若無法。名字為誰而和合。是則無名字。復次若諸法實有。不應以心識故知有。若以心識故[3]知有。是則非有。如地堅相。以身根身識知故有。若無身根身識知則無堅相。問曰。身根身識若知若不知。而地常是堅相。答曰。若先自知有堅相。若從他聞則知有堅相。若先不知不聞則無堅相。

简体字   正體字

and deceptive and do not correspond to reality. If in reality a given characteristic actually possesses existence, then it should not be the case that it could become nonexistent. Why? If something now becomes nonexistent which previously was existent, this falls into the domain of the annihilationist view. If one adopts an annihilationist stance, then this is an erroneous position.

5. The Role of Naming in Imputing Existence to Dharmas

Moreover, it is on account of a naming-based unification that one imputes existence to dharmas. It is on account of this that dharmas produced by nominal unification cannot finally be gotten at.

Question: Although dharmas which are the product of this name-based unification cannot finally be gotten at, [is it not the case that] one does still have this naming and the corresponding unification?

Response: If there is no dharma [corresponding to this artificial name-based unification], by whose action of naming could there be such unification? In such a case, the naming itself would be nonexistent as well.

Again, if dharmas actually existed, it should not be the case that one knows of their existence solely through the mind's consciousness. If it is simply on account of the mind's consciousness that one comprehends their existence, this does not in itself qualify them as possessing a [genuine] existence.

Take for example the earth's characteristic of solidity. It is on account of the body's faculty of touch and the awareness on the part of the body's tactile consciousness that it is supposed to exist. If there were no bodily faculty of touch and no awareness on the part of the body's tactile consciousness, then there could be no characteristic feature of solidity.

6. Mutability of Characteristics as a Signifier of Unreality

Question: Whether or not there is a knowing awareness produced through the body's faculty of touch and the body's tactile consciousness, [is it not the case that] the earth element nonetheless remains eternally characterized by solidity?

Response: It may be that one already knows for himself that there exists the characteristic of solidity. Or else it may be that, having heard it from someone else, one knows there exists a characteristic of solidity. If one did not previously know it for himself and had not previously heard of it from someone else, then there would be no [basis for imputing the existence of a] characteristic of solidity.

复次地若常是坚相。不应舍其相。如凝酥蜡蜜树胶。融则舍其坚相堕湿相中。金银铜铁等亦尔。如水为湿相。寒则转为坚相。如是等种种悉皆舍相。复次诸论议师辈。有能令无。无能令有。诸贤圣人坐禅人。能令地作水水作地。如是等诸法皆可转。如十一切入中说。复次是有见。为贪欲瞋恚愚痴结缚斗诤故生。若有生此欲恚等处。是非佛法。何以故。佛法相善净故。以是故非实。复次一切[4]法有二种。色法无色法。色法分析乃至微尘散灭无馀。如檀波罗蜜品破施物中说。无色法五情所不[5]知故。意情生住灭时观故。知心有分。有分故无常。无常故空。

复次地若常是堅相。不應捨其相。如凝酥蠟蜜樹膠。融則捨其堅相墮濕相中。金銀銅鐵等亦爾。如水為濕相。寒則轉為堅相。如是等種種悉皆捨相。復次諸論議師輩。有能令無。無能令有。諸賢聖人坐禪人。能令地作水水作地。如是等諸法皆可轉。如十一切入中說。復次是有見。為貪欲瞋恚愚癡結縛鬪諍故生。若有生此欲恚等處。是非佛法。何以故。佛法相善淨故。以是故非實。復次一切[4]法有二種。色法無色法。色法分析乃至微塵散滅無餘。如檀波羅蜜品破施物中說。無色法五情所不[5]知故。意情生住滅時觀故。知心有分。有分故無常。無常故空。

简体字　　　　　　　　　正體字

Moreover, if it were the case that earth was eternally character-ized by solidity, it should not be the case that it could relinquish its characteristic. Take for example congealed curds, wax, honey or the pitch from trees. When they melt they lose their characteristic of solidity and so fall within the characteristic of liquidity. Gold, sil-ver, copper, iron, and so forth are also like this. As another example, take water which is characterized by liquidity. If it becomes cold, it may then transform so that it becomes characterized by solidity. There are all sorts of other examples such as these wherein in every case the characteristic features are relinquished.

Additionally, dialecticians are able to cause that which exists to become nonexistent and are able to cause that which is nonexis-tent to become existent. The Worthies, the Āryas, and those who sit in dhyāna meditation are able to cause earth to become water and water to become earth. All other sorts of dharmas such as these can be transformed. This is as discussed in the treatment of the ten universal bases (*kṛtsnāyatana*).

7. THE AFFLICTION-BASED NATURE OF EXISTENCE-AFFIRMING VIEWS

Furthermore, this view which holds to the validity of "existence" is produced on account of greed, hatred, stupidity, the fetters, and disputation. If something is held to exist which is produced on these bases of greed, hatred, and so forth, this does not qualify as the Dharma of the Buddha. Why is this the case? This is because the characteristic features of the Dharma of the Buddha are good-ness and purity. Hence such doctrinal positions do not correspond to reality.

8. UNREALITY OF BOTH FORM AND FORMLESS DHARMAS

Also, all dharmas are subsumed within two categories: form dhar-mas and formless dharmas. Form dharmas may be analyzed down to the tiniest particles and thus may be so destroyed through disper-sion that nothing remains. This is just as explained in the chapters on Dāna Pāramitā wherein we set forth a refutation of the existence of material objects given as gifts.

As for formless dharmas, [they cannot be said to exist] because they are not known by the five basic sense faculties. Also, because the observation on the part of the intellectual mind faculty occurs even as it undergoes arising, dwelling, and destruction, one knows that thought itself is divided into parts. Because thoughts are divided into parts, they are therefore impermanent. Because they are impermanent, they are therefore empty of any inherent

空故非有。弹指[6]顷有六十
时。一一时中心有生灭。相
续生故。知是贪心[7]是瞋心
是[171b]痴心是信心清净智慧
禅定心。行者观心生灭。如
流水灯焰。此名入空智门。
何以故。若一时生馀时中灭
者。此心应常。何以故。此
极少时中无灭故。若一时中
无灭者。应终始无灭。复次
佛说有为法皆有三相。若极
少时中生而无灭者是为非有
为法若极少时中心生住灭
者。何以但先生而后灭。不
先灭而后生。复次若先有心
后有生。则心不待生。何以
故。先[8]已有心故。若先有
生则生无所生。又生灭性相
违。生[9]则不应有

空故非有。彈指[6]頃有六十
時。一一時中心有生滅。相
續生故。知是貪心[7]是瞋心
是[171b]癡心是信心清淨智慧
禪定心。行者觀心生滅。如
流水燈焰。此名入空智門。
何以故。若一時生餘時中滅
者。此心應常。何以故。此
極少時中無滅故。若一時中
無滅者。應終始無滅。復次
佛說有為法皆有三相。若極
少時中生而無滅者是為非有
為法若極少時中心生住滅
者。何以但先生而後滅。不
先滅而後生。復次若先有心
後有生。則心不待生。何以
故。先[8]已有心故。若先有
生則生無所生。又生滅性相
違。生[9]則不應有

existence. Because they are empty of any inherent existence, they do not qualify as "existent."

9. The Unreality of Production and Extinction

There are sixty "instants" which transpire during a single finger snap. During each one of those instants, thought undergoes a production and an extinction. It is on account of the continuity occurring among these production events that one develops an awareness of whether one is dealing with a greed-related thought, a hate-related thought, a delusion-related thought, a faith-filled thought, or a thought characterized by purity, wisdom, or dhyāna absorption.

The practitioner contemplates the production and extinction of thought as being like flowing water or the flame of a lamp. This constitutes entry into the gateway of the wisdom of emptiness. How is this so? If it were in fact the case that any given thought was produced at one moment and then only destroyed during another subsequent moment, this thought should be possessed of permanence. How could this be so? It is because no destruction whatsoever took place during this extremely brief prior moment. If it were the case that no destruction took place during that single moment, it should be the case that there should never be any [subsequent] destruction either.

Then again, the Buddha stated that conditioned dharmas possess the three characteristic features [of production, dwelling, and extinction]. If during the most extremely brief moment there was production but no destruction, this would have to be an unconditioned dharma.

On the other hand, if it were the case that during the most extremely brief moment a thought was produced, dwelt and was then extinguished, how could one claim that production occurred first and extinction occurred later rather than [the alternative proposition where] extinction might occur first, followed by production?

Alternately, if it were the case that first there was the thought and afterwards there was the production, then the thought would not be dependent upon its production. Why? Because there would previously already be the existence of the thought. If, on the other hand, the production already existed previously, then production would have nothing which it subsequently produced.

Additionally, the natures of production and extinction are mutually opposed. When there is production, then there ought not to

灭。灭时不应有生。以是故一时不可得。异亦不可得。是即无生。若无生则无住灭。若无生住灭则无心数法。无心数法则无心不相应。诸行色无色法无故。无为法亦无。何以故因有为故有无为。若无有为则亦无无为。复次见作法无常故。知不作法常。若然者。今见作法是有法。不作法应是无法。以是故常法不可得。复次外道及佛弟子。说常[10]法有同有异。同者虚空涅盘。外[11]道有神时方微尘冥初。如是等名为异。[12]又佛弟子说非数缘灭[13]是常。又[14]复言[15]灭因缘法常。因缘生法无常。摩诃衍中。常[16]法法性如真际。

滅。滅時不應有生。以是故一時不可得。異亦不可得。是即無生。若無生則無住滅。若無生住滅則無心數法。無心數法則無心不相應。諸行色無色法無故。無為法亦無。何以故因有為故有無為。若無有為則亦無無為。復次見作法無常故。知不作法常。若然者。今見作法是有法。不作法應是無法。以是故常法不可得。復次外道及佛弟子。說常[10]法有同有異。同者虛空涅槃。外[11]道有神時方微塵冥初。如是等名為異。[12]又佛弟子說非數緣滅[13]是常。又[14]復言[15]滅因緣法常。因緣生法無常。摩訶衍中。常[16]法法性如真際。

简体字   正體字

be extinction. When there is extinction, then there ought not to be production. For these reasons, simultaneousness in this cannot be shown to be the case. But neither can a difference in time be shown to be the case either.

10. Consequence: All Dharma Categories Are Realized as Nonexistent

This then just amounts to the nonexistence of production. If there is no production, then there is no dwelling or extinction either. If there is no production, dwelling, or extinction, then there are no dharmas belonging to the mind. If there are no dharmas belonging to the mind (*caitasikadharma*), then there are no [formative factor dharmas] not associated with the mind (*cittaviprayuktasaṃskāradharma*). If all formative factor dharmas (*saṃskāradharma*), form dharmas (*rūpadharma*), and formless dharmas (*arupadharma*) are nonexistent, then unconditioned dharmas (*asaṃskṛtadharma*) must also be non-existent. Why? It is on account of the conditioned (*saṃskṛta*) that one has the unconditioned (*asaṃskṛta*). If there are no conditioned [dharmas], then there are no unconditioned [dharmas] either.[26]

11. Refutation of Eternally-Existent Dharmas

Additionally, it is on account of observing that created dharmas are impermanent that one comes to know dharmas which are not created to be eternally existent. This being the case, when one now observes that created dharmas are existent dharmas, one should realize that dharmas which are not created are nonexistent dharmas. It is on account of this that no eternal dharma can be found.

Furthermore, in their discussions of "eternally-existent" dharmas, non-Buddhists (*tīrthika*) and disciples of the Buddha have those which they hold in common and those over which they differ. Those which they hold in common are empty space (*ākāśa*) and nirvāṇa. The non-Buddhists have a "soul" (*ātman*), time, direction, extremely minute particles (*paramāṇu*), and "the primordial source" (*tamas*). These are categories over which they differ.

Additionally, there are disciples of the Buddha who claim that cessation not achieved through comprehension (*apratisaṃkhyā-nirodha*) is eternal and who further claim that the dharmas involving the extinguishing of causes and conditions are eternally-abiding whereas dharmas which are the product of causes and conditions are impermanent.

As for the dharmas which are considered eternally-abiding by proponents of the *Mahāyāna*, we have the nature of dharmas (*dharmatā*),[27] suchness (*tathatā*), ultimate reality (*bhūtakoṭi*), and all

如是[17]等种种。名为常法虚空涅盘。如先赞菩萨品中说。神及时方微尘亦如上说。以是故不应言诸法有。若诸法无者。有二种。一者常无。二者断灭故无。若先有今无若今有后无是则断灭。若然者则无因缘。无因缘者应一物中出一切物。亦应一[18]切物中都无所出。后世中亦如是。若断罪福因缘。则不应有贫富[171c]贵贱之异及堕恶道畜生中。若言常无则无苦集[19]灭道。若无四谛则无法宝。[20]若无法宝则无八贤圣道。若无法宝僧宝则无佛宝。若如是者则破三宝。复次若一切法实空者。则无罪福亦无父母亦无世间礼法亦无善无恶。然则善恶同门是非一贯。一切物

简体字

如是[17]等種種。名為常法虛空涅槃。如先讚菩薩品中說。神及時方微塵亦如上說。以是故不應言諸法有。若諸法無者。有二種。一者常無。二者斷滅故無。若先有今無若今有後無是則斷滅。若然者則無因緣。無因緣者應一物中出一切物。亦應一[18]切物中都無所出。後世中亦如是。若斷罪福因緣。則不應有貧富[171c]貴賤之異及墮惡道畜生中。若言常無則無苦集[19]滅道。若無四諦則無法寶。[20]若無法寶則無八賢聖道。若無法寶僧寶則無佛寶。若如是者則破三寶。復次若一切法實空者。則無罪福亦無父母亦無世間禮法亦無善無惡。然則善惡同門是非一貫。一切物

正體字

sorts of other [synonymous] concepts that are held to be eternally-abiding dharmas. As for empty space and *nirvāṇa*, they are as discussed previously in the section in praise of the bodhisattvas. The "soul" (*ātman*) as well as time, direction and the most minute particles are also as discussed previously. It is for these reasons that one should refrain from claiming that any dharma actually exists.

12. Reductio Ad Absurdum Refutation of "Nonexistence" Claims

As for the nonexistence of dharmas, it is of two sorts. The first is eternal nonexistence. The second is nonexistence achieved through severance [of a prior existence]. In a case where something previously existent now becomes nonexistent or something now existent later becomes nonexistent, this is extinction through severance.

If this were actually the case, then this involves the nonexistence of any associated causes and conditions. If there were no associated causes and conditions, then it ought to be the case that all things should be able to come forth from any single thing and it should also be the case that no thing could come forth from any other things.

This would also be the case for future existences. If there were a severance of the causes and conditions associated with karmic punishments and blessings, then there should no longer exist any of the differences involved in poverty versus wealth or nobility versus baseness. Neither could there be any falling into the wretched destinies or, in particular, an animal-realm rebirth.

If one claims that there is such a thing as eternal nonexistence, then there would be no suffering, no accumulation, no cessation, and no Path. If there were none of these four truths, then there could be no Dharma Jewel. If there were no Dharma Jewel, then there could be no path of the Eight stations of the Worthies and the Āryas. If there were no Dharma jewel and also no Sangha Jewel, then there could be no Buddha Jewel, either. If this were actually the case, then one would thereby achieve the destruction of the Three Jewels.

13. Non-Ultimacy of Emptiness Claims

Furthermore, if all dharmas were actually empty, then there would be no karmic offenses or blessings, nor would there be one's father and mother, nor would there be any of the world's ceremonial observances or laws, nor would there be any good or any evil. In that case then, good and bad would possess the same entryway and right and wrong would be of the same strand. All things would be

尽无。如梦中所见。若言实
无有如是失。此言谁当信
者。若言颠倒故见有者。当
见一人时。何以不见二三。
以其实无而颠倒见故。若不
堕此有无见。得中道实[21]
相。云何知实。如过去恒河
沙等诸佛菩萨所知所说。未
来恒河沙等诸佛菩萨所知所
说。现在恒河沙等诸佛菩萨
所知所说。信心大故不疑不
悔。信力大故能持能受。是
名法忍。复次禅定力故。心
柔软清净闻诸法实相应心
与会。信着深入无疑无[22]
悔。所以者何。疑悔是欲界
系法。麤恶故。不入柔软心
中。是名法忍。复次智慧力
故。于一切诸法中。种种观
无有一法可得者。是法能忍
能受不疑不悔。是名法忍。
复次菩萨思惟。凡夫人以无
明毒故。

简体字

just as nonexistent as the things seen in a dream. If one claims that all [dharmas] are actually nonexistent, such a claim is possessed of these faults. Who would believe this statement?

If one states that it is on account of inverted views that one sees things as existing, then when one sees a single person, why does one not see two or three since in reality they do not exist and are only seen on account of inverted views?

14. Six Additional Bases of "Patience with Respect to Dharmas"
    a. Realization of the True Character of the Middle Way

If one does not fall into these views [which insist on the reality] of existence or nonexistence, one may gain realization of the true character of the Middle Way. How does one know what is real? It is as known and proclaimed by all of the Ganges' sands number of buddhas and bodhisattvas of the past, as known and proclaimed by all of the Ganges' sands number of buddhas and bodhisattvas of the future, and as known and proclaimed by the Ganges' sands number of buddhas and bodhisattvas of the present. Because one's mind of faith is great, one does not have doubts and one does not have regrets. Because the power of one's faith is great, one is able to uphold [their Dharma] and is able to accept it. This is what is known as "patience with respect to dharmas."

b. Meditation's Role Fathoming of the True Character of Dharmas

Additionally, through the power of dhyāna absorption, one's mind becomes so pliant and pure that, when one hears of the true character of dharmas, this resonates with one's own mind and one integrates that realization. One grasps it through faith, deeply enters into it, and has no doubts and no regrets. Why? Doubts and regrets are dharmas bound to the desire realm. Because they are coarse and unwholesome, they do not enter into a pliant mind. This is what is meant by "patience with respect to dharmas."

c. Acquiescence in Unfindability of Dharmas

Moreover, on account of the power of wisdom, one subjects all dharmas to the scrutiny of all sorts of contemplations and finds that there is not a single dharma which can be gotten at. One is able to have patience with this dharma and is able to accept it without having doubts or regrets. This is what is known as "patience with respect to dharmas."

d. Realization of Ārya Wisdom Destroys Delusion's Poison

Additionally, the bodhisattva considers, "It is on account of the poison of ignorance that common people transform [through inverted

于一切诸法中作转相。非常
作常想苦作乐想。无我有我
想空谓有实。非有为有有为
非有。如是等种种法中作转
相。得圣实智慧破无明毒。
知诸法实相。得无常苦空无
我智慧。弃舍不着。是法能
忍是名法忍。复次观一切诸
法。从本已来常空今世亦
空。是法能信能受是为法
忍。问曰。若从本已来常空
今世亦空。是为恶邪。云何
言法忍。答曰。若观诸法毕
竟空。取相心着[172a]是为恶
邪见。若观空不着不生邪
见。是为法忍。如偈说。

诸法性常空　心亦不着空。
如是法能忍　是佛道初相。

[172a05]　　如是等种种入智慧
门。观诸法实相心不退不悔
不随诸观。

於一切諸法中作轉相。非常
作常想苦作樂想。無我有我
想空謂有實。非有為有有為
非有。如是等種種法中作轉
相。得聖實智慧破無明毒。
知諸法實相。得無常苦空無
我智慧。棄捨不著。是法能
忍是名法忍。復次觀一切諸
法。從本已來常空今世亦
空。是法能信能受是為法
忍。問曰。若從本已來常空
今世亦空。是為惡邪。云何
言法忍。答曰。若觀諸法畢
竟空。取相心著[172a]是為惡
邪見。若觀空不著不生邪
見。是為法忍。如偈說。

諸法性常空　心亦不著空。
如是法能忍　是佛道初相。

[172a05]　　如是等種種入智慧
門。觀諸法實相心不退不悔
不隨諸觀。

简体字   正體字

views] the characteristics of all dharmas, imagining the impermanent to be permanent, imagining that which is suffering to be blissful, imagining that which is non-self to embody a self, holding the opinion that [dharmas] empty of inherent existence possess a reality, taking that which is nonexistent to be existent, and taking that which is existent to be being nonexistent. In a manner such as this they transform the characteristics of all sorts of dharmas."

He gains the genuine wisdom of the Āryas and destroys the poison of ignorance. He realizes the true character of dharmas. He gains the wisdom cognizing that which is impermanent, empty, and not self. He gets rid of [the poison of ignorance] and retains no attachment to it. It is by virtue of his ability to course in patience with respect to these dharmas that he qualifies as possessing "patience with respect to dharmas."

e. Contemplation of Dharmas as Eternally Empty

Furthermore, he contemplates all dharmas as having been eternally empty from their origin on up to the present and as remaining empty in the present era as well. He is able to have faith with respect to this dharma and is able to accept it. This constitutes "patience with respect to dharmas."

Question: If [one were to hold that] they were eternally empty from their origin on up to the present and are empty in the present era as well, this would be an egregious error. How can you speak of it as "patience with respect to dharmas?"

Response: If in contemplating all dharmas as being ultimately empty one seizes upon this characteristic and one's mind becomes attached this *does* constitute an egregious error. However, if in contemplating emptiness one does not become attached and does not bring forth erroneous views, this *does* constitute "patience with respect to dharmas." This is as explained in a verse:

> The nature of dharmas is that they are eternally empty,
> And yet the mind still does not attach to emptiness.
> If one is able to maintain patience with such dharmas,
> This is the characteristic sign of the Buddha Path's beginning.

f. Non-Retreat from Reality; Imperturbability; Universal Benefit

Through all sorts of concepts such as these one enters the gateway to wisdom. When one is able to contemplate in accordance with reality the true character of dharmas while one's mind does not retreat from it, does not have regrets, does not stray off along the

亦无所忧。能得自利利他。
是名法忍。是法忍有三种。
行清净不见忍辱法。不见己
身。不见骂辱人。不戏诸
法。是时名清净法忍。以是
事故说菩萨住般若波罗蜜中
能具足羼提波罗蜜。不动不
退故。云何名不动不退。瞋
恚不生不出恶言。身不加恶
心无所疑。菩萨知般若波罗
蜜实相。不见诸法心无所着
故。若人来骂若加楚毒杀
害。一切能忍。以是故说住
般若波罗蜜中。能具足羼提
波罗蜜。

简体字

亦無所憂。能得自利利他。
是名法忍。是法忍有三種。
行清淨不見忍辱法。不見己
身。不見罵辱人。不戲諸
法。是時名清淨法忍。以是
事故說菩薩住般若波羅蜜中
能具足羼提波羅蜜。不動不
退故。云何名不動不退。瞋
恚不生不出惡言。身不加惡
心無所疑。菩薩知般若波羅
蜜實相。不見諸法心無所著
故。若人來罵若加楚毒殺
害。一切能忍。以是故說住
般若波羅蜜中。能具足羼提
波羅蜜。

正體字

course of the contemplations, and still does not have anything about which it is distressed—if one is also able to succeed in benefiting oneself while benefiting others as well—this is what is referred to as "patience with respect to dharmas."

I. Concluding Statement on Patience with Respect to Dharmas

This patience with respect to dharmas has three bases by which its practice qualifies as pure: One does not perceive the existence of any dharma of patience itself. One does not perceive the existence of one's own person. One does not perceive the existence of a person who is scolding and subjecting one to insult.

Additionally, one refrains from frivolous dialectical discourse regarding any of the dharmas. It is at this time that one's practice qualifies as the pure practice of "patience with respect to dharmas." It is with regard to these very factors that it is said that the bodhisattva who abides in the *prajñāpāramitā* (the perfection of wisdom) is able to completely perfect *kṣānti pāramitā* (the perfection of patience). This is because [his mind] does not move and does not retreat.

What precisely is meant by "does not move and does not retreat"? Hatefulness does not arise. One does not utter any harsh words. One's body does not inflict any harm. One's mind remains free of doubts. The bodhisattva knows in accordance with reality the true character [of dharmas as beheld by] the *prajñāpāramitā* (the perfection of wisdom). He does not engender any perception of the existence of any dharma. This because his mind remains free of anything to which it is attached.

Consequently, even if a person comes along and curses him, even if someone subjects him to extremely toxic poison, and even if someone kills or injures him, he nonetheless remains able to have patience with it all. It is for this reason that it is said that one who abides in the *prajñāpāramitā* (the perfection of wisdom) is able to completely perfect *kṣānti pāramitā* (the perfection of patience).

Part Three Endnotes

1. These reduced-font parenthetical notes are all integral to the received Chinese text preserved in the *Taisho* Tripiṭaka. It may or may not be that they originate with Kumārajīva's oral explanations to his translation scribes.

2. Merit and wisdom are the two "provisions" (*saṃbhāra*) required for realization of buddhahood. See my Kalavinka Press translations of Nāgārjuna's *Bodhisaṃbhāra Śastra* (with my complete translation of the only extant early Indian commentary) and *Ratnāvalī* for extensive treatments of this topic.

3. The "three seals of Dharma" refers to all karmic formative factors (*saṃskāra*) being impermanent, all dharmas being devoid of an inherently-existing self, and nirvāṇa being a genuine dharma characterized by quiescent cessation. (They are mentioned again below at 170a.)

4. In the acquisition of the Path, there are basically eight patiences and eight knowledges. The more provisional levels of abhidharmic interpretation posit that the former are causes for effects manifest as the latter. Higher tenets tend to interpret the two as different facets of the same highly-realized psycho-spiritual capacity.

5. This short section consists of terse and cryptic abhidharma-speak. Because I am not an Abhidharma specialist, the translation of the above few paragraphs must remain somewhat tentative for now. As always, specialists are invited to offer improvements for credited inclusion in subsequent editions.

6. A *dānapati* is a layperson who provides material support to the monastic community.

7. A species of rose apple.

8. A *vihāra* is a monastic dwelling.

9. "Floral Appearance" (Utpalavarṇā) was a nun as well as an arhat.

10. The five "relentless" (*ānantarya*) transgressions are: patricide; matricide; killing an arhat; creating a schism in a harmoniously-dwelling community of the monastic Sangha; and spilling the blood of a buddha. The Chinese term used in this text literally means "traitorous" or "unfilial." I have chosen to ignore it in favor of its antecedent Sanskrit term (also commonly employed in other sino-Buddhist texts). The Sanskrit term connotes immediacy, unavoidability, and relentlessness of hell-bound retribution. These transgressions are discussed in *Abhidharma-kośa-bhāṣyam*, Ch. 4.

11. An *araṇya* is a secluded hermitage.

12. The Vasu gods are a particular category of gods ruled over by Śakra Devānām Indra.

13. This is a reference to the fire which arises at the end of each eon (*kalpa*), burning up everything in the realm of desire even on up to the first dhyāna heavens.

14. This section was originally written specifically to counteract vulnerability to sexual desire in celibate male renunciants or in men contemplating taking up the monk's life. Nāgārjuna devotes his arguments in this section to inspiring path-acquisition by monks through a "counteractive" teaching aimed at defeating affection for women. He chose here as didactic examples the least edifying behaviors of the least virtuous women, confident that women would not be reading this text. (In 200 CE, women were neither taught to read nor allowed to sit in on monastery lectures devoted to discourses on these topics.) Obviously, the author did not feel that a balanced presentation on the nature of women would advance the entirely valid intended effect of this teaching.

    For a female renunciant audience such as might be found in a Buddhist nunnery, Nāgārjuna would have marshaled a similar list of short-comings focused specifically upon the numerous unedifying behaviors of the least virtuous men. Women wishing to brave this section might consider envisioning a similar male-focused discussion so as to derive the same attachment-defeating benefit. Suggested examples of the least edifying behaviors of the least virtuous men might include: the tendency of such men to view women primarily as objects for sexual gratification; the tendency to treat women as menial domestic servants; the tendency to pursue affairs outside of the marriage or to disappear altogether once the wife has become pregnant or has grown less beautiful with age; the tendency to engage in domestic verbal and physical abuse; the tendency to become so obsessed with career success and wealth accumulation that they virtually abandon the family; the tendency to instigate and endlessly pursue wars; and the tendency to fail utterly as regards loving-kindness and compassion, so much so that they remain unmoved even in the face of preventable famine, plague, and genocide.

    In any case, it should be noted that, whenever referencing ultimate truth, Nāgārjuna does not even admit any ultimate reality of gender, let alone positive or negative attributes of gender. This passage is a deliberately "antidotal" or "counteractive" prescription intended to effect a cure of specific male attachments. It is certainly *not* a reflection of his realization of ultimate truth or of his many pronouncements devoted to it.

15. "Five destinies" refers to rebirth among the gods and demi-gods (*asuras*), humans, animals, hungry ghosts, and hells. Lest one be confused by references elsewhere to "six destinies," one should

understand that the alternate designation is merely a consequence of the somewhat more usual taxonomic convention of treating "gods" and "demi-gods" as two separate rebirth destinies.

16. This refers to a Jātaka tale related earlier in the *Exegesis* in which the Buddha predicts the far, far distant future buddhahood of a pigeon.

17. This is probably a reference to the story of a rishi who, harassed by people seeking spiritual favors, swore a hateful oath on everyone in the country. Because he possessed the five superknowledges, this caused all of the citizens to fall dead.

18. For those unfamiliar with doctrinal terms, it may help to understand that "dharmas" in this context are synonymous with "aspects of existence," or "phenomena." As for "patience" as the term is used in this type of context, it is often synonymous with "acquiescence" achieved through deep understanding of the true nature of such phenomena.

19. The basis for classifying these two sub-types appears to be that the former involves aversion-related afflictions, whereas the latter involves attachment-related afflictions. In the case of the examples given for the latter category, the objects of attachment are: a) objects of sensual desire; and b) a false conception of the existence of a "self" and, secondarily, attachment to the supposed importance of that "self."

20. By "neutral mind," Nāgārjuna means to refer to a mind free of two things: 1) mental afflictions (such as hatred); 2) the intention to take a life. One should not be so naive and deluded as to propose that this "neutral mind" is somehow a reference to retaining the psychopath's complete disinterest in the evil of his deeds and the suffering wrought by them.

21. The eight worldly dharmas, also known as the "eight winds" (for their tendency to buffet the mind), are: gain and loss; disgrace and esteem; praise and blame; suffering and happiness. Lest it not be readily evident, the difference between the second and third pairs is that the former refers to the current general state of one's social standing, whereas the latter refers to any given present-moment circumstance wherein someone is either praising or scolding.

22. The reason that Nāgārjuna brings up the karmic vulnerabilities of taking rebirth in the heavens is to remind the practitioner that this human rebirth, trying as it may be, is the only circumstance in which one is able to successfully cultivate and gain success in the path of spiritual liberation. Celestial rebirth is so blissful that one is robbed of any motivation to cultivate. Lower-realm rebirth involves so much suffering and difficulty that it is impossible to cultivate the Path in those realms. Hence human rebirth is actually the ideal circumstance for cultivating the Path.

23. The "fourteen difficult questions":

   (1-4) Are the world and the self eternal, non-eternal, both, neither?

   (5-8) Are the world and the self finite, non-finite, both, neither?

   (9-12) Does the Tathāgata (the Buddha) exist after death, not exist after death, both, neither?

   (13-14) Is the life force (*jīva*) identical with the body or not?

24. Nāgārjuna refers here to his extensive discussion in Fascicle One of "four doctrinal perspectives" (*siddhānta*) which illustrate the four stances from which the Buddha's teachings are presented (worldly, individually-tailored, counteractive, and ultimate truth).

25. Note the completely deceptive punctuation in the *Taisho* Chinese text. "The emptiness of emptiness" is the fourth of the eighteen emptinesses, Nāgārjuna's discussion of which comprises the entirety of Fascicle Thirty-one.

26. Nāgārjuna has effectively done away with all dharmas at this point. We realize this because we know that all traditional comprehensive listings of dharmas fall under five categories: mind dharmas; dharmas belonging to the mind (which include many of the formative-factor dharmas); form dharmas; formative-factor dharmas not associated with the mind; and unconditioned dharmas.

27. It is this *dharmatā* ("the nature of dharmas" or "things as they really are") which is the Sanskrit antecedent for most of the occasions in which Kumārajīva gives us the loose Chinese equivalent of *zhu fa shi xiang* (諸法實相). I ofen translate this as "true character of dharmas," or "dharmas as they really are."

[164n06] 義第二十四 = 義 [元], = 上第十九 [宮] [石], (義第二十四) - [明]

[164n07] ([經]) - [宋] [宮] [石]

[164n08] ([論]) - [宋] [宮] [石]

[164n09] 秦 = 此 [明]

[164n10] 心 = 法 [石]

[164n11] 名 + （為）[宋] [元] [明] [宮]

[164n12] 軟 = 濡 [宮]

[164n13] 瘡 = 創 [宮]* [* 1]

[164n14] 淨清 = 清淨 [宋] [元] [明] [宮]

[164n15] 簡 = 揀 [宋] [元] [明] [宮]

[164n16] 戚 = 族 [宋] [元] [明] [宮]

[164n17] 曇 + （彌）[石]

[164n18] 汝 = 以 [宋] [元] [明]

[164n19] 敬 = 以 [宋] [元] [明] [宮]

[164n20] (受) - [石]

[164n21] 旦 = 怛 [宋] [元] [明] [宮]

[164n22] 嬰 = 瓔 [宋] [元] [宮]

[164n23] 唉 = 嗽 [元] [明] [宮], = [口*束] [石]

[164n24] 奈 = 李 [宮] [石]

[164n25] 大立 = 立大 [宋] [元] [明] [宮]

[165n01] 爪 = [打 - 丁+瓜] [宋] [宮]

[165n02] 到 + （於）[宋] [元] [明] [宮]

[165n03] 應當 = 當應 [宋] [元] [明] [宮]

[165n04] (為人敬養) - [宋] [宮] [石]

[165n05] 惟 + （便）[石]

[165n06] 食 = 服 [石]

[165n07] 勸 = 勤 [石]

[165n08] 雖 + （欲）[宋] [元] [明] [宮]

[165n09] 滋味 = 味味 [宋]

[165n10] 患 = 惡 [宋] [元] [明] [宮]

[165n11] 玉 = 王 [石]

[165n12] 各 = 名 [石]

[165n13] 好黑好白 = 好白好黑 [宋] [元] [明] [宮]

[165n14] 一一 = 二 [宮]

[165n15] 睫嫈娺 = [月*妾]嫈娺 [宮], = [月*妾][月*(䁋/安)][目*音] [石]

[165n16] 近 = 迎 [宋] [元] [明] [宮]

[165n17] 逼 = 遍 [石]

[165n18] 命 = 帝 [宋] [元] [明] [宮]

[165n19] 日 = 月 [宋] [元] [明] [宮] [石]

[165n20] 昱爍 = 煜爟 [元] [明]

[165n21] 傾 = 輕 [宮]

[165n22] (最) - [石]

[166n01] 視 = 親 [元] [明]* [* 1]

[166n02] 德 = 慧 [石]

[166n03] 染 = 深 [石]

[166n04] 恥 = 慚 [宋] [元] [明] [宮] [石]

[166n05] 網 = 細 [石]

[166n06] 眄 = [目*子] [石]

[166n07] 應不 = 不應 [宋] [元] [明] [宮]

[166n08] (人如) - [石]

[166n09] 要 = 惡 [宋] [元] [明] [宮] [石]

[166n10] (人) - [石]

[166n11] 政 = 正 [宋] [元] [明] [宮]

[166n12] (女) - [宋] [元] [明] [宮] [石]

[166n13] 述婆伽 = 怵波伽 [宋] [元] [明] [宮], = 床婆伽 [石]

[166n14] 美 = 鳥 [宋] [元] [明] [宮] [石]

[166n15] 世 = 施 [宋] [元] [明] [宮]

[166n16] (忍) - [石]

[166n17] 遊 = 採 [宋] [元] [明] [宮]

[166n18] 亂 + （人）[石]

[166n19] 悲 = 慈 [宋] [元] [明] [宮]

[166n20] 迫 = 逼 [宋] [元] [明] [宮] [石]

[166n21] 加 = 以 [宋] [元] [明] [宮] [石]

[167n01] 興 = 與 [石]

[167n02] (惱) - [宋] [元] [明] [宮]

[167n03] (我) - [宋] [元] [明] [宮]

[167n04] (辱) - [石]

[167n05] 佛 + （佛答）[宋] [元] [宮]

[167n06] (偈) - [宋] [元] [明] [宮]

[167n07] 利 = 我 [石]

[167n08] (之) - [宋] [元] [明] [宮]

[167n09] 瞋 + （之）[宋] [元] [明] [宮]

[167n10] 煉 = 鍊 [宋] [元] [明] [宮]

[167n11] 猶 = 有 [宋] [元] [明] [宮] [石]

[167n12] 大 = 火 [宮]

[167n13] 輪 = 輸 [石]

[167n14] 告 + （之）[宋] [元] [明] [宮]

[167n15] 汝諸乃至重十六字宋元明宮四本俱作長行

[167n16] 火出燒身 = 云何瞋靜 [石]

[167n17] 能 = 忍 [石]

[167n18] 輕 = 輙 [石]
[167n19] 智 = 知 [宋] [元] [明] [宮]
[167n20] (行) - [宋] [元] [明] [宮] [石]
[167n21] 燔 = 煏 [宋] [元] [明] [宮]
[167n22] (者) - [宋] [元] [明] [宮] [石]
[168n01] 愈 = 逾 [宋] [元] [明] [宮]
[168n02] [衝 - 重+素] = 禦 [宋] [元] [明] [宮], = 御 [石]
[168n03] 累 = 壘 [宋] [元] [明] [宮]
[168n04] 墼 = 塹 [宮]
[168n05] (行) - [石]
[168n06] (境) + 界 [宋] [元] [明] [宮]
[168n07] 度 + (經) [石]
[168n08] 法忍義 = 下 [宋] [元] [宮] [石], = 之餘 [明]
[168n09] (第二十五) - [元] [明],第二十五 = 第二十 [宮], 第二十五 + (之餘) [石]
[168n10] 後秦 = 姚秦 [宋] [元] [明] [宮]
[168n11] (龜茲國) - [宋] [元] [明] [宮] [石]
[168n12] 藏 + (法師) [宋] [元] [明] [宮] [石]
[168n13] (奉詔) - [宋] [元] [明] [宮] [石]
[168n14] 鞊 = 詰 [宋] [元] [明] [宮]* [* 1]
[168n15] 住 = 作 [宋] [元] [明] [宮] [石]
[168n16] (心) - [宋] [宮] [石]
[168n17] (無) - [石]
[168n18] (諸) - [宋] [元] [明] [宮]
[168n19] (先) - [宋] [元] [明] [宮]
[168n20] (而) - [宋] [元] [明] [宮]
[168n21] (以是故) - [宋] [元] [明] [宮] [石]
[168n22] 畏怖 = 怖畏 [宋] [元] [明] [宮]
[168n23] 烏 = 鳥 [宋] [宮]
[168n24] 人 + (先) [宋] [元] [明] [宮] [石]
[168n25] (得道) - [宋] [元] [明] [宮]
[169n01] 小 + (苦) [宋] [元] [明] [宮]
[169n02] (我) - [宋] [元] [明] [宮]
[169n03] 悔 = 為 [宋] [宮]
[169n04] 蔑人 = 憍慢 [宋] [元] [明] [宮]
[169n05] 楯 = 盾 [宋] [元] [明] [宮]
[169n06] 哀 = 請 [宋] [元] [明] [宮] [石]
[169n07] (值) - [宋] [元] [明] [宮] [石]
[169n08] 相 + (法) [宋] [元] [明] [宮] [石]
[169n09] (有人言) - [宋] [元] [明] [宮] [石]

[169n10] (萬) - [宮]
[169n11] 切 + (法) [宋] [元] [明] [宮] [石]
[169n12] 二 = 一 [宮]
[169n13] (或) - [宋] [元] [明] [宮]
[170n01] (難) - [宮] [石]
[170n02] (此) - [宋] [元] [明] [宮]
[170n03] 汝答 = 若為 [石]
[170n04] 欲 = 次 [石]
[170n05] 一心 = 心一 [宋] [元] [明] [宮] [石]
[170n06] 不至 = 至不 [石]
[170n07] 新新 = 漸漸 [宮]
[170n08] (能) - [宋] [元] [明] [宮]
[170n09] (欲) - [宋] [元] [明] [宮]
[170n10] 法 + (得) [宋] [元] [明] [宮] [石]
[170n11] 有 + (後) [宋] [元] [明] [宮]
[170n12] 則 = 即 [宋] [元] [明] [宮]* [* 1]
[170n13] 損 = 積 [宮] [石]
[170n14] (德) - [宋] [元] [明],德 = 業 [宮] [石]
[170n15] 常 + (相) [宋] [元] [明]
[170n16] (說) - [宋] [元] [明] [宮]
[170n17] 緣 + (有者) [宋] [元] [明] [宮]
[170n18] (有老) - [宮]
[170n19] (為) - [宋] [元] [明] [宮]
[170n20] (是) - [宋] [元] [明] [宮]
[171n01] (若實) - [宋] [元] [明] [宮]
[171n02] 先 + (相) [石]
[171n03] (知) - [宋] [元] [明] [宮] [石]
[171n04] 法有 = 有法 [宋] [元] [明] [宮] [石]
[171n05] 知 = 得 [石]
[171n06] 頃 = 頂 [元]
[171n07] (是) - [宋] [元] [明] [宮]
[171n08] 已 = 以 [宋] [元] [明] [宮]
[171n09] 則 = 相 [石]
[171n10] 法 + (法) [宋] [元] [明] [宮]
[171n11] 道 + (言) [元] [明]
[171n12] 又 = 有 [宋] [元] [明] [宮] [石]
[171n13] (是) - [宋] [元] [明] [宮] [石]
[171n14] (復) - [宋] [元] [明] [宮] [石]
[171n15] (滅) - [宋] [宮] [石]
[171n16] (法) - [石]

[171n17] (等) - [宋] [元] [明] [宮]
[171n18] (切) - [宋] [元] [明] [宮]
[171n19] 滅 = 盡 [宋] [元] [明] [宮] [石]
[171n20] (若無法寶) - [宋] [元] [明] [宮]
[171n21] (相) - [宮] [石]
[171n22] (惱) + 悔 [宋],悔 = 惱 [宮]

Part Four:

THE PERFECTION OF VIGOR

(Chapters 26–27)

Part Four Contents

NĀGĀRJUNA ON THE PERFECTION OF VIGOR

[1]大智[2]度论释初品中毗梨耶波罗蜜[3]义第二十六。

[0172a18] [4]【经】身心精进不懈[5]息故[6]应具足毗梨耶波罗蜜。

[0172a19] [7]【论】[8]毗梨耶（秦言精进）问曰。如精进。是一切善法本。应最在初。今何以故第四。答曰。布施持戒忍辱世间常有。如客主之义法应供给。乃至畜生亦知布施。或有人种种因缘故能布施。若为今世若为后世。若为道故布施。不须精进。如持戒者。见为恶之人王法治罪。便自畏惧不敢为非。或有性善不作诸恶。有人闻今世作恶后世受罪。而以怖畏故能持戒。有人闻持戒因缘故得离生老病死。是中心生口言。我从今日不复杀生。

简体字

[1]大智[2]度論釋初品中毗梨耶波羅蜜[3]義第二十六。

[0172a18] [4]【經】身心精進不懈[5]息故[6]應具足毗梨耶波羅蜜。

[0172a19] [7]【論】[8]毗梨耶（秦言精進）問曰。如精進。是一切善法本。應最在初。今何以故第四。答曰。布施持戒忍辱世間常有。如客主之義法應供給。乃至畜生亦知布施。或有人種種因緣故能布施。若為今世若為後世。若為道故布施。不須精進。如持戒者。見為惡之人王法治罪。便自畏懼不敢為非。或有性善不作諸惡。有人聞今世作惡後世受罪。而以怖畏故能持戒。有人聞持戒因緣故得離生老病死。是中心生口言。我從今日不復殺生。

正體字

THE PERFECTION OF VIGOR

By Ārya Nāgārjuna

Chapter 26: The Meaning of the Perfection of Vigor

Sutra text: It is through being vigorous in body and mind and refraining from indolence or resting that one perfects *vīrya pāramitā* (the perfection of vigor).

Exegesis:

I. INTRODUCTORY DISCUSSION OF THE PERFECTION OF VIGOR

Vīrya (Chinese textual note: In our language, one says "vigor")[1] ....

A. WHY VIGOR IS FOURTH AMONG THE SIX PERFECTIONS

Question: Something like vigor, the basis of all good dharmas, should be listed as foremost among the perfections. Why is it now only placed as the fourth among them?

1. WHY VIGOR IS NOT REQUIRED FOR THE FIRST THREE PERFECTIONS

Response: Giving, moral virtue, and patience are eternally-existing ideas in the world. For instance, the standard of propriety between guests and hosts calls for the presenting of gifts. Even animals know to engage in giving.

There may be all sorts of reasons why a person is able to engage in giving. Perhaps it is for the sake of the present life. Perhaps it is for the sake of future lives. Or perhaps one gives for the sake of the Path. One does not require vigor in such cases.

As for the upholding of the moral precepts, because one observes that those who commit evil deeds meet with punishment through royal law, one becomes fearful [of such consequences] and thus doesn't dare do what is wrong. In other cases, there are those who are good by their very nature and so refrain from all evil deeds. There are also those people who hear that if one does evil in the present life, one will undergo punishment in future lives. Because they are frightened by such a prospect, they are able to abide by the moral precepts.

There are still others who hear that one may transcend birth, aging, sickness, and death through the causal circumstances associated with observing the moral precepts. Then, on account of this, they resolve with their minds and declare with their words: "From this very day on, I will never again kill any beings."

如是等即是戒。岂须精进波罗蜜[172b]而能行耶。如忍辱中。若骂若打若杀。或畏故不报。或少力或畏罪或修善人法或为求道故默然不报。皆不必须精进波罗蜜乃能忍也。今欲得知诸法实相。行般若波罗蜜故修行禅定。禅定是实智慧之门。是中应懃修精进一心行禅。复次布施持戒忍辱。是大福德安隐快乐。有好名誉。所欲者得。既得知此福利之味。今欲增进更得妙胜禅定智慧。譬如穿井已见湿泥。转加增进必望得水。又如钻火已得见烟。倍复力励必望得火。欲成佛道凡有二门。一者福德。二者智慧。行施戒忍是为福德门。知一切诸法实相摩诃般若波罗蜜。是为智慧门。菩萨入福德门。除一切罪所愿皆得。

简体字

如是等即是戒。豈須精進波羅蜜[172b]而能行耶。如忍辱中。若罵若打若殺。或畏故不報。或少力或畏罪或修善人法或為求道故默然不報。皆不必須精進波羅蜜乃能忍也。今欲得知諸法實相。行般若波羅蜜故修行禪定。禪定是實智慧之門。是中應懃修精進一心行禪。復次布施持戒忍辱。是大福德安隱快樂。有好名譽。所欲者得。既得知此福利之味。今欲增進更得妙勝禪定智慧。譬如穿井已見濕泥。轉加增進必望得水。又如鑽火已得見煙。倍復力勵必望得火。欲成佛道凡有二門。一者福德。二者智慧。行施戒忍是為福德門。知一切諸法實相摩訶般若波羅蜜。是為智慧門。菩薩入福德門。除一切罪所願皆得。

正體字

These sorts of instances are synonymous with observance of the moral precepts. How then would one have any particular need of the *pāramitā* of vigor to practice them?

As for the sphere of patience, even when subjected to scolding, striking, or even murder, one may still remain silent and refrain from retaliating, doing so on account of fearfulness, lesser strength, dread of punishment, because one cultivates the dharmas of a good person, or because one seeks realization of the Path. None of these circumstances require the *pāramitā* of vigor as an essential condition for being able to practice patience.

2. Why Vigor is Essential to Dhyāna and Prajñā

One now desires to succeed in accordance with reality the true character of dharmas (*dharmatā*). In order to course in *prajñāpāramitā* (the perfection of wisdom), one cultivates dhyāna absorption. Dhyāna absorption is the gateway to genuine wisdom. It is herein that one should diligently cultivate vigor, thereby becoming single-minded in the practice of dhyāna meditation.

3. Two Analogies: Well Drilling and Fire Starting

Moreover, giving, moral virtue, and patience produce the peace, security, and happiness associated with great merit. One thereby enjoys a fine reputation and obtains whatever one desires. Having gained these, one then knows the flavor of the benefits of merit.

Now, however, one wishes to advance beyond this so that one might develop marvelously supreme dhyāna absorption and wisdom. This is analogous to digging a well. When one has already discovered wet mud, one then adds increased effort, for one has just then experienced a definite hope that water will be found. This is also comparable to "drilling" to ignite a fire once has already seen smoke beginning to come forth. One then redoubles his efforts and enthusiasm based on a definite hope that a fire will soon start.

4. Two Gates to Buddhahood: Merit and Wisdom

When one desires to achieve buddhahood, there are generally two gateways involved in gaining entry: The first of them is merit and the second is wisdom. Practicing giving, observing the moral precepts, and implementing patience collectively serve as the gateway to the acquisition of merit. The *mahāprajñāpāramitā* which knows in accordance with reality the true character of dharmas—this is the gateway to the acquisition of wisdom.

When the bodhisattva passes through the gateway of merit, he gets rid of all karmic offenses and succeeds in gaining whatever he

若不得愿者。以罪垢遮故。
入智慧门则不厌生死。不乐
涅盘。二事一故。今欲出生
摩诃般若波罗蜜。般若波罗
蜜。要因禅定门。[9]禅定门
必须大精进力。何以故[10]散
乱心。不能得见诸法实相。
譬如风中然灯不能照物。灯
在密屋明必能照。是禅定智
慧。不可以福愿求。亦非麁
观能得。要须身心精懃急着
不懈尔乃成办。如佛所说。
血肉脂髓皆使竭尽。但[11]
令皮骨筋在不舍精进。如是
乃能得禅定智慧。得是二事
则众事皆办。以是故精进第
四。名为禅定实智慧之根。
上三中虽有精进少故不说。
问曰。有人言。但行布施持
戒忍辱故得

若不得願者。以罪垢遮故。
入智慧門則不厭生死。不樂
涅槃。二事一故。今欲出生
摩訶般若波羅蜜。般若波羅
蜜。要因禪定門。[9]禪定門
必須大精進力。何以故[10]散
亂心。不能得見諸法實相。
譬如風中然燈不能照物。燈
在密屋明必能照。是禪定智
慧。不可以福願求。亦非麁
觀能得。要須身心精懃急著
不懈爾乃成辦。如佛所說。
血肉脂髓皆使竭盡。但[11]
令皮骨筋在不捨精進。如是
乃能得禪定智慧。得是二事
則眾事皆辦。以是故精進第
四。名為禪定實智慧之根。
上三中雖有精進少故不說。
問曰。有人言。但行布施持
戒忍辱故得

简体字 　　　　　　　　　 正體字

wishes. If he does not realize his wishes, it is because the defilement of offenses continues to block further progress.

Once he passes on through the gateway of wisdom, he no longer harbors any particular abhorrence for cyclic birth and death, nor does he take any particular delight in nirvāṇa. This is because he realizes that these two matters are actually one.

5. Wisdom's Basis in Dhyāna Meditation

One wishes now to give birth to the *mahāprajñāpāramitā*. The *prajñā-pāramitā's* essential cause is the gateway of dhyāna absorption. Entry into gateway of dhyāna absorption definitely requires the power of great vigor. Why [are they essential]? It is because the scattered and chaotic mind is unable to succeed in perceiving the true character of dharmas in accordance with reality.

a. Analogy: A Lamp's Illumination

This circumstance is analogous to that of a lamp which, when burning in the wind, is unable to illuminate things. When the lamp abides in a closed room, its brightness becomes definitely able to produce illumination.

b. The Irrelevance of Merit to Dhyāna and Wisdom

This dhyāna absorption and wisdom cannot be hoped for or sought out through merit. Nor is it the case that they can be gained through coarse contemplations. It is an essential that one be intensely diligent in body and mind, urgently adhering to such practice without becoming lax. It is only through such efforts that success will be realized. This is as described by the Buddha when he said, "Even though my blood, flesh, fat, and marrow were completely wasted away to the point where there remained only skin, bone, and sinews, I still did not relinquish the practice of vigor."

6. Summation: Vigor is Essential to Dhyāna and Wisdom.

It is only in this manner that one will be able to gain dhyāna absorption and wisdom. Once one has succeeded in these two matters, all of the many endeavors will have reached their completion. It is for these reasons that vigor is placed fourth among the perfections. It is the very root of dhyāna absorption and wisdom. Although the previous three perfections do involve a measure of vigor, because less is required therein, we have not yet discussed it.

7. Challenge: Merit Alone is Adequate for Dhyāna and Wisdom

Question: There are those who claim: "One need only practice giving, upholding of precepts, and patience. Based on that, one gains

大福德。福德力故所願皆
得。禅定智慧自然而至。复
何用精进波罗蜜[12]为。答
曰。佛道甚深难得。虽有布
施持戒忍辱力。要须精[172c]
进。得甚深禅定实智慧及无
量诸佛法。若不行精进则不
生禅定。禅定不生则不得生
梵天王处。何况欲求佛道。
复次有人。如民大居士等欲
得无量宝物则应意皆得。如
顶生王王四天下。[13]天雨七
宝及所须之物。释提婆那民
分座与坐。虽有是福然不能
得道。如罗频珠比丘。虽得
阿罗汉道乞食七日不得空钵
而还。后以禅定火自烧其身
而般涅盘。以是故知。非但
福德力故得道。欲成佛道要
须懃大精进。

大福德。福德力故所願皆
得。禪定智慧自然而至。復
何用精進波羅蜜[12]為。答
曰。佛道甚深難得。雖有布
施持戒忍辱力。要須精[172c]
進。得甚深禪定實智慧及無
量諸佛法。若不行精進則不
生禪定。禪定不生則不得生
梵天王處。何況欲求佛道。
復次有人。如民大居士等欲
得無量寶物則應意皆得。如
頂生王王四天下。[13]天雨七
寶及所須之物。釋提婆那民
分座與坐。雖有是福然不能
得道。如羅頻珠比丘。雖得
阿羅漢道乞食七日不得空鉢
而還。後以禪定火自燒其身
而般涅槃。以是故知。非但
福德力故得道。欲成佛道要
須懃大精進。

简体字 | 正體字

great merit. Through the power of merit, everything one wishes for will be achieved. Hence dhyāna absorption and wisdom will naturally develop." If this is so, what further use might there be for the *pāramitā* of vigor?

8. REFUTATION: NO SUCH RESULT WITHOUT VIGOR

Response: The Buddha Path is extremely profound and difficult to bring to realization. Even though one may possess the power of giving, moral virtue, and patience, still, as an essential condition, one must nonetheless incorporate vigor in order to obtain the extremely deep dhyāna absorptions, genuine wisdom, and the incalculable number of dharmas associated with buddhahood. If one fails to practice vigor, then one will not succeed in bringing forth dhyāna absorption. If one does not bring forth dhyāna absorption, then one cannot even succeed in being reborn in the domain of a Brahma Heaven king. How much the less might one hope to gain realization of the path to buddhahood?

a. EVIDENCE CITED AGAINST ADEQUACY OF MERIT ALONE

Moreover, there are persons such as the layman Meṇḍaka who [possessed so much merit that], whenever he wished to acquire countless precious things, could obtain them as a spontaneous result of merely thinking about them. For others such as King "Born From the Crown," ruler over the four continents, the heavens rained down the seven precious things as well as anything else he wanted. He was a man with whom Śakra Devānām Indra divided his throne so that they both sat together on it. Although these men possessed such great karmic blessings as this, they still could not succeed in gaining [the fruits of] the Path.

b. EVIDENCE FOR VIGOR: LOSAKA-TIṢYA

[On the other hand], there are examples such as the Bhikshu Losaka-tiṣya. Although he was able even to achieve the path of arhatship, [his merit had become so deficient that] he went on the alms round for seven days in a row, received nothing, and was forced in each case to return with an empty bowl. Later, however, he was able to use the fire of dhyāna absorption to incinerate his own body and then enter nirvāṇa. On account of this, one knows that it is not solely on the basis of the power of blessings that one gains the Path. If one wishes to perfect the Buddha Path, as an essential condition one must be diligent in the application of great vigor.

问曰。菩萨观精进有何利益。而懃修不懈。答曰。一切今世后世道德利益皆由精进得。复次若人欲自度身。尚当懃急精进。何况菩萨誓愿欲度一切。如赞精进偈中说。

[14]有人不惜身　智慧心决定。
如法行精进　所求事无难。

如农失懃修　所收必丰实。
亦如涉远路　懃[15]则必能达。

若得生天上　及得涅盘乐。
如是之因缘　皆由精进力。

非天非无因　自作故自得。
谁有智慧人　而不自勉励。

三界火炽然　譬如大[16]炎火。
有智决断人　乃能得免离。

以是故佛告　阿难正精进。
如是不懈[17]怠　直至于佛道。

勉强而懃修　穿地能通泉。

問曰。菩薩觀精進有何利益。而懃修不懈。答曰。一切今世後世道德利益皆由精進得。復次若人欲自度身。尚當懃急精進。何況菩薩誓願欲度一切。如讚精進偈中說。

[14]有人不惜身　智慧心決定。
如法行精進　所求事無難。

如農失懃修　所收必豐實。
亦如涉遠路　懃[15]則必能達。

若得生天上　及得涅槃樂。
如是之因緣　皆由精進力。

非天非無因　自作故自得。
誰有智慧人　而不自勉勵。

三界火熾然　譬如大[16]炎火。
有智決斷人　乃能得免離。

以是故佛告　阿難正精進。
如是不懈[17]怠　直至於佛道。

勉強而懃修　穿地能通泉。

简体字   正體字

B. QUESTION: WHAT ARE THE BENEFITS OF VIGOR?

Question: When the bodhisattva contemplates vigor, what benefits does he perceive it to possess that he then diligently cultivates it without becoming lax?

a. ALL PATH BENEFITS FLOW FORTH FROM VIGOR

Response: All of the virtues associated with the Path and all of the benefits in present and future existences are gained on account of vigor. Moreover, if one wished only to succeed in bringing himself across to liberation, he should still be diligently and urgently vigorous. How much the more so is this the case with the bodhisattva who has made vows with the desire of bringing all beings across to liberation. This is as described in a verse in praise of vigor:

b. VERSE IN PRAISE OF VIGOR

There are persons who don't indulge cherishing of the body
And whose mind of wisdom is resolute and fixed.
Practicing vigor in accordance with Dharma,
They find no difficulty in gaining whatever is sought.

They are like the farmer[2] who diligently cultivates his fields.
His harvest will definitely be abundantly substantial.
They are also like one who travels the road to a distant place.
If diligent, they certainly succeed in reaching the destination.

Whether it be the achievement of rebirth in the heavens
Or whether it be gaining the bliss of nirvāṇa,
Such causes and conditions as these
All arise on account of the power of vigor.

Such results aren't bestowed by a god nor devoid of cause.
Because one's created them himself, he himself is the beneficiary.
Whosoever is a person possessed of wisdom,
And yet fails to urge himself on with exhortations–

Should realize the fire of the three realms is burning
Like a great blazing conflagration.
Only a person possessed of wisdom and decisiveness
Is able to avoid it and make good his escape.

It is for this reason that the Buddha proclaimed
Right vigor for the sake of Ānanda.
If in this manner one refrains from being lax or idle,
One will arrive directly at realization of the Buddha Path.

If one exhorts oneself intensely and labors at it diligently,
He may burrow into the ground and be able to reach a spring.

精进亦如是　无求而不得。
能如行道法　精进不懈者。
无量果必得　此报终不失。

[0173a02] 复次精进法。是一切
诸善[1]法之根本。能出生一
切诸道法乃至阿耨多罗三藐
三菩提。何况[2]于小利。如
毘尼中说。一切诸善法乃至
阿耨多罗三藐三菩提。皆从
精进不放逸生。复次精进能
动发先世福德。如雨润种能
令必生此亦如是。虽有先世
福德因缘。若无精进则不能
生。乃至今世利尚不能得。
何况佛道。复次诸大菩萨荷
负众生。受一切苦乃至阿鼻
泥犁中苦。心亦不懈。是为
精进。复次一切众事。若无
精进则不能成。譬如下药以
巴豆为主。若除巴豆则无下
力。如是意止神足根力觉道
必待精进。若无精进则众事
不办。如戒唯在八道不在馀
处。信在

精進亦如是　無求而不得。
能如行道法　精進不懈者。
無量果必得　此報終不失。

[0173a02] 復次精進法。是一切
諸善[1]法之根本。能出生一
切諸道法乃至阿耨多羅三藐
三菩提。何況[2]於小利。如
毘尼中說。一切諸善法乃至
阿耨多羅三藐三菩提。皆從
精進不放逸生。復次精進能
動發先世福德。如雨潤種能
令必生此亦如是。雖有先世
福德因緣。若無精進則不能
生。乃至今世利尚不能得。
何況佛道。復次諸大菩薩荷
負眾生。受一切苦乃至阿鼻
泥犁中苦。心亦不懈。是為
精進。復次一切眾事。若無
精進則不能成。譬如下藥以
巴豆為主。若除巴豆則無下
力。如是意止神足根力覺道
必待精進。若無精進則眾事
不辦。如戒唯在八道不在餘
處。信在

简体字　　　　　　　　　　正體字

The case with vigor is just the same as this.
There is nothing sought which will not then be gained.

If one is able to accord with Dharma in practicing the Path,
Whoever then is vigorous and thus refrains from indolence
Will definitely succeed in garnering innumerable fruits
And such rewards as these will then never be lost.

C. VIGOR'S ASPECTS DISCUSSED
1. VIGOR AS THE ROOT OF ALL GOOD DHARMAS

Moreover, the dharma of vigor is the root and foundation for all of the good dharmas. It is able to produce all of the dharmas of the Path even up to *anuttarasamyaksaṃbodhi*, how much the more is this the case with minor benefits. This is as described in the Vinaya: "All good dharmas including even *anuttarasamyaksaṃbodhi* are born from being vigorous and from not being neglectful."

2. VIGOR AS THE ACTIVATOR OF KARMIC BLESSINGS FROM THE PAST

Moreover, vigor is able to activate the blessings from previous existences just as rain moistening seeds surely causes them to grow. This is just the same. Although one may possess the causes and conditions of merit from previous existences, if one is not vigorous, then it will not be able to come forth. Thus one will be unable to gain any benefit even in the present life, how much the less will one succeed in realizing the path to buddhahood.

3. BODHISATTVA VIGOR DOES NOT FEAR HELLS

Furthermore, the great bodhisattvas take on the burdens of beings, undergoing all of the sufferings including even the sufferings in the *avīci niraya* (the uninterrupted hells). Nor do their minds become lax. This constitutes vigor.

4. VIGOR'S IMPORTANCE IN COMPLETING ENDEAVORS

Moreover, in all of the manifold endeavors, if one has no vigor, then they will not be able to be completed. This is analogous to purgative medicines taking *Croton tiglium* as what is primary. If one leaves out the *Croton tiglium*, then they have no purgative power. In this same manner, the foundations of mindfulness, the bases of spiritual power, the roots, the powers, the wings of enlightenment and the Path are all dependent upon vigor. If one has no vigor, then the manifold endeavors are not completed.

5. VIGOR'S PRESENCE IN ALL PATH-PRACTICE CATEGORIES

As a point of comparison, the moral precepts are only found in the eightfold Path and are not found in other places. Faith is found in the

根力餘处则无。如精进者无处不有。既总众法而别自有门。譬如无明使遍在一切诸使中。而别有不共无明。问曰。菩萨欲得一切佛法。欲度一切众生。欲灭一切烦恼。皆得如意。云何增益。精进而能得佛。譬如小火不能烧大林。火势增益能烧一切。答曰。菩萨从初发心作誓愿。当令一切众生得欢乐。常为一切不自惜身。若惜身者于诸善法不能成办。以是故增益精进。复次菩萨种种因缘呵懈怠心。令乐着精进。懈怠黑云覆诸明慧。吞灭功德增长不善。懈怠之人。初虽小乐后则大苦。譬如毒食。初虽香美久则杀人。懈怠之心烧诸功德譬如大火烧诸林野。

简体字

根力餘處則無。如精進者無處不有。既總眾法而別自有門。譬如無明使遍在一切諸使中。而別有不共無明。問曰。菩薩欲得一切佛法。欲度一切眾生。欲滅一切煩惱。皆得如意。云何增益。精進而能得佛。譬如小火不能燒大林。火勢增益能燒一切。答曰。菩薩從初發心作誓願。當令一切眾生得歡樂。常為一切不自惜身。若惜身者於諸善法不能成辦。以是故增益精進。復次菩薩種種因緣呵懈怠心。令樂著精進。懈怠黑雲覆諸明慧。吞滅功德增長不善。懈怠之人。初雖小樂後則大苦。譬如毒食。初雖香美久則殺人。懈怠之心燒諸功德譬如大火燒諸林野。

正體字

roots and the powers, but if one looks in the other places, then they are not to be found. But, as for vigor, there is no place where it does not exist. Not only does it generally subsume the many dharmas, but it also constitutes an entryway [to Dharma] in its own right.

6. ANALOGY: THE PRESENCE OF IGNORANCE IN ALL DEFILEMENTS

This is analogous to the defilement (*anuśaya*) of ignorance. It is universally present in all of the other defilements and still, aside from all such instances there exists yet another specific category of "exclusively abiding" ignorance (*āveṇikī avidyā*).

7. QUESTION: HOW DOES ONE INCREASE VIGOR?

Question: The bodhisattva wishes to gain all of the buddha dharmas, desires to bring all beings across to liberation, desires to extinguish all of the afflictions, and wishes to have everything manifest in accordance with his aspirations. How does one go about increasing and enhancing vigor so as to be able to gain buddhahood? This would be comparable to a small fire being unable to burn down a great forest, but when the intensity of the fire increases and becomes augmented it is able to burn everything.

a. THROUGH THE ALTRUISTIC VOW

Response: From the time of his first bringing forth the resolve to attain bodhi, the bodhisattva makes the vow that he will cause all beings to gain happiness and that for the sake of everyone, he will not indulge any cherishing regard for his own body. If one indulges a cherishing regard for his own body, then one will be unable to be successful in bringing all good dharmas to completion. It is on account of this that one is able to increase one's vigor.

b. THROUGH RENOUNCING INDOLENCE

Additionally, for all manner of reasons the bodhisattva renounces the mind of indolence (*kausīdya*) and causes himself to become blissfully adherent to vigor. The black clouds of indolence cover over brilliant wisdom, swallow up and destroy meritorious qualities, and increase that which is not good.

1) INDOLENCE ANALOGIES: POISONED FOOD AND FIRE

Although the person who is indolent initially enjoys a minor measure of happiness, he later undergoes great suffering. This is analogous to poisoned food. Although it may initially be fragrant and exquisite, after a time, it kills a person.

The mind of indolence burns up all meritorious qualities just like a great fire burns up an entire forest wilderness. A person who

懈怠之人失诸功德。譬如被贼无复遗馀。如偈说。

[173b]
应得而不得　已得而复失。
既自轻其身　众人亦不敬。

常处大暗中　无有诸威德。
尊贵智慧法　此事永以失。

闻诸妙道法　不能以益身。
如是之过失　皆由懈怠心。

虽闻增益法　不能得上及。
如是之过罪　皆由懈怠心。

生业不修理　不入于道法。
如是之过[3]失　皆由懈怠心。
上智所弃远　中人时复近。
下[4]愚为之没　如猪乐在溷。

若为世中人　三事皆废失。
欲乐及财利　福德亦复没。

若为出家人　则不得二事。
生天及涅盘　名誉二俱失。

如是诸废失　欲知其所由。

简体字

懈怠之人失諸功德。譬如被賊無復遺餘。如偈說。

[173b]
應得而不得　已得而復失。
既自輕其身　眾人亦不敬。

常處大闇中　無有諸威德。
尊貴智慧法　此事永以失。

聞諸妙道法　不能以益身。
如是之過失　皆由懈怠心。

雖聞增益法　不能得上及。
如是之過罪　皆由懈怠心。

生業不修理　不入於道法。
如是之過[3]失　皆由懈怠心。
上智所棄遠　中人時復近。
下[4]愚為之沒　如猪樂在溷。

若為世中人　三事皆廢失。
欲樂及財利　福德亦復沒。

若為出家人　則不得二事。
生天及涅槃　名譽二俱失。

如是諸廢失　欲知其所由。

正體字

is indolent loses all meritorious qualities just as there is nothing which remains when a person has been attacked by thieves. This is as set forth in a verse:

2) Verse in Warning Against Indolence

One ought to gain it, and yet one does not gain it.
One has already gained it, but then one loses it again.
Having already taken himself lightly,
Everyone else also fails to respect him.

One constantly dwells in the great darkness.
One has none of the awesome virtues.
As for the venerable and noble dharma of wisdom,
This matter is eternally lost thereby.

Though one has heard the marvelous Dharma of the Path,
One is unable to use it to benefit himself.
Transgressions and mistakes of this sort,
All come forth from the indolent mind.

Although one has heard the Dharma which leads to increase,
One is unable to succeed in ascending to reach it.
Transgressions and offenses of this sort
All come forth from the indolent mind.

The work of this life is not cultivated or regulated,
One does not enter into the Dharma of the Path.
Transgressions and mistakes of this sort
All come forth from the indolent mind.

It is cast off and distanced by those of superior wisdom.
Middling persons at times draw close to it again.
The inferior and stupid are submerged by it
And are like pigs taking pleasure in the sty.

If one is a person of the world,
Three things waste away and are lost:
Desired pleasures, the benefits of wealth—
One's karmic blessings sink away as well.

If one is a person who has left the home life,
Then one fails to gain two matters:
Birth in the heavens as well as nirvāṇa.
For both of these persons, one's reputation is entirely lost.

Matters of this sort are all wasted and lost.
If one wishes to know their origin,

一切诸贼中　无过懈怠贼。
以是众罪故　懒心不应作。
马井二比丘　懈怠坠恶道。
虽见佛闻法　犹亦不自[5]免。

[0173b22] 如是等种种。观懈怠之罪精进增长。复次观精进之益。今世后世佛道涅盘之利皆由精进。复次菩萨知一切诸法皆空无所有。而不证涅盘。怜愍众生集诸善法。是精进波罗蜜力。复次菩萨一人独无等侣。以精进福德力故。能破魔军及结使贼得成佛道。既得佛道。于一切诸法一相无相其实皆空。而为众生说诸法种种名字种种方便。[173c]度脱众[6]生老病死苦。将灭度时以法身。与弥勒菩萨摩诃[7]萨迦叶阿难等。然后入金刚三昧。自碎身骨令如芥子。以度众生而不舍精进力。复次如阿难。为诸比丘说七觉[8]意。

一切諸賊中　無過懈怠賊。
以是眾罪故　懶心不應作。
馬井二比丘　懈怠墜惡道。
雖見佛聞法　猶亦不自[5]免。

[0173b22] 如是等種種。觀懈怠之罪精進增長。復次觀精進之益。今世後世佛道涅槃之利皆由精進。復次菩薩知一切諸法皆空無所有。而不證涅槃。憐愍眾生集諸善法。是精進波羅蜜力。復次菩薩一人獨無等侶。以精進福德力故。能破魔軍及結使賊得成佛道。既得佛道。於一切諸法一相無相其實皆空。而為眾生說諸法種種名字種種方便。[173c]度脫眾[6]生老病死苦。將滅度時以法身。與彌勒菩薩摩訶[7]薩迦葉阿難等。然後入金剛三昧。自碎身骨令如芥子。以度眾生而不捨精進力。復次如阿難。為諸比丘說七覺[8]意。

简体字　　　　　　　　　　　　　　　正體字

Among all of the thieves,
None surpass the thief of indolence.

On account of these manifold defects,
One should not develop a mind of indolence.

The two bhikshus, Aśvaka and Punarvasuka,
Were indolent and so fell into the wretched destinies.
Although they had seen the Buddha and heard the Dharma,
Still, they were unable themselves to avoid such a fate.

There are all sorts of bases such as these whereby one contemplates the faults inherent in laziness and whereby one's vigor increases.

c. THROUGH CONTEMPLATING THE BENEFITS

Additionally, one contemplates the increase accruing from vigor. All of the benefits of the Buddha Path and nirvāṇa in present and future lifetimes all come forth from vigor. Moreover, the bodhisattva knows all dharmas as empty, knows that there is nothing whatsoever therein which exists, and so does not opt for the realization of nirvāṇa. His acting out of pity for beings and his accumulation of good dharmas is on account of the power of the *pāramitā* of vigor.

1) THE VIGOR OF SHAKYAMUNI

Additionally, on account of the power of vigor and merit, the Bodhisattva [Shakyamuni], single-handedly and without the aid of any comrades, was able to destroy the demon armies as well as the thieves of the fetters and so then succeeded in gaining the Buddha Path. Having gained the Buddha Path, though he perceived all dharmas as being of a singular characteristic, as being without characteristics and as being in reality entirely empty, nonetheless, for the sake of beings, he spoke of all sorts of names for the dharmas, and employed all sorts of skillful means to bring beings across to liberation from the sufferings of birth, aging, sickness, and death.

When he was about to cross on over into cessation, he passed on his Dharma corpus to the likes of Maitreya Bodhisattva Mahāsattva, Kāśyapa, Ānanda, and others. Afterwards, he entered the *vajra* samādhi, crushed his own bones into fragments the size of mustard seeds which he employed to bring beings across to liberation, and so did not even then relinquish the power of vigor.

2) STORY: BUDDHA PRAISES VIGOR TO ĀNANDA

Then again, for example, when Ānanda was discoursing on the seven limbs of enlightenment (*saṃbodhyaṅga*) for the sake of the

至精进觉意。佛问阿难。汝说精进觉意耶。阿难言说精进觉意。如是三问三答。佛即从坐起告阿难。人能爱乐修行精进。无事不得得至佛道终不虚也。如是种种因缘。观精进利而得增益。如是精进。佛有时说为[9]欲。或时说精进。有时说不放逸。譬如人欲远行。初欲去时是名为欲。发行不住是为精进。能自劝励不令行事稽留。是为不放逸。以是故知欲生精进。精进生故不放逸。不放逸故能生诸法。乃至得成佛道。复次菩萨欲脱生老病死[10]亦欲度脱众生。常应精进一心不放逸。如人擎油钵行大众中。现前一心不放逸故大得名利。

至精進覺意。佛問阿難。汝說精進覺意耶。阿難言說精進覺意。如是三問三答。佛即從坐起告阿難。人能愛樂修行精進。無事不得得至佛道終不虛也。如是種種因緣。觀精進利而得增益。如是精進。佛有時說為[9]欲。或時說精進。有時說不放逸。譬如人欲遠行。初欲去時是名為欲。發行不住是為精進。能自勸勵不令行事稽留。是為不放逸。以是故知欲生精進。精進生故不放逸。不放逸故能生諸法。乃至得成佛道。復次菩薩欲脫生老病死[10]亦欲度脫眾生。常應精進一心不放逸。如人擎油鉢行大眾中。現前一心不放逸故大得名利。

简体字   正體字

Bhikshus, he came to the "vigor" limb of enlightenment and the Buddha then asked Ānanda, "Are you explaining the vigor limb of enlightenment?"

Ānanda replied, "I am indeed explaining the vigor limb of enlightenment."

And so this continued with three questions and three answers, after which the Buddha got up from his seat and told Ānanda, "If a person is able to love and take pleasure in cultivating vigor, there is no endeavor in which he will not be successful. He will succeed in arriving at the Buddha Path and in the end, it will not have been in vain."

Based on all sorts of causes and conditions such as these one contemplates the benefits of vigor and succeeds in making it increase.

8.   Dharmas Linked to Vigor: Zeal, Vigor, Non-negligence

Vigor of this sort was referred to by the Buddha at some times as being "zeal" (*chanda*), at some times as being "vigor" (*vīrya*) and at some times as being "non-negligence" (*apramāda*).

a.   Analogy: Like Going on a Trip

This may be well illustrated by the case of a man who is about to travel far. At the beginning, when he is desirous of leaving, this is what is referred to as "zeal." When, having begun his journey, he refrains from stopping [at some point along the way], this is what constitutes "vigor." When he is able to keep exhorting himself, thus preventing any interruptions in the tasks he must carry out on his journey, this is what is intended by "non-negligence."

From this, one can know that zeal generates vigor. Because vigor has been brought forth one is non-negligent. Because one is non-negligent one is able to bring forth all dharmas on up to and including the Buddha Path.

Furthermore, the bodhisattva who wishes to gain liberation from birth, aging, sickness, and death while also desiring to cross over beings to liberation should constantly be vigorous and should be single-minded in his non-negligence.

b.   Analogy: Like Not Spilling a Bowl of Oil

He should be like the man who was able to carry a bowl of oil through a great crowd [without spilling a drop, lest he be subjected to capital punishment by his king]. Because he was able to manifest single-mindedness and non-negligence, he gained great fame and benefit.

又如偏阁嶮道若[11]悬绳若[12]乘山[13]羊。此诸恶道以一心不放逸故。身得安隐。今世大得名利。求道精进亦复如是。若一心不放逸所愿皆得。复次譬如水流能决大石。不放逸心亦复如是。专修方便。常行不废。能破烦恼诸结使山。复次菩萨有三种思惟。若我不作不得果报。若我不自作不从他来。若我作者终不失。如是思惟当必精进。为佛道故懃修专精而不放逸。如一小阿兰若。独在林中坐禅而生懈怠。林中有神是佛弟子。入一死尸骨中。歌儛而来。说此偈言。

[174a]

林中小比丘　何以生懈废。
昼来若不畏　夜复如是来。

[0174a03] 是比丘惊怖起坐内自思惟。中夜复睡。是神复现

简体字

又如偏閣嶮道若[11]懸繩若[12]乘山[13]羊。此諸惡道以一心不放逸故。身得安隱。今世大得名利。求道精進亦復如是。若一心不放逸所願皆得。復次譬如水流能決大石。不放逸心亦復如是。專修方便。常行不廢。能破煩惱諸結使山。復次菩薩有三種思惟。若我不作不得果報。若我不自作不從他來。若我作者終不失。如是思惟當必精進。為佛道故懃修專精而不放逸。如一小阿蘭若。獨在林中坐禪而生懈怠。林中有神是佛弟子。入一死屍骨中。歌儛而來。說此偈言。

[174a]

林中小比丘　何以生懈廢。
晝來若不畏　夜復如是來。

[0174a03] 是比丘驚怖起坐內自思惟。中夜復睡。是神復現

正體字

c. Analogy: Like Traversing Precipitous Terrain

This is also just like when traveling on an extremely precipitous and difficult route: Whether one uses suspended ropes or rides on a mountain goat, on all such bad pathways as these, it is on account of being single-minded and non-negligent that one succeeds in preserving one's physical safety while also being able in this very life to gain great fame and benefit.

The vigor employed in seeking the Path is just the same. If one is single-minded and non-negligent, one gains everything which one wishes for.

d. Analogy: Like Flowing Water Cutting Through Stone

Then again, just as flowing water is able to cut through a huge boulder, so, too, it is with the non-negligent mind. If one engages in focused cultivation of skillful means which one constantly carries forward and does not desist from, then one will be able to smash the mountain of the afflictions and fetters.

9. Three Vigor-Generating Reflections

Moreover, the bodhisattva engages in three sorts of analyses: "If I do not accomplish this, then I will not be able to gain the resultant reward. If I don't go ahead and do it myself, then it won't be the case that it shall somehow manifest through the efforts of others. If I do accomplish this, then it can never be lost." When one contemplates in this way, then he will certainly become vigorous and, for the sake of the Buddha Path, he shall diligently cultivate, shall remain focused and attentive to detail, and shall avoid falling into negligence.

10. Story: The Lazy Forest Monk

These ideas are illustrated by the case of a minor *āraṇyaka*[3] who sat alone in dhyāna in the forest and became lazy. There was a spirit in the forest who was a disciple of the Buddha who [noticed this and thus] entered the skeleton of a corpse and came forth, singing and dancing, and then uttered this verse:

> Little bhikshu in the forest,
> Why have you become lazy and neglectful?
> If when I come in the daytime you do not fear me,
> I will come again like this at night.

This bhikshu was shocked and frightened, took up his sitting again, and then carried on with his inward contemplations. In the middle of the evening, he fell back to sleep again. This spirit manifested yet

十头口中出火牙爪如剑眼赤
如炎。顾语将从捉此懈怠比
丘。此处不应懈怠。何以
故尔。[1]是比丘大怖即起思
惟。专精念法得阿罗汉道。
是名自强精进不放逸力能得
道果。复次是精进不自惜身
而惜果报。于身四仪坐卧行
[2]住常懃精进。宁自失身不
废道业。譬如失火以瓶水[3]
投之。唯存灭火而不惜瓶。
如仙人师教弟子说偈言。

决定心悦豫　如获大果报。
如愿事得时　乃知此最妙。

[0174a15] 如是种种因缘。观精
进之利。能令精进增益。复
次菩萨修诸苦行。若有人来
求索头目髓脑尽能与之。而
自念言。我有忍辱精进智慧
方便之力受之尚苦。何况愚
駭

again, this time with ten heads each spewing fire from its mouth, each with fangs like swords, and each with eyes as red as flames. He spoke gravely, followed after and then seized this lazy bhikshu, saying, "You should not be lazy in this place! Why are you being this way?"

This bhikshu became filled with great terror and immediately resumed his contemplations. He became focused and precise in his mindfulness of the Dharma and consequently gained the path of arhatship. This is what is meant by forcing oneself to become vigorous. Through the power of being non-negligent, one is able to gain the fruition of the Path.

11. CHERISHING THE RESULT OVER PHYSICAL COMFORT

Moreover, in this practice of vigor one does not indulge any particular cherishing regard for his own body but rather cherishes a regard for the resultant retribution. Thus one is constantly diligent and vigorous in the four physical postures of sitting, lying down, walking, and standing. One would rather lose his own body than diminish the quality of his path-associated karma.

a. ANALOGY: SACRIFICING A VASE TO EXTINGUISH FIRE

This is analogous to when a fire has gotten out of control and one throws a vase full of water at it. One only bears in mind the idea of putting out the fire and so does not continue to cherish the vase.

b. VERSE CITATION

This principle is also illustrated by the verse spoken by a rishi in instructing his disciple:

> The mind which is resolute experiences pleasure.
> It's just as when garnering a great reward,
> Or when something wished for is finally gained.
> It is then that one realizes this is the most marvelous thing.

Focusing on all sorts of reasons such as these, one contemplates the benefits of vigor and is able thereby to cause one's vigor to increase and become enhanced.

12. THE ALTRUISTIC DETERMINATION TO BRING ABOUT LIBERATION

Additionally, the bodhisattva cultivates all manner of ascetic practices. If a person comes seeking his head, eyes, marrow or brains, he is able to give them all to him while thinking to himself, "Even though I have the power of patience, vigor, wisdom, and skillful means, enduring this still involves suffering, how much the more so would this be the case for deluded and foolish beings who inhabit

三涂众生。我当为此众生故。懃修精进早成佛道而度脱之。

大智度论卷第十五。

简体字

三塗眾生。我當為此眾生故。懃修精進早成佛道而度脱之。

大智度論卷第十五。

正體字

the three wretched destinies. For the sake of these beings I should diligently cultivate vigor, gain an early realization of the Buddha Path, and then cross them over to liberation."

大智度论释初品中毘梨耶波罗蜜[4]义第二十七(卷第十六)。

[*]龙树菩萨造。[*]后秦龟兹国三藏鸠摩罗什[*]奉诏译。

[0174a29] 问曰。云何名精进相。答曰。于事必能起发无难。志意坚强心无疲惓所作究竟。[5]以此五事为精进相。复次如佛所说。精进相者。身心不息故。譬如释迦[6]牟尼佛。先世曾作贾客主。将诸贾人入嶮难处。是中有罗刹鬼。以手遮之言。汝住莫动不听汝去。贾客主即以右拳击[*]之。拳即着鬼挽不可离。复[7]以左拳击之亦不可离。以右足蹴之足复粘着。复以左足蹴之亦复如是。以头冲之头即复着。鬼问言。汝今如是欲作何等心[8]休息未。答言。虽复五事被系。我心终不为汝[9]息也。当以精进力。与汝相击要不懈退。鬼时欢喜心念。此人胆力极大。即语人言。汝精进力大。

简体字

大智度論釋初品中毘梨耶波羅蜜[4]義第二十七(卷第十六)。

[*]龍樹菩薩造。[*]後秦龜茲國三藏鳩摩羅什[*]奉詔譯。

[0174a29] 問曰。云何名精進相。答曰。於事必能起發無難。志意堅強心無疲惓所作究竟。[5]以此五事為精進相。復次如佛所說。精進相者。身心不息故。譬如釋迦[6]牟尼佛。先世曾作賈客主。將諸賈人入嶮難處。是中有羅刹鬼。以手遮之言。汝住莫動不聽汝去。賈客主即以右拳擊[*]之。拳即著鬼挽不可離。復[7]以左拳擊之亦不可離。以右足蹴之足復粘著。復以左足蹴之亦復如是。以頭衝之頭即復著。鬼問言。汝今如是欲作何等心[8]休息未。答言。雖復五事被繫。我心終不為汝[9]息也。當以精進力。與汝相擊要不懈退。鬼時歡喜心念。此人膽力極大。即語人言。汝精進力大。

正體字

Chapter 27: Specific Aspects of the Perfection of Vigor

II. THE CHARACTERISTIC FEATURES OF VIGOR

   A. THE FIVE CHARACTERISTIC FEATURES OF VIGOR

Question: What are the characteristic features of vigor?

Response: With regard to endeavors, one has the attitude that he is certainly able to succeed. In taking them up, one finds no difficulty. One's determination and intentions are solid and strong. One's mind is free of weariness. Whatever is engaged in is carried through to the end. These five factors constitute the characteristics of vigor.

   B. BUDDHA'S STATEMENT ON THE MARKS OF VIGOR

Then again, according to what the Buddha said, the marks of vigor consist in the body and mind not resting.

   C. STORY: THE FEARLESS LEADER JATAKA

This is illustrated by Shakyamuni Buddha in a previous life when he was the leader of a group of merchants. He led the merchants into a precipitous and difficult place. There happened to be a *rākṣasa* ghost there who blocked their way, holding up his hands and saying, "You must stop. Don't move. I will not permit you to go."

The leader of the merchants then hit [the ghost] with his right fist. The fist immediately stuck to the ghost such that he was unable to pull it away. Next, he hit it with his left fist and was also unable to pull it away. He kicked him with his right foot and it, too, became stuck. Next he kicked it with his left foot and the same thing happened. He used his head to butt it, whereupon it immediately became stuck as well.

The ghost then asked, "Now that you are in this fix, what do you propose to do next? Has your mind given up or not?"

He replied, "Although I continue to be bound up in these five ways, my mind will never be forced by you to cease its determination. I will use the power of vigor to carry on the fight with you. I'm determined not to retreat."

The ghost then felt delighted and thought, "This man's really got guts." He then told the man, "Your power of vigor is immense. You

必不休息放汝令去。行者如是。于善法中初夜中夜后夜诵经坐禅求诸法实相。不为诸结使所覆身心不懈。是名精进相。是精进名心数法懃行不住相。随心行共心生。或有觉有观或无觉有观或无觉无观。如阿毘昙法广说。于一切善法中懃修不懈。是名精进相。于五根中名精进根。根增长名精进力。心能开悟名精进觉。能到佛道涅盘城。是名正精进。四念处中能懃系心。是精进分。四正懃是精进门。四如意足中。欲精进[10]即是精进。六波罗蜜中名精进波罗蜜。问曰。汝先赞精进。今说精进相。是名何精进。答曰。是一切善法精进中相。

简体字

必不休息放汝令去。行者如是。於善法中初夜中夜後夜誦經坐禪求諸法實相。不為諸結使所覆身心不懈。是名精進相。是精進名心數法懃行不住相。隨心行共心生。或有覺有觀或無覺有觀或無覺無觀。如阿毘曇法廣說。於一切善法中懃修不懈。是名精進相。於五根中名精進根。根增長名精進力。心能開悟名精進覺。能到佛道涅槃城。是名正精進。四念處中能懃繫心。是精進分。四正懃是精進門。四如意足中。欲精進[10]即是精進。六波羅蜜中名精進波羅蜜。問曰。汝先讚精進。今說精進相。是名何精進。答曰。是一切善法精進中相。

正體字

are someone who definitely will not give up. I'll turn you loose and allow you to leave."

D. Description of the Vigorous Practitioner

The practitioner is just like this. With respect to good dharmas, in the beginning, middle and end of the night he recites scriptures, sits in dhyāna, and seeks to know in accordance with reality the true character of dharmas. He is not covered over by the fetters and he does not become lazy in either body or mind. These are the characteristics of vigor.

E. According to the Abhidharma

This vigor is a dharma belonging to the mind. It is characterized by diligence in practice and by non-stopping. It accompanies the actions of the mind and arises in conjunction with the mind. It may be that there are both primary ideation (*vitarka*) and mental discursion (*vicāra*). It may be that it remains free of initial ideation yet involves mental discursion. Or it may be that there is neither initial ideation nor mental discursion. This is as extensively explained in the *Abhidharma's* discussion of dharmas.

F. Vigor's Presence Throughout Buddha's Teachings

To diligently cultivate all good dharmas without becoming lazy— this is the characteristic feature of vigor. Vigor is one of the five roots. When this root increases and grows, it becomes that power of vigor [counted among the five powers]. When the mind is able to become awakened, it is known as the vigor limb of enlightenment [among the seven limbs of enlightenment]. When one is able to reach to the Buddha Path's city of nirvāṇa, this is known as the right vigor [counted among the eight-fold Path]. Within the sphere of the four foundations of mindfulness, the ability to diligently anchor the mind [to the object of mindfulness] is the part played by vigor. The four right efforts are gateways [for the application] of vigor. Among the four bases of psychic power, zeal and vigor are [both] just [different aspects of] vigor. Among the six *pāramitās*, it is the *pāramitā* of vigor.

G. Questions on the Characteristics of Vigor

Question: You first praised vigor. Now you speak of the characteristics of vigor. What sort of vigor are you referring to?

Response: We refer here to the characteristics of vigor as it manifests in the midst of all good dharmas.

问曰。今说摩诃般若波罗蜜
论议中。应说精进波罗蜜。
何以[11]故。说一切善法中精
进。答曰。初发心菩萨于一
切善法中精进。渐渐次第得
精进波罗蜜。问曰。一切善
法[174c]中精进多。今说精进
波罗蜜。已入一切善法精进
中。答曰。为佛道精进名为
波罗蜜。诸馀善法中精进。
但名精进。不名波罗蜜。问
曰。一切善法中懃何以不名
精进波罗蜜。而独名菩萨精
进为波罗蜜。答曰。波罗蜜
名到彼岸。世间人及声闻辟
支佛。不能具足行[12]诸波罗
蜜。是故不名为[13]精进波罗
蜜。复次是人无大慈大悲。
弃舍众生不求十力四无所畏
十八不共法一切智及无碍解
脱无量身无量光明无量音声
无量持戒禅定[14]智慧。以是
故是人精进不名波罗蜜。复
次菩萨精进不休不息一心求
佛道。如是行者名为精进波
罗蜜。如好施菩萨。求如意
珠抒大海水。正使筋骨枯尽
终不懈

簡体字

問曰。今說摩訶般若波羅蜜
論議中。應說精進波羅蜜。
何以[11]故。說一切善法中精
進。答曰。初發心菩薩於一
切善法中精進。漸漸次第得
精進波羅蜜。問曰。一切善
法[174c]中精進多。今說精進
波羅蜜。已入一切善法精進
中。答曰。為佛道精進名為
波羅蜜。諸餘善法中精進。
但名精進。不名波羅蜜。問
曰。一切善法中懃何以不名
精進波羅蜜。而獨名菩薩精
進為波羅蜜。答曰。波羅蜜
名到彼岸。世間人及聲聞辟
支佛。不能具足行[12]諸波羅
蜜。是故不名為[13]精進波羅
蜜。復次是人無大慈大悲。
棄捨眾生不求十力四無所畏
十八不共法一切智及無礙解
脫無量身無量光明無量音聲
無量持戒禪定[14]智慧。以是
故是人精進不名波羅蜜。復
次菩薩精進不休不息一心求
佛道。如是行者名為精進波
羅蜜。如好施菩薩。求如意
珠抒大海水。正使筋骨枯盡
終不懈

正體字

Question: Now we are discussing the doctrinal meaning of the *mahāprajñāpāramitā* (the perfection of wisdom). One should be explaining here the *pāramitā* of vigor. Why then are you discussing vigor as it manifests in the midst of all good dharmas?

Response: The bodhisattva who has first brought forth the resolve to gain realization of bodhi practices vigor in the midst of all good dharmas and so gradually and sequentially achieves the *pāramitā* of vigor.

Question: There is an abundance of vigor implicitly present within all good dharmas. Now you embark on a discussion of the *pāramitā* of vigor even though it is already subsumed within that vigor already present in all good dharmas. [Why?]

Response: Vigor which is adopted for the sake of realizing the Buddha Path is referred to as "*pāramitā.*" The vigor present in all other wholesome dharmas is referred to simply as "vigor" and is therefore not referred to as "*pāramitā.*"

Question: Why is it that diligence in all other good dharmas is not referred to as the *pāramitā* of vigor and why does only qualify the bodhisattva's vigor as exemplifying "*pāramitā*"?

H. Vigor *Pāramitā*'s Distinguishing Characteristics

Response: "*Pāramitā*" means "reaching to the other shore." Worldly people, the Śrāvaka disciples, and the Pratyekabuddhas are unable to completely perfect the practice of the *pāramitās*. Therefore it is not referred to in such cases as the "*pāramitā*" of vigor.

Additionally, these people do not have the great kindness and the great compassion. They cast off and abandon beings. They do not seek the ten powers, the four fearlessnesses, the eighteen special dharmas, all-knowledge, the unobstructed liberations, innumerable bodies, innumerable radiances, innumerable sounds and voices, innumerable observances of the moral precepts, innumerable dhyāna absorptions, or innumerable manifestations of wisdom. It is for these reasons that the vigor of these persons is not referred to as exemplifying "*pāramitā.*"

Additionally, the vigor of the bodhisattva is unrelenting and unresting as he single-mindedly seeks the Buddha Path. In the case of those who practice in this way, it qualifies as consitituting the *pāramitā* of vigor. This is exemplified by Grand Giving Bodhisattva (Mahātyāgavat) who in seeking the wish-fulfilling gem searched through all the waters of the great oceans. Even when this endeavor caused his sinews and bones to atrophy, he never rested or

废。得如意珠以给众生济其身苦。菩萨如是难为能为。是为菩萨精进波罗蜜。复次菩萨以精进力为首。行五波罗蜜。是时名为菩萨精进波罗蜜。譬如众药和合能治重病。菩萨精进亦如是。但行精进不能行五波罗蜜。是不名菩萨精进波罗蜜。复次菩萨精进。不为财利富贵力势。亦不为身不为生天转轮[15]王梵释天王。亦不自为以求涅盘。但为佛道利益众生。如是相名为菩萨精进波罗蜜。复次菩萨精进。修行一切善法大悲为首。如慈父[16]爱子。唯有一子而得重病。一心求药救疗其[17]病。菩萨精进以慈为首亦复如是。救疗一切心无暂舍。复次菩萨精进。以实相智慧为首。行六波罗蜜。是名菩萨精进波罗蜜。问曰。诸法实相无为无[175a]作。精进有为有作相。云何以实相为首。答曰。虽知诸法实相无为无作。

廢。得如意珠以給眾生濟其身苦。菩薩如是難為能為。是為菩薩精進波羅蜜。復次菩薩以精進力為首。行五波羅蜜。是時名為菩薩精進波羅蜜。譬如眾藥和合能治重病。菩薩精進亦如是。但行精進不能行五波羅蜜。是不名菩薩精進波羅蜜。復次菩薩精進。不為財利富貴力勢。亦不為身不為生天轉輪[15]王梵釋天王。亦不自為以求涅槃。但為佛道利益眾生。如是相名為菩薩精進波羅蜜。復次菩薩精進。修行一切善法大悲為首。如慈父[16]愛子。唯有一子而得重病。一心求藥救療其[17]病。菩薩精進以慈為首亦復如是。救療一切心無暫捨。復次菩薩精進。以實相智慧為首。行六波羅蜜。是名菩薩精進波羅蜜。問曰。諸法實相無為無[175a]作。精進有為有作相。云何以實相為首。答曰。雖知諸法實相無為無作。

简体字 　　　　　　　　　正體字

diminished his efforts. Thus he found the wish-fulfilling gem and used it to supply the needs of beings and rescue them from physical suffering. In this way the bodhisattva is able to do what is difficult to do. This constitutes the bodhisattva's *pāramitā* of vigor.

Moreover, the bodhisattva takes the power of vigor as foremost and so proceeds in this way as he practices the other five *pāramitās*. When done in this way one's practice qualifies as the bodhisattva's *pāramitā* of vigor. This is analogous to a severe illness being curable only by a combination of numerous different medicinal ingredients. The bodhisattva's vigor is just like this. If he only practiced vigor, yet was be unable to practice the other five *pāramitās*, then this could not qualify as the bodhisattva's *pāramitā* of vigor.

Furthermore, the bodhisattva's vigor is not for the sake of valuables, benefits, wealth, noble status, or power. Nor is it for the sake of his own person, for the sake of being reborn in the heavens, for the sake of becoming a wheel-turning king, or for the sake of becoming a king of the gods such as Brahmā or Śakra Devānām Indra. Nor is it for the sake of gaining nirvāṇa for himself. It is solely for the sake of the Buddha Path and the benefit of beings. Such characteristics as these qualify as constituting the bodhisattva's *pāramitā* of vigor.

Then again, the bodhisattva's vigor is such that, in cultivating all good dharmas, the great compassion is taken as foremost. It is as if there was a lovingly-kind father who cherished his son. He has only the one son and this son comes down with a serious disease. He single-mindedly seeks for medicines to save his son from the disease. The bodhisattva's taking of kindness as foremost in his practice of vigor is just like this. In his rescuing and treating of everyone, his mind does not forsake them for even a moment.

Then again, the vigor of the bodhisattva takes the reality-concordant wisdom cognizant of the true character [of dharmas] as foremost in his practice of the six *pāramitās*. This is what qualifies as the bodhisattva's *pāramitā* of vigor.

I. The Pāramitā of Vigor's Orientation to Ultimate Reality

Question: The reality-concordant true character of dharmas is unconditioned and within the sphere of the wishless (*apraṇihita*). Vigor is characterized by being conditioned and in the sphere of [goal-oriented] wishes. How is it then that [the bodhisattva's *pāramitā* of vigor] can take the true character of dharmas as foremost?

Response: Although one is aware that the reality-concordant true character of dharmas is unconditioned and in the sphere of the

以本愿大悲欲度众生故。于无作中以精进力度脱一切。复次若诸法实相无为无作如涅盘相。[1]无一无二。汝云何言实相与精进相异耶。汝即不解诸法相。复次[2]尔时菩萨[3]观三界五道众生[4]各失所乐。无色界天乐定心着。不觉命尽。堕在欲界中受禽兽形。色界诸天亦复如是。从清净处堕。还受婬欲在不净中。欲界六天乐着五欲。还堕地狱受诸苦痛。见人道中。以十善福贸得人身。人身多苦少乐寿尽多堕恶趣中。见诸畜生受诸苦恼。鞭杖驱驰负重涉远。项领穿坏热铁烧[5]烁。此人宿行因缘。以系缚众生鞭杖苦恼。如是等种种因缘故。受

以本願大悲欲度眾生故。於無作中以精進力度脫一切。復次若諸法實相無為無作如涅槃相。[1]無一無二。汝云何言實相與精進相異耶。汝即不解諸法相。復次[2]爾時菩薩[3]觀三界五道眾生[4]各失所樂。無色界天樂定心著。不覺命盡。墮在欲界中受禽獸形。色界諸天亦復如是。從清淨處墮。還受婬欲在不淨中。欲界六天樂著五欲。還墮地獄受諸苦痛。見人道中。以十善福貿得人身。人身多苦少樂壽盡多墮惡趣中。見諸畜生受諸苦惱。鞭杖驅馳負重涉遠。項領穿壞熱鐵燒[5]爍。此人宿行因緣。以繫縛眾生鞭杖苦惱。如是等種種因緣故。受

簡体字　　　　　　　　　　　正體字

wishless, on account of a desire to bring beings across to liberation which is rooted in the great compassion and in one's original vows, even in the midst of wishlessness, one employs the power of vigor to bring everyone over to liberation.

Also, if the true character of dharmas is unconditioned, wishless, and characterized by being like nirvāṇa, it is neither singular nor dual. Why then do you say that the true character [of dharmas] is conceptually incompatible with character of vigor? You simply do not understand the true character of dharmas.

J. The Bodhisattva's Contemplations of Cyclic Existence

Additionally, the bodhisattva contemplates the beings of the three realms and five paths, observing that they each lose that in which they find pleasure.

1. The Celestial Realms

The gods of the formless realms take pleasure in the absorptions and their minds are attached. They fail to realize that their lives are coming to an end. They fall into the desire realm wherein they take on the forms of birds and beasts.

The gods of the form realm are also just like this. They fall from a pure place and once again undergo sexual desire and abide in the midst of impurity.

The gods of the six desire heavens are blissfully attached to the five desires there and then fall back down again, plummeting into the hells where they undergo all manner of suffering and pain.

2. The Human Realm

He also observes that within the realm of humans, beings have traded the karmic blessings arising from the ten good deeds for the body of a human being. The human body is characterized by much suffering and only a little bliss. When the human life comes to an end, the majority of them fall down into the wretched destinies.

3. The Animal Realm and Antecedent Causes

He also observes that the animals undergo all manner of suffering and torment. They are whipped and beaten, driven along, forced to run fast, burdened with heavy loads, and compelled to travel far. Their necks are injured by yokes and they are burned by hot metal brands. The past-life causal circumstances for this individual consisted in tying up beings, whipping and flogging them, and thus causing them suffering and torment. On account of all sorts of causal circumstances such as these, one then takes on the form of

象马牛羊麞鹿畜兽之形。婬
欲情重无明偏多。受鹅鸭孔
雀鸳鸯鸠鸽鸡[6]鹙鹦鹉百舌
之属。受此众鸟种类百千。
婬行罪故。身生毛羽[7]隔诸
细滑。嘴[8]［口*(甚-其+庚)］
麃[9]［革*昂］不别触味。瞋恚
偏多。受毒蛇蝮[10]蝎蚑蜂百
足含毒之虫。愚痴多故。受
蚓蛾蜣蜋蚁蝼𫇭[11]鹙角鸱之
属诸駮虫鸟。憍慢瞋[12]恚多
故。受师子虎豹诸猛兽身。
邪慢缘故。受生驴猪骆驼之
中。悭贪嫉妒轻躁[13]短促
故。受猕猴[14]［狂-王+哥］玃
熊罴之形。邪贪憎嫉业因缘
故。受猫狸土虎诸兽之身。
无愧无惭[15]饕餮因缘故。受
乌鹊鸱鹫诸鸟之形。轻慢善
人故。受鸡狗野干等身。

象馬牛羊麞鹿畜獸之形。婬
欲情重無明偏多。受鵝鴨孔
雀鴛鴦鳩鴿鷄[6]鷲鸚鵡百舌
之屬。受此眾鳥種類百千。
婬行罪故。身生毛羽[7]隔諸
細滑。嘴[8]［口*(甚-其+庚)］
麃[9]［革*卬］不別觸味。瞋恚
偏多。受毒蛇蝮[10]蝎蚑蜂百
足含毒之虫。愚癡多故。受
蚓蛾蜣蜋蟻蝼𫇭[11]鷲角鴟之
屬諸駮虫鳥。憍慢瞋[12]恚多
故。受師子虎豹諸猛獸身。
邪慢緣故。受生驢猪駱駝之
中。慳貪嫉妒輕躁[13]短促
故。受獼猴[14]［狂-王+哥］玃
熊羆之形。邪貪憎嫉業因緣
故。受貓狸土虎諸獸之身。
無愧無慚[15]饕餮因緣故。受
烏鵲鴟鷲諸鳥之形。輕慢善
人故。受鷄狗野干等身。

简体字　　　　　　正體字

such domestic and wild animals as elephants, horses, cattle, sheep, roebucks, and deer.

a. On Account of Lust

For those whose lustful feelings are heavy and whose ignorance is especially great, they take on birth as a goose, duck, peacock, mandarin duck, turtledove, pigeon, chicken, wild duck, parrot, or blackbird. They take on the form of these hundreds of thousands of different kinds of birds. On account of offenses committed within the sphere of sexual activity, their bodies grow forth down and feathers which cut off erotic sensations. Their bills and claws are coarse and hard and do not distinguish tactile subtleties.

b. On Account of Hatred

Those whose hatred has been especially great take on rebirths as poisonous snakes, vipers, scorpions, spiders, wasps, centipedes, and other venomous insects.

c. On Account of Stupidity

Those whose stupidity has been great take on rebirths among worms, moths, dung beetles, ants, mole crickets, *syou-lyou* (*Scops chinensis*) owls, horned owls, and other dull-witted insects and birds.

d. On Account of Arrogance and Haughtiness

Those who have been excessively arrogant and hateful take on birth in the bodies of lions, tigers, leopards, and other fierce beasts. On account of having been perversely haughty, one may take on birth among donkeys, pigs, or camels.

e. On Account of Miserliness, Jealousy, Shamelessness, etc.

On account of being miserly, greedy, and jealous, while also being agitated and skittish, one may take on the form of a monkey, baboon, or bear. On account of the causal circumstances of the karma of being perversely greedy and hatefully jealous one may take on the body of a wildcat, "earth-tiger," or other such animal. On account of the causal circumstances associated with being devoid of a sense of blame or a sense of shame in one's gluttony, one takes on the form of a crow, magpie, owl, or vulture.

f. On Account of Slighting the Good

On account of slighting good people, one takes on the body of such beasts as chickens, dogs, and coyotes.

简体字	正體字
大作布施瞋恚曲心。以此因缘故受诸龙身。大修布施心高陵[16]疟苦恼众生。受金翅鸟形。如是等种种结[175b]使业因缘故。受诸畜生禽兽之苦。菩萨得天眼观众生轮转五道迴旋其中。天中死人中生。人中死天中生。天中死生地狱中。地狱中死生天上。天上死生饿鬼中。饿鬼中死还生天上。天上死生畜生中。畜生中死生天上。天上死还生天上地狱饿鬼畜生亦如是欲界中死色界中生。色界中死欲界中生。欲界中死无色界中生。无色界中死欲界中生。欲界中死欲界中生。色界无色界亦如是。活地狱中死黑绳地狱中生。黑绳地狱中死	大作布施瞋恚曲心。以此因緣故受諸龍身。大修布施心高陵[16]瘧苦惱眾生。受金翅鳥形。如是等種種結[175b]使業因緣故。受諸畜生禽獸之苦。菩薩得天眼觀眾生輪轉五道迴旋其中。天中死人中生。人中死天中生。天中死生地獄中。地獄中死生天上。天上死生餓鬼中。餓鬼中死還生天上。天上死生畜生中。畜生中死生天上。天上死還生天上地獄餓鬼畜生亦如是欲界中死色界中生。色界中死欲界中生。欲界中死無色界中生。無色界中死欲界中生。欲界中死欲界中生。色界無色界亦如是。活地獄中死黑繩地獄中生。黑繩地獄中死

g. ON ACCOUNT OF GIVING MARKED BY HATEFULNESS, ETC.

If one performs a lot of giving with a hateful and devious mind, on account of these causal circumstances, one takes on the body of a dragon. If one cultivates great giving, but one's mind is nonetheless imperious in carrying out the persecution of beings in a state of suffering and torment, one takes on the form of the golden-winged [*garuḍa*] bird.

On account of the karmic causal circumstances of all sorts of fetters such as these, one undergoes the suffering of the animal realm's birds and beasts.

4. CYCLIC EXISTENCE AS SEEN BY THE BODHISATTVA'S HEAVENLY EYE

When the bodhisattva gains the heavenly eye, he contemplates [the fashion in which beings] course along in a cyclic manner throughout the five destinies of rebirth.

a. WITHIN THE FIVE DESTINIES

They go through cycles therein wherein having died in the heavens, they are born among humans, having died among humans, they are born in the heavens. Having died in the heavens, they are reborn in the hells. Having died in the hells, they are reborn in the heavens. Having died in the heavens, they are reborn among hungry ghosts. Having died among hungry ghosts, they may return again to rebirth in the heavens. Having died in the heavens, they are then reborn among animals. Having died among animals, they may be reborn in the heavens. Having died in the heavens, they may return to rebirth again in the heavens. [The rebirth circumstances associated with] the hells, the hungry ghosts and the animals are also just like this.

b. WITHIN THE THREE REALMS

Having died in the desire realm, one may be reborn in the form realm. Having died in the form realm, one may be reborn in the desire realm. Having died in the desire realm, one may be reborn in the formless realm. Having died in the formless realm, one may be reborn in the desire realm. Having died in the desire realm, one may be reborn yet again in the desire realm. [The rebirth circumstances associated with] the form realm and the formless realm are also just like this.

c. WITHIN THE HELL REALMS

Having died in the Living (*saṃjīva*) Hells, one may be reborn in the Black Line (*kālasūtra*) Hells. Having died in the Black Line Hells, one

活地狱中生。活地狱中死还生活地狱中。合会地狱乃至阿鼻地狱亦如是。炭坑地狱中死。沸屎地狱中生。沸屎地狱中死。炭坑地狱中生。炭坑地狱中死。还生炭坑地狱中。烧林地狱乃至摩诃波头摩地狱亦如是。展转生其中。卵生中死胎生中生。胎生中死卵生中生。卵生中死还生卵[17]生中。胎生湿生化生亦如是。阎浮提中死弗婆提中生。弗婆提中死阎浮提中生。阎浮提中死还生阎浮提中。[18]劬陀尼欝怛罗越亦如是。四天处死[19]三十三天中生。[*]三十三天中死四天处生。四天处死还生四天处。[*]三十三天乃至他化自在天亦如是。梵众天中死梵辅天中生。梵辅天中死梵众天中生。梵众天中死

活地獄中生。活地獄中死還生活地獄中。合會地獄乃至阿鼻地獄亦如是。炭坑地獄中死。沸屎地獄中生。沸屎地獄中死。炭坑地獄中生。炭坑地獄中死。還生炭坑地獄中。燒林地獄乃至摩訶波頭摩地獄亦如是。展轉生其中。卵生中死胎生中生。胎生中死卵生中生。卵生中死還生卵[17]生中。胎生濕生化生亦如是。閻浮提中死弗婆提中生。弗婆提中死閻浮提中生。閻浮提中死還生閻浮提中。[18]劬陀尼欝怛羅越亦如是。四天處死[19]三十三天中生。[*]三十三天中死四天處生。四天處死還生四天處。[*]三十三天乃至他化自在天亦如是。梵眾天中死梵輔天中生。梵輔天中死梵眾天中生。梵眾天中死

简体字　　　　　　　　　　　　　　正體字

may be reborn in the Living Hells. Having died in the Living Hells, one may return to be reborn in the Living Hells. From the Uniting (*saṃghāta*) Hells to the Avīci Hells, it is just the same as this.

Having died in the Charcoal Pit (*kukūla*) Hells, one may be reborn in the Boiling Excrement (*kuṇapa*) Hells. Having died in the Boiling Excrement Hells, one may be reborn in the Charcoal Pit Hells. Having died in the Charcoal Pit Hells, one may then return to be reborn in the Charcoal Pit Hells. From the Burning Forest (*ādīptavana*) Hells to the Mahāpadma ("Great Lotus") Hells, it is just the same as this as one goes through cycles of rebirth therein.

d. WITHIN THE FOUR CATEGORIES OF BIRTH

Having died in the realm of the egg-born (*aṇḍaja*), one may then be reborn in the realm of the womb-born (*jarāyuja*). Having died in the realm of the womb-born, one may then be reborn in the realm of the egg-born. Having died in the realm of the egg-born, one may then return to be reborn among the egg-born. It is just the same as this with the womb-born, moisture-born (*saṃsvedaja*), and transformationally-born (*upapāduka*).

e. IN THE FOUR CONTINENTS

Having died in the continent of Jambudvīpa, one may be reborn in Pūrvavideha. Having died in Pūrvavideha, one may be reborn in Jambudpvīpa. Having died in Jambudvīpa, one may then return to be reborn in Jambudvīpa. It is just the same as this with regard to the continents of Aparagodānīya and Uttarakuru.

f. IN THE DESIRE REALM HEAVENS

Having died in the station of the Four Heavenly Kings (*cāturmahārājika*), one may be reborn in the Heaven of the Thirty-three (*trāyastriṃśa*). Having died in the Heaven of the Thirty-three, one may be reborn in the station of the Four Heavenly Kings. Having died in the station of the Four Heavenly Kings, one may then be reborn again in the station of the Four Heavenly Kings. The circumstances [associated with rebirth] are just the same from the Heaven of the Thirty-three on up to the Heaven of Independence Through Transformation of Others (*paranirmitavaśavartin*).

g. IN THE FORM AND FORMLESS HEAVENS

Having died in the Assembly of Brahmā Heaven (*brahmakāyika*), one may be reborn in the Ministers of Brahmā Heaven (*brahmapurohita*). Having died in the Ministers of Brahmā Heaven, one may be reborn in the Assembly of Brahmā Heaven. Having died in the Assembly

还生梵众天中。梵辅天少光
[20]天无量光光音少净无量净
遍净何那跋罗伽得生。大果
虚空处。识处。无所有处。
非有想非无想处。亦如是。
非有想非无想天中死阿鼻地
狱中生。如是展转生五道
中。菩萨见是已生大悲心。
我于众生为无所益。[175c]虽
与世乐乐极则苦。当以佛道
涅盘常乐益于一切。云何而
益。当懃大精进乃得实智
慧。得实智慧知诸法实相。
以馀波罗蜜助成以益众生。
是为菩萨精进波罗蜜。见饿
鬼中饥渴故两眼陷毛发长。
东西驰走若欲趣水。护水诸
鬼以铁杖逆打。设无守鬼水
自然竭。或时天雨雨化为
炭。或有饿鬼常被火烧。如
劫尽时诸山火出。或有饿鬼
羸瘦狂走。毛发[21]蓬乱以覆
其身。

還生梵眾天中。梵輔天少光
[20]天無量光光音少淨無量淨
遍淨何那跋羅伽得生。大果
虛空處。識處。無所有處。
非有想非無想處。亦如是。
非有想非無想天中死阿鼻地
獄中生。如是展轉生五道
中。菩薩見是已生大悲心。
我於眾生為無所益。[175c]雖
與世樂樂極則苦。當以佛道
涅槃常樂益於一切。云何而
益。當懃大精進乃得實智
慧。得實智慧知諸法實相。
以餘波羅蜜助成以益眾生。
是為菩薩精進波羅蜜。見餓
鬼中飢渴故兩眼陷毛髮長。
東西馳走若欲趣水。護水諸
鬼以鐵杖逆打。設無守鬼水
自然竭。或時天雨雨化為
炭。或有餓鬼常被火燒。如
劫盡時諸山火出。或有餓鬼
羸瘦狂走。毛髮[21]蓬亂以覆
其身。

简体字   正體字

of Brahmā heaven, one may then be reborn again in the Assembly of Brahmā Heaven. From the Ministers of Brahmā Heaven, the Lesser Light Heaven, the Immeasurable Light Heaven, the Light and Sound Heaven, the Lesser Purity Heaven, the Immeasurable Purity Heaven, the Universal Purity Heaven, or the Anabhraka Heaven, one may then succeed in being reborn in the Great Fruition (*bṛhatphala*) heaven.

[The rebirth circumstances in] the Station of Limitless Space, the Station of Limitless Consciousness, the Station of Nothing Whatsoever, and the Station of Neither Perception nor Non-perception are just the same as this. Having died in the Station of Neither Perception nor Non-perception, one may then be reborn in the Avīci Hells. It is in this manner that one courses through cycles of rebirths throughout the five destinies.

h. THE BODHISATTVA'S CONTEMPLATION-BASED CONCLUSION

After the bodhisattva sees this, he brings forth a thought of great compassion, thinking, "I have been of no benefit to beings. Although I might bestow worldly bliss upon them, when that bliss reaches its culmination, then it just results in suffering. I should use the eternal bliss of the Buddha Path and nirvāṇa to benefit everyone."

How then does one accomplish benefit? One should be diligent in great vigor. Then and only then does one achieve true wisdom. When one gains true wisdom, one knows in accordance with reality the true character of dharmas. Thus one employs the other *pāramitās* to assist in achieving benefit for beings. It is this which constitutes the bodhisattva's *pāramitā* of vigor.

i. THE BODHISATTVA'S OBSERVATIONS AMONG HUNGRY GHOSTS

He also sees that among the hungry ghosts (*preta*) they have become so afflicted by hunger and thirst that their eyes have become sunken and their hair has grown long. They run hurriedly off to the east and to the west. Whenever they move towards a source of water, the ghosts who guard the water use iron clubs to beat them back away from it. In the event that there is no guardian ghost, the water spontaneously dries up of itself. There may be times when it rains whereupon the rainwater transforms into charcoal.

Other hungry ghosts are constantly burned by fire, just as when, at the end of the kalpa, all of the mountains spew forth fire. There are some hungry ghosts who are emaciated and thin and who run about crazily. The hair of their bodies and heads has become tangled and disheveled and has grown to cover their entire bodies.

或有饿鬼常食屎尿涕唾[22]欧吐盪涤馀汁。或时至厕溷边立伺求不净[23]汁。或有饿鬼常求产妇藏血饮之。形如烧树咽如针孔。若与其水千岁不足或有饿鬼。自破其头以手取脑而舐。或有饿鬼形如黑山铁锁锁颈叩头求哀归命狱卒。或有饿鬼先世恶口。好以麁语加[24]彼众生。众生憎恶见之如雠。以此罪故堕饿鬼中。如是等种种罪故。堕饿鬼趣中受无量苦痛。见八大地狱苦毒万端。活大地狱中诸受罪人各各共斗。恶心瞋[25]诤手捉利刀互相割剥。以[26]槊相刺。铁[27]叉相[*]叉。铁棒相棒。铁杖相捶。铁[28]铲相贯。而以利刀互相切脍。又以铁爪而相殴裂。各[29]以身血而相涂漫。痛毒逼切闷无所觉。宿业因缘冷风来吹。狱卒唤之[30]咄诸罪人还活。以是故名

或有餓鬼常食屎尿涕唾[22]歐吐盪滌餘汁。或時至廁溷邊立伺求不淨[23]汁。或有餓鬼常求產婦藏血飲之。形如燒樹咽如針孔。若與其水千歲不足或有餓鬼。自破其頭以手取腦而舐。或有餓鬼形如黑山鐵鎖鎖頸叩頭求哀歸命獄卒。或有餓鬼先世惡口。好以麁語加[24]彼眾生。眾生憎惡見之如讎。以此罪故墮餓鬼中。如是等種種罪故。墮餓鬼趣中受無量苦痛。見八大地獄苦毒萬端。活大地獄中諸受罪人各各共鬪。惡心瞋[25]諍手捉利刀互相割剝。以[26]槊相刺。鐵[27]叉相[*]叉。鐵棒相棒。鐵杖相捶。鐵[28]鑱相貫。而以利刀互相切膾。又以鐵爪而相毆裂。各[29]以身血而相塗漫。痛毒逼切悶無所覺。宿業因緣冷風來吹。獄卒喚之[30]咄諸罪人還活。以是故名

简体字   正體字

There are also hungry ghosts who constantly eat feces, urine, tears, spittle, vomit, and rinse water. Sometimes they go alongside latrines and stand there longing to partake of the impure fluids. There are some hungry ghosts who seek after and drink the internal blood from birthing women. Their forms are like burning trees and their throats are like the eye of a needle. In the event that they do encounter their fluid of choice, even in ten thousand years they would not be filled to satisfaction.

There are some hungry ghosts who break open their own heads and, using their hands, scoop out their own brains and then feast upon them.

Yet other hungry ghosts shaped like a black mountain have had iron locks latched on their necks and prostrate themselves before the hell guardians, seeking mercy and paying homage.

And then there are hungry ghosts who in the previous lifetime engaged in harsh speech, taking pleasure at inflicting coarse language on beings such that the beings detested and abhorred them and looked upon them like enemies. On account of these offenses, they fell into rebirth among the hungry ghosts. On account of all sorts of other offenses such as these, one may fall into the path of the hungry ghosts and undergo immeasurable bitterness and pain.

5. THE BODHISATTVA'S OBSERVATIONS WITHIN THE HELLS

He also sees the myriad forms of cruel suffering endured within the eight great hells.

a. THE GREAT LIVING HELLS

In the Great Living Hells, all of those persons who are undergoing punishment each fight with one another. With evil intent they struggle hatefully, taking up sharp knives which they use to slice and skin each other. They use spears to impale each other. They use iron forks to spear one another. They use iron truncheons to beat one another. They use iron staves to cudgel one another. They use iron lances to run each other through and then take sharp knives to slice and mince each other. They also take up iron claws with which they rip and rend each other. They gush forth blood and smear each other with the blood from their bodies.

When the deleterious effects of the pain are pushed to extreme intensity, they faint and cannot be revived. Then a cold wind originating in the causes and conditions of past-life actions comes along and blows. The guardians of hell yell at them, cursing the offenders, whereupon they return to life. It is for this reason that it is referred

活地狱。即时平复复受苦
毒。此中众生以宿行因缘好
杀物命。牛羊禽兽。为田业
舍宅奴婢妻子国土钱财故而
相杀害。如是等种种杀业报
故。受此剧罪。见黑绳大地
狱中罪人。为恶罗刹狱卒鬼
匠。常以[176a]黑热铁绳。拼
度罪人。以狱中铁斧[1]煞之
斫之。长者令短短者令长。
方者使圆圆者使方。斩截四
[2]肢却其耳鼻落其手足。以
大铁锯解析[3]揣截。破其肉
分脔脔称之。此人宿行因缘
谗贼[4]忠良。妄语恶口两舌
[5]无义语枉杀无辜。或作奸
吏酷暴侵害。如是等种种恶
口谗贼[6]故受此罪。见合会
大地狱中。恶罗刹狱卒作种
种形。牛马猪羊麋鹿狐狗
虎狼师子六驳大[7]鸟雕鹫鹑
鸟。作此种种诸鸟兽头。而
来吞噉龁[8]啮[齿*齐]掣罪
人。

活地獄。即時平復復受苦
毒。此中眾生以宿行因緣好
殺物命。牛羊禽獸。為田業
舍宅奴婢妻子國土錢財故而
相殺害。如是等種種殺業報
故。受此劇罪。見黑繩大地
獄中罪人。為惡羅刹獄卒鬼
匠。常以[176a]黑熱鐵繩。拼
度罪人。以獄中鐵斧[1]煞之
斫之。長者令短短者令長。
方者使圓圓者使方。斬截四
[2]肢却其耳鼻落其手足。以
大鐵鋸解析[3]揣截。破其肉
分臠臠稱之。此人宿行因緣
讒賊[4]忠良。妄語惡口兩舌
[5]無義語枉殺無辜。或作奸
吏酷暴侵害。如是等種種惡
口讒賊[6]故受此罪。見合會
大地獄中。惡羅刹獄卒作種
種形。牛馬猪羊麋鹿狐狗
虎狼師子六駁大[7]鳥鵰鷲鶉
鳥。作此種種諸鳥獸頭。而
來吞噉齘[8]嚙[齒*齊]掣罪
人。

简体字   正體字

to as the "Living" Hell. They immediately return to normal and then undergo yet again their excruciating sufferings. The beings herein have as causes and conditions of their previous life the taking of pleasure in killing animals, whether cattle or sheep, birds or beasts. They engaged in killing in the course of farm work or else killed and injured each other whilst contending for houses, slaves and servants, wives and sons, countries and territories, money and wealth. They undergo this intense punishment as retribution for all sorts of such killing karma as this.

b. The Great Black Line Hells

He also sees those transgressors within the Great Black Line Hells who are set upon by fearsome *rākṣasas*, hell soldiers, and worker ghosts who constantly go about using hot black iron cords to lay out their work on those offenders. They then use the iron hell axes and, stretching [the lines] tight, [and snapping them to mark a line], they proceed to go about chopping them up. Those who are long-shaped are made short. Those who are short in appearance are made long. Those who are angular are caused to become round and those who are round are caused to become angular. The [hell workers] cut off the four limbs, slice away the ears and nose, and lop off the hands and feet. They use a great iron saw to slice and section [the offenders] into approximate sizes. They cut up their flesh and weigh it out, slice by slice.

The previous life causes and conditions of these people was such that they spoke maliciously, attacking those who were faithful and good. They engaged in lying, harsh speech, divisive speech, and unprincipled speech. They brought about the unjust execution of those who had committed no crimes. In some cases, they had served as wicked officials wreaking cruelty and violence as they encroached on and injured their victims. They undergo these punishments on account of all sorts of instances of harsh speech and harms wrought through slander.

c. The Great Unification Hells

He also sees the Great Unification Hells wherein fearsome *rākṣasas* and hell soldiers manifest in many different forms, in the guise of all sorts of different cattle, horses, pigs, sheep, roebucks, foxes, dogs, tigers, wolves, lions, the six sorts of domestic animals, as great birds, as eagles, vultures, and quail. They appear with the heads of all of these sorts of birds and animals and come forth to seize and attack the offender with their jaws, gulping and chomping and

两山相合大热铁轮轹诸罪人令身破碎。热铁臼中捣之令碎。如[9]竿蒲[10]桃亦如压油。譬如蹂场聚肉成［廿/积］。积头如山。血流成池。雕鹫虎狼各来[11]诤掣。此人宿业因缘多杀牛马猪羊麞鹿狐兔虎狼师子六驳大[*]鸟众鸟。[12]如是等种种鸟兽[13]多残贼故还[14]为此众鸟兽头来害罪人。又以力势相陵枉[15]压赢弱。受两山相合罪。悭贪瞋恚愚痴怖畏故。断事轻重不以正理。或破正道转易正法。受热铁轮轹热铁臼捣。第四第五名叫唤大叫唤。此大地狱其中罪人罗刹狱卒头黄如金。眼中火出着[16]赤色衣。身肉坚劲走疾如风。手足长大口出恶声。捉三股[*]叉箭。堕如雨刺射罪人。罪人狂怖叩头求哀。[17]小见放舍小见怜愍。

两山相合大熱鐵輪轢諸罪人令身破碎。熱鐵臼中搗之令碎。如[9]竿蒲[10]桃亦如壓油。譬如蹂場聚肉成［廿/積］。積頭如山。血流成池。鵰鷲虎狼各來[11]諍掣。此人宿業因緣多殺牛馬猪羊麞鹿狐兔虎狼師子六駁大[*]鳥眾鳥。[12]如是等種種鳥獸[13]多殘賊故還[14]為此眾鳥獸頭來害罪人。又以力勢相陵枉[15]壓羸弱。受兩山相合罪。慳貪瞋恚愚癡怖畏故。斷事輕重不以正理。或破正道轉易正法。受熱鐵輪轢熱鐵臼搗。第四第五名叫喚大叫喚。此大地獄其中罪人羅刹獄卒頭黃如金。眼中火出著[16]赤色衣。身肉堅勁走疾如風。手足長大口出惡聲。捉三股[*]叉箭。墮如雨刺射罪人。罪人狂怖叩頭求哀。[17]小見放捨小見憐愍。

简体字   正體字

chewing. Then two mountains rush together and a huge hot iron wheel rolls over all of the offenders, thereby causing their bodies to burst and be broken apart.

In a hot iron mortar, a pestle causes them to be crushed into pieces. It is as if one were crushing grapes or pressing oil. On what is comparable to a trampling ground, their flesh is all gathered together in a heap. The heads are piled up like a mountain. The blood flows down and forms a lake.

The eagles and vultures and tigers and wolves each come and struggle to strike at the offenders. The past life karmic causes and conditions of these persons was such that they engaged in much killing of cattle, horses, pigs, sheep, roebucks, foxes, rabbits, tigers, wolves, lions, the six domestic animals, great birds, and flocks of birds. Because they engaged in many injurious attacks upon all sorts of birds and animals such as these, these offending individuals are subjected in return to these many sorts of bird and animal heads coming at them and injuring them.

Additionally, on account of employing the power of their strength to persecute the frail and weak and subject them to its unjust crushing effects, they undergo the punishment of two mountains coming together. On account of allowing miserly greed, hatred, stupidity, or fear to influence them to adjudicate the severity of punishment of cases in a way which does not accord with correct principle, or on account of being instrumental in destroying the correct Path and altering right Dharma, they undergo as retribution the punishment of being rolled over by a hot metal wheel and being put through the hot metal mortar and pestle.

d. The Screaming and Great Screaming Hells

The fourth and the fifth hells are known as the Screaming and Great Screaming Hells. In these immense hells those offenders therein are set upon by *rākṣasa* hell soldiers whose heads are yellow like gold, whose eyes shoot forth fire and who wear red-colored robes. The flesh on their bodies is hard and tough and they run about with the speed of the wind. Their hands and feet are long and large and a fearsome voice issues from their mouths. They wield three-pronged lances and fall like rain, piercing and impaling the offenders. The offenders become crazy with fright and bow down seeking mercy, but only rarely are they set loose and only rarely are they the objects of pity.

即时将入热铁地狱纵广百由
旬。驱打驰走足皆焦然。脂
髓流出如[*]筈苏油。铁棒棒
头头破脑出如破酪瓶。斫[18]
锉割剥身体糜烂。而复将入
铁阁。屋间黑烟来熏。互相
推[19]压更相怨毒。皆言何以
压我[20]才欲求[176b]出其门[21]
以闭。大声[22]嗥呼音常不
绝。此人宿行因缘。皆由[23]
斗秤欺诳非法断事。受寄不
还。侵陵下劣。恼诸穷贫令
其号哭。破他城郭坏人聚落
伤害劫剥。室家怨毒举城叫
[24]唤。有时[25]谲诈欺诳诱
之。令出而复害之。如是等
种种因缘故。受如此罪。大
叫唤地狱中人。皆坐熏杀穴
居之类。幽闭囹圄或暗烟窟
中而熏杀之。或投井中劫夺
他财。如是等种种因缘。受
大叫唤地狱罪。

即時將入熱鐵地獄縱廣百由
旬。驅打馳走足皆焦然。脂
髓流出如[*]筈蘇油。鐵棒棒
頭頭破腦出如破酪瓶。斫[18]
剉割剝身體糜爛。而復將入
鐵閣。屋間黑烟來熏。互相
推[19]壓更相怨毒。皆言何以
壓我[20]纔欲求[176b]出其門[21]
以閉。大聲[22]嗥呼音常不
絕。此人宿行因緣。皆由[23]
斗秤欺誑非法斷事。受寄不
還。侵陵下劣。惱諸窮貧令
其號哭。破他城郭壞人聚落
傷害劫剝。室家怨毒舉城叫
[24]喚。有時[25]譎詐欺誑誘
之。令出而復害之。如是等
種種因緣故。受如此罪。大
叫喚地獄中人。皆坐熏殺穴
居之類。幽閉囹圄或闇烟窟
中而熏殺之。或投井中劫奪
他財。如是等種種因緣。受
大叫喚地獄罪。

简体字   正體字

e. THE HOT METAL HELLS

Then the offenders are suddenly taken into the Hot Metal Hells which are a hundred yojanas in length and breadth. They are driven along with blows and move along quickly with their feet in flames. Their fat and marrow flows out just as when one expresses *perilla ocimoides* oil. Iron truncheons are used to strike blows upon their heads. Their heads break open and their brains burst forth just as when one shatters a vase full of curds. They are chopped into mince meat after being sliced and skinned. Their bodies break down into a gruel-like consistency whereupon they are next brought into an iron pavilion. Black smoke comes up and smokes them within the rooms. They crush against one another intensifying the poison of mutual animosity. They all call out, "Why are you crushing me?" and then seek to get out. Because the door has been closed upon them there is a loud noise of calling out, the sound of which is constant and unending.

The causes and conditions of the past life actions of these people was such that they cheated on weights and measures and decided matters in a way contrary to Dharma. They held valuables in trust for others but then refused to return them. They encroached on and persecuted those of inferior social station. They tormented the poverty-stricken so severely as to cause them to cry out and weep. They broke down the city walls of others, destroyed people's villages, inflicted injury, and pillaged and stripped [the inhabitants]. The poison of animosity which they inflicted on homes and families was such that the entire city cried out and howled. Sometimes they would cleverly deceive the inhabitants and thus induce them to come forth. Having caused them to come out, they then set about inflicting harm on them once again. On account of all sorts of other such similar causes and conditions they undergo punishments of this sort.

f. GREAT SCREAMING HELL CAUSALITY

The people in the Great Screaming Hells are all undergoing punishment for inflicting death through fumigation on those types of beings who live in caves. They shut others up in dark places and imprisoned them or else placed them in dark smoky caves and then proceeded to kill them with smoke. Or perhaps they threw them into wells and stole their valuables. On account of all sorts of other such causes and conditions as these they undergo punishment in the Great Screaming Hells.

第六第七热大热地狱。中有
二大铜镬。一名难陀二名跋
难陀[26]（秦言喜大喜也）醎沸
水[27]满中。罗刹鬼狱卒以罪
人投中。如厨士烹肉。人在
镬中脚上头下。譬如煮豆熟
烂。骨节解散皮肉相离。知
其已烂以[*]又[*]又出。行业
因缘冷风吹活。复投炭坑[28]
中。或着沸[29]屎中。譬如鱼
出于水而着热沙中。又以[30]
浓血[31]而自煎熬。从炭坑中
出。投之焰床强驱令坐。眼
耳鼻口及诸毛孔一切火出。
此人宿世恼乱父母师长沙门
婆罗门。[32]于诸好人福田中
恼令心热。以此罪故受热地
狱罪。或有宿世煮生茧。或
生[33]炙猪羊。或以木贯人而
生炙之。或焚烧山野及诸聚
落佛图精舍。[34]及天神等。
或推众生着火坑中。如是等
种种因缘。生此地狱中。

第六第七熱大熱地獄。中有
二大銅鑊。一名難陀二名跋
難陀[26]（秦言喜大喜也）醎沸
水[27]滿中。羅刹鬼獄卒以罪
人投中。如廚士烹肉。人在
鑊中腳上頭下。譬如煮豆熟
爛。骨節解散皮肉相離。知
其已爛以[*]又[*]又出。行業
因緣冷風吹活。復投炭坑[28]
中。或著沸[29]屎中。譬如魚
出於水而著熱沙中。又以[30]
濃血[31]而自煎熬。從炭坑中
出。投之焰床強驅令坐。眼
耳鼻口及諸毛孔一切火出。
此人宿世惱亂父母師長沙門
婆羅門。[32]於諸好人福田中
惱令心熱。以此罪故受熱地
獄罪。或有宿世煮生繭。或
生[33]炙豬羊。或以木貫人而
生炙之。或焚燒山野及諸聚
落佛圖精舍。[34]及天神等。
或推眾生著火坑中。如是等
種種因緣。生此地獄中。

简体字   正體字

g. THE HOT AND GREATLY HOT HELLS

The sixth and the seventh hells are the Hot and Greatly Hot Hells. Within them there are two immense copper cauldrons, one of which is called Nanda and the other of which is called Upananda. (Chinese textual note: "In our language, these mean 'joy' and 'great joy.'") They are filled to the top with boiling salt water. *Rākṣasa* ghost hell soldiers throw the offenders into them, working like chefs boiling meat. The people in the cauldrons become, from feet to head, like beans which have been completely cooked to the point of disintegration. The bones and joints come apart and scatter. The skin and flesh separate from each other. Once it has become apparent that [the offenders] have decomposed, they then use forks to pitch them out. On account of the causes and conditions of the karma which they have committed, a cold wind comes up and by its blowing brings them back to life.

Next they are pitched into the charcoal pit or else placed in boiling excrement. They become then like fish which have been pulled out of the water and then placed on hot sand. They may also be stewed in thick blood. They are pulled forth from the charcoal pit and thrown onto a flaming bed where they are driven with force to sit upon it. Fire then shoots forth from their eyes, ears, nose, mouth, and all of their hair pores.

In past lives, these people tormented and created chaos in the lives of their fathers, mothers, teachers, elders, śramaṇas and brahmans. With respect to fine people and those persons who constitute fields of merit, they tormented them and caused their minds to become inflamed. On account of these offenses they undergo punishment in the hot hells. Or perhaps in previous lives they boiled live silkworm cocoons or perhaps roasted live pigs and sheep or perhaps skewered people on a wooden pole and roasted them alive, or perhaps they set fire to and burned the mountains and wilderness, or villages, or Buddhist stupas, or monastic dwellings, or those dedicated to gods, spirits and so forth. Or else they may have pushed beings into a fire pit. It is on account of all sorts of causes and conditions such as these they are born into this hell.

h. THE AVĪCI HELLS

He also sees the Avīci Hells which in length and breadth are four thousand miles (*li*) and which are surrounded by an iron wall. Compared to the other seven hells, this is the deepest. Hell-soldier *rākṣasas* use huge hammers to hammer those offenders, just as

见阿鼻地狱。纵广四千里周
迴铁壁。于七地狱其处最
深。狱卒罗刹以大铁[35]椎椎
诸罪人。如锻师打铁。从头
剥皮乃至其足。以五百钉钉
[36]挓其身如[*]挓牛皮。互相
掣[37]挽应手破裂。热铁火车
以轹其身驱入火坑。令[38]
抱炭[176c]出热沸屎河驱令入
中。[39]有铁[*]嘴毒虫。从鼻
中入脚底出。从足下入口中
出。竖剑道中驱令驰走。足
下破碎如厨脍肉。利刀剑[*]
槊飞入身中。譬如霜树落叶
随风乱坠。罪人手足耳鼻支
节。皆被[40]斫剥割截在地流
血成池。二大恶狗一名赊摩
二名赊婆罗。铁口猛毅[41]
破人筋骨。力逾虎豹猛如师
子。有大刺林驱逼罪人强令
上树。[42]罪人上时刺便下
向。下时刺便上向。大身毒
蛇蝮蝎恶虫竞来齧之。大鸟
长嘴破头嗽脑。入醎河中随
流上下。出则蹈热铁地行铁
刺上。或坐铁[43]杌杌从下
入。以钳开口灌以洋铜。吞
热铁丸入口。口焦入咽咽烂
入腹。腹然五藏皆焦

简体字

見阿鼻地獄。縱廣四千里周
迴鐵壁。於七地獄其處最
深。獄卒羅刹以大鐵[35]椎椎
諸罪人。如鍛師打鐵。從頭
剝皮乃至其足。以五百釘釘
[36]挓其身如[*]挓牛皮。互相
掣[37]挽應手破裂。熱鐵火車
以轢其身驅入火坑。令[38]
抱炭[176c]出熱沸屎河驅令入
中。[39]有鐵[*]嘴毒虫。從鼻
中入腳底出。從足下入口中
出。竪劍道中驅令馳走。足
下破碎如廚膾肉。利刀劍[*]
槊飛入身中。譬如霜樹落葉
隨風亂墜。罪人手足耳鼻支
節。皆被[40]斫剝割截在地流
血成池。二大惡狗一名賒摩
二名賒婆羅。鐵口猛毅[41]
破人筋骨。力踰虎豹猛如師
子。有大刺林驅逼罪人強令
上樹。[42]罪人上時刺便下
向。下時刺便上向。大身毒
蛇蝮蝎惡虫競來齧之。大鳥
長嘴破頭嗽腦。入醎河中隨
流上下。出則蹈熱鐵地行鐵
刺上。或坐鐵[43]杌杌從下
入。以鉗開口灌以洋銅。吞
熱鐵丸入口。口焦入咽咽爛
入腹。腹然五藏皆焦

正體字

when a blacksmith pounds iron. They then peel off [the offenders'] skin from the head on down to the feet and use five hundred nails to nail and stretch it just as one stretches the skin of an ox. They struggle with each other for possession of [the hell-dweller] and, as soon as they lay hands on him, quickly pull his body apart.

A hot iron "fire vehicle" rolls over the bodies, driving them to plunge into a pit of fire. They are forced to carry coals as they come forth. They are then driven along and caused to plunge into a river of boiling excrement. There are iron-billed poisonous worms who enter through the nose and emerge from the bottom of the feet and who enter from the bottom of the feet and emerge from the mouth. [Those offenders] are driven along and caused to run down a road of vertical sword blades. Their feet burst open and are shredded like minced meat from the kitchen. Sharp knives and sword-tipped lances fly through the air and plunge into their bodies, falling down in a chaotic torrent just as leaves fall from a frost-bitten tree by the force of the wind. The hands, feet, ears, noses, and extremities of the offenders are all thereby chopped, flayed, cut, and sliced off by them.

The flowing blood forms a lake on the ground. Two huge and fearsome dogs, the first named Śyāma and the second named Śabala, use their jaws of iron and fierce strength to shatter the bones of [the offenders'] limbs. They are more powerful than tigers and leopards and more fierce than lions.

There is a great forest of spiked trees. The offenders are driven along and forced to climb the trees. When the offenders climb upwards, the spikes then point downward. When they climb down, the spikes then point upwards. Huge poisonous snakes, scorpions, and toxic insects struggle in haste to come at and bite them. Immense birds with long bills break open their heads, gulping and swallowing their brains.

[The offenders] are plunged into a river of brine and are swept up and down by the currents. When they get out, they tread upon hot iron ground and walk over iron spikes. Or perhaps they sit upon iron stakes and the stakes enter them from below. Pliers are used to open their mouths whereupon molten copper is then poured down their mouths. They swallow hot metal pellets which pour into their mouths. The mouth is burned whereupon they plunge into the throat. The flesh of the throat disintegrates from whence they then enter the belly. The belly is burned. The five organs are all scorched

直过堕地。但见恶色恒闻臭气常触麁澁遭诸苦痛迷闷[44]委顿。或狂逸[45]唐突或藏窜投掷或[46]颠匐堕落。此人宿行多造大恶五逆重罪。断[47]诸善根法言非法非法言[48]法。破因破果憎嫉善人。以是罪故入此地狱受罪最剧。如是等种种八大地狱[49]周围其外复有十六小地狱为眷属。八寒冰八炎火。其中罪毒不可见闻。八炎火地狱者。一名炭坑二名沸屎三名烧林四名剑林五名刀道六名铁刺林七名醎河八名铜橛。是为八。八寒冰地狱者。一名頞浮陀(少多有孔)二名尼罗浮陀(无[50]孔)三名[51]阿罗罗[177a](寒[1]战声也)四名阿婆婆(亦患寒声)五名睺睺(亦[2]是患寒声)六名沤波罗(此地狱外壁似青[3]莲花[4]也)

简体字

直過墮地。但見惡色恒聞臭氣常觸麁澁遭諸苦痛迷悶[44]委頓。或狂逸[45]唐突或藏竄投擲或[46]顛匐墮落。此人宿行多造大惡五逆重罪。斷[47]諸善根法言非法非法言[48]法。破因破果憎嫉善人。以是罪故入此地獄受罪最劇。如是等種種八大地獄[49]周圍其外復有十六小地獄為眷屬。八寒冰八炎火。其中罪毒不可見聞。八炎火地獄者。一名炭坑二名沸屎三名燒林四名劍林五名刀道六名鐵刺林七名醎河八名銅橛。是為八。八寒冰地獄者。一名頞浮陀(少多有孔)二名尼羅浮陀(無[50]孔)三名[51]阿羅羅[177a](寒[1]戰聲也)四名阿婆婆(亦患寒聲)五名睺睺(亦[2]是患寒聲)六名漚波羅(此地獄外壁似青[3]蓮花[4]也)

正體字

whereupon [those pellets] plunge straight through and fall out onto the ground.

[The offenders] see only horrible forms, constantly smell stinking vapors, constantly rub against rough surfaces, encounter bitter pain, and become confused, faint, and exhausted. Some of them become crazed and flee, bursting away from their ranks. Others attempt to run and hide. Yet others throw themselves down or tumble and fall down.

The past-life actions of these people included the committing of many great evils including the five nefarious and grave offenses. They cut off all roots of goodness, said of Dharma that it was non-Dharma, said of non-Dharma that it was Dharma, attempted to refute cause, attempted to refute effect, and were hateful and jealous of good people. On account of these offenses, they entered these hells and so undergo punishments of the most intense sort.

All sorts of circumstances such as these characterize the eight great hells. Surrounding them externally there are sixteen more lesser hells which are subsidiary to these. They are the eight cold ice hells and the eight blazing flame hells. The cruelty of their punishments is such as one cannot bear to see or bear to hear reported.

i. The Eight Blazing Flame Hells

As for the eight blazing flame hells, the first type are known as the Charcoal Pit Hells. The second type are known as Boiling Excrement Hells. The third type are known as the Burning Forest Hells. The fourth type are known as the Forest of Swords Hells. The fifth type are known as the Road of Knives Hells. The sixth type are known as the Forest of Iron Spikes Hells. The seventh type are known as the River of Brine Hells. The eighth type are known as the Copper Stake Hells. These constitute those eight hells.

j. The Eight Cold Ice Hells

As for the eight types of cold ice hells, the first are known as the Arbuda Hells. (Ch. text note: "[Means]: Possessing some measure of openings.") The second type are known as the Nirarbuda Hells. (Ch. text note: "[Means]: No opening.") The third type are known as the Aṭaṭa Hells. (Ch. text note: "[Means]: The sound of shivering.") The fourth type are known as the Hahava Hells. (Ch. text note: "[Means]: Also a sound of being afflicted by cold.") The fifth type are known as the Huhuva Hells. (Ch. text note: "[Means]: Also a sound of being afflicted by cold.") The sixth type are known as the Utpala Hells. (Ch. text note: "[Means]: The outer wall of this hell is like a green lotus

七名波头摩（红莲[5]花罪人
生中受苦[*]也）八名摩诃波
头摩。是为八。若破清净戒
出家法。令白衣轻贱佛道。
或[6]排众生着火坑中。或众
生命未尽顷于火上炙之。如
是等种种因缘。堕炭坑地狱
中。大火炎炭至膝烧罪人
身。若沙门婆罗门福田食。
以不净手触。或先噉或以不
净物着中。或以热沸屎灌他
身破净命。以邪命自活。如
是等种种因缘。堕沸屎地狱
中。沸屎深广如大海水。中
有[7]虫以铁为嘴破罪人头噉
脑破骨食髓。若焚烧草木伤
害诸虫。或烧林大猎为害弥
广。如是等种种因缘。堕
烧林地狱中。草木火然以
烧罪人。若执[8]持刀剑闘诤
伤杀。若斫树[9]压人以报宿
怨。若人以忠信诚告而密

简体字

七名波頭摩（紅蓮[5]花罪人
生中受苦[*]也）八名摩訶波
頭摩。是為八。若破清淨戒
出家法。令白衣輕賤佛道。
或[6]排眾生著火坑中。或眾
生命未盡頃於火上炙之。如
是等種種因緣。墮炭坑地獄
中。大火炎炭至膝燒罪人
身。若沙門婆羅門福田食。
以不淨手觸。或先噉或以不
淨物著中。或以熱沸屎灌他
身破淨命。以邪命自活。如
是等種種因緣。墮沸屎地獄
中。沸屎深廣如大海水。中
有[7]虫以鐵為嘴破罪人頭噉
腦破骨食髓。若焚燒草木傷
害諸虫。或燒林大獵為害彌
廣。如是等種種因緣。墮
燒林地獄中。草木火然以
燒罪人。若執[8]持刀劍闘諍
傷殺。若斫樹[9]壓人以報宿
怨。若人以忠信誠告而密

正體字

flower.") The seventh type are known as the Padma Hells. (Ch. text note: "[Means]: red lotus flower. Those with offenses are born into them and there undergo their sufferings.") The eighth type are known as the Mahāpadma Hells. These constitute the eight.

k. DESCRIPTION OF THE EIGHT BLAZING FLAME HELLS
1) THE CHARCOAL PIT HELLS

If one breaks the pure precepts and the dharma of the monastic, or if one causes the "white-robed" ones (the laity) to make light of the Buddha Path and subject it to derision, or perhaps if one pushes beings into a pit of fire or perhaps if before a being's life has ended, one tips them into the fire and burns them—on account of all sorts of causes and conditions such as these, one falls into the Charcoal Pit Hells. The Great Blazing Flames and coals reach up to the knees and burn the bodies of those with offenses.

2) THE BOILING EXCREMENT HELLS

If one touched the food of such fields of merit as the śramaṇas or brahmans with unclean hands, or perhaps first chewed it oneself, or perhaps put impure things into it, or perhaps if one poured boiling hot excrement onto another's body, or perhaps destroyed the purity of another's life, or perhaps sustained one's life through a deviant livelihood—on account of all sorts of causes and conditions such as these, one falls into the boiling excrement hells.

The boiling excrement is as deep and as vast as the waters of the great ocean. There are therein insects with bills made of iron which break open the skulls of the offenders and then chew and gulp their brains while also breaking open their bones and eating out their marrow.

3) THE BURNING FOREST HELLS

If one set fire to grasslands and forests, harming and injuring all of the insects, or perhaps if one set fire to a forest in the course of hunting, thereby committing injury on a vast scale—on account of all sorts of causal circumstances as these, one falls into the Burning Forest Hells. The grasslands and forests [in these hells] are ablaze and thus thereby burn those with offenses.

4) THE FOREST OF SWORDS HELLS

If one has wielded knives or swords and entered into battling which brought injury and death, if one chopped down a tree to crush other people in revenge for old animosities, or if, when others, out of loyalty and trust, have made reports in confidence, one secretly

相中陷。如是等种种因缘。堕剑林地狱中。此地狱罪人入中。风吹剑叶割截手足耳鼻皆令堕落。是时林中有[10]乌鹫恶狗来食其肉。若以利刀刺人。若橛若[11]枪伤人。若断截[12]道路[13]拨彻桥梁。破正法道示以非法道。如是等种种因缘。堕[14]利刀道地狱中。[*]利刀道地狱[15]者。于绝壁狭道中。[16]竖利刀令罪人行上而过。若犯邪婬侵他妇女贪受乐触。如是等种种因缘。堕铁刺林地狱中。刺树高一由旬。上有大毒蛇化作美女身。唤此罪人上来共汝作乐。狱卒驱之令上。刺皆下向贯刺罪人。身被刺害入骨彻髓。既至[17]林上化女还复蛇身。破头入腹处处穿穴皆悉破烂。[177b]忽复还活身体平复。化

简体字

相中陷。如是等種種因緣。墮劍林地獄中。此地獄罪人入中。風吹劍葉割截手足耳鼻皆令墮落。是時林中有[10]烏鷲惡狗來食其肉。若以利刀刺人。若橛若[11]槍傷人。若斷截[12]道路[13]撥徹橋樑。破正法道示以非法道。如是等種種因緣。墮[14]利刀道地獄中。[*]利刀道地獄[15]者。於絕壁狹道中。[16]竪利刀令罪人行上而過。若犯邪婬侵他婦女貪受樂觸。如是等種種因緣。墮鐵刺林地獄中。刺樹高一由旬。上有大毒蛇化作美女身。喚此罪人上來共汝作樂。獄卒驅之令上。刺皆下向貫刺罪人。身被刺害入骨徹髓。既至[17]林上化女還復蛇身。破頭入腹處處穿穴皆悉破爛。[177b]忽復還活身體平復。化

正體字

awaited the opportunity to entrap them thereby—on account of all sorts of causal factors such as these, one falls into the Forest of Swords Hells.

When those with offenses enter into this hell, the wind blows about the sword-like leaves which then slice off the hands, feet, ears, and nose, thus causing them all to fall away. At this time, there are crows, vultures, and horrific dogs within the forest which come and consume [the offenders'] flesh.

5) The Road of Sharp Knives Hells

If one has used sharp knives to stab people, or if one has used stakes or spears to injure people, or if one has cut off paths and roads or destroyed bridges, or if one has destroyed the pathway of right Dharma and has shown people a way which is contrary to Dharma—on account of all sorts of causal factors such as these, one falls into the Road of Sharp Knives Hells. As for basis of the name of the Road of Sharp Knives Hell, sharp knives are set up vertically on a narrow path lined with steep walls and those with karmic offenses are compelled to walk on over and beyond them.

6) The Forest of Iron Spikes Hells

If one has committed sexual misconduct wherein one has attacked the wives or daughters of others in one's lust to experience erotic physical contact—on account of all sorts of causal factors as these, one falls into the Forest of Iron Spikes Hell where there are trees bristling with spikes one yojana in height. In the top of each of them, there is a huge venomous serpent which has transformed into the body of a beautiful maiden and which calls out to this person with offenses, "Come on up here and I will join together with you in enjoying mutual pleasures."

The hell guardians then drive him on up, compelling him to ascend. The spikes [on the trees] then all point downwards and impale the person with karmic offenses. His body thus is injured by their impaling him, driving even into his bones and all the way to the marrow.

When the transgressor reaches the top of the tree, the transformationally-produced maiden's body turns back into the body of the serpent. It then breaks open his head and plunges down into [the offender's] belly and, in place after place, burrows through it so that [his body] becomes entirely destroyed and broken down.

Next, [the offender] suddenly returns to life with his body restored to normal, whereupon the transformationally-produced

女复在树下唤之狱卒以箭仰
射呼之令下刺复仰刺。既得
到地化女身[18]复毒蛇破罪
人身。如是久久从热铁刺林
出。遥见河水清凉快乐。走
往趣之入中变成热沸醎水。
罪人在中须臾之顷。皮肉离
散骨立水中。狱卒罗刹以[*]
叉钩出[19]之。持着岸上。此
人宿行因缘。伤杀水性鱼鼋
之属。或时[20]排人及诸众生
令没水中。或投之沸汤或投
之冰水。如是等种种恶业因
缘故[21]受此罪。若在铜橛
地狱。狱卒罗刹问诸罪人。
汝何处来。答言。我苦闷不
知来处。但患饥渴若言渴。
是时狱卒即驱逐罪人令坐热
铜橛上。以铁钳开口灌以洋
铜。若言饥坐之铜橛吞以铁
丸入口。口焦入咽咽烂入
腹。[22]腹然五藏烂坏直过堕
地。

女復在樹下喚之獄卒以箭仰
射呼之令下刺復仰刺。既得
到地化女身[18]復毒蛇破罪
人身。如是久久從熱鐵刺林
出。遙見河水清涼快樂。走
往趣之入中變成熱沸醎水。
罪人在中須臾之頃。皮肉離
散骨立水中。獄卒羅剎以[*]
叉鉤出[19]之。持著岸上。
此人宿行因緣。傷殺水性魚
鼋之屬。或時[20]排人及諸眾
生令沒水中。或投之沸湯或
投之冰水。如是等種種惡業
因緣故[21]受此罪。若在銅橛
地獄。獄卒羅剎問諸罪人。
汝何處來。答言。我苦悶不
知來處。但患飢渴若言渴。
是時獄卒即驅逐罪人令坐熱
銅橛上。以鐵鉗開口灌以洋
銅。若言飢坐之銅橛吞以鐵
丸入口。口焦入咽咽爛入
腹。[22]腹然五藏爛壞直過墮
地。

简体字　　　　　　　正體字

maiden manifests there yet again, but this time she stands at the base of the tree calling up to him. The hell guardians use arrows which they shoot upwards, yelling at him and ordering him to descend whereupon the spikes again face upwards. Once he has reached the ground, the transformationally-produced maiden's body transforms again into that of a venomous snake that proceeds [once again] to destroy the body of the person with karmic offenses. [These punishments continue] in this fashion for a long time, after which the offender emerges from the forest of hot iron spikes.

7) THE RIVER OF BRINE HELLS

Off in the distance, [offenders] see a river of cool and pleasant waters. They run to it and jump in, whereupon it transforms into boiling hot brine. When offenders have been in it for only a moment, the skin and flesh separate and fall apart, leaving the skeletons standing there in the water. The hell guardian *rākṣasas* then use a pitch fork to gaff them out of the water and affix them on the bank.

The causal circumstances of these people's past-life actions was that they injured and killed water-going creatures such as fish and turtles, or perhaps at times they pushed people or other beings, causing them to drown in the water, or perhaps they threw them into boiling broth, or perhaps they threw them into ice water. On account of all sorts of evil karmic causes and conditions such as these, they undergo such punishments [in the River of Brine Hells].

8) THE COPPER STAKE HELLS

If one is in the Copper Stake Hells, the hell guardian *rākṣasas* demand of the offender, "Where did you come from?"

He replies by saying, "I have been through such suffering that I lost consciousness and do not know where I came from. I know only that I am afflicted by hunger." [Alternatively, he may say], "I am afflicted by thirst." If he says that he is thirsty, the hell guardian then immediately chases along after the transgressor and forces him to sit down on hot copper spikes, uses iron pliers to [wrench] open the mouth, and then pours molten copper into it.

If [the offender] says that he is hungry, he is sat down on copper spikes and is forced to gulp [intensely hot] iron pellets which are poured into his mouth. After the mouth has been scorched, they enter the throat. Then, after the throat has disintegrated, they move on into the belly. The belly burns and the five organs are thus disintegrated and ruined. Then [the hot iron pellets] plunge straight through and fall out onto the ground.

此人宿行因缘劫盗他财以自
供口。诸出家人或时诈病多
求[23]酥油石蜜。或无戒无禅
无有智慧。而多受人施或恶
口伤人。如是等种种宿业因
缘。堕铜橛地狱。若人堕頞
浮陀地狱中。其处积氷毒风
来吹。令诸罪人皮毛裂落筋
肉断绝骨破髓出。即复完坚
受罪如初。此人宿业因缘。
寒月剥人或劫盗冻人薪火。
或作恶龙瞋毒忿恚。放大雹
雨氷冻害人。或轻贱谤毁若
佛及佛弟子持戒之人。或口
四业作众重罪。如是等种种
因缘。堕[24]頞浮陀地狱中。
尼罗浮陀亦如是。頞浮陀少
[25]多有孔时得出入。尼罗波
绝无孔罅无出入处。[26]呵婆
婆呵罗罗睺睺此三地狱。寒
风噤[27]战口不能

简体字

此人宿行因緣劫盜他財以自
供口。諸出家人或時詐病多
求[23]酥油石蜜。或無戒無禪
無有智慧。而多受人施或惡
口傷人。如是等種種宿業因
緣。墮銅橛地獄。若人墮頞
浮陀地獄中。其處積氷毒風
來吹。令諸罪人皮毛裂落筋
肉斷絕骨破髓出。即復完堅
受罪如初。此人宿業因緣。
寒月剥人或劫盜凍人薪火。
或作惡龍瞋毒忿恚。放大雹
雨氷凍害人。或輕賤謗毀若
佛及佛弟子持戒之人。或口
四業作眾重罪。如是等種種
因緣。墮[24]頞浮陀地獄中。
尼羅浮陀亦如是。頞浮陀少
[25]多有孔時得出入。尼羅波
絕無孔罅無出入處。[26]呵婆
婆呵羅羅睺睺此三地獄。寒
風噤[27]戰口不能

正體字

This person's past life karmic causes and conditions were such that he robbed or pilfered the valuables of others, using them to supply the appetites of his own mouth. Among monastics, it may have been the case that there were times when they feigned illness and thus sought to obtain a greater measure of ghee or rock honey. Or perhaps they were devoid of any observance of the moral precepts or devoid of any practice of dhyāna meditation or were devoid of any development of wisdom and yet nonetheless accepted a great measure of people's donations. Or else they may have injured people with harsh speech. On account of all sorts of past life karmic causes and conditions such as these, they came to fall into these Copper Stake Hells.

l. Description of the Eight Cold Ice Hells

1) The Arbuda Hells

If a person falls into the Arbuda Hells, he abides on a mass of ice. A fierce wind comes up and blows, causing the skin and hair of all of those offenders to split open and fall away while their sinews and flesh snap apart and their bones burst open and the marrow comes forth. They are then immediately restored to wholeness and solidity again, whereupon they undergo punishments just as before.

The past life karmic causes and conditions of these people were such that, during the cold months, they forced people to be stripped, or perhaps they stole the fuel and fire of people who were cold, or perhaps they had been evil dragons who, [acting under the influence of] the poison of hatred, had unleashed their anger and had let fall great hail and rainstorms, thus causing ice and cold to injure people. Or perhaps they had slighted or derided or slandered or besmirched the reputation of either a buddha, a buddha's disciples, or people who uphold the moral precepts. Or perhaps through the four unwholesome karmic actions of the mouth they committed manifold severe offenses. On account of all sorts of causes and conditions such as these, one falls into the Arbuda Hells.

2) The Nirarbuda Hells

The Nirarbuda Hells are also like this. Although the Arbuda Hells have some openings whereby one may sometimes succeed in coming and going, the Nirarbuda Hells have absolutely no openings or cracks and thus have no place whereby one may come and go.

3) The Aṭaṭa, Hahava, and Huhuva Hells

In the three hells known as Aṭaṭa, Hahava, and Huhuva, the cold wind inflicts a silencing shivering that prevents the mouth from

开 。 因 其 呼 声 而 以 名
狱。**[177c]** 沤波罗狱中。冻冰
[28]浃渫有似青莲花。波头摩
状。如此间赤莲花。摩呵波
头摩。是中拘**[29]**迦离住处。
有智之人闻是惊言。咄以此
无明恚爱法故。乃受此苦。
出而复入无穷无已。菩萨见
此如是思惟。此苦业因缘皆
是无明诸烦恼所作。我当精
进懃修六度集诸功德。断除
众生五道中苦。兴发大哀增
益精进。如见父母幽闭囹圄
[30]拷掠搒笞忧毒万端。方
便求救心不暂舍。菩萨见诸
众生受五道苦念之如父亦复
如是。复次菩萨精进世世勤
修。求诸财宝给施众生心无
懈废。自有财物能尽施与心
亦不懈。

開 。 因 其 呼 聲 而 以 名
獄。**[177c]** 漚波羅獄中。凍冰
[28]浃渫有似青蓮花。波頭摩
狀。如此間赤蓮花。摩呵波
頭摩。是中拘**[29]**迦離住處。
有智之人聞是驚言。咄以此
無明恚愛法故。乃受此苦。
出而復入無窮無已。菩薩見
此如是思惟。此苦業因緣皆
是無明諸煩惱所作。我當精
進懃修六度集諸功德。斷除
眾生五道中苦。興發大哀增
益精進。如見父母幽閉囹圄
[30]拷掠搒笞憂毒萬端。方
便求救心不暫捨。菩薩見諸
眾生受五道苦念之如父亦復
如是。復次菩薩精進世世勤
修。求諸財寶給施眾生心無
懈廢。自有財物能盡施與心
亦不懈。

简体字   正體字

opening. The hells are named after the sounds emitted [by those hell-dwellers].

4) THE UTPALA, PADMA, AND MAHĀPADMA HELLS

In the Utpala ("Blue Lotus") Hells, the freezing of the ice creates formations which are like the blossom of a blue lotus. In the Padma ("Lotus") Hells, the shape [created by the ice] resembles that of our red lotus blossoms. The Mahāpadma ("Great Lotus") Hells are the dwelling place of Kokālīka, [the slanderer of Śāriputra and Maudgalyāyana].

6. HOW THE WISE REACT TO OBSERVING SUCH SUFFERINGS

A person possessed of wisdom hears this and exclaims in alarm, "Alas! On account of these dharmas of ignorance, anger, and lust, one then undergoes such suffering as this. One gets out and then enters it again, doing so endlessly and never being able to bring it to a halt."

7. HOW THE BODHISATTVA REACTS TO OBSERVING SUCH SUFFERINGS

The bodhisattva observes this and considers thus, "The causes and conditions of this suffering karma are all created from ignorance and afflictions. I should vigorously and diligently cultivate the six perfections and amass all manner of merit so as to cut off and get rid of these sufferings encountered by beings within the five destinies." He then lets flourish a sentiment of great empathy which increases and augments his vigor.

It is as if he were seeing his own parents being confined to a dark cell in prison and as if he were watching them being beaten and flogged. He experiences the intense pangs of worry in a myriad forms and, through skillful means, seeks to save them, never forsaking them in his thoughts for even a moment. When the bodhisattva observes beings undergoing the sufferings of the five rebirth destinies, he remains mindful of them in this fashion, just as he would in the case of his own father.

K. THE BODHISATTVA'S VIGOR IN THE OTHER PERFECTIONS
1. THE BODHISATTVA'S VIGOR IN GIVING

Moreover, the vigor of the bodhisattva is diligently cultivated in life after life. He seeks after valuables and jewels with which to provide for and make gifts to beings while he is not lazy in mind and does not allow his practice to diminish. When he himself possesses valuable material objects, he is able give exhaustively of all of them with no retreating from this even in his mind.

复次精进持戒。若大若小一切能受。一切能持不毁不犯。大如毛发。设有违失即时发露初不覆藏。复次懃修忍辱。若人刀杖打害骂詈毁辱及恭敬供养。一切能忍不受不着。于深法中其心不没亦不疑悔。复次专精一心修诸禅定。能住能[31]守得五神通及[32]四等心胜处背舍十一切[33]处。具诸功德得四念[34]处及诸菩萨见佛三昧。复次菩萨精进求法不懈。身心懃力供养法师。种种恭敬供给给[35]使。初不违失亦不废退。不惜身命以为法故。诵读问答。初中后夜思惟

復次精進持戒。若大若小一切能受。一切能持不毀不犯。大如毛髮。設有違失即時發露初不覆藏。復次懃修忍辱。若人刀杖打害罵詈毀辱及恭敬供養。一切能忍不受不著。於深法中其心不沒亦不疑悔。復次專精一心修諸禪定。能住能[31]守得五神通及[32]四等心勝處背捨十一切[33]處。具諸功德得四念[34]處及諸菩薩見佛三昧。復次菩薩精進求法不懈。身心懃力供養法師。種種恭敬供給給[35]使。初不違失亦不廢退。不惜身命以為法故。誦讀問答。初中後夜思惟

简体字　　　　　　　　　　　　正體字

2. The Bodhisattva's Vigor in Moral Virtue

Furthermore, he is vigorous in his upholding of the precepts. Whether they are major or whether they are minor, he is able to accept them all. He is able to uphold them all without doing damage to them or breaking them. Even in the case of those which in the degree of their significance are comparable to a strand of hair— if he has an instance of erring and contravening, he immediately reveals this [and repents], never at any point concealing his errors.

3. The Bodhisattva's Vigor in Patience

Additionally, he is diligent in his cultivation of patience. Whether people use knives or staves to beat and injure him, whether they scold and revile him, whether they besmirch his reputation and insult him, or whether they offer him reverential respect and offerings, he is able to have patience with all of it. He neither accepts it [as constituting reality] nor becomes attached to any of it. With respect to profound dharmas, his mind does not become sunken [in discouragement] by them. Nor does he experience doubts or regrets regarding them.

4. The Bodhisattva's Vigor in Cultivation of Dhyāna Meditation

Then again, he is focused and precise in his cultivation of the dhyāna absorptions. He is able to abide in them and is able to guard them. He gains the five superknowledges (*abhijñā*) as well as the four minds of equal regard (*apramāṇacitta*), the liberations (*vimokṣa*), the bases of ascendancy (*abhibhvāyatana*), and the ten universal bases (*kṛtsnāyatana*). He brings to perfection every sort of merit, gains the four stations of mindfulness (*smṛtyupasthāna*) as well as the samādhi wherein the bodhisattva is able to see the Buddhas.

5. The Bodhisattva's Vigor in Cultivation of the Perfection of Wisdom

Furthermore, the bodhisattva vigorously seeks the Dharma without being lazy in this endeavor. In both body and mind, he employs the power of diligence in making offerings to masters of the Dharma. He manifests every sort of respect, reverence, and offering to supply their needs and render them service. Even from the outset, he does not err by acting in a way contrary to what is proper, nor does he allow his efforts to diminish or retreat in their consistency. For the sake of the Dharma, he refrains from indulging any cherishing regard for even his own body and life.

He recites, reads, inquires, and offers answers. In the beginning, middle and later periods of the night, he cogitates upon it, bears it

忆念筹量分别。求其因缘选
择同异。欲知实相一切诸法
自相异相总相别相一相有相
无相如实相。诸佛菩萨无
量智慧[36]心[37]不没不退。
是名菩萨精进。如是等种
种因缘。能生能办种种善
法。是故名为精进波罗蜜。
波罗蜜义如先说。复次菩
萨精进。[38]名为精进波罗
蜜。[178a]馀人精进不名波罗
蜜。问曰。云何为精进满
足。答曰。菩萨生身法性身
能具功德。是为精进波罗蜜
满足。满足义如上说。身心
精进。不废息故。问曰。精
进是心数法。[1]经何以名身
精进。答曰。精进虽是心数
法。从身力出[2]故名为身精
进。如受是心数法。[3]而有
五识相应受。

憶念籌量分別。求其因緣選
擇同異。欲知實相一切諸法
自相異相總相別相一相有相
無相如實相。諸佛菩薩無
量智慧[36]心[37]不沒不退。
是名菩薩精進。如是等種
種因緣。能生能辦種種善
法。是故名為精進波羅蜜。
波羅蜜義如先說。復次菩
薩精進。[38]名為精進波羅
蜜。[178a]餘人精進不名波羅
蜜。問曰。云何為精進滿
足。答曰。菩薩生身法性身
能具功德。是為精進波羅蜜
滿足。滿足義如上說。身心
精進。不廢息故。問曰。精
進是心數法。[1]經何以名身
精進。答曰。精進雖是心數
法。從身力出[2]故名為身精
進。如受是心數法。[3]而有
五識相應受。是

简体字　　　　　　　　　　　　　　正體字

in mind, assesses it, and draws distinctions with regard to it. He seeks [to understand] its causes and conditions and analyzes its identities and differences.

He desires to know the true character of all dharmas in accordance with reality, including their individual characteristics, their differentiating characteristics, their general characteristics, their special characteristics, their characteristics of singularity, their characteristics of existence, their characteristics of nonexistence, and the characteristics whereby they accord with reality. In his pursuit of the immeasurable wisdom of the Buddhas and the Bodhisattvas, he does not allow his mind to become submerged [in discouragement], nor does he allow himself to retreat from his efforts.

L. The Nature of the Bodhisattva's Vigor

This is what is known as the vigor of the bodhisattva. On account of all sorts of different causes and conditions such as these, he is able to bring forth and bring to completion all manner of good dharmas. It is for this reason that it is known as the *pāramitā* of vigor. The meaning of *pāramitā* is as previously explained.

Moreover, it is this vigor of the bodhisattva which qualifies as the *pāramitā* of vigor whereas the vigor of other people does not qualify as "*pāramitā.*"

M. How One Perfects the *Pāramitā* of Vigor

Question: How does one go about accomplishing the complete perfection of vigor?

Response: In both his birth body and his Dharma-nature body, the bodhisattva is able to bring merit to perfection. This constitutes the complete perfection of the *pāramitā* of vigor. The meaning of "complete perfection" is as stated above [in the Sutra text beginning this chapter]: "[It is through] being vigorous in body and mind and refraining from indolence or resting [that one perfects *vīrya pāramitā*]."

N. Physical Vigor versus Mental Vigor

Question: Vigor is a dharma belonging to the mind. Why then does the Sutra refer to vigor of the body?

Response: Although vigor is a dharma belonging to the mind, because it comes forth through the power of the body, one therefore also refers to "vigor of the body." It is just as with "feeling." It, too, is a dharma belonging to the mind. But still, there do exist feelings (i.e. "sensations") corresponding to the five consciousnesses. These

是名身受[4]有意识相应受是
为心受。精进亦如是。身力
勲修若手布施。口诵法言。
若讲说法。如是等名为身[5]
口精进。复次行布施持戒。
是为身精进。忍辱禅定智慧
是名心精进。复次外事勲修
是为身精进。内自专精是为
心精进。麁精进名为身。细
精进名为心。为福德精进名
为身。为智慧精进是为心。
若菩萨初发心乃至得无生
忍。[6]于是中间名身精进。
生身未舍故得无生忍。舍肉
身得法性身。乃至成佛。是
为心精进。复次菩萨初发心
时功德未足故。种三福因
缘。布施持戒善心渐得福
报。以施众生。众生未足。
更广修福发大悲心。一切众
生不足于财多作众恶。我以
少财不能满足其意。其意不

名身受[4]有意識相應受是為
心受。精進亦如是。身力勲
修若手布施。口誦法言。若
講說法。如是等名為身[5]口
精進。復次行布施持戒。是
為身精進。忍辱禪定智慧是
名心精進。復次外事勲修是
為身精進。內自專精是為心
精進。麁精進名為身。細精
進名為心。為福德精進名為
身。為智慧精進是為心。
若菩薩初發心乃至得無生
忍。[6]於是中間名身精進。
生身未捨故得無生忍。捨肉
身得法性身。乃至成佛。是
為心精進。復次菩薩初發心
時功德未足故。種三福因
緣。布施持戒善心漸得福
報。以施眾生。眾生未足。
更廣修福發大悲心。一切眾
生不足於財多作眾惡。我以
少財不能滿足其意。其意不

簡体字　　　　　　　　　　　　　　　　正體字

are referred to as "physical feeling." There are feelings which correspond to the intellectual consciousness. These constitute "mental feelings." The circumstance in the case of vigor is just like this.

When one uses physical effort in diligent cultivation, as for instance when the hands present a gift, when the mouth carefully recites words of Dharma, or when one delivers lectures in explanation of Dharma, such instances qualify as vigor of the body and mouth.

Moreover, when one practices giving or upholds the precepts, these constitute examples of vigor of the body. Patience, dhyāna absorption, and wisdom qualify as instances of vigor of the mind.

Then again, [one may say that] the diligent cultivation of outward endeavors constitutes vigor of the body while when one is focused and precise inwardly, this constitutes vigor of the mind. Coarse vigor is corresponds to that which is physical whereas refined vigor corresponds to that which is mental. Vigor which is implemented for the sake of producing merit corresponds to that which is physical whereas that vigor which is taken up for the sake of wisdom corresponds to that which is mental.

That [vigor] which is employed by the bodhisattva from the time of bringing forth the initial resolve [to become a buddha] on up until he realizes the unproduced-dharmas patience (*anutpattikadharmakṣānti*) corresponds to vigor of the body, this on account of his not yet having relinquished the physical birth body. When he realizes the unproduced-dharmas patience, he then relinquishes the fleshly body and gains the Dharma-nature body. From that very point on through to the realization of buddhahood corresponds to vigor on the part of the mind.

Then again, [one may also explain that] when the bodhisattva first brings forth the resolve, because his merit is not yet complete, he engages in planting the causes and conditions of the three kinds of merit, namely giving, upholding of precepts, and the mind imbued with goodness, and so gradually gains merit in reward. As he goes about giving to beings, beings are not yet fulfilled, and so he cultivates merit even more vastly and brings forth the mind of great compassion.

Because all beings are inadequately equipped with wealth, they tend more towards the commission of the many varieties of evil. [Thus he thinks], "If I resort to a lesser quantity of valuables, I shall be unable to satisfy their aspirations. If their aspirations are not

满不能懃受教诲。不受道教
不能得脱生老病死。我当作
大方便给足于财令其充满。
便入大海求诸异宝。登山履
危以求妙药。入深石窟求诸
异物石汁珍宝以给众生。或
作萨陀婆冒涉崄道。劫贼师
子虎狼恶兽。为布施众生
故。懃求财宝不以为难。药
草呪术能令铜变为金。如是
种种变化致诸财物。及四方
无主物以给众生。是为身
精进。得五[178b]神通能自变
[7]化作诸美味。或至天上取
自然食。如是等名为心精
进。能集财宝以用布施。是
为身精进。以是布施之德。
得至佛道。是为心精进。生
身菩萨行六波罗蜜。是为身
精进。法性身菩萨行六波罗
蜜。是为心精进(未得法身
心则随身。已得法

满不能懃受教诲。不受道教
不能得脱生老病死。我當作
大方便給足於財令其充滿。
便入大海求諸異寶。登山履
危以求妙藥。入深石窟求諸
異物石汁珍寶以給眾生。或
作薩陀婆冒涉崄道。劫賊師
子虎狼惡獸。為布施眾生
故。懃求財寶不以為難。藥
草呪術能令銅變為金。如是
種種變化致諸財物。及四方
無主物以給眾生。是為身
精進。得五[178b]神通能自變
[7]化作諸美味。或至天上取
自然食。如是等名為心精
進。能集財寶以用布施。是
為身精進。以是布施之德。
得至佛道。是為心精進。生
身菩薩行六波羅蜜。是為身
精進。法性身菩薩行六波羅
蜜。是為心精進(未得法身
心則隨身。已得法

简体字 　　　　　　正體字

fulfilled, they will be unable to be diligent in their taking on of instruction. If they do not accept instruction in the Path, they will be unable to succeed in gaining liberation from birth, aging, sickness, and death. I should therefore create a grand skillful means whereby I may be able to completely supply them all with valuables and thus cause them to become entirely satisfied."

Consequently he then goes out on the great sea, seeking to obtain all manner of exotic jewels. He climbs mountains and passes, going through dangerous situations, all in order to seek for marvelous medications. He enters deep rock caves, seeking for all sorts of exotic material objects as well as the precious jewels which constitute the essences of stone, all in order to use them to supply the needs of beings.

In some instances, he may become a *sārthavāha* (a caravan traveler) who travels along precipitous pathways subjecting himself to the depredations of robbers, thieves, lions, tigers, wolves, and malevolent beasts. For the sake of giving to beings, he is diligent in seeking out valuables and jewels and does not take that endeavor to be a difficult one.

Through the use of herbs and spells, he seeks to be able even to cause copper to turn into gold. Employing all sorts of transformations such as these, he causes there to be all manner of valuable objects, this while also availing himself of those objects throughout the four directions which have no owner, using them to supply the needs of beings. Activities of these sorts constitute vigor of the body.

He gains the five superknowledges and is thus enabled to perform transformations whereby he creates all manner of delectable flavors, in some instances even going up to the heavens to obtain their spontaneously appearing cuisine. All sorts of cases such as these constitute vigor on the part of the mind.

He is able to accumulate wealth and jewels which he uses in his giving. This constitutes vigor on the part of the body. Employing the merit from this giving, he then becomes able to succeed in reaching the Buddha Path. This constitutes vigor on the part of the mind. The birth-body bodhisattva's cultivation of the six *pāramitās* constitutes vigor on the part of the body. The Dharma-nature body bodhisattva's cultivation of the six *pāramitās* constitutes vigor on the part of the mind. (Ch. text note: If one has not yet gained the Dharma body, the mind follows the body. If one has already gained the Dharma

身则心不随身。身不累心
也。）

[0178b07] 复次一切法中皆能
成办不惜身命。是为身精
进。求一切禅定智慧时心不
懈惓。是为心精进。复次身
精进者。受诸懃苦终不[8]懈
废。如说。波罗奈国梵摩达
王。游猎于[9]野林中见二鹿
群。群各有主。一主有五百
群鹿。一主身七宝色。是释
迦[10]牟尼菩萨。一主是提婆
达多。菩萨鹿王见[11]人王大
众杀其部党。起大悲心迳到
王前。王人竞射飞矢如雨。
王见此鹿直进趣已无所忌
惮。勅诸从人摄汝弓[12]矢无
得断其来意。鹿王既至跪白
[13]人王。君以嬉游逸乐小事
故。群鹿一时皆受死苦。若
以供膳[14]辄当差次日送一鹿
以供王厨。王善其言听如其
[15]意。于是二鹿群主大集差
次各当一日[16]送应次者。

身則心不隨身。身不累心
也。）

[0178b07] 復次一切法中皆能
成辦不惜身命。是為身精
進。求一切禪定智慧時心不
懈惓。是為心精進。復次身
精進者。受諸懃苦終不[8]懈
廢。如說。波羅奈國梵摩達
王。遊獵於[9]野林中見二鹿
群。群各有主。一主有五百
群鹿。一主身七寶色。是釋
迦[10]牟尼菩薩。一主是提婆
達多。菩薩鹿王見[11]人王大
眾殺其部黨。起大悲心逕到
王前。王人競射飛矢如雨。
王見此鹿直進趣已無所忌
憚。勅諸從人攝汝弓[12]矢無
得斷其來意。鹿王既至跪白
[13]人王。君以嬉遊逸樂小事
故。群鹿一時皆受死苦。若
以供膳[14]輒當差次日送一鹿
以供王廚。王善其言聽如其
[15]意。於是二鹿群主大集差
次各當一日[16]送應次者。

简体字　　　　　　　　正體字

body, then the mind does not follow the body. The body then no longer acts as a burden to the mind.)

Then again, [one may explain that] when one becomes able to succeed in bringing all dharmas to completion while refraining from indulging any cherishing regard for his own body or life, this constitutes vigor on the part of the body. While seeking to develop all of the types of dhyāna absorptions and wisdom, one's mind refrains from indulging any laziness or weariness, this constitutes vigor on the part of the mind.

1. Story: The Deer King Jataka Tale

Moreover, as for vigor on the part of the body, one takes on all manner of hardship through diligence yet never succumbs to laziness or diminishment of one's endeavors. This is as told [in the *jātaka* tale of] Brahmadatta, the King of the state of Vārāṇasī. He was roaming and hunting in the wilderness forests where he observed that there were two herds of deer. The herds each had a ruler and each herd consisted of five hundred deer. One of the rulers [of the deer] possessed a coloration resembling the seven kinds of precious things. This was Shakyamuni [in a past life] as a bodhisattva. The other ruler [of the deer] was Devadatta.

The bodhisattva deer king observed a large group of followers of the human king killing his clan, brought forth the mind of great compassion, and proceeded to go directly before the King. [As it drew closer], the King's men attempted to shoot it. The flying arrows fell like rain. After the King saw that this deer was advancing fearlessly straight towards him, he ordered all of his followers, "Halt the shooting of your arrows! Don't interfere with his intentions in coming forth."

When the king of the deer had arrived, he knelt and addressed the king of the humans, saying, "On account of what for your Lordship is but a minor matter of unrestrained pleasure in the enjoyment of sport, the [entire] herd of deer at once undergoes the suffering of death. How would it be if we instead offered for his meals, regularly and in accord with our own sequence, one deer to be sent each day as an offering to the kitchen of the King?" The King approved of his words and permitted it to be as he intended.

At this point the two rulers of the deer herds convened a great meeting [of the herds] to determine the order by which they would be sent. Each of them took on the responsibility whereby one of them would be sent forth every day in accord with the proper order.

是[17]时提婆达多鹿群中。有
一鹿怀[18]子来白其主。我身
今日[19]当应送死。而我怀
子子非次也。乞垂料理使死
者得次生者不滥。鹿王怒之
言。谁不惜命。次来但去何
得辞也。鹿母思惟。我王不
仁不以理恕不察我辞。横见
瞋怒不足告也。即至菩萨王
所以情具白。王问此鹿。汝
主何言。鹿曰。我主不仁。
不见料理而见瞋怒。大王仁
及一切故来归命。如我今日
天地虽旷无所控告。菩萨思
[178c]惟。此甚可愍。若我不
理抂杀其子。若非次更差次
未及之。如何可遣。唯有我
当代之思。之[20]既定。即自
送身遣鹿母还。我今代汝汝
勿忧也。鹿王迳到王门。众
人见之怪其自来以事白王。
王亦怪之而命令前问言。诸
鹿尽耶。汝何以来。

是[17]時提婆達多鹿群中。有
一鹿懷[18]子來白其主。我身
今日[19]當應送死。而我懷
子子非次也。乞垂料理使死
者得次生者不濫。鹿王怒之
言。誰不惜命。次來但去何
得辭也。鹿母思惟。我王不
仁不以理恕不察我辭。橫見
瞋怒不足告也。即至菩薩王
所以情具白。王問此鹿。汝
主何言。鹿曰。我主不仁。
不見料理而見瞋怒。大王仁
及一切故來歸命。如我今日
天地雖曠無所控告。菩薩思
[178c]惟。此甚可愍。若我不
理抂殺其子。若非次更差次
未及之。如何可遣。唯有我
當代之思。之[20]既定。即自
送身遣鹿母還。我今代汝汝
勿憂也。鹿王逕到王門。眾
人見之怪其自來以事白王。
王亦怪之而命令前問言。諸
鹿盡耶。汝何以來。

简体字   正體字

There was a deer at this time within Devadatta's herd which was pregnant with a fawn and which consequently came forward and addressed her ruler, saying, "Today, it is I myself who should be sent forth to die. However, I am pregnant with a fawn. It is not the case that it is the fawn's turn to go. I beg that you will dispense your calculations in managing this in such a way that whosoever dies does so according to the proper order while also ensuring that he who is yet to be born will not become involved in it."

The King of that herd of deer became angry at her and said, "Who does not cherish his own life? When the sequence comes up, one just goes. How could there be any withdrawing from it?"

The pregnant doe thought, "My king is not humane. He does not extend empathy in accord with principle. He will not countenance my withdrawal and so precipitously falls into a rage over it. He is not even worthy to hear my case." She then immediately went to the bodhisattva [deer] king and set forth all of her sentiments.

The [deer] king asked this deer, "What did your lordship say?"

The deer said, "My lord did not respond humanely. He has not seen fit to apply his imagination to managing this matter. On the contrary, he become enraged at me. Because the great king's humanity extends to everyone, I came here to seek refuge in him. Although heaven and earth are vast, today those such as myself are bereft of any forum to present our case."

The bodhisattva [deer] thought, "This is extremely pitiable! If I do not bring order to this matter, there will occur an unprincipled slaughter of her fawn. If it is not done according to sequence, this by changing the order of selection, then [slaughter] shall fall upon one whose turn has not yet come. How then could such a one be sent off? There is only myself who would be appropriate to take her place."

When his consideration of the matter had been decided, he immediately went along himself, dispatching the mother deer to return [to the herd], saying, "I am now going to substitute for you. You have nothing to worry about."

The deer king then went directly to the gate of the king. When the group of people there saw him, they were amazed that he himself had come and so informed the King of this matter. The King was amazed at this as well and so ordered that [the deer king] be brought forward. He then inquired, "Have the deer all come to an end? Why is it that you yourself have come?"

鹿王言。大王仁及群鹿人无犯者。但有滋茂何有尽时。我以异部群中有一鹿怀子。以子垂产身当[21]俎割子亦[22]并命。归告于我我以愍之。非分更差是亦不可。若归而不救无异木石。是身不久必不免死。慈救苦厄功德无量。若人无慈[23]与虎狼[24]无异。王闻是言即从坐起。而说偈[25]言。

我实是畜[26]兽　名曰人头鹿。
汝虽是鹿身　名为鹿头人。

以理而言之　非以形为人。
若能有慈惠　虽兽实是人。

我从今日始　不食一切肉。
我以无畏施　且可安汝意。

[0178c20] 诸鹿得安王得仁信。复次如[27]爱法梵志。十二岁遍阎浮提。求知圣法而不能得。时世无佛

简体字

鹿王言。大王仁及群鹿人無犯者。但有滋茂何有盡時。我以異部群中有一鹿懷子。以子垂產身當[21]俎割子亦[22]併命。歸告於我我以愍之。非分更差是亦不可。若歸而不救無異木石。是身不久必不免死。慈救苦厄功德無量。若人無慈[23]與虎狼[24]無異。王聞是言即從坐起。而說偈[25]言。

我實是畜[26]獸　名曰人頭鹿。
汝雖是鹿身　名為鹿頭人。

以理而言之　非以形為人。
若能有慈惠　雖獸實是人。

我從今日始　不食一切肉。
我以無畏施　且可安汝意。

[0178c20] 諸鹿得安王得仁信。復次如[27]愛法梵志。十二歲遍閣浮提。求知聖法而不能得。時世無佛

正體字

The deer king explained, "The humanity of the great King has extended to the entire herd of deer. Among men, there are none who have transgressed it. There is only flourishing. How could there be a time when [the deer] would come to an end? I have come because there is a doe within the other herd which is pregnant with fawn. As the fawn is about to be born just when [the doe's] body should be put to death, the fawn is threatened with having to share the same fate. Consequently [the doe] took refuge in me, telling me of her plight.

"It is on account of that circumstance that I took pity on her. Nor could I allow a change in the sequence such that it would fall on one who should have no part in it. Given that she took refuge in me, were I to fail to rescue [her fawn], I would be no different from a tree or a stone. This body of mine will not endure long [in any case]. It is certain that one cannot avoid death. To bring forth kindness and rescue someone from suffering and misery results in measureless merit. If a person has no kindness, then he is no different from a tiger or a wolf."

When the King heard these words, he immediately arose from his throne and uttered a verse, saying:

In truth it is I who am the beast
And who may thus be called a human-headed deer.
Although you possess the body of a deer,
You may be called a deer-headed human.

To speak of it according to the principle,
It is not that it is by one's form that one becomes human.
If one is able to possess kindness and generosity,
Although one may be a beast, in truth he is human.

For my own part, beginning with this very day,
I shall no longer eat any sort of flesh.
I will make a gift of fearlessness,
And so shall be able to put your mind at peace.

The deer thereafter achieved a state of peace while the King himself succeeded in realizing his own humanity and trustworthiness.

2. Story: The Sacrifice of the Brahmacārin Lover of Dharma

Then again, this is exemplified by the case of the *brahmacārin* known as "Lover of Dharma." For twelve years he went everywhere in Jambudvīpa searching for knowledge of the Dharma of the sages but still was unable to find it. There was no buddha in the world

佛法亦尽。有一婆罗门言。
我有圣法一偈若实爱法当以
与汝。答言。实爱法。婆罗
门言。若实爱法当以汝皮为
纸以身骨为笔以血书之。当
以与汝。即如其言破骨剥皮
以血写[28]偈。

如法应修行　非法不应受。
今世[29]亦后世　行法者安隐。

[0178c29] 复次昔野火烧林。林
中有一雉懃身自力。[179a]飞
入水中渍其毛羽来灭大火。
火大水少往来疲乏不以为
苦。是时天帝释来问之言。
汝作何等。答言。我救此林
愍众生故。此林荫育处广清
凉快乐。我诸种类及诸宗亲
并诸众生皆依仰此。我有身
力云何懈怠而不救之。天帝
问言。汝乃精懃当至几时。
雉言。以死为期。天帝言。
汝心虽尔谁证知者。

佛法亦盡。有一婆羅門言。
我有聖法一偈若實愛法當以
與汝。答言。實愛法。婆羅
門言。若實愛法當以汝皮為
紙以身骨為筆以血書之。當
以與汝。即如其言破骨剝皮
以血寫[28]偈。

如法應修行　非法不應受。
今世[29]亦後世　行法者安隱。

[0178c29] 復次昔野火燒林。林
中有一雉懃身自力。[179a]飛
入水中漬其毛羽來滅大火。
火大水少往來疲乏不以為
苦。是時天帝釋來問之言。
汝作何等。答言。我救此林
愍眾生故。此林蔭育處廣清
涼快樂。我諸種類及諸宗親
并諸眾生皆依仰此。我有身
力云何懈怠而不救之。天帝
問言。汝乃精懃當至幾時。
雉言。以死為期。天帝言。
汝心雖爾誰證知者。

简体字　　　　　　　　　　　　　　正體字

at that time. The Dharma of the Buddha had disappeared as well. There was a brahman who said, "I possess one verse of the Dharma of the Āryas. If you are truly one who loves the Dharma, I will give it to you."

He replied, "I truly do love the Dharma."

The Brahman said, "If you truly do love the Dharma, then you ought to use your skin as paper, ought to use the bones of your body as a pen, and ought to use your blood [as ink] to write it down. Then I will give it to you."

[Lover of Dharma] then did as he had been requested to do, breaking his bones, stripping off his skin, and writing down this verse with his blood:

> In accordance with Dharma one should cultivate.
> That which is non-Dharma one should not accept.
> In the present life and in the future life as well,
> He who practices Dharma is peaceful and secure.

3. Story: The Bird That Tried to Save a Burning Forest

Then again, once upon a time in the past there was a wildfire which was burning up a forest. There was a pheasant in that forest which, with diligent physical efforts, used his own strength to fly into the water, soak his feathers, and then fly forth, attempting thereby to extinguish the great blaze. The fire was great and water was but little. It flew back and forth repeatedly and, even though it became exhausted, it did not find that to be suffering. The god Śakradevendra manifested at that time, coming forth to ask [the bird], "Just what is it that you are trying to do, anyway?"

It replied, "I am [attempting to] save this forest out of pity for the beings in it. The area nurtured by the shade of this forest is vast, refreshingly cool, and blissful. All of our species—all of our lineages and relatives as well as all of the other beings rely upon this forest. As long as I have any remaining physical strength, how could I be lazy and so fail to rescue it?"

That lord of the heavens asked it, "As for your being so energetic and diligent, how much longer do you suppose you can continue this way?"

The pheasant said, "I take the point of my death as the appointed hour."

That lord of the heavens then asked, "Although your intentions may be so, who would be able to verify and really know that [what you claim is true]?"

即自立誓。我心至诚信不虚者火即当灭。是时净居天。知菩萨弘誓。即为灭火。自古及今唯有此林。[1]常独蔚茂不为火烧。如是等种种。宿世所行难为能为。不惜身命国财妻子象马七珍头目[2]骨髓勤施不倦。如说。菩萨为诸众生。一日之中千死千生如檀尸忍禅。般若波罗蜜中所行如是。菩萨本生经中种种因缘相。是为身精进。于诸善法修行。信乐不生疑悔而不懈怠。从一切贤圣。下至凡[3]人求法无厌。如海吞流。是为菩萨心精进。问曰。心无厌足是事不然。所以者何。若所求事办所愿[4]已成是则应足。若理不可求事不可办。亦应舍废。

即自立誓。我心至誠信不虛者火即當滅。是時淨居天。知菩薩弘誓。即為滅火。自古及今唯有此林。[1]常獨蔚茂不為火燒。如是等種種。宿世所行難為能為。不惜身命國財妻子象馬七珍頭目[2]骨髓勤施不倦。如說。菩薩為諸眾生。一日之中千死千生如檀尸忍禪。般若波羅蜜中所行如是。菩薩本生經中種種因緣相。是為身精進。於諸善法修行。信樂不生疑悔而不懈怠。從一切賢聖。下至凡[3]人求法無厭。如海吞流。是為菩薩心精進。問曰。心無厭足是事不然。所以者何。若所求事辦所願[4]已成是則應足。若理不可求事不可辦。亦應捨廢。

简体字   正體字

[The pheasant] then immediately set forth a vow, stating "My mind is ultimately sincere. If in its trustworthiness it is free of any falseness, may it be that this blaze should be immediately extinguished."

At this very time, the gods of the Pure Dwelling Heaven became aware of the bodhisattva's vow and then immediately extinguished the fire for its sake. From ancient times on up to the present, it is only this one forest which has always been growing luxuriantly and which has remained unburned by any fires.

4. SUMMATION ON PHYSICAL VIGOR

All sorts of other cases such as these illustrate that, in that which has been carried out in practice in his previous lifetimes, he has been able to do what is difficult to do. He has not indulged any cherishing regard even for his own body and life, his country, his wealth, wives, sons, elephants, horses, the seven precious things, his head, eyes, bones, or his marrow. He has been diligent in giving without weariness.

As the saying goes, "For the sake of beings, the bodhisattva would undergo in a single day even a thousand deaths and a thousand births." The practices undertaken in perfecting the *pāramitās* of *dāna*, *śīla*, patience, dhyāna and prajñā are of this same sort. The characteristic features of what is intended by "vigor associated with the body" are as illustrated by all sorts of causal circumstances described in the *Sutra on the Past Lives of the Bodhisattva*.

5. SUMMATION ON MENTAL VIGOR

The carrying on of cultivation in all good dharmas while maintaining faith and happiness, while not generating doubts or regrets, while not falling into laziness, and while continuing to seek the Dharma insatiably from all of the Worthies, the Āryas, and everyone on down even to the common people, doing so in a manner comparable to the sea's swallowing up of everything flowing into it—it is this which constitutes the mental vigor of the bodhisattva.

O. CHALLENGE: ISN'T UNREMITTING VIGOR A FALLACIOUS CONCEPT?

Question: For the mind to be insatiable is a situation which does not exist. Why? If that endeavor which one seeks [to accomplish] is finished and if that which one wishes for has already been completed, then one ought to be satisfied. If there is some principle which cannot be sought out or some endeavor which cannot be finished, then it ought to be the case that one relinquishes it and thus diminishes

[5]云何恒无厌足。如人穿井求泉。用功转多。转无水相。则应止息。亦如行道。已到所在不应复行。云何恒无厌足。答曰。菩萨精进。不可以世间譬喻为比。如穿井力少则不能得水。非无水也。若此处无水馀处必有如有所至。[6]必求至佛至佛无厌诲人不倦。故言无厌。复次菩萨精进志愿弘旷。誓度一切[7]而众生无尽。是故精进亦不可尽。汝言事办应止是事不然。虽得至佛众生[179b]未尽不应休息。譬如火相若不灭终[8]不冷。菩萨精进亦复如是。未入灭度终不休息。以是故十八不共法中。欲及精进二事常修。复次菩萨不住法住般若波罗蜜中不废精进。是菩萨精进非佛精进。复次菩萨未得菩萨道。生死身

[5]云何恒無厭足。如人穿井求泉。用功轉多。轉無水相。則應止息。亦如行道。已到所在不應復行。云何恒無厭足。答曰。菩薩精進。不可以世間譬喻為比。如穿井力少則不能得水。非無水也。若此處無水餘處必有如有所至。[6]必求至佛至佛無厭誨人不倦。故言無厭。復次菩薩精進志願弘曠。誓度一切[7]而眾生無盡。是故精進亦不可盡。汝言事辦應止是事不然。雖得至佛眾生[179b]未盡不應休息。譬如火相若不滅終[8]不冷。菩薩精進亦復如是。未入滅度終不休息。以是故十八不共法中。欲及精進二事常修。復次菩薩不住法住般若波羅蜜中不廢精進。是菩薩精進非佛精進。復次菩薩未得菩薩道。生死身

简体字

正體字

one's efforts. How could one be eternally insatiable? It is just as with a person who digs a well or seeks for a spring: If one invests ever more effort at the task and there are fewer and fewer signs of water, then one ought to stop and desist. This is also comparable to when one travels a road: Once one has reached his destination, he needn't travel further. How could it be that one might remain eternally insatiable?

P. Response: Not So, for Vigor Continues On, Unabated

Response: One cannot employ worldly analogies in making comparisons about the vigor of the bodhisattva. Indeed, it *is* just as with the digging of a well. If one's strength is only slight, then one remains unable to find water. It is not the case that there is no water. If there is no water in this place, then it certainly does exist somewhere else. It is also just as when one has some place to which one is going. One must certainly continue seeking buddhahood until one has successfully reached it. Even once one reaches buddhahood, one does not indulge any weariness. One never tires of teaching people. It is on this basis that one speaks of "insatiability."

Moreover, the vigor of the bodhisattva entails determination and aspiration which are immense and vast. He vows to cross everyone over to liberation, this even though beings are inexhaustible in number. Therefore the vigor itself must also be inexhaustible. When you claim that once one has expended effort in the carrying out of an endeavor, it ought to be allowed to come to an end, this is incorrect. Although one [eventually] succeeds in reaching buddhahood, because even then beings have not yet been brought to an end, one still should not rest.

This is analogous to the characteristic nature of fire which, if not extinguished, never grows cold. The vigor of the bodhisattva is just like this. So long as he has not yet crossed on over into a liberation involving cessation, he refrains from resting. It is for this reason that the eternal cultivation of zeal and vigor are qualities contained among the eighteen dharmas exclusive to a buddha.

Furthermore, [as stated in the Sutra]: "It is by resort to the dharma of non-abiding that the bodhisattva abides in the *prajñāpāramitā*." Thus he does not allow his cultivation of vigor to diminish. And this vigor practiced by the bodhisattva is still not that of a buddha.

Q. Examples of the Unremitting Nature of the Bodhisattva's Vigor

Furthermore, so long as the bodhisattva has not yet gained realization of the path of the bodhisattva, he continues to employ that body

以好事施众生。众生反更以
不善事加之。或有众生。菩
萨赞美反更毁辱。菩萨恭敬
而反轻慢。菩萨慈念反求其
过。谋欲中伤。此众生等无
有[9]力势来恼菩萨。菩萨于
此众生发弘誓愿。我得佛道
要当度此恶中之恶诸众生
辈。于此恶中其心不懈生大
悲心。譬如慈母怜其子病忧
念不舍如是相是为菩萨精
进。复次行布施波罗蜜时。
十方种种乞儿来欲求索。不
应索者皆来索之。及[10]所
爱重难舍之物。语菩萨言。
与我两眼。与我头脑骨髓爱
重妻子及诸贵价珍宝。如是
等难舍之物。乞者强索。其
心不动悭瞋不起。见疑心不
生。一心为佛道故布施。

以好事施眾生。眾生反更以
不善事加之。或有眾生。菩
薩讚美反更毀辱。菩薩恭敬
而反輕慢。菩薩慈念反求其
過。謀欲中傷。此眾生等無
有[9]力勢來惱菩薩。菩薩於
此眾生發弘誓願。我得佛道
要當度此惡中之惡諸眾生
輩。於此惡中其心不懈生大
悲心。譬如慈母憐其子病憂
念不捨如是相是為菩薩精
進。復次行布施波羅蜜時。
十方種種乞兒來欲求索。不
應索者皆來索之。及[10]所
愛重難捨之物。語菩薩言。
與我兩眼。與我頭腦骨髓愛
重妻子及諸貴價珍寶。如是
等難捨之物。乞者強索。其
心不動慳瞋不起。見疑心不
生。一心為佛道故布施。

简体字   正體字

subject to birth and death in providing those fine things which he endeavors to bestow on beings.

It may be that, contrary to what might be expected, beings [not only do not respond in kind], they go so far as to afflict him with circumstances which are not good. [For instance], there may be beings who, when the bodhisattva praises their fine qualities, they proceed in contrary fashion to besmirch his reputation and heap abuse upon him. It may also be that, even though the bodhisattva may be respectful and reverential [to beings], they nonetheless respond by acting in such a contrary fashion that they slight him and treat him with condescension. There may also be times when, although the bodhisattva remains motivated by kindness in his mindfulness of others, still, they counter this by seeking out his faults and plotting to do him harm.

[In spite of all this], these beings are nonetheless all equally bereft of any power whereby they might visit torment on the bodhisattva. The bodhisattva has brought forth a great vow with respect to these beings, "When I gain the path to buddhahood, I must cross on over to liberation even these beings who belong to the class of the most evil among the evil." Even in the midst of all this evil, his mind still does not become indolent. Consequently he continues to bring forth the mind of great kindness. In doing so, he is like the lovingly-kind mother who feels pity for her son in his illness, who is beset with worry about him, who continues to remain mindful of him, and who never forsakes him. Characteristic features such as these are emblematic of that vigor in which the bodhisattva engages.

Moreover, when one practices the *pāramitā* of giving, all sorts of beggars come from the ten directions, seeking things and making demands. Even that which they should not demand. they nonetheless come and demand while also demanding those things which one loves most intensely. They say to the bodhisattva, "Give me both of your eyes. Give me your head, brains, bones, marrow, the wife and son which you love so dearly, and also give me all of your extremely valuable precious jewels."

Those beggars forcefully demand such difficult to relinquish things as these. Nonetheless, his mind does not move and neither miserliness nor hatred arise in him in response to these circumstances. The mind which indulges views or doubts does not develop in him. He proceeds to make such gifts single-mindedly and for the sake of realizing the path to buddhahood. Thus in his actions, he

譬如须弥山四方风吹所不能动。如是种种相。是名精进波罗蜜。复次菩萨精进。遍行五波罗蜜。是为精进波罗蜜。问曰。若行戒波罗蜜时。若有人来乞三衣鉢[11]盂。若与之则毁戒。[12]何以故佛不听故。若不与则破檀波罗蜜。精进云何遍行五事。答曰。若新行菩萨。则不能一世一时遍行五波罗蜜。如菩萨行檀波罗蜜时。见饿虎饥急欲食其子。菩萨是时兴大悲心即以身施。菩萨父母以失子故。忧愁懊恼两目失明。虎杀菩萨亦应得罪而[179c]不筹量。父母忧苦虎得杀罪。但欲满檀自得福德。又如持戒比丘。随事轻重摈。诸犯法。

简体字

譬如須彌山四方風吹所不能動。如是種種相。是名精進波羅蜜。復次菩薩精進。遍行五波羅蜜。是為精進波羅蜜。問曰。若行戒波羅蜜時。若有人來乞三衣鉢[11]盂。若與之則毀戒。[12]何以故佛不聽故。若不與則破檀波羅蜜。精進云何遍行五事。答曰。若新行菩薩。則不能一世一時遍行五波羅蜜。如菩薩行檀波羅蜜時。見餓虎飢急欲食其子。菩薩是時興大悲心即以身施。菩薩父母以失子故。憂愁懊惱兩目失明。虎殺菩薩亦應得罪而[179c]不籌量。父母憂苦虎得殺罪。但欲滿檀自得福德。又如持戒比丘。隨事輕重擯。諸犯法。

正體字

is comparable to Mount Sumeru which, when the four directions' winds blow, cannot be moved by them. All sorts of characteristic features such as these are emblematic of the *pāramitā* of vigor.

Furthermore, the vigor of the bodhisattva is universally active throughout his practice of the other five *pāramitās*. It is this which constitutes the *pāramitā* of vigor.

R. CHALLENGE: ONE PERFECTION CAN'T BE OPERATIVE IN THE OTHERS

Question: If when one is practicing the *pāramitā* of vigor, someone comes and begs one's three robes and bowl, if one gives them to him, he will break the precepts, [thus failing in the *pāramitā* of moral virtue]. How is this so? It is because the Buddha did not permit [one to part with the robes or the bowl]. If one fails to give, however, one thereby destroys the *pāramitā* of vigor. How then can vigor be universally operative in the other five endeavors?

S. RESPONSE: INDEED, IT *IS* IMPOSSIBLE FOR ONE NEW TO THE PRACTICE

Response: [In fact], if one is a bodhisattva new in his practice, then he will *not* be able to make [the perfection of vigor] universally operative in the other five *pāramitās* in a way which is simultaneous even across the course of a single lifetime.

1. STORY: SHAKYAMUNI'S PAST-LIFE GIFT TO THE TIGRESS

This point is well illustrated by that time when the [past-life Shakyamuni] Bodhisattva was practicing the *pāramitā* of vigor and observed a starving tigress whose hunger had become so urgent that she was about to eat her cubs. The Bodhisattva then let flourish the mind of great compassion and immediately made a gift [to the tigress] of his body.

Because the Bodhisattva's father and mother had lost their son, their distress and grief were such that they lost the vision in both eyes. It should also be the case that the tigress must have incurred a karmic offense associated with the killing of the Bodhisattva. Nonetheless, he failed to take into account the grief-caused suffering on the part of his parents or the tigress's incurring of the offense of killing. He wished only to perfect the practice of *dāna* and thus realize for himself the associated merit.

2. EXAMPLE: SO, TOO, THE BHIKSHU OBSERVING MORAL VIRTUE

This is also exemplified by the bhikshu who upholds the precepts. No matter what the situation, whether it might involve a minor or a major regulation, he rejects anyone with whom a transgression might occur. Even though the person who is rejected might

被擯之人愁苦懊恼。但欲持戒不愍其苦。或时行世俗般若息慈悲心。如释迦[13]牟尼菩萨。宿世为大国王太子。父王有梵志[14]师不食[15]五谷。众[16]人敬信以为奇特。太子思惟人有四体[17]必资五谷。而此人不食必是曲取人心非[18]真法也。父母告子此人精进不食[19]五谷是世希有。汝何愚甚而不敬之。太子答言。愿小留意。此人不久证验自出。是时太子求其住处至林树间。问林中牧牛人。此人何所食噉。牧牛者答言。此人夜中少多服[20]酥以自全命。太子知已还宫欲出其证验。即以种种诸下药草熏青莲华。

简体字

被擯之人愁苦懊惱。但欲持戒不愍其苦。或時行世俗般若息慈悲心。如釋迦[13]牟尼菩薩。宿世為大國王太子。父王有梵志[14]師不食[15]五穀。眾[16]人敬信以為奇特。太子思惟人有四體[17]必資五穀。而此人不食必是曲取人心非[18]真法也。父母告子此人精進不食[19]五穀是世希有。汝何愚甚而不敬之。太子答言。願小留意。此人不久證驗自出。是時太子求其住處至林樹間。問林中牧牛人。此人何所食噉。牧牛者答言。此人夜中少多服[20]酥以自全命。太子知已還宮欲出其證驗。即以種種諸下藥草熏青蓮華。

正體字

experiences the anguish of distress and grief [at his refusal to accede to precept-threatening conduct], he strives only to uphold the precepts and does not take pity on the sufferings of others which might arise as a consequence.

T. Bodhisattvas Focus at Times Solely on Worldly Prajñā

It may be in some instances that because one is focused on the practice of the common prajñā of the world, one sets aside the mind of kindness and compassion.

1. Example: Buddha's Past Life as a Doubting Prince

This is well illustrated by the case of Shakyamuni when, as a bodhisattva in a previous life, he was a prince, the son of a great country's king. His father, the King, had taken as his own guru a *brahmacārin* who [claimed] to refrain from eating any of the five types of grains. The masses generally revered him, esteemed him with their faith, held him up as marvelously special.

The Prince pondered this matter, reflecting, "Men all possess [a body with] the four limbs. They must sustain it with the five types of grains, and yet this man [supposedly] does not eat. It must certainly be the case that he has seized the minds of the population through deviousness. He must not be one who is possessed of the genuine Dharma."

His father and mother spoke to their son, saying "This man is intensely vigorous [in his spiritual cultivation]. He does not eat the five types of grains and thus is a person only rarely encountered in this world. How can it be that you persist in being so extremely foolish that you do not respect him?"

The Prince replied by saying, "I pray that you may devote a little attention to this matter. It will not be long before this man's verification will naturally emerge." The Prince then sought out [the Guru's] dwelling place and went into the adjoining forest where he proceeded to inquire of the woodland cowherds, asking, "Well, just what is it that this fellow eats, anyway?"

The cowherds replied, "At night, this man eats a greater or lesser measure of curds, relying on this as the means by which to sustain his life." When the Prince became aware of this, he returned to the palace with the desire to bring forth his verification of the facts. He then used a variety of purgative medicinal herbs and caused them to permeate some blue lotus blossoms.

清旦梵志入宫坐王边。太子
手执此花来供养之拜已授
与。梵志欢喜自念。王及夫
人内外大小皆服事我。唯太
子不见敬信。今日以好华供
养甚善无量。得此好华敬所
来处。举以向鼻嗅之。华中
药气入腹。须臾腹内药作欲
求下处。太子言。梵志不食
何缘向厕。急捉之须臾便吐
王边。吐中纯[*]酥。证验现
已。王与夫人乃知其诈。太
子言。此人真贼求名故以诳
一国。如是行世俗般若。但
求满智。寝怜愍心不畏人
瞋。或时菩萨行出世间般
若。于持戒布施心不染着。
何以故施者受者所施财物。
于罪不罪于瞋不瞋。于进于
怠摄心散心不可得故。复次
菩萨行精进波罗蜜。于一切
[21]法不生不灭非常非无常
非苦非乐非空非实非我非无
[180a]我非一非异非有非无。

清旦梵志入宮坐王邊。太子
手執此花來供養之拜已授
與。梵志歡喜自念。王及夫
人內外大小皆服事我。唯太
子不見敬信。今日以好華供
養甚善無量。得此好華敬所
來處。舉以向鼻嗅之。華中
藥氣入腹。須臾腹內藥作欲
求下處。太子言。梵志不食
何緣向廁。急捉之須臾便吐
王邊。吐中純[*]酥。證驗現
已。王與夫人乃知其詐。太
子言。此人真賊求名故以誆
一國。如是行世俗般若。但
求滿智。寢憐愍心不畏人
瞋。或時菩薩行出世間般
若。於持戒布施心不染著。
何以故施者受者所施財物。
於罪不罪於瞋不瞋。於進於
怠攝心散心不可得故。復次
菩薩行精進波羅蜜。於一切
[21]法不生不滅非常非無常
非苦非樂非空非實非我非無
[180a]我非一非異非有非無。

简体字　　　　　　　正體字

Early the next morning, that brahmacārin [guru] entered the palace [once again] and sat down alongside the King. The Prince then took up these flower blossoms in his hands and came forward to make an offering to [the Guru]. After having bowed before him, he presented [the flowers] to him. The Brahmacārin was delighted and thought to himself, "The King, his wife, those within and those without, the great ones, the lesser ones—they all make obeisance to me and serve me.

"Heretofore it has only been the Prince from whom I received neither reverence nor faith. Today, however, he makes an offering of beautiful flowers to me. This is extremely fine, immeasurably so."

Having received these beautiful flower blossoms, as a demonstration of respect for the place from which they came, he then raised them to his nose and inhaled [their fragrance]. The medicinal vapors within the blossoms then entered his belly. In but an instant, the medicine went to work in his belly. He was seized by the need to find a place to stoop down. The Prince then said, "The Brahmacārin does not eat. Why then does he now move towards the toilet?" [As he said this], he held [the Brahmacārin] tightly and in but a moment [that guru] vomited there alongside the King.

[As it turned out], the vomit was composed entirely of curds. When this verification of the facts had been revealed, the King and his wife both realized how he had deceived them. The Prince then said, "This man is truly a thief. Out of a desire for fame, he has cheated an entire country."

So it was that he devoted himself to the cultivation of common worldly prajñā, seeking only to fulfill his wisdom. Thus, in doing so, he set aside the mind of sympathy and pity and did not fear incurring the hatred of others.

2. Bodhisattvas Focus on World-Transcending Prajñā

At other times, the bodhisattva practices world-transcending prajñā. In upholding precepts and bestowing gifts, his mind remains free of defiling attachment. Why? Because the donor, the recipient, the valuable gift, offense, non-offense, hatred, non-hatred, vigor, laziness, the focused mind, and the scattered mind—none of these are apprehensible. Moreover, in practicing the *pāramitā* of vigor, the bodhisattva takes all dharmas to be neither produced nor destroyed, neither eternal nor non-eternal, neither suffering nor blissful, neither empty nor real, neither self nor non-self, neither singular nor different, and neither existent nor nonexistent.

尽知一切诸法因缘和合。但有名字实相不可得。菩萨作如是观。知一切有为皆是虚诳心息无为。欲灭其心唯以寂灭为安隐。尔时念本愿怜愍众生故。还行菩萨法集诸功德。菩萨自念我虽知诸法虚诳。众生不知是事。于五道中受诸苦痛。我今当具足行六波罗蜜。菩萨[1]报得神通。亦得佛道三十二相八十种好。一切智慧大慈大悲无碍解脱。十力四无所畏十八不共法三达等无量诸佛法。得是法时一切众生皆得信净。皆能受行爱乐佛法能办是事。皆是精进波罗蜜力。是为精进波罗蜜。如佛所说。[2]尔时菩萨精进不见身不见心。身无所作心无所念。身心一等而无分别。所求佛道以度众生。不见众生为此岸。

簡体字

盡知一切諸法因緣和合。但有名字實相不可得。菩薩作如是觀。知一切有為皆是虛誑心息無為。欲滅其心唯以寂滅為安隱。爾時念本願憐愍眾生故。還行菩薩法集諸功德。菩薩自念我雖知諸法虛誑。眾生不知是事。於五道中受諸苦痛。我今當具足行六波羅蜜。菩薩[1]報得神通。亦得佛道三十二相八十種好。一切智慧大慈大悲無礙解脫。十力四無所畏十八不共法三達等無量諸佛法。得是法時一切眾生皆得信淨。皆能受行愛樂佛法能辦是事。皆是精進波羅蜜力。是為精進波羅蜜。如佛所說。[2]爾時菩薩精進不見身不見心。身無所作心無所念。身心一等而無分別。所求佛道以度眾生。不見眾生為此岸。

正體字

He completely realizes that all dharmas are but a conjunction of causes and conditions, that they possess only names, and that no characteristic of ultimate reality can be found in them. The bodhisattva carries on this sort of contemplation and so realizes that everything which is conditioned is in fact false and deceptive. He lets his mind rest in the unconditioned and desires to bring his thoughts to cessation, [realizing that] it is only by resort to quiescent cessation that one achieves peaceful security.

He then calls to mind his original vows and, on account of sympathy and pity for beings, returns to the practice of the dharmas of the bodhisattva and so proceeds to accumulate every sort of merit. The bodhisattva then thinks to himself, "Although I realize that all dharmas are false and deceptive, beings are unaware of this matter. Within the five destinies of rebirth, they endure all manner of suffering and pain. I should now completely perfect the practice of the six *pāramitās*."

U. SUMMATION: THE BODHISATTVA'S PERFECTION OF VIGOR *PĀRAMITĀ*

The bodhisattva gains as karmic reward the superknowledges and also gains the Buddha Path, including the thirty-two major marks, the eighty subsidiary characteristics, all types of wisdom, the great kindness, the great compassion, unobstructed liberation, the ten powers, the four fearlessnesses, the eighteen dharmas exclusive to the Buddha, the three clarities (*trividyā*) and the immeasurable number of other dharmas associated with buddhahood. Once he succeeds in realizing these dharmas, subsequent occurrences wherein all beings may gain the purification of faith, may all be enabled to take on the practice, may all be able to feel affection for and bliss in the Dharma of the Buddha, and may all be enabled to carry out this same endeavor themselves—all of this is a product of the power of the *pāramitā* of vigor.

This is what constitutes the *pāramitā* of vigor. It is just as has been stated by the Buddha: "At that time, the vigor of the bodhisattva becomes such that he does not even perceive [the existence of] a body and does not even perceive [the existence of] a mind. His body has nothing whatsoever which it engages in doing and the mind has nothing whatsoever which it bears in mind. The body and mind become as one and the same and thus there is no making of such distinctions in this regard." In that path to buddhahood which is sought for the sake of bringing beings to deliverance, one does not perceive beings as constituting this shore, nor does he perceive the

佛道为彼岸。一切身心所
作放舍。如梦所为觉无所
作。[3]是名寂灭。诸精进故
名为波罗蜜。所以者何。知
一切精进皆是邪伪故。以一
切作法皆是虚妄不实。如梦
如幻。诸法平等是为真实。
平等法中不应有所求索。是
故知一切精进皆是虚妄。虽
知精进虚妄。而常成就不
退。是名菩萨[4]真实精进。
如佛言。我于无量劫中。头
目髓脑以施众生令其愿满。
持戒忍辱禅定时。在山林中
身体干枯。或持斋节食。或
绝诸色味或忍[5]骂辱刀杖之
患。是故身体焦枯。又常坐
禅曝露懃苦以求智慧。诵读
思惟问难讲说。一切诸法以
智分别好恶麁细虚实多少。
供养无量诸佛。懃懃精进求
此功德。欲具[180b]足五波罗
蜜。我是时[6]无所得。不得
檀尸羼精进禅智慧波罗蜜。

佛道為彼岸。一切身心所
作放捨。如夢所為覺無所
作。[3]是名寂滅。諸精進故
名為波羅蜜。所以者何。知
一切精進皆是邪偽故。以一
切作法皆是虛妄不實。如夢
如幻。諸法平等是為真實。
平等法中不應有所求索。是
故知一切精進皆是虛妄。雖
知精進虛妄。而常成就不
退。是名菩薩[4]真實精進。
如佛言。我於無量劫中。頭
目髓腦以施眾生令其願滿。
持戒忍辱禪定時。在山林中
身體乾枯。或持齋節食。或
絕諸色味或忍[5]罵辱刀杖之
患。是故身體焦枯。又常坐
禪曝露懃苦以求智慧。誦讀
思惟問難講說。一切諸法以
智分別好惡麁細虛實多少。
供養無量諸佛。懃懃精進求
此功德。欲具[180b]足五波羅
蜜。我是時[6]無所得。不得
檀尸羼精進禪智慧波羅蜜。

简体字   正體字

Buddha Path as constituting the opposite shore. Everything done by the body and mind are set aside and relinquished as if they were mere dream-state endeavors which are realized on waking to have not involved the accomplishment of any endeavors at all.

This is what qualifies as quiescent cessation. It is with reference to this that all instances of vigor qualify as constituting *"pāramitā."* How is this so? One realizes that all instances of vigor involve a coursing in [dharmas which by their very character involve] error and deceptiveness. This is because all created dharmas are empty, false, and unreal. They are like a dream and like a magically-conjured illusion.

All dharmas are uniformly equal. This is what is genuinely real. Among these dharmas which are of a single uniform equality, one should not have those which one seeks to obtain. One therefore realizes that all instances of vigor involve that which is empty and false. Although one realizes that vigor involves that which is empty and false, still, he constantly works at perfecting it and does not retreat from engaging in it. This is what qualifies as the genuine vigor of the bodhisattva.

As stated by the Buddha, "Throughout an incalculable number of kalpas I gave my head, eyes, marrow, and brain to beings so as to allow them to fulfill their wishes. When practicing the upholding of precepts, patience, and dhyāna, I dwelt in the mountains and forests wherein my body became dehydrated and emaciated. At times I fasted, reducing the intake of food. At times I cut off all taste for any form of sensual experience. At times I endured the calamities of scolding, vilification, knives and clubs. On these accounts my body became haggard and emaciated.

"Additionally, I constantly sat in dhyāna meditation and so was exposed to the elements and endured intense suffering, this for the sake of seeking wisdom. I recited, studied, pondered upon, asked about, and delivered explanations on [Dharma]. I employed wisdom in reference to each and every dharma, making distinctions with regard to good, evil, coarse, fine, false, real, greater, and lesser.

"I made offerings to an incalculable number of buddhas. I was assiduous and diligent in applying vigor to the seeking of these forms of merit, wishing to completely perfect the other five *pāramitās.* However, throughout this entire time, nothing whatsoever was obtained by me. I did not obtain the *pāramitās* of *dāna, śīla, kṣānti,* vigor, dhyāna, or wisdom.

见然灯佛以五华散佛。布发泥中。得无生法忍。即时六波罗蜜满。于空中立[7]偈赞然灯佛。见十方无量诸佛。是时得实精进身。精进平等故得心平等。心平等故得一切诸法平等。如是种种因缘相。名为精进波罗蜜。

大智度论卷第十六

見然燈佛以五華散佛。布髮泥中。得無生法忍。即時六波羅蜜滿。於空中立[7]偈讚然燈佛。見十方無量諸佛。是時得實精進身。精進平等故得心平等。心平等故得一切諸法平等。如是種種因緣相。名為精進波羅蜜。

大智度論卷第十六

简体字

正體字

"When I encountered Burning Lamp (Dīpaṃkara) Buddha, I scattered five blossoms over the Buddha, laid my hair down in the mud [that he might cross], and gained right then the unproduced-dharmas patience (*anutpattikadharmakṣānti*). The six *pāramitās* were then straightaway fulfilled. I stood there in empty space, praised Burning Lamp Buddha with verses, and then beheld the immeasurable number of buddhas throughout the ten directions. It was at that time that I gained that body which is endowed with genuine vigor."

It is on account of one's vigor being uniformly equal [in its application to all dharmas] that one gains the mind which itself is uniform in its equality. It is on account of one's mind being uniform in its quality that one achieves [that state] wherein all dharmas are [realized as] uniform in their equality.

All sorts of causes, conditions, and characteristics such as these constitute what is meant by "the *pāramitā* of vigor."

Part Four Endnotes

1. These reduced-font parenthetical notes are integral to the Chinese
    text as preserved in the *Taisho* edition of the Buddhist Canon. It is pos-
    sible that they were added by the editorial assistants to the translator,
    Kumārajīva, this in an effort to make the text more intelligible to the
    400 CE-era Chinese audience.

2. Substituting the 夫 of my woodblock edition for the obvious scribal
    error (失) contained in *Taisho*.

3. An *āraṇyaka* is a cultivator of the Path who dwells in the forest.

Part Four Variant Readings from Other Chinese Editions

[174n04] 義第二十七 = 下第二十七 [宋], = 下 [元], = 之餘 [明], = 下第二十二 [宮] [石]

[174n05] 以此五事為 = 如是等名 [宋] [元] [明] [宮] [石]

[174n06] 牟 = 文 [宋] [元] [明] [宮] [石]

[174n07] 以 = 次 [宋] [元] [明] [宮] [石]

[174n08] 休息 = 首伏 [石]

[174n09] 息 = 伏 [宋] [元] [明] [宮] [石]

[174n10] (即) - [宋] [元] [明] [宮]

[174n11] (故) - [宋] [元] [明] [宮] [石]

[174n12] 諸波羅蜜 = 精進 [宋] [元] [明] [宮]

[174n13] (精進) - [宋] [元] [明] [宮] [石]

[174n14] 智慧 + (等諸善法) [宋] [元] [明] [宮] [石]

[174n15] (聖) + 王 [宋] [元] [明] [宮] [石]

[174n16] 愛子 = 母 [宋] [元] [明] [宮] [石]

[174n17] 病 = 疾 [宋] [元] [明] [宮] [石]

[175n01] (無一) - [宮]

[175n02] (爾時) - [宋] [元] [明] [宮] [石]

[175n03] 觀 + (得神通力見) [宋] [宮] [石], (得神通力以天眼見) [元] [明]

[175n04] 各失所樂 = 以失樂為苦 [宋] [元] [明] [宮] [石]

[175n05] 爍 = 烙 [元] [明]

[175n06] 鷟 = 鴡 [宋] [宮], = 鷟 [元] [明], = [矛*鳥] [石]

[175n07] 隔 = 翻 [宋] [宮]

[175n08] [口*(甚-其+庚)] = 距 [宋] [元] [明] [宮] [石]

[175n09] [革*卬] = 鞭 [宋] [元] [明] [宮]

[175n10] 蝎 = 蠍 [元] [明]

[175n11] 鷟 = 鵰 [宋] [元] [明] [宮], = [矛*鳥] [石]

[175n12] (恚) - [宋] [元] [明] [宮]

[175n13] 短 = 施 [石]

[175n14] [狂-王+哥]獲 = [聲-耳+加]獲 [石]

[175n15] 饕 = 餐 [石]

[175n16] 瘧 = 虐 [宋] [元] [明] [宮]

[175n17] 生中 = 中生 [宋] [元] [宮]

[175n18] 劬 = 瞿 [宋] [元] [明] [宮]

[175n19] 三十三天 = 忉利天 [宋] [元] [明] [宮] [石]* [* 1 2]

[175n20] (天) - [宋] [元] [明] [宮]

[175n21] 蓬 = 鬆 [宋] [元] [明] [宮]

[175n22] 歐 = 嘔 [宋] [元] [明] [宮]

[175n23] (汁) - [宋] [元] [明] [宮] [石]

[175n24] 彼 = 被 [宋] [元] [明] [宮] [石]

[175n25] 諍 = 爭 [宋] [元] [明] [宮]*

[175n26] 槊 = 稍 [宋] [元] [明] [宮], = 梢 [石]* [* 1]

[175n27] 又 = 釵 [宋] [宮] [石]* [* 1 2 3 4 5]

[175n28] 鑕 = 弗 [宋] [元] [明] [宮]

[175n29] 以 = 把 [宋] [元] [明] [宮] [石]

[175n30] 咄 = 啜 [石]

[176n01] 煞之 = 教人 [宋] [元] [明] [宮] [石]

[176n02] 肢 = 支 [宋] [元] [明] [宮]

[176n03] 揣 = 剬 [宋] [元] [明] [宮]

[176n04] 忠 = 中 [宋] [宮] [石]

[176n05] 無義 = 綺 [宋] [元] [明] [宮] [石]

[176n06] 故 = 故故 [宋] [元] [明] [宮]

[176n07] 鳥 = 象 [宋] [元] [明] [宮] [石]* [* 1]

[176n08] 嚙[齒*齊] = 齧[齒*查] [宋] [元] [明] [宮]

[176n09] 笮 = 迮 [石]* [* 1]

[176n10] 桃 = 萄 [宋] [元] [明] [宮], = 陶 [石]

[176n11] 諍 = 爭 [元] [明]

[176n12] (多殘賊) + 如 [宋] [石], (多相殘賊) + 如 [元] [明]

[176n13] (多殘賊) - [宋] [元] [明] [宮] [石]

[176n14] 為 = 受 [宋] [元] [明] [宮]

[176n15] 壓 = 押 [宋] [元] [明] [宮] [石]

[176n16] 赤 = 赭 [宋] [元] [明] [宮] [石]

[176n17] (大將軍) + 小 [宋] [元] [明]

[176n18] 剉 = 刺 [宋] [元] [明] [宮] [石]

[176n19] 壓 = 庘 [石]

[176n20] 纔 = 裁 [元] [宮] [石]

[176n21] 以 = 已 [宋] [元] [明] [宮] [石]

[176n22] 嘷 = 號 [宋] [元] [明] [宮]

[176n23] 斗秤 = 斗秤 [宋] [元] [宮], = 斗稱 [明] [石]

[176n24] 唤 = 呼 [宋] [元] [明] [宮] [石]
[176n25] 譎 = 決 [宋] [宮], (譎) - [石]
[176n26] (秦言喜大喜也) - [明]
[176n27] 滿中 = 中滿 [石]
[176n28] (中) - [宋] [元] [明] [宮] [石]
[176n29] 屎 = 灰 [元] [明] [宮] [石]
[176n30] 濃 = 膿 [元] [明]
[176n31] 而自 = 自而 [石]
[176n32] (於諸) - [宋] [宮] [石]
[176n33] 炙 = 燀 [宋] [元] [明] [宮], = 爛 [石]
[176n34] (及天神) - [宋] [元] [明] [宮] [石]
[176n35] 椎椎 = 槌槌 [宋] [元] [明] [宮]
[176n36] 挓 = [序-予+(扗-(打-丁))] [宋] [宮], = 磔 [元] [明]* [* 1]
[176n37] 挽 = 椀 [宋]
[176n38] 抱 = 把 [宮]
[176n39] (中) + 有 [宋] [元] [明] [宮] [石]
[176n40] 斫 = 破 [石]
[176n41] 破 + (碎) [宋] [元] [明] [宮] [石]
[176n42] (罪人) - [石]
[176n43] 杙杙 = 弋弋 [宋] [元] [明] [宮]
[176n44] 委頓 = 萎熟 [宋] [宮] [石], = 萎頓 [元] [明]
[176n45] 唐突 = 唐突 [宋] [元] [明] [宮]
[176n46] 顛蹟 = 蹟仆 [宋] [宮], = 顛仆 [元] [明]
[176n47] (諸) - [宋] [宮] [石]
[176n48] 法 + (實言非實非實言實) [宋] [元] [明] [宮] [石]
[176n49] (周圍其外) - [宋] [元] [明] [宮] [石]
[176n50] 孔 + (也) [石]
[176n51] 阿 = 呵 [宋] [元] [明] [宮]
[177n01] 戰 = 顫 [宋] [元] [明] [宮]
[177n02] (是) - [明]
[177n03] 蓮 = 黄 [元]
[177n04] 也 = 色 [宋], (也) - [石]* [* 1]
[177n05] 花 + (色) [明]
[177n06] 排 = 推 [宋] [元] [明] [宮]*
[177n07] (細) + 虫 [宋] [元] [明] [宮] [石]
[177n08] 持 = 打 [宮]
[177n09] 壓 = 押 [宋] [宮]
[177n10] 鳥 = 鳥 [宋] [元] [明] [宮] [石]
[177n11] 槍 = 鏘 [宋] [元] [明] [宮] [石]

[177n12] 道 = 通 [宮] [石]
[177n13] 撥徹 = 發撤 [元] [明]
[177n14] (利) - [宋] [元] [明] [宮] [石]* [* 1]
[177n15] 者 = 中 [宋] [元] [明] [宮] [石]
[177n16] 竪 = 堅 [石]
[177n17] 林 = 樹 [宋] [元] [明] [宮]
[177n18] 復 + (作) [宋] [元] [明] [宮] [石]
[177n19] (之) - [宋] [元] [明] [宮] [石]
[177n20] 排 = 推 [宋] [元] [明]
[177n21] 受此 = 此受 [石]
[177n22] 腹 = 焦 [宋] [元] [明] [宮]
[177n23] 酥 = 蘇 [宋] [元] [宮]
[177n24] 頌 = 阿 [宋] [元] [明] [宮] [石]
[177n25] ((多有…處))十八字 = ((時有間暫得休息尼羅浮陀無間無休息時))十七字 [宋] [元] [明] [宮] [石]
[177n26] 呵 = 阿 [明]
[177n27] 戰 = 顫 [宋] [元] [明] [宮]
[177n28] 浹 = [泳-永+甲] [石]
[177n29] 迦 = 伽 [宋] [元] [明] [宮]
[177n30] 拷 = 栲 [宋] [元] [宮]
[177n31] 守 = 學 [元] [明]
[177n32] 四等心勝處 = 四無量心八勝處八 [宋] [元] [明] [宮] [石]
[177n33] 處 = 入 [宋] [元] [宮], 處 + (入) [石]
[177n34] 處 = 止 [宮] [石]
[177n35] 使 = 施 [明]
[177n36] (心) - [宋] [宮] [石]
[177n37] 不沒不退 = 不退不沒 [宋] [元] [明] [宮]
[177n38] 名 + (名) [宮]
[178n01] (經) - [宋] [宮] [石]
[178n02] (故) - [宋] [元] [明] [宮]
[178n03] (而有) - [宮] [石]
[178n04] (有) - [宋] [元] [明] [宮] [石]
[178n05] (口) - [元] [明] [宮] [石]
[178n06] 於 = 從 [宋] [元] [明] [宮] [石]
[178n07] 化 = 作 [宋] [元] [明] [宮]
[178n08] 懈廢 = 癈懈 [石]
[178n09] (野) - [宋] [元] [明] [宮]
[178n10] 牟尼 = 文 [宋] [元] [明] [宮] [石]
[178n11] 人 = 又 [石]
[178n12] 矢 = 箭 [宋] [元] [明] [宮] [石]

[178n13] 人王 = 王言 [宋] [元] [明] [宮]
[178n14] 輒當 = 當自 [宋] [元] [明] [宮] [石]
[178n15] 意 = 言 [宮]
[178n16] (送應次者) - [宋] [元] [明] [宮] [石]
[178n17] (時) - [宋] [元] [明] [宮] [石]
[178n18] 子 + (次至應送) [宋] [元] [明] [宮] [石]
[178n19] 當應 = 應當 [宋] [元] [明] [宮]
[178n20] 既 = 明 [石]
[178n21] 俎 = 俎 [宋] [元] [明] [宮]
[178n22] 併 = 并 [宋] [元] [明] [宮]
[178n23] 與 + (夫) [石]
[178n24] 無 = 亦何 [宋] [元] [明] [宮], = 亦何以 [石]
[178n25] 言 = 曰 [明]
[178n26] 獸 = 生 [宋] [元] [明] [宮]
[178n27] 愛法 = 法愛 [宋] [宮]
[178n28] 偈 = 之 [宮]
[178n29] 亦 = 及 [宋] [元] [明] [石], = 乃 [宮]
[179n01] 常 = 當 [宋] [元] [明] [宮]
[179n02] 骨髓 = 髓惱 [宋] [宮], = 髓腦 [明] [石]
[179n03] 人 = 夫 [宋] [元] [明] [宮]
[179n04] 已 = 以 [宋] [宮] [石]
[179n05] (云何恒無厭足) - [宮] [石]
[179n06] 必求至佛至佛 = 必至得佛以此 [石], = 得佛為到以此 [宮]
[179n07] (而) - [宋] [元] [明] [宮] [石]
[179n08] 不冷 = 無不燒 [宋] [元] [明] [宮] [石]
[179n09] (力) - [宮]
[179n10] 所愛 = 索所 [宋] [元] [明] [宮] [石]
[179n11] 盂 = 扞 [石]
[179n12] (何以故佛不聽故) - [宮] [石]
[179n13] 牟 = 文 [宋] [元] [明] [宮] [石]
[179n14] 師 + (詐以) [宋] [元] [明] [宮] [石]
[179n15] 五穀 = 惑物 [宮] [石]
[179n16] 人 = 生 [宮]
[179n17] 必資五穀 = 要必有食 [宮] [石]
[179n18] 真 = 其 [石]
[179n19] (五穀) - [宋] [元] [明] [宮] [石]

[179n20] 酥 = 蘇 [宋] [元] [宮]* [* 1]
[179n21] 法 = 諸法 [宋] [元] [明] [宮] [石]
[180n01] 報得 = 得生報 [宋] [元] [明] [宮] [石]
[180n02] (爾時) - [宋] [元] [明] [宮]
[180n03] (是名寂) - [石]
[180n04] (真) - [宋] [宮] [石]
[180n05] 罵 = 詈 [宋] [元] [明] [宮]
[180n06] 無 = 未有 [宋] [元] [明] [宮], (無) - [石]
[180n07] (偈) - [宋] [元] [明] [宮] [石]

Part Five:

THE PERFECTION OF DHYĀNA MEDITATION

(Chapter 28)

Part Five Contents

Nāgārjuna on the Perfection of Dhyāna Meditation

大智度论释初品中禅波罗蜜[8]第二十[9]八[10]（卷第十七）

[*]龙树菩萨造。

[*]后秦龟兹国三藏鸠摩罗什[*]奉诏译。

[0180b17]　　[11]【经】不乱不味故。应具足禅波罗蜜。

[0180b17]　　[12]【论】问曰。菩萨法以度一切众生为事。何以故。闲坐林泽静默山间。独善其身弃舍众生。答曰。菩萨身虽远离众生心常不舍。静处求定[13]得实智慧以度一切。譬如服药将身权息[14]家务。气力平健则修业如故。菩萨宴寂亦复如是。以禅定力[15]故服智慧药。得神通力还在众生。或作父母妻子。或[16]作师徒宗长。或天或人下至畜生。种种语言方便开导。复次菩萨行布施持戒忍辱[17]是三事。名为福德门。于无量世中。作天王释提桓因转轮圣王阎浮提王。

简体字

大智度論釋初品中禪波羅蜜[8]第二十[9]八[10]（卷第十七）

[*]龍樹菩薩造。

[*]後秦龜茲國三藏鳩摩羅什[*]奉詔譯。

[0180b17]　　[11]【經】不亂不味故。應具足禪波羅蜜。

[0180b17]　　[12]【論】問曰。菩薩法以度一切眾生為事。何以故。閑坐林澤靜默山間。獨善其身棄捨眾生。答曰。菩薩身雖遠離眾生心常不捨。靜處求定[13]得實智慧以度一切。譬如服藥將身權息[14]家務。氣力平健則修業如故。菩薩宴寂亦復如是。以禪定力[15]故服智慧藥。得神通力還在眾生。或作父母妻子。或[16]作師徒宗長。或天或人下至畜生。種種語言方便開導。復次菩薩行布施持戒忍辱[17]是三事。名為福德門。於無量世中。作天王釋提桓因轉輪聖王閻浮提王。

正體字

THE PERFECTION OF DHYĀNA MEDITATION
By Ārya Nāgārjuna

Chapter 28: The Perfection of Dhyāna Meditation

Sutra text: It is through being neither mentally distracted nor indulging of enjoyment that one should perfect dhyāna *pāramitā*.

Exegesis text:

I. INTRODUCTORY DISCUSSION

    A. QUESTION: WHY DOES THE BODHISATTVA MEDITATOR ABANDON BEINGS?

Question: The Dharma of the bodhisattva takes the spiritual liberation of all beings as the work to be done. Why then does he sit at leisure in forests or marshes, or abide, still and silent in the mountains, solely benefiting himself, casting aside and forsaking beings?

    B. RESPONSE: TO GAIN WISDOM VIA ABSORPTIONS, WITH ALTRUISTIC INTENT

Response: Although the bodhisattva may be physically far apart from beings, still, his mind never forsakes them. Residing in a quiet location, he strives to develop the meditative absorptions and thus obtain actual wisdom, this in order to [eventually] deliver everyone to liberation.

        1. ANALOGY: LIKE TAKING MEDICINE TO CURE A MALADY

This is analogous to when one takes medicine to tend to the body and, as an expedient, sets aside household responsibilities. When one's energy and strength return to their normally healthful state, then one takes up one's work again just as before. The bodhisattva's indulgence in stillness is just like this. He employs the power of dhyāna absorption to ingest the medicine of wisdom and then gains the power of the superknowledges.

He then returns to be among beings, becoming perhaps a father, mother, wife, or son, perhaps a master, student, or lineage elder, perhaps a god, perhaps a human, or on down even to becoming an animal. He employs all manner of speech and skillful means to instruct and lead.

        2. BODHISATTVA PRACTICES THREE MERIT-GENERATING ALTRUISTIC GATEWAYS

Furthermore, the bodhisattva practices giving, observance of the moral precepts, and patience. These three endeavors are known as "the gateways to meritorious qualities." During the course of an incalculable number of lifetimes, he then becomes a heavenly king, a Śakradevendra, a wheel-turning sage king, the king of Jambudvīpa.

常施众生七宝衣服。五情所
欲今世后世皆令具足。如经
中说。转轮圣王以十善教
民。后世皆生天上。世世利
益众生令得快乐。此乐无常
还复受苦。菩萨因此发大悲
心。欲以常乐涅盘利益众
生。此常乐涅盘。从实智慧
生实智慧从一心禅定生。譬
如然灯。[18]灯虽能照在大风
中不能为用。若置之密[19]宇
其用乃全。散心中智慧亦如
是。若无禅定静室。虽有智
慧其用不全。得禅定则实智
慧生。以是故菩萨虽离众生
远在静处求得禅定。以禅定
清净故智慧亦净。譬如油[20]
炷净故其明亦净。以是故欲
得净智慧者。行此禅定。复
次若求世间近事。不能专心
则事业不成。何况甚深佛道
而不用禅定。禅定名摄诸乱
心。乱心轻飘甚于鸿毛。驰
散不停驶过疾风。不可制止

常施眾生七寶衣服。五情所
欲今世後世皆令具足。如經
中說。轉輪聖王以十善教
民。後世皆生天上。世世利
益眾生令得快樂。此樂無常
還復受苦。菩薩因此發大悲
心。欲以常樂涅槃利益眾
生。此常樂涅槃。從實智慧
生實智慧從一心禪定生。譬
如然燈。[18]燈雖能照在大風
中不能為用。若置之密[19]宇
其用乃全。散心中智慧亦如
是。若無禪定靜室。雖有智
慧其用不全。得禪定則實智
慧生。以是故菩薩雖離眾生
遠在靜處求得禪定。以禪定
清淨故智慧亦淨。譬如油[20]
炷淨故其明亦淨。以是故欲
得淨智慧者。行此禪定。復
次若求世間近事。不能專心
則事業不成。何況甚深佛道
而不用禪定。禪定名攝諸亂
心。亂心輕飄甚於鴻毛。馳
散不停駛過疾風。不可制止

简体字　　　　　　　　正體字

He constantly makes gifts to beings of the seven precious things, clothing, and the objects of the five desires.[1] In the present life and in future lives, he insures that they are all abundantly available. As it says in a scripture, "The wheel-turning sage king teaches the ten good deeds to the people.[2] In future lives they are all reborn in the heavens."

In life after life, he works for the benefit of beings and causes them to experience bliss. This bliss, however, is impermanent and so they come back yet again and are forced to undergo suffering. Because of this, the bodhisattva generates thoughts imbued with the great compassion and wishes then to benefit beings with the constant bliss of nirvāṇa. This constant bliss of nirvāṇa is born of actual wisdom. Actual wisdom is born of single-minded dhyāna absorption.

3. ANALOGY: A LANTERN BECOMES BRIGHT IN A STILL ROOM

This is analogous to a burning lantern. Although the lantern is capable of providing illumination, it cannot be useful in a stiff breeze. However, if one places it in a closed room, its usefulness then becomes completely manifest. Wisdom in the context of a scattered mind is just like this. Although one may possess wisdom, without the still room of dhyāna absorption, its usefulness is incomplete. If one gains dhyāna absorption, then genuine wisdom comes forth.

It is on this account that, even though he is apart from beings and far away in a quiet place, the bodhisattva is nonetheless striving to gain dhyāna absorption. It is by virtue of purity in dhyāna absorption that his wisdom becomes pure as well. This is analogous to an oil lamp. Because it is clean, its brightness is also immaculate. Because of this, one who wishes to gain pure wisdom cultivates this dhyāna absorption.

4. THE NECESSITY OF MENTAL FOCUS

Furthermore, even when one is merely striving at worldly endeavors close at hand, if he is unable to focus his mind, then such endeavors will not be successful. How much the more so would this be the case where one wishes to realize the extremely profound path of the Buddha while failing to avail himself of dhyāna absorption.

a. SIMILES FOR UNFOCUSED THOUGHT: DOWN; WIND; MONKEY; LIGHTNING

Dhyāna absorption refers to the focusing of thought which has become chaotic. Chaotic thoughts float lightly about even more readily than goose down. They gallop along and scatter ceaselessly, moving faster than a swift wind. Their uncontrollability

剧于猕猴。暂现转灭甚于掣
电。心相如是不可禁止。若
欲制之非禅不定。如偈说。

禅为守智藏。功德之福田。
禅为清净水。能洗诸欲尘。

禅为金[21]刚铠。能遮烦恼箭。
虽未得无馀。涅盘分已得。

得金刚三昧。摧碎结使山。
得六神通力。能度无量人。

嚣尘蔽天日。大雨能[22]淹之。
觉观风散心。禅定能灭之。

[0180c26] 复次禅定难得。行者
一心专求不废乃[23]当得之。
诸天及神仙[24]犹尚不能得。
何况凡夫懈怠[25]心者。如佛
在尼拘卢树下坐禅。魔王三
女。说偈问言。

独坐林树间。六根常寂默。
有若失重宝。无援愁苦[181-1]
毒。

劇於獼猴。暫現轉滅甚於掣
電。心相如是不可禁止。若
欲制之非禪不定。如偈說。

禪為守智藏。功德之福田。
禪為清淨水。能洗諸欲塵。

禪為金[21]剛鎧。能遮煩惱箭。
雖未得無餘。涅槃分已得。

得金剛三昧。摧碎結使山。
得六神通力。能度無量人。

囂塵蔽天日。大雨能[22]淹之。
覺觀風散心。禪定能滅之。

[0180c26] 復次禪定難得。行者
一心專求不廢乃[23]當得之。
諸天及神仙[24]猶尚不能得。
何況凡夫懈怠[25]心者。如佛
在尼拘盧樹下坐禪。魔王三
女。說偈問言。

獨坐林樹間。六根常寂默。
有若失重寶。無援愁苦[181-1]
毒。

简体字

正體字

and unstoppability are more extreme than that of monkeys. [The suddenness of] their momentary appearance and disappearance exceeds that of lightning bolts.

b.   THE NECESSITY OF EMPLOYING DHYĀNA TO FOCUS THOUGHT

It is the characteristic of thought to be unrestrictable and unstoppable like this. If one does wish to bring it under control, then, in the absence of dhyāna, one will be unable to achieve absorption. This is as stated in a verse:

5.   THE BENEFITS OF DHYĀNA MEDITATION

a.   A VERSE ON THE BENEFITS OF DHYĀNA MEDITATION

Dhyāna is the treasury for the retaining of wisdom
And the field of merit for qualities which are worthy.
Dhyāna serves as the waters which are pure.
It is able to wash away the dusts of the desires.

Dhyāna is the armor made of *vajra*.
It's able to ward off the arrows of affliction.
Although one's not yet reached [nirvāṇa] "without residue",
A share in nirvāṇa nonetheless has been attained.

One succeeds in gaining the *vajra* samādhi,
Smashing then and shattering the mountain of the fetters.
One attains the power of six superknowledges,
And is able to deliver a number of people beyond count.

Dust raised by tumult may obscure the sky and sun,
Yet a heavy rain may soak it all away.
The winds of ideation and deliberation scatter the mind,
Nonetheless, dhyāna absorption is able to extinguish them.

b.   THE NECESSITY OF VIGOROUS EFFORT TO MEDITATIVE DEVELOPMENT

Furthermore, dhyāna absorption is difficult to attain. Only if the practitioner single-mindedly and exclusively strives without stint will he attain it. Even the gods and spirits and rishis are unable to attain it, how much the less lazy-minded ordinary fellows.

c.   STORY: MĀRA'S DAUGHTERS INTERVIEW THE BUDDHA

When the Buddha was sitting in dhyāna beneath the *nyagrodha* tree, the three daughters of the King of the Māras set forth a question in verse, saying:

Sitting alone amongst the forest trees,
The six-fold faculties always still and quiet—
It seems as if you've lost a precious jewel,
Yet are free of pain from suffering wrought by anguish.

容[2]颜世无比。而常闭目坐。
我等心有疑。何求而在此。

[0181a05]　　尔时世尊。以偈答曰。

我得涅盘味。不乐处染爱。
内外贼[3]已除。汝父亦灭退。

我得甘露味。安乐坐林间。
恩爱之众生。为之起[4]慈心。

[0181a10] 是时三女。心生惭愧而自说言。此人离欲不可动也。即灭去不现。问曰。行何方便得禅波罗蜜。答曰。却五事[5]（五尘）[6]除五法[7]（五盖）行五[8]行。云何[*]却五事当呵责五欲。哀哉众生常为五欲所恼而犹求之不已。此五欲者得之转剧。如火炙疥。五欲无益如狗龂骨。五欲增[9]诤如鸟竞肉。五欲烧人如逆风执炬。五欲害人如践恶蛇。五欲无实如

容[2]顏世無比。而常閉目坐。
我等心有疑。何求而在此。

[0181a05]　　爾時世尊。以偈答曰。

我得涅槃味。不樂處染愛。
內外賊[3]已除。汝父亦滅退。

我得甘露味。安樂坐林間。
恩愛之眾生。為之起[4]慈心。

[0181a10] 是時三女。心生慚愧而自說言。此人離欲不可動也。即滅去不現。問曰。行何方便得禪波羅蜜。答曰。却五事[5]（五塵）[6]除五法[7]（五蓋）行五[8]行。云何[*]却五事當呵責五欲。哀哉眾生常為五欲所惱而猶求之不已。此五欲者得之轉劇。如火炙疥。五欲無益如狗齩骨。五欲增[9]諍如鳥競肉。五欲燒人如逆風執炬。五欲害人如踐惡蛇。五欲無實如

简体字　　　　　　　　　正體字

> In all the World, your visage has no peer,
> And yet you always sit with your eyes closed.
> The thoughts of each of us possess a doubt:
> "What do you seek by dwelling in this place?"

At that time, the Bhagavan replied with a verse:

> As I have found the flavor of nirvāṇa,
> I don't find pleasure dwelling in tainted love.
> Within, without, the thieves have been expelled.
> Your father too: destroyed and sought retreat.

> I have discovered the flavor of sweet-dew ambrosia (*amṛta*),
> In peace and bliss, I sit within the forest.
> As for the beings immersed in fond affections—
> For all their sakes, I raise compassionate thoughts.

At this time, the three daughters felt ashamed and said to themselves, "This man has transcended desire and cannot be moved." They then disappeared and showed themselves no more.

II. The Means by Which One Succeeds in Dhyāna Meditation

A. Question: What Means are Used to Succeed in Dhyāna Meditation?

Question: What skillful means does one implement in order to achieve dhyāna *pāramitā*?

B. Response: Renounce Desires; Eliminate Hindrances; Adopt Practices

Response: One renounces five classes of phenomena (the five sense objects),[3] eliminates five dharmas (the five hindrances), and adopts five practices.

1. Renunciation of the Five Desires

What is meant by "renouncing five phenomena"? This means that one should condemn the five desires. How pitiful! Beings are constantly afflicted by the five desires and yet they still continue to seek after them endlessly.

a. Faults Inherent in Pursuing Desires: Ten Analogies

As for these five desires, one obtains them and they become more severe. This is just as when one uses fire to cauterize an itch. Pursuing the five desires is a useless endeavor comparable to a dog's gnawing away at a bone. Pursuing the five desires increases disputation, just as when birds fight with each other over carrion. The five desires burn people in the same way as happens when carrying a torch into an opposing wind. The five desires harm a person just as when one steps on a poisonous snake. The five desires are insubstantial like

梦所得。五欲不久如假借须
臾。世人愚惑贪着五欲至死
不舍。为之后世受无量苦。
譬如愚人贪着好果。上树食
之不肯时下。人伐其树树倾
乃堕身首毁坏痛恼而死。又
此五欲得时须臾。乐失时为
大苦。如蜜涂刀舐者。贪甜
不知伤舌。五欲法者与畜生
共。有智者识之能自远离。
如说。有一优婆塞。与众估
客远出治生。是时寒雪夜行
失伴。在一石窟中住。时山
神变为一女。来欲试之。说
此偈言。

白雪覆山地。鸟兽皆隐藏。
我独无所恃。[10]惟愿见愍伤。

[0181b01]   优婆塞两手掩耳。
而答偈言。

无羞弊恶人。[11]说此不净言。
水漂火烧去。不欲闻[12]汝声。

有妇心不欲。何况造邪婬。
诸欲乐甚浅。大苦患甚深。

梦所得。五欲不久如假借須
臾。世人愚惑貪著五欲至死
不捨。為之後世受無量苦。
譬如愚人貪著好果。上樹食
之不肯時下。人伐其樹樹傾
乃墮身首毀壞痛惱而死。又
此五欲得時須臾。樂失時為
大苦。如蜜塗刀舐者。貪甜
不知傷舌。五欲法者與畜生
共。有智者識之能自遠離。
如說。有一優婆塞。與眾估
客遠出治生。是時寒雪夜行
失伴。在一石窟中住。時山
神變為一女。來欲試之。說
此偈言。

白雪覆山地。鳥獸皆隱藏。
我獨無所恃。[10]惟願見愍傷。

[0181b01]   優婆塞兩手掩耳。
而答偈言。

無羞弊惡人。[11]說此不淨言。
水漂火燒去。不欲聞[12]汝聲。

有婦心不欲。何況造邪婬。
諸欲樂甚淺。大苦患甚深。

简体字　　　　　　　　正體字

something obtained in a dream. Satisfaction from the five desires is short-lived and is as if borrowed for only an instant. Worldly people deludedly lust for and attach to the five desires, not forsaking them even unto death. On account of them, in later lives, they undergo immeasurable suffering.

This is analogous to a stupid person greedily attached to a type of fine fruit who climbs up the tree and feasts upon them, but cannot bring himself to descend in time. Someone then chops down the tree, causing the tree to tilt over whereupon he falls, his body and head are mangled, and he then dies an agonizing death.

Moreover, these five desires, when attained, are blissful only for a moment. When lost, there is great suffering. This is comparable to when a person licks away at a honey-smeared blade. In his greed for the sweetness, he is unaware of injuring his tongue. The rituals involved in pursuing the five desires are held in common with animals. One who is wise is well aware of this and thus is naturally able to distance himself from them.

b. STORY: THE MOUNTAIN SPIRIT TESTS THE TRAVELING LAYMAN

This is illustrated by the tale told of an *upāsaka* who, together with a group of traders, traveled afar in the course of their business. It happened to be cold and snowy at the time. When they were traveling along at night, he lost touch with his companions and took shelter in a stone cave. A mountain spirit, desirous of testing him, then transformed into a maiden who appeared in his presence. She uttered this verse, saying:

> The white snow covers the mountainous ground.
> The birds and beasts all hide themselves away.
> I, alone, have no one to indulge my needs.
> I pray only to experience your kindness in my plight.

The *upāsaka* covered his ears with both hands and replied with a verse in which he said:

> You shameless and base person—
> You speak to me these words about impure actions.
> Would that water could rinse or fire burn them away.
> I have no desire to further hear your voice.

> I have a wife, but my mind does not course in desire.
> How much the less would I engage in sexual misconduct.
> The bliss afforded by all desires is extremely shallow,
> The calamity brought by its great suffering is extremely profound.

诸欲得无厌。失之为大苦。
未得愿欲得。得之为所恼。

诸欲乐甚少。忧苦毒甚多。
为之失身命。如蛾赴灯火。

[0181b10]　山神闻此偈已。即擎此人送至伴中。是为智者呵欲不可。[13]着五欲者。名为妙色声香味触。欲求禅定皆应弃之。云何弃色。观色之患。若人着色诸结使火。尽皆炽然烧害人身。如火烧金银。煮沸热蜜虽有色味烧身烂口。急应舍之。若人染着妙色美味亦复如是。复次好恶在人色无定也。何以知之。如遥见所爱之人即生喜爱心。若遥见怨家恶人即生[14]怒害心。若见中人则无怒无喜。

简体字

諸欲得無厭。失之為大苦。
未得願欲得。得之為所惱。

諸欲樂甚少。憂苦毒甚多。
為之失身命。如蛾赴燈火。

[0181b10]　山神聞此偈已。即擎此人送至伴中。是為智者呵欲不可。[13]著五欲者。名為妙色聲香味觸。欲求禪定皆應棄之。云何棄色。觀色之患。若人著色諸結使火。盡皆熾然燒害人身。如火燒金銀。煮沸熱蜜雖有色味燒身爛口。急應捨之。若人染著妙色美味亦復如是。復次好惡在人色無定也。何以知之。如遙見所愛之人即生喜愛心。若遙見怨家惡人即生[14]怒害心。若見中人則無怒無喜。

正體字

All the desires, once gained, then bring no satiation.
When one loses them, this makes for great suffering.
When not yet obtained, one prays that one might obtain them.
Once one's obtained them, one becomes tormented by them.

The bliss afforded by all of the desires is extremely slight.
The poison of distress and suffering is so very much.
For the sake of them, one may lose one's body and life.
Just like the moth which casts itself into the lantern fire.

Once the mountain spirit had listened to this verse, she immediately lifted him up in her arms and transported him back into the midst of his companions. This is a case of one with wisdom renouncing desires, [realizing that] one cannot indulge attachment to them.

c. RENUNCIATION OF VISIBLE FORMS

As for the five desires, they refer to pleasing visible forms, sounds, smells, tastes, and touchables. All who desire to seek dhyāna absorptions should reject them.

1) THE CALAMITOUS NATURE OF ATTACHMENT TO PLEASING FORMS

How does one renounce [these pleasing] visible forms? One contemplates the calamity inherent in [the pursuit of] visible forms. If a person becomes attached to such visible forms, the fire of all the fetters blazes up furiously, burning and injuring his person.

2) TWO ANALOGIES: MOLTEN GOLD OR SILVER; BOILING HONEY

This is just as when one uses fire to melt gold or silver and just as when one brings hot honey to the boil. Although those substances still manifest their typical appearance and flavor, they sear the body and ruinously scorch the mouth. Then one is compelled to immediately cast them aside. If a person has developed a defiling attachment to marvelous visible forms and fine flavors, the circumstance is just the same.

3) NON-INHERENCY OF BEAUTY AND UGLINESS

Moreover, [perceptions of] "beauty" and "ugliness" are such as reside with the person. Visible forms themselves are unfixed in this regard. How does one know this? Take for instance when one sees from afar a person of whom one is fond: One immediately brings forth thoughts of delight and fondness. If, on the other hand, one sees from afar an evil person who is one's adversary, one immediately generates hateful thoughts inclined towards inflicting injury. When one observes a person towards whom one's feelings are neutral, one experiences neither rage nor delight.

若欲弃此喜怒。当除邪念及
色一时俱舍。譬如洋金烧
身。若欲除之。不得但欲弃
火而留金。要当金火俱弃。
如频婆娑罗王。以色故身入
敌国。独在婬女阿梵婆罗房
中。忧填王以色染故。截五
百仙人手足。如是等种种因
缘。是名呵色欲。云何呵
声。声相不停暂闻即灭。愚
痴之人不解声相无常变失
故。于音声中妄生好乐。于
已过之声念而生着。如五百
仙人在山中住。甄陀罗女于
雪山池中浴。闻其歌声即失
禅定。心醉狂逸不能自持。
譬如大风吹诸林树。闻此细
妙歌声柔软清净。生邪念
想。是故不觉心狂。

若欲棄此喜怒。當除邪念及
色一時俱捨。譬如洋金燒
身。若欲除之。不得但欲棄
火而留金。要當金火俱棄。
如頻婆娑羅王。以色故身入
敵國。獨在婬女阿梵婆羅房
中。憂填王以色染故。截五
百仙人手足。如是等種種因
緣。是名呵色欲。云何呵
聲。聲相不停暫聞即滅。愚
癡之人不解聲相無常變失
故。於音聲中妄生好樂。於
已過之聲念而生著。如五百
仙人在山中住。甄陀羅女於
雪山池中浴。聞其歌聲即失
禪定。心醉狂逸不能自持。
譬如大風吹諸林樹。聞此細
妙歌聲柔軟清淨。生邪念
想。是故不覺心狂。

簡体字   正體字

4) RENUNCIATION OF ERRONEOUS THOUGHT AND MISTAKEN PERCEPTION

If one wishes to renounce [this tendency to respond with either] "delight" or "rage," then one must get rid of the erroneous thoughts as well as the [perceptions imputed on their corresponding] forms, simultaneously relinquishing them both entirely.

5) ANALOGY: AVOIDING BOTH FIRE AND MOLTEN METAL

This is analogous to an instance wherein one exposed to molten metal which burns the body. If one wishes to get rid of that circumstance, it will not do to simply seek the rejection of the fire alone while still retaining that [molten] metal. It is essential then that one should cast aside both the [molten] metal and the fire as well.

6) CITATIONS: DANGERS RISKED THROUGH ATTACHMENT TO FORMS

[The negative effect of attachment to pleasing visible forms] is exemplified by the case of King Bimbisāra who, on account of such visible forms forms, personally went into an enemy country where he remained, unaccompanied, in the room of the courtesan Āmrapālī. [Additionally, there was the case of] King Udayana who, on account of being mentally defiled by [attachment to] such visible forms, cut off the hands and feet of five hundred rishis. All sorts of causes and conditions such as these serve to illustrate what is meant by renouncing the desire for "forms."

d. RENUNCIATION OF SOUNDS

1) THE NATURE OF ATTACHMENT TO SOUNDS AND THE LIABILITIES

Why must one renounce sounds? It is the characteristic of sounds that they do not abide. One hears them only momentarily and then they immediately disappear. Because foolish people do not understand a sound's characteristic of being impermanent and disappearing, they erroneously develop fondness for and pleasure in sounds. They retain in their minds sounds which have already passed and then generate attachment to them.

2) STORY: THE *KINNARA* MAIDEN'S SINGING DISTURBS THE RISHIS

This is illustrated by the the five hundred rishis who dwelt in the mountains. The *kinnara* maiden was bathing in a pool in the Snow Mountains. When they heard the sound of her singing, they immediately lost their dhyāna absorptions. Their minds became drunken, crazed, and so unrestrained that they were unable to control themselves. It was as if a great wind had begun to blow through the forest trees. When they heard this subtle and marvelous voice so soft and pure, they thought indecent thoughts. Because of this, without their even being aware of it, their minds became deranged.

今世失诸功德。后世当堕恶
道。有智之人观声。[15]念念
生灭前后不俱。无相及者。
作如是知则不生染着。若
斯[16]人者诸天音乐尚不能
乱。何况人声。如是等种种
因缘。是名呵声欲。云何呵
香。人谓着香少罪。染爱于
香开结使门虽复百岁持戒能
一时坏之。如[17]一阿罗汉。
常入龙宫食已以钵授[18]与沙
弥令洗。钵中有残饭数粒。
沙弥嗅之大香。食之甚美。
便作方便入师绳床下。两手
捉绳床脚。其师[19]至时与绳
床俱入龙宫。龙言。此未得
道何以将来。师言。不觉。
沙弥得饭食[20]之。又见龙女
身体

今世失諸功德。後世當墮惡
道。有智之人觀聲。[15]念念
生滅前後不俱。無相及者。
作如是知則不生染著。若
斯[16]人者諸天音樂尚不能
亂。何況人聲。如是等種種
因緣。是名呵聲欲。云何呵
香。人謂著香少罪。染愛於
香開結使門雖復百歲持戒能
一時壞之。如[17]一阿羅漢。
常入龍宮食已以鉢授[18]與沙
彌令洗。鉢中有殘飯數粒。
沙彌嗅之大香。食之甚美。
便作方便入師繩床下。兩手
捉繩床腳。其師[19]至時與繩
床俱入龍宮。龍言。此未得
道何以將來。師言。不覺。
沙彌得飯食[20]之。又見龍女
身體

简体字   正體字

Thus it is that one may lose one's meritorious qualities in the present life and even become bound in later lives to fall into the wretched destinies.

3) SOUNDS AS PERCEIVED BY THE WISE

A person possessed of wisdom contemplates sounds and perceives that, in every new thought-moment, they are produced and destroyed, that the prior and latter sounds are not mutually inclusive, and that they do not even extend to reach each other. If one is able to develop such an understanding, then one does not develop defiling attachments [rooted in imputing meaning onto adjacent but unrelated sound vibrations]. Whoever becomes like this is unable to become disoriented even by the music of the gods, how much the less by the voices of humans. All sorts of causes and conditions such as these serve to illustrate what is meant by renouncing the desire for sounds.

e. RENUNCIATION OF FRAGRANCES
1) THE LIABILITIES INVOLVED IN ATTACHMENT TO FINE FRAGRANCES

Why must one renounce fragrances? People are of the opinion that having an attachment to fragrances is but a minor offense. However, a defiling attachment to fragrances may open the door to the fetters. Then, although one may have accumulated a hundred years in the observance of the moral precepts, one is nonetheless able to ruin it all in a single moment.

2) STORY: FRAGRANCES PULL A NOVICE AWAY FROM THE PATH

Take for instance the arhat who regularly entered the dragon palace. After eating, he took his bowl and gave it to his *śramaṇera* [attendant], ordering him to wash it. There were a few leftover grains of rice in the bowl. The *śramaṇera* smelled them, found them magnificently fragrant, and then ate them, finding them to be extremely delectable.

He then devised a clever technique through which he inserted himself in the under part of his master's rope-mesh sedan chair. By gripping the legs of the rope-mesh sedan chair with his two hands, when his master went forth, he entered the dragon palace right along with the rope-mesh sedan chair.

The Dragon later asked him, "Why did you bring along this person who has not yet realized the Path?"

The Master said, "I did not realize [he came with me]."

The Śramaṇera thus obtained some of that rice and ate it. He also became able to lay eyes on the daughter of the dragon whose body

端正香妙无比心大染着。即
作要愿。我当作福夺此龙处
居其宫殿。龙言。后莫将此
沙弥来。沙弥还已一心布施
持戒。专求所愿。愿早作
龙。是时遶寺足下水出。自
知必得作龙。[21]径至师本
入处大池边。以袈裟覆头而
入。即死变为大龙。福德大
故即杀彼龙举池尽赤。未尔
之前诸师及僧呵之。沙弥
言。我心已定心相已出。[22]
时师将诸众僧就池观之。如
是因缘由着香故。复次有一
比丘。在林中莲华池边经
行。闻莲华香[23]其心悦乐过
而心爱。池神语[*]之言。汝
何以[24]故舍彼林[25]下禅净坐
处而偷我香。以着香故诸结
使卧者[26]皆起。时更有一人
来入池中。多取其花掘挽

简体字

端正香妙無比心大染著。即
作要願。我當作福奪此龍處
居其宮殿。龍言。後莫將此
沙彌來。沙彌還已一心布施
持戒。專求所願。願早作
龍。是時遶寺足下水出。自
知必得作龍。[21]徑至師本
入處大池邊。以袈裟覆頭而
入。即死變為大龍。福德大
故即殺彼龍舉池盡赤。未爾
之前諸師及僧呵之。沙彌
言。我心已定心相已出。[22]
時師將諸眾僧就池觀之。如
是因緣由著香故。復次有一
比丘。在林中蓮華池邊經
行。聞蓮華香[23]其心悅樂過
而心愛。池神語[*]之言。汝
何以[24]故捨彼林[25]下禪淨坐
處而偷我香。以著香故諸結
使臥者[26]皆起。時更有一人
來入池中。多取其花掘挽

正體字

was beautiful and whose perfume was incomparably marvelous. His mind then developed an immense defiled attachment for her. He then immediately made a vow, "I should create enough merit that I will be able to seize this dragon's dwelling and then live here myself."

The Dragon requested, "In the future, when you come here, do not bring this śramaṇera along with you."

After the Śramaṇera had returned, he single-mindedly devoted himself to the practice of giving and to observance of the moral precepts. He sought exclusively to bring about that result which he had vowed to obtain. He wished to soon become a dragon. Then, whenever he performed his circumambulations in the monastery, water gushed forth from beneath his feet. He knew then that he would certainly be successful in becoming a dragon.

He next went directly to the place alongside the great pond where his master had originally entered it. He then covered his head with his *kāṣāya* robe and plunged in. He immediately died and changed into a great dragon. Because his accumulated merit was so abundant, he was then able to quickly slay the other dragon. At that point, the entire pond turned red in color.

Before the situation had come to this, all of his masters and the other members of the Sangha had scolded him. He had replied, "My mind has already become fixed on this and the characteristic features of the desired result have already begun to manifest in my mind."

The Master then led the assembly of Sanghans to the edge of the pool to observe this. Even such causal circumstances such as these may be brought about on account of an attachment to fragrances.

3) Story: A Spirit Rebukes a Bhikshu for Enjoying Fragrances

Additionally, there was a bhikshu who was walking next to a lotus pool in the forest. When he smelled the fragrance of the lotus blossoms, his mind was pleased and so experienced a feeling of enjoyment. Having passed on by, his mind developed a fondness for it.

The pond spirit then spoke to him, saying, "Why is it that you have forsaken that spot beneath the trees where you sit purely in dhyāna meditation, preferring instead to come forth and steal these fragrances of mine? It is on account of attachment to fragrances that dormant fetters may be influence to manifest again."

Then, yet another person came along. He went right into the pool and pulled up many of its flowers. He then started digging, pulling

根茎狼籍而去。池神默无所
言。比丘言。此人破汝池取
汝花。汝都无言。我但池岸
边行。便见呵骂[27]言偷我
香池神言。世间恶人常在罪
垢粪中不净没头。我不共语
也。汝是禅行好人。而着此
香破汝好事。是故呵汝。譬
如白[182-1]叠鲜净。而有黑物
点污众人皆见。彼恶人者。
譬如黑衣点墨人所不见。谁
问之者。如是等种种因缘。
是名呵香欲。云何呵味。当
自觉悟。我但以贪着美味故
当受众苦。洋铜灌口噉烧
铁丸。若不观食[2]法嗜心坚
着。堕不净虫中。如一沙弥
心常爱酪。诸檀越饷僧酪。
时沙弥每得残分。心中爱着
乐喜不离。命终之后生此残
酪瓶中。沙弥师得

根莖狼籍而去。池神默無所
言。比丘言。此人破汝池取
汝花。汝都無言。我但池岸
邊行。便見呵罵[27]言偷我
香池神言。世間惡人常在罪
垢糞中不淨沒頭。我不共語
也。汝是禪行好人。而著此
香破汝好事。是故呵汝。譬
如白[182-1]疊鮮淨。而有黑物
點污眾人皆見。彼惡人者。
譬如黑衣點墨人所不見。誰
問之者。如是等種種因緣。
是名呵香欲。云何呵味。當
自覺悟。我但以貪著美味故
當受眾苦。洋銅灌口噉燒
鐵丸。若不觀食[2]法嗜心堅
著。墮不淨虫中。如一沙彌
心常愛酪。諸檀越餉僧酪。
時沙彌每得殘分。心中愛著
樂喜不離。命終之後生此殘
酪瓶中。沙彌師得

简体字

正體字

forth roots and stems, created a disorderly mess, and then left. The pond spirit remained silent, not saying anything at all.

The Bhikshu then said, "This person destroyed your pond and took your flowers. Yet, you didn't say anything to him. However, when I merely passed by the pond bank, I suffered your rebuke and a scolding wherein you claimed I had stolen your fragrances."

The pond spirit said, "The evil people of the world constantly immerse their heads in the excrement of offense-related defilement. I do not even bother to speak to them. You, however, are a fine person who engages in the practice of dhyāna meditation. Thus, when you become attached to these fragrances, it destroys your fine endeavors. This is why I scolded you.

"This is analogous to a white cloth which is fresh and pure but then gets a spot where it has become stained by something black. Everyone observes it. In the case of those who are evil persons, it is comparable to an already blackened robe becoming spotted with some ink. It is such as people would not even notice. So, who would even bother to bring it up?"

All sorts of causal circumstances such as this demonstrate what is meant by renouncing the desire for fragrances.

f. RENUNCIATION OF TASTES

1) THE LIABILITIES INVOLVED IN ATTACHMENT TO FINE FLAVORS

Why must one renounce tastes? One ought to realize that, "Solely on account of desirous attachment to fine flavors, I may become bound to undergo a multitude of sufferings, may have molten copper poured down my throat, and may be forced to consume burning hot iron pellets."

If one fails to observe the Dharma in its applications to eating, and if one's thoughts of particular fondness become solidly attached, one may even fall down amongst the worms which abide in the midst of impurities.

2) STORY: A NOVICE FALLS AWAY DUE TO ATTACHMENT TO TASTES

Such a situation is exemplified by the case of a particular śrāmaṇera whose mind became obsessively fond of curds. Whenever the dānapati benefactors made an offering of curds to the Sangha, the portion which was left over would always be passed on to that śrāmaṇera. His thoughts became affectionately attached to its flavor, taking such pleasure and delight that he was unable to let go of it.

When his life came to an end, he was reborn in this vase which held the leftover curds. The guru of that śrāmaṇera had gained

阿罗汉道。僧分酪时语言。
徐徐莫伤此爱酪沙弥。诸人
言。[3]此是虫何以言爱酪沙
弥。答言。此虫本是我沙弥
但坐贪爱残酪故生此瓶中。
师得酪分虫在中来。师言。
爱酪人汝何以来。即以酪与
之。复次如一[4]国王名月分
王。有太子爱着美味。王守
园者日送好菓。园中有一大
树。树上有鸟养子。[5]常飞
至香山中。取好香果以养其
子。众子争之一果堕地。守
园人晨朝见之。奇[6]其非常
即送与王。王珍此果香色殊
异。太子见之便索。王爱其
子即以与之。太子食果得其
气味。染心深着日日欲得。
王即召园人问其所由。守园
人言。此果无种从地得之。
不知所由来也。太子啼[7]哭
不食。王催责园人仰汝得
之。园人至得果处。见有鸟
巢知鸟衔来。翳身树上伺欲
取之。鸟母

阿羅漢道。僧分酪時語言。
徐徐莫傷此愛酪沙彌。諸人
言。[3]此是虫何以言愛酪沙
彌。答言。此虫本是我沙彌
但坐貪愛殘酪故生此瓶中。
師得酪分虫在中來。師言。
愛酪人汝何以來。即以酪與
之。復次如一[4]國王名月分
王。有太子愛著美味。王守
園者日送好菓。園中有一大
樹。樹上有鳥養子。[5]常飛
至香山中。取好香果以養其
子。眾子爭之一果墮地。守
園人晨朝見之。奇[6]其非常
即送與王。王珍此果香色殊
異。太子見之便索。王愛其
子即以與之。太子食果得其
氣味。染心深著日日欲得。
王即召園人問其所由。守園
人言。此果無種從地得之。
不知所由來也。太子啼[7]哭
不食。王催責園人仰汝得
之。園人至得果處。見有鳥
巢知鳥銜來。翳身樹上伺欲
取之。鳥母

简体字   正體字

the way of arhatship. When the Sangha divided up the curds, he said to them, "Be careful, be careful. Don't injure the curd-loving *śrāmaṇera.*"

Everyone said, "But this is just a worm. Why do you refer to it as 'the curd-loving *śrāmaṇera*'?"

He replied, "Originally, this worm was my *śrāmaṇera* [attendant]. Because he only sat there immersed in a gluttonous affection for leftover curds, he came to be reborn in this vase. When the master received his share of the curds, the worm came along with it. The master said, "Curd-loving fellow. Why did you come here?" He then gave it the curds.

3) Story: A Prince's Fatal Attachment to Fine Flavors

This [issue of attachment to fine flavors] is also illustrated by the case of a king known as "Partial Moon King" (Candrabhāga). He had a son who was a prince affectionately attached to delectable flavors. Every day the royal gardener brought fine fruits. There was a large tree within the garden. Up in the top of the tree, there was a bird carrying on with raising its young. It often flew off into the Fragrant Mountains from which it brought back a type of fine, aromatic fruit as nourishment for its young. The clutch of young birds happened to struggle over one of them so much that a fruit came tumbling on down to the ground.

Early in the morning, the gardener noticed it, was amazed by its unusual appearance, and so immediately took it to the King. The King valued this fruit for its unusual fragrance and appearance. The Prince noticed it and asked to have it. The King loved his son and so immediately gave it to him. The Prince ate the fruit, experienced its bouquet and flavor, and was overcome with thoughts tainted by profound attachment. Consequently he sought to receive it again, day after day.

The King immediately summoned the gardener and asked into its origins. The gardener said, "This fruit has no seed. It was obtained from off of the ground. I do not know from whence it came." The Prince wailed and cried and stopped eating. The King forced upon the gardener the responsibility for this, saying, "We look to you to find more of it."

The gardener went to the place where he had found the fruit, saw that there was a bird's nest, and realized that the bird had carried it hence. He camouflaged himself up in the tree and waited with the intention of seizing one [of the fruits]. When the mother

来时即夺得果送。日日如是。鸟母怒之于香山中取毒果。其香味色全似前者。园人夺得输王。王与太子。食之未久身肉烂坏而死。[8]着味如是有失身之苦。如是等种种因缘。是名呵着味欲。云何呵触。此触是生诸结使之[9]火因。系缚心之根本。何以故。馀四情[10]则各当其分。此则遍满身识。生处广故多生染着。此着难离。何以知之。如人着色。观身不净三十六种则生[11]厌心。若于触中生着虽知不净。贪其细软观[12]不净无所益。是故难离。复次以其难舍故。为之常作重罪。若堕地狱。地狱有二部。一名寒氷二名焰火。此二狱中皆以身触受罪苦毒万端。此触名为大黑暗处。危难之险道也。

來時即奪得果送。日日如是。鳥母怒之於香山中取毒果。其香味色全似前者。園人奪得輸王。王與太子。食之未久身肉爛壞而死。[8]着味如是有失身之苦。如是等種種因緣。是名呵著味欲。云何呵觸。此觸是生諸結使之[9]火因。繫縛心之根本。何以故。餘四情[10]則各當其分。此則遍滿身識。生處廣故多生染著。此著難離。何以知之。如人著色。觀身不淨三十六種則生[11]厭心。若於觸中生著雖知不淨。貪其細軟觀[12]不淨無所益。是故難離。復次以其難捨故。為之常作重罪。若墮地獄。地獄有二部。一名寒氷二名焰火。此二獄中皆以身觸受罪苦毒萬端。此觸名為大黑闇處。危難之險道也。

简体字

正體字

bird arrived, he immediately forcibly seized one of the fruits so as to deliver it forth.

This happened every day in the same way. The mother bird became furious at this and so returned with a poisonous fruit from the Fragrant Mountains which in fragrance, flavor, and appearance was identical to the previously delivered variety. The gardener seized it and took it forth as tribute to the King. The King gave it to the Prince. Not long after [the prince] had eaten it, the flesh of his body rotted away and he died.

In just such a manner, attachment to tastes possesses the [potential] to precipitate the suffering of losing one's life. All sorts of causal circumstances such as these illustrate what is meant by renouncing the desire involved in attachment to tastes.

g. Renunciation of Touchables
1) The Nature of Attachment to Touchables and its Liabilities

Why must one renounce touch? This touch is the cause for the production of the fire of the fetters and is the root of the bondage of the mind. How is this so? The other four sense faculties each occupy their own particular area. This one, however, involves a consciousness which pervades the entire body. Because the area from which it may arise is extensive, it more commonly [serves as the basis for] generating defiled attachment.

This attachment is difficult to abandon. How does one know this? Take for example a person attached to [sensual] forms. [Ordinarily], if one contemplates the thirty-six categories of impurity in the body, one generates a mind of renunciation. If, however, one has developed an attachment to touch, even though one may then become aware of the impurity, one may nonetheless continue to crave its [sensations of] subtle softness. At this point, contemplation of impurity may not provide any benefits. It is for this reason that it is difficult to relinquish.

Additionally, because it is so difficult to relinquish, one may continue on this account to regularly generate grave karmic transgressions. If one falls into the hells, those hells have two regions: The first is known as "cold ice." The second is known as "blazing fire." In both of these hells, [sensations associated with] physical touch are employed to cause one to undergo punishments inflicting a myriad forms of suffering-generating cruelty. This "touch" is known as the place of the great darkness. It is a precipitous path attended by danger and difficulty.

复次如罗睺罗母本生经中
说。释迦文菩萨有二夫人。
一名[13]劬毘耶。二名耶输
陀罗。耶输陀罗罗睺罗母
也。[*]劬毘耶是宝女故不孕
子。耶输陀罗以菩萨出家
夜。自觉[14]妊身。菩萨出
家六年苦行。耶输陀罗[15]
亦六年怀[*]妊不产。诸释诘
之。菩萨出家[16]何由有此。
耶输陀罗言。我无他罪。我
所怀子实是太子体胤。诸释
言。何以久而不产。答言。
非我所知。诸释集议。闻
王欲如法治罪。[*]劬毘耶白
王。愿宽恕之。我常与耶输
陀罗共住。我为其证知其无
罪。待其子生知似父不治之
无晚。王即宽置。佛六年苦
行既满。初成佛时其夜生罗
睺罗。王见其似父爱乐忘
忧。语群臣言。我儿虽去今
得其子。与儿在无异。耶输
陀罗。虽免罪黜恶声满国。
耶输陀罗欲除恶名。佛成道
已。还迦毘罗婆度诸释子。
时净饭王及耶输陀罗。常

復次如羅睺羅母本生經中
說。釋迦文菩薩有二夫人。
一名[13]劬毘耶。二名耶輸
陀羅。耶輸陀羅羅睺羅母
也。[*]劬毘耶是寶女故不孕
子。耶輸陀羅以菩薩出家
夜。自覺[14]妊身。菩薩出
家六年苦行。耶輸陀羅[15]
亦六年懷[*]妊不產。諸釋詰
之。菩薩出家[16]何由有此。
耶輸陀羅言。我無他罪。我
所懷子實是太子體胤。諸釋
言。何以久而不產。答言。
非我所知。諸釋集議。聞
王欲如法治罪。[*]劬毘耶白
王。願寬恕之。我常與耶輸
陀羅共住。我為其證知其無
罪。待其子生知似父不治之
無晚。王即寬置。佛六年苦
行既滿。初成佛時其夜生羅
睺羅。王見其似父愛樂忘
憂。語群臣言。我兒雖去今
得其子。與兒在無異。耶輸
陀羅。雖免罪黜惡聲滿國。
耶輸陀羅欲除惡名。佛成道
已。還迦毘羅婆度諸釋子。
時淨飯王及耶輸陀羅。常

简体字　　　　　　　　　　　正體字

2) STORY: YAŚODHARĀ AND THE BUDDHA

a) SUBSTORY ONE: YAŚODHARĀ'S DIFFICULTY PREGNANCY

Then again, this is as described in the *Sutra on the Previous Lives of Rāhula's Mother.* As the Bodhisattva, Shakyamuni had two consorts. The first was named Gopiyā. The second was named Yaśodharā. Yaśodharā was the mother of Rāhula. Because Gopiyā was a barren woman, she did not become pregnant with child. It was on the night that the Bodhisattva left behind the home life that Yaśodharā realized that she was pregnant.

The Bodhisattva [Shakyamuni] engaged in ascetic practices for six years. For six full years, Yaśodharā remained pregnant without giving birth. All of the Shakyans inquired of her, "The Bodhisattva has left behind the home life. How is it that this could occur?"

Yaśodharā said, "I have committed no offenses with others. The child with which I am pregnant is truly a scion of the Prince."

The Shakyans said, "How is it then that it has now been so long and yet it still has not been born?"

She replied, "This is a matter not even I understand."

The Shakyans assembled and conferred on the matter. When she heard that the King wished to carry out a lawful punishment of offenses, Gopiyā addressed the King, "I pray that, out of sympathy for her, you will be lenient. I have dwelt together with Yaśodharā constantly. I can certify for her that I know she is free of transgressions. Wait for her child to be born. Then you will be able to know if it resembles the father or not. It would not be too late then to carry out punishments."

The King then allowed leniency. When the Buddha's six years of ascetic practices had been fulfilled, on the very night when he achieved buddhahood, she gave birth to Rāhula. The King observed that he resembled his father, felt affection and delight, and forgot his worries. He spoke to the group of ministers, saying, "Although my son has gone away, I have now gained his son. It is no different than if my son was here."

Although Yaśodharā had avoided the punishment of being cast out, she had nonetheless acquired a bad reputation which spread throughout the country. Yaśodharā wished to get rid of the stain on her reputation.

After the Buddha had gained realization of the Path, he returned to Kapilavastu in an attempt to cross over the sons of the Shakyans to liberation. At that time King Śuddhodana and Yaśodharā regularly

请佛入宫食。是时耶输陀罗持[17]一[18]鉢百味欢喜丸。与罗睺罗令持上佛。是时佛[19]以神力。变五百阿罗汉。[20]皆如佛身无有别异。罗睺罗以七岁身持欢喜丸。径至佛前奉进世尊。是时佛摄神力。诸比丘身复如故。皆空鉢而坐。唯佛鉢中盛满欢喜丸。耶输陀罗即白王言。以此证验我无罪也。耶输陀罗即问佛言。我有何因缘怀[*]妊六年佛言。汝子罗睺罗。过去久远世时曾作国王。时有一五通仙人来入王国。语王言。王法治贼请治我罪。王言。汝有何罪。答言。我入王国犯不与取。辄饮王水用王杨枝。王言。我以相与何罪之有。我初登王位。皆以水及杨枝施于一切。仙人言。王虽已施我心疑悔罪不除也。愿今见治无令后罪。王言。若必欲尔。小停待我入还。王入宫中六日不出。此仙人在王园中

简体字

請佛入宮食。是時耶輸陀羅持[17]一[18]鉢百味歡喜丸。與羅睺羅令持上佛。是時佛[19]以神力。變五百阿羅漢。[20]皆如佛身無有別異。羅睺羅以七歲身持歡喜丸。徑至佛前奉進世尊。是時佛攝神力。諸比丘身復如故。皆空鉢而坐。唯佛鉢中盛滿歡喜丸。耶輸陀羅即白王言。以此證驗我無罪也。耶輸陀羅即問佛言。我有何因緣懷[*]妊六年佛言。汝子羅睺羅。過去久遠世時曾作國王。時有一五通仙人來入王國。語王言。王法治賊請治我罪。王言。汝有何罪。答言。我入王國犯不與取。輒飲王水用王楊枝。王言。我以相與何罪之有。我初登王位。皆以水及楊枝施於一切。仙人言。王雖已施我心疑悔罪不除也。願今見治無令後罪。王言。若必欲爾。小停待我入還。王入宮中六日不出。此仙人在王園中

正體字

invited the Buddha to come to the palace for meals. At one such time Yaśodharā took a bowl of "hundred-flavored delightful dumplings," handed it to Rāhula, and then directed him to take it up and offer them to the Buddha.

The Buddha then resorted to his spiritual powers to transform all five hundred arhats so that they all appeared identical to the Buddha, showing no differences at all. The seven-year-old Rāhula carried the delightful dumplings forward, went straight before the Buddha himself, and then offered them up to the Bhagavan.

[The Buddha] then withdrew his spiritual powers whereupon all of the bhikshus were restored to their original physical appearance. They were all sitting there with empty bowls. Only the Buddha's bowl was full of delightful dumplings. Yaśodharā then addressed the King, saying, "Let this serve as verification that I have remained free of any transgressions."

b) Substory Two: Origins of Yaśodharā's Difficult Pregnancy

Yaśodharā then inquired of the Buddha, "What is the causal basis behind my remaining pregnant for a period of six years?"

The Buddha said, "Long ago, in a lifetime far off in the past, your son Rāhula was the king of a country. There was a rishi possessed of the five superknowledges who came at that time and entered that king's country. He spoke to the King, saying, "It is the royal law to punish thieves. I request that you punish me for my offenses."

The King said, "But what offenses have you committed?"

He replied, "I entered the King's country and transgressed by taking what had not been given. I have repeatedly drunk the King's water and used the King's willow branches [as tooth brushes]."

The King said, "But I have already given those things [to the people]. What transgression could there be in this? When I first ascended to the position of king, I bestowed the use of both water and willow branches universally on everyone."

The Rishi said, "Although the King has already made a gift of them, my mind is nonetheless afflicted by doubts and regrets. Thus the offense is not yet expiated. I pray that I will now undergo corrective measures so as to prevent being subjected to [karmic] punishments later."

The King said, "If you must insist, wait a little bit for me to go on in and come back out again."

The King then entered the palace. Even after six days, he still had not emerged again. The Rishi stayed in the King's garden enduring

六日饥渴。仙人思惟。此王
正以此治我。王过六日而出
辞谢仙人。我便相忘莫见咎
也。以是因缘故。受五百世
三恶道罪。五百世常六年在
母胎中。以是证故。耶输陀
罗无有罪也。是时世尊。食
已出去。耶输陀罗心生悔
恨。如此好人世所希有。我
得遭遇而今永失。世尊坐时
谛视不眴。世尊出时寻后观
之远没乃止。心大懊恨。每
一思至躄地气绝。傍人以水
灑之乃得苏息。常独思惟。
天下谁能善为呪术。能转其
心令复本意欢乐如初。即以
七宝名珠着金[21]盘上以持募
人。有一梵志应之言。我能
呪之令其意转。当作百味欢
喜丸。以药草和之。以呪语
禁之。其心便转必来无疑。
耶输陀罗受其教法。遣人请
佛。愿与圣众俱屈威神。佛
入王宫。[1]耶输陀罗即

简体字

六日飢渴。仙人思惟。此王
正以此治我。王過六日而出
辭謝仙人。我便相忘莫見咎
也。以是因緣故。受五百世
三惡道罪。五百世常六年在
母胎中。以是證故。耶輸陀
羅無有罪也。是時世尊。食
已出去。耶輸陀羅心生悔
恨。如此好人世所希有。我
得遭遇而今永失。世尊坐時
諦視不眴。世尊出時尋後觀
之遠沒乃止。心大懊恨。每
一思至躄地氣絕。傍人以水
灑之乃得蘇息。常獨思惟。
天下誰能善為呪術。能轉其
心令復本意歡樂如初。即以
七寶名珠著金[21]槃上以持募
人。有一梵志應之言。我能
呪之令其意轉。當作百味歡
喜丸。以藥草和之。以呪語
禁之。其心便轉必來無疑。
耶輸陀羅受其教法。遣人請
佛。願與聖眾俱屈威神。佛
入王宮。[183-1]耶輸陀羅即

正體字

hunger and thirst for those six days. The Rishi thought to himself, "This King is just now using this situation to punish me."

After six days had gone by, the King came out and released the Rishi, saying, "I completely forgot about this. Do not hold it against me." On account of this causal circumstance, he underwent five hundred lifetimes of punishment in the three wretched destinies and then for five hundred lifetimes always remained in his mother's womb for a period of six years. On account of this verifying evidence, [we should realize that] Yaśodharā was free of transgressions.

c) Substory Three: Yaśodharā's Attempt to Bring Back the Buddha

At this time, after he had finished his meal, the Bhagavān departed. Yaśodharā's thoughts were full of regret, "Such a fine man as this, rare in all the world—I succeeded in encountering him, but now have lost him forever."

When the Bhagavān sat down, she gazed at him intently without even blinking. When the Bhagavān departed, her gaze followed along after him so intently that only when [his silhouette] sank away on the horizon did she finally desist. Her thoughts were full of grief and regret. Every time she thought of it, she would collapse and go into a faint. Her attendants would sprinkle her with water. Only then did she revive and breath normally again.

She constantly remained alone, pondering, "Who in all the world is so good at the skill of casting spells that he might be able to turn [the Buddha's] mind around, causing him to return to his original state of mind, thus allowing us to once again be as delighted and happy as before?" She then placed the seven precious things and other rare jewels into a gold tray and, taking it up, went forth to enlist the services of someone [who could help her do this].

There was one *brahmacarin* who responded to her by saying, "I am able to cast a spell upon him which will cause his mind to turn back. You must make hundred-flavored delightful dumplings in which you mix together herbs. Use the phrases of the spell to capture him. His mind will then turn around and he will certainly come. Of this there is no doubt."

Yaśodharā followed his instructions and then sent others to invite the Buddha, saying, "Pray may you, together with the assembly of Āryas, deign to bend down from your [heights of] awesome spirituality [and honor us with your presence]." The Buddha then came and entered into the King's palace. Yaśodharā immediately

[2]遣百味欢喜丸着佛鉢中。佛既食之。耶输陀罗冀想如愿欢娱如初。佛食无异心[3]目澄静。耶输陀罗言。今不动者药力未行故耳。药势发时必如我愿。佛饭食讫而呪愿已从座起去。耶输陀罗冀药力晡时日入当发必还宫中。佛食如常身心无异。诸比丘明日食时。着衣持鉢入城乞食。具闻此事增益恭敬。佛力无量神心难测不可思议。耶输陀罗药欢喜丸其力甚大。而世尊食之身心无异。诸比丘食已出城。以是事具白世尊。佛告诸比[4]丘。此耶输陀罗。非但今世以欢喜丸惑我。乃往过去世时。亦以欢喜丸惑我。尔时世尊。为诸比丘说本生因缘。过去久远世时。[5]婆罗奈国山中有仙人。以仲[6]春之月于澡[*]盘中小便。见鹿麚麀合会。婬心即动精流[*]盘中。麀鹿饮之即时有[7]娠。满月生

[2]遣百味歡喜丸著佛鉢中。佛既食之。耶輸陀羅冀想如願歡娛如初。佛食無異心[3]目澄靜。耶輸陀羅言。今不動者藥力未行故耳。藥勢發時必如我願。佛飯食訖而呪願已從座起去。耶輸陀羅冀藥力晡時日入當發必還宮中。佛食如常身心無異。諸比丘明日食時。著衣持鉢入城乞食。具聞此事增益恭敬。佛力無量神心難測不可思議。耶輸陀羅藥歡喜丸其力甚大。而世尊食之身心無異。諸比丘食已出城。以是事具白世尊。佛告諸比[4]丘。此耶輸陀羅。非但今世以歡喜丸惑我。乃往過去世時。亦以歡喜丸惑我。爾時世尊。為諸比丘說本生因緣。過去久遠世時。[5]婆羅奈國山中有仙人。以仲[6]春之月於澡[*]槃中小便。見鹿麚麀合會。婬心即動精流[*]槃中。麀鹿飲之即時有[7]娠。滿月生

简体字　　　　　　　　　　　　　正體字

sent forth the hundred-flavored delightful dumplings and had them placed in the Buddha's bowl. When the Buddha had eaten them, Yaśodharā hoped that, in accordance with her wish, they would be able to share joy together again just as before. The Buddha ate them, yet appeared no different, his mind and eyes remaining clear and quiet.

Yaśodharā said, "That he does not now move is just because the power of the potion has not yet become active, that's all. Once the strength of the potion has taken effect, events will certainly turn out just as I have wished."

When the Buddha had finished eating and had uttered the [meal-ending] mantra and prayer, he arose from his seat and left. Yaśodharā hoped the power of the potion would take effect in the late afternoon and that it would then become active, certainly causing him to return then to the palace. However, the Buddha remained then just the same as ever, no different in either body or mind.

When it came time on the next day for the Bhikshus to take their meal, they put on their robes, took up their bowls, and then went forth into the city to seek alms. They all then heard of this event and were thus moved to increased reverence, thinking, "The powers of the Buddha are immeasurable. His spirit and mind are difficult to fathom. They are inconceivable and indescribable. The power of Yaśodharā's delightful dumplings was extremely great and yet the Bhagavan ate them with no difference being effected on either his body or mind."

When the Bhikshus had finished eating and had gone forth from the city, they reported the entire matter to the Bhagavan.

d) Substory Four: The Buddha's Past Life as a One-Horned Rishi

The Buddha told the Bhikshus, "As for this Yaśodharā, it is not just in this present life that she has used the delightful dumplings to confuse me. Once before, during a past life, she also used the delightful dumplings to confuse me."

The Bhagavan then described the past-life causes and conditions behind this, saying, "In a time long ago and far off in the past, there was a rishi in the mountains of the state of Benares who, in mid-spring was relieving himself into a basin when he observed a buck and a doe mating. Lustful thoughts suddenly arose in him, whereupon his semen flowed into the basin.

The doe happened to drink from that basin and became pregnant. When the months of pregnancy were complete, she gave birth

子形类如人。唯头有一角其
足似鹿。鹿当产时至仙人[8]
菴边而产。见子是人。以付
仙人而去。仙人出时见此鹿
子。自念本缘。知是己儿取
已养育。及其年大勲教学
问。通十八种大经。又学
坐禅行四无量心[9]即得五神
通。一时上山值大雨。泥滑
其足不便。躄地破其[10]鍕
持。又伤其足。便大瞋恚。
以[*]鍕持盛水呪令不雨。仙
人福德诸龙鬼神皆为不雨。
不雨故五谷五果尽皆不生。
人民穷乏无复生路。[*]婆罗
奈[11]国王忧愁懊恼。命诸大
[12]官集议雨事。明者议言。
我[13]曾传闻。仙人山中有
一角仙人。以足不便故。上
山躄地伤足。瞋呪此雨令十
二年不堕。王思惟言。若十
二年不雨我国了矣。无复人
民。王即开募。其有能令仙
人失五通。属我为民者。

子形類如人。唯頭有一角其
足似鹿。鹿當產時至仙人[8]
菴邊而產。見子是人。以付
仙人而去。仙人出時見此鹿
子。自念本緣。知是己兒取
已養育。及其年大勲教學
問。通十八種大經。又學
坐禪行四無量心[9]即得五神
通。一時上山值大雨。泥滑
其足不便。躄地破其[10]鍕
持。又傷其足。便大瞋恚。
以[*]鍕持盛水呪令不雨。仙
人福德諸龍鬼神皆為不雨。
不雨故五穀五果盡皆不生。
人民窮乏無復生路。[*]婆羅
奈[11]國王憂愁懊惱。命諸大
[12]官集議雨事。明者議言。
我[13]曾傳聞。仙人山中有
一角仙人。以足不便故。上
山躄地傷足。瞋呪此雨令十
二年不堕。王思惟言。若十
二年不雨我國了矣。無復人
民。王即開募。其有能令仙
人失五通。屬我為民者。

简体字   正體字

to a fawn with the appearance of a man. There were only [the differences of] a single horn on the head and feet like those of a deer. When the deer was about to fawn, she went to a place alongside the rishi's hut and gave birth. She saw that her fawn was a person and so entrusted it to the rishi and left.

When the Rishi came out, he saw this progeny of the deer, recalled to himself the original conditions, knew that it was his own son, and so took him and raised him. As [the son] grew to adulthood, [the Rishi] was diligent in instructing him in the topics of study so that he was able to penetrate the eighteen great classics. Additionally, [the son] studied sitting in dhyāna meditation, practiced the four immeasurable minds, and then straightaway gained realization of the five superknowledges.

Once, [once the son had grown up and become a rishi in his own right], he was climbing up the mountain and happened to encounter a great rainstorm. The mud became slippery, causing him to lose his footing, fall to the ground, damage his ewer, and injure his foot. He reacted by becoming greatly enraged. With a ewer full of water, he then cast a spell intended to cause all rains to cease. Due to the influence of the meritorious qualities possessed by this rishi, the dragons, ghosts, and spirits acted on his behalf to ensure that no more rain would fall.

Because it did not rain, the five types of grains and the five types of fruit all failed to grow. The populace became impoverished, destitute, and without any way whereby they might go on living. The king of the state of Benares was distressed, worried, and tormented by grief. He ordered all of the great officials to convene and discuss the rainfall situation.

One of the intelligent ones among them offered an opinion, saying, "I have heard it rumored that up in the Rishi Mountains there is a one-horned rishi who, on account of losing his footing, fell down as he ascended the mountain, injuring his foot. He cast a hateful spell on these rains whereby he caused them to not fall for a period of twelve years."

The King thought to himself, "If it goes twelve years without raining, my country will surely be finished. There will be no people left at all."

The King then issued an appeal, stating, "Could it be that there is someone who is able to cause a rishi to lose his five superknowledges and who will then instruct me in how to do this for the sake

当与分国半治。是[*]婆罗奈
国有婬女。名曰扇陀。端正
[14]无双。来应王募问诸人
言。此是人非[15]人。众人
言。是人耳。仙人所生。婬
女言。若是人者我能坏之。
作是语已取金[*]盘盛好宝
物。语[*]国王言。我当骑此
仙人项来。婬女即时求五百
乘车载五百美女。[16]五百鹿
车载种种欢喜丸。皆以众[17]
药和之。以[18]众彩画之令似
杂果及持种种大力美酒色味
如水。服树皮衣草[19]衣。
行林树间[20]以像仙人。于仙
人[*]菴边作草庵而住。一角
仙人游行见之。诸女皆出迎
逆。好华[21]好香供养仙人。
仙人大喜。诸女[22]皆以美言
敬辞问讯仙人。将入房中坐
好床蓐。与好[23]净酒以为净
水。与欢喜丸以为果蓏。食
饮饱已语诸女言。我从生已
来初未得如此好果好水。诸
女言。我[24]以一心行善故天
与我。愿得此[25]好果好水。
仙人问诸女。汝何以故肤色
肥盛。答言。我曹食此好
果。饮此美水故肥

當與分國半治。是[*]婆羅奈
國有婬女。名曰扇陀。端正
[14]無雙。來應王募問諸人
言。此是人非[15]人。眾人
言。是人耳。仙人所生。婬
女言。若是人者我能壞之。
作是語已取金[*]槃盛好寶
物。語[*]國王言。我當騎此
仙人項來。婬女即時求五百
乘車載五百美女。[16]五百鹿
車載種種歡喜丸。皆以眾[17]
藥和之。以[18]眾彩畫之令似
雜果及持種種大力美酒色味
如水。服樹皮衣草[19]衣。
行林樹間[20]以像仙人。於仙
人[*]菴邊作草庵而住。一角
仙人遊行見之。諸女皆出迎
逆。好華[21]好香供養仙人。
仙人大喜。諸女[22]皆以美言
敬辭問訊仙人。將入房中坐
好床蓐。與好[23]淨酒以為淨
水。與歡喜丸以為果蓏。食
飲飽已語諸女言。我從生已
來初未得如此好果好水。諸
女言。我[24]以一心行善故天
與我。願得此[25]好果好水。
仙人問諸女。汝何以故膚色
肥盛。答言。我曹食此好
果。飲此美水故肥

简体字   正體字

of the people? I will divide the country so that each of us will then be rulers over half of it."

In this country of Benares, there was a courtesan by the name of Śāntā who was incomparably beautiful. She came in response to the King's appeal and asked everyone there, "Is this individual a man or is it someone who is not really a man?"

Everyone replied, "He is a man, that's all. He was born as the son of a rishi."

The courtesan said, "If he is a man, I will be able to destroy him." After she had said this, she took up a tray made of gold filled up with fine and precious objects, and told the king of the country, "I will come back here mounted on the neck of this rishi."

The courtesan then immediately sought to assemble five hundred carriages carrying five hundred beautiful maidens and five hundred deer-carts carrying all sorts of delightful morsels all of which had been admixed with many herbs. She used many different hues to color them so that they appeared like various kinds of fruits and then took all sorts of greatly powerful fine liquors which, in appearance and flavor, were identical to water.

They dressed in tree bark clothing and grass clothing and traveled into the forest, appearing thereby as if they were rishis themselves. They set up grass huts off to one side of the Rishi's hut and then took up residence there. The one-horned rishi was wandering about and observed them. The maidens all came out and welcomed him. They used beautiful flowers and fine incenses as offerings to the Rishi. The Rishi was greatly delighted.

All of the maidens used lovely words and respectful phrases in greeting the Rishi. They took him on into their quarters and sat with him on fine bedding. They gave him fine clear liquor which he took to be pure water. They gave him delightful morsels which he took to be fruit. After he had feasted and drunk his fill, he told the maidens, "From the time of my birth on up to the present, this is a first. I have never yet had such choice fruit and such fine water."

The maidens said, "It is because we have been single-minded in our practice of goodness that the gods fulfill our wishes to obtain these choice fruits and fine water."

The Rishi asked the maidens, "How is it that your complexions and bodies are so full and flourishing?"

They replied, saying, "It is because we eat these fine fruits and drink this marvelous water that our bodies are so full and flourishing

[26]盛如此。女白仙人言。
汝何以不在此间住。答曰。
亦可住耳。女言。可共澡洗
即亦可之。女手柔软触之心
动。便复与诸[27]美女更互相
洗。欲心转生遂成婬事。即
失神通天为大雨七日七夜。
令得欢[28]喜饮食。七日[29]
已后酒[30]果皆尽。继以山水
木果。其味不美更索前者。
答言。已尽今当共行。去此
不远有可得处。仙人言。随
意。即便共出。[31]婬女知去
城不远。女便在道中卧言。
我极不能复行。仙人言。汝
不能行者。骑我项上当[32]项
汝去。女先遣信白王。王可
观我智能。王勅严驾出而观
之。问言。何由得尔。女白
王言。我以方便力故今已如
此。无所复能。令住城中好
供养恭敬之。[33]足五所欲。
拜为大臣住城少日。身转羸
瘦。念

简体字

[26]盛如此。女白仙人言。
汝何以不在此間住。答曰。
亦可住耳。女言。可共澡洗
即亦可之。女手柔軟觸之心
動。便復與諸[27]美女更互相
洗。欲心轉生遂成婬事。即
失神通天為大雨七日七夜。
令得歡[28]喜飲食。七日[29]
已後酒[30]果皆盡。繼以山水
木果。其味不美更索前者。
答言。已盡今當共行。去此
不遠有可得處。仙人言。隨
意。即便共出。[31]婬女知去
城不遠。女便在道中臥言。
我極不能復行。仙人言。汝
不能行者。騎我項上當[32]項
汝去。女先遣信白王。王可
觀我智能。王勅嚴駕出而觀
之。問言。何由得爾。女白
王言。我以方便力故今已如
此。無所復能。令住城中好
供養恭敬之。[33]足五所欲。
拜為大臣住城少日。身轉羸
瘦。念

正體字

as this." The maidens addressed the Rishi, saying, "Why don't you come and live here among us?"

He replied, saying, "I, too, could abide here."

The maidens said, "We could even bathe together." He then assented to that as well. The hands of the maidens were soft and tender. When they touched him, his mind moved. He then continued to bathe together with the beautiful maidens. Desirous thoughts began to develop and consequently he engaged in sexual intercourse. He immediately lost his superknowledges, whereupon the heavens made a great downpour of rain which went on for seven days and seven nights allowing them the opportunity to [remain indoors], devoting themselves to the delights of food and drink.

After the seven days had passed, the liquor and fruit were all gone, whereupon they continued to supply their needs with the waters of the mountain and the fruits from the trees. However, their flavors were not so marvelous, and so [the Rishi] sought more of what they had before.

She replied to him, saying, "They are already used up. We must now go together to a place, not far from here, where such things can be obtained."

The Rishi said, "We can do as you wish." They then went off together. The courtesan knew when they had come to a spot not far from the city. The maiden then lay down in the middle of the road and said, "I'm exhausted. I can't walk any further."

The Rishi said, "If it's the case that you cannot walk, sit up on my shoulders and I will carry you forth."

The maiden had already sent along beforehand a letter to the King in which she told the King, "The King will now be able to observe my intelligence and abilities."

The King ordered up his official carriage and went forth to observe them. He inquired of her, "How did you manage to bring this about?"

The maiden addressed the King, saying, "It is on account of the power of expedient means that I have now already caused the situation to develop in this way. I have no abilities beyond this. Order him to live within the city. Make fine offerings to him and pay respects to him. Keep him satisfied with the five objects of desire."

The King honored him with the status of a great official. [The Rishi] had dwelt in the city for only a short span of days when his body became haggard and emaciated. He remembered the mental

禅定心乐厌此世欲。王问仙人。汝何不乐身转羸瘦。仙人答王。我虽得五欲。常自忆念林间闲静诸仙游处不能去心。王自思惟。若我强违其志。违志为苦苦极则死。本以求除旱患。今已得之。当复何缘强夺其志。即发遣之。既还山中精进不久还得五通。佛告诸比丘。一角仙人我身是也。婬女者耶输陀罗是。尔时以欢喜丸惑我。我未断结为之所惑。今复欲以药欢喜丸惑我不可得也。以是事故知。细软触法能动仙人。何况愚夫。如是种种因缘。是名呵细滑欲。如是呵五欲除五盖[34]者。复次贪欲[35]之人去道甚远。所以者何。欲为种种恼乱住处。若心着贪欲无由近道。如除欲盖偈所说。

入道惭愧人。持钵福众生。
云何纵尘欲。沈没于五情。

簡体字

禪定心樂厭此世欲。王問仙人。汝何不樂身轉羸瘦。仙人答王。我雖得五欲。常自憶念林間閑靜諸仙遊處不能去心。王自思惟。若我強違其志。違志為苦苦極則死。本以求除旱患。今已得之。當復何緣強奪其志。即發遣之。既還山中精進不久還得五通。佛告諸比丘。一角仙人我身是也。婬女者耶輪陀羅是。爾時以歡喜丸惑我。我未斷結為之所惑。今復欲以藥歡喜丸惑我不可得也。以是事故知。細軟觸法能動仙人。何況愚夫。如是種種因緣。是名呵細滑欲。如是呵五欲除五蓋[34]者。復次貪欲[35]之人去道甚遠。所以者何。欲為種種惱亂住處。若心著貪欲無由近道。如除欲蓋偈所說。

入道慚愧人。持鉢福眾生。
云何縱塵欲。沈沒於五情。

正體字

bliss of dhyāna absorptions and so grew disgusted with these worldly desires. The King asked the Rishi, "How is it that you have become so unhappy that your body has now become so haggard and emaciated?"

The Rishi replied to the King, "Although I have gained the five desires, I constantly recall the leisure and stillness in the forest, the wandering place of all the rishis. I cannot get it out of my mind."

The King thought to himself, "If I force him to go against his aspirations, such a contravention of one's aspirations entails suffering. If the suffering reaches an extreme, then he will die. Originally, this was on account of seeking to get rid of the calamity of drought. Now I have already succeeded in that. Why should I continue to forcibly keep him from his aspirations?" Hence [the King] then released him.

After he had returned to the mountains, he had not applied himself vigorously for so very long before he regained once again the five superknowledges.

The Buddha told the Bhikshus, "The one-horned rishi was myself. The courtesan was Yaśodharā. At that time she succeeded in deceiving me with the delightful dumplings. I had not yet cut off the fetters and so was tricked by her. Now she again wished to use the delightful dumplings to trick me but was unable to succeed."

On account of this matter one knows that the dharma of subtle and tender touch is able to move even a rishi, how much the more would this be so of any foolish common person. All sorts of causes and conditions such as these illustrate what is meant by renouncing the desire for [sensations of] subtle smoothness. In this fashion one renounces the five desires.

2. ELIMINATING THE FIVE HINDRANCES

a. ELIMINATING SENSUAL DESIRE

As for eliminating the five hindrances, again, a person who indulges sensual desire (*kāma-chanda*), departs extremely far from the Path. How is this so? Sensual desire is the abiding place of all sorts of torment and chaos. If the mind is attached to sensual desire, one has no way to approach the Path. This is as described in the verse on banishing the hindrance of sensual desire:

A person with a sense of shame and blame who's entered the Path
And who holds up his bowl so as to provide blessings for beings—
How could he give free reign to desire for the sense objects
And thus become sunken down amidst the five sense faculties?

着铠持刀杖。见敌而退走。
如是[36]怯弱人。举世所轻笑。

比丘为乞士。除发着袈裟。
五情马所制。取笑亦如是。

又如豪贵人。盛服以严身。
而行乞衣食。取笑于众[184-1]
人。

比丘除饰好。毁形以摄心。
而更求欲乐。取笑亦如是。

已舍五欲乐。弃之而不顾。
如何还欲得。如愚自食吐。

如是[2]贪欲人。不知观本愿。
亦不识好丑。狂醉于渴爱。

惭愧尊重法。一切皆[3]已弃。
贤智所不亲。愚騃所爱近。

诸欲求时苦。得之多怖畏。
失时怀热恼。一切无乐时。

诸欲患如是。以何当舍之。
得诸禅定乐。则不为所欺。

欲乐着无厌。以何能灭除。

着铠持刀杖。见敌而退走。
如是[36]怯弱人。举世所轻笑。

简体字

著鎧持刀杖。見敵而退走。
如是[36]怯弱人。舉世所輕笑。

比丘為乞士。除髮著袈裟。
五情馬所制。取笑亦如是。

又如豪貴人。盛服以嚴身。
而行乞衣食。取笑於眾[184-1]
人。

比丘除飾好。毀形以攝心。
而更求欲樂。取笑亦如是。

已捨五欲樂。棄之而不顧。
如何還欲得。如愚自食吐。

如是[2]貪欲人。不知觀本願。
亦不識好醜。狂醉於渴愛。

慚愧尊重法。一切皆[3]已棄。
賢智所不親。愚騃所愛近。

諸欲求時苦。得之多怖畏。
失時懷熱惱。一切無樂時。

諸欲患如是。以何當捨之。
得諸禪定樂。則不為所欺。

欲樂著無厭。以何能滅除。

正體字

To put on the armor and brandish both sword and truncheon,
[Only to] retreat and run away at the sight of the enemy,
Such a timid and faint-hearted man
Is such as the entire world slights and laughs at.

The bhikshu is an almsman
He gets rid of his hair and dons the *kāṣāya* robe
If he is so controlled as this by the horse of the five sense faculties,
He brings on laughter in just this same way.

If he is also like an aristocratic noble
Who adorns himself in formal attire
And then goes about begging for clothing and food,
He thus draws forth the laughter of everyone.

The bhikshu gets rid of adornment with finery.
He neglects his appearance in order to focus his mind.
If he continues to seek for the pleasures of sensual desire,
He brings on laughter in just this way.

He's already forsaken the pleasures of the five desires,
Casting them off without looking back.
Why then would he still desire to obtain them,
Like a stupid person who feasts on his own vomit?

People such as these who engage the sensual desires
Do not know to contemplate their original vows,
Nor do they distinguish between the good and the bad.
They've become crazed and drunken with craving.

One with a sense of shame and blame who deeply reveres Dharma
Has already entirely cast aside everything.
That which the worthy and wise do not grow close to,
Is that which the foolish and stupid approach with affection.

All of the sensual desires, when sought, inflict suffering.
Once one's obtained them, there's much fear [they may be lost].
When they're lost, one is beset by agitation and torment.
Thus there is never a time in which one abides in bliss.

If the sensual desires bring calamities of this sort
How can one succeed in forsaking them?
If one gains the bliss of the dhyāna absorptions,
Then one will not be cheated by them.

If one is insatiably attached to the pleasures of sensual desire,
How is one able to extinguish and get rid of them?

若得不净观。此心自然无。

着欲不自觉。以何悟其心。
当观老病死。尔乃出四渊。

诸欲难放舍。何以能远之。
若能乐善法。此欲自然息。

诸欲难可解。何以能释之。
观身得实相。则不为所缚。

如是诸观法。能灭诸欲火。
譬如大澍雨。野火无[4]在者。

[0184a25] 如是等种种因缘。灭除欲盖。瞋恚盖者。失诸善法之本。堕诸恶道之因。[5]诸乐之怨家。善心之大贼。种种恶口之府藏。如佛教瞋弟子偈言。

汝当知思惟。受身及处胎。
秽恶之幽苦。既生之艰难。

既思得此意。而复不灭瞋。
则当知此辈。则是无心人。

若无罪[6]报果。亦无诸呵责。
犹[7]当应慈忍。何况苦果剧。

若得不淨觀。此心自然無。

著欲不自覺。以何悟其心。
當觀老病死。爾乃出四淵。

諸欲難放捨。何以能遠之。
若能樂善法。此欲自然息。

諸欲難可解。何以能釋之。
觀身得實相。則不為所縛。

如是諸觀法。能滅諸欲火。
譬如大澍雨。野火無[4]在者。

[0184a25] 如是等種種因緣。滅除欲蓋。瞋恚蓋者。失諸善法之本。墮諸惡道之因。[5]諸樂之怨家。善心之大賊。種種惡口之府藏。如佛教瞋弟子偈言。

汝當知思惟。受身及處胎。
穢惡之幽苦。既生之艱難。

既思得此意。而復不滅瞋。
則當知此輩。則是無心人。

若無罪[6]報果。亦無諸呵責。
猶[7]當應慈忍。何況苦果劇。

简体字   正體字

If one succeeds in the contemplation of impurity,
Thoughts of this sort then naturally disappear.

If one remains attached to desire without being aware of it oneself,
How can one succeed in awakening his own mind?
He should contemplate aging, sickness, and death.
Doing so, he then becomes able to escape those four abysses.[4]

The sensual desires are difficult to put down and relinquish.
How is one able to distance oneself from them?
If one is able to find pleasure in good dharmas,
This sensual desire will naturally be put to rest.

The sensual desires are difficult to untie.
How is one able to let loose of them?
If one contemplates the body and realizes its true character,
Then one will not be tied up by them.

Dharmas of contemplation such as these
Are able to extinguish the fires of the sensual desires
Just as when, with the coming of the great seasonal rains,
The wildfires no longer continue to burn.

All sorts of causal bases such as these illustrate what is meant by extinguishing and eliminating the hindrance of sensual desire.

b. ELIMINATING ILL-WILL

As for the hindrance of ill-will (*vyāpāda*), it is the basis for losing all good dharmas, the cause for falling into the wretched destinies, the enemy of all forms of bliss, the great thief preying on the wholesome mind, and the repository of all manner of harsh speech. This is illustrated in a verse spoken by the Buddha to instruct disciples under the influence of hatefulness:

You should be aware of and contemplate this:
In taking on a body and dwelling in the womb,
The suffering of confinement in defiled and fearsome straights,
And then, once born, the intense difficulty which ensues.

If one has contemplated this and then realized its import,
And yet still not extinguishe ill-will,
Then one should understand that those of this ilk
Are people devoid of [humane] thoughtfulness.

Even if there were no resultant retribution for the offense,
And, even if there were no rebuke and scolding as a result,
One should still be able to stop it through kindness and patience.
How much the more so, given the intensity of its bitter fruits?

当观老病死。一切无[8]免者。
当起慈悲心。云何恶加物。

众生相怨贼。斫刺受苦毒。
云何修善人。而复加恼害。

常当行慈悲。定心修诸善。
不当怀恶意。侵害于一切。

若勤修道法。恼害则不行。
善恶势不竝。如水火相背。

瞋恚来覆心。不知别好丑。
亦不识利害。不知畏恶道。

不计他苦恼。不觉身心疲。
先自受苦因。然后及他人。

若欲灭瞋恚。当思惟慈心。
独处自清闲。息事灭因缘。

当畏老病死。九种瞋恼除。
如是思惟慈。则得灭瞋毒。

[0184b22]　如是等种种因缘。
除瞋恚盖。睡眠盖者。能破
今世三事欲乐利乐福德。能
破

當觀老病死。一切無[8]免者。
當起慈悲心。云何惡加物。

眾生相怨賊。斫刺受苦毒。
云何修善人。而復加惱害。

常當行慈悲。定心修諸善。
不當懷惡意。侵害於一切。

若勤修道法。惱害則不行。
善惡勢不竝。如水火相背。

瞋恚來覆心。不知別好醜。
亦不識利害。不知畏惡道。

不計他苦惱。不覺身心疲。
先自受苦因。然後及他人。

若欲滅瞋恚。當思惟慈心。
獨處自清閑。息事滅因緣。

當畏老病死。九種瞋惱除。
如是思惟慈。則得滅瞋毒。

[0184b22]　如是等種種因緣。
除瞋恚蓋。睡眠蓋者。能破
今世三事欲樂利樂福德。能
破

简体字　　　　　　　　　　　正體字

One ought to contemplate aging, sickness, and death.
There is no one who is able to avoid it.
One should bring forth thoughts of kindness and compassion.
How could one inflict evil deeds on other beings?

Beings act like thieves who are enemies each to the other,
Hacking and stabbing each other, undergoing intense suffering.
How could one be a person who cultivates goodness
And yet still inflict even more torment and injury on others?

One should always embody kindness and compassion,
And fix one's mind on cultivating every form of goodness.
One must not cherish malicious intentions,
Whereby one attacks others and wreaks widespread harm.

If one diligently cultivates the dharmas of the Path,
Then one will not practice torment and injury.
The power of good and evil are incompatible,
Just as water and fire are opposed to one another.

Hatefulness comes and covers over the mind,
One doesn't know then to distinguish between good and bad,
Nor is one aware of what benefits or injures.
One doesn't know then to fear the wretched destinies.

One does not reckon the suffering and torment of others.
One does not realize the wearying effect on body and mind.
One first takes on the cause of suffering,
And then afterwards visits it upon other people.

If one wishes to extinguish ill-will,
One ought to contemplate with the mind of kindness,
And dwell alone in self-purifying leisure,
Putting aside endeavors and extinguishing its causal bases.

One ought to know fear of aging, sickness, and death,
And get rid of the nine kinds of hatefulness and torment.
If, in this manner, one contemplates with kindness,
Then one will succeed in extinguishing the poison of hatefulness.

All sorts of causal bases such as these illustrate the means for getting rid of the hindrance of ill-will.

c. ELIMINATING LETHARGY-AND-SLEEPINESS

As for the hindrance of lethargy-and-sleepiness (*styāna-middha*), it is able to destroy three features of the present existence: the happiness associated with the various desires, the happiness associated with wealth, and one's stock of merit. It is able to destroy the most

今世后世究竟乐。与死无
异。唯有气息。如一菩萨以
偈呵[9]眠睡弟子言。

汝起勿抱臭身卧。
种种不净假名人。
如得重病箭入体。
诸苦痛集安可眠。
一切世间死火烧。
汝当求出安可眠。
如人被缚将去杀。
灾害垂至安可眠。
结贼不灭害未除。
如共毒蛇同室宿。
亦如临阵白刃间。
尔时安可而睡眠。
眠为大暗无所见。
日日[10]侵诳夺人明。
以眠覆心无所识。
如是大失安可眠。

[0184c05] 如是等种种因缘。呵
睡眠盖。[11]掉悔盖者。[*]掉
之为法破出家心。如[12]人摄
心犹不能住。何况[*]掉散。[*]
掉散之人如无钩醉象[13]决鼻
骆驼。不可禁制。如偈说。

汝已剃头着染衣。
执持瓦钵行乞食。
云何乐着戏[*]掉法。
既无法利失世乐。

[0184c11] 悔[14]法者。如犯大
罪人常怀畏怖。悔箭

今世後世究竟樂。與死無
異。唯有氣息。如一菩薩以
偈呵[9]眠睡弟子言。

汝起勿抱臭身臥。
種種不淨假名人。
如得重病箭入體。
諸苦痛集安可眠。
一切世間死火燒。
汝當求出安可眠。
如人被縛將去殺。
災害垂至安可眠。
結賊不滅害未除。
如共毒蛇同室宿。
亦如臨陣白刃間。
爾時安可而睡眠。
眠為大闇無所見。
日日[10]侵誑奪人明。
以眠覆心無所識。
如是大失安可眠。

[0184c05] 如是等種種因緣。呵
睡眠蓋。[11]掉悔蓋者。[*]掉
之為法破出家心。如[12]人攝
心猶不能住。何況[*]掉散。[*]
掉散之人如無鉤醉象[13]決鼻
駱駝。不可禁制。如偈說。

汝已剃頭著染衣。
執持瓦鉢行乞食。
云何樂著戲[*]掉法。
既無法利失世樂。

[0184c11] 悔[14]法者。如犯大
罪人常懷畏怖。悔箭

简体字

正體字

ultimate forms of bliss enjoyed in both present and future lives. It is no different from death and differs from it only in that breathing is still present. This is as illustrated by a verse spoken by a bodhisattva in scolding his sleepy disciple:

> You! Get up! Don't lay there hugging that stinking body
> That is all sorts of impurities falsely referred to as a "person."
> It's as if you've gotten a grave illness or been shot with an arrow.
> With the pain of suffering accumulating, how then can you sleep?

> The entire world is being burned up by the fire of death.
> You should be seeking means of escape. How then can you sleep?
> Just as when someone bound and taken off for execution,
> With grievous injury about to befall you, how can you sleep?

> With insurgent fetters not yet quelled and harm not yet averted,
> It's as if one were sleeping in a room with a venomous snake,
> And is as if one had met up with the gleaming blades of soldiers.
> At such a time, how could it be that you now can still sleep?

> Sleep is a great darkness in which nothing is visible.
> With every day, it invades and deceives, stealing a person's vision.
> When sleep blankets the mind, one is not aware of anything.
> With such great faults as these, how then can you sleep?

All sorts of causal bases such as these illustrate the need to eliminate the hindrance of lethargy-and-sleepiness.[5]

d. ELIMINATING EXCITEDNESS-AND-REGRETFULNESS

As for the hindrance of "excitedness-and-regretfulness," (*auddhatya-kaukṛtya*), it is the action of "excitedness" as a dharma that it destroys the mind of one who has left the home life. If a person focuses his mind, it may still not remain in one place, how much the less if one is excited and scattered. A person who is excited and scattered is like a drunken elephant unmanaged by [the elephant keeper's] hook and like a camel whose nose has just been pierced. He cannot be controlled. This is as set forth in a verse:

> You've already shaved your head and donned the dyed robe.
> Taking up the clay bowl, you go out on the alms round.
> How can you delight in clinging to ways of frivolity and agitation?
> Having gained no Dharma benefit, you lose worldly bliss as well.

As for the dharma of regretfulness, it is just as with a person who has committed a great transgression and so constantly embraces fearfulness on that account. In such a case, the arrow of regretfulness

入心坚不可拔。如偈说。

不应作而作。应作而不作。
悔恼火所烧。后世堕恶道。

若人罪[15]能悔。已悔则放舍。
如是心安乐。不应常念着。

若有二种悔。不作若已作。
以是悔着心。是则愚人相。

不以心悔故。不作而能作。
诸恶事[16]已作。不能令不作。

[0184c21] 如是等种种因缘。呵
[*]掉[17]悔盖。疑盖者。以疑
覆[18]心故。于诸法中不得定
心。定心无故。于佛法中空
无所得。譬如人入宝山。若
无手者无所能取。如说疑义
偈言。

如人在岐道。疑惑无所趣。
诸法实相中。疑亦复如是。

疑故不懃求。诸法之实相。
是疑从痴生。恶中之弊恶。

入心堅不可拔。如偈說。

不應作而作。應作而不作。
悔惱火所燒。後世墮惡道。

若人罪[15]能悔。已悔則放捨。
如是心安樂。不應常念著。

若有二種悔。不作若已作。
以是悔著心。是則愚人相。

不以心悔故。不作而能作。
諸惡事[16]已作。不能令不作。

[0184c21] 如是等種種因緣。呵
[*]掉[17]悔蓋。疑蓋者。以疑
覆[18]心故。於諸法中不得定
心。定心無故。於佛法中空
無所得。譬如人入寶山。若
無手者無所能取。如說疑義
偈言。

如人在岐道。疑惑無所趣。
諸法實相中。疑亦復如是。

疑故不懃求。諸法之實相。
是疑從癡生。惡中之弊惡。

简体字   正體字

has plunged so deeply into his mind and stuck so so firmly that it cannot be pulled out. This is as described in a verse:

> One ought not to have done it and yet one did it.
> One ought to have done it and yet one did not do it.
> One is burned by the fire of regretful torment.
> And in later lives falls into the wretched destinies.

> If a person is able to feel regret for an offense,
> Having regretted it, one should then put it down and let it go.
> A mind like this abides in happiness.
> One should not constantly remain attached to it in one's thoughts.

> If one has the two kinds of regretfulness,
> Having not done and having already done it,
> Because this regretfulness attaches to the mind,
> This then is the mark of a foolish person.

> It is not the case that by means of the mind's feeling regret
> That which one didn't do will still be able to be done.
> [As for] the evil endeavors one has already committed,
> One is unable to cause them to be undone.

All sorts of causal bases such as these illustrate the necessity of eliminating the hindrance of excitedness-and-regretfulness.[6]

e. ELIMINATING THE HINDRANCE OF DOUBTFULNESS

As for the hindrance of doubtfulness (*vicikitsā*), because doubtfulness covers over the mind, one is unable to achieve a resolutely fixed mind with respect to any dharma. Because one remains without any definite resolve, one's endeavors in the Buddha's Dharma are useless and one gains nothing whatsoever. This is analogous to a person who enters into a mountain full of jewels. If he has no hands, he remains unable to take anything with him. This is as set forth in a verse on the meaning of doubtfulness:

> It is just as when a person on a forked road
> Is so confused by doubtfulness that he goes nowhere at all,
> In [seeking realization] of the true character of dharmas,
> Doubtfulness acts in just this same way.

> Because one remains doubtful, one does not seek diligently
> [To realize] the true character of dharmas.
> This doubt comes forth from stupidity,
> Among those [mental factors] which are bad, it is the most inferior.

善不善法中。生死及涅盘。
定实真有法。于中莫生疑。

汝若生疑心。死王狱吏缚。
如师子搏鹿。不能得解脱。

在世虽有疑。当随妙善法。
譬如观岐道。利好者应逐。

[0185a06] 如是等种种因缘故。
应舍疑[185-1]盖。弃是五盖。
譬如负[2]债得脱。重病得[3]
差。饥饿之地得至豐国。如
从狱得出。如于恶贼中得自
[*]免济安隐无患。行者亦如
是。除却五盖其心安隐清净
快乐。譬如日月以五事覆
曀。烟云尘雾罗睺。阿修罗
手障则不能明照。人心亦如
是。为五盖所覆自不能利。
亦不能益人。若能呵五欲除
五盖。行五法。欲精进念巧
慧一心。行此五法得五[4]支
成就。初禅欲名欲。于欲界
中出欲。得初禅

善不善法中。生死及涅槃。
定實真有法。於中莫生疑。

汝若生疑心。死王獄吏縛。
如師子搏鹿。不能得解脫。

在世雖有疑。當隨妙善法。
譬如觀岐道。利好者應逐。

[0185a06] 如是等種種因緣故。
應捨疑[185-1]蓋。棄是五蓋。
譬如負[2]債得脫。重病得[3]
差。飢餓之地得至豐國。如
從獄得出。如於惡賊中得自
[*]免濟安隱無患。行者亦如
是。除却五蓋其心安隱清淨
快樂。譬如日月以五事覆
曀。煙雲塵霧羅睺。阿修羅
手障則不能明照。人心亦如
是。為五蓋所覆自不能利。
亦不能益人。若能呵五欲除
五蓋。行五法。欲精進念巧
慧一心。行此五法得五[4]支
成就。初禪欲名欲。於欲界
中出欲。得初禪

简体字　　　　　　　　　　正體字

Among the wholesome and unwholesome dharmas,
Cyclic birth-and-death as well as nirvāṇa
Are definitely real and truly-existent dharmas.
Do not give rise to doubtfulness with respect to them.

If you give rise to thoughts of doubtfulness,
The King of Death's hell minions will tie you up.
Just as when a lion pounces on a deer,
You will be unable to succeed in escaping.

Although one may possess doubts as one abides in the world,
One should still accord with the sublime and wholesome Dharma,
Just as when one contemplates a road which comes to a fork,
One should follow the one which leads to fine benefits.

On account of all sorts of causal bases such as these, one should eliminate the hindrance of doubtfulness.

f. The Benefits of Eliminating the Five Hindrances (Five Similes)

When one gets rid of these five hindrances, it is analogous to paying off a debt and being released from it, like gaining a cure for a serious disease, like leaving behind a place of famine and reaching a country of abundance, like getting out of prison, like being rescued from the midst of evil bandits so that one is peaceful, secure, and free of calamity. It is just like this for the practitioner. When he gets rid of the five hindrances, his mind becomes peaceful, secure, pure, and blissful.

g. Analogy: The Negative Effect of the Hindrances on the Mind

It is just as with the sun and moon which may be obscured by five things: When they are blocked by smoke, clouds, dust, fog, or the hand of Rāhu the *asura*, they are unable to shine brightly. So too it is with a person's mind is. When it is covered over by the five hindrances, one remains unable to benefit oneself and also unable to be of help to others.

3. Practicing the Five Dharmas: Zeal; Vigor; Mindfulness; etc.

Where one is able to renounce the five desires and eliminate the five hindrances, one then takes up the practice of five dharmas, namely zeal, vigor, mindfulness, discerning knowing, and single-mindedness. If one practices these five dharmas, then one succeeds in gaining the five component aspects [of the first dhyāna] and thus proceeds to perfect one's realization of the first dhyāna.

"Zeal" (*chanda*) refers to the desire to escape from the desires of the desire realm and gain realization of the first dhyāna.

精进。名离家持戒。初夜后
夜专精不懈。节食摄心不令
[5]驰散念。名念初禅乐。知
欲界不净狂惑可贱。初禅为
尊重可贵。巧慧名观察筹量
欲界乐。初禅乐轻重得失一
心。名[6]常系心缘中不令分
散。复次专求初禅放舍欲
乐。譬如患怨常欲灭除。则
不为怨之所害也。如佛为着
欲婆罗门说。我本观欲。欲
为怖畏忧苦因缘。欲为少乐
[7]其苦甚多。欲为魔网缠绵
难出。欲为烧热乾竭诸乐。
譬如[8]树林四边火起。欲为
如临火坑甚可怖畏。如逼毒
蛇。如怨贼拔刀。如恶罗
刹。如恶毒入口。如吞[9]销
铜。如三流狂象。如临大深
坑。如师子断道。如摩竭鱼
开口。诸欲亦如是甚可怖
畏。若着诸欲令人恼苦。着
欲之人亦如狱因。如鹿在
围。如鸟入网。

简体字

精進。名離家持戒。初夜後
夜專精不懈。節食攝心不令
[5]馳散念。名念初禪樂。知
欲界不淨狂惑可賤。初禪為
尊重可貴。巧慧名觀察籌量
欲界樂。初禪樂輕重得失一
心。名[6]常繫心緣中不令分
散。復次專求初禪放捨欲
樂。譬如患怨常欲滅除。則
不為怨之所害也。如佛為著
欲婆羅門說。我本觀欲。欲
為怖畏憂苦因緣。欲為少樂
[7]其苦甚多。欲為魔網纏綿
難出。欲為燒熱乾竭諸樂。
譬如[8]樹林四邊火起。欲為
如臨火坑甚可怖畏。如逼毒
蛇。如怨賊拔刀。如惡羅
刹。如惡毒入口。如吞[9]銷
銅。如三流狂象。如臨大深
坑。如師子斷道。如摩竭魚
開口。諸欲亦如是甚可怖
畏。若著諸欲令人惱苦。著
欲之人亦如獄因。如鹿在
圍。如鳥入網。

正體字

"Vigor" (*vīrya*) refers to abandoning the home life, observing the moral-virtue precepts, remaining exclusively focused and not lax in the beginning of the night and in the end of the night, being measured in eating, and focusing the mind in a way in which it is not allowed to run off and become scattered.

"Mindfulness" (*smṛti*) refers to being mindful of the bliss of the first dhyāna, being aware that the desire realm is impure, deceptive and worthy of being seen as base whereas the first dhyāna is honorable, to be esteemed, and worthy of being seen as noble.

"Discerning knowing" (*samprajñāna*) refers to contemplating, investigating, and taking the measure of the bliss of the desire realm as compared with the bliss of the first dhyāna, thus realizing then their relative importance and benefits.

"Single-mindedness" (*citta-eka-agra*) refers to constantly anchoring the mind in the midst of specific objective conditions while not allowing it to split off and become scattered.

4. Renunciation of Desire: 43 Analogies Leading to First Dhyāna

Moreover, one seeks exclusively to gain the first dhyāna and, in doing so, renounces the pleasures of desire. By way of analogy, it is as if one were obsessed with worry over a particular enemy and so constantly sought to eliminate him. This being the case, that enemy would have no opportunity to bring him harm.

This is illustrated by what the Buddha said to the Brahman who was attached to desire: "I originally contemplated desire and realized that desire constitutes a cause and condition for apprehensiveness, distress, and suffering. Desire brings only few pleasures, whereas its sufferings are extremely numerous."

Desire is the net of the demons and an entangling web from which it is difficult to escape. Desire is a burning heat drying up all bliss. It is like being in a forest with flames rising on all four sides. Desire, as when approaching a fiery pit, is extremely fearsome. It is like cornering a venomous snake, like an enemy invader brandishing a knife, like an evil *rākṣasa* ghost, like deadly poison entering the mouth, like swallowing molten copper, like three columns of crazed elephants, like approaching an extremely deep abyss, like a lion blocking the path, like the Makara fish-monster opening its maw. All desires are like this and are very much worthy of being feared. The desires cause people to undergo tormenting suffering.

Those people who are attached to desire are like convicts in a prison, like deer caught in a corral-trap, like birds snared in a net,

如鱼吞钩。如[10]豺搏狗。如乌在[11]鵄群。如蛇值野猪。如鼠在猫中。如群盲[12]人临坑。如蝇着热油。如[13]〔病-丙+宁〕人在阵。如躄人遭火。如入沸醶河。如舐蜜涂刀。如四衢脔肉。如薄覆刀[14]林。如华覆不净。如蜜涂毒甕。如毒蛇箧。如梦虚诳。如假借当归。如幻诳小儿。如焰无实。如没大水。如船入摩竭鱼口。如雹害谷。如[15]霹雳临人。诸欲亦如是。虚诳无实无牢无强。乐少苦多。欲为魔军破[16]诸善功德。常为劫害众生故。出如是等种种诸喻。呵五欲除五盖行五法。得至初禅。问曰。八背舍八胜处十一切入四无量心诸定三昧。如是等种种定。不名波罗蜜。何以但言禅波罗蜜。答曰。此诸定功德。都是思惟修。禅[17]秦言思惟修。言禅波罗蜜一切皆摄。复次禅最大如王。说禅则摄

如魚吞鉤。如[10]豺搏狗。如烏在[11]鵄群。如蛇值野猪。如鼠在貓中。如群盲[12]人臨坑。如蠅著熱油。如[13]〔病-丙+寧〕人在陣。如躄人遭火。如入沸醶河。如舐蜜塗刀。如四衢臠肉。如薄覆刀[14]林。如華覆不淨。如蜜塗毒甕。如毒蛇篋。如夢虛誑。如假借當歸。如幻誑小兒。如焰無實。如沒大水。如船入摩竭魚口。如雹害穀。如[15]霹靂臨人。諸欲亦如是。虛誑無實無牢無強。樂少苦多。欲為魔軍破[16]諸善功德。常為劫害眾生故。出如是等種種諸喻。呵五欲除五蓋行五法。得至初禪。問曰。八背捨八勝處十一切入四無量心諸定三昧。如是等種種定。不名波羅蜜。何以但言禪波羅蜜。答曰。此諸定功德。都是思惟修。禪[17]秦言思惟修。言禪波羅蜜一切皆攝。復次禪最大如王。說禪則攝

简体字   正體字

like fish who have swallowed a hook, like a dog pounced upon by a leopard, like a crow amidst a band of owls, like a snake which has run up against a wild boar, and like a mouse among cats. They are like blind men approaching an abyss, like a fly caught in hot oil, like a peaceful man caught up in military combat, like a lame person who has entered a conflagration, like one who has entered a river of boiling brine, like one who licks a honey-smeared blade, and like one [sentenced to be] sliced to ribbons in the city square.

The desires are like a thinly covered grove of knives, like flowers covering filth, like a jar of honey mixed with poison, and like a basket of venomous snakes. They are like the falseness and deception of a dream, like a debt which must be repaid, and like a conjuration which deceives a small child. In their lack of substantiality, they are like the flames of a fire. [Involvement with them] is like being drowned in a great body of water and like when a boat enters into the gullet of the Makara fish-monster.

They are like a hailstorm destroying crops, like crashing thunder and lightning striking right next to a person. The desires are just like this. They are false, deceptive, devoid of substantiality, devoid of durability, devoid of potency, possessing only few pleasures, but many sufferings. The desires constitute an army of demons smashing all of one's goodness and merit.

It is because they constantly serve to plunder and injure beings that we present all sorts of analogies such as these. If one renounces the five desires, gets rid of the five hindrances, and practices the five dharmas, one may then succeed in reaching the first dhyāna.

5. QUESTION: WHY IS "DHYĀNA" THIS *PĀRAMITĀ'S* DESIGNATION?

Question: The absorptions and samādhis such as the eight liberations (*vimokṣa*), the eight bases of ascendancy (*abhibhvāyatana*), the ten universal bases (*kṛtsnāyatana*), and the four immeasurable minds (*apramāṇacitta*)—all sorts of other absorptions such as these are not referred to here as "*pāramitā.*" Why is it that one speaks only of "dhyāna" *pāramitā*?

6. RESPONSE: "DHYĀNA" SUBSUMES ALL MEDITATIVE PRACTICES

Response: The meritorious qualities of all of these absorptions in every case involve the cultivation of contemplative thought. (Ch. text note: In our language, "dhyāna" means "the cultivation of contemplative thought.") When one speaks of "the *pāramitā* of dhyāna," all of these are subsumed. Moreover, "dhyāna" is the greatest among them and so is like a king. When one speaks of "dhyāna," then this subsumes

一切。说馀定则不摄。何以
故。是四禅中智定等而乐。
未到地中间地智多而定少。
无色界定多而智少。是处非
乐。譬如车一轮强一轮弱则
不安隐。智定不等亦如是。
复次是四禅处有四等心。五
神通背舍胜处。一切处无诤
三昧。愿智顶禅自在定练
禅。十四变化心般舟般。诸
菩萨三昧首楞严等。略说则
百二十。诸佛三昧不动等。
略说则百八。及佛得道舍
寿。如是等种种功德妙定皆
在禅中。以是故禅名波罗
蜜。[18]馀定不名波罗蜜。问
曰。汝先言呵五欲除五盖。
行五法得初禅。修何事依何
道能得初禅。答曰。依不净
观安那般那[19]念等诸

一切。說餘定則不攝。何以
故。是四禪中智定等而樂。
未到地中間地智多而定少。
無色界定多而智少。是處非
樂。譬如車一輪強一輪弱則
不安隱。智定不等亦如是。
復次是四禪處有四等心。五
神通背捨勝處。一切處無諍
三昧。願智頂禪自在定練
禪。十四變化心般舟般。諸
菩薩三昧首楞嚴等。略說則
百二十。諸佛三昧不動等。
略說則百八。及佛得道捨
壽。如是等種種功德妙定皆
在禪中。以是故禪名波羅
蜜。[18]餘定不名波羅蜜。問
曰。汝先言呵五欲除五蓋。
行五法得初禪。修何事依何
道能得初禪。答曰。依不淨
觀安那般那[19]念等諸

简体字　　　　　　　　　正體字

all of them. When one speaks of any of the other absorptions, then one does not thereby subsume the rest. Why is this? Within these four dhyānas, wisdom and meditative absorption are equal and so they are blissful. At the stage of "the preliminary ground" (*anāgamya*, a.k.a. "access concentration"), wisdom is greater and meditative absorption is lesser. In the formless realm, absorption is greater whereas wisdom is lesser. Such stations as these are not blissful. They are analogous to a carriage on which one wheel is strong and one wheel is weak. If this is the case, then one is not peaceful or secure. When wisdom and absorption do not abide in equal balance, then it is just like this.

Moreover, in the stations of these four dhyānas, there exist the four immeasurable minds (lit. "minds of equal regard"), the five superknowledges, the liberations, the bases of ascendancy, the universal bases, the samādhi of non-contention (*araṇā-samādhi*), the knowledge arising through resolution (*praṇidhi-jñāna*), the summit-reaching dhyāna (*prāntakoṭika-dhyāna*), the sovereign-independence absorption, the refining dhyānas, the fourteen transformation-generating mind states [contained within the four dhyānas], the *pratyutpanna-samādhi*, the samādhis of the bodhisattvas, the foremost *śuraṅgama*, and so forth. Generally-described, there are one hundred and twenty.

Generally-described, the samādhis of the Buddhas such as the "immovable" [samādhi] number one hundred and eight. These reach even to those achieved by the Buddhas when they gain realization of the Path and when they relinquish their lives. All sorts of other such marvelous absorptions possessed of meritorious qualities are contained within "dhyāna." It is for this reason that "dhyāna" is referred to as the [emblematic designation for] the *"pāramitā"* [associated with meditative discipline] whereas the other absorptions do not serve as the basis for referring to *"pāramitā."*

7. QUESTION: WHICH PRACTICES BRING ABOUT THE FIRST DHYĀNA?

Question: You stated earlier that, if one renounces the five desires, gets rid of the five hindrances, and cultivates five dharmas, then one gains the first dhyāna. Precisely which endeavors does one actually cultivate and which path does one base oneself on so that one then becomes able to reach the first dhyāna?

8. RESPONSE: IMPURITY, BREATH, ETC., PER THE *DHYĀNA SUTRA* VERSE

Response: One relies upon the contemplation of impurity, the *ānāpāna* mindfulness (of respiration), and other such methods of

定门。如禅经禅义偈中说。

离欲及恶法。有觉并有观。
离生得喜乐。是人入初禅。

已得离婬火。则获清凉定。
如人大热闷。入冷[20]池则乐。

如贫得宝藏。大喜觉动心。
分别则为观。入初禅亦然。

知二法乱心。虽善而应离。
如大水澄静。波荡亦无见。

譬如人大极。安隐睡卧时。
若有唤呼声。其心大恼乱。

摄心入禅时。以觉观为恼。
是故除觉观。得入一识处。

内心清净故。定生得喜乐。
得入此二禅。喜勇心大悦。

摄心第一定。寂然无所念。
患喜欲弃之。亦如舍觉观。

由受故有喜。失喜则生忧。
离喜乐身受。舍念及方便。

定門。如禪經禪義偈中說。

離欲及惡法。有覺并有觀。
離生得喜樂。是人入初禪。

已得離婬火。則獲清涼定。
如人大熱悶。入冷[20]池則樂。

如貧得寶藏。大喜覺動心。
分別則為觀。入初禪亦然。

知二法亂心。雖善而應離。
如大水澄靜。波蕩亦無見。

譬如人大極。安隱睡臥時。
若有喚呼聲。其心大惱亂。

攝心入禪時。以覺觀為惱。
是故除覺觀。得入一識處。

內心清淨故。定生得喜樂。
得入此二禪。喜勇心大悅。

攝心第一定。寂然無所念。
患喜欲棄之。亦如捨覺觀。

由受故有喜。失喜則生憂。
離喜樂身受。捨念及方便。

简体字   正體字

access to absorption. This is as set forth in the *Dhyāna Sutra*'s verse on the meaning of dhyāna:

> One leaves behind desire as well as evil dharmas.
> There exist "ideation" as well as "mental discursion."
> This abandonment generates "joy" and "bliss" which are realized.
> This person gains entry into the first dhyāna.
>
> When one has already succeeded in leaving behind the fire of lust,
> Then one gains this clear and cool "concentration,"
> Just as if a person oppressed by great heat,
> On entering a cool water pool, then enjoys bliss.
>
> This is just as when a poor person gains a treasury of jewels:
> "Ideation" full of great delight moves his mind.
> As he proceeds with discriminations, that is "mental discursion."
> Entering the first dhyāna is just like this.
>
> One realizes that these two dharmas bring chaos to the mind
> And that, although wholesome, they, too, must be abandoned,
> This is just as with a large pool of still and clear water:
> When waves wash across it, one cannot see down into it.
>
> It is analogous to a person who, greatly exhausted,
> Once safe and secure, lays down to sleep:
> If then there is the noise of someone calling out to him,
> His mind feels greatly tormented and chaotic.
>
> When one focuses one's mind and enters dhyāna,
> One takes "ideation" and "mental discursion" to be tormenting.
> Therefore one eliminates this ideation and mental discursion,
> And succeeds in reaching the station of singular consciousness.
>
> Because, inwardly, one's mind is pure,
> "Concentration" arises and one gains "joy" and "bliss".
> When one succeeds in entering the second dhyāna,
> The joy is intensely strong and one's mind is greatly pleased.
>
> Focusing the mind, one enters the foremost level of concentration,
> One abides in stillness and has nothing of which one thinks.
> One sees "joy" as calamitous and desires to eliminate it,
> Just as one has done with "ideation" and "mental discursion."
>
> It is through feeling that one experiences "joy."
> If one loses "joy," then one falls prey to distress.
> One abandons "joy" and experiences "physically-based bliss."
> One relinquishes thoughts as well as that which facilitates them.

圣人得能舍。馀人舍为难。
若能知乐患。见不动大安。

忧喜先已除。苦乐今亦断。
舍念清净心。入第四禅中。

第三禅中乐。无常动故苦。
欲界中断忧。初二禅除喜。

是故佛世尊。第四禅中说。
先已断忧喜。今[21]则除苦乐。

[0185c28] 复次持戒清净闲居独处。守摄诸根初夜后夜专精思惟。弃舍外乐以禅自娱。离诸欲不善法。依未到地得初禅。初禅如阿毗昙说。禅有四种。一味相应。二净三无漏。四初禅所摄报得五众。是中行者入净无漏。二禅三禅四禅亦如是。如佛所说。若有比丘离诸欲及恶不善法。有觉有观。离生喜乐入初禅。

聖人得能捨。餘人捨為難。
若能知樂患。見不動大安。

憂喜先已除。苦樂今亦斷。
捨念清淨心。入第四禪中。

第三禪中樂。無常動故苦。
欲界中斷憂。初二禪除喜。

是故佛世尊。第四禪中說。
先已斷憂喜。今[21]則除苦樂。

[0185c28] 復次持戒清淨閑居獨處。守攝諸根初夜後夜專精思惟。棄捨外樂以禪自娛。離諸欲不善法。依未到地得初禪。初禪如阿毗曇說。禪有四種。一味相應。二淨三無漏。四初禪所攝報得五眾。是中行者入淨無漏。二禪三禪四禪亦如是。如佛所說。若有比丘離諸欲及惡不善法。有覺有觀。離生喜樂入初禪。

简体字   正體字

Āryas may acquire it and still maintain equanimity towards it,
But other persons find it difficult to relinquish.
If one is able to realize the calamity inherent in "bliss,"
One may then experience the great peace of immovability.

Having already eliminated both distress and "joy,"
One now also severs both suffering and bliss.
One relinquishes thought and, with a mind which is pure,
One enters into the fourth dhyāna.

As for the bliss experienced in the third dhyāna,
Since one is moved by its impermanence, it involves suffering.
As for what exists in the desire realm, one severs their distress.
As for aspects of the first and second dhyāna, one eliminates "joy."

It is for these reasons that the Buddha, the Bhagavan,
Expounded [the Dharma] from within the fourth dhyāna.
Having earlier cut off both distress and joy.
There, one now eliminates both "suffering" and "bliss."

a. THE FIRST DHYĀNA

Moreover, when one has upheld the precepts purely, dwells in leisure in a solitary place, guards and draws in the sense faculties, endeavors exclusively and precisely in the cultivation of contemplative thought during both the earlier and later periods of the night, abandons external pleasures, finds one's pleasure in dhyāna, and abandons all of the unwholesome dharmas associated with desire, basing one's practice on the preliminary ground (*anāgamya*), one then proceeds to gain the first dhyāna.

The first dhyāna is as discussed in the Abhidharma. Dhyāna may fall into any of four general categories: The first is that experienced as "enjoyable" [due to intense bliss] (*āsvādana*); the second is pure (*śuddhaka*); the third is free of all outflow impurities (*anāsrava*); the fourth is the five aggregates gained in the first dhyāna [heavens] as karmic retribution (*vipākaja*). Among these, the practitioner strives for entry into those which are "pure" and "free of outflow impurities." The [categorizations and aims] are the same with respect to the second dhyāna, the third dhyāna, and the fourth dhyāna.

According to the explanation set forth by the Buddha:

> If there is a bhikshu who abandons the desires as well as evil and unwholesome dharmas, while possessing "ideation" (*vitarka*) and possessing "mental discursion" (*vicāra*), this abandonment generates "joy" (*prīti*) and "bliss" (*prasrabdhi-sukha*). Thus it is as he gains entry into the first dhyāna.[7]

诸欲者。所爱着色等五欲。思惟分别呵欲如先说。恶不善法者。贪欲等五盖。离此内外二事故得初禅。初禅相有觉有观喜乐一心。有觉有观者。得初禅中未曾所得善法功德故。心大惊悟常为欲火所烧。得初禅时如入清凉池。又如贫人卒得宝藏。行者思惟分别欲界过罪。知初禅利益功德甚多。心大欢喜。是名有觉有观。问曰。有觉有观为一[186-1]法是二法耶。答曰。二法。麁心初念是名为觉。细心分别是名为观。譬如撞钟初声大时名为觉。后声[2]微细名为观。

简体字

諸欲者。所愛著色等五欲。思惟分別呵欲如先說。惡不善法者。貪欲等五蓋。離此內外二事故得初禪。初禪相有覺有觀喜樂一心。有覺有觀者。得初禪中未曾所得善法功德故。心大驚悟常為欲火所燒。得初禪時如入清涼池。又如貧人卒得寶藏。行者思惟分別欲界過罪。知初禪利益功德甚多。心大歡喜。是名有覺有觀。問曰。有覺有觀為一[186-1]法是二法耶。答曰。二法。麁心初念是名為覺。細心分別是名為觀。譬如撞鐘初聲大時名為覺。後聲[2]微細名為觀。

正體字

As for "the desires," this refers to those five objects of sensual desire to which one is affectionately attached. They are inclusive of "visible forms," and so forth. The contemplation, analysis, and renunciation of desire are as discussed earlier. The "evil and unwholesome dharmas" refers to the five hindrances which include sensual desire and the other [four hindrances]. Because one leaves these behind these issues both inwardly and outwardly, one then succeeds in gaining the first dhyāna.

The characteristics of the first dhyāna are that there exist "ideation" (*vitarka*), "mental discursion" (*vicāra*), "joy" (*prīti*), "bliss" (*prasrabdhi-sukha*), and "single-mindedness" (*citta-eka-agratā*). As for "possessing 'ideation' and possessing 'mental discursion,'" upon entering the first dhyāna, on account of realizing the qualities of those good never before experienced, one's mind is profoundly startled and awakened. [Heretofore], one has constantly been subjected to being burned by the fires of desire. Then, on gaining the first dhyāna, it is like entering a clear and cool pool of water. This circumstance is also analogous to the experience of a poor person suddenly gaining a treasury full of jewels.

The practitioner then contemplates and makes analytic discriminations regarding the faults of desire-realm existence and thus realizes that the benefits of [having moved beyond it into] the first dhyāna are extremely numerous. Consequently his mind experiences profound delight. This is what is intended when [the scriptures] speak of being possessed of ideation and being possessed of mental discursion therein.

1) QUESTION: ARE "IDEATION" AND "DISCURSION" ONE OR TWO?

Question: Are "being possessed of ideation" and "being possessed of mental discursion" references to a single dharma or are they instead references to two [distinctly separate] dharmas?

2) RESPONSE: THEY ARE TWO DISTINCTLY DIFFERENT PHENOMENA

Response: They are two dharmas. The coarse mind's first thought is referred to as "ideation." [Subsequent] analytic discriminations made by the subtle mind are referred to as "mental discursion." They are analogous to when one strikes a gong. At the beginning, when the sound is most loud, this corresponds to what is referred to as "ideation." Afterwards, when the sound has become more faint and subtle, this corresponds to what is referred to as "mental discursion."

问曰。如阿毘昙说。欲界乃
至初禅。一心中觉观相应。
今云何言麁心初念名为觉细
心分别名为观。答曰。二法
虽在一心二相不俱。觉时观
不明了。观时觉不明了。譬
如日出众星不现。一切心心
数法随时受名。亦复如是。
如佛说若断一法我证汝得阿
那含。一法者。所谓悭贪。
实应说五下分结尽得阿那
含。云何言[3]但断一法。以
是人悭贪偏多。诸馀结使皆
从而生。是故悭尽馀结亦
断。觉观随时受名。亦复如
是。行者知是觉观虽是善法
而娆乱定心。心欲离故呵是
觉观作是念。觉观娆动

問曰。如阿毘曇說。欲界乃
至初禪。一心中覺觀相應。
今云何言麁心初念名為覺細
心分別名為觀。答曰。二法
雖在一心二相不俱。覺時觀
不明了。觀時覺不明了。譬
如日出眾星不現。一切心心
數法隨時受名。亦復如是。
如佛說若斷一法我證汝得阿
那含。一法者。所謂慳貪。
實應說五下分結盡得阿那
含。云何言[3]但斷一法。以
是人慳貪偏多。諸餘結使皆
從而生。是故慳盡餘結亦
斷。覺觀隨時受名。亦復如
是。行者知是覺觀雖是善法
而嬈亂定心。心欲離故呵是
覺觀作是念。覺觀嬈動

简体字

正體字

3) Challenge: Abhidharma Claims They Exist in One Thought

Question: According to the Abhidharma, within the desire realm, up to and including the first dhyāna, ideation and mental discursion correspond to one single thought. Why then do you now claim that the coarse mind's first thought is referred to as "ideation" and that analytic discriminations performed by the subtle mind are referred to as "mental discursion"?

4) Response: Though Present in One Thought, They Are Distinct

Response: Although the two dharmas may indeed exist within the course of a single thought, those two characteristics are not simultaneously present therein. At the time of ideation, mental discursion is not completely and clearly manifest. At the time of mental discursion, ideation is not completely and clearly manifest. This is analogous to the circumstance which occurs when the sun comes up and the many stars then no longer manifest their appearance. All mind dharmas and dharmas belonging to the mind receive their designation in accordance with the time in which they manifest in just such a fashion.

This is exemplified by the Buddha's saying, "If you cut off one single dharma, I will certify that you have attained the station of the *anāgāmin,* [the third-stage arhat]. As for that one dharma, it is the so-called 'miserliness' (*mātsarya*)." As a matter of fact, one should say that, when one brings to an end the five lower increments of the fetters, it is then that one attains the station of an *anāgāmin.* Why then did he say that he needed to cut off only one single dharma? It is because this one person's miserliness was especially excessive. All of his other fetters were arising from it. Therefore, once the miserliness had been brought to an end, the other fetters would also be cut off.

In this very same way, ideation and mental discursion receive their designations in correspondence to [their relative prominence at] any given time.

b. The Second Dhyāna

The practitioner should realize that, although this ideation and mental discursion may be [devoted to] wholesome dharmas, still, they disturb and bring chaos to a mind [focused on gaining] meditative absorption.

Because one's mind wishes to abandon them, one renounces these ideations and mental discursions and takes up mindful contemplations such as this: "Ideation and mental discursion disturb

禅心。譬如清水波盪则无所见。又如疲极之人得息欲睡。傍人唤呼种种恼乱。摄心内定觉观娆动。亦复如是。如是等种种因缘呵觉观。觉观灭内清净[4]系心一处。无觉无观定生喜乐入二禅。既得二禅。得二禅中未曾所得无比喜乐。觉观灭者。知觉观过罪故灭。内清净者。入深禅定。信舍初禅觉观所得利重所失甚少所获大多。系心一缘故。名内清净。行者观喜之过亦如觉观。随所喜处多喜多忧。所以者何。如贫人得宝欢喜无量。一旦失之其忧亦深。喜即转而

简体字

禪心。譬如清水波盪則無所見。又如疲極之人得息欲睡。傍人喚呼種種惱亂。攝心內定覺觀嬈動。亦復如是。如是等種種因緣呵覺觀。覺觀滅內清淨[4]繫心一處。無覺無觀定生喜樂入二禪。既得二禪。得二禪中未曾所得無比喜樂。覺觀滅者。知覺觀過罪故滅。內清淨者。入深禪定。信捨初禪覺觀所得利重所失甚少所獲大多。繫心一緣故。名內清淨。行者觀喜之過亦如覺觀。隨所喜處多喜多憂。所以者何。如貧人得寶歡喜無量。一旦失之其憂亦深。喜即轉而

正體字

and move the mind immersed in dhyāna. This is analogous to a clear pool of water. If it becomes agitated by the rippling action of waves, then one cannot see anything [contained in it]. This is also just the same as when an extremely fatigued man gains the opportunity to take a nap and is on the verge of falling asleep, but then is subjected to all manner of torment and disturbance by someone else who starts yelling and calling out to him."

The circumstance is the same in the case of the disturbance and agitation inflicted by ideation and mental discursion upon the mind focused inwardly on meditative absorption. It is for all manner of reasons such as these that one renounces ideation and mental discursion.

[According to the explanation set forth by the Buddha]:

When ideation and mental discursion are caused to cease and one is "possessed of inward purity" (*adhyātma-saṃprasāda*), one is able to "anchor the mind in a single place" (*citta-eka-agratā*). With no ideation and no mental discursion, there exist "joy" (*prīti*) and "bliss" (*sukha*) which are generated by this concentration. Thus it is that one gains entry into the second dhyāna.[8]

When one reaches the second dhyāna, one gains the incomparably delightful bliss of the second dhyāna which is such as one has never achieved before. As for "the cessation of ideation and mental discursion," because one realizes the faults inherent in ideation and mental discursion, one therefore causes them to cease.

As for being "inwardly pure" (*adhyātma-saṃprasāda*), when one enters deep dhyāna absorption, one possesses the faith that the benefits of relinquishing the ideation and mental discursion of the first dhyāna are of great importance, that those things lost thereby will be but few whereas one's gains will be extremely numerous. It is through being able to anchor the mind on a single objective condition that one refers here to the gaining of "inward purity."

c. THE THIRD DHYĀNA

The practitioner's contemplation of the faults of joy is just the same as was his contemplation of ideation and mental discursion. Wherever one experiences joy, there is both an abundance of joy and an abundance of distress. Why is this the case? This is analogous to when a poor person obtains a treasure and consequently experiences an immeasurable amount of joyfulness, but then finds one day that he has lost it. In such a circumstance, his distress is also profound. It is simply through the sudden reversal of joy that

成忧。是故当舍离此喜。故行舍念智受身乐。是乐圣人能得能舍。一心在乐入第三禅。舍者舍喜心不复悔。念智者既得三禅中乐。不令于乐生患。受身乐者。是三禅乐遍身皆受。圣人能得能舍者。此乐世间第一能生心着。凡夫少能舍者。以是故佛说。行慈果报遍净地中第一。行者观乐之失。亦如观喜。知心不动处最为第一。若有动处是则有苦。行者以第三禅乐动故求不动处。以断苦乐先灭忧喜。故

成憂。是故當捨離此喜。故行捨念智受身樂。是樂聖人能得能捨。一心在樂入第三禪。捨者捨喜心不復悔。念智者既得三禪中樂。不令於樂生患。受身樂者。是三禪樂遍身皆受。聖人能得能捨者。此樂世間第一能生心著。凡夫少能捨者。以是故佛說。行慈果報遍淨地中第一。行者觀樂之失。亦如觀喜。知心不動處最為第一。若有動處是則有苦。行者以第三禪樂動故求不動處。以斷苦樂先滅憂喜。故

简体字   正體字

one thereby creates distress. Hence one should establish oneself in equanimity and abandon one's indulgence of joyfulness.

Consequently, [according to the Buddha's explanation]:

> One develops: "equanimity in the sphere of the formative-factors aggregate" (*saṃskāra-upekṣa*); "mindfulness" (*smṛti*); "discerning knowing" (*samprajñāna*); and "physically-based bliss" (*sukhā-vedanā*). As for this "bliss," āryas are able to acquire it and are able to maintain equanimity towards it. In a state of "single-mindedness" (*citta-eka-agratā*) and abiding in bliss, one enters the third dhyāna.[9]

As for "equanimity," one maintains equanimity with respect to the [the absence of the recently-abandoned] "joy" and thus the mind does not return to it with a feeling of regretfulness.

As for "mindfulness," and "discerning knowing," [these are the factors by which], having now gained the bliss of the third dhyāna, one does not allow oneself to experience calamitous distress associated with such bliss [at those times when it does not happen to be manifesting].

As for "experiencing physically-based bliss," this bliss of the third dhyāna is experienced everywhere throughout the body. As for "āryas are able to acquire it and yet are still able to maintain equanimity towards it," this bliss is of the sort which is most able to cause those who abide in the world to become mentally attached to it. Among common people, only a few are able to maintain equanimity towards it. Therefore the Buddha said, "As for the retribution gained as an effect from the practice of kindness, that enjoyed at the station of universal purity is supreme."

d. THE FOURTH DHYĀNA

The practitioner's contemplations of the faults inherent in experiencing this [physically-based] bliss (*sukhā-vedanā*) are just the same as were his [earlier] contemplations of [the faults of] "joy" (*prīti*). He realizes that the mind's establishment in the station of immovability is the most supreme priority. [He also realizes that], if one has a circumstance wherein one may be moved, then one is bound to be afflicted with suffering. On account of being moved by the bliss of the third dhyāna, the practitioner seeks a station at which he is not subject to being moved.

[According to the explanation set forth by the Buddha]:

> Through cutting off both suffering and bliss and having earlier put an end to both distress and joy, one consequently enters

不苦不乐舍念清净入第四
禅。是四禅中无苦无乐。但
有不动智慧。以是故说第四
禅舍念清净。第三禅乐动故
说苦。是故第四禅中说断苦
乐。如佛说。过一切色相不
念别相。灭有对相得入无边
虚空处。行者作是念。若无
色则无饥渴寒热之苦。是身
色麁重弊恶虚诳非实。先世
因缘和合报得此身。种种
苦恼之所住处。云何当得[*]
免此身患。当观此[5]身中虚
空。常观身空如[6]笼如甄。
常念不舍则得度色不复见
身。如内[7]身空外色亦尔。
是时能观无量无边空。得此
观已无苦无乐其心转增。如
鸟闭着瓶中瓶破得出。是名
空处定。是空无量无边。

不苦不樂捨念清淨入第四
禪。是四禪中無苦無樂。但
有不動智慧。以是故說第四
禪捨念清淨。第三禪樂動故
說苦。是故第四禪中說斷苦
樂。如佛說。過一切色相不
念別相。滅有對相得入無邊
虛空處。行者作是念。若無
色則無飢渴寒熱之苦。是身
色麁重弊惡虛誑非實。先世
因緣和合報得此身。種種
苦惱之所住處。云何當得[*]
免此身患。當觀此[5]身中虛
空。常觀身空如[6]籠如甄。
常念不捨則得度色不復見
身。如內[7]身空外色亦爾。
是時能觀無量無邊空。得此
觀已無苦無樂其心轉增。如
鳥閉著瓶中瓶破得出。是名
空處定。是空無量無邊。

简体字   正體字

into the fourth dhyāna wherein "one experiences neither suffering nor bliss" (*aduḥkha-asukha*) and abides in "pure equanimity" (*upekṣa-pariśuddhi*) and in "pure mindfulness" (*smṛti-
pariśuddhi*).[10]

In this fourth dhyāna, there is neither suffering nor bliss. There
is only unmoving wisdom. It is therefore said that, in the fourth
dhyāna, one abides in "pure equanimity" and "pure mindfulness."
Because the bliss of the third dhyāna causes one to be moved, one
speaks of its being associated with suffering. Therefore, in the fourth
dhyāna, one speaks of having cut off both suffering and bliss.

9. THE FOUR FORMLESS ABSORPTIONS
a. THE BOUNDLESS SPACE ABSORPTION

As the Buddha stated, "One transcends [the perception of] all characteristics of physical forms and thus does not bear in mind any
such distinguishing characteristics. One ceases [any perception of]
the marks of duality (as with the subject-object duality of sense faculties versus sense objects) and succeeds then in entering 'the station of boundless space.'"

The practitioner takes up this contemplation, "If there is no physical form, then neither do there exist any of its associated sufferings
involving hunger, thirst, cold, or heat. This physical form is coarse,
heavy, base, bound up with evil, false, deceptive, and unreal. It is
as retribution from the coming together of previous life causes and
conditions that one gains this body. It is the abiding place for all
manner of suffering and torment. How can one succeed in avoiding
these physical calamities?"

One should contemplate the empty space within this body. One
constantly contemplates the body as being empty like a basket or
clay pot. When one constantly carries on this mindfulness without
relinquishing it, one then succeeds in going beyond form so that
one no longer perceives a body. Just as it is with the emptiness of
one's own body, so too it is with respect to objective form.

At this point, one becomes able to contemplate immeasurable
and boundless space. Once one has developed this contemplation,
there is neither suffering nor bliss and, as a result, one's mind gains
enhanced capacities. This is comparable to the circumstance of a bird
which has been confined in a vase when the vase is finally broken
and it makes its escape. This is referred to as "the absorption associated with the station of [boundless] space (*ākāśa-anantya-āyatana-
samāpatti*)." The space herein is immeasurable and unbounded.

[8]以识缘之缘多则散能破于定。行者观虚空。缘受想识。如病如痛如疮如刺。无常苦空无我。欺诳和合则有非是实也。如是念已。舍虚空缘但缘识。云何而缘现前识。缘过去未来无量无边识。是识无量无边。如虚空无量无边。是名识处定。是识无量无边。以识缘之识多则散能破于定。行者观是缘识。受想行识如病如痛如疮如刺。无常苦空无我。欺诳和合而有非实有也。如是观已则破识相。是呵

简体字

[8]以識緣之緣多則散能破於定。行者觀虛空。緣受想識。如病如癲如瘡如刺。無常苦空無我。欺誑和合則有非是實也。如是念已。捨虛空緣但緣識。云何而緣現前識。緣過去未來無量無邊識。是識無量無邊。如虛空無量無邊。是名識處定。是識無量無邊。以識緣之識多則散能破於定。行者觀是緣識。受想行識如病如癲如瘡如刺。無常苦空無我。欺誑和合而有非實有也。如是觀已則破識相。是呵

正體字

When one employs consciousness to take [boundless space] as an objective condition. If one's focuses on it extensively, one may tend toward [having one's absorption] becoming scattered. This is a circumstance that has the capacity to destroy one's meditative absorption. As the practitioner is contemplating empty space, he then takes the feeling, perception, formative-factor, and consciousness [aggregates] as objective conditions and contemplates them as being like a sickness, like a boil, like an ulcer, like thorns, as impermanent, suffering, empty, and devoid of self, as deceptive, as existing [only] through the conjunction of [conditions], and as being inherently unreal.

b. The Boundless Consciousness Absorption

After having borne those [objective conditions] in mind in this manner, he relinquishes the practice of taking empty space as an objective condition. He then takes only consciousness itself as the objective condition which is contemplated.

How then is it that one can take the presently manifest consciousness as the objective condition and also take the immeasurable and boundless consciousness of the past and the future as objective conditions? This consciousness is immeasurable and unbounded. In fact, it is just as immeasurable and unbounded as was the case with the empty space [taken as the focus of the previous absorption]. This is referred to as "the absorption associated with the station of [boundless] consciousness (*vijñāna-anantya-āyatana-samāpatti*)."

This consciousness is immeasurable and unbounded. When one employs one's consciousness to take consciousness as an objective condition, since these [manifestations of] consciousness are many, one then tends towards [having one's absorption] become scattered. This is a circumstance which has the capacity to bring about the destruction of one's meditative absorption.

The practitioner contemplates this taking of consciousness as the objective condition [as well as the aggregates of] feeling, perception, formative factors and consciousness [regards them all as being] like a sickness, like a boil, like an ulcer, like thorns, as impermanent, suffering, empty and devoid of self, as deceptive, as existing [only] through the conjunction of conditions, and as being not really existent.

c. The Nothing-Whatsoever Absorption

After having engaged in this contemplation, he then demolishes the distinguishing characteristics of consciousness. This renunciation

识处赞无所有处。破诸识相系心在无所有中。是名无所有处[9]定。无所有处缘受想行识。如病如痈如疮如刺。无常苦空无我。欺诳和合而有非实有也。如是思惟。无想处如痈。有想处如病如痈如疮如刺。第一妙处是非有想非无想[10]处。问曰。非有想非无想处。有受想行识。云何言非有想非无想。答曰。是中有想微细难觉故。谓为非有想。有想故非无想。凡夫心谓得诸法实相。是为涅盘。佛法中虽知有想。因其本名。名为非有想非无想处。问曰。云何是无想。

識處讚無所有處。破諸識相繫心在無所有中。是名無所有處[9]定。無所有處緣受想行識。如病如癰如瘡如刺。無常苦空無我。欺誑和合而有非實有也。如是思惟。無想處如癰。有想處如病如癰如瘡如刺。第一妙處是非有想非無想[10]處。問曰。非有想非無想處。有受想行識。云何言非有想非無想。答曰。是中有想微細難覺故。謂為非有想。有想故非無想。凡夫心謂得諸法實相。是為涅槃。佛法中雖知有想。因其本名。名為非有想非無想處。問曰。云何是無想。

简体字   正體字

of the station of [boundless] consciousness and the praising of the station of nothing whatsoever—this demolition of the distinguishing characteristics of consciousness and the anchoring of the mind in nothing whatsoever—this is referred to as "the absorption of the station of nothing whatsoever (*akiṃcanya-āyatana-samāpatti*)."

In the station of nothing whatsoever, one takes as objective conditions [the aggregates of] feeling, perception, formative factors, and consciousness and regards them as being like a sickness, like a boil, like an ulcer, like thorns, as being impermanent, suffering, empty and devoid of self, as deceptive, as [only] existing through the conjunction of conditions, and as not being really existent.

d. The Neither-Perception-nor-Nonperception Absorption

He contemplates them in this manner, thinking, "Stations characterized by non-perception are like a boil. Stations wherein perception does exist are like a sickness, like a boil, like an ulcer, and like thorns. The most sublime of stations is the station of neither perception nor non-perception (*naiva-saṃjñā-nāsaṃjñā-āyatana*)."

1) Question: "Neither Perception nor Non-perception"?

Question: In the station of neither perception nor non-perception, there exist [the aggregates of] feeling, perception, formative factors, and consciousness. How then can it be said that there is "neither perception nor non-perception"?

2) Response: Perception Is Subtle and Not Utterly Non-Existent

Response: It is because there exists therein a perception which is so faint, subtle, and difficult to be aware of that it is commonly referred to as not having any perception, [hence the designation "neither perception..."]. It is because perception actually does exist, [albeit feebly], that it is also referred to as not being devoid of perception either, [hence the designation "...nor non-perception"].

[When this absorption develops in] the mind of a common person, he believes that he has gained reality-concordant realization of the true character of dharmas and that this constitutes nirvāṇa. Within the Dharma of the Buddha, although we are aware that perception does exist there, because [that absorption] already possesses this designation, we [acquiesce in] referring to it as "the station of neither perception nor non-perception."

3) Question: How May One Be Deemed "Devoid of Perception"?

Question: How is it that someone may be [deemed to be] devoid of perception?

答曰。无想有三种。一无想定。二灭[11]受定。三无想天。凡夫人欲灭心入无想定。佛弟子欲灭心入灭受定。是诸禅定有二种。若有漏若无漏。有漏即是凡夫所行如上说。无漏[12]是十六圣行。若有漏道。依上地边离下地欲。若无漏道。离自地欲及上地。以是故凡夫于有顶处不得离欲。更无上地边故。若佛弟子欲离欲界欲欲界烦恼。思惟断九种上中下。上上．上中．上下．中上．中中．中下．下上．下中．下下。断此九种故。佛弟子若依有漏道欲得初禅。

简体字

答曰。無想有三種。一無想定。二滅[11]受定。三無想天。凡夫人欲滅心入無想定。佛弟子欲滅心入滅受定。是諸禪定有二種。若有漏若無漏。有漏即是凡夫所行如上說。無漏[12]是十六聖行。若有漏道。依上地邊離下地欲。若無漏道。離自地欲及上地。以是故凡夫於有頂處不得離欲。更無上地邊故。若佛弟子欲離欲界欲欲界煩惱。思惟斷九種上中下。上上．上中．上下．中上．中中．中下．下上．下中．下下。斷此九種故。佛弟子若依有漏道欲得初禪。

正體字

4) Response: "Non-Perception" is of Three Types, as Follows:

Response: Being free of perceptive thought is of three types: The first is the no-thought absorption (*asaṃjñi-samāpatti*); the second is the cessation-of-[both-perception-and-] feeling absorption (*saṃjñā-vedayita-nirodha-samāpatti*); and the third is the no-thought heaven (*asaṃjñi-deva*). Common people wish to extinguish perceptive thought and enter the no-thought absorption. The disciples of the Buddha wish to cause cessation of perceptive thought and enter into the cessation-of-[both-perception-and-] feeling absorption.

III. Important Issues Involved in Cultivation of Dhyāna

A. Outflow Versus Non-Outflow Cultivation: Details and Implications

All of these dhyāna absorptions fall into two categories: those possessed of outflow impurities (*sāsrava*) and those devoid of outflow impurities (*anāsrava*). Those possessed of outflow impurities are just those which are practiced by the common person and are as previously discussed. Those which are devoid of outflow impurities are those corresponding to the sixteen practice-aspects of the [four truths as realized by] āryas.

If one is on the outflow path, then one depends upon the preliminary concentration of the immediately superior station in order to be able to renounce desires associated with the lower station [upon which one abides]. In the case of the non-outflow path, one renounces the desires associated with one's own station and then goes on from there to reach the immediately superior station. It is for this reason that, at the summit of existence, the common person becomes unable to renounce the desires [associated with the station on which he then abides]. This is because there are no more preliminary concentrations associated with an immediately superior station.

In the case of the disciples of the Buddha, they seek to renounce the desire-realm desires and the desire-realm afflictions. In the course of the practice of meditative discipline, they must sever nine grades [of these defilements] which are of relatively major, intermediate, and minor grade. Specifically, they are: major-major; intermediate-major; minor-major; major-intermediate; intermediate-intermediate; minor-intermediate; major-minor; intermediate-minor; and minor-minor.

Because one must sever these nine [grades of defilements],[11] if a disciple of the Buddha based in the "path of outflows" (*sāsrava-mārga*) wishes to succeed in reaching the first dhyāna, he must

是时于未到地。九无碍道八解脱道中。现在修有漏道。未来修有漏无漏道。第九解脱道中。于未到地现在修有漏道。未来修未到地有漏无漏道及初禅边地有漏。若无漏道欲得初禅亦如是。若依有漏道离初禅欲。于第二禅边地。九无[187-1]碍道八解脱道中。现在修二禅边地有漏。未来修二禅边地有漏道。亦修无漏初[2]禅及眷属。第九解脱道中。[3]于第二禅边地。现在修二禅边地有漏道。未来修二禅边地初禅无漏及眷属二禅净无漏。若无漏道离初禅欲。九无[*]碍道八

是時於未到地。九無礙道八解脱道中。現在修有漏道。未來修有漏無漏道。第九解脱道中。於未到地現在修有漏道。未來修未到地有漏無漏道及初禪邊地有漏。若無漏道欲得初禪亦如是。若依有漏道離初禪欲。於第二禪邊地。九無[187-1]礙道八解脱道中。現在修二禪邊地有漏。未來修二禪邊地有漏道。亦修無漏初[2]禪及眷屬。第九解脱道中。[3]於第二禪邊地。現在修二禪邊地有漏道。未來修二禪邊地初禪無漏及眷屬二禪淨無漏。若無漏道離初禪欲。九無[*]礙道八

简体字 正體字

proceed from the "preparatory station concentration" (*anāgamya*) to implement nine [successive acts of "counteractive abandonment" (*prahāṇa-pratipakṣa*)] associated with the "uninterrupted path" (*ānantarya-mārga*) and must also implement eight [corresponding successive acts of "counteractive conservation" (*adhāra-pratipakṣa*)] associated with the "path of liberation" (*vimukti-mārga*), cultivating during the present via the path of outflows, and cultivating them in the future via either the outflow path or via the non-outflow path.

As for the ninth [of the acts of counteractive conservation] associated with the path of liberation, it is cultivated initially in the preparatory station concentration (*anāgamya*) via the outflow path and then later it may be cultivated in the preparatory station concentration via either the outflow path or via the non-outflow path. One's reaching of the preliminary concentration (*sāmantaka*) of the first dhyāna, [otherwise known as the "preparatory station" (*anāgamya*)], it is accomplished via the outflow path.

In the case of one wishing to succeed in gaining the first dhyāna via the non-outflow path, it is also done in this same manner.

In the case of one who relies upon the non-outflow path to abandon the desires associated with the first dhyāna, in the preliminary concentration of the second dhyāna, implementing nine [acts of abandonment] associated with the uninterrupted path and eight [acts of conservation] associated with the path of liberation, he cultivates the preliminary concentration of the second dhyāna in accordance with the outflow path. Later, he cultivates the preliminary concentration of the second dhyāna in accordance with the outflow path, and also cultivates the first dhyāna and its concomitants in accordance with the non-outflow path.

In implementing the ninth [of the acts of conservation] associated with the path of liberation, in the preliminary concentration of the second dhyāna, he initially cultivates the preliminary concentration of the second dhyāna according to the outflow path. Later, he cultivates the preliminary concentration of the second dhyāna and the first dhyāna according to the non-outflow path and, as for the concomitants of the second dhyāna, he cultivates them via the pure or non-outflow paths.

In the case of one who, in accordance with the non-outflow path, abandons the desires associated with the first dhyāna, in implementing the nine [acts of abandonment] associated with the uninterrupted path and the eight [acts of conservation] associated with

解脱道中。现在修自地无漏道。未来修初禅及眷属有漏无漏道。第九解脱道中。现在修自地无漏道。未来修初禅及眷属有漏无漏道。及修二禅净无漏乃至无所有处离欲时亦如是。非有想非无想处离欲时。九无[*]碍道八解脱道中。[4]但修一切无漏道。第九解脱道中。修三界善根及无漏道。除无心定。修有二种。一得修二行修。得修名本所不得而今得。未来世修自事亦修馀事。行修名曾得于现前修。未来亦尔不修馀。

简体字

解脫道中。現在修自地無漏道。未來修初禪及眷屬有漏無漏道。第九解脫道中。現在修自地無漏道。未來修初禪及眷屬有漏無漏道。及修二禪淨無漏乃至無所有處離欲時亦如是。非有想非無想處離欲時。九無[*]礙道八解脫道中。[4]但修一切無漏道。第九解脫道中。修三界善根及無漏道。除無心定。修有二種。一得修二行修。得修名本所不得而今得。未來世修自事亦修餘事。行修名曾得於現前修。未來亦爾不修餘。

正體字

the path of liberation, he initially cultivates the station on which he currently abides in accordance with the non-outflow path and in the future cultivates the first dhyāna and its concomitants via the outflow path or the non-outflow path.

In implementing the ninth of the mental actions associated with the uninterrupted path, he initially cultivates the station on which he abides in accordance with the non-outflow path and then later cultivates the first dhyāna and its concomitants according to the outflow path or the non-outflow path. Then, as for the cultivation of the second dhyāna, that is in accordance with the pure or non-outflow paths.

This process continues thus even on up to the station of nothing whatsoever, with instances of abandoning desires involving the same approach as has been described here.

At the station of neither perception nor non-perception, in abandoning desires, when implementing the nine [acts of abandonment] associated with the uninterrupted path and when implementing the eight [acts of conservation] associated with the path of liberation, one can cultivate all of these only in accordance with the non-outflow path.

When it comes to implementing the ninth [act of conservation] associated with the path of liberation, one's cultivation avails itself of the roots of goodness developed in the three realms and in accordance with the non-outflow path. [This is the manner in which] one dispenses with the no-thought absorption.

B. Analytic Discussions of the Meditation-Practice Path

1. Two Basic Categories of Meditation Cultivation

There are two categories of cultivation [involved in acquiring and consolidating stations gained through dhyāna meditation]. In the case of the first, that is "acquisition-based cultivation." As for the second, that is "practice-based cultivation."

"Acquisition-based cultivation" simply refers to now gaining the realization of [stations] one has not already realized earlier. In future lives, one cultivates one's own naturally acquired [meditation-related] circumstances and then will also cultivate other [meditation-related] circumstances as well.

"Practice-based cultivation" refers to cultivating in the present the practice of [those meditation stations] one has already gained while proceeding in the future in the same manner, refraining from cultivating other topics.

如是等种种诸禅定中修。复次禅定相略说有二十三种。八味八净七无漏。复有六因。相应因．共因．相似因．遍因．报因．名因。一一无漏。七无漏因是相似因。自地中增相应[5]因共有因初味定初味定因乃至后味定后味定因。净亦如是。四缘因缘．次第缘．缘缘．增上缘。因缘[6]者如上说。初禅无漏定

如是等種種諸禪定中修。復次禪定相略說有二十三種。八味八淨七無漏。復有六因。相應因．共因．相似因．遍因．報因．名因。一一無漏。七無漏因是相似因。自地中增相應[5]因共有因初味定初味定因乃至後味定後味定因。淨亦如是。四緣因緣．次第緣．緣緣．增上緣。因緣[6]者如上說。初禪無漏定

简体字   正體字

One thus proceeds in this manner with the cultivation of all different sorts of dhyāna absorptions.

2. GENERAL TYPES AND SUBTYPES OF MEDITATIVE CONCENTRATIONS

Additionally, there are in general twenty-three types of meditative concentrations. Of these, eight of them belong to the category of those which are focused on enjoyment (*āsvādana*), eight of them belong to the category of those which are pure (*śuddhaka*), and seven of them belong to the category of those which are devoid of outflow impurities (*anāsrava*).

3. THE SIX TYPES OF CAUSES ASSOCIATED WITH THE STAGES OF MEDITATION

Additionally, there are six types of causes. They are: associated causes (*samprayuktaka-hetu*); coexistent causes (*sahabhū-hetu*); similar causes (*sabhāga-hetu*); universal causes (*sarvatraga-hetu*); retributive causes (*vipāka-hetu*); and nominal causes for existence (*kāraṇa-hetu*, a.k.a.: *nāma-hetu*). Each and every one of the non-outflow [dharmas], the seven non-outflow causes, are themselves "similar" causes. [Actions taken on] the very station on which one abides may serve to increase associated causes and coexistent causes [for continuing to abide on that station].

Hence abiding on the first of the concentrations focused on "enjoyment" may serve as the cause for [continuance of] that very first of the concentrations focused on enjoyment. This may also be the case on forward even to the circumstance where abiding in the very last of the concentrations focused on enjoyment may serve as the cause for [continuance of] that very last among the concentrations focused on enjoyment. This would also equally be true in the case of the category of concentrations referred to as "pure" (*śuddhaka*) concentrations.

4. THE FOUR CONDITIONS

There are four types of conditions (*pratyaya*). They are: conditions serving as causes (*hetu-pratyayatā*); equal and immediately antecedent conditions (*samanantara-pratyayatā*); conditions serving as objective conditions (*ālambana-pratyayatā*); and predominant conditions (*adhipata-pratyayatā*).

a. CONDITIONS SERVING AS CAUSES

As for "conditions serving as causes," this is as discussed earlier.

b. EQUAL AND IMMEDIATELY ANTECEDENT CONDITIONS

[As for "equal and immediately antecedent conditions"], the first dhyāna in the non-outflow path may serve as the equal and

次第生六种定。一初禅净二
无漏。二禅三禅亦如是。二
禅无漏定次第生八种定。自
地净无漏初禅净无漏。三禅
四禅亦如是。三禅无漏定次
第生十种。自地二下地四上
地四。第四禅空处亦如是。
识处无漏定次第生九种。自
地二下地四上地三。无所有
处无漏定次第生七种。自地
二下地四上地一。非有想非
无想处[7]净次第生六心。自
地二下地四。诸净地亦如
是。

次第生六種定。一初禪淨二
無漏。二禪三禪亦如是。二
禪無漏定次第生八種定。自
地淨無漏初禪淨無漏。三禪
四禪亦如是。三禪無漏定次
第生十種。自地二下地四上
地四。第四禪空處亦如是。
識處無漏定次第生九種。自
地二下地四上地三。無所有
處無漏定次第生七種。自地
二下地四上地一。非有想非
無想處[7]淨次第生六心。自
地二下地四。諸淨地亦如
是。

简体字   正體字

immediately antecedent condition for the generation of six different types of concentrations. These are, first, the "pure" first dhyāna, second, the "non-outflow" first dhyāna, and, in the same manner, [the "pure" and "non-outflow" concentrations associated with] the second dhyāna and [the "pure" and "non-outflow" concentrations associated with] the third dhyāna.

The second dhyāna may serve as the equal and immediately antecedent condition for the generation of eight different types of concentrations. These are: the pure and non-outflow concentrations associated with its own station; the pure and non-outflow concentrations associated with the first dhyāna; and, similarly, [the pure and non-outflow concentrations associated with] the third dhyāna and the fourth dhyāna as well.

The third dhyāna in the non-outflow path may serve as the equal and immediately antecedent condition for the generation of ten different types of concentrations. These are: the two associated with its own station; the four associated with the [two] immediately inferior stations; and the four associated with the [two] immediately superior stations.

The circumstances are the same for the fourth dhyāna and for the concentration associated with the station of limitless space.

The non-outflow concentration associated with the station of limitless consciousness may serve as the equal and immediately antecedent condition for the generation of nine kinds [of concentrations]. They are: the two associated with its own station; the four associated with the [two] immediately inferior stations; and the three associated with the [two] immediately superior stations.

The non-outflow concentration associated with the station of nothing whatsoever may serve as the equal and immediately antecedent condition for the generation of seven kinds [of concentrations]. They are: the two associated with its own station; the four associated with the [two] immediately inferior stations; and the one associated with the immediately superior station.

The pure concentration corresponding to the station of neither perception nor non-perception may serve as the equal and immediately antecedent condition for the generation of six mental states. They are: the two associated with its own station and the four associated with the [two] immediately inferior stations.

The scenarios are the same with respect to each of the pure concentration stations as well.

又皆益自地味。初禅味次第
二种味净。乃至非想非非想
处味亦如是。净无漏禅一切
处缘味禅。缘自地中味。亦
缘净爱。无无漏缘故[8]不缘
无漏。净无漏根本无色定。
不缘下地有漏。名因增上
缘。通一切四无量心[9]三背
舍八胜处。八一切处皆缘欲
界五神通。缘欲色界。馀
各随[10]所缘。灭受想定无
所缘。[11]一切四禅中有练
法。[12]以无漏练有漏故。得
四禅心自在。能以无漏第四
禅。练有漏第四禅。然后第
三

又皆益自地味。初禪味次第
二種味淨。乃至非想非非想
處味亦如是。淨無漏禪一切
處緣味禪。緣自地中味。亦
緣淨愛。無無漏緣故[8]不緣
無漏。淨無漏根本無色定。
不緣下地有漏。名因增上
緣。通一切四無量心[9]三背
捨八勝處。八一切處皆緣欲
界五神通。緣欲色界。餘
各隨[10]所緣。滅受想定無
所緣。[11]一切四禪中有練
法。[12]以無漏練有漏故。得
四禪心自在。能以無漏第四
禪。練有漏第四禪。然後第
三

简体字   正體字

Additionally, in every case, [each of these concentrations serves as the equal and immediately antecedent conditions for generation of] an increase in [the quality of the concentrations focused on] enjoyment associated with their own stations. Hence the concentration focused on enjoyment (*āsvādana*) associated with first dhyāna serves as the equal and immediately antecedent condition for the generation of the two categories of dhyāna consisting in the concentration focused on enjoyment and the pure (*śuddhaka*) concentration. And so it goes on up to the concentration focused on enjoyment associated with the station of neither perception nor non-perception for which the circumstances are also just the same.

c. Objective Conditions and Predominant Conditions

The "pure" and "non-outflow" categories of dhyāna take the "enjoyment-focused" concentrations as objective conditions on all of the stations. They take the enjoyment-focused concentration associated with their own stations as an objective condition and also take the craving for purity (*viśuddha-tṛṣṇā*) as an objective condition. Because there are no non-outflow states which serve as conditions for them, they do not take non-outflow states as objective conditions.

The pure concentrations, the non-outflow concentrations, and the basic formless absorptions do not take any of the lower outflow-associated stations as objective conditions.

Nominal cause and predominant conditions are operative in regard to all of the four immeasurable minds, three of the eight liberations, the eight bases of ascendancy, and eight of the [ten] universal bases. In every case, [these concentrations] take as conditions five of the superknowledges as operative in the desire realm. So, too, do they take the desire realm and the form realm as conditions. As for the rest, these vary in accordance with what might be taken as conditions.

The absorption involving cessation of feeling and perception has nothing which it takes as an objective condition.

5. The Dharma of Refinement

All four of the dhyānas involve dharmas of "refinement" (*vardhana-dharma*). Through employing that which is characterized by the absence of outflow impurities to refine that which possesses outflow impurities, one succeeds in gaining sovereign independence of mind in the four dhyānas. One is able to employ the non-outflow fourth dhyāna to refine the fourth dhyāna associated with outflow impurities. Subsequently, one proceeds similarly with the third, the

第二第一禅。皆以自地无漏练自地有漏。问曰。何以名练禅。答曰。诸圣人乐无漏定不乐有漏。离欲时[*]净有漏不乐。而自得今欲除其滓秽故。以无漏练之。譬如[13]炼金[14]去其秽无漏练有漏亦复如是。从无漏禅起入净禅。如是数数。是名为炼。复次诸禅中有顶禅。何以故名顶有二种。阿罗汉坏法不坏法。不坏法阿罗汉。于一切深禅定得自在。能起顶禅。得是顶禅能转寿为富转富为寿。复有愿智四辩无诤三昧。愿智者。愿欲知三世事。随所愿则知。此愿

第二第一禪。皆以自地無漏練自地有漏。問曰。何以名練禪。答曰。諸聖人樂無漏定不樂有漏。離欲時[*]淨有漏不樂。而自得今欲除其滓穢故。以無漏練之。譬如[13]煉金[14]去其穢無漏練有漏亦復如是。從無漏禪起入淨禪。如是數數。是名為煉。復次諸禪中有頂禪。何以故名頂有二種。阿羅漢壞法不壞法。不壞法阿羅漢。於一切深禪定得自在。能起頂禪。得是頂禪能轉壽為富轉富為壽。復有願智四辯無諍三昧。願智者。願欲知三世事。隨所願則知。此

简体字   正體字

second, and the first dhyānas, in all cases employing any given station's non-outflow concentration to refine that same station's concentration which is associated with outflow impurities.

Question: What is meant by "refining" (*vardhana*) dhyāna?

Response: All of the Āryas are pleased by whatsoever is free of outflow impurities and are not pleased by that which is associated with outflow impurities. In their renunciation of desires, they are not pleased by those concentrations which, though categorized as "pure," are nonetheless still "associated with outflow impurities." Still, these are "naturally acquired." Consequently, they now strive to eliminate the associated defiling impurities, employing [concentrations] free of outflow impurities to refine them away.

This is analogous to the process of smelting gold whereby one does away with any impurities it might contain. The resorting to non-outflow concentrations to refine those associated with outflow impurities is a process of this very same sort. They arise from non-outflow dhyāna and enter directly into the corresponding "pure" dhyāna, performing this same action many times. This is what is meant by "refinement."

6. The Summit-Reaching Dhyāna

Additionally, among all of the dhyānas there is that known as the "summit-reaching dhyāna" (*prāntakoṭika-dhyāna*). Why is it referred to as "summit-reaching"? There are two categories of arhats, those whose dharmas makes them "vulnerable to suffering a loss" (*parihāṇa-dharma arhat*) and those whose dharmas make them "invulnerable to suffering a loss (*aparihāṇa-dharma-arhat*)."

Those arhats who are invulnerable to suffering a loss have gained sovereign independence in their cultivation of all of the deep dhyāna absorptions. They are able to generate the "summit-reaching dhyāna." One who has gained this "summit-reaching dhyāna" is able to transform lifespan into wealth and is able to transform wealth into lifespan.

7. Knowledge via Resolve, Unimpeded Knowledges, Non-Disputation

Additional topics to be considered include the knowledge generated through resolve (*praṇidhi-jñāna*), the four types of unobstructed knowledge (*pratisaṃvid*), and the non-contention samādhi (*araṇā-samādhi*).

As for "knowledge generated through resolve" (*praṇidhi-jñāna*), if one wishes to know matters associated with the three periods of time, whatsoever one wishes to know, one then knows it. This

智二处摄。欲界第四禅四辩
者。法辩辞辩二处摄。欲界
[15]初禅。馀二辩九地摄。
欲界四禅四无色定。无诤三
昧者。令他心不起诤。五处
摄。欲界及四禅。问曰。得
诸禅更有馀法耶。答曰。味
定生亦得退亦得。净禅生时
得。离欲时得无漏。离欲时
得。退时得九地无漏定。四
禅三无色定未到地禅中间能
断结使。未到地禅中间舍根
相应。若人成就禅下地变化
心亦成就。如初禅成就。有
[16]二种变化心。一者初禅。
二者欲界。二禅三种三禅四
种四禅五种。若二禅三禅四
禅中。欲闻见

願智二處攝。欲界第四禪四
辯者。法辯辭辯二處攝。欲
界[15]初禪。餘二辯九地攝。
欲界四禪四無色定。無諍三
昧者。令他心不起諍。五處
攝。欲界及四禪。問曰。得
諸禪更有餘法耶。答曰。味
定生亦得退亦得。淨禪生時
得。離欲時得無漏。離欲時
得。退時得九地無漏定。四
禪三無色定未到地禪中間能
斷結使。未到地禪中間捨根
相應。若人成就禪下地變化
心亦成就。如初禪成就。有
[16]二種變化心。一者初禪。
二者欲界。二禪三種三禪四
種四禪五種。若二禪三禪四
禪中。欲聞見

简体字 正體字

"knowledge generated through resolve" is subsumed within two stations, namely the desire realm and the fourth dhyāna.

As for the four types of unobstructed knowledge, unobstructed knowledge of dharmas (*dharma-pratisaṃvid*) and unobstructed knowledge in all aspects of speech (*nirukta-pratisaṃvid*) are subsumed within two stations, namely the desire realm and the first dhyāna. The other two types of unobstructed knowledge—[the one with respect to the meanings of things (*artha-pratisaṃvid*) and the other with respect to eloquent expression (*pratibhāna-pratisaṃvid*)]—they are common to nine stations, namely the desire realm, the four dhyānas, and the four formless absorptions.

As for the non-contention samādhi, it is that by which one causes others' minds to not generate disputation. It is subsumed within five stations, namely the desire realm and the four dhyānas.

8. Additional Dhyāna-Related Dharmas

Question: Are there yet more dharmas associated with the realization of the dhyānas?

Response: In the case of the concentrations focused on enjoyment (*āsvādana*), they may also be gained either through rebirth or through retreat [from superior stations]. The pure concentrations (*śuddhaka*) may be gained through rebirth or through renunciation of desires. As for those which are free of outflow impurities (*anāsrava*), they may be gained through renunciation of desires or through retreat [from superior stations].

One may cut off fetters in non-outflow concentrations associated with any of the nine grounds, namely the four dhyānas, three of the formless absorptions, the preparatory station (*anāgamya*), and the "intermediate dhyāna" (*dhyāna-anantara*).

The preparatory station and the intermediate dhyāna are states associated with the faculty of equanimity (*upekṣā-indriya*) [in relation to the feeling aggregate].

If one perfects a given dhyāna, he perfects the transformation-generating mind in relation to lower stations as well. For instance, if one perfects the first dhyāna, then that involves two types of transformation-generating mind: first, the first dhyāna; and second, the desire realm. Hence there are three types corresponding to acquisition of the second dhyāna, four types corresponding to the third dhyāna, and five types corresponding to the fourth dhyāna.

In an instance where one abides in the second dhyāna, the third dhyāna, or the fourth dhyāna, when one wishes to hear, see, or

触时皆用梵世识。[17]识灭时则止。四无量意五神通八背舍八胜处十一切入九次第定九[18]相十想三三昧三解脱门三无漏根三十七品。如是等诸功德。皆禅波罗蜜中生。是中应广说。问曰。应说禅波罗蜜。何以但说禅。答曰。禅是波罗蜜之本。得是禅已怜愍众生。内心中有种种禅定妙乐而不知求。乃在外法不净苦中求乐。如是观已生大悲心立弘誓愿。我当令众生皆得禅定内乐离不净乐。依此禅乐已。次令得佛道乐。是时禅[19]定得名波罗蜜。复次于此禅中。不受味不求报不随报生。为调心故入禅。以智慧方便还生欲界。度脱一切众生。是时禅名为波罗蜜。复次菩萨入深禅定。一切天人不能知其心。所依

觸時皆用梵世識。[17]識滅時則止。四無量意五神通八背捨八勝處十一切入九次第定九[18]相十想三三昧三解脫門三無漏根三十七品。如是等諸功德。皆禪波羅蜜中生。是中應廣說。問曰。應說禪波羅蜜。何以但說禪。答曰。禪是波羅蜜之本。得是禪已憐愍眾生。內心中有種種禪定妙樂而不知求。乃在外法不淨苦中求樂。如是觀已生大悲心立弘誓願。我當令眾生皆得禪定內樂離不淨樂。依此禪樂已。次令得佛道樂。是時禪[19]定得名波羅蜜。復次於此禪中。不受味不求報不隨報生。為調心故入禪。以智慧方便還生欲界。度脫一切眾生。是時禪名為波羅蜜。復次菩薩入深禪定。一切天人不能知其心。所依

简体字　　　　　　　　　　　　　正體字

touch, in every case, one may avail oneself of the Brahmaloka consciousness [corresponding to a first dhyāna realm]. When that consciousness disappears, then [such abilities] cease functioning.

The four immeasurable minds, the five superknowledges, the eight liberations, the eight bases of ascendancy, the ten universal bases, the nine sequential absorptions, the nine reflections, the ten recollections, the three samādhis, the three gates to liberation, the three non-outflow faculties, the thirty-seven wings of enlightenment and other such meritorious qualities as these are all generated from within dhyāna *pāramitā*. They should be extensively discussed herein [in the following chapters].

IV. The Perfection of Dhyāna Meditation

Question: One should be discussing dhyāna *pāramitā* (the perfection of dhyāna meditation). Why then do you speak only of aspects of dhyāna meditation *per se*?

A. The Bodhisattva's Practice of Dhyāna Meditation

Response: [Acquisition of] the dhyānas constitutes the very root of *"pāramitā."* Having already succeeded in these dhyānas, one feels pity for beings, this because they realize that beings possess the marvelous bliss of all sorts of dhyāna absorptions right within their own minds, yet they do not know to seek for them. Consequently they seek for pleasure in the impurity and suffering associated with outward dharmas.

After one has contemplated such circumstances, one brings forth the mind of great compassion and sets forth a vast vow, declaring, "I will cause all beings to gain the inward bliss of dhyāna absorption whereby they may then separate from impure pleasures. Based on this dhyāna bliss, I will next influence them to gain the bliss of the Buddha Path." It is at this time that dhyāna absorption succeeds in qualifying as *"pāramitā."*

Moreover, when in the midst of these dhyānas, one does not indulge in those focused on enjoyment (*āsvādana*), does not seek karmic rewards, and does not allow himself to take on rebirth [in celestial realms] corresponding to such karmic rewards. It is for the sake of training the mind that one enters into the dhyānas. One avails oneself of wisdom and skillful means and so returns to be reborn in the desire realm to bring all beings across to liberation. It is at this time that dhyāna may qualify as *"pāramitā."*

Then again, when the bodhisattva enters deep dhyāna absorption, no gods or men are able to know his mind, what he relies

所缘见闻觉知法中心不动。如毘摩罗[188-1]鞊经中。为舍利弗说[2]宴坐法。不依身不依心不依三界。于三界中不得身心。是为[*]宴坐。复次若人闻禅定乐胜于人天乐。便舍欲乐求禅定。是为自求乐利不足奇也。菩萨则不[3]然。但为众生[4]欲令慈悲心净。不舍众生菩萨禅。禅中皆发大悲心。禅有极妙内乐。而众生舍之而求外乐。譬如大富盲人。多有伏藏不知不见而行乞求。智者愍[5]其自有妙物不能知见而从他乞。众生亦如是。心中自有种种禅定乐。而不知发反求外乐。复次菩萨[6]知诸法实相故。入禅中心安隐不着味。诸馀外道虽入禅定[7]心不安隐。不知诸法实故着禅味。

简体字

所緣見聞覺知法中心不動。如毘摩羅[188-1]鞊經中。為舍利弗說[2]宴坐法。不依身不依心不依三界。於三界中不得身心。是為[*]宴坐。復次若人聞禪定樂勝於人天樂。便捨欲樂求禪定。是為自求樂利不足奇也。菩薩則不[3]然。但為眾生[4]欲令慈悲心淨。不捨眾生菩薩禪。禪中皆發大悲心。禪有極妙內樂。而眾生捨之而求外樂。譬如大富盲人。多有伏藏不知不見而行乞求。智者愍[5]其自有妙物不能知見而從他乞。眾生亦如是。心中自有種種禪定樂。而不知發反求外樂。復次菩薩[6]知諸法實相故。入禪中心安隱不著味。諸餘外道雖入禪定[7]心不安隱。不知諸法實故著禪味。

正體字

upon, or what he takes as an objective condition. In the midst of the dharmas of perceiving, hearing, being aware, and realizing, his mind does not move.

This is illustrated in the *Vimalakīrti Sutra* where it is explained to Śāriputra that, in the dharma of happily abiding in sitting meditation, "One does not rely on the body, does not rely on the mind, and does not rely on the three realms. In the midst of the three realms he does not apprehend the existence of either body or mind. This is what constitutes happily abiding in sitting meditation."

Additionally, if a person hears that the bliss of dhyāna absorption is superior to the bliss of men or gods and then relinquishes the bliss of desires in order to seek dhyāna absorption, this constitutes a personal seeking for one's own bliss and benefit and is inadequate to be considered noteworthy. The bodhisattva is not like this. It is only for the sake of beings that he wishes to cause his mind of kindness and compassion to become pure. He does not forsake beings.

As for the dhyāna of the bodhisattva, even when in the midst of the dhyānas, he in every case brings forth the mind of great compassion. Dhyāna is possessed of the most ultimately marvelous inward bliss and yet beings forsake it and then instead seek after outward pleasures.

This is analogous to an extremely rich man who is blind. Although he owns much wealth which is hidden away, he remains unaware of it, fails to see it, and so is moved then to taking up begging. The wise pity such a person because, even though he already has marvelous possessions of his own, because he is unable to be aware of or see them, he is provoked to go about begging from others. Beings are just like this. Within their own minds, they themselves already possess all kinds of bliss associated with the dhyāna absorptions. Nonetheless, they do not realize how to bring it forth. Hence, paradoxically, they then go about seeking after outward sources of pleasure.

Moreover, because the bodhisattva has realized the true character of dharmas, even though he experiences peace and security when he enters into dhyāna, still, he does not allow himself to become attached to its enjoyability. Although when all of the non-Buddhists enter into dhyāna absorption, their minds do not actually abide in peace and security, still, because they have not realized the true character of dharmas, they become attached to the enjoyment of dhyāna.

问曰。阿罗汉辟支佛俱不着
味。何以不得禅波罗蜜。答
曰。阿罗汉辟支佛虽不着
味。无大悲心故不名禅波罗
蜜。又复不能尽行诸禅。菩
萨尽行诸禅。麁细大小深浅
内缘外缘一切尽行。以是故
菩萨心中名禅波罗蜜。馀人
但名禅。复次外道声闻菩萨
皆得禅定。而外道禅中有三
种患。或味着或邪见或憍
慢。声闻禅中慈悲薄。于诸
法中[8]不以利智贯达诸法实
相。独善其身断诸佛种。菩
萨禅[9]中无此事。欲集一切
诸佛法故。于诸禅中不忘众
生。乃至[10]昆虫常加慈念。
如释迦文尼佛。本为螺[11]髻
仙人。名尚阇[12]利。常行第
四禅。出入息断在一树下坐
[13]兀然不动。鸟见如此谓之
为木。即于髻中生卵。是菩
萨从禅觉知[14]头上有鸟卵。

問曰。阿羅漢辟支佛俱不著
味。何以不得禪波羅蜜。答
曰。阿羅漢辟支佛雖不著
味。無大悲心故不名禪波羅
蜜。又復不能盡行諸禪。菩
薩盡行諸禪。麁細大小深淺
內緣外緣一切盡行。以是故
菩薩心中名禪波羅蜜。餘人
但名禪。復次外道聲聞菩薩
皆得禪定。而外道禪中有三
種患。或味著或邪見或憍
慢。聲聞禪中慈悲薄。於諸
法中[8]不以利智貫達諸法實
相。獨善其身斷諸佛種。菩
薩禪[9]中無此事。欲集一切
諸佛法故。於諸禪中不忘眾
生。乃至[10]昆虫常加慈念。
如釋迦文尼佛。本為螺[11]髻
仙人。名尚闍[12]利。常行第
四禪。出入息斷在一樹下坐
[13]兀然不動。鳥見如此謂之
為木。即於髻中生卵。是菩
薩從禪覺知[14]頭上有鳥卵。

简体字   正體字

B. WHY ARE NOT ARHAT AND PRATYEKABUDDHA DHYĀNA "PERFECTIONS"?

Question: Both the arhats and pratyekabuddhas refrain from attachment to the enjoyment [of dhyāna]. Why then does their circumstance not qualify as "*pāramitā*"?

C. RESPONSE: DUE TO DEFICIENT COMPASSION AND INCOMPLETE PRACTICE

Response: Although the arhats and pratyekabuddhas do not become attached to such enjoyment, because they do not have the mind of great compassion, they do not qualify as having reached the *pāramitā* of dhyāna. Furthermore, they are not able to completely practice all of the dhyānas. The Bodhisattva completely practices all of the dhyānas. The coarse, the subtle, the major, the minor, the deep, the shallow, those focused on inward objective conditions, and those focused on outward objective conditions—these are all thoroughly practiced by him. Therefore, as practiced within the mind of the bodhisattva, it qualifies as dhyāna "*pāramitā*," whereas, as practiced by others, it only qualifies to be termed "dhyāna."

Additionally, non-Buddhists, Śrāvaka-disciples, and bodhisattvas all achieve dhyāna absorption. However there are three sorts of calamitous circumstances within the dhyāna of the non-Buddhists: In some cases, they are attached to its enjoyment, in others, they hold to erroneous views, and in yet others, they are afflicted with arrogance and pridefulness.

Within the dhyāna of the Śrāvaka-disciples, kindness and compassion are but scant. They do not employ sharp wisdom to penetrate through to the true character of dharmas. They exclusively devote themselves to benefiting their own persons and so are party to severing the lineage of the Buddhas.

D. THE KINDNESS OF THE BODHISATTVA

The dhyāna of the Bodhisattvas is free of such issues. Because they wish to accumulate the Dharma of all Buddhas, even in the midst of the dhyānas, they do not forget beings. Thus they constantly retain a lovingly-kind mindfulness regarding even the smallest insects.

E. STORY: SHAKYAMUNI AS A BODHISATTVA RISHI

This is illustrated by Shakyamuni Buddha who, in a previous life, was the conch-haired rishi named Śaṅkhācārya who constantly cultivated the fourth dhyāna wherein breathing in and out stops completely. He was sitting, erect and unmoving, beneath a tree. A bird saw him like this, took him to be a tree, and then laid its eggs in his hair. This bodhisattva eventually came out of his dhyāna absorption and realized a bird's eggs had been laid on his head.

即自思惟。若我起动鸟母必
不复来。鸟母不来鸟卵必
坏。即还入禅。至鸟子飞去
尔乃起。复次除菩萨。馀人
欲界心不得次第入禅。菩萨
行禅波罗蜜。于欲界心次第
入禅。何以故。菩萨世世修
诸功德。结使心薄心柔软
故。复次馀人得总相智慧。
能离欲如无常观苦观不净
观。菩萨于一切法中能别相
分别离欲。如五百仙人飞行
时。闻[15]甄陀罗女歌声。心
着狂醉皆失神足一时堕地。
如声闻闻紧陀罗王屯[16]仑摩
弹琴歌声以诸法实相赞佛。
是时须弥山及诸树木皆动。
大迦叶等诸大弟子皆于座上
不能自安。天[17]须菩萨问
大迦叶。汝最耆年行头陀第
一。今何故不能制心自安。
大迦叶答曰。我于人天诸欲
心不倾动。

即自思惟。若我起動鳥母必
不復來。鳥母不來鳥卵必
壞。即還入禪。至鳥子飛去
爾乃起。復次除菩薩。餘人
欲界心不得次第入禪。菩薩
行禪波羅蜜。於欲界心次第
入禪。何以故。菩薩世世修
諸功德。結使心薄心柔軟
故。復次餘人得總相智慧。
能離欲如無常觀苦觀不淨
觀。菩薩於一切法中能別相
分別離欲。如五百仙人飛行
時。聞[15]甄陀羅女歌聲。心
著狂醉皆失神足一時墮地。
如聲聞聞緊陀羅王屯[16]崙摩
彈琴歌聲以諸法實相讚佛。
是時須彌山及諸樹木皆動。
大迦葉等諸大弟子皆於座上
不能自安。天[17]須菩薩問
大迦葉。汝最耆年行頭陀第
一。今何故不能制心自安。
大迦葉答曰。我於人天諸欲
心不傾動。

He then thought to himself, "If I get up and move about, the mother bird will certainly not come back again. If the mother bird does not return, the bird's eggs will certainly be ruined." He then went back into dhyāna again. He remained there until the young birds had flown away. Then and only then did he get up from his meditation spot.

F. The Bodhisattva's Correct Acquisition and Practice of Dhyāna

Moreover, with the exception of the bodhisattva, the minds of others in the desire realm are unable to sequentially enter the dhyāna absorptions. When the bodhisattva practices the *pāramitā* of dhyāna within the desire realm, his mind sequentially enters the dhyāna absorptions. How is this the case? In life after life, the bodhisattva cultivates all manner of merit [facilitating easy access to the dhyāna absorptions even when resident in the desire realm]. Because his mind consequently abides in a state of pliancy, thoughts freighted with fetters are but scant in him.

Additionally, others may gain a wisdom with respect to general characteristics whereby they are able to transcend desire through contemplation of impermanence, contemplation of suffering, and contemplation of impurity. The bodhisattva is able to distinguish the specific characteristics of all dharmas and becomes able thereby to transcend desire.

G. Story: Five Hundred Rishis; Mahākāśyapa Moved by Music

This is illustrated by the case of the five hundred rishis who, when they were flying along, heard the sound of the *kinnara* maidens singing. Their minds became attached, crazed, and so intoxicated that they all lost their foundations of spiritual power and simultaneously fell back to earth.

It is also illustrated by the case of the Śrāvakas who heard Druma, the King of the Kinnaras, strumming his lute and praising the Buddha by singing about the true character of dharmas. At this time, even Mount Sumeru and all of the trees quaked. Mahākāśyapa and the other great disciples could not remain still in their seats.

Devapuṣpāgra Bodhisattva[12] asked Mahākāśyapa, "You are the most senior in years and are foremost in the observance of the *dhūta* ascetic practices. Why then do you now remain unable to control your mind and remain at peace?"

Mahākāśyapa replied, "I am not even slightly moved by any of the thoughts of desire associated with men or gods. This bodhisattva possesses a sound which is the reward for an immeasurable

是菩萨无量功德报声。又复
以智慧变化作声。所不能
忍。若八方风起。不能令须
弥山动。劫尽时毘蓝风至。
吹须弥山[18]令如腐草。以是
故知。菩萨于一切法中。别
相观得离诸欲。诸馀人等但
得禅之名字。不得波罗蜜。
复次馀人知菩萨入出禅心。
不能知住禅心所缘所到知诸
法深浅。阿罗汉辟支佛尚不
能知。何况馀人。譬如象王
渡水。入时出时足迹可见。
在水中时不可得知。若得初
禅同得初禅人能知。而不能
知菩萨入初禅。有人得二
禅。观知得初禅心了了知。
不能知菩萨入初禅心。乃至
非有想非无想处亦如是。复
次超越三昧中。从初禅起入
第三禅。[19]第三禅中起入
虚空处。虚空处起入无所有
处。[20]二乘唯能[21]超一不能
[*]超二。

是菩薩無量功德報聲。又復
以智慧變化作聲。所不能
忍。若八方風起。不能令須
彌山動。劫盡時毘藍風至。
吹須彌山[18]令如腐草。以是
故知。菩薩於一切法中。別
相觀得離諸欲。諸餘人等但
得禪之名字。不得波羅蜜。
復次餘人知菩薩入出禪心。
不能知住禪心所緣所到知諸
法深淺。阿羅漢辟支佛尚不
能知。何況餘人。譬如象王
渡水。入時出時足跡可見。
在水中時不可得知。若得初
禪同得初禪人能知。而不能
知菩薩入初禪。有人得二
禪。觀知得初禪心了了知。
不能知菩薩入初禪心。乃至
非有想非無想處亦如是。復
次超越三昧中。從初禪起入
第三禪。[19]第三禪中起入
虛空處。虛空處起入無所有
處。[20]二乘唯能[21]超一不能
[*]超二。

简体字   正體字

amount of merit. Moreover, he employs a wisdom-generated transformation to create these sounds. Hence they are such as one is
unable to endure. Even if the eight winds come up, they are unable
to cause Mount Sumeru to move. But at the end of the kalpa, the
vairambhavāyu winds come and blow upon Mount Sumeru, causing it to be just as vulnerable to the winds as a blade of withered
grass."

On account of this, one may realize that the bodhisattva employs
a contemplation of the particular characteristics of all dharmas and
so is able to transcend all desires. The practice of all other persons
is only deserving of being called "dhyāna." It does not reach to the
level of "*pāramitā.*"

H. The Untraceable Nature of the Bodhisattva's Dhyāna *Pāramitā*

Moreover, other persons may be able to know the mind of the bodhisattva as he enters and leaves dhyāna, but they are unable to know
his mind as he dwells in dhyāna, what it takes as its objective conditions, where it goes, or its depth in knowing all dharmas. Not even
arhats and pratyekabuddhas are able to know these matters, how
much the less might other people be able to do so. This is analogous
to when the king of the elephants crosses a body of water. When
he enters and when he leaves, his tracks may be visible. However,
when he is out in the water, one is unable perceive such things.

If one gains the first dhyāna, those who have had the same
achievement in the first dhyāna are able to know it, but they are
unable to be aware of the bodhisattva's entry into the first dhyāna.
In the case of persons who have reached the second dhyāna, they
may contemplate and know the mind which has gained the first
dhyāna, knowing it utterly and completely. Still, they remain
unable to know the bodhisattva's mind even in its entry into the
first dhyāna. This continues to be just the same even on up to and
including the station of neither perception nor non-perception.

I. The Superior Ability of the Bodhisattva in "Overstepping" Stations

Additionally, in the "overstepping" samādhi (*vyutkrāntaka-samādhi*),
one may arise from the first dhyāna and enter the third dhyāna,
may arise from the midst of the third dhyāna and enter the station
of limitless space, or may arise from the station of limitless space
and enter the station of nothing whatsoever. Two Vehicles' practitioners are only able to leap over one station, but are not able to leap
over two.

With sovereign independence, the bodhisattva may arise from

菩萨自在超。从初禅起或入
三禅如常法。或时入第四
禅。或入空处识处无所有处
或非有想非无想处。或入灭
受想定。灭受想定起或[22]入
无所有处或识处空处四禅乃
至初禅。或时[*]超一或时超
二。乃至超九。声闻不[23]能
超二。何以故。智慧功德禅
定力薄故。譬如二种师子。
一黄师子。二白[24]发师子。
黄师子虽亦能[25]超。不如
白[*]发师子王。如是等种种
因缘分别禅波罗蜜。复次尔
时菩萨常入禅定。摄心不动
不生觉观。亦能为十方一切
众生以无量音声说法而度脱
之。是名禅波罗蜜。问曰。
如经中说。先有觉观思惟然
后[26]能说法。入禅定中无语
觉观。不应得说法。汝今云
何言常在禅定中不生觉观而
为众生说法。答曰。生死人
法入禅定。先

菩薩自在超。從初禪起或入
三禪如常法。或時入第四
禪。或入空處識處無所有處
或非有想非無想處。或入滅
受想定。滅受想定起或[22]入
無所有處或識處空處四禪乃
至初禪。或時[*]超一或時超
二。乃至超九。聲聞不[23]能
超二。何以故。智慧功德禪
定力薄故。譬如二種師子。
一黃師子。二白[24]髮師子。
黃師子雖亦能[25]超。不如
白[*]髮師子王。如是等種種
因緣分別禪波羅蜜。復次爾
時菩薩常入禪定。攝心不動
不生覺觀。亦能為十方一切
眾生以無量音聲說法而度脫
之。是名禪波羅蜜。問曰。
如經中說。先有覺觀思惟然
後[26]能說法。入禪定中無語
覺觀。不應得說法。汝今云
何言常在禪定中不生覺觀而
為眾生說法。答曰。生死人
法入禪定。先

简体字   正體字

the first dhyāna and leap over into the third dhyāna in accordance with the normal procedure. Alternately, he may sometimes instead enter into the fourth dhyāna or may enter into the station of limitless space, the station of limitless consciousness, the station of nothing whatsoever, or perhaps may enter even into the station of neither perception nor non-perception. Again, perhaps he may enter into the absorption of the extinction of feeling and perception and, arising from the absorption of the extinction of feeling and perception, he may enter into the station of nothing whatsoever, the station of limitless consciousness, the station of limitless space, or the fourth dhyāna, and so forth, even on down to the first dhyāna.

He may sometimes leap over one station or sometimes leap over two stations, and so forth on up to leaping over nine stations. The Śrāvaka-disciples are unable to leap over two stations. Why is this? It is because the power of their wisdom, merit, and dhyāna absorption are slight. This is analogous to two kinds of lion: the first being the yellow lion and the second being the white-haired lion. Although the yellow lion is able to leap, he is unable to compare to the white-haired king of lions in this respect. All sorts of causes and conditions such as these served to distinguish the *pāramitā* of dhyāna.

J. THE DHARMA-BODY BODHISATTVA'S ALTRUISTIC WORKS EVEN IN SAMĀDHI

Furthermore, [as stated in the scriptures], "At that time, the bodhisattva constantly enters into dhyāna absorption, focuses his mind, remains unmoving, does not give rise to either ideation or mental discursion, and yet he is still able to employ an incalculable number of sounds and voices to speak Dharma for all of the beings of the ten directions and so brings them across to liberation." This is what is referred to dhyāna *pāramitā*.

Question: According to what is set forth in the Sutras, one first possesses ideation, mental discursion, and the process of contemplation, after which one is then enabled to expound the Dharma. When one enters dhyāna absorption, one is free of verbally-based ideation and mental discursion and thus then should not be able to expound the Dharma. Why do you now say that [the bodhisattva] is constantly abiding in dhyāna absorption, that he does not give rise to ideation or mental discursion, and that he is still able to proclaim the Dharma for the benefit of beings?

Response: It is the dharma of persons subject to cyclic birth-and-death that, having entered into dhyāna absorption, they first

以语觉观然后说法。法身菩萨离生死身。知一切[27]诸法。常住如禅定相。不见有乱。法身菩萨变化无量身。为众生说法。而菩萨心无所分别。如[28]何修罗琴。常自出声随意而作无[29]人弹者。此亦无散心亦无摄心。是福德报生故。随人意出声。法身菩萨亦如是。无所分别亦无散心。亦无说法相。是无量福德禅定智慧因缘故。是法身菩萨。种种法音随应而出。悭贪心多闻说布施之声。破戒瞋恚懈怠乱心愚痴之人。各各闻说持戒忍辱禅定智慧之声。闻是法已各各思惟。渐以三乘而得度脱。复次菩萨观一切法。若乱若定皆是不二相。馀人[30]除乱求定。何以故。以乱法中起瞋想。

以語覺觀然後說法。法身菩薩離生死身。知一切[27]諸法。常住如禪定相。不見有亂。法身菩薩變化無量身。為眾生說法。而菩薩心無所分別。如[28]何修羅琴。常自出聲隨意而作無[29]人彈者。此亦無散心亦無攝心。是福德報生故。隨人意出聲。法身菩薩亦如是。無所分別亦無散心。亦無說法相。是無量福德禪定智慧因緣故。是法身菩薩。種種法音隨應而出。慳貪心多聞說布施之聲。破戒瞋恚懈怠亂心愚癡之人。各各聞說持戒忍辱禪定智慧之聲。聞是法已各各思惟。漸以三乘而得度脫。復次菩薩觀一切法。若亂若定皆是不二相。餘人[30]除亂求定。何以故。以亂法中起瞋想。

简体字　　　　　　　　　　　　　　　　正體字

resort to verbally-based ideation and mental discursion, and afterwards expound on Dharma. The Dharma-body bodhisattva has left behind [that series of] bodies which are subject to cyclic birth-and-death, knows all dharmas, and is marked by constantly abiding in a manner the same as one immersed in dhyāna absorption. He is no longer vulnerable to any confusion.

The Dharma-body bodhisattva creates through his powers of transformation an incalculable number of bodies. He speaks Dharma for the sake of beings and yet this bodhisattva's mind has nothing with respect to which it makes discriminations. It is like the lute of the *asuras* which constantly and spontaneously emits sounds. It creates them in responsive accordance with the individual's intentions. Nobody strums it. This takes place independently of any scattering of mind or concentration of mind. This arises as a karmic retribution for merit. It accords with one's individual wishes in its creation of music.

The Dharma-body bodhisattva is also like this. He has nothing which is the object of discriminations. Nor does he experience any scattering of mind. What's more, he has none of the characteristic signs of [the ordinary person's] expounding of the Dharma. This is on account of the causes and conditions associated with immeasurable merit, with dhyāna absorption, and with wisdom. In the case of this Dharma-body bodhisattva, all sorts of Dharma sounds are put forth according to what is appropriate. For one whose mind is characterized by much miserliness and greed, he hears a voice which speaks of giving. For those persons who break precepts, are hateful, are lazy, are chaotic-minded or who are foolish, each accordingly will hear a voice speaking of upholding precepts, patience, [vigor], dhyāna, or wisdom. Having heard this Dharma, each of them ponders upon it and gradually takes up cultivation within the Three Vehicles teachings and thence succeeds in crossing over to liberation.

K. The Bodhisattva's Transcendence of Dual Modes

Additionally, as the bodhisattva contemplates all dharmas, whether they be those associated with mental scattering or whether they be those associated with the concentration, in every case he realizes that they are non-dual in character. Other persons apply themselves to getting rid of mental scattering and seeking the concentrations. Why is this? It is because, in the midst of dharmas associated with scattering, their thoughts tend towards hatefulness whereas, in the

于定法中生着想。如欎陀罗伽仙人。得五通日日飞到[189-1]国王宫中食。王大夫人如其国法[2]捉足而礼。夫人手触即失神通。从王求车乘驾而出。还其本处入林树间。更求五通一心专至。垂当得时有鸟在树上。急鸣以乱其意。舍树至水边求定。复闻鱼斗动水之声。此人求禅不得。即生瞋恚。我当尽杀鱼鸟。此人久后思惟得定。生非有想非无想处。于彼寿尽下生作飞狸。杀诸鱼鸟作无量罪堕三恶道。是[3]为禅定[4]中着心因缘。外道如此。佛弟子中亦有一比丘。得四禅生增上慢谓得四道。得初禅时谓是须陀洹。第二禅时谓是斯陀含。第三禅时谓是

於定法中生著想。如欎陀羅伽仙人。得五通日日飛到[189-1]國王宮中食。王大夫人如其國法[2]捉足而禮。夫人手觸即失神通。從王求車乘駕而出。還其本處入林樹間。更求五通一心專至。垂當得時有鳥在樹上。急鳴以亂其意。捨樹至水邊求定。復聞魚鬥動水之聲。此人求禪不得。即生瞋恚。我當盡殺魚鳥。此人久後思惟得定。生非有想非無想處。於彼壽盡下生作飛狸。殺諸魚鳥作無量罪墮三惡道。是[3]為禪定[4]中著心因緣。外道如此。佛弟子中亦有一比丘。得四禪生增上慢謂得四道。得初禪時謂是須陀洹。第二禪時謂是斯陀含。第三禪時謂是

简体字   正體字

midst of dharmas associated with concentration, their thoughts tend towards attachment.

1. STORY: UDRAKA, THE RISHI

This is illustrated by the case of Udraka, the rishi. He had gained the five superknowledges. Every day he flew to the palace of the King where he took his meal.

On one occasion, according with the traditions of her country, the wife of the King made obeisance to him, grasping his feet as she did so. When the wife's hands touched him, he immediately lost his spiritual powers. He [was forced to] seek a carriage from the King. He got into the carriage and left, returning to his original dwelling place.

He then went into the forest and sought once again the five super-knowledges, applying himself to the endeavor single-mindedly and exclusively. Just when he was about to gain them again, there was a bird up in a tree which started calling out urgently, thus causing his mind to become scattered.

He then left that tree behind and went to the shore of a lake and sought absorption there. He then repeatedly heard the splashing sound of a fish jumping. This man was then unsuccessful in seeking to enter dhyāna and then became enraged, swearing "I ought to kill every one of the fish and the birds, too!"

Much later, this man's cultivation of contemplative thought resulted in his gaining the absorptions. He was reborn in the station of neither perception nor non-perception. When that lifetime came to an end, he fell down into rebirth as a flying fox which killed birds and fish, thus creating an incalculable number of karmic offenses. As a result, he then fell into successive rebirths in the three wretched destinies.

This is a set of causal circumstances associated with a mind attached to the dhyāna absorptions.

2. STORY: THE BHIKSHU WHO MISTOOK THE DHYĀNAS FOR ARHATSHIP

Non-Buddhists are prone to circumstances of this sort. Among the disciples of the Buddha there is also the example of a bhikshu who had gained the fourth dhyāna and had developed such extreme arrogance that he was of the opinion that he had gained the four-fold path [of the arhats]. When he had gained the first dhyāna, he thought it was the station of the *srota-āpanna*. When he gained the second dhyāna, he thought it was the station of the *sakṛdāgāmin*. When he gained the third dhyāna, he thought it was the station of

阿那含。第四禅时谓得阿罗汉。恃是而止不复求进。命欲尽时见有四禅中阴相来。便生邪见。谓无涅盘佛为欺我。恶邪生故失四禅中阴。便见阿鼻泥[5]犁中阴相。命终即生阿鼻地狱。诸比丘问佛。某甲比丘阿兰若命终生何处。佛言。是人生阿鼻泥[*]犁中。诸比丘皆大惊怪。此人坐禅持戒所由尔耶。佛言。此人增上慢。得四禅时谓得四道故。临命终时见四禅中阴相。便生邪见谓无涅盘。我是阿罗汉今还复生。佛为虚诳。是时即见阿鼻泥[*]犁中阴相。命终即生阿鼻地狱中。是时佛说偈言。

多闻持戒禅。未得无漏法。
虽有此功德。此事不可信。

[0189a28] 是比丘受是恶道苦。是故知。取乱相能生瞋等烦恼。

简体字

the *anāgāmin*. When he gained the fourth dhyāna, he thought he had gained arhatship.

Based on this, he stopped applying himself and did not seek to advance any further. When his life was about to come to an end, he saw the signs of the arrival of the intermediary aggregates bringing rebirth in the fourth dhyāna [heavens]. He reacted to this with a wrong view whereby he thought, "There is no such thing as nirvāṇa. The Buddha has cheated me."

On account of generating this maliciously perverse idea, he lost the intermediary aggregates leading to rebirth in the fourth dhyāna realms and next saw the signs of the arrival of the intermediary aggregates associated with the Avīci hells. As a consequence, when his life ended, he was immediately reborn in the Avīci hells.

The Bhikshus asked the Buddha, "When bhikshu so-and-so, the *āraṇya* hermitage dweller, finally died, where then was he reborn?"

The Buddha said, "This man was reborn in the Avīci hells."

The Bhikshus were all greatly startled and amazed, exclaiming "This man sat in dhyāna meditation and upheld the precepts. Could it be this serves as the basis for such a resulting circumstance?"

The Buddha said, "This man was extremely arrogant. This happened because when he gained the four dhyānas, he believed he had actually gained the four-fold path [of the arhats]. Then, when his life was coming to its end, he saw the signs of the fourth dhyāna intermediary aggregates and generated a wrong view, thinking, 'There is no such thing as nirvāṇa. I am an arhat and yet I am now returning to be born yet again. The Buddha's teachings are false and deceptive.'

"At this very time, he immediately saw the signs of the intermediary aggregates of the Avīci hells. When his life ended, he was immediately reborn in the Avīci hells." The Buddha then uttered a verse, saying:

> One may be learned, uphold the precepts, and be adept at dhyāna,
> While not yet realizing the dharma free of outflow impurities.
> Although one may possess these meritorious qualities,
> This circumstance is one on which one cannot base one's trust.

3. The Bodhisattva Realizes a Singular Nature in Dual Phenomena

This bhikshu consequently underwent this sort of suffering in the wretched destinies. One may realize from this that if one grasps at the characteristic of being mentally scattered, one may develop towards it hate-filled thoughts and other such afflictions. If one

取定相能生着。菩萨不取乱相。亦不取禅定相。乱定相一故是名禅波罗蜜。如初禅相。离欲除盖摄心一处。是菩萨利根智慧观故。于五盖无所舍。于禅定相无所取。诸法[6]相空故。云何于五盖无所舍。贪欲盖非内非外亦不两中间。何以故。若内法有不应待外生。若外法有于我亦无患。若两中间有两间则无[7]处。亦不从先世来。何以故。一切法无来故。如童子无有欲。若先世有者小亦应有。以是故知先世不来。亦不至后世。不从诸方来。亦不常自有。[8]不一分中。非遍身中。[9]二亦不从五尘来。亦不从五情出。无所从生无所从灭。

简体字

取定相能生著。菩薩不取亂相。亦不取禪定相。亂定相一故是名禪波羅蜜。如初禪相。離欲除蓋攝心一處。是菩薩利根智慧觀故。於五蓋無所捨。於禪定相無所取。諸法[6]相空故。云何於五蓋無所捨。貪欲蓋非內非外亦不兩中間。何以故。若內法有不應待外生。若外法有於我亦無患。若兩中間有兩間則無[7]處。亦不從先世來。何以故。一切法無來故。如童子無有欲。若先世有者小亦應有。以是故知先世不來。亦不至後世。不從諸方來。亦不常自有。[8]不一分中。非遍身中。[9]二亦不從五塵來。亦不從五情出。無所從生無所從滅。

正體字

seizes upon the characteristic of abiding in concentration, then one may then develop attachments with respect to that.

The bodhisattva does not seize upon the characteristic of mental scattering nor does he seize upon the characteristic of abiding in dhyāna concentration. This is because the characteristics of scattering and the characteristic of abiding in concentration are ultimately of a single character. It is this realization which qualifies as concordant with dhyāna *pāramitā*.

L. The Bodhisattva's Wisdom-Based Transcendence of the Hindrances

Take for example the characteristic features of the first dhyāna consisting of separating from desires, of eliminating the hindrances, and of focusing the mind in a single place. These bodhisattvas, on account of their sharp faculties and wisdom-based contemplations regarding the five hindrances have nothing whatsoever which they eliminate, and with respect to the characteristic features of the dhyāna concentrations, they have nothing whatsoever which is seized upon. This is because the characteristic features of all dharmas are empty of inherent existence.

How is it that, with respect to the five hindrances, there is nothing whatsoever which is eliminated? The hindrance of sensual desire does not abide inwardly, does not abide outwards, and does not abide anywhere between the two. How is that? If it existed as an inward dharma, it should not have to depend on any outward phenomenon for its arising. If it abides instead as an outwardly-existent dharma, then it should not present any calamity to oneself. If it were the case that it resided somewhere between the two, then it would in effect be devoid of any real location at all.

Nor does it come [forward into the present] from previous existences. How is that? All dharmas are devoid of any coming. Take for example a young child. He is free of sensual desire. If it were the case that it existed based upon previous existences, then one should possess it even when very young. For this reason, one should know that it does not come forth from earlier existences. Nor does it proceed on into later existences. Nor does it come from any of the directions. Nor does it constantly exist just spontaneously.

It does not exist in any one part [of the body]. It is not the case that it is pervasive throughout the entire body. Being singular,[13] it does not come from the five different sense objects, nor does it come forth from the five different sense faculties. It has no place from which it arises nor does it have any place wherein it is extinguished.

是贪欲若先生若后生若一时
生。是事不然。何以故。若
先有生后有贪欲。是中不应
贪欲生。未有贪欲故。若后
有生先有贪欲。则生无所
生。若一时生则无生者无生
处。生者生处无分别故。复
次是贪欲贪欲者不一不异。
何以故。离贪欲贪欲者不可
得。离贪欲者贪欲不可得。
是但从和合因缘生。和合因
缘生法即是自性空。如是贪
欲贪欲者异不可得。若一贪
欲贪欲者则无分别。如是等
种种因缘贪欲生不可得。若
法无生是法亦无灭。不生不
灭故则无定无乱。如是观贪
欲盖。则与禅为一。馀盖亦
如是。若得诸法实相观五盖
则无所有。是时便知五盖实
相即是禅实[*]相。禅实[*]相
即是五盖。菩萨如是能知五
欲及五盖禅

是貪欲若先生若後生若一時
生。是事不然。何以故。若
先有生後有貪欲。是中不應
貪欲生。未有貪欲故。若後
有生先有貪欲。則生無所
生。若一時生則無生者無生
處。生者生處無分別故。復
次是貪欲貪欲者不一不異。
何以故。離貪欲貪欲者不可
得。離貪欲者貪欲不可得。
是但從和合因緣生。和合因
緣生法即是自性空。如是貪
欲貪欲者異不可得。若一貪
欲貪欲者則無分別。如是等
種種因緣貪欲生不可得。若
法無生是法亦無滅。不生不
滅故則無定無亂。如是觀貪
欲蓋。則與禪為一。餘蓋亦
如是。若得諸法實相觀五蓋
則無所有。是時便知五蓋實
相即是禪實[*]相。禪實[*]相
即是五蓋。菩薩如是能知五
欲及五蓋禪

简体字

正體字

Whether one posits this desire as having a prior production, a later production, or as existing simultaneously with its production, none of these are the case, either. How is this so? If it was the case that there was first a production and later the existence of desire, there should not be the production of desire, this because [effective causes of] desire had not yet had any prior existence.

[On the other hand], if it was the case that only later was there its "production" while the desire itself had existed previously already, then the "production" should not really have anything new which it was producing.

If it was the case that [desire and its production] arose simultaneously, then there would be neither a producer nor a basis from which it was produced. This is because the entity produced and the basis of production would be indistinguishable.

Moreover, this desire and the individual who desires are neither one nor different. How is this so? No individual who desires can be found apart from desire. No desire can be found apart from the individual who desires. This phenomenon is produced solely from the coming together of causes and conditions. Dharmas which are produced from the coming together of causes and conditions are themselves empty of any inherently existent nature.

When seen in this manner, no difference can be found between desire itself and the individual who desires. If they were identical, then desire and the one who desires would be indistinguishable. Due to all sorts of causal bases such as these, the production of desire cannot be gotten at. If a dharma has no production, then this dharma has no destruction either. Since it is neither produced nor destroyed, then neither meditative concentration nor mental distraction can be said to exist.

When one contemplates the hindrance of desire in this manner, then it is found to be essentially identical with dhyāna. The other hindrances are also just like this.

M. The Ultimate Reality Based Identity of Dhyāna and Hindrances

In the case of one who has realized the true character of dharmas, on contemplating the five hindrances, he finds that they have no inherent existence at all. He then realizes that the true character of the five hindrances is identical with the true character of dhyāna and that the true character of dhyāna is identical with that of the five hindrances. In this way the bodhisattva is able to realize that the five desires as well as the five hindrances, the dhyāna

定及[10]支[11]一相无所依入
禅定。是为禅波罗蜜。复次
若菩萨行禅波罗蜜时。五波
罗蜜和合助成。是名禅波罗
蜜。复次菩萨以禅波罗蜜力
得神通。一念之顷不起于
定。能供养十方诸佛。华香
珍宝种种供养。复次菩萨以
禅波罗蜜力变身无数。遍入
五道以三乘法教化众生。复
次菩萨入禅波罗蜜中。除诸
恶不善法。入初禅乃至非有
想非无想定。其心调柔一一
禅中行大慈[12]大悲。以慈悲
因缘。拔无量劫中罪。得诸
法实相智故。为十方诸佛及
大菩萨所念。复次菩萨入禅
波罗蜜中。以天眼观十方五
道中众生。见生色界中者受
禅定乐味。还堕禽兽中受种
种苦。

定及[10]支[11]一相無所依入
禪定。是為禪波羅蜜。復次
若菩薩行禪波羅蜜時。五波
羅蜜和合助成。是名禪波羅
蜜。復次菩薩以禪波羅蜜力
得神通。一念之頃不起於
定。能供養十方諸佛。華香
珍寶種種供養。復次菩薩以
禪波羅蜜力變身無數。遍入
五道以三乘法教化眾生。復
次菩薩入禪波羅蜜中。除諸
惡不善法。入初禪乃至非有
想非無想定。其心調柔一一
禪中行大慈[12]大悲。以慈悲
因緣。拔無量劫中罪。得諸
法實相智故。為十方諸佛及
大菩薩所念。復次菩薩入禪
波羅蜜中。以天眼觀十方五
道中眾生。見生色界中者受
禪定樂味。還墮禽獸中受種
種苦。

简体字   正體字

concentrations as well as their component factors—they are all of a single character. Thus, without depending on anything whatsoever, he is able to enter dhyāna absorption. It is this which qualifies as dhyāna *"pāramitā."*

N. Dhyāna Pāramitā's Interactive Influence on the Other Pāramitās

Moreover, when the bodhisattva practices the *pāramitā* of dhyāna, the other five *pāramitās* are all comprehensively assisted in their completion. It is this which qualifies as dhyāna *"pāramitā."*

O. Dhyāna Pāramitā as the Basis for Acquisition of Superknowledges

Furthermore, the bodhisattva employs the power of dhyāna *pāramitā* to gain the superknowledges. In only a single thought-moment, even while not emerging from absorption, he is able to make offerings of flowers, incense and all sorts of precious treasures to the Buddhas of the ten directions.

Additionally, the bodhisattva employs the power of the dhyāna *pāramitā* to transformationally create innumerable bodies which universally enter into the five destinies and which employ the Dharma of the Three Vehicles to teach and transform beings.

P. Dhyāna Pāramitā as Basis for Riddance of Unwholesome Dharmas

Moreover, when the bodhisattva has entered into the *pāramitā* of dhyāna, he gets rid of all evil and unwholesome dharmas. Entering the first dhyāna and so forth until we come to the absorption of neither perception nor non-perception, his mind is well-regulated and pliant. In each and every one of the dhyānas, he practices the great kindness and the great compassion. On account of the causes and conditions associated with [practicing] kindness and compassion, he is able to remove the offenses accumulated throughout the course of an incalculable number of kalpas. On account of having gained the reality-concordant wisdom cognizing the true character of dharmas, he is borne in mind by the Buddhas and great Bodhisattvas of the ten directions.

Q. How Dhyāna Pāramitā and the Heavenly Eye Enhance Compassion

Furthermore, the bodhisattva who has entered into dhyāna *pāramitā* employs the heavenly eye and contemplates the beings within the five destinies throughout the ten directions. He observes that there are those who have been born in the form realm who indulge themselves therein in the enjoyment-focused dhyāna concentrations. He sees that they then fall back into the realms of birds and beasts and then consequently undergo all sorts of associated sufferings.

复见欲界诸天七宝池中华
香自娱。后堕醶沸屎地狱
中。[13]见[14]人中多闻世智
辩聪。不得道故。还堕猪羊
畜兽中无所别知。如是[15]等
种种。失大乐得大苦。失大
利得大衰。失尊贵得卑贱。
于此众生生悲心。渐渐增广
得成大悲不惜身命。为众生
故懃行精进以求佛道。复次
不乱不味故。名禅波罗蜜。
如佛告舍利弗。菩萨般若波
罗蜜中住。具足禅波罗蜜。
不乱不味故。问曰。云何名
[16]乱。乱有二种。一者微二
者麁微者有三种。一爱多[17]
二慢多三见多。云何爱多。
得禅定乐其心乐着[18]爱味。
云何慢多。得禅[19]定时自谓
难事已得而以自高。云何见
多。以我见等入禅定。分别
取相。是实馀妄语。

復見欲界諸天七寶池中華
香自娛。後墮醶沸屎地獄
中。[13]見[14]人中多聞世智
辯聰。不得道故。還墮豬羊
畜獸中無所別知。如是[15]等
種種。失大樂得大苦。失大
利得大衰。失尊貴得卑賤。
於此眾生生悲心。漸漸增廣
得成大悲不惜身命。為眾生
故懃行精進以求佛道。復次
不亂不味故。名禪波羅蜜。
如佛告舍利弗。菩薩般若波
羅蜜中住。具足禪波羅蜜。
不亂不味故。問曰。云何名
[16]亂。亂有二種。一者微二
者麁微者有三種。一愛多[17]
二慢多三見多。云何愛多。
得禪定樂其心樂著[18]愛味。
云何慢多。得禪[19]定時自謂
難事已得而以自高。云何見
多。以我見等入禪定。分別
取相。是實餘妄語。

简体字   正體字

Additionally, he sees gods of the desire realm who take their pleasure amidst flowers and incenses in pools lined with the seven precious things and then afterwards fall into the hell of brine and boiling excrement.

He observes those among humans who are very learned and possessed of worldly wisdom, eloquence, and intelligence who, on account of not having gained the Path, fall back again among the pigs, sheep, and other domestic animals wherein they have nothing whatsoever in the way of discriminating awareness.

He observes all sorts of cases such as these wherein beings lose great bliss and obtain great suffering, lose great profit and obtain great decline, and lose honorable and noble status and obtain low and base social station. He develops a mind of compassion for these beings which gradually increases and broadens and succeeds in developing into the great compassion. He then refrains from any cherishing of his own body or life. For the sake of beings, he proceeds with diligence in seeking realization of the Buddha Path.

V. Summation of Key Factors in Realization of Dhyāna *Pāramitā*

Moreover, "it is through being neither mentally distracted nor indulging enjoyment" that one defines dhyāna *pāramitā*. As the Buddha told Śāriputra, "The bodhisattva abides in the Prajñāpāramitā. It is through being neither mentally distracted nor indulging enjoyment that one should perfect dhyāna *pāramitā*."

Question: What is meant by being "mentally distracted"?

Response: There are two kinds of "mental distraction." The first is subtle. The second is coarse. Among the subtle there are three types. The first is where there is much desire. The second is where there is much arrogance. The third is where there are many views.

What is meant by that type which is characterized by "much desire"? Having obtained the bliss of dhyāna absorption, one's mind becomes blissfully attached and desires the enjoyment of it.

What is meant by that type in which there is "much arrogance"? This refers to when one has achieved dhyāna absorption and is of the opinion that a difficult endeavor has already been achieved and so, on account of that, one elevates oneself.

What is meant by that type in which there are "many views"? On account of the view which seizes upon the existence of a self and other such views, having entered into dhyāna absorption, one makes discriminations and so seizes upon different characteristics, claiming, "This is what is real. All else is but a pack of lies."

是三名为微细乱。从是因缘于禅定退起三毒。是为麁乱。味者初得禅定一心爱[20]着是为味。问曰。一切烦恼皆能染着。何以[21]故但名爱为味。答曰。爱与禅相似。何以故。禅则摄心坚住爱亦专着难舍。又初求禅时。心专欲得。爱之为性欲乐专求。欲与禅定不相[190-1]违故。既得禅定[2]深着不舍则坏禅定。譬如施人物。必望现报则无福德。于禅[3]受味爱着于禅。亦复如是。是故但以爱名味。不以馀结为味。

大智度论卷第十七。

简体字

是三名為微細亂。從是因緣於禪定退起三毒。是為麁亂。味者初得禪定一心愛[20]著是為味。問曰。一切煩惱皆能染著。何以[21]故但名愛為味。答曰。愛與禪相似。何以故。禪則攝心堅住愛亦專著難捨。又初求禪時。心專欲得。愛之為性欲樂專求。欲與禪定不相[190-1]違故。既得禪定[2]深著不捨則壞禪定。譬如施人物。必望現報則無福德。於禪[3]受味愛著於禪。亦復如是。是故但以愛名味。不以餘結為味。

大智度論卷第十七。

正體字

These three are referred to as "subtle" mental distraction. Stemming from these causal factors, one withdraws from dhyāna absorption and develops the three poisons. This then constitutes what is termed "coarse mental distraction."

As for "indulging enjoyment," this refers to when one first succeeds in gaining dhyāna concentration and then indulges a single-minded desire-based attachment to it. This is what constitutes "indulging enjoyment."

Question: All of the afflictions are able to result in defilement and attachment. Why does one only refer here to "desire" as the basis for indulging "enjoyment"?

Response: "Desire" and dhyāna are similar. How is this so? In the case of dhyāna, one focuses the mind so that it abides solidly. In the case of desire, one also becomes exclusively attached so that one relinquishes [attachment to its objects] only with difficulty. Also, when one first seeks dhyāna, one's mind becomes exclusively focused on the wish to gain it. "Desire" exclusively seeks for the bliss associated with the indulgence of sensual desires. Because sensual desire and dhyāna concentration are [in this sense] not opposed [as regards the nature of the motivations involved], when one has already gained dhyāna concentration, if one indulges deep attachment to it and does not relinquish it, then one consequently proceeds to destroy the dhyāna concentration.

This is analogous to making gifts of things to people. If one insists on hoping for a present reward, then there is no karmic merit which results from it. In the case of dhyāna, when one indulges in enjoyment-focused mind states and becomes desirously attached to dhyāna, it is just the same as this. It is for this reason that we only cite "desire" as the basis of the enjoyment-focused meditation and do not cite any of the other fetters as associated with such enjoyment.

Part Five Endnotes

1. The five desires: visual forms, sounds, smells, tastes, touchables.

2. The ten good deeds refer to avoidance of ten karmic errors, three physical (killing, stealing, sexual misconduct), four verbal (lying, harsh speech, divisive speech, frivolous speech [usually interpreted as "useless and/or lewd" speech]), and three mental (greed, hatred, erroneous views).

3. These reduced-font parenthetical statements are part of the Taisho text and may or may not originate with the original translation editors.

4. This refers to birth, aging, sickness, and death.

5. On the question of why "lethargy-and-sleepiness" is a dual-component hindrance, Vasubandhu indicates (in Chapter Five of his *Treasury of Analytic Knowledge*) that it is because both "lethargy" and "sleepiness" are nourished by the same five factors (bad omens seen in dreams [*tandrī*]; unhappiness [*arati*]; physical exhaustion [*vijṛmbhikā*]; uneven consumption of food [*bhakte'samatā*]; mental depression [*cetaso līnatva*]), are starved by the same single factor (illuminated perception [*āloka-saṃjñā*]), and are productive of the same result of mental languor. This per Pruden, *Abhidharma-kośa-bhāṣyam* (851–2).

6. On the question of why "excitedness-and-regretfulness" is a dual-component hindrance, Vasubandhu indicates (in Chapter Five of his *Treasury of Analytic Knowledge*) that it is because both "excitedness" and "regretfulness" are nourished by the same four factors (ideation regarding relatives, land, immortals, previous pleasures and the associated companions), are starved by the same single factor (calmness), and are productive of the same result of mental agitation. This per Pruden, *Abhidharma-kośa-bhāṣyam* (852).

7. The four aspects contained in quotation marks together with *samādhi* constitute the five component factors present in the second dhyāna. These block-set quotations derive, sometimes loosely, from the *Dhyāna Sūtra*. The long verse quoted above and attributed by Nāgārjuna to this same scripture, serves as the narrative outline for Nāgārjuna's entire treatment of the four dhyānas in this section.

8. The four aspects contained in quotation marks are the four component factors present in the second dhyāna.

9. The five aspects contained in quotation marks are the five component factors present in the third dhyāna.

10. The three aspects contained in quotation marks together with *samādhi* constitute the four component factors present in the fourth dhyāna.

11. In fact there are nine such successively graded defilements occurring in relation to each of nine stations which include the preliminary ground *anāgamya*, the four dhyānas, and the four *samāpattis*.

12. "Devapuṣpāgra" is my so-far unattested reconstruction for the Chinese which appears somewhat tentatively to mean "Celestial Floral Pistil," the apparent allusion being to the bodhisattva's constantly residing on a lotus.

13. This alternate reading of "singular" found in five editions has been preferred here for the Taisho text's "dual."

Part Five Variant Readings in Other Chinese Editions

[180n08] (第二十八)－[元][明]
[180n09] 八＝三[宮][石]
[180n10] (卷第十七)－[石]
[180n11] ([經])－[宋][宮]
[180n12] ([論])－[宋][宮]
[180n13] (獲)＋得[宋][
元][明],(定)＋得[宮]
[180n14] 家＝眾[元][明]
[180n15] (故)－[元][明][宮][石]
[180n16] (作)－[宋][元][明][宮][石]
[180n17] (是)－[宋][元][明][宮][石]
[180n18] (燈)－[石]
[180n19] 宇＝室[元][明][石]
[180n20] 炷＝性[石]
[180n21] 剛＝[金*剛][石]
[180n22] 淹＝掩[宋][宮][石]
[180n23] 當＝思[宮]
[180n24] (猶)－[宋][元][明][宮][石]
[180n25] (心)－[宋][元][明][宮][石]
[181n01] 毒＝庸[宋][元][明][宮]
[181n02] 顏＝貌[宋][元][明][宮]
[181n03] 已＝以[石]
[181n04] 慈＝悲[宋][元][明][宮][石]
[181n05] (五塵)－[宋][宮][石]
[181n06] ((除五…行))八字＝((
除五蓋行五法))六字[宮]
[181n07] (五蓋)－[宋][宮][石]
[181n08] 行＋(初禪五支)[元][明]
[181n09] 諍＝爭[宋][元][明][宮]
[181n10] 惟＝唯[宋][元][明][宮]
[181n11] 說＝設[宋][元][宮][石]
[181n12] 汝＝此[宋][元][明][宮]
[181n13] (著)－[宋][宮][石]
[181n14] 怒＝怨[宋][元][明][宮]
[181n15] (念念)－[宋][宮][石]
[181n16] 人＝智[元][明]
[181n17] (一)－[宋][元][明][宮][石]
[181n18] (與)－[宋][元][明][宮]
[181n19] 至＝去[元][明]
[181n20] (之)－[宋][元][
明][宮][石]* [* 1]
[181n21] 徑＝經[宮]
[181n22] (時師)－[宋][宮][石]
[181n23] ((其心…愛))八字＝((鼻受
心著))四字[宋][元][明][宮][石]
[181n24] (故)－[宋][元][明][宮][石]
[181n25] 下＝中[宋][元][明][宮]
[181n26] 皆＝今皆覺[宋][
元][明][宮][石]
[181n27] 言偷我＝云我瑜[
宋][元][明][宮][石]
[182n01] 疊＝[疊*毛][宋][元][明][宮]
[182n02] (法)－[宋][元][明][宮][石]
[182n03] (此是虫)－[宋][宮][石]
[182n04] 國＋(土)[宋][元][明][宮]
[182n05] (鳥母)＋常[元][明]
[182n06] 其＝甚[宋][元][明][宮]
[182n07] 哭＝泣[宋][元][明][宮][石]
[182n08] (着味…苦)九字－[
宋][元][明][宮][石]
[182n09] 火＝大[宋][元][明][宮][石]
[182n10] (則)－[宋][元][明][宮]
[182n11] 厭心＝心厭[宋][宮]
[182n12] (不淨)－[宋][元][明][宮][石]
[182n13] 劬＝瞿[宋][元][明][宮]* [* 1 2]
[182n14] 妊＝任[石]* [* 1 2]
[182n15] (亦)－[宋][元][明][宮]
[182n16] 何＝所[石]
[182n17] (一鉢)－[石]
[182n18] (鉢)－[宋][宮]
[182n19] 以神力＝神力以[
宋][元][明][宮]
[182n20] 皆＝令[宋][元][明][宮][石]
[182n21] 槃＝盤[宋][元][
明][宮]* [* 1 2 3]
[183n01] (時)＋耶[宋][元][明][宮]
[183n02] 遣＝進[宋][元][明][宮][石]
[183n03] 目＝自[宋][元][明][宮][石]
[183n04] 丘＋(汝欲聞不諦聽之)[元][明]
[183n05] 婆＝波[元][明]* [* 1 2]
[183n06] 春＝秋[宋][宮][石]
[183n07] 娠＝身[宋][元][明][宮][石]
[183n08] 菴＝庵[宋][元][明][宮]* [* 1]
[183n09] (即)－[宋][元][明][宮]
[183n10] 鍾＝軍[宋][元][明][宮]* [* 1]

[183n11] (國)－[宋] [元] [
明] [宮] [石]* [* 1]
[183n12] 官＝臣 [元] [明]
[183n13] (曾)－[宋] [元] [明] [宮] [石]
[183n14] 無雙＝巨富 [宋] [宮] [石]
[183n15] (人)－[石]
[183n16] 五百＝百五 [石]
[183n17] 藥＋(草) [宋] [元] [明] [宮] [石]
[183n18] 眾彩畫之＝彩畫 [
宋] [元] [明] [宮] [石]
[183n19] (衣)－[石]
[183n20] 以＝似 [元] [明]
[183n21] 好＝妙 [宋] [元] [明] [宮] [石]
[183n22] (皆)－[宋] [元] [明] [宮]
[183n23] 淨＝清 [宋] [元] [明] [宮] [石]
[183n24] (以)－[宋] [元] [明] [宮] [石]
[183n25] 好果好水＝好水好
果 [宋] [元] [明] [宮] [石]
[183n26] (盛)－[宋] [元] [明] [宮] [石]
[183n27] (美)－[宋] [元] [明] [宮] [石]
[183n28] 喜＝樂 [宋] [元] [明] [宮] [石]
[183n29] 已＝以 [宋] [元] [明] [宮] [石]
[183n30] 果＝食 [宋] [元] [明] [宮] [石]
[183n31] (媱女知)－[宋] [
元] [明] [宮] [石]
[183n32] 項＝擔 [宋] [元] [明] [宮] [石]
[183n33] 足五所＝給足五 [元] [明]
[183n34] (者)－[宋] [元] [明] [宮] [石]
[183n35] 之人＝蓋者 [宋] [
元] [明] [宮] [石]
[183n36] 怯＝性 [石]
[184n01] 人＝生 [石]
[184n02] 貪欲＝欲貪 [宋] [宮]
[184n03] 已＝以 [宋] [元] [明] [宮] [石]
[184n04] 在者＝不滅 [宋] [元] [明]
[184n05] 諸＝法 [元] [明]
[184n06] 報果＝果報 [宋] [元] [明] [宮]
[184n07] 當＝尚 [元] [明]
[184n08] 免＝勉 [石]* [* 1 2]
[184n09] 眠睡＝睡眠 [宋] [
元] [明] [宮] [石]
[184n10] 侵＝欺 [元] [明]
[184n11] 掉＝挑 [石]* [* 1 2 3 4 5]
[184n12] 人＋(睡) [宮]
[184n13] 決＝缺 [宋] [宮],＝穴 [元] [明]

[184n14] (法)－[宋] [元] [明] [宮] [石]
[184n15] 能＝雖 [宮]
[184n16] 已＝以 [宋] [宮]
[184n17] (悔)－[宮]
[184n18] (心)－[宋] [元] [明] [宮]
[185n01] (蓋)－[宋] [元] [明] [宮] [石]
[185n02] 債＝責 [石]
[185n03] 差＝瘥 [宋] [元] [明] [宮]
[185n04] 支＝枝 [宋] [元] [
明] [宮] [石]下同
[185n05] 馳＝持 [宮]
[185n06] 常＝當 [宮]
[185n07] 其苦甚多＝多苦 [宋] [明] [
石],＝多若 [元],＝多苦甚多 [宮]
[185n08] 樹林＝林樹 [石]
[185n09] 銷＝洋 [宋] [元] [明] [宮]
[185n10] 豺＝豹 [宋] [元] [明] [宮]
[185n11] 鵁＝鶁 [宋] [宮],＝鵰 [元] [明]
[185n12] (人)－[宋] [石] [明] [宮] [石]
[185n13] [病-丙+寧]＝儜 [
宋] [元] [明] [宮]
[185n14] 林＝杖 [宋] [元] [宮] [石]
[185n15] 霹靂＝霹靂 [宋] [元] [明] [宮]
[185n16] (諸)－[宋] [元] [明] [宮]
[185n17] 秦＝此 [明]
[185n18] (餘定不名波羅蜜)－[宮] [石]
[185n19] (念)－[宋] [元] [明] [宮] [石]
[185n20] 池＝地 [宋] [元] [明] [宮]
[185n21] 則＝得 [宋] [元] [明] [宮]
[186n01] 法＋(為) [宋] [元] [明] [宮] [石]
[186n02] 微細＝細微 [宋] [元] [明] [宮]
[186n03] 但＝俱 [宋] [宮]
[186n04] 繫＝擊 [明]
[186n05] 身＋(身) [宋] [元] [明] [宮] [石]
[186n06] 籠＝筵 [宋] [宮] [石]
[186n07] (身)－[宋] [元] [明] [明] [石]
[186n08] 以＝行 [宋] [宮]
[186n09] (定)－[宋] [元] [明] [宮] [石]
[186n10] (處)－[宮] [石]
[186n11] 受＋(想) [宋] [元] [明] [宮]
[186n12] 是＝行 [宋] [元] [
明] [宮],＝所 [石]
[187n01] 礙＝閡 [石]* [* 1 2]
[187n02] 禪＋(無漏) [宋] [元] [明] [宮]
[187n03] (於)－[石]

[187n04] (但)－[石]

[187n05] (因)－[宋][元][明][宮]

[187n06] (者)－[宋][元][明][宮][石]

[187n07] (淨)－[宋][元][明][宮]* [* 1]

[187n08] (不緣無漏)－[宋][宮][石]

[187n09] 三＝八[石]

[187n10] 所＝名[宮]

[187n11] (一切)－[宋][元][明][宮][石]

[187n12] (以)－[宋][宮]

[187n13] 煉＝練[宋][元][明][宮][石]

[187n14] (去其…是)十二字－[
宋][元][明][宮][石]

[187n15] (初)－[宋][宮]

[187n16] 二＝種[元][明]

[187n17] (識)－[石]

[187n18] 相＝想[元][明][宮]

[187n19] (定)－[宋][元][明][宮]

[188n01] 鞊＝詰[宋][元][明][宮]

[188n02] 宴＝燕[石]* [* 1]

[188n03] 然＝殺[石]

[188n04] 欲令＝故今[石],欲
＝故[宋][元][明][宮]

[188n05] 其＝之其人[宋][元][
明],＝之其[宮],＝之其某[石]

[188n06] 知＝如[宋][宮]

[188n07] 心不＝不心[石]

[188n08] 不＋(能)[宋][元][明][宮]

[188n09] 中＝定[宮]

[188n10] 昆＝鯤[宋][元][明][宮]

[188n11] 瞖＝結[石]

[188n12] 利＝梨[宋][元][明][宮][石]

[188n13] 兀＝無[石]

[188n14] 頭＝頂[宋][元][明][宮][石]

[188n15] 甄＝緊[宋][元][明][宮]

[188n16] 崙＝嶮[宮]

[188n17] 須＝鬚[宋][宮][
石],＝鬘[元][明]

[188n18] 令＝今[石]

[188n19] (第)－[宋][元][明][宮][石]

[188n20] (二乘)－[石]

[188n21] 超＝起[石]* [* 1 2]

[188n22] (入)－[宮][石]

[188n23] (能)－[元][宮][石]

[188n24] 髮＝毛[宋]*,＝髦[元][明]* [* 1]

[188n25] 超＝踔[元][明]

[188n26] (能)－[宋][元][明][宮][石]

[188n27] 諸＝語[石]

[188n28] 何＝阿[宋][元][明][宮]

[188n29] 人＝又[元]

[188n30] 除＝於[元][明]

[189n01] (國)－[宋][元][明][宮]

[189n02] 捉＝接[元][明]

[189n03] 為＋(為)[宋][宮]

[189n04] 中＋(亂)[元][明]

[189n05] 犁＝[黍-禾+利][石]* [* 1 2]

[189n06] (相)－[宋],[宮][石]* [* 1 2]

[189n07] 處＋(所)[宋][元][明]

[189n08] 不＝非[元][明]

[189n09] (二)－[宋][元][明][宮][石]

[189n10] 支＝枝[宋][元][明][宮][石]

[189n11] (一)－[元][明]

[189n12] (大)－[宋][元][明][宮]

[189n13] (又)＋見[宋][元][明]

[189n14] 人中＝中人[宋]

[189n15] 等＋(身)[宋][元][明]

[189n16] 亂＋(答)[宋][元][明][宮]

[189n17] 二＝三[明]

[189n18] 愛＝受[石]

[189n19] (定)－[宋][元][明][宮][石]

[189n20] 著＝樂[宋][元][明][宮]

[189n21] (故)－[宋][元][明][宮][石]

[190n01] 違＝逆[宮]

[190n02] 深＝染[宋][元][明][宮][石]

[190n03] 受味＝愛身[元][石]

Part Six:

THE PERFECTION OF WISDOM

(Chapters 29-30)

Part Six Contents

NĀGĀRJUNA ON THE PERFECTION OF WISDOM

大智[190-4]度论释初品中般若波罗蜜[5]第二十[6]九（卷第十八）。

[*]龙树菩萨造。

[*]后秦龟兹国三藏鸠摩罗什[*]奉诏译。

[0190a15]　　[7]【经】于一切法不着故。应具足般若波罗蜜。

[0190a16]　　[8]【论】问曰。云何名般若波罗蜜。答曰。诸菩萨从初发心。求一切种智。于其中间知诸法实相慧是般若波罗蜜。问曰。若尔者不应名为波罗蜜。何以故。未到智慧边故。答曰。佛所得智慧是实波罗蜜。因是波罗蜜故。菩萨所行亦名波罗蜜。因中说果故。是般若波罗蜜在佛心中变名为一切种智。菩萨行智慧求度彼岸故。名波罗蜜。佛已度彼岸故。名一切种智。问曰。佛一切诸烦恼及习已断智慧眼净。应如实得诸法实相。诸法实相

简体字

大智[190-4]度論釋初品中般若波羅蜜[5]第二十[6]九（卷第十八）。

[*]龍樹菩薩造。

[*]後秦龜茲國三藏鳩摩羅什[*]奉詔譯。

[0190a15]　　[7]【經】於一切法不著故。應具足般若波羅蜜。

[0190a16]　　[8]【論】問曰。云何名般若波羅蜜。答曰。諸菩薩從初發心。求一切種智。於其中間知諸法實相慧是般若波羅蜜。問曰。若爾者不應名為波羅蜜。何以故。未到智慧邊故。答曰。佛所得智慧是實波羅蜜。因是波羅蜜故。菩薩所行亦名波羅蜜。因中說果故。是般若波羅蜜在佛心中變名為一切種智。菩薩行智慧求度彼岸故。名波羅蜜。佛已度彼岸故。名一切種智。問曰。佛一切諸煩惱及習已斷智慧眼淨。應如實得諸法實相。諸法實相

正體字

THE PERFECTION OF WISDOM

By Ārya Nāgārjuna

Chapter 29: On the Meaning of the Perfection of Wisdom

Sutra text: It is through refraining from attachment to any dharma that one should perfect *prajñāpāramitā* (the perfection of wisdom).[1]

Exegesis text:

I. ON THE MEANING OF THE PERFECTION OF WISDOM
  A. *PRAJÑĀPĀRAMITĀ* DEFINED
    1. QUESTION: WHAT IS MEANT BY *"PRAJÑĀPĀRAMITĀ"*?

Question: What is meant by *"prajñāpāramitā?"*

    2. RESPONSE: THE BODHISATTVA'S REALITY-COGNIZING WISDOM

Response: All bodhisattvas, from the time of first bringing forth the resolve to realize bodhi (enlightenment), seek to gain the "knowledge of all modes" (*sarva-ākāra-jñatā*).[2] In the interim period, that wisdom which knows in accordance with reality the true character of dharmas (*dharmatā*)[3] is what qualifies as *"prajñāpāramitā."*

    3. CHALLENGE: BUT THAT IS NOT ULTIMATE AND SHOULD NOT QUALIFY

Question: If that is the case, then it ought not to be referred to as *"pāramitā."* Why? Because they have not yet reached to the limits of wisdom.

    4. RESPONSE: THIS DESCRIBES THE CAUSE IN TERMS OF ITS EFFECT

Response: The wisdom realized by the Buddha is genuinely *"pāramitā"* (perfected). Because the cause itself is *"pāramitā,"* the practice of the bodhisattva also qualifies as *"pāramitā."* This is because, in the sphere of the causes, one speaks in terms of the fruit [which they bring forth].

Within the mind of a Buddha, *prajñāpāramitā* changes in name and is referred to then as the "knowledge of all modes." Because in the bodhisattva's practice of wisdom he seeks to [perfect it by] "bringing it across to the other shore," it is referred to as *"pāramitā."*[4] Because the Buddha has already "brought it across to the other shore," it is then referred to as "the knowledge of all modes."

      a. CHALLENGE: BODHISATTVAS HAVE IMPURITIES AND IMPERFECT WISDOM

Question: The Buddha has already cut off all afflictions (*kleśa*) and habitual propensities (*vāsanā*) and has purified the eye of wisdom (*prajñā-cakṣus*). He should therefore have already realized the true character of dharmas in accordance with reality. The true character

即是般若波罗蜜。菩萨未尽
诸漏慧眼未净。云何能得诸
法实相。答曰。此义后品中
当广说。今但略说。如人入
海。有始入者。有尽其源底
者。深浅虽异俱名为入。佛
菩萨亦如是。佛则穷尽其
底。菩萨未断诸烦恼习。势
力少故不能深入如后品中
说。譬喻如人于暗室然灯。
照诸器物皆悉分了。更有大
灯益复明审。则知后灯所破
之暗。与前灯合住。前灯虽
与暗共住而亦能照物。若前
灯无暗则后灯无所增益。诸
佛菩萨智慧亦如是。菩萨智
慧虽与烦恼习合而能得诸法
实相。亦如前灯亦能照物。
佛智慧尽诸烦恼习。亦得诸
法实相。如后灯倍复明了。
问曰。云何是诸法实相。

简体字

即是般若波羅蜜。菩薩未盡
諸漏慧眼未淨。云何能得諸
法實相。答曰。此義後品中
當廣說。今但略說。如人入
海。有始入者。有盡其源底
者。深淺雖異俱名為入。佛
菩薩亦如是。佛則窮盡其
底。菩薩未斷諸煩惱習。勢
力少故不能深入如後品中
說。譬喻如人於闇室然燈。
照諸器物皆悉分了。更有大
燈益復明審。則知後燈所破
之闇。與前燈合住。前燈雖
與闇共住而亦能照物。若前
燈無闇則後燈無所增益。諸
佛菩薩智慧亦如是。菩薩智
慧雖與煩惱習合而能得諸法
實相。亦如前燈亦能照物。
佛智慧盡諸煩惱習。亦得諸
法實相。如後燈倍復明了。
問曰。云何是諸法實相。

正體字

of dharmas is just [as perceived with] *prajñāpāramitā*. The bodhi-sattva has not yet exhausted all outflow impurities (*āsrava*). His eye of wisdom has not yet been purified. How then could he succeed in realizing the true character of dharmas?

b. Response: They Have Already Entered and Hence Qualify
1) Analogy: Just As When Entering the Sea to Varying Depths

Response: This meaning will be extensively discussed in a later chapter. Now it shall only be discussed in brief. It is comparable to when a person enters the sea. There are those who have just begun to enter it. Then again, there are those who have gotten entirely to the bottom at its deepest point. Although there are differences in depth, they are both described as having "entered" it. It is just the same with Buddhas and bodhisattvas. In the case of the Buddha, he has reached to the very bottom of it. The bodhisattvas have not yet cut off all afflictions or habitual propensities. Because their strength is less, they are unable to enter deeply.

2) Analogy: Just as with Lamps of Varying Brightness

As stated in a later chapter, this is analogous to a case where one person lights a lamp in a dark room which illuminates all of the material objects such that one is entirely able to distinguish between them. Then yet another large lamp is introduced which increases even more the clarity of visible detail. When this happens, one realizes that the darkness dispersed by the latter lamp dwelt together in the company of the prior lamp. Although the prior lamp dwelt together with a measure of darkness, still, it was nonetheless also able to illuminate things. Then again, if there had been no darkness with the prior lamp, then the later lamp would have afforded no increased benefit.

The wisdom of the Buddhas and bodhisattvas is just the same as this. Although the wisdom of the bodhisattva does coexist with afflictions and habitual propensities, still, it is nonetheless able to achieve a realization of the true character of dharmas in just the same manner as the prior lamp was still able to illuminate things. The wisdom of the Buddhas has put an end to all afflictions and habitual propensities and so has also achieved realization of the true character of dharmas in just the same manner as the later lamp was doubly bright in the degree of its illumination.

c. Question: What is Meant by the "True Character of Dharmas"?

Question: Just what is meant by "the true character of dharmas"?

答曰。众人各各说诸法实相
自以为[9]实。此中实相者。
不可破坏。常住不异无能作
者。如后品中。佛语须菩
提。若菩萨观一切法。非常
非无常。非苦非乐。非我非
无我。非有非无等。亦不作
是观。是名菩萨行般若波罗
蜜。是义舍一切观。灭一切
言语离诸心行。从本已来不
生不灭如涅盘相。一切诸法
相亦如是。是名诸法实相。
如赞般若波罗蜜偈[10]说。

般若波罗蜜。实法不颠倒。
念想观已除。言语法亦灭。

无量众罪除。清净心常一。
如是尊妙人。则能见般若。

如虚空无染。无戏无文字。
若能如是观。是即为见佛。

若如法观佛。般若及涅盘。
是三则一相。其实无有异。

答曰。眾人各各說諸法實相
自以為[9]實。此中實相者。
不可破壞。常住不異無能作
者。如後品中。佛語須菩
提。若菩薩觀一切法。非常
非無常。非苦非樂。非我非
無我。非有非無等。亦不作
是觀。是名菩薩行般若波羅
蜜。是義捨一切觀。滅一切
言語離諸心行。從本已來不
生不滅如涅槃相。一切諸法
相亦如是。是名諸法實相。
如讚般若波羅蜜偈[10]說。

般若波羅蜜。實法不顛倒。
念想觀已除。言語法亦滅。

無量眾罪除。清淨心常一。
如是尊妙人。則能見般若。

如虛空無染。無戲無文字。
若能如是觀。是即為見佛。

若如法觀佛。般若及涅槃。
是三則一相。其實無有異。

简体字

正體字

d. Response: The Irrefutable, Eternally-Abiding, Noncomposite, etc.

Response: When each person speaks of "the true character of dharmas," he takes his own position on the matter as constituting what is genuine. The "true character" of which we speak here is beyond refutation. It is eternally abiding, undifferentiated, and not such as anyone can create.

e. Citation: Buddha's Statement to Śāriputra

It is as described by the Buddha to Śāriputra in a later chapter [of the Sutra], "When the bodhisattva contemplates all dharmas, they are perceived as neither permanent nor impermanent, neither suffering nor blissful, neither self nor non-self, neither existent nor nonexistent, and so forth, and yet he still does not actually [intentionally have to] carry out such a contemplation."

This is what is meant by the bodhisattva's practice of *prajñā-pāramitā*. The meaning of this is such that it involves the relinquishing of all [intentionally-initiated] contemplations, the extinguishing [of the utility] of any words or speech, and the transcendence of all actions undertaken by the mind. From its very origin on up until the present, it has been neither produced nor destroyed and has been characterized by being like nirvāṇa. The character of each and every dharma is precisely thus. This is what is meant by the "true character of dharmas." This is as described in a verse in praise of *prajñāpāramitā*:

B. A Verse in Praise of the Perfection of Wisdom

The *prajñāpāramitā*
Is a dharma conveying reality, not an inverted view.
Conceptual contemplations have been dispensed with.
The dharma of words and speech has been extinguished as well.

An incalculable number of offenses have been gotten rid of.
The pure mind is constantly unified.
If one is such a venerable and marvelous person,
Then one is able to perceive prajñā.

Like empty space, it is devoid of stains,
It is free of frivolousness and involves no words.
If one is able to contemplate in this manner,
This is identical to seeing the Buddha.

If, in accord with Dharma, one contemplates the Buddha,
And prajñā, and nirvāṇa,
These three are found to be singular in characteristic.
In their reality, there is no difference.

诸佛及菩萨。能利益一切。
般若为之母。能出生养育。

佛为众生父。般若能生佛。
是则为一切。众生之祖母。

般若是一法。佛说种种名。
随诸众生力。为之立异字。

若人得般若。议论心皆灭。
譬如日出时。朝露一时失。

般若之威德。能动二种人。
无智者恐怖。有智者欢喜。

若人得般若。则为般若主。
般若中不着。何况于馀法。

般若无所来。亦复无所去。
智者一切处。求之不能得。

若不见般若。是则为被缚。
若人见般若。是亦名被缚。

若人见般若。是则得解脱。
若不见般若。是亦得解脱。

是事为希有。甚深有大名。
譬如幻化物。见而不可见。

諸佛及菩薩。能利益一切。
般若為之母。能出生養育。

佛為眾生父。般若能生佛。
是則為一切。眾生之祖母。

般若是一法。佛說種種名。
隨諸眾生力。為之立異字。

若人得般若。議論心皆滅。
譬如日出時。朝露一時失。

般若之威德。能動二種人。
無智者恐怖。有智者歡喜。

若人得般若。則為般若主。
般若中不著。何況於餘法。

般若無所來。亦復無所去。
智者一切處。求之不能得。

若不見般若。是則為被縛。
若人見般若。是亦名被縛。

若人見般若。是則得解脫。
若不見般若。是亦得解脫。

是事為希有。甚深有大名。
譬如幻化物。見而不可見。

简体字　　　　　　　　　　　　　　　正體字

The Buddhas as well as the Bodhisattvas
Are able to bring benefit to all.
Prajñā serves as a mother to them.
It is able to give birth to and raise them.

The Buddha serves as the father of beings.
Prajñā is able to give birth to the Buddha.
This being so, it serves for all
As the grandmother of beings.

Prajñā is a singular dharma.
The Buddha speaks forth all sorts of names.
According with the strengths of beings,
He establishes for them different designations.

If a person realizes prajñā,
All thoughts of dialectical discourse are extinguished.
This is comparable to when the sun rises.
All at once, the morning dew is made to disappear.

The awesome qualities of prajñā
Are able to move two kinds of people.
The one who is devoid of wisdom is frightened.
The one possessed of wisdom is delighted.

If one realizes prajñā,
He then becomes a master of prajñā.
He is not attached to anything within prajñā,
How much the less to any other dharma.

Prajñā has no coming from anywhere,
Nor does it have any going to anywhere.
For one who is wise, in any place
He seeks for it, he is still unable to find it.

If one does not perceive prajñā,
This then is to be in bondage.
If one does perceive prajñā,
This, too, qualifies as bondage.

If a person perceives prajñā,
This then is the gaining of liberation.
If one does not perceive prajñā,
This, too, is the achievement of liberation.

This phenomenon is one which is rare,
It is extremely profound and greatly renowned.
Like something magically conjured,
It is perceived, yet imperceptible.

诸佛及菩萨。声闻辟支佛。
解脱涅盘道。皆从般若得。

言说为世俗。怜愍一切故。
假名说诸法。虽说而不说。

般若波罗蜜。譬如大火焰。
四边不可取。无取亦不取。

一切取已舍。是名不可取。
不可取而取。是即名为取。

般若无坏相。过一切言语。
适无所依[11]止。谁能赞其德。

般若虽叵赞。我今能得赞。
虽未脱死地。则为已得出。

諸佛及菩薩。聲聞辟支佛。
解脫涅槃道。皆從般若得。

言說為世俗。憐愍一切故。
假名說諸法。雖說而不說。

般若波羅蜜。譬如大火焰。
四邊不可取。無取亦不取。

一切取已捨。是名不可取。
不可取而取。是即名為取。

般若無壞相。過一切言語。
適無所依[11]止。誰能讚其德。

般若雖叵讚。我今能得讚。
雖未脫死地。則為已得出。

简体字

正體字

For the Buddhas and the Bodhisattvas,
For the Śrāvakas and the Pratyekabuddhas,
The path of liberation and nirvāṇa,
In every case, is gained from prajñā.

The verbal discourse is for the common people of the World,
And is engaged in on account of pity for all.
Employing false names, he speaks about dharmas.
Although he speaks, he still does not speak.

The *prajñāpāramitā*
Is comparable to a great fiery blaze.
It cannot be grasped from any of four sides.
In it there is neither grasping nor non-grasping.

All grasping has already been relinquished.
This is what is meant by its being "ungraspable."
It is ungraspable, and yet one grasps it.
It is just this that is meant by "grasping" it.

Prajñā is characterized by indestructibility.
It goes beyond all words and speech.
Fittingly, it has nothing upon which it depends.
Who then could be able to praise its qualities?

Although prajñā cannot become an object of praise,
I am able now to proceed with praising it.
Although not yet liberated from the mortal ground,
One succeeds thereby in moving beyond it.

[191-1]大智度论[2]释般若相义[3]第三十。

[0191a03]　问曰。何以[4]独称般若波罗蜜为摩诃。而不称五波罗蜜。答曰。摩诃[5]秦言大。般若言慧。波罗蜜言到彼岸。以其能到智慧大海彼岸。到[6]诸一切智慧边穷尽其极故。名到彼岸。一切世间[7]中十方三世诸佛第一大。次有菩萨辟支佛声闻。是四大人皆从般若波罗蜜[*]中生。是故名为大。复次能与众生大果报。无量无尽常不变异。所谓涅盘。馀五波罗蜜不能尔。布施等离般若波罗蜜。但能与世间果报。是故不得名大。问曰。何者是智慧。答曰。般若波罗蜜摄一切智[8]慧。所以者何。菩萨求佛道。应当学一切法得一切智慧。所谓声闻辟支佛佛智慧。是智慧有三种。学无学

简体字

[191-1]大智度論[2]釋般若相義[3]第三十。

[0191a03]　問曰。何以[4]獨稱般若波羅蜜為摩訶。而不稱五波羅蜜。答曰。摩訶[5]秦言大。般若言慧。波羅蜜言到彼岸。以其能到智慧大海彼岸。到[6]諸一切智慧邊窮盡其極故。名到彼岸。一切世間[7]中十方三世諸佛第一大。次有菩薩辟支佛聲聞。是四大人皆從般若波羅蜜[*]中生。是故名為大。復次能與眾生大果報。無量無盡常不變異。所謂涅槃。餘五波羅蜜不能爾。布施等離般若波羅蜜。但能與世間果報。是故不得名大。問曰。何者是智慧。答曰。般若波羅蜜攝一切智[8]慧。所以者何。菩薩求佛道。應當學一切法得一切智慧。所謂聲聞辟支佛佛智慧。是智慧有三種。學無學

正體字

Chapter 30: The Aspects and Import of Prajñā

II. The Aspects and Import of Prajñā
  A. The Exalted Nature of the *Mahāprajñāpāramitā*
    1. Question: Why is *Prajñāpāramitā* Alone Considered "Great"?

Question: Why is the *prajñāpāramitā* (the perfection of wisdom) alone called the *"Mahā" prajñāpāramitā* (the *great* perfection of wisdom) in a manner not matching [the names of] the other five *pāramitās*?

    2. Response: It Gives Birth to the Great Ones and the Great Result

Response: (Chinese text note: In our language, *"mahā"* means "great." *"Prajñā"* means "wisdom." *"Pāramitā"* means "reaching to the other shore.")[5] Because it is able to reach to the other shore of the great sea of wisdom and because it reaches to its very boundaries and utterly exhausts its most ultimate limits, it qualifies as "perfect" in its "reaching to the other shore." In all the worlds, the Buddhas of the ten directions and three periods of time are the greatest. Next in order come the Bodhisattvas, the Pratyekabuddhas and the Śrāvaka-disciples. These four classes of great persons are all born from *prajñāpāramitā*. It is for this reason that it qualifies as "great."

Additionally, it is able to bestow on beings a great resultant reward which is incalculable, inexhaustible, and eternally unchanging, namely "nirvāṇa." The other five *pāramitās* cannot do this. "Giving" and the others, in the absence of the *prajñāpāramitā*, are only able to bring resultant rewards on the worldly plane. It is for this reason that they cannot, [in and of themselves], qualify as "great."

  B. On the Various Levels of Genuine Wisdom
    1. Question: What is Meant Here by "Wisdom"?

Question: What is meant by "wisdom"?

    2. Response: It Subsumes All Other Forms of Wisdom...

Response: *Prajñāpāramitā* subsumes all forms of wisdom. How is this so? While pursuing the Buddha Path, the bodhisattva should study all dharmas and realize all forms of wisdom, namely the wisdom of Śrāvaka-disciples, Pratyekabuddhas, and the Buddhas.

    a. The Wisdom of the Śrāvaka disciples

This wisdom [of the Śrāvaka disciples] is of three kinds: that of those "still subject to training" (*śaikṣa*), that of those "beyond training"

非学非无学。非学非无学。智者如乾慧地不净安那般那欲界系四念处[9]煖法顶法忍法世间第一法等。学智者苦法智忍慧乃至向阿罗汉第九无[10]碍道中金刚三昧慧。无学智者阿罗汉第九解脱智。从是[11]已后一切无学智。如尽智无生智等。[12]是为无学智求辟支佛道智慧亦如是。问曰。若辟支佛道亦如是者。云何分别声闻辟支佛。答曰。道虽一种而用智有异。若诸佛不出佛法已灭。是人先世因缘故。独出智慧不从他闻。自以智慧得道。

简体字

非學非無學。非學非無學。智者如乾慧地不淨安那般那欲界繫四念處[9]煖法頂法忍法世間第一法等。學智者苦法智忍慧乃至向阿羅漢第九無[10]礙道中金剛三昧慧。無學智者阿羅漢第九解脫智。從是[11]已後一切無學智。如盡智無生智等。[12]是為無學智求辟支佛道智慧亦如是。問曰。若辟支佛道亦如是者。云何分別聲聞辟支佛。答曰。道雖一種而用智有異。若諸佛不出佛法已滅。是人先世因緣故。獨出智慧不從他聞。自以智慧得道。

正體字

(*aśaikṣa*), and that of those "neither subject to further training nor beyond further training" (*naiva-śaikṣa-nāśaikṣa*).

As for the wisdom of those "neither subject to further training nor beyond further training," it refers to such categories as the ground of "dry wisdom" (*śukla-vidarśana-bhūmi*), the contemplation on the unlovely (*aśubha-bhāvanā*), *ānāpāna-[smṛti]* (mindfulness of the breath), the four stations of mindfulness (*smṛti-upāsthanā*) in connection to the desire realm, the dharma of heat (*uṣmagata*), the dharma of summits (*mūrdhan*), the dharma of patience (*kṣānti*), the foremost worldly dharmas (*laukika-agra-dharma*), and other such dharmas.

As for the wisdom of those "still subject to training," it refers to such categories as the patience associated with the dharma knowledge of suffering (*duḥkhe-dharma-jñāna-kṣānti*), and so forth on to the wisdom of the *vajropama-samādhi* of one verging on arhatship at the point of the ninth [act of counteractive abandonment (*prahāṇa-pratipakṣa*)] on the "uninterrupted path" (*ānantarya-mārga*).

As for the wisdom of those "beyond training," this refers to the arhat's wisdom arising with the ninth [act of "counteractive conservation" (*adhāra-pratipakṣa*)] on the "path of liberation" (*vimukti-mārga*). From this point on, everything qualifies as the wisdom of those "beyond training." For instance: the knowledge of destruction (*kṣaya-jñāna*), the knowledge of non-production (*anutpāda-jñāna*), and so forth. This is what constitutes the wisdom of those beyond training. In the course of seeking the way of pratyekabuddhahood, the levels of wisdom are the same as these.

b.   The Wisdom of the Pratyekabuddhas

1)   Pratyekabuddhas Versus Śrāvakas: What's the Difference?

Question: If the path of a pratyekabuddha is just the same [as that of an arhat], on what basis could one distinguish between śrāvaka-disciples and pratyekabuddhas?

2)   Pratyekabuddhas Awaken With No Present-Life Instruction

Response: Although their paths are of a single type, still, their uses of wisdom have their differences. In a case where buddhas have not come forth [into the world] or else the Dharma of any given buddha has already become extinct, this person, on account of causal factors associated with previous lifetimes, brings forth wisdom on his own and does not do so based on hearing it [directly, in this life], from anyone else. On his own, he employs wisdom to gain realization of the Path.

如一国王出在园中游戏。清
朝见林树华菓蔚茂甚可爱
乐。王食已而卧。王诸夫人
婇女。皆共取华毁折林树。
王觉已见林毁坏而自觉悟。
一切世间无常变坏皆亦如
是。思惟是已无漏道心生断
[13]诸结使得辟支佛道。具
六神通即飞到闲静林间。如
是等因缘。先世福德愿行果
报。今世见少因缘。成辟支
佛道如是为异。复次辟支佛
有二种。一名独觉。二名因
缘觉。因缘觉如上说。独觉
者。是人今世成道。自觉不
从他闻。是名独觉辟支迦
佛。独觉辟支迦佛有二种。
一本是学人在人中生。是时
无佛佛法灭。是须陀洹已满
七生。不应第八生自得成
道。是

简体字

如一國王出在園中遊戲。清
朝見林樹華菓蔚茂甚可愛
樂。王食已而臥。王諸夫人
婇女。皆共取華毀折林樹。
王覺已見林毀壞而自覺悟。
一切世間無常變壞皆亦如
是。思惟是已無漏道心生斷
[13]諸結使得辟支佛道。具
六神通即飛到閑靜林間。如
是等因緣。先世福德願行果
報。今世見少因緣。成辟支
佛道如是為異。復次辟支佛
有二種。一名獨覺。二名因
緣覺。因緣覺如上說。獨覺
者。是人今世成道。自覺不
從他聞。是名獨覺辟支迦
佛。獨覺辟支迦佛有二種。
一本是學人在人中生。是時
無佛佛法滅。是須陀洹已滿
七生。不應第八生自得成
道。是

正體字

3) STORY: THE KING ENLIGHTENED BY IMPERMANENCE

This is illustrated by an instance in which the king of a country had gone out into his gardens to wander about and enjoy himself. As he observed in the early morning the blossoming of the grove's trees and the flourishing abundance of fruit, he was struck by how extremely lovely and pleasurable they were. After the King had eaten, he then lay down to take a nap. Meanwhile, the wives and female entertainers of the King all went about picking flowers and, in the process, damaged the trees by breaking off branches.

After the King awoke, he observed the destruction in the grove and became spontaneously enlightened to the fact that all worlds are impermanent and bound to destruction in just this same way. After he had contemplated this, the mind of the non-outflow path (*anāsrava-mārga*) arose in him, he cut off the fetters, gained the way of the pratyekabuddha, perfected the six superknowledges, and flew off into an unoccupied and quiet area of the forest.

On account of causal circumstances such as these which arise as karmic reward for previous-life meritorious deeds, vows, and practices, one may need in this life only to observe a minor cause or condition and then be able as a result to perfect the path of the pratyekabuddha. It is factors such as these which constitute the difference [between the paths of a pratyekabuddha and an arhat].

a) TWO PRATYEKABUDDHAS: SOLITARILY OR CONDITIONS-ENLIGHTENED

Again, there are two kinds of pratyekabuddhas. One of them is referred to as "solitarily enlightened." A second type is referred to as "awakened by causes and conditions." To be "awakened by causes and conditions" is as related above. As for being "solitarily enlightened," this refers to a person who completes the Path in the present life, achieving a spontaneous enlightenment not involving hearing teachings from anyone else. This is what is meant by the "solitarily enlightened" pratyekabuddha.

b) THE TWO SUBTYPES OF SOLITARILY-ENLIGHTENED PRATYEKABUDDHA
i) SOLITARY SUBTYPE ONE: THE "LESSER" PRATYEKABUDDHA

The "solitarily enlightened" pratyekabuddha is of two types. The first is one who originally was on the path still subject to training (*śaikṣa*) and who was then reborn among people. There was no buddha in the world at this time and that buddha's Dharma had already become extinct. This *srota-āpanna* ("stream-enterer") had already fulfilled seven subsequent rebirths, should not have taken an eighth rebirth, but then spontaneously became enlightened. This

人不名佛。不名阿罗汉。名为小辟支迦佛。与阿罗汉无异。或有不如舍利弗等大阿罗汉者。[14]大辟支佛[15]亦于[16]一百劫中。作功德增长智慧。得三十二相分。或有三十一相或[17]三[18]十二十九相乃至一相。于九种阿罗汉中。智慧利胜于诸深法中总相别相。能入久修习定。常乐独处。如是相名为大辟支迦佛。以是为异。求佛道者从初发心作愿。愿我作佛度脱众生。得一切佛法行六波罗蜜。破魔军众及诸烦恼。得一切智成佛道。乃至入无余涅盘。随本愿行。从是中间所有智慧总相别相一切尽知。是名佛道智慧。是三种智慧尽能知尽到其边。以是故言到智慧边。问曰。若如所说一切智慧。尽应入若世间若出世间。何以但言

人不名佛。不名阿羅漢。名為小辟支迦佛。與阿羅漢無異。或有不如舍利弗等大阿羅漢者。[14]大辟支佛[15]亦於[16]一百劫中。作功德增長智慧。得三十二相分。或有三十一相或[17]三[18]十二十九相乃至一相。於九種阿羅漢中。智慧利勝於諸深法中總相別相。能入久修習定。常樂獨處。如是相名為大辟支迦佛。以是為異。求佛道者從初發心作願。願我作佛度脫眾生。得一切佛法行六波羅蜜。破魔軍眾及諸煩惱。得一切智成佛道。乃至入無餘涅槃。隨本願行。從是中間所有智慧總相別相一切盡知。是名佛道智慧。是三種智慧盡能知盡到其邊。以是故言到智慧邊。問曰。若如所說一切智慧。盡應入若世間若出世間。何以但言

简体字

正體字

person is not properly referred to as either a buddha or as an arhat, but is instead referred to as a "lesser" pratyekabuddha. In fact, he is no different from an arhat. In some cases, they may not be comparable to the great arhats such as Śāriputra.

ii) SOLITARY SUBTYPE TWO: THE "GREAT" PRATYEKABUDDHA

A "great" pratyekabuddha creates merit and increases his wisdom across the course of a hundred kalpas and gains a number of the thirty-two marks. He may possess thirty-one marks or perhaps thirty, twenty-nine, or even on down to just one of the marks. Compared to the nine types of arhats, the acuteness of his wisdom is superior. He is able to fathom the general and specific characteristics of profound dharmas. He cultivates the absorptions for extended periods of time. He constantly takes pleasure in dwelling alone. One who has characteristics such as these is referred to as a "great" pratyekabuddha. It is characteristics such as these which constitute the differences [between arhats and pratyekabuddhas].

c. THE WISDOM OF THE BUDDHAS

One who seeks the Path of the Buddha, from the time of first bringing forth the resolve to [to realize complete enlightenment], makes a vow, "I vow that I will become a Buddha and cross the beings over to liberation, that I will succeed in realizing all of the Buddha dharmas, that I will practice the six *pāramitās*, that I will smash the hordes of demon armies as well as all of the afflictions, that I will gain the knowledge of all modes, that I will realize the Buddha Path, and that I shall ultimately gain entry into the nirvāṇa without residue."

One then practices in accord with his original vows. From this time on, during the interim, all of the wisdom which one accumulates—that which knows entirely all of the general characteristics and specific characteristics [of all dharmas]—this is what is meant by the wisdom of the Buddha Path.

One is exhaustively able to know everything within the sphere of these three levels of wisdom and is able to reach all the way to its very boundaries. Hence it is said that one reaches to the very limits of wisdom.

C. NON-BUDDHIST WISDOM IS ARTIFICIAL AND FALLACY-RIDDEN

1. OBJECTION: WHY RECOMMEND ONLY THREE-VEHICLES WISDOM?

Question: If it were to be as stated here, then one ought to explore all of the classes of wisdom, whether they be worldly wisdom or world-transcending wisdom. Why then do you only speak of reaching to

三乘智慧尽到其边不说馀
智。答曰。三乘是实智慧。
馀者皆是虚妄。菩萨虽知而
不专行。如除摩[19]梨山一
切无出栴檀木。若馀处或有
好语。皆从佛法中得自非佛
法。初闻似好久则不妙。譬
如牛乳驴乳。其色虽同牛乳
[20]攒则成[21]酥。驴乳[*]攒则
成[22]尿。佛法语及外道语。
不杀不盗慈愍众生摄心离欲
观空虽同。然外道语初虽似
妙。穷尽所归则为虚诳。一
切外道皆着我见。若实有我
应堕二种。若坏相若不坏
相。若坏相应如牛皮。若不
坏相应如虚空。此二处无杀
罪无不杀福。若如虚空雨露
不能润。风热不能乾。

三乘智慧盡到其邊不說餘
智。答曰。三乘是實智慧。
餘者皆是虛妄。菩薩雖知而
不專行。如除摩[19]梨山一
切無出栴檀木。若餘處或有
好語。皆從佛法中得自非佛
法。初聞似好久則不妙。譬
如牛乳驢乳。其色雖同牛乳
[20]攢則成[21]酥。驢乳[*]攢則
成[22]尿。佛法語及外道語。
不殺不盜慈愍眾生攝心離欲
觀空雖同。然外道語初雖似
妙。窮盡所歸則為虛誑。一
切外道皆著我見。若實有我
應墮二種。若壞相若不壞
相。若壞相應如牛皮。若不
壞相應如虛空。此二處無殺
罪無不殺福。若如虛空雨露
不能潤。風熱不能乾。

简体字   正體字

the very boundaries of the wisdom of the Three Vehicles while failing to mention the other classes of wisdom?

2. RESPONSE: ONLY THE THREE VEHICLES REFLECT GENUINE WISDOM

Response: That of the Three Vehicles is genuine wisdom. Any others are all empty and false. Although the bodhisattva is aware of them, he does not focus on practicing them.

1) ANALOGY: MT. MALAYA AS THE SOURCE OF SANDALWOOD.

It is just as with Mount Malaya. No place else produces sandalwood trees. If it is the case that other sources possess fine discourses, it is because, in all such cases, they were originally obtained from within the Dharma of the Buddha. They themselves, however, do not accord with the Dharma of the Buddha. When one first hears them, they may seem to be good, but if one listens longer, they turn out not to be so fine.

2) ANALOGY: COW MILK VERSUS DONKEY MILK

This is analogous to the difference between cow milk and donkey milk. Although they are the same in color, if one churns cow milk, it turns into butter, whereas if one churns donkey milk, it becomes like urine.

3. THE SIMILARITIES ARE FALSE AND HENCE DECEPTIVE

Although the Dharma of the Buddha as well as that of non-Buddhist paths may seem to be the same as regards not killing, not stealing, having kindness and pity for beings, focusing the mind, transcending desire, and contemplating emptiness, still, in the case of the discourse of non-Buddhist paths, although they may initially seem as if they are marvelous, if one follows them out to the end point to which they lead, they are then found to be false and deceptive.

4. FALLACIES UNDERGIRDING NON-BUDDHIST CONCEPTS OF WISDOM
  a. REFUTATION OF NON-BUDDHIST "SELF" AND KARMA EFFICACY

All of the non-Buddhist paths are attached to the view of a self. If it was actually the case that a self existed, then it ought to fall into one or the other of two categories. Either it is characterized by destructibility or else it is characterized by indestructibility. If it is characterized by destructibility, then it ought to be something like a cow hide. If it is characterized by indestructibility, then it ought to be comparable to empty space. In the case of both of these positions, they are both such as would involve no offense entailed in killing and would involve no merit in refraining from killing.

If it were like empty space, then neither rain nor dew would be able to moisten it and neither wind nor heat would be able to dry

是则堕常相。若常者苦不能恼乐不能悦。若不受苦乐。不应避祸就福。若如牛皮[23]则为风雨所坏[24]若坏则堕无常。若无常则无罪福。外道语若实如是。何有不杀为福杀生为罪。问曰。外道戒福所失如是。其禅定智慧复云何。答曰。外道以我心逐禅故。多爱见慢故。不舍一切法故。无有实智慧。问曰。汝言外道观空。观空则舍一切法。云何言不舍一切法故。无有实智慧。答曰。外道虽观空。而取空相。虽知诸法空。而不自知我空。爱着观空智慧故。

简体字

是則墮常相。若常者苦不能惱樂不能悅。若不受苦樂。不應避禍就福。若如牛皮[23]則為風雨所壞[24]若壞則墮無常。若無常則無罪福。外道語若實如是。何有不殺為福殺生為罪。問曰。外道戒福所失如是。其禪定智慧復云何。答曰。外道以我心逐禪故。多愛見慢故。不捨一切法故。無有實智慧。問曰。汝言外道觀空。觀空則捨一切法。云何言不捨一切法故。無有實智慧。答曰。外道雖觀空。而取空相。雖知諸法空。而不自知我空。愛著觀空智慧故。

正體字

it out. If this were the case, then it would fall into the category of something which is permanent. If it were permanent, then suffering would be unable to torment it and happiness would be unable to please it. If it thus was something which did not experience suffering or happiness, then it ought not to be concerned with avoiding evil and striving to perform deeds which generate merit.

If it was comparable to a cow hide, then it would be such as might be destroyed by wind and rain. If it was destructible, then it would fall into the category of something which is impermanent. If it were impermanent, then there could be neither [future punishments resulting from] offenses nor [future blessings resulting from] engaging in meritorious karmic deeds.

If in fact the discourse of the non-Buddhist traditions corresponds to these characterizations, then what would be the point in having the teaching that refraining from killing is karmically meritorious and that engaging in killing constitutes a karmic offense?

b. OBJECTION: BUT NON-BUDDHIST ABSORPTIONS SURELY QUALIFY?

Question: Although the [teachings on] moral restrictions and karmic merit of these non-Buddhists may involve such fallacies, what about [the quality of] their dhyāna absorptions and wisdom?

c. RESPONSE: EVEN THERE, ATTACHMENTS DISQUALIFY THEM

Response: Because non-Buddhist paths pursue the cultivation of dhyāna meditation with a mind which holds to the existence of a self, because they are excessive in affection, views, and arrogance, and because they fail to relinquish all dharmas, they do not possess any genuine wisdom.

d. OBJECTION: SURELY THEIR "EMPTINESS" TRANSCENDS DHARMAS?

Question: You admit that non-Buddhist paths contemplate emptiness. If one contemplates emptiness, then one relinquishes all dharmas. How then can you say that, because they do not relinquish all dharmas, they therefore possess no actual wisdom?

e. RESPONSE: THEY ARE ATTACHED EVEN TO EMPTINESS

Response: Although non-Buddhist paths do contemplate emptiness, still, they seize upon that characteristic of being empty. Although they may be aware that dharmas are empty, still, they are unaware that the self itself is empty. [They are dismissed herein as not having relinquished all dharmas and as possessing no actual wisdom precisely] because their "wisdom" is wedded to a cherishing attachment to the contemplation of emptiness.

问曰。外道有无想定。心心数法都灭。都灭故无有取相爱着智慧咎。答曰。无想定力强令心灭。非实智慧力。又于此中生涅盘[25]想。不知是和合作法。以是故堕颠倒中。是中心虽暂灭。得因缘还生。譬如人无梦睡时心想不行[26]悟则还有。问曰无想定其失如是。更有非有想非无想定。是中无一切妄想。亦不如强作无想定灭想。是中以智慧力故无想。答曰。是中有想细微故不觉若无想佛弟子。复何缘更求实智慧。佛法中是非有想非无想中识。依[192-1]四众住。是四众属因缘故无常。无常故苦。无常苦故空。空故无

简体字

問曰。外道有無想定。心心數法都滅。都滅故無有取相愛著智慧咎。答曰。無想定力強令心滅。非實智慧力。又於此中生涅槃[25]想。不知是和合作法。以是故墮顛倒中。是中心雖暫滅。得因緣還生。譬如人無夢睡時心想不行[26]悟則還有。問曰無想定其失如是。更有非有想非無想定。是中無一切妄想。亦不如強作無想定滅想。是中以智慧力故無想。答曰。是中有想細微故不覺若無想佛弟子。復何緣更求實智慧。佛法中是非有想非無想中識。依[192-1]四眾住。是四眾屬因緣故無常。無常故苦。無常苦故空。空故無

正體字

f. OBJECTION: THEIR "NO-THOUGHT ABSORPTION" MUST QUALIFY?

Question: Non-Buddhist paths do possess the no-thought absorption (*asaṃjñā-samāpatti*) in which the mind dharmas as well as the dharmas associated with the mind are all extinguished. Because they are entirely extinguished, there is no fault therein involving a class of wisdom typified by cherishing attachment and seizing on particular characteristics.

g. RESPONSE: IT IS MERELY AN ARTIFICIALLY-PRODUCED DHARMA

Response: The power of the no-thought absorption resides in forcing the mind to enter extinction. It is not the case that it is based on the power of actual wisdom. Additionally, they are of the opinion that this actually constitutes nirvāṇa while remaining unaware that it is merely a compositely created dharma. On account of this, they fall into inverted views. Although thought is temporarily extinguished herein, nonetheless, when one encounters the appropriate causes and conditions, it will arise yet again. This situation is analogous to that of a person who has fallen into a dreamless sleep in which the thoughts of the mind are not manifesting activity. Still, when such a person reawakens, they do manifest their existence yet again.

h. OBJECTION: PEAK OF EXISTENCE, *BHAVĀGRA*, MUST BE WISDOM-BASED?

Question: Even if the faults of the no-thought absorption are as you describe here, still there is the additional absorption of "neither perception nor non-perception" (*naiva-saṃjñā-nāsaṃjñā-samāpatti*). There is no erroneous thought therein, nor does one extinguish thought in the manner of the artificially-created no-thought absorption. In this latter circumstance, it is by resort to the power of wisdom that one comes to be free of thought.

i. RESPONSE: SUBTLE THOUGHT STILL REMAINS EVEN THERE

Response: Even in this situation, thought is still present. It is simply because it is subtle that one remains unaware of it. If it was the case that it really was free of thought, why then would the disciples of the Buddha go beyond it in seeking to realize actual wisdom?

In the Dharma of the Buddha, this consciousness associated with the absorption of neither perception nor non-perception [is seen to] abide in dependence upon the other four aggregates. Because these four aggregates are subsumed within the sphere of causes and conditions, they are therefore impermanent. Because they are impermanent, they are therefore associated with suffering. Because they are impermanent and hence associated with suffering, they are therefore empty. Because they are empty, they are therefore devoid

我。空无我故可舍。汝等爱
着智慧故不得涅盘。譬如尺
蠖屈安后足然后进前足。所
缘尽无复进处而还。外道依
止初禅舍下地欲。乃至依非
有想非无想处。舍无所有
处。上无所复依。[2]故不能
舍非有想非无想处。以更无
依处恐惧失我。畏堕无所得
中故。复次外道经中。有听
杀盗婬妄语饮酒言。为天祠
呪杀无罪。为行道故。若遭
急难欲自全身。而杀小人无
罪。又有急难为行道故。除
金馀者得盗取以自全济。后
当除此殃罪。

我。空無我故可捨。汝等愛
著智慧故不得涅槃。譬如尺
蠖屈安後足然後進前足。所
緣盡無復進處而還。外道依
止初禪捨下地欲。乃至依非
有想非無想處。捨無所有
處。上無所復依。[2]故不能
捨非有想非無想處。以更無
依處恐懼失我。畏墮無所得
中故。復次外道經中。有聽
殺盜婬妄語飲酒言。為天祠
呪殺無罪。為行道故。若遭
急難欲自全身。而殺小人無
罪。又有急難為行道故。除
金餘者得盜取以自全濟。後
當除此殃罪。

简体字   正體字

of self. Because they are empty and devoid of self, they are therefore such as may appropriately be renounced.

1)   ATTACHMENTS IN *BHAVĀGRA* PREVENT GENUINE NIRVĀṆA

It is because you and those like you maintain a cherishing attachment for this sort of wisdom that you do not succeed in reaching nirvāṇa.

2)   ANALOGY: LIKE A DEAD-ENDED LOOPER CATERPILLAR

This [circumstance wherein one abides in the neither perception nor non-perception absorption] is analogous to that of the looper caterpillar which arches to position its hind legs [thus drawing them forward] and then, afterwards, extends its front legs on ahead. When it runs out of space, as there is no further place to which it can advance, it then returns back again.

Non-Buddhists resort to abiding in the first dhyāna in order to relinquish the desires associated with lower stations. This process goes on until they resort to abiding in the station of neither perception nor non-perception in order to relinquish the station of nothing whatsoever. On account of the fact that there is nothing above it to which they might resort, they remain unable to relinquish the station of neither perception nor non-perception. This is because they have no further place upon which to rely, becausee they are terrified at the prospect of losing the self, and because they fear falling into that circumstance wherein there is nothing whatsoever which can be gotten at.

j.   NON-BUDDHIST CONCEPTIONS OF MORALITY ARE FAULTY

Additionally, in the scriptures of the non-Buddhists, there are statements permitting of killing, stealing, sexual misconduct, false speech, and the consumption of intoxicants.

[For instance], when employed for the purpose of making sacrifices to gods, [they claim that] resorting to incantations to kill carries no offense because it is done in service of practicing the Path. In the event that one encounters urgent difficulties and wishes to preserve one's own physical life and so kills a person of lesser station, they maintain that there is no offense in this so long as it is done for the sake of practicing their path.

Also, if there are urgent difficulties and it is for the sake of practicing their path, [they claim] one may steal anything but gold in order to save oneself from those circumstances. [This is based on the opinion that], later on, one will be able to get rid of this disastrous offense.

除师妇国王夫人善知识妻童女。馀者逼迫急难得邪婬。为师及父母为[3]身为牛为媒故。听妄语。寒乡听饮石蜜酒。天祠中或听[4]尝一[5]渧二[6]渧酒。佛法中则不然。于一切众生慈心等视。乃至蚁子亦不夺命。何况杀人。一针一缕不取。何况多物无主。婬女不以指触何况人之[7]妇女。戏笑不得妄语。何况故作妄语。一切酒一切时常不得饮。何况寒乡天祠。汝等外道与佛法悬殊有若天地。汝等外道法。是生诸烦恼处。佛法则是灭诸烦恼处。是为大异。诸佛法无量有若大海。随众生意故种种说法。或说有或说无或说常或

除師婦國王夫人善知識妻童女。餘者逼迫急難得邪婬。為師及父母為[3]身為牛為媒故。聽妄語。寒鄉聽飲石蜜酒。天祠中或聽[4]嘗一[5]渧二[6]渧酒。佛法中則不然。於一切眾生慈心等視。乃至蟻子亦不奪命。何況殺人。一針一縷不取。何況多物無主。婬女不以指觸何況人之[7]婦女。戲笑不得妄語。何況故作妄語。一切酒一切時常不得飲。何況寒鄉天祠。汝等外道與佛法懸殊有若天地。汝等外道法。是生諸煩惱處。佛法則是滅諸煩惱處。是為大異。諸佛法無量有若大海。隨眾生意故種種說法。或說有或說無或說常或

简体字   正體字

[They also claim that], aside from womenfolk associated with one's teachers, the wife of the King, the wife of one's spiritual master, and virgin girls, one may engage in sexual misconduct with any others when encountering pressing and urgent difficulties.

If it is for the sake of one's teachers, one's father or mother, one's own person, for the sake of a cow, or for the sake of a matchmaker, they allow that one may engage in false speech. In cold regions, it is permitted that one may drink liquor made from rock honey. In the course of making sacrifices to a god, it is considered permissible that one may taste one or two drops of liquor.

k. BUDDHIST MORALITY PERMITS NO SUCH ERRORS

In the Dharma of the Buddha, it is not this way. In regard to all beings, one maintains a mind of kindness and looks upon them equally, even to the point that one does not take the life of even an ant. How much the less might one kill a person? One does not take even a needle or a thread. How much the less might one take objects of greater value? One may not even lay a finger on a woman not under the protection of another and may not so much as touch even a courtesan. How much the less might one be able to touch a man's wife or daughter?

Even in joking, one may not engage in false speech. How much the less may one deliberately tell a lie? One may never drink any liquor at any time. How much the less might one do so on account of residing in a cold region or on account of performing a sacrifice to a god?

5. SUMMARY DISMISSAL OF NON-BUDDHIST TRADITIONS

[The beliefs of] you and other non-Buddhists like you are so extremely different from the Buddha's Dharma as to be as far apart as heaven and earth. Your dharmas and that of other non-Buddhists like you is a place for the production of afflictions. In the case of the Dharma of the Buddha, it is a place for the doing away with afflictions. This constitutes a great difference.

D. DESCRIPTION OF THE DHARMA OF THE BUDDHA

The dharmas of the Buddha are countless and comparable in vastness to a great sea. It was on account of according with the minds of beings that there are all sorts of different articulations of Dharma. Sometimes they speak of existence, sometimes they speak of nonexistence, sometimes they speak of permanence, sometimes they speak of impermanence, sometimes they speak of suffering, sometimes

说无常或说苦或说乐或说我
或说无我或说懃行三业摄诸
善法或说一切诸法无作相。
如是等种种异[8]说。 无智[9]
闻之谓为乖错。智者入三种
法门。观一切佛语。皆是实
法不相违背。何等是三门。
一者蜫勒门。二者阿毘昙
门。三者空门。问曰。云何
名蜫勒。云何名阿毘昙。云
何名空门。答曰。蜫勒有三
百二十万言。佛在世时大迦
[10]栴延之所造。佛灭度后
人寿转减。忆识力少不能广
诵。诸得道人撰为三十八万
四千言。若人入蜫勒门论议
则无穷。其中有随相门对治
门等种种诸门。随相门者。
如佛说偈。

诸恶莫作。诸善奉行。
自净其意。是诸佛教。

[0192b11] 是中心数法尽应说。
今但说自净其意。则知

说無常或說苦或說樂或說我
或說無我或說懃行三業攝諸
善法或說一切諸法無作相。
如是等種種異[8]說。 無智[9]
聞之謂為乖錯。智者入三種
法門。觀一切佛語。皆是實
法不相違背。何等是三門。
一者蜫勒門。二者阿毘曇
門。三者空門。問曰。云何
名蜫勒。云何名阿毘曇。云
何名空門。答曰。蜫勒有三
百二十萬言。佛在世時大迦
[10]栴延之所造。佛滅度後
人壽轉減。憶識力少不能廣
誦。諸得道人撰為三十八萬
四千言。若人入蜫勒門論議
則無窮。其中有隨相門對治
門等種種諸門。隨相門者。
如佛說偈。

諸惡莫作。諸善奉行。
自淨其意。是諸佛教。

[0192b11] 是中心數法盡應說。
今但說自淨其意。則知

简体字   正體字

they speak of bliss, sometimes they speak of self, sometimes they speak of no self, sometimes they speak of diligently cultivating the three modes of karmic action and accumulating all manner of good dharmas, and sometimes they speak of all dharmas as characterized by being in the sphere of the wishless (*apraṇihita*).

1. THE THREE GATEWAYS TO THE DHARMA

Upon hearing all of these different explanations, one without wisdom would be of the opinion that they are perverse and erroneous. One who is wise, however, enters three types of gateways to Dharma and, in contemplating all of the discourses of the Buddha, finds that they are genuine and are not contradictory. What are the three gateways? The first is the *Piṭaka* gateway. The second is the Abhidharma gateway. The third is the emptiness gateway.

Question: What is meant by the "*Piṭaka*" gateway? What is meant by the "Abhidharma" gateway? What is meant by the "emptiness" gateway?

a. THE PIṬAKA UPADEŚA GATEWAY

Response: The *Piṭaka* [-*upadeśa*] has three million, two hundred thousand words. It was created by [Mahā]kātyāyana when the Buddha was still in the World. After the Buddha crossed into cessation, the human lifespan gradually diminished and the strength of people's memories become reduced to the point that they were no longer able to perform vast recitations. Those who had gained the Path condensed it into three hundred and eighty-four thousand words. If a person enters through the *Piṭaka* [-*upadeśa*] gateway, the dialectical discussions are endless. There are contained within it the gateway of according with characteristics, the counteractive gateway, and all sorts of other gateways as well.

1) THE PIṬAKA UPADEŚA'S "CHARACTERISTICS" GATEWAY

As for the gateway of according with characteristics, it is as illustrated by a verse spoken by the Buddha:

Do not do any evil.
Uphold the practice of every good.
Each should purify his own mind.
This is the teaching of all Buddhas.

At this point one should discuss all of the mental dharmas associated with the mind (*caitasika-dharma*). Now, when he only speaks of "each purifying his own mind," one knows then that he has [implicitly] spoken of all mental dharmas associated with the mind. How

诸心数法已说。何以故。同相同缘故。如佛说四念处。是中不离四正懃四如意足五根五力。何以故。四念处中四种精进则是四正懃四种定是为四如意足。五种善法是为五根五力。佛虽不说馀门但说四念处。当知已说馀门。如佛于四谛中或说一谛或二或三。如马星比丘为舍利弗说偈。

诸法从缘生。
是法缘及尽。
我师大圣[11]王。
是义如[12]是说。

[0192b21] 此偈但说三谛。当知道谛已在中不相离故。譬如一人犯事举家受罪。如是等名为随相门。对治门者。如佛但说四颠倒。常颠倒乐颠倒我颠倒净颠倒。是中虽不说四念处。当知已有四念处义。譬如说药已知其病说病则知其药。若说

简体字

諸心數法已說。何以故。同相同緣故。如佛說四念處。是中不離四正懃四如意足五根五力。何以故。四念處中四種精進則是四正懃四種定是為四如意足。五種善法是為五根五力。佛雖不說餘門但說四念處。當知已說餘門。如佛於四諦中或說一諦或二或三。如馬星比丘為舍利弗說偈。

諸法從緣生。
是法緣及盡。
我師大聖[11]王。
是義如[12]是說。

[0192b21] 此偈但說三諦。當知道諦已在中不相離故。譬如一人犯事舉家受罪。如是等名為隨相門。對治門者。如佛但說四顛倒。常顛倒樂顛倒我顛倒淨顛倒。是中雖不說四念處。當知已有四念處義。譬如說藥已知其病說病則知其藥。若說

正體字

is this so? It is because they share the same characteristics and the same conditions.

For instance, when the Buddha speaks of the four stations of mindfulness, there is in that no departure from the four right efforts, the four bases of psychic power, the five root-faculties and the five powers. How is this so? There are four kinds of vigor contained right within the four stations of mindfulness. These then are just the four right efforts. There are four kinds of absorption. These are the four bases of psychic power. There are five kinds of good dharmas. These are the five root-faculties and the five powers.

Although the Buddha did not discuss the other gateways [at that time] and so only spoke of the four stations of mindfulness, one should realize that he had already [implicitly] spoken of the other gateways. This is just as with the Buddha and the four truths wherein he would sometimes speak of one truth, sometimes speak of two, and sometimes speak of three. This is exemplified in the verse spoke by Bhikshu Aśvajit (Lit. "Horse Star") for Śāriputra:

All dharmas arise from conditions.
These dharmas' conditions then meet their end.
My master, the great king of the Āryas
Explains this meaning thus.

This verse only refers to three of the truths. One should realize that the truth of the Path is already implicitly contained among them. This is because it is not apart from them. This is analogous to that circumstance wherein, when only a single person commits an offense, the entire family nonetheless endures the punishment. Cases such as these indicate what is meant by the "according with characteristics" gateway.

2) The Piṭaka Upadeśa's "Counteractive" Gateway

As for the counteractive gateway, this is exemplified by the Buddha's only speaking of the four inverted views: the inverted view imputing permanence, the inverted view imputing blissfulness, the inverted view imputing a self, and the inverted view imputing purity. Although he did not speak herein of the four stations of mindfulness, one should realize that it already possesses the meaning of the four stations of mindfulness.

This is comparable to when, with the mentioning of a particular medicine, one thereby immediately knows of the associated sickness and when one mentions a particular sickness, one immediately knows of its associated medicine. So, too, if one speaks of the

四念处则知已说四倒。四倒则是邪相。若说四倒则已说诸结。所以者何。说其根本则知枝条皆得。如佛说一切世间有三毒。说三毒当知已说三分八正道。若说三毒当知已说一切诸烦恼毒。十五种爱是贪欲毒。[13]十五种瞋是瞋恚毒。十五种无明是愚痴毒。诸邪见憍慢疑属无明。如是一切[14]结使皆入三毒。以何灭之。三分八正道。若说三分八正道。当知已说一切三十七品。如是等种种相名为对治门。[15]如是等诸法名为蜫勒门。云何名阿毘昙门。或佛自说诸法义。或佛自说诸法名。诸弟子种种集述解其义。如佛说。[16]若有比丘于诸有为法不能正忆念。欲得世间第一法无有是处。若不得世间第一法。欲入正位中无有是处。若不入正位。欲

简体字

four stations of mindfulness, then one knows that one has already implicitly spoken of the four inverted views.

If one brings up the four inverted views, then these are just characteristics of erroneous understanding. If one speaks of the four inverted views then one has already implicitly mentioned the fetters. How is this the case? If one speaks of something's roots, then one thereby also gains knowledge of its branches.

For example, the Buddha said that all worlds contain three poisons. In speaking of the three poisons, one should know that he has already implicitly mentioned three [countervailing] components of the eight-fold right path. If he speaks of the three poisons, one should know that he has already thereby implicitly mentioned the poisons involved in all of the afflictions.

The fifteen kinds of affection constitute the poison of desire. The fifteen kinds of hatefulness constitute the poison of hatred. The fifteen kinds of ignorance constitute the poison of delusion. All of the erroneous views, arrogance, and doubt are subsumed within ignorance. In this manner, all of the fetters are entirely subsumed within the three poisons. What then does one employ to destroy them? It is those three component aspects of the eight-fold right path, [the three trainings of moral virtue, concentration, and wisdom].

If someone speaks of the three [countervailing] component aspects of the eight-fold right path, then one should realize that he has already thereby implicitly mentioned all of the thirty-seven wings of enlightenment. All sorts of characteristic features such as these indicate what is meant by the "counteractive gateway."

Dharmas such as have been described above constitute what is referred to as the "*Piṭaka* [*-upadeśa*]" gateway.

b. The "Abhidharma" Gateway

What then is meant by the "Abhidharma" gateway? In some cases, the Buddha himself explained the meanings of dharmas. In some cases the Buddha himself explained the names of dharmas. Still, the disciples engaged in the creation of all sorts of compilations and exegeses explaining his meaning. For instance, the Buddha said:

> If there were a bhikshu who was unable to correctly bear in mind conditioned dharmas who nonetheless wished to gain the foremost worldly dharma, this would be impossible. If one fails to gain the foremost worldly dharma and yet still wishes to enter into the midst of the "correct" stage (*samyaktva niyāma*), this would be impossible to accomplish. If one wished to gain

得须陀洹斯陀含阿那含阿罗
汉无有是处。有比丘于诸有
为法。正忆念得世间第一法
斯有是处。若得世间第一法
入正位。入正位得须陀洹斯
陀含阿那含阿罗汉必有是
处。如佛直说。世间第一法
不说相义。何界系何因[17]何
缘何果报。从世间第一法。
种种声闻所行法乃至无馀涅
盘。一一分别相义。[18]如
是等是名阿毗昙门。空门者
生空法空。如频婆娑罗王迎
经中。佛告大王。色生时但
空生。色灭时但空灭。诸行
生时但空生。灭时但空灭。
是中无吾我。无人无神。无
人从今世至后世。除因缘和
合名字等众生。凡夫愚人逐
名求实。如是等经中佛说生
空。

得須陀洹斯陀含阿那含阿羅
漢無有是處。有比丘於諸有
為法。正憶念得世間第一法
斯有是處。若得世間第一法
入正位。入正位得須陀洹斯
陀含阿那含阿羅漢必有是
處。如佛直說。世間第一法
不說相義。何界繫何因[17]何
緣何果報。從世間第一法。
種種聲聞所行法乃至無餘涅
槃。一一分別相義。[18]如
是等是名阿毗曇門。空門者
生空法空。如頻婆娑羅王迎
經中。佛告大王。色生時但
空生。色滅時但空滅。諸行
生時但空生。滅時但空滅。
是中無吾我。無人無神。無
人從今世至後世。除因緣和
合名字等眾生。凡夫愚人逐
名求實。如是等經中佛說生
空。

简体字   正體字

the realization of a *srota-āpanna*, a *sakṛdāgāmin*, an *anāgāmin*, or an arhat, this, too, would be impossible.

If there were a bhikshu who, possessed of right mindfulness with respect to conditioned dharmas, gained the foremost worldly dharma, this is possible. If one had gained the foremost worldly dharma and then succeeded in entering into the "correct stage," if one had entered into the correct stage and then succeeded in gaining the realization of a *srota-āpanna*, a *sakṛdāgāmin*, an *anāgāmin*, and an arhat, this is definitely possible.

As for what the Buddha directly explained herein, he did not mention the characteristics and meaning of the foremost worldly dharma. He did not describe the realms to which it belongs, what its causes are, what its conditions are, and which karmic effects occur as a result. The discriminating explanation of the characteristics and meanings of all of the sorts of dharmas practiced by the Śrāvakas—those dharmas consisting of the foremost worldly dharma and so forth on through to the nirvāṇa without residue—explanations such as these comprise what falls within the sphere of the "Abhidharma" gateway.

c. The "Emptiness" Gateway

As for the "emptiness" gateway, it refers to the emptiness of beings (*pudgala-śūnyatā*) and the emptiness of dharmas (*dharma-śūnyatā*).

1) The Emptiness of Beings

[In the case of the first], take for example this passage from the *Sutra on the Encounter with King Bimbasāra* (*Bimbasāra-rāja-pratyud-gamana-sūtra*):

> The Buddha told the great king: When form is produced, it is only emptiness which is being produced. When form is destroyed, it is only emptiness which is being destroyed. When karmic formative factors (*saṃskāra*) are produced, it is only emptiness which is being produced. When they are destroyed, it is only emptiness which is being destroyed.
>
> There is herein no self (*ātman*), no person (*pudgala*), and no spiritual soul (*puruṣa*). There is no person who goes from this life on into the later life aside from a conjunction of causes and effects, a being consisting only of names and such. The foolish common person pursues reality by chasing after names.

It was in sutras such as these that the Buddha explained the emptiness of beings.

法空者。如佛说大空经中。
十二因缘无明乃至老死。若
有人言是老死。若言谁老死
皆是邪见。生有取[19]爱受
触六入名色识行无明亦如
是。若有人言身即是神。若
言身异于神。是二虽异同为
邪见。佛言。身即是神。如
是邪见非我弟子。身异于神
亦是邪见。非我弟子。是经
中佛说法空。若说谁老死。
当知是虚妄是名生空。若说
是老死当知是虚妄是名法
空。乃至无明亦如是。复次
佛说梵网经中六十二见。若
有人言。神常世间亦常。是
为邪见。若言神无常世间无
常是亦邪见。神及世间常亦
无常。神及世间非常亦非非
常。皆是邪见。以是故知诸
法皆空是为实。

法空者。如佛說大空經中。
十二因緣無明乃至老死。若
有人言是老死。若言誰老死
皆是邪見。生有取[19]愛受
觸六入名色識行無明亦如
是。若有人言身即是神。若
言身異於神。是二雖異同為
邪見。佛言。身即是神。如
是邪見非我弟子。身異於神
亦是邪見。非我弟子。是經
中佛說法空。若說誰老死。
當知是虛妄是名生空。若說
是老死當知是虛妄是名法
空。乃至無明亦如是。復次
佛說梵網經中六十二見。若
有人言。神常世間亦常。是
為邪見。若言神無常世間無
常是亦邪見。神及世間常亦
無常。神及世間非常亦非非
常。皆是邪見。以是故知諸
法皆空是為實。

简体字   正體字

2) Śrāvaka-Level Emptiness of Dharmas

As for the emptiness of dharmas, take for example the *Great Emptiness Sutra* (*Mahā-śūnyatā-sūtra*) wherein the Buddha stated:

> Within the twelve causes and conditions, from ignorance on through to old age and death, if there is a person who says that there is an old age or a death, or if he says that there is someone who grows old or someone who dies—in every such instance— these are erroneous views. The same is true [for such statements] with regard to birth, becoming, grasping, craving, feeling, contact, the six sense entrances, name-and-form, consciousness, karmic formative factors (*saṃskāra*) and ignorance.
>
> If there is a person who says that the body is just the spiritual soul or if there is someone who says that the body is different from the spiritual soul—although these two are different, they are identical in that they are both erroneous views.

The Buddha said, "To say that the body is just the spiritual soul…. [Anyone positing] erroneous views such as these is not my disciple. To say that the body is different from the spirit is also an erroneous view. [Anyone proposing this] is not my disciple." In this part of the Sutra, the Buddha was speaking of the emptiness of dharmas.

When he said, "…if there is a person who says that there is someone who grows old or who dies…," one should know that this fallacy was brought up in relation to the emptiness of beings.

Where he said, "If there is a person who claims that there is an old age or a death…," one should know that this fallacy was brought up in relation to the emptiness of dharmas. This is also the case with the other references up to and including the above reference to "ignorance."

Additionally, the Buddha discussed the sixty-two wrong views in the *Brahmā's Net Sutra* (*Brahma-jāla-sūtra*), saying:

> If there is a person who claims that the spiritual soul is permanent and that the world is permanent, these are erroneous views. If one claims that the spiritual soul is impermanent and that the world is impermanent, these, too, are erroneous views. To claim that the spiritual soul and the world are both permanent and impermanent or to claim that the spiritual soul and the world are neither permanent nor impermanent—In each of these cases, these are erroneous views.

Therefore one should know that all dharmas are empty. This is what is actually the case.

问曰。若言神常应是邪见。
何以故。神性无故。若言世
间常亦应是邪见。何以故。
世间实皆无常。颠倒故言有
常。若言神无常亦应是邪
见。何以故。神性无故。不
应言无常。若言世间无常不
应是邪见。何以故。一切有
为法性实皆无常。答曰。若
一切法实皆无常。佛云何说
世间无常是名邪见。是故可
知非实是无常。问曰。佛处
处说观有为法无常苦空无我
令人得道。云何言无常堕邪
见。答曰。佛处处说无常。
处处说不灭。如摩诃男释王
来至佛所白佛言。是迦毗罗
人众殷多。我或值奔车逸马
狂象鬪人时。便失念佛心。
是时自念。我今若死当生何
处。

問曰。若言神常應是邪見。
何以故。神性無故。若言世
間常亦應是邪見。何以故。
世間實皆無常。顛倒故言有
常。若言神無常亦應是邪
見。何以故。神性無故。不
應言無常。若言世間無常不
應是邪見。何以故。一切有
為法性實皆無常。答曰。若
一切法實皆無常。佛云何說
世間無常是名邪見。是故可
知非實是無常。問曰。佛處
處說觀有為法無常苦空無我
令人得道。云何言無常墮邪
見。答曰。佛處處說無常。
處處說不滅。如摩訶男釋王
來至佛所白佛言。是迦毘羅
人眾殷多。我或值奔車逸馬
狂象鬪人時。便失念佛心。
是時自念。我今若死當生何
處。

简体字   正體字

a) Objection: On Soul-permanence, World Impermanence

Question: If one claims that the spiritual soul is permanent, this ought to be an erroneous view. Why? Because a [self-existent] nature of any such "spiritual soul" is nonexistent.

If one claims that the world is permanent, this, too, ought to be a false view. Why? The world is actually entirely impermanent. It is on account of inverted views that one speaks of the world as permanent.

If one says that the spiritual soul is impermanent, this, too, ought to be an erroneous view. Why? One should not say that the spiritual soul is impermanent simply because it is devoid of a [self-existent] nature.

If one says that the world is impermanent, it should not be that this is an erroneous view. Why? It is the nature of all conditioned dharmas that they are in fact impermanent.

b) Response: World Impermanence Really Is False

Response: If it is actually the case that all dharmas are impermanent, why did the Buddha say, "To say that the world is impermanent is an erroneous view."? Therefore one can know that it is not actually the case that it is impermanent.

c) Objection: How Can You Claim Impermanence is False?

Question: In place after place, the Buddha instructed one to contemplate conditioned dharmas as impermanent, suffering, empty, and devoid of self, thus causing people to gain the Path. How then can you state that, when one posits the reality of "impermanence," that constitutes an erroneous view?

d) Response: Such Teachings Merely Accord with Circumstances

Response: In place after place, the Buddha spoke of impermanence and in place after place, he spoke of [certain factors] "not being destroyed."

e) Story: Buddha's Teaching of King Mahānāman

Take for instance when the Shākyan King, Mahānāman, came to where the Buddha dwelt:

> [King Mahānāman] addressed the Buddha, saying, "The population of Kapilavastu is huge. Sometimes when I encounter a speeding chariot, a runaway horse, a crazed elephant or battling people, I lose the thought focused on mindfulness of the Buddha. At these times, I think to myself, 'If I died now, where would I be reborn?'"

佛告摩诃男。汝勿怖勿畏。
汝是时不生恶趣必至善处。
譬如树常东向曲。若有斫者
必当东倒。善人亦如是。若
身坏死时。善心意识长夜以
信戒闻施慧熏[193-1]心故。必
得利益上生天上。若一切法
念念生灭无常。佛云何言诸
功德[2]熏心故[3]必得上生。
以是故知非无常性。问曰。
若无常不实。佛何以说无
常。答曰。佛随众生所应
而说法。[4]破常颠倒故说无
常。以人不知不信后世故。
说心去后世上生天上。罪福
业因缘百千万劫不失。是对
治悉檀。非第一义悉檀。诸
法实相非常非无常。佛亦处
处说诸法空。诸法空中亦无
无常。以是故说

佛告摩訶男。汝勿怖勿畏。
汝是時不生恶趣必至善處。
譬如樹常東向曲。若有斫者
必當東倒。善人亦如是。若
身壞死時。善心意識長夜以
信戒聞施慧熏[193-1]心故。必
得利益上生天上。若一切法
念念生滅無常。佛云何言諸
功德[2]熏心故[3]必得上生。
以是故知非無常性。問曰。
若無常不實。佛何以說無
常。答曰。佛隨眾生所應
而說法。[4]破常顛倒故說無
常。以人不知不信後世故。
說心去後世上生天上。罪福
業因緣百千萬劫不失。是對
治悉檀。非第一義悉檀。諸
法實相非常非無常。佛亦處
處說諸法空。諸法空中亦無
無常。以是故說

简体字

正體字

The Buddha told Mahānāman, "You should not be frightened. Do not fear. At such a time, you would not be reborn in one of the wretched destinies. You would certainly proceed to a good place. This is analogous to a tree which has always leaned well to the east. If there is someone who cuts it down, it will certainly fall toward the east.

"The situation is identical in the case of a person who is good. In an instance where the body is destroyed and one then dies, because throughout the long night [of time], the mental consciousness of the wholesome mind has imbued the mind with faith, moral virtue, learning, giving, and wisdom, one will certainly gain the benefit of it and thus achieve rebirth in the heavens."

f) Hence Dharmas Aren't Inherently Impermanent

If it was the case that all dharmas are impermanent by virtue of being produced and destroyed in every thought moment, why did the Buddha say that, because all of the meritorious qualities permeate the mind, one will certainly gain a superior rebirth? On account of this, one should realize that [dharmas] are not impermanent by nature.

g) Objection: Why Then Did the Buddha Teach "Impermanence"?

Question: If impermanence is not actually the case, why did the Buddha speak of impermanence?

h) Response: "Impermanence" is Only a Provisional Teaching

Response: The Buddha accorded with what was appropriate for particular beings and so spoke that dharma for their sakes. It was in order to refute the inverted view imputing permanence that he spoke of impermanence.

[In the opposite case], because people were unaware of or did not believe in later existences, he spoke of the mind going on into a later existence and being reborn in the heavens, explaining that the karmic causes and conditions of offenses and merit are not lost even in a million kalpas.

These are instances of the counteractive *siddhānta* (doctrinal perspective). They do not reflect [the ultimate truth of] the supreme meaning *siddhānta*. The true character of dharmas does not involve either the concept of permanence or the concept of impermanence.

Then, too, the Buddha spoke in place after place of the emptiness of dharmas. In the emptiness of dharmas, even impermanence itself is nonexistent. It is for these reasons that it is stated here that

世间无常是邪见。是故名为
法空。复次毘耶离梵志名论
力。诸[5]梨昌等大[6]雇其宝
物令与佛论。取其[7]雇已。
即以其夜思撰五百难。明
旦与诸[*]梨昌至佛所。问佛
言。一究竟道为众多究竟
道。佛言。一究竟道无众多
也。梵志言。佛说一道。诸
外道师各各有究竟道。是为
众多非一。佛言。是虽[8]各
有众多皆非实道。何以故。
一切皆以邪见着故。不名究
竟道。佛问梵志。鹿头梵志
得道不。答言。一切得道中
是为第一。是时长老鹿头梵
志比丘在佛后扇佛。佛问梵
志。汝识是比丘不。梵志识
之惭愧低头。是时佛说义品
偈。

各各谓究竟。而各自爱着。
各自是非彼。是皆非究竟。

是人入论众。辩明义理时。
各各相是非。胜负怀忧喜。

世間無常是邪見。是故名為
法空。復次毘耶離梵志名論
力。諸[5]梨昌等大[6]雇其寶
物令與佛論。取其[7]雇已。
即以其夜思撰五百難。明
旦與諸[*]梨昌至佛所。問佛
言。一究竟道為眾多究竟
道。佛言。一究竟道無眾多
也。梵志言。佛說一道。諸
外道師各各有究竟道。是為
眾多非一。佛言。是雖[8]各
有眾多皆非實道。何以故。
一切皆以邪見著故。不名究
竟道。佛問梵志。鹿頭梵志
得道不。答言。一切得道中
是為第一。是時長老鹿頭梵
志比丘在佛後扇佛。佛問梵
志。汝識是比丘不。梵志識
之慚愧低頭。是時佛說義品
偈。

各各謂究竟。而各自愛著。
各自是非彼。是皆非究竟。

是人入論眾。辯明義理時。
各各相是非。勝負懷憂喜。

简体字   正體字

to claim that the world is impermanent is an erroneous view. Hence one refers here to the emptiness of dharmas.

i) Dharmas' Emptiness Story: Buddha's Debate with Vivādabala

Furthermore, there is the case of the *brahmacārin* from Vaiśāli known as Vivādabala (lit. "Power of Debate"). The Licchavis had given him many precious things to obtain his services in debating the Buddha. Having accepted his fee for service, he proceeded that night to contemplate and select five hundred challenging debate topics. Then, early the next morning, he went with the Licchavis to the place where the Buddha dwelt:

> [Vivādabala] asked the Buddha, "Is there one ultimate path or are there many ultimate paths?"
>
> The Buddha replied, "There is one ultimate path, not many."
>
> The Brahmacārin said, "The Buddha claims that there is one path, yet all of the non-Buddhist masters each have an ultimate path. These constitute 'many,' not just 'one.'"
>
> The Buddha said, "Although each has his own and there are many of them, in every case, they are not the actual path. Why? It is because all of them are attached to erroneous views that they do not qualify as the ultimate path."
>
> The Buddha then asked the Brahmacārin, "Has the *brahmacārin* Mṛgaśiras (lit. "Deer Head") realized the Path or not?"
>
> He replied, "That individual is the one foremost among all who have realized the Path."
>
> It just so happened that the elder *brahmacārin* Mṛgaśiras was just then standing as a bhikshu behind the Buddha, fanning the Buddha. The Buddha then asked the Brahmacārin, "Do you recognize this bhikshu here, or not?"
>
> The Brahmacārin then recognized him and, struck with shame, lowered his head.

The Buddha next uttered this verse found in the *Categories of Meaning* (*Arthavarga*):

> Everyone is of the opinion that he [possesses] the ultimate,
> And so each to his own is cherishingly attached.
> Each sees himself as right and attributes faults to others.
> In every case, these do not qualify as "ultimate."
>
> These people enter into the debate assembly.
> As they make distinctions among meanings and principles,
> Each points out the rights and wrongs of the other.
> Victor and vanquished then embrace either distress or delight.

胜者堕憍坑。负者[9]堕忧狱。
是故有智者。不随此二法。
论力汝当知。我诸弟子法。
无虚亦无实。汝欲何所求。
汝欲坏我论。终已无此处。
一切智难胜。适足自毁坏。

[0193c01]　如是等处处声闻经中
说诸法空。摩诃衍空门者。
一切诸法性常自空。不以智
慧方便观故空。如佛为须菩
提说色。色自空受想行识识
[10]自空。十二入十八界十二
因缘三十七品十力四无所畏
十八不共法大慈大悲萨婆若
乃至阿耨多罗三藐三菩提皆
自空。问曰。若一切诸法性
常自空[11]真空无所有者。云
何不堕邪见。邪见名无罪无
福无今世后世与此无异。

勝者墮憍坑。負者[9]墮憂獄。
是故有智者。不隨此二法。
論力汝當知。我諸弟子法。
無虛亦無實。汝欲何所求。
汝欲壞我論。終已無此處。
一切智難勝。適足自毀壞。

[0193c01]　如是等處處聲聞經中
說諸法空。摩訶衍空門者。
一切諸法性常自空。不以智
慧方便觀故空。如佛為須菩
提說色。色自空受想行識識
[10]自空。十二入十八界十二
因緣三十七品十力四無所畏
十八不共法大慈大悲薩婆若
乃至阿耨多羅三藐三菩提皆
自空。問曰。若一切諸法性
常自空[11]真空無所有者。云
何不墮邪見。邪見名無罪無
福無今世後世與此無異。

简体字   正體字

> The victor falls into the pit of arrogance.
> The loser then falls into a hell of distress.
> Therefore, in an instance involving one who is wise,
> He does not go along with either of these two dharmas.

[The Buddha then continued with more verses directed specifically at Vivādabala]:

> Vivādabala, you ought to know that,
> Among my disciples and within my Dharma,
> There is nothing held to be [ultimately] "false" or "real."
> What then is it that you are now seeking to accomplish?

> If you are wishing to destroy my discourse on doctrine,
> It is ultimately impossible to succeed in such an endeavor.
> For it is difficult to vanquish the knowledge of all modes,
> This would be tantamount to destroying your own doctrine.

In place after place within the sutras of the Śrāvakas are discussions such as these which explain the emptiness of all dharmas.

3) The Mahāyāna Emptiness of Dharmas

As for the Mahāyāna gateway to emptiness, all dharmas, by their very nature, are eternally and intrinsically empty. It is not merely on account of some contemplation arising from wisdom-based skillful means that they are found to be empty. As the Buddha explained to Subhūti:

> Form is inherently empty of form. [The same is true for] feeling, perception, karmic formative factors, and consciousness which, just so, is inherently empty of consciousness. The twelve sense bases, the eighteen sense realms, the twelve causes and conditions, the thirty-seven wings of enlightenment, the ten powers, the four fearlessnesses, the eighteen exclusive dharmas, the great kindness, the great compassion, *sarvajñāna* (omniscience), and so forth until we come to *anuttarasamyaksaṃbodhi* (perfect enlightenment)—they are all entirely inherently empty.

a) Objection: How is "Emptiness" not an Erroneous View?

Question: If [one claims that] all dharmas, by their very nature, are eternally and intrinsically empty and that, in true emptiness, nothing whatsoever exists, how does this not amount to falling into an erroneous view? By "erroneous view," we refer here to [the belief that] there is neither offense nor merit and that there is no present life or later life. [Those erroneous views] are no different from this [concept you propose].

答曰。无罪无福人。不言无今世。但言无后世。如草木之类自生自灭。或人生或人杀。止于现在更无后世生。而不知观身内外所有自相皆空以是为异。复次邪见人多行众恶断诸善事。观空人善法尚不欲作。何况作恶。问曰。邪见有二种。有破因破果。有破果不破因。如汝所说破果不破因。破果破因者。言无因无缘无罪无福则是破因。无今世后世罪福报是则破果。观空人言皆空。则罪福因果皆无。与此有何等异。答曰。邪见人于诸法断灭令空。摩诃衍人知诸法真空不破不坏。

答曰。無罪無福人。不言無今世。但言無後世。如草木之類自生自滅。或人生或人殺。止於現在更無後世生。而不知觀身內外所有自相皆空以是為異。復次邪見人多行眾惡斷諸善事。觀空人善法尚不欲作。何況作惡。問曰。邪見有二種。有破因破果。有破果不破因。如汝所說破果不破因。破果破因者。言無因無緣無罪無福則是破因。無今世後世罪福報是則破果。觀空人言皆空。則罪福因果皆無。與此有何等異。答曰。邪見人於諸法斷滅令空。摩訶衍人知諸法真空不破不壞。

简体字   正體字

b) Response: This Characterization is Wrong, As Follows...

Response: A person who [claims that] there is no offense nor merit does not claim that there is no present lifetime. He only claims that there are no later lifetimes [and that people are] the same as such things as grasses and trees which are naturally born and which naturally die. [He claims that] a certain person is born [and then] a certain person is killed and that it all ceases within the present, beyond which there is no additional later lifetime into which one is subsequently reborn. But they do not know to contemplate everything to do with the person both inwardly and outwardly [and realize that], in every case, it is empty of any inherently existent characteristics. It is this which constitutes the difference.

Additionally, people holding erroneous views are inclined for the most part toward engaging in manifold evils and ceasing all wholesome endeavors. People contemplating emptiness do not wish even to engage in the activity involved in wholesome dharmas. How much the less would they wish to engage in evil deeds?

c) Objection: Isn't Emptiness Just Causality Refutation?

Question: There are two type of erroneous views. There are those which attempt to refute "cause" and also to refute "effect" and then there are those which attempt to refute effect but which do not attempt to refute cause. Those corresponding to your description attempt to refute effect but not cause.

As for those which attempt to refute effect and also to refute cause, if one claims that there are no causes, no conditions, no offenses, and no merit, then this constitutes an attempt to refute cause. If one claims that there are no retributions associated with karmic offenses and meritorious karmic deeds in present and later lives, then this constitutes at attempt to refute effects.

Now, the person who contemplates emptiness claims that, in every case, they are empty. If this is the case, then karmic offenses and meritorious karmic deeds as well as causes and effects—all of them are entirely nonexistent.

This being the case, what differences exist among such claims?

d) Response: Mahāyana Emptiness Doesn't Imply Acausality

Response: Those who hold to erroneous views resort to annihilationism to arrive at the emptiness of all dharmas. A proponent of the Mahāyana realizes the true emptiness of all dharmas but still does not engage in any such refutations or attempts to demolish [causality tenets].

问曰。是邪见三种。一者破罪福报不破罪福。破因缘果报不破因缘。破后世不破今世。二者破罪福报亦破罪福。破因缘果报亦破因缘。破后世亦破今世。不破一切法。三者破一切法皆令无所有。观空人亦言真空无所有。[12]与第三邪[13]见有何等异。答曰。邪见破诸法令空。观空人知诸法真空不破不坏。复次邪见人言诸法皆空无所有。取诸法空相戏论。观空人知诸法空不取相不戏论。复次邪见人虽口说一切空。然于爱处生爱。瞋处生瞋。

問曰。是邪見三種。一者破罪福報不破罪福。破因緣果報不破因緣。破後世不破今世。二者破罪福報亦破罪福。破因緣果報亦破因緣。破後世亦破今世。不破一切法。三者破一切法皆令無所有。觀空人亦言真空無所有。[12]與第三邪[13]見有何等異。答曰。邪見破諸法令空。觀空人知諸法真空不破不壞。復次邪見人言諸法皆空無所有。取諸法空相戲論。觀空人知諸法空不取相不戲論。復次邪見人雖口說一切空。然於愛處生愛。瞋處生瞋。

简体字

正體字

e)   Objection: Emptiness Embraces the Three Erroneous Views

Question: These erroneous views are of three types: The first is typified by one who attempts to refute the retribution for karmic offenses and meritorious karmic deeds but does not attempt to refute such offenses and meritorious deeds. He attempts to refute effect-associated retribution from causes and conditions but does not attempt to refute causes and conditions. He attempts to refute the existence of later lifetimes but does not attempt to refute the existence of the present lifetime.

The second is typified by one who attempts to refute both the retribution associated with offenses and merit as well as offenses and merit themselves, who attempts to refute the existence of effect-associated retribution from causes and conditions as well as the causes and conditions themselves, and who attempts to refute the existence of later lifetimes as well as the present lifetime. Still, he does not attempt to refute all dharmas.

The third is typified by one who attempts to refute all dharmas, claiming that, in every case, they may be shown to be entirely non-existent. The person who contemplates emptiness also speaks of true emptiness and claims that there is nothing whatsoever which exists. What difference is there then between this and the third type of erroneous view?

f)   Response: Again, Emptiness Doesn't Involve Acausality

Response: The one who holds to erroneous views brings about emptiness through the refutation of all dharmas. The person who contemplates emptiness realizes that dharmas are themselves truly empty and does not engage in refutations or attempt to demolish [the causality tenets to which you refer].

Moreover, the person who holds to erroneous views claims that all dharmas are entirely empty and that there is nothing whatsoever which exists. [As a consequence of that approach], he seizes upon dharmas' characteristic of being empty and engages in frivolous debates. The person who contemplates emptiness realizes that all dharmas are themselves empty, but in doing so, does not seize upon that characteristic or engage in such frivolous debates.

g)   Attachment to Emptiness Still Involves Afflictions

Furthermore, although those who seize upon erroneous views claim that everything is empty, still, where one might be prone to desire, they still give rise to desire. Where one might be prone to hatefulness, they still become hateful. Where one might be prone

慢处生慢。痴处生痴。自诳其身。如佛弟子实知空心不动。一切结使生处不复生。譬如虚空烟火不能染大雨不能湿。如是观空。种种烦恼不复着其心。复次邪见人言无所有。不从[194-1]爱因缘出。真空名从[*]爱因缘生是为异。四无量心诸清净法。以所缘不实故。犹尚不与真空智慧等。何况此邪见。复次是见名为邪见。真空见名为正见。行邪见人今世[2]为弊恶人。后世[3]当入地狱。行真空智慧人今世致誉后世得作佛。譬如水火之异。亦如甘露毒药天食须陀以比臭粪。

慢處生慢。癡處生癡。自誑其身。如佛弟子實知空心不動。一切結使生處不復生。譬如虛空烟火不能染大雨不能濕。如是觀空。種種煩惱不復著其心。復次邪見人言無所有。不從[194-1]愛因緣出。真空名從[*]愛因緣生是為異。四無量心諸清淨法。以所緣不實故。猶尚不與真空智慧等。何況此邪見。復次是見名為邪見。真空見名為正見。行邪見人今世[2]為弊惡人。後世[3]當入地獄。行真空智慧人今世致譽後世得作佛。譬如水火之異。亦如甘露毒藥天食須陀以比臭糞。

简体字　　　　　　　　正體字

to arrogance, they still become arrogant. And where one might be prone to delusion, they still become deluded. They each deceive themselves.

h) Buddhists Realizing Emptiness Transcend Afflictions.

In the case of the disciples of the Buddha realizing emptiness in accordance with reality, their minds do not move. In every circumstance wherein one might be prone to the arising of the fetters, they no longer arise. They become like empty space which even a smoky fire remains unable to stain and which even a great rain is unable to drench. In the case of whoever contemplates emptiness in this way, all of the various sorts of afflictions are no longer able to attach to their minds.

i) Erroneous Views Involve Submersion in Desire

Additionally, even though people seizing on erroneous views may claim there is nothing whatsoever which exists, they still haven't freed themselves from the causes and conditions of desire. [Correct understanding of] true emptiness refers to a circumstance wherein one has already emerged from any causes and conditions associated with desire.[6] These [distinctions as set forth above] constitute the difference [between inverted views and the correct understanding of emptiness].

j) Realization of True Emptiness Involves Transcendence

Not even the pure dharmas of the four immeasurable minds are able to match the wisdom realizing true emptiness. This is because the objects upon which they focus are unreal. How much the less could those erroneous views be able to match it?

k) Three Analogies: Distinctions in Life Quality and Destiny

Also, these views [discussed above] all qualify as erroneous views. Views based on realization of true emptiness, however, qualify as right views. Those who course in erroneous views are base and evil people in the present lifetime and then become bound to fall into the hells in later lifetimes.

One who courses in wisdom founded on true emptiness gains a good reputation in the present life and then succeeds in later lives in realizing buddhahood. The difference here is like that between water and fire. The differences are so great that trying to compare them would be like comparing lethal poison to sweet-dew ambrosia (*amṛta*) or like trying to compare stinking feces to that food of the gods known as *sudhā*.

复次真空中有空空三昧。邪[4]见空虽有空而无空空三昧。复次观[5]真空人。先有无量布施持戒禅定。其心柔软。诸结使薄。然后得真空。邪见中无此事。但欲以忆想分别邪心取空。譬如田舍人。初不识盐。见[6]贵人以盐着种种肉菜中而食。问言。何以故尔。语言此盐能令诸物味美故。此人便念此盐能令诸物美自味必多。便空抄盐满口食之醎苦伤口。而问言。汝何以言盐能作美。[*]贵人言。痴人。此当筹量多少和之令美。云何纯食盐。无智人闻空解脱门不行诸功德。但欲得空。是为邪见断诸善根。如是等义名为空门。

復次真空中有空空三昧。邪[4]見空雖有空而無空空三昧。復次觀[5]真空人。先有無量布施持戒禪定。其心柔軟。諸結使薄。然後得真空。邪見中無此事。但欲以憶想分別邪心取空。譬如田舍人。初不識鹽。見[6]貴人以鹽著種種肉菜中而食。問言。何以故爾。語言此鹽能令諸物味美故。此人便念此鹽能令諸物美自味必多。便空抄鹽滿口食之醎苦傷口。而問言。汝何以言鹽能作美。[*]貴人言。癡人。此當籌量多少和之令美。云何純食鹽。無智人聞空解脫門不行諸功德。但欲得空。是為邪見斷諸善根。如是等義名為空門。

简体字　　　　　　　　　　　　　　正體字

l) TRUE EMPTINESS INVOLVES EVEN EMPTINESS-OF-EMPTINESS

Moreover, when coursing in the realization of true emptiness, one has access to the "emptiness of emptiness" samādhi. In the case of that type of "emptiness" based only on erroneous views, although there is an emptiness [to which one refers], still, there is no actual coursing in the emptiness-of-emptiness samādhi.

m) EMPTINESS REALIZATION ENTAILS GIVING, VIRTUE, DHYĀNA

Furthermore, a person who contemplates true emptiness has first gone through an incalculable amount of giving, upholding of precepts, and dhyāna absorption. His mind is gentle and pliant and his afflictive fetters are but scant. Afterwards, he gains the realization of true emptiness. In the case of one who courses in erroneous views, there have been none of these endeavors. He simply wishes to seize upon emptiness by resort to erroneous thoughts linked to speculations and discriminations.

n) STORY: THE COUNTRY BUMPKIN INFATUATED WITH SALT

This is comparable to the man of rural origins who had never before seen salt. He happened to observe a man of noble status flavoring various meat and vegetable dishes with salt before eating them. He asked, "Why do you do that?"

The other man replied, "It is because this salt is able to make everything taste delectable."

This man then thought, "If this salt is able to cause everything to taste delectable, then its own flavor must be even more delicious." He then scooped up only the salt, filled his mouth with it, and swallowed it down. The intensity of the saltiness injured his mouth after which he exclaimed, "Why did you claim that salt is able to make for delectability?"

The man of noble background said, "You fool! With something like this, you must carefully calculate how much to mix in to achieve delectability. How could you even contemplate just eating salt by itself?"

d. SUMMARY STATEMENT ON THE EMPTINESS GATEWAY TO DHARMA

One who is deficient in wisdom hears of the emptiness gateway to liberation but fails to also cultivate all manner of meritorious qualities. He wishes only to realize emptiness. This is a case of maintaining erroneous views and thereby cutting off one's own roots of goodness.

Concepts such as these illustrate what is meant by "the gateway of emptiness."

若人入此三门则知佛法义不
相违背。能知是事即是般若
波罗蜜力。于一切法无所罣
碍。若不得般若波罗蜜法。
入阿毗昙门则堕有中。若入
空门则堕无中。若入蜫勒门
则堕有无中。复次菩萨摩诃
萨。行般若波罗蜜。虽知诸
法一相亦能知一切法种种
相。虽知诸法种种相亦能知
一切法一相。菩萨如是智慧
名为般若波罗蜜。问曰。菩
萨摩诃萨。云何知一切法种
种相。云何知一切法一相。
答曰。菩萨观诸法[7]相。所
谓有相。因是[8]有诸法中有
心生。如是等一切有。问
曰。无法中云何有心生。
答曰。若言无是事即是有[9]
法。复次菩萨观一切法一
相。所谓无相。

若人入此三門則知佛法義不
相違背。能知是事即是般若
波羅蜜力。於一切法無所罣
礙。若不得般若波羅蜜法。
入阿毗曇門則墮有中。若入
空門則墮無中。若入蜫勒門
則墮有無中。復次菩薩摩訶
薩。行般若波羅蜜。雖知
諸法一相亦能知一切法種種
相。雖知諸法種種相亦能知
一切法一相。菩薩如是智慧
名為般若波羅蜜。問曰。菩
薩摩訶薩。云何知一切法種
種相。云何知一切法一相。
答曰。菩薩觀諸法[7]相。所
謂有相。因是[8]有諸法中有
心生。如是等一切有。問
曰。無法中云何有心生。
答曰。若言無是事即是有[9]
法。復次菩薩觀一切法一
相。所謂無相。

简体字   正體字

2. Summary Statement on the Three Gateways to Dharma

If one enters into these three gateways [of the *Piṭaka-upadeśa*, of the Abhidharma, and of emptiness], then he will realize that the principles contained in the Dharma of the Buddha are not mutually contradictory. The origin of one's ability to realize this concept is just the power of *prajñāpāramitā*. As a result, one has no hangups or obstructions with respect to any dharma.

If one does not succeed in realizing the dharma of *prajñāpāramitā*, then, on entering the Abhidharma gateway, one falls into [a view seizing on] existence. Upon entering into the emptiness gateway, one falls into [a view seizing on] nonexistence. And when one enters into the *Piṭaka* [-*upadeśa*] gateway, one falls into [a view seizing on] both existence and nonexistence.

Additionally, in his practice of *prajñāpāramitā*, although the bodhisattva *mahāsattva* knows the identical characteristics among all dharmas, he is also able to know all of the differing characteristics of all dharmas. Although he knows all of the differing characteristics of all dharmas, he is also able to know the identical characteristics among all dharmas. It is this class of bodhisattva wisdom which qualifies as "*prajñāpāramitā*."

E. The Bodhisattva's Use of *Prajñāpāramitā* in Contemplations

1. Question: How Does the Bodhisattva Know Aspects of Dharmas?

Question: How is it that the bodhisattva, *mahāsattva* knows all of the different characteristics of all dharmas? How is it that he knows the identical characteristics among dharmas?

2. Response: He May Contemplate Them As "Existent"

Response: The bodhisattva contemplates [any given] characteristic of dharmas, [for instance], the so-called "existence" characteristic. On account of this "existence," in the midst of all dharmas, thoughts which correspond to "existence" arise. It is in a manner such as this that everything [may be said to] "exist."

3. Question: How Is "Existence" Imputed to Non-Existents?

Question: How is it that among "nonexistent" dharmas, thoughts imputing "existence" might arise?

4. Response: "Nonexistence" is just a Reflection of "Existence"

Response: If one speaks of "nonexistence," this very matter is itself just [a reflection of] the dharma of "existence."

Additionally, the bodhisattva may contemplate an identical characteristic among all dharmas, the so-called characteristic of

如牛中无羊相羊中无牛相。
如是[10]等诸法中各各无他
相。如先言因有故有心生。
是法异于有。异故应无。若
有法是牛羊亦应是牛。何以
故。有法不异故。若异则
无。如是等一切皆无。复次
菩萨观一切法一因。是一法
诸法中一心生诸法各各有一
相。合众一故名为二名为
三。一为实。二三为虚。复
次菩萨观诸法有所因故有。
如人身无常。何以故。生灭
相故。一切法皆如是有所因
故有。复次一切[11]诸法无所
因故有。如人身无常

简体字

如牛中無羊相羊中無牛相。
如是[10]等諸法中各各無他
相。如先言因有故有心生。
是法異於有。異故應無。若
有法是牛羊亦應是牛。何
以故。有法不異故。若異則
無。如是等一切皆無。復次
菩薩觀一切法一因。是一法
諸法中一心生諸法各各有一
相。合眾一故名為二名為
三。一為實。二三為虛。復
次菩薩觀諸法有所因故有。
如人身無常。何以故。生滅
相故。一切法皆如是有所因
故有。復次一切[11]諸法無所
因故有。如人身無常

正體字

"nonexistence." This is just as with the case of cows wherein the characteristic of "being a sheep" is nonexistent and is also just as with the case of sheep wherein the characteristic of "being a cow" is also nonexistent. In a just the same manner, among all dharmas, each and every one of them is devoid of the characteristics of that which is "other."

Just as mentioned previously, it is on account of "existence" that thoughts corresponding to "existence" may arise. In the case of these dharmas, however, we speak of that which is different from what may be said to "exist." Because it is different, then it ought to be the case that it is "nonexistent."

[Given the aforementioned], if it were actually the case that the dharma of existence [could be] represented by the cow, [for example], then it ought [by force of logic] to also be the case that the sheep, too, is just a cow. Why? Because, in the case of both of them, the dharma of "existence" is no different. If it were different, then it would be the case, [again, by force of logic], that it would be "nonexistent." In this same manner, everything [which is "other"] would, [logically-speaking], be entirely "nonexistent."

5. The Bodhisattva May Contemplate Dharmas As "Singular," etc.

Then again, the bodhisattva may contemplate all dharmas in terms of their singularity. Based on this dharma of singularity, even in the midst of all dharmas, thoughts reflecting the concept of "singularity" may arise in him. Each and every dharma can be said to possess the mark of singularity. It is through the coming together of multiple instances of such "singularity" that one then refers to "two" or then refers to "three." It is [solely] the "one" which is [accorded the status of being] "real," whereas the "two" and the "three" are [simply] false [composites of singularity].

6. He May Contemplate Dharmas As "Caused"

Then again, the bodhisattva contemplates dharmas as existing through having that by which they are caused. As in the case of the human body, they are impermanent. Why is this? This is because they are characterized by the processes of production and extinction. All dharmas are just like this. This is because their existence occurs through having that by which they are caused.

7. He May Contemplate Dharmas As "Causeless"

Yet again, [however, it may be said that] it is on account of having no cause that any dharma [can be supposed to] "exist." Taking for example the human body, its impermanence occurs by virtue of

生灭故。因生灭故知无常。此因复应有因。如是则无穷。若无穷则无因。若是因更无因是无常。因亦非因。如是等一切无因。复次菩萨观一切法有相。无有法无相者。如地坚重相水冷湿相火热照相风轻动相虚空容受相。分别觉知是为识相。有此有彼是为方相。有久有近是为时相。浊恶心恼众生是为罪相。净善心愍众生是为福相。着诸法是为缚相。不着诸法是为解脱相。现前知一切法无碍是为佛相。如是等一切各有相。复次菩萨观一切法皆无相。是诸相从因缘和合生。无自性故无。如地色香味触四法和合故名地。不

简体字

生滅故。因生滅故知無常。此因復應有因。如是則無窮。若無窮則無因。若是因更無因是無常。因亦非因。如是等一切無因。復次菩薩觀一切法有相。無有法無相者。如地堅重相水冷濕相火熱照相風輕動相虛空容受相。分別覺知是為識相。有此有彼是為方相。有久有近是為時相。濁惡心惱眾生是為罪相。淨善心愍眾生是為福相。著諸法是為縛相。不著諸法是為解脫相。現前知一切法無礙是為佛相。如是等一切各有相。復次菩薩觀一切法皆無相。是諸相從因緣和合生。無自性故無。如地色香味觸四法和合故名地。不

正體字

its being produced and then destroyed. It is on account of its being produced and destroyed that one knows that it is impermanent. This cause itself ought additionally to have its own cause. If this were the case, then this would be a case of infinite regression. If this [tracing back of causation is in fact] endless, then this [becomes tantamount to] being devoid of any cause.

If this cause has no additional [prior] cause [to which it can be traced], then the cause of this circumstance of "impermanence" is really a case of being devoid of cause. [When contemplated] in this manner, [one finds that] everything is devoid of any cause.

8. He May Contemplate Dharmas As "Having Aspects"

Additionally, the bodhisattva contemplates all dharmas as possessing particular characteristics. There are no existent dharmas which are entirely devoid of characteristics. For instance, earth is characterized by solidity and heaviness. Water is characterized by coolness and moistness. Fire is characterized by heat and illumination. Wind is characterized by lightness and movement. Empty space is characterized by the ability to envelop things and take them in. Discrimination, awareness, and knowing constitute the characteristics of consciousness.

Having a "this" and a "that" constitutes the characteristic of spatiality. Having a "long ago" and a "more recent" constitutes the characteristic of time. Possession of a turbid and evil mind together with the tormenting of beings constitute the characteristics of karmic offenses. Possessing a pure and good mind which pities beings constitute the characteristics of meritorious karma. Being attached to dharmas constitutes the characteristic feature of bondage. Not being attached to any dharma whatsoever constitutes the characteristic feature of liberation. Direct and unimpeded knowing of all dharmas constitutes the characteristic feature of buddhahood.

In like fashion, each and every phenomenon possesses its own particular characteristic features.

9. He May Contemplate Dharmas as "Devoid of Aspects"

Then again, the bodhisattva contemplates all dharmas as being in every case devoid of characteristics. All of these characteristics are produced from the coming together of causes and conditions. Because they are devoid of any inherently existent nature, they are therefore nonexistent. Take for instance the case of [the element] "earth." It is referred to as "earth" on account of the conjunction of the four dharmas of forms, smells, tastes, and touchables. It is not

但色故名地。亦不但香但味
但触故名为地。何以故。若
但色是地。馀三则不应是
地。地则无香味触。香味触
亦如是。复次是四法云何为
一法。一法云何为四法。以
是故不得以四为地。亦不得
离四为地。问曰。我不以四
为地。但因四法故地法生。
此地在四法中住。答曰。若
从四法生地。地与四法异。
如父母生子子则异父母。若
尔者今眼见色鼻知香舌知味
身知触。地若异此四法者。
应更有异根异识知。若更无
异根异识知则无有地。问
曰。若上说地相有失。

但色故名地。亦不但香但味
但觸故名為地。何以故。若
但色是地。餘三則不應是
地。地則無香味觸。香味觸
亦如是。復次是四法云何為
一法。一法云何為四法。以
是故不得以四為地。亦不得
離四為地。問曰。我不以四
為地。但因四法故地法生。
此地在四法中住。答曰。若
從四法生地。地與四法異。
如父母生子子則異父母。若
爾者今眼見色鼻知香舌知味
身知觸。地若異此四法者。
應更有異根異識知。若更無
異根異識知則無有地。問
曰。若上說地相有失。

solely on the basis of form that it is referred to as "earth." Nor is it solely on the basis of smells, solely on the basis of tastes, or solely on the basis of touchables that it is therefore referred to as "earth."

How is this the case? If it was solely forms which constituted earth, then wherever the other three [component aspects] were present, it should not be that it would then qualify as "earth." In such a case, earth would then be devoid of the aspects of smell, taste, and tangibility. The circumstantial permutations would hold in just the same fashion for the other aspects consisting of smells, tastes, and touchables.

Again, how is it that these four dharmas could constitute a single dharma? How is it that a single dharma could be comprised of four dharmas? On account of this [inherent contradiction], one cannot take four [dharmas] as constituting earth nor can one have [the element] "earth" apart from these four aspects.

10. Objection: But These Four Dharmas Don't Constitute "Earth"

Question: I do not take these four aspects as constituting "earth." It is simply that it is on account of these four dharmas that the dharma of earth is produced. This "earth" then dwells among these four dharmas.

11. Response: This is a Fallacy, Refuted as Follows...

Response: If it was actually true that earth was produced from four dharmas, then earth itself would be different from these four dharmas in just the same way that when a father and mother give birth to a son, the son is then different from the father and the mother.

If it was the case that earth was different from these four dharmas, then in just the same manner as the eye perceives forms, as the nose is aware of smells, as the tongue is aware of tastes, and as the body is aware of touchables, there should then exist an additional and different sense faculty together with a different associated consciousness which perform the function of being aware [of this distinctly different objective entity known as "earth"].

If there is in fact no such additional and different sense faculty with its associated consciousness which perform the function of being aware [of the sense-object known as "earth"], then there could be no earth [under the theoretical circumstance you posit].

12. Objection: If Fallacious, then the Abhidharma Offers Clarity

Question: If the above-proposed statement about the characteristics of earth indeed possesses such faults, then the actual circumstance

应如阿毘昙说地相。地名四
大造色。但地种是坚相。地
是可见色。答曰。若地但是
色先已说失。又地为坚相。
但眼见色如水中月镜中像草
木影。则无坚相。坚[12]则身
根触知故。复次若眼见色是
地坚相。是地种眼见色。亦
是水火湿热相。是水火种。
若尔者风风种亦应分别而不
分别如说何等是风风种。何
等风种风。若是一物不应作
二种。答若是不异者。地及
地种不应异。问曰。是四大
各各不相离。地中有四种。
水火风各有四种但地中地多
故。以地为名。水火风亦
尔。答曰。不然。何以故。
若火中有四大应都是热。无
不热火故。若三大

應如阿毘曇說地相。地名四
大造色。但地種是堅相。地
是可見色。答曰。若地但是
色先已說失。又地為堅相。
但眼見色如水中月鏡中像草
木影。則無堅相。堅[12]則身
根觸知故。復次若眼見色是
地堅相。是地種眼見色。亦
是水火濕熱相。是水火種。
若爾者風風種亦應分別而不
分別如說何等是風風種。何
等風種風。若是一物不應作
二種。答若是不異者。地及
地種不應異。問曰。是四大
各各不相離。地中有四種。
水火風各有四種但地中地多
故。以地為名。水火風亦
爾。答曰。不然。何以故。
若火中有四大應都是熱。無
不熱火故。若三大

简体字   正體字

should accord with the Abhidharma's discussion of the characteristics of earth wherein it states that "earth" refers to a type of form created from the four great [elements], that it is solely the element earth which is characterized by solidity, and that "earth" constitutes a visible form.

13. RESPONSE: THIS, TOO, HAS FAULTS, AS FOLLOWS...

Response: As for the claim that earth is only form, we have already discussed that fallacy. Additionally, as for this claim that earth is characterized by solidity, if it were the case that it need only be the eye which perceives form, it should be like the moon reflected in water, like an image in a mirror, or like the shadows of shrubs and trees. In such a circumstance, there would be no quality of solidity [of which one might speak] for it is through the sense faculty of physical touch that solidity is perceived.

Moreover, if one posits that the form seen by the eye is earth's characteristic of solidity, [this fails to acknowledge that] this earth-element form which is seen by the eye is also characterized by the moistness of water and the heat of fire. But these are the elements of water and fire [and hence are not "earth"].

If this was actually the case, then one should also be able to [visually] distinguish the wind element in wind, but one is not actually able thereby to distinguish it. If it were as you claim, then, which is the wind element in the wind and which is the wind in the wind element? If there is only a single thing which is involved, then it should not be the case that it acts through the agency of two distinct elements. If one were to respond that they are not actually different, then it should not be the case that earth and the element of earth are different, either.

14. OBJECTION: EACH OF THE ELEMENTS CONTAINS THE OTHERS

Question: As for these four elements, each and every one of them does not exist separately from the others. Within earth, there exist the rest of the four elements. Water, fire and wind each possess the rest of the four elements. It is just that, in the case of "earth," it is because the earth element is dominant in it that it is referred to as "earth." The circumstance is the same with water, fire, and wind.

15. RESPONSE: THAT IS A FALLACY, AS FOLLOWS...

Response: That is not so. Why? If it was actually the case that the four great elements all exist within fire, it should be then that they are all hot, this because there is no fire which is not hot. If there were such a circumstance wherein any of the other three elements

在火中。不热则不名为火。
若热则舍自性皆名为火。若
谓细故不可知则与无无异。
若有麁可得则知有细。若无
麁亦无细。如是种种因缘地
相不可得。若地相不可得。
一切法相亦不可得。是故一
切法皆一相。问曰。不应言
无相。何以故。于诸法无相
即是相。若无无相则不[195-1]
可破一切法相。何以故。无
无相故。若有是无相则不应
言一切法无相。答曰。以无
相破诸法相。若有无相相则
堕诸法相中。若不入诸法[2]
相中则不应难无相。皆破诸
法相亦自灭相。譬如前火木
然诸薪已亦复自然。是故圣
人行无相。无相三昧破无相
故。复次菩萨。观一切法不
合不散无色无形

简体字

在火中。不熱則不名為火。
若熱則捨自性皆名為火。若
謂細故不可知則與無無異。
若有麁可得則知有細。若無
麁亦無細。如是種種因緣地
相不可得。若地相不可得。
一切法相亦不可得。是故一
切法皆一相。問曰。不應言
無相。何以故。於諸法無相
即是相。若無無相則不[195-1]
可破一切法相。何以故。無
無相故。若有是無相則不應
言一切法無相。答曰。以無
相破諸法相。若有無相相則
墮諸法相中。若不入諸法[2]
相中則不應難無相。皆破諸
法相亦自滅相。譬如前火木
然諸薪已亦復自然。是故聖
人行無相。無相三昧破無相
故。復次菩薩。觀一切法不
合不散無色無形

正體字

existed within fire and they were not hot, then one could not refer to it as fire. If they were in fact hot, then they would relinquish their own particular natures and would then all be referred to as fire.

If one were to claim that it is because they are so subtle that one is unable to perceive them, then that would be no different from their being entirely nonexistent therein. If it were the case that there was something coarse which could be gotten at, then one could know that there is actually something existing therein which is subtle. If there is nothing which is coarse therein, then there is nothing which is subtle therein, either.

On account of all sorts of cause and conditions such as these, the characteristics of earth cannot be gotten at. If it is the case that one cannot get at the characteristics of earth, then the characteristics of all other dharmas cannot be gotten at, either. Therefore all dharmas have this single characteristic [of inapprehensibility of signs].

16. Objection: Nonexistence of Aspects is itself an Aspect

Question: One should not claim that they are devoid of characteristics. Why? If all dharmas are devoid of characteristics, this is in itself a characteristic. If there were no "nonexistence of characteristics," then one could not refute the characteristics of all dharmas. How is this so? Because there would be no "nonexistence of characteristics." If this "nonexistence" characteristic does exist, then one ought not to say that all dharmas are devoid of characteristics.

17. Response: That is Only a Means for Refuting Aspects

Response: One employs the nonexistence of characteristics to refute the characteristics of dharmas. If there existed a "nonexistence of characteristics" characteristic, then one would fall into [a position affirming the existence of] the characteristics of dharmas. If one did not thereby enter into [a position affirming the existence of] the characteristics of dharmas, then it should not be the case that one questions the nonexistence of characteristics.

As it is employed as a universal refutation of the characteristics of dharmas it demolishes its own characteristics as well. This is analogous to a burning log already present in a fire which, after igniting all fuel added to it, incinerates itself as well. Thus it is that the ārya courses in signlessness. This is because the signlessness samādhi serves to demolish even the characteristic of nonexistence.

18. Additional Prajñā-Based Bodhisattva Contemplations

Also, the bodhisattva contemplates all dharmas as neither conjoined nor dispersed, as being without form, without shape, non-

无对无示无说一相。所谓无相。如是等诸法一相。云[3]何观种种相。一切法摄入二法中。所谓名色色无色可见不可见有对无对有漏无漏有为无为等。二百二法门如千难品中说。复次有二法。忍辱柔和。又二法亲敬供养。二施财施法施。二力慧分别力修道力。二具足戒具足正见具足。二相质直相柔软相。二法定智。二法明解[4]说。二法世间法第一义法。二法念巧[5]慧。二谛世谛第一义谛。二解脱待时解脱不坏心解脱。二种涅盘有馀涅盘无馀涅盘。二究竟事究竟愿究竟。二见知见断见。二具足义具足语具足。二法少欲知足。二法易养易满。二法法随法行。二智尽智无生智。

無對無示無說一相。所謂無相。如是等諸法一相。云[3]何觀種種相。一切法攝入二法中。所謂名色色無色可見不可見有對無對有漏無漏有為無為等。二百二法門如千難品中說。復次有二法。忍辱柔和。又二法親敬供養。二施財施法施。二力慧分別力修道力。二具足戒具足正見具足。二相質直相柔軟相。二法定智。二法明解[4]說。二法世間法第一義法。二法念巧[5]慧。二諦世諦第一義諦。二解脫待時解脫不壞心解脫。二種涅槃有餘涅槃無餘涅槃。二究竟事究竟願究竟。二見知見斷見。二具足義具足語具足。二法少欲知足。二法易養易滿。二法法隨法行。二智盡智無生智。

简体字　　　　　　　　　正體字

dual, as indemonstrable, as ineffable, and as having but a single characteristic, namely signlessness.

Discussions such as these speak in terms of a singular mark of dharmas. How is it that one contemplates all of the different sorts of marks possessed by dharmas?

a. Two-fold Categorizations

All dharmas may be subsumed within two-fold categorizations of dharmas, in particular: name and form; form and formless; visible and invisible, involving [sense-faculty–sense-object] opposition (*pratigha*) and not involving such opposition (*sapratigha*); possessing outflow impurities and being free of outflow impurities, conditioned and unconditioned, and so forth.[7] There are two hundred different two-fold dharma categorizations as discussed in the "Thousand Difficult Questions" chapter.

Additionally, there are the two-fold dharmas of patience and pliant harmoniousness. There are also: the two-fold dharmas of personal reverence and the making of offerings; the two types of giving, the giving of wealth and the giving of Dharma; the two powers, the power of wise analysis and the power of cultivation of the Path; the two completions, completeness in precepts and completeness in correct views; the two characteristics, the characteristic of straightforwardness and the characteristic of pliancy; the two dharmas of meditative concentration and wisdom; the two dharmas of knowing (*vidyā*) and liberation (*vimukti*); the two dharmas, worldly dharmas and dharmas of the supreme meaning; and the two dharmas of mindfulness and discerning wisdom.

There are also: the two truths, worldly truth and the truth of the supreme meaning; the two liberations, temporary liberation (*sāmayikī vimukti*) and indestructible liberation of mind (*akopya-ceto-vimukti*); the two kinds of nirvāṇa, nirvāṇa with residue and nirvāṇa without residue; the two types of ultimate fulfillment, ultimate fulfillment of endeavors and ultimate fulfillment of vows; the two types of seeing, seeing arrived at through knowledge and seeing arrived at through severance; two kinds of completeness, completeness in meaning and completeness in discourse; the two dharmas of having but few desires and knowing when enough is enough; the two dharmas of ease in nourishing and ease of fulfillment; the two dharmas of accordance with Dharma and implementation of Dharma; and the two types of knowledge, the knowledge of destruction and the knowledge of non-production. In a manner

如是等[6]分别无量二法门。复[7]次[8]知三道。见道修道无学道。三性断性离性灭性。三修戒修定修慧修。三菩提佛菩提辟支迦佛菩提声闻菩提。[9](更不复学智满足之名也)三乘佛乘辟支迦佛乘声闻乘。三归依佛法僧。三住梵住天住圣住。三增上自增上他增上法增上。诸佛三不护身业不护口业不护意业不护。三福处[10]布施持戒善心。三器杖闻器杖离欲器杖慧器杖。三轮变化轮示他心轮教化轮。三解脱门空解脱门无相解脱门无作解脱门。如是等无量三法门。复知四法。四念处四正懃四如意足四圣谛四圣种

简体字

如是等[6]分別無量二法門。復[7]次[8]知三道。見道修道無學道。三性斷性離性滅性。三修戒修定修慧修。三菩提佛菩提辟支迦佛菩提聲聞菩提。[9](更不復學智滿足之名也)三乘佛乘辟支迦佛乘聲聞乘。三歸依佛法僧。三住梵住天住聖住。三增上自增上他增上法增上。諸佛三不護身業不護口業不護意業不護。三福處[10]布施持戒善心。三器杖聞器杖離欲器杖慧器杖。三輪變化輪示他心輪教化輪。三解脫門空解脫門無相解脫門無作解脫門。如是等無量三法門。復知四法。四念處四正懃四如意足四聖諦四聖種

正體字

such as this, one may make distinctions with regard to an incalculable number of two-fold gateways to Dharma.

b. Three-fold Dharma Categorizations

Furthermore, he knows: the three paths consisting of the path of seeing, the path of meditation (lit. "path of cultivation"), and the path of those beyond training; the three natures consisting of the nature realized through severance, the nature realized through abandonment, and the nature realized through cessation; the three trainings consisting of training in the moral-virtue prohibitions, training in meditative concentration, and training in wisdom; the three types of bodhi consisting of the bodhi of the Buddhas, the bodhi of the Pratyekabuddhas, and the bodhi of the Śrāvaka-disciples (Chinese textual note: This refers to being beyond further training and being complete in wisdom.); the Three Vehicles consisting of the Buddha Vehicle, the Pratyekabuddha Vehicle, and the Śrāvaka-disciple Vehicle; the Three Refuges consisting of refuge in the Buddha, refuge in the Dharma and refuge in the Sangha; and the three classes of [meditative] abodes consisting of those correlating to the [four-immeasurables] abodes of Brahmā, those correlating to the [dhyāna-heaven] abodes of the gods, and the [affliction-free] abodes of the Āryas; the three bases of authority consisting of authority rooted in oneself, authority based on others, and authority based in the Dharma.

He also knows: the three types of unguardedness on the part of buddhas consisting of unguardedness with respect to actions of the body, unguardedness with respect to actions of the mouth, and unguardedness with respect to actions of the mind; the three bases for the production of merit consisting of giving, upholding of moral precepts, and cultivation of the wholesome mind; the three staves consisting of the staff of listening, the staff of abandoning desires, and the staff of wisdom; the three modes (lit. "wheels") consisting of the mode of manifesting supernatural transformations, the mode of reading others' minds, and the mode of teaching and transforming beings; and the three gates to liberation consisting of the emptiness gate to liberation, the signlessness gate to liberation, and the wishlessness gate to liberation. There are an incalculable number of three-fold gateways to Dharma such as these.

c. Four-fold Dharma Categorizations

Additionally, he knows the four-fold dharmas: the four station of mindfulness; the four right efforts; the four foundations of psychic power; the four truths of the Āryas; the four lineage-bases of the

四沙门果四知[11]四信四道四
摄法四依四通达善根四道四
天人轮四坚法四无所畏四无
量心。如是等无量四法门。
复知五无学众五出性五解脱
处五根五力五大施五智五阿
那含五净居天处五治[12]道五
智三昧五圣分[13]支三昧五
如法语道。如是等无量五法
门。复知六舍法六爱敬法六
神通六种阿罗汉六地见谛道
六随顺念六三昧六定六波罗
蜜。如是等无量六法门。复
知七觉意七财七依止七想定
七妙法七知七善人去处七净
七财福七非财福七助定法。
如是等无量七法门。复知八
圣道分八背舍八胜处八大人
念八种精进八丈夫八阿罗汉
力。如是等无量八法门。

四沙門果四知[11]四信四道四
攝法四依四通達善根四道四
天人輪四堅法四無所畏四無
量心。如是等無量四法門。
復知五無學眾五出性五解脫
處五根五力五大施五智五阿
那含五淨居天處五治[12]道五
智三昧五聖分[13]支三昧五
如法語道。如是等無量五法
門。復知六捨法六愛敬法六
神通六種阿羅漢六地見諦道
六隨順念六三昧六定六波羅
蜜。如是等無量六法門。復
知七覺意七財七依止七想定
七妙法七知七善人去處七淨
七財福七非財福七助定法。
如是等無量七法門。復知八
聖道分八背捨八勝處八大人
念八種精進八丈夫八阿羅漢
力。如是等無量八法門。

简体字   正體字

Āryas; the four fruits of the śramaṇa; the four knowledges; the four faiths; the four paths; the four means of attraction; the four reliances; the four roots of goodness conducive to penetrating understanding; [an additional set of] four paths; the four "wheels" of gods and men; the four dharmas in which one develops solidity;[8] the four fearlessnesses; and the four immeasurable minds. There are an incalculable number of four-fold gateways to Dharma such as these.

d. Five-fold Dharma Categorizations

Also, he knows the five groups of those beyond training, the five transcendent natures, the five bases of liberation, the five root-faculties, the five powers, the five types of great giving, the five types of knowledges, the five types of anāgāmin, the five abodes of the pure-dwelling gods, the five types of counteractive paths, the five knowledge-based samādhis, the five-component samādhis of the Āryas, and the five methods of discourse according with Dharma. There are an incalculable number of five-fold gateways to Dharma such as these.

e. Six-fold Dharma Categorizations

Furthermore, he knows the six dharmas of relinquishment, the six dharmas of affectionate respect, the six superknowledges, the six kinds of arhats, the six stations on the path of seeing the truth, the six recollections, the six samadhis, the six absorptions, and the six *pāramitās*. There are an incalculable number of six-fold gateways to Dharma such as these.

f. Seven-fold Dharma Categorizations

Additionally, he knows the seven limbs of enlightenment, the seven forms of wealth, the seven supports, the seven absorptions associated with thought, the seven sublime dharmas, the seven knowledges, the seven destinies of good people, the seven forms of purity, the seven forms of merit associated with wealth, the seven forms of merit not associated with wealth, and the seven absorption-assisting dharmas. There are an incalculable number of seven-fold gateways to Dharma such as these.

g. Eight-fold Dharma Categorizations

Also, he knows the eight-fold path of the Āryas, the eight liberations, the eight bases of ascendancy, the eight realizations of great men, the eight forms of vigor, the eight types of great men, and the eight powers of the arhat. There are an incalculable number of eight-fold gateways to Dharma such as these.

复知九次第定九名色等[14]减[15]（从名[16]色至生死为[17]九）九无漏智[18]得尽智故除等智也。九无漏地[19]六禅三无色九地思惟道

[0195b24] 如是等无量九法门。复知十无[20]学法十想十智十一切入十善大地佛十力。如是等无量十法门。复知十一助圣道法。复知十二因缘法。复知十三出法。十四变化心。十五心见谛道。十六安那般那行。十[21]七圣行。[22]十八不共法。十九离地[23]思惟道中一百六十二道。[24]能破烦恼贼。[25]一百七十八沙门果。八十九有为果。八十九无为果。如是等种种无量异相法。生灭增减得失垢净悉能知之。菩萨摩诃萨知是诸法已。能令诸法入自性空而于诸法无所着。过声闻辟支佛地。入菩萨位中。

简体字

復知九次第定九名色等[14]減[15]（從名[16]色至生死為[17]九）九無漏智[18]得盡智故除等智也。九無漏地[19]六禪三無色九地思惟道

[0195b24] 如是等無量九法門。復知十無[20]學法十想十智十一切入十善大地佛十力。如是等無量十法門。復知十一助聖道法。復知十二因緣法。復知十三出法。十四變化心。十五心見諦道。十六安那般那行。十[21]七聖行。[22]十八不共法。十九離地[23]思惟道中一百六十二道。[24]能破煩惱賊。[25]一百七十八沙門果。八十九有為果。八十九無為果。如是等種種無量異相法。生滅增減得失垢淨悉能知之。菩薩摩訶薩知是諸法已。能令諸法入自性空而於諸法無所著。過聲聞辟支佛地。入菩薩位中。

正體字

h. Nine-fold Dharma Categorizations

Furthermore, he knows the nine sequential absorptions, the nine "reduced-format" [links in the chain of causality from] name-and-form and so forth (Chinese textual note: "From name-and-form to birth and death makes nine."), the nine knowledges free of outflow impurities, this because, in gaining the knowledge associated with cessation, one eliminates the "equal" knowledge [from among the ten types knowledge], the nine stations free of outflow impurities, six dhyāna-related stations together with three formless absorptions, and the nine stations on the path of meditation.[9] There are an incalculable number of nine-fold gateways to Dharma such as these.

i. Ten-fold Dharma Categorizations

Additionally, he knows the ten dharmas of those beyond study, the ten reflections, the ten knowledges, the ten universal bases, the ten goods, the ten grounds,[10] and the ten powers of a buddha. There are an incalculable number of ten-fold gateways to Dharma such as these.

j. Additional Dharma Categorizations

He also knows the eleven dharmas which assist the path of an ārya, also knows the dharma of the twelve causes and conditions, also knows the thirteen transcendent dharmas, the fourteen transformative minds, the fifteen mental events on the path of seeing the truths, the sixteen-fold practice of *ānāpāna*, the seventeen practices of the Āryas, the eighteen dharmas exclusive to the Buddha, the nineteen stations of abandonment, the one hundred and sixty-two path-events on the path of meditation which are able to demolish the insurgents of the afflictions, the one hundred and seventy-eight fruits of the śramaṇa, [comprised of] the eighty-nine conditioned fruits and the eighty-nine unconditioned fruits. There are an incalculable number of dharmas such as these which possess differing characteristics. [Whether they are] produced or destroyed, increased or decreased, conducing to gain or loss, or are pure or impure, he is able to utterly know them all.

19. All Such Contemplation Objects Are Reduced to Emptiness

After the bodhisattva, *mahāsattva* has come to know these dharmas, he is able to cause all dharmas to enter into the emptiness of inherent existence. And so it is he retains no attachment to any dharma.

F. The Bodhisattva's Extensive Adoption of Teaching Expedients

He goes beyond the stations of the Śrāvaka-disciples and the Pratyekabuddhas and enters into the bodhisattva position

入菩萨位中已。以大悲怜愍故。以方便力分别诸法种种名字。度众生令得三乘。譬如工巧之人。以药力故。能令银变为金金变为银。问曰。若诸法性真空。云何分别诸法种种名字。何以不但说真空性。答曰。菩萨摩诃萨。不说空是可得可着。若可得可着。不应说诸法种种异相。不可得空者无所罣碍。若有罣碍是为可得。非不可得空。若菩萨摩诃萨。知不可得空。还能分别诸法。怜愍度脱众生。是为般若波罗蜜力。取要言之诸法实相。是般若波罗蜜。问曰。一切世俗经书。及九十六种出家经中。皆说有诸法实相。又声闻法三藏中。亦有诸法实相。何以不名为般若波罗蜜。而此经中诸法实相。独名般若波罗蜜。

入菩薩位中已。以大悲憐愍故。以方便力分別諸法種種名字。度眾生令得三乘。譬如工巧之人。以藥力故。能令銀變為金金變為銀。問曰。若諸法性真空。云何分別諸法種種名字。何以不但說真空性。答曰。菩薩摩訶薩。不說空是可得可著。若可得可著。不應說諸法種種異相。不可得空者無所罣礙。若有罣礙是為可得。非不可得空。若菩薩摩訶薩。知不可得空。還能分別諸法。憐愍度脫眾生。是為般若波羅蜜力。取要言之諸法實相。是般若波羅蜜。問曰。一切世俗經書。及九十六種出家經中。皆說有諸法實相。又聲聞法三藏中。亦有諸法實相。何以不名為般若波羅蜜。而此經中諸法實相。獨名般若波羅蜜。

简体字   正體字

(*samyaktva niyāma*). After he has entered into the bodhisattva position, on account of great compassion and pity for beings, he employs the power of expedients to explain the distinctions implicit in the names of the various dharmas and thus brings beings across to liberation, causing them to succeed in gaining the Three Vehicles. In doing this, he is like a skillful craftsman who, on account of the power of herbal potions, is able to cause silver to change into gold and gold to change into silver.

    1. Objection: If Empty, Why Make Distinctions?

Question: If it is the case that the nature of all dharmas is true emptiness, why would he make distinctions among all of the various names of dharmas? Why would he not just speak of the true emptiness?

    2. Response: Abiding in Emptiness, One Refrains from Attachment

Response: The bodhisattva, *mahāsattva* does not speak of emptiness as something which may be obtained or attached to. If it could be obtained or attached to, he should not then discuss all of the various sorts of different characteristics. As for the emptiness which cannot be obtained, one remains free of any hangups or obstructions with respect to it. If there were any hangups or obstructions, then it would be something which could be obtained and thus it would not be the emptiness which cannot be obtained.

    In the case of the bodhisattva, *mahāsattva*, he has realized the emptiness which cannot be obtained and yet is still able to make distinctions with respect to dharmas, is still able to feel compassion for beings, and is still able to take them across to liberation. This is the power of *prajñāpāramitā*. To state it in a way which grasps the essential point: It is [direct and correct perception of] the true character of dharmas which constitutes the essence of *prajñāpāramitā*.

    G. On the Exclusive Definition of *Prajñāpāramitā*
    1. Objection: Why Such Exclusivity in Defining *Prajñāpāramitā*?

Question: All of the worldly and common classics as well as all of the ninety-six types of monastic scriptures claim that they embody [the correct understanding of] the true character of dharmas. Additionally, the three-fold canon of the Śrāvaka-disciples' Dharma also is held to embody [the direct and correct perception of] the true character of dharmas. Why then do they not also qualify as embodying *prajñāpāramitā*? Why is it claimed here that the true character of dharmas as presented in this sutra is alone in qualifying as embodying *prajñāpāramitā*?

答曰。世俗经书中。为安国全家身命寿乐故非实。外道出家堕邪见法中。心爱着故是亦非实。声闻法中虽有四谛。以无常苦空无我观诸法实相。以智慧不具足不利。不能为一切众生。不为得佛法故。虽有实智慧。不名般若波罗蜜。如说佛入出诸三昧。舍利弗等乃[26]至不闻其名。何况能知。何以故。诸阿罗汉辟支佛初发心时。无大愿无大慈大悲。不求一切诸功德。不供养一切三世十方佛。不审谛求知诸法实相。但欲求脱老病死苦[196-1]故。诸菩萨从初发心弘大誓愿有大慈悲。求一切诸功德。供养一切三世十方诸佛。有大利智求诸法实相。除种种诸观。所谓净观不净观常观无常观乐观苦观空观

简体字

答曰。世俗經書中。為安國全家身命壽樂故非實。外道出家墮邪見法中。心愛著故是亦非實。聲聞法中雖有四諦。以無常苦空無我觀諸法實相。以智慧不具足不利。不能為一切眾生。不為得佛法故。雖有實智慧。不名般若波羅蜜。如說佛入出諸三昧。舍利弗等乃[26]至不聞其名。何況能知。何以故。諸阿羅漢辟支佛初發心時。無大願無大慈大悲。不求一切諸功德。不供養一切三世十方佛。不審諦求知諸法實相。但欲求脫老病死苦[196-1]故。諸菩薩從初發心弘大誓願有大慈悲。求一切諸功德。供養一切三世十方諸佛。有大利智求諸法實相。除種種諸觀。所謂淨觀不淨觀常觀無常觀樂觀苦觀空觀

正體字

2. RESPONSE: DUE TO WORLDLINESS, WRONG VIEWS, AND SHORTCOMINGS

Response: The worldly and common classics are not reflective of genuine reality because they are dedicated to the establishment of the state, the preservation of the family, the person, longevity, and pleasure. Because the non-Buddhist monastics fall into the dharmas of erroneous views whereby their minds are affectionately attached, they, too, are not reflective of genuine reality.

Although the Dharma of the Śrāvaka-disciples does contain the four truths and although they do employ impermanence, suffering, emptiness, and non-self in the contemplation of the true character of dharmas, because their wisdom is incomplete and is not acutely sharp, they remain unable to act on behalf of all beings. Although they do possess genuine wisdom, because it is not employed for the sake of succeeding in the dharma of buddhahood, it does not qualify as "*prajñāpāramitā*."

For example, Sariputra and the others have not even heard the names of the various samādhis which the Buddha enters and exits. How much the less have they been able to know them directly? Why is this the case? When the Arhats and the Pratyekabuddhas first generated their resolve, they had no great vows and they had no great kindness or great compassion. They have not sought to create all forms of merit. They have not made offerings to all of the Buddhas of the three periods of time throughout the ten directions. They have not sought to know the true character of dharmas in a way which utterly fathoms the truth. This is because they have sought only to gain liberation from the sufferings of aging, sickness, and death.

H. THE DISTINGUISHING FEATURES OF THE BODHISATTVA'S PRACTICE

From the time they first formulated the resolve to realize bodhi, the bodhisattvas have possessed vast and magnificent vows. They have possessed the great kindness and compassion, have sought to create all forms of merit, and have made offerings to all of the Buddhas of the three periods of time throughout the ten directions. They possess great sharp wisdom with which they have sought [to fathom] the true character of dharmas.

They have dispensed with all of the various kinds of contemplations such as the so-called contemplation of purity, the contemplation of impurity, the contemplation of permanence, the contemplation of impermanence, the contemplation of blissfulness, the contemplation of suffering, the contemplation of emptiness, the

实观我观无我观。舍如是等
妄见心力诸观。但观外缘中
实相。非净非不净非常非非
常非乐非苦非空非实非我非
无我。如是等诸观不着不得
世俗法故。非第一[2]义周遍
清净不破不坏。诸圣人行
处。是名般若波罗蜜。问
曰。已知般若体相是无相无
得法。行者云何能得是法。
答曰。佛以方便说法。行者
如所说行则得。譬如绝崖嶮
道假梯能上。又如深水因船
得[3]渡。初发心菩萨。若从
佛闻若从弟子闻若于经中
闻。一切法毕竟空。无有决
定性可取可着。第一实法灭
诸戏论。涅盘相是最安隐。
我欲度脱一切众生。

實觀我觀無我觀。捨如是等
妄見心力諸觀。但觀外緣中
實相。非淨非不淨非常非非
常非樂非苦非空非實非我非
無我。如是等諸觀不著不得
世俗法故。非第一[2]義周遍
清淨不破不壞。諸聖人行
處。是名般若波羅蜜。問
曰。已知般若體相是無相無
得法。行者云何能得是法。
答曰。佛以方便說法。行者
如所說行則得。譬如絕崖嶮
道假梯能上。又如深水因船
得[3]渡。初發心菩薩。若從
佛聞若從弟子聞若於經中
聞。一切法畢竟空。無有決
定性可取可著。第一實法滅
諸戲論。涅槃相是最安隱。
我欲度脫一切眾生。

简体字

正體字

contemplation of substantiality, the contemplation of self, and the contemplation of the absence of self.

They have relinquished all such contemplations as these which involve the powers of a mind beset by erroneous views, which merely contemplate the true character [of dharmas] in the context of outward conditions, and which [focus on concepts such as] neither pure nor impure, neither permanent nor impermanent, neither blissful nor suffering, neither empty nor substantial, and neither self nor devoid of self.

They have refrained from attachment to any such contemplations as these and have refrained from couching their realizations in them, this because [those contemplations] are inherently linked to mundane worldly dharmas. [Those contemplations] do not correspond to the supreme meaning with its universally pervasive purity, irrefutability, and infallibility, [and hence they do not correspond to] that place in which the Āryas course. These are the considerations which determine what qualifies as "*prajñāpāramitā.*"

1. QUESTION: HOW THEN DOES ONE REALIZE *PRAJÑĀPĀRAMITĀ*?

Question: We already know that the substance and characteristics of *prajña* constitute a dharma which is devoid of characteristics and which cannot be "obtained." How then is the practitioner able to succeed in "obtaining" realization of this Dharma?

2. RESPONSE: PRACTICE IN ACCORD WITH THE SKILLFUL-MEANS INSTRUCTIONS

Response: The Buddha uses skillful means to explain the Dharma. If the practitioner practices in a way which accords with those explanations, he will succeed in obtaining realization of it.

3. ANALOGIES: ASCENDING A CLIFF; CROSSING THE WATERS

This is comparable to being faced with a dangerous path up a precipitous cliff. If one follows the steps, one will in fact be able to ascend it. It is also just as with a deep body of water. It is through the use of a boat that one succeeds in crossing on over it.

I. THE BODHISATTVA'S ADOPTION OF SIX-PERFECTIONS PRACTICE

Whether he has learned from the Buddha, his disciples, or the Sutras, the bodhisattva newly established in his resolve [should contemplate] thus: "All dharmas are ultimately empty and devoid of any fixed nature amenable to either grasping or attachment. The dharma of supreme reality puts an end to all frivolous discourse. Nirvāṇa has the character of being the most conducive to peace and security. It is my aspiration to bring all beings across to liberation.

云何独取涅盘。我今福德智慧神通力未具足故。不能引导众生。当具足是诸因缘。行布施等五波罗蜜。财施因缘故得大富。法施因缘故得[4]大智慧。能以此二施引导贫穷众生令入三乘道。以持戒因缘[5]故。生人天尊贵。自脱三恶道。亦令众生免三恶道。以忍辱因缘故。障瞋恚毒得身色端政威德第一。见者欢喜敬信心伏。况复说法。以精进因缘故。能破今世后世福德道法懈怠。得金刚身不动心。以是身心破凡夫憍慢。令得涅盘。以禅定因缘故。破散乱心离五欲罪。乐能为众生说离[6]欲法。禅是般若波罗蜜依止处。

简体字

云何獨取涅槃。我今福德智慧神通力未具足故。不能引導眾生。當具足是諸因緣。行布施等五波羅蜜。財施因緣故得大富。法施因緣故得[4]大智慧。能以此二施引導貧窮眾生令入三乘道。以持戒因緣[5]故。生人天尊貴。自脫三惡道。亦令眾生免三惡道。以忍辱因緣故。障瞋恚毒得身色端政威德第一。見者歡喜敬信心伏。況復說法。以精進因緣故。能破今世後世福德道法懈怠。得金剛身不動心。以是身心破凡夫憍慢。令得涅槃。以禪定因緣故。破散亂心離五欲罪。樂能為眾生說離[6]欲法。禪是般若波羅蜜依止處。

正體字

How then could I seize upon nirvāṇa for myself alone? Because the power of my merit, wisdom and superknowledges is not yet complete, I am as yet unable to lead beings forth. I should therefore perfect these causes and conditions by cultivating giving as well as the other five *pāramitās*."

1. The Practice of Giving and Its Effects

On account of the causes and conditions associated with the giving of material wealth, one gains great riches. On account of the causes and conditions associated with the giving of Dharma, one gains great wisdom. One is able then to employ these two types of giving to lead forth poor and destitute beings and cause them to enter the path of the Three Vehicles.

2. The Practice of Moral Virtue and Its Effects

On account of the causes and conditions associated with upholding the precepts, one is reborn among men or gods as one who is honored and noble. And one succeeds oneself in becoming liberated from the three wretched destinies while also causing other beings to avoid the three wretched destinies.

3. The Practice of Patience and Its Effects

On account of the causes and conditions associated with patience, one blocks off the poison of hatred, gains a physical body which is handsome, and becomes foremost in awesome virtue. Whosoever sees such a person becomes delighted, respectful, faithful, and humble in mind. One is then well able to speak Dharma for their benefit.

4. The Practice of Vigor and Its Effects

On account of the causes and conditions associated with vigor, one is able to destroy that laziness with respect to the Dharma of the Path [which commonly accompanies] merit-based karmic rewards in the present and future lifetimes. One succeeds then in obtaining the *vajra* body and an unmoving mind. One employs this body and mind to shatter the arrogance typical of the common person, thereby bringing about the realization of nirvāṇa.

5. The Practice of Dhyāna and Its Effects

On account of the causes and conditions associated with dhyāna, one demolishes the scattered mind, separates from the offenses associated with the five desires, and finds happiness in being able to explain for beings the dharma of transcending desire. Dhyāna is the station upon which *prajñāpāramitā* depends and in which it

依是禅般若波罗蜜自然而生。如经中说。比丘一心专定能观诸法实相。复次知欲界中多以悭贪罪业闭诸善门。行檀波罗蜜时。破是二事开诸善门。欲令常开故。行十善道。尸罗波罗蜜未得禅定智慧。未离欲故。破尸罗波罗蜜。以是故行忍辱。知上三事能开福门。又知是福德果报无常。天人[7]中受乐还复堕苦。厌是无常福德故。求实相般若波罗蜜。是云何当得。必以一心乃当可得。如贯龙王宝珠。一心观察能不触龙。则[8]得价直阎浮提。一心禅定除却五欲五盖。欲得心乐大用精进。是故次忍辱说精进波罗蜜。

依是禪般若波羅蜜自然而生。如經中說。比丘一心專定能觀諸法實相。復次知欲界中多以慳貪罪業閉諸善門。行檀波羅蜜時。破是二事開諸善門。欲令常開故。行十善道。尸羅波羅蜜未得禪定智慧。未離欲故。破尸羅波羅蜜。以是故行忍辱。知上三事能開福門。又知是福德果報無常。天人[7]中受樂還復墮苦。厭是無常福德故。求實相般若波羅蜜。是云何當得。必以一心乃當可得。如貫龍王寶珠。一心觀察能不觸龍。則[8]得價直閻浮提。一心禪定除却五欲五蓋。欲得心樂大用精進。是故次忍辱說精進波羅蜜。

简体字　　　　　　　　　　　正體字

abides. It is in reliance upon dhyāna that *prajñāpāramitā* is spontaneously produced. This is as explained in the Sutras: "The bhikshu singlemindedly devoting himself to meditative concentration becomes able thereby to contemplate the true character of dharmas."

6. THE FIRST THREE PERFECTIONS AS CRUCIAL TO GAINING MERIT

Additionally, one realizes that, within the desire realm, the gateway to all forms of goodness is for the most part closed on account of the offense karma associated with miserliness and greed. When one cultivates *dāna pāramitā*, one demolishes these two phenomena and opens up the gateway to all forms of goodness. Out of a desire to keep it open forever, one cultivates the way of the ten good karmic deeds.

As for [the cultivation of] the *pāramitā* of *śīla* (the perfection of moral virtue), when one has not yet gained dhyāna absorption or wisdom, because one has not yet left behind desire, one is liable to destroy the *pāramitā* of *śīla*. For this reason, one engages in the cultivation of patience. When one develops a knowing awareness of these three endeavors [devoted to giving, moral virtue, and patience], one becomes able to open up the gateway to merit.

7. THE FUTILITY OF FOCUSING SOLELY ON MERIT

One additionally knows that the rewards gained as effects from these karmically meritorious actions are impermanent. One may enjoy the bliss among gods and men but then may once again fall back down into suffering. On account of having had one's fill of these impermanent rewards for meritorious deeds, one then seeks to realize the *prajñāpāramitā* [which correctly perceives] the true character [of dharmas].

8. THE FACTORS CRUCIAL TO REALIZING *PRAJÑĀPĀRAMITĀ*

a. THE CLOSE RELATIONSHIP BETWEEN VIGOR, DHYĀNA, AND *PRAJÑĀPĀRAMITĀ*

How, then does one go about bringing it to realization? It is essential that one employ single-mindedness. Then and only then will one be able to gain it. This is analogous to seizing the precious pearl of the dragon king. One must be single-mindedly observant and must also be able to avoid touching the dragon. If one can succeed in this, then one gains something which is as valuable as [the entire continent of] Jambudvīpa.

In one's single-minded devotion to dhyāna absorption, one gets rid of the five desires and the five hindrances. Striving to succeed in gaining the bliss of the mind, one makes great use of vigor. It is for this reason that, after patience, it is the *pāramitā* of vigor which

如经中说。行者端身直坐系念在前。专精求定正使肌骨枯朽终不[9]懈退。是故精进修禅。若有财而施不足为难。畏堕恶道恐失好名。持戒忍辱亦不为难。以是故上三度中不说精进。今为般若波罗蜜实相从心求定。是事难故应须精进。如是行能得般若波罗蜜。问曰。要行五波罗蜜然后得般若波罗蜜。亦有行一二波罗蜜。得般若[10]波罗蜜耶。答曰。诸波罗蜜有二种。一者一波罗蜜中相应随行。具诸波罗蜜。二者随时别行波罗蜜。多者受名。譬如四大共合

如經中說。行者端身直坐繫念在前。專精求定正使肌骨枯朽終不[9]懈退。是故精進修禪。若有財而施不足為難。畏墮惡道恐失好名。持戒忍辱亦不為難。以是故上三度中不說精進。今為般若波羅蜜實相從心求定。是事難故應須精進。如是行能得般若波羅蜜。問曰。要行五波羅蜜然後得般若波羅蜜。亦有行一二波羅蜜。得般若[10]波羅蜜耶。答曰。諸波羅蜜有二種。一者一波羅蜜中相應隨行。具諸波羅蜜。二者隨時別行波羅蜜。多者受名。譬如四大共合

简体字

正體字

is next explained. This is as stated in the Sutras: "The practitioner makes his body erect and sits straight up with his attention fixed directly before him. He devotes himself exclusively to seeking meditative concentration, doing so with such determination that, even if he were to cause his own flesh and bones to become withered and emaciated, he would still never desist or retreat from the endeavor."

b. WHY VIGOR ISN'T EMPHASIZED WITH THE FIRST THREE PERFECTIONS

It is for this reason that one practices vigor as one pursues the cultivation of dhyāna. If one happened to possess wealth and then engage in giving, this would not be sufficient to constitute any real difficulty. If one happened to fear falling into the wretched destinies or if one happened to feel anxiety about the possibility of losing one's fine reputation and then, based on that, one decided to engage in observance of the moral precepts or in the practice of patience, this would not really qualify as something of any particular difficulty, either. It is for this reason that, within the sphere of the first three of the perfections discussed above, one does not yet speak of the practice of vigor.

c. WHY VIGOR IS ESSENTIAL TO REALIZATION OF *PRAJÑĀPĀRAMITĀ*

Now, however, one is seeking to develop meditative concentration from within his own mind, this for the sake of *prajñāpāramitā* and [perception of] the true character [of dharmas]. Because this is an endeavor which is so difficult, one must realize that vigor is essential to success. If one then cultivates in this manner, one will become able to gain the realization of *prajñāpāramitā*.

d. QUESTION: ARE ALL FIVE *PĀRAMITĀS* PREREQUISITES FOR *PRAJÑĀPĀRAMITĀ*?

Question: Is it essential to cultivate the other five *pāramitās* after which, only then one gains realization of *prajñāpāramitā*? Or might it also be possible that one could cultivate only one or two of the other *pāramitās* and then succeed in realizing *prajñāpāramitā*?

e. RESPONSE: NOT FIXED, AS EACH SUBSUMES ALL OTHERS

Response: With respect to the *pāramitās*, there are two types [of cultivation]. As for the first, within a practice which corresponds to and accords with a single *pāramitā*, there are contained all of the other *pāramitās*.

As for the second approach, one accords with the time, and, [as appropriate], specifically cultivates a given *pāramitā*. [One's practice] then takes on the name of the one which currently predominates. This is analogous to the case with the four great elements when

虽不相离以多者为名。相应
随行者。一波罗蜜中具五波
罗蜜是不离五波罗蜜。得般
若波罗蜜。随时得名者。或
因一因[11]一得般若波罗蜜。
若人发阿耨多罗三藐三菩提
心布施。是时求布施相。不
一不异非常非无常非有非无
等。如[12]破布施中说。因布
施实相解。一切法亦如是。
是名因布施得般若波罗蜜。
或有持戒不恼众生心无有
悔。若取相生着则起诤[13]
竞。是人虽先不瞋众生。于
法有憎爱心故而瞋众生。是
故若欲不恼众生。当行诸法
平等。若分别是罪是无罪则
非行尸罗

简体字

雖不相離以多者為名。相應
隨行者。一波羅蜜中具五波
羅蜜是不離五波羅蜜。得般
若波羅蜜。隨時得名者。或
因一因[11]一得般若波羅蜜。
若人發阿耨多羅三藐三菩提
心布施。是時求布施相。不
一不異非常非無常非有非無
等。如[12]破布施中說。因布
施實相解。一切法亦如是。
是名因布施得般若波羅蜜。
或有持戒不惱眾生心無有
悔。若取相生著則起諍[13]
競。是人雖先不瞋眾生。於
法有憎愛心故而瞋眾生。是
故若欲不惱眾生。當行諸法
平等。若分別是罪是無罪則
非行尸羅

正體字

they exist in combination. Then, although they are not separated from each other, it is the one which predominates in any given circumstance which determines the designation which is applied.

In the case of the practice which corresponds to and accords with a single *pāramitā*, the other five *pāramitās* are contained right within it. In a case such as that, one does not abandon the other five *pāramitās* as one proceeds with acquisition of *prajñāpāramitā*. In the circumstance where the designation corresponds to the particular practice adopted at any given time, it may be that it is on account of one particular [*pāramitā*] or on account of two[11] [*pāramitās*] that one succeeds in the acquisition of *prajñāpāramitā*.

f. REALIZATION OF *PRAJÑĀPĀRAMITĀ* THROUGH GIVING

Take for example the case of one who has set his mind on *anuttara-samyak-saṃbodhi* and has thus embarked on the cultivation of giving, he may seek at this time to discover just what constitutes the characteristics of giving, only to find then that those characteristics are neither singular nor different, that they are neither permanent nor impermanent, that they are neither existent nor nonexistent, and so forth. This is as discussed in the section on the analysis of the components of giving.[12]

Based on his understanding of the true character [of the dharmas involved in practicing the perfection] of giving, he then comes to understand all dharmas in this very same way. This is what is meant by achieving realization of *prajñāpāramitā* (the perfection of wisdom) through one's cultivation of the practice of giving.

g. REALIZATION OF *PRAJÑĀPĀRAMITĀ* THROUGH MORAL VIRTUE

Or perhaps in other cases there are those who undertake the observance of the moral precepts, refrain from tormenting beings, and who then find that the mind becomes free of regrets. If, in such a case, one were to seize upon the specific features [of the precepts] and then become attached to them, then one would be prone to initiate disputes. Such a person, although initially not cherishing any hatred towards beings, may consequently engender hatred towards other beings on account of thoughts of hatred and affection linked to particular dharmas.

Therefore, if one desires to refrain from tormenting beings, one should cultivate a stance of uniformly-equal regard in the midst of all dharmas. If, [failing to do so], one makes discriminations whereby one regards this as an offense and regards that as being free of offense, then this is not a practice which accords with *śīla*

波罗蜜。何以故。憎罪爱不
罪。心则自高还堕恼众生道
中。是故菩萨。观罪者不罪
者心无憎爱。如是观者。是
为但行尸罗波罗蜜。得般若
波罗蜜。菩萨作是念若不得
法忍则不能常忍。一切众生
未有逼迫能忍。苦来切已则
不能忍。譬如囚畏杖楚而就
死苦。以是因缘故。当生法
忍。无有打者骂[14]者亦无受
者。但从先世颠倒果报因缘
故。名为受。是时不分别是
忍事忍。[15]法者深入毕竟空
故。是名法忍。得是法忍。
常不复瞋恼众生。法忍相应
慧。是般若波罗蜜。精进常
在一切善法中。能成就一切
善法。若智慧筹量分别诸
法。通达法性。是时精进助
成智慧。

简体字

波羅蜜。何以故。憎罪愛不
罪。心則自高還墮惱眾生道
中。是故菩薩。觀罪者不罪
者心無憎愛。如是觀者。是
為但行尸羅波羅蜜。得般若
波羅蜜。菩薩作是念若不得
法忍則不能常忍。一切眾生
未有逼迫能忍。苦來切已則
不能忍。譬如囚畏杖楚而就
死苦。以是因緣故。當生法
忍。無有打者罵[14]者亦無受
者。但從先世顛倒果報因緣
故。名為受。是時不分別是
忍事忍。[15]法者深入畢竟空
故。是名法忍。得是法忍。
常不復瞋惱眾生。法忍相應
慧。是般若波羅蜜。精進常
在一切善法中。能成就一切
善法。若智慧籌量分別諸
法。通達法性。是時精進助
成智慧。

正體字

pāramitā. Why is this so? It is because, if one detests offenses and feels affection for the absence of offenses, then one elevates oneself and falls yet again into the path of tormenting other beings.

Therefore, when the bodhisattva contemplates those who commit offenses and those who do not commit offenses, his mind remains free of both detestation and affection. If one carries on one's contemplations in this fashion, this is an instance of the singular practice *śīla pāramitā* resulting in the realization of *prajñāpāramitā*.

h. REALIZATION OF *PRAJÑĀPĀRAMITĀ* THROUGH PATIENCE

The bodhisattva takes up this contemplation: "If one fails to acquire the patience with respect to dharmas, then he will not be able to be constant in his practice of patience. There has not otherwise yet been a being who has been able to maintain patience when subjected to coercive force. If it comes to the point where one's agony becomes intense, then one becomes unable to endure it any longer." This is analogous to the circumstance of a convict who, terrorized by beatings, prefers the suffering of death [by suicide].

It is for this reason that one must develop the patience with respect to dharmas. [Once this patience has been perfected], there no longer exists any being who physically beats or curses someone. Nor does there exist anyone undergoing such acts. It is solely on account of past-life actions based on inverted views producing [present-life] karmic retribution that one speaks of "undergoing" [such abuses].

At this point, one no longer makes any such discriminations whereby there exists anyone who possesses patience with respect to such circumstances which might require patience. As for patience with respect to dharmas, it is on account of having deeply entered into their ultimate emptiness that it then qualifies as "patience with respect to dharmas." When one acquires this patience with respect to dharmas, one is never again prone to becoming hateful towards other beings. That wisdom which corresponds to the "patience with respect to dharmas" is just this "*prajñāpāramitā*."

i. REALIZATION OF *PRAJÑĀPĀRAMITĀ* THROUGH VIGOR

As for vigor, one constantly abides in the midst of good dharmas and is able to bring all good dharmas to completion. In an instance where one employs wisdom to analyze and make distinctions with respect to dharmas, one then develops a penetrating understanding of the nature of dharmas. It is at this point that vigor then serves to assist the realization of wisdom.

又知精进实相离身心如实不动。如是精进能生般若波罗蜜。馀精进如幻如梦。虚诳非实是故不说。若深心摄念。能如实见诸法实相。诸法实相者。不可以见闻念知能得。何以故。六情六尘皆是虚诳因缘果报。是中所知所见皆亦虚诳。是虚诳知都不可信。所可信者。唯有诸佛于阿僧只劫所得实相智慧。以是智慧依禅定一心观诸法实相。是名禅定中生般若波罗蜜。或有离五波罗蜜。但闻读[197-1]诵思惟筹量。通达诸法实相。是方便智中。生般若波罗蜜。或从二或三四波罗蜜。生般若波罗蜜。如闻说一谛而成道果。或闻二三四谛而得道果。有人于苦谛多惑故。为

简体字

又知精進實相離身心如實不動。如是精進能生般若波羅蜜。餘精進如幻如夢。虛誑非實是故不說。若深心攝念。能如實見諸法實相。諸法實相者。不可以見聞念知能得。何以故。六情六塵皆是虛誑因緣果報。是中所知所見皆亦虛誑。是虛誑知都不可信。所可信者。唯有諸佛於阿僧祇劫所得實相智慧。以是智慧依禪定一心觀諸法實相。是名禪定中生般若波羅蜜。或有離五波羅蜜。但聞讀[197-1]誦思惟籌量。通達諸法實相。是方便智中。生般若波羅蜜。或從二或三四波羅蜜。生般若波羅蜜。如聞說一諦而成道果。或聞二三四諦而得道果。有人於苦諦多惑故。為

正體字

Additionally, one realizes that the true character [of the dharma] of vigor transcends both body and mind, corresponds to reality, and involves no movement. It is in a manner such as this that vigor may enable the generation of *prajñāpāramitā*. All other manifestations of vigor are like mere conjurations and are like experiences taking place in a dream. Because they are false, deceptive, and unreal, we do not discuss them here.

j. Realization of *Prajñāpāramitā* through Dhyāna Meditation

If one employs a deep mind to focus one's thoughts, one becomes able to perceive the true character of dharmas in accordance with reality. As for the true character of dharmas, it is not such as can be realized through seeing, hearing, bearing concepts in mind, or through knowing. Why is this so? The six sense faculties and the six sense objects all fall within the sphere of effect-related retributions associated with false and deceptive causes and conditions. Herein everything one knows and perceives is also entirely false and deceptive. All of these instances of false and deceptive knowing are such as cannot be trusted.

As for that which actually *can* be trusted, it is only that wisdom cognizing the true character [of dharmas] acquired by the buddhas across the course of *asaṃkhyeya* kalpas. Because this wisdom is anchored in single-minded contemplation of the true character of dharmas while in the midst of dhyāna concentration, it is this circumstance which constitutes the development of *prajñāpāramitā* from within the practice of dhyāna meditation.

k. *Prajñāpāramitā* Realization Independent of the Other Perfections

In some cases, there may be those who gain a penetrative understanding of the true character of dharmas entirely apart from the practice of the other five *pāramitās*, this being accomplished simply through listening, reading, reciting, contemplating, and analyzing. In a case such as this, it is based on these provisional approaches to developing wisdom that *prajñāpāramitā* is born.

l. Realization of *Prajñāpāramitā* through any Number of Perfections

In other cases, it may be that *prajñāpāramitā* is born from within two or three or four other *pāramitās*. This is analogous to those cases wherein someone hears just one of the Truths and then succeeds in completely gaining the fruits of the Path or someone else hears two, three, or four of the Truths and then gains the fruits of the Path.

There are those persons who, for the most part, are greatly deluded with respect to the truth of suffering, but for whom one

说苦谛而得道。馀三谛亦如是。或有都惑四谛故。为说四谛而得道。如佛语比丘。汝若能断贪欲。我保汝得阿那含道。若断贪欲当知恚痴亦断。六波罗蜜中亦如是。为破多悭贪故。说布施法。当知馀恶亦破。为破杂恶故具为说六。是故或一一行。或合行普为一切人故。说六波罗蜜。非为一人。复次若菩萨不行一切法不得一切法故得般若波罗蜜。所以者何。诸行皆虚妄不实。或近有过或远有过。如不善法近有过罪。善法久后变异时。着者能生忧苦。是远有过罪。譬如美食恶食俱有杂毒。食恶食即时不悦。食美食即时甘悦。久后俱

簡体字

說苦諦而得道。餘三諦亦如是。或有都惑四諦故。為說四諦而得道。如佛語比丘。汝若能斷貪欲。我保汝得阿那含道。若斷貪欲當知恚癡亦斷。六波羅蜜中亦如是。為破多慳貪故。說布施法。當知餘惡亦破。為破雜惡故具為說六。是故或一一行。或合行普為一切人故。說六波羅蜜。非為一人。復次若菩薩不行一切法不得一切法故得般若波羅蜜。所以者何。諸行皆虛妄不實。或近有過或遠有過。如不善法近有過罪。善法久後變異時。著者能生憂苦。是遠有過罪。譬如美食惡食俱有雜毒。食惡食即時不悅。食美食即時甘悅。久後俱

正體字

need only explain the truth of suffering, whereupon they then succeed in gaining the Path. The circumstances may be just the same in relation to the other three of the Truths. In other cases, it may be that there is someone who is entirely deluded with respect to all four of the Truths, but once one explains all four truths for them, they straightaway gain realization of the Path.

For example, the Buddha once told the Bhikshus, "If you are able to cut off desire, I guarantee that you will realize the path of the *anāgāmin*." One should realize from this that, if one simply succeeds in cutting off desire, hatred and stupidity will then be cut off as well.

Within the six *pāramitās*, the circumstance is just the same. It is for the sake of demolishing excessive miserliness that one speaks of the dharma of giving. One should know that the other evils also become demolished thereby.

It is for the sake of demolishing all of the various evils that a complete discussion of all six is presented. Therefore, since some practice each one singularly and others pursue a comprehensive practice of them all, all six *pāramitās* have been explained here so as to universally address the needs of everyone. It is not the case that they are set forth only to address the needs of a single class of individuals.

m. Realization of *Prajñāpāramitā* through no Seizing on Practices

Then again, if the bodhisattva refrains from taking up the practice of any particular dharma, because he does not apprehend any dharma whatsoever, he may thereby succeed in realizing *prajñāpāramitā*. How can this be the case? All practices are essentially false and unreal. In some cases, they possess faults in the near term. In other cases, they possess faults in the more distant term.

In the case of unwholesome dharmas, in the near term, they are involve karmic transgressions. In the case of good dharmas, there may be a time when, after a long while, they become so transformed that one becomes attached to them and thus generates distressful suffering on their account. In that case, they involve karmic transgressions in the distant term.

These circumstances are analogous to the certain cases involving both fine food and bad food, both of which have been mixed with poison. When one eats the bad food, one immediately becomes displeased. When one eats the fine food, although one will immediately be pleased, still, after a long while, in both cases, one's life will

夺命故。二不应食。善恶诸行亦[2]复如是。问曰。若尔者佛何以说三行梵行天行圣行。答曰。行无行故名为圣行。何以故。一切圣行中。不离三解脱门故。梵行天行中因取众生相故生。虽行时无过后皆有失。又即今求实皆是虚妄。若贤圣以无着心行此二行则无咎。若能如是行无行法皆无所得。颠倒虚妄烦恼毕竟不生。如虚空清净故。得诸法实相。以无所得为得。如无所得般若中说。色等法。非以空故空从本已来常自空。色等法。[3]不以智慧不及故无所得。从本已来常自无所得。

奪命故。二不應食。善惡諸行亦[2]復如是。問曰。若爾者佛何以說三行梵行天行聖行。答曰。行無行故名為聖行。何以故。一切聖行中。不離三解脫門故。梵行天行中因取眾生相故生。雖行時無過後皆有失。又即今求實皆是虛妄。若賢聖以無著心行此二行則無咎。若能如是行無行法皆無所得。顛倒虛妄煩惱畢竟不生。如虛空清淨故。得諸法實相。以無所得為得。如無所得般若中說。色等法。非以空故空從本已來常自空。色等法。[3]不以智慧不及故無所得。從本已來常自無所得。

be stolen away. In fact, neither of the two should be eaten. All good and bad practices are comparable to these circumstances.

1) Objection: Why Did Buddha Explain Three Classes of Practice?

Question: If this is the case, why did the Buddha speak of the three classes of practice: the practice of Brahmā; the practice of the gods; and the practice of the Āryas?

2) Response: All Except that of the Āryas Involve Faults

Response: The "practice of the Āryas" qualifies as such on account of being free of [attachment to] any practice. How is this so? In all of the practices of the Āryas, one does not depart from the three gateways to liberation [consisting of emptiness, signlessness, and wishlessness].

In the case of "the practice of Brahmā" and "the practice of the gods," however, they are both generated on the basis of a seizing on the mark of the existence of a being. Although at the time of engaging in such practices, they are free of any particular faults, in every case, they later involve defects. Moreover, even in the very present, if one seeks to discover their reality, one discovers in every case that they are essentially false.

In the case of the Worthies and Āryas, because they would practice these two sorts of practice with an unattached mind, they themselves would in fact be free of any sort of fault in that connection.

3) In "No-practice" Practice, Nothing Whatsoever is Obtained

If one is able to practice the dharma of "no practice" in this manner, in every case, nothing whatsoever is gained. Inverted views, falseness, and afflictions are finally not produced at all. Because one remains as pure as empty space, one succeeds then in realizing the true character of dharmas. One takes having nothing whatsoever which is gained as that which is gained. This is as discussed in the section devoted to "the prajñā of non-attainment."

In the case of form and other such dharmas, it is not on account of being made empty that they are empty. Rather, it is the case that, from their very origin on forward to the present, they have always been inherently empty.

In the case of form and other such dharmas, it is not on account of one's wisdom somehow failing to extend to include them that there is nothing whatsoever which is gained. Rather, it is the case that, from their very origin on forward to the present, they have always been inherently devoid of anything whatsoever which can be gotten at.

是故不应问行几波罗蜜得般若[4]波罗蜜。诸佛怜愍众生随俗故。说行非第一义。问曰。若无所得无所行。行者何以求之。答曰。无所得有二种。一者世间欲。有所求不如意。是无所得。二者诸法实相中。[5]受决定相。不可得故。名无所得。非无有福德智慧增益善根。如凡夫人分别世间法故有所得。诸善功德亦如是。随世间心故说有所得。诸佛心中则无所得。是略说般若波罗蜜义。后当广说。

大智[6]度论卷第十八。

简体字

是故不應問行幾波羅蜜得般若[4]波羅蜜。諸佛憐愍眾生隨俗故。說行非第一義。問曰。若無所得無所行。行者何以求之。答曰。無所得有二種。一者世間欲。有所求不如意。是無所得。二者諸法實相中。[5]受決定相。不可得故。名無所得。非無有福德智慧增益善根。如凡夫人分別世間法故有所得。諸善功德亦如是。隨世間心故說有所得。諸佛心中則無所得。是略說般若波羅蜜義。後當廣說。

大智[6]度論卷第十八。

正體字

Therefore one should not be asking, "How many *pāramitās* does one practice in order to gain *prajñāpāramitā*?" It is because, out of pity for beings, the Buddhas accord with mundane conventions and thus then speak of "practice." It is not the case that this really represents the ultimate meaning.

4)   QUESTION: IF SO, HOW CAN *PRAJÑĀPĀRAMITĀ* BE SOUGHT?

Question: If there is nothing whatsoever gained and nothing whatsoever practiced, how can the practitioner seek for it?

5)   RESPONSE: DIFFERENTIATION OF THE CONCEPT OF "GAIN"

Response: Having "nothing whatsoever which is gained" is of two different sorts. As for the first, it refers to the realm of worldly desires where, when there is that which is sought and it does not end up according with one's intentions, this constitutes having "nothing whatsoever which is gained." As for the second, it is because no fixed characteristics can be gotten at in the true character of dharmas that one then speaks of having "nothing whatsoever which is gained."

It is not the case that there is actually an absence of meritorious qualities, wisdom, or superior roots of goodness. It is on account of being like the common person who engages in making discriminations with respect to worldly dharmas that there might be anything at all which might be gained. So, too, it is with respect to all of the meritorious qualities associated with goodness. It is only on account of according with the minds of those in the world that one speaks of having anything which might be gained. Within the mind of the Buddhas, there is nothing whatsoever which is gained.

J.   CONCLUDING STATEMENT ON THIS EXPLANATION OF *PRAJÑĀPĀRAMITĀ*

This has been but a summary explanation of *"prajñāpāramitā."* It shall be discussed more extensively in due course.

Part Six Endnotes

1. The reader may wish at this point to review Nāgārjuna's six-page introductory discussion on the meaning of the perfection of wisdom. That discussion comprises the whole of Exegesis Chapter 17 where it serves as the introduction to Nāgārjuna's treatment of the the six perfections in aggregate and the perfection of giving in particular. That "introductory chapter" is the very first chapter in this book.

2. This is the third of three types of knowledge. It refers explicitly and exclusively to the endless categories of knowledge possessed only by a fully enlightened Buddha.

3. It is probable that Kumārajīva's "true character of dharmas" (諸法實相) translates the Sanskrit *dharmatā*, though in some cases Kumārajīva also renders *dharma-svabhāva* and *bhūta-naya* in this way. It really just means "dharmas as they really are" when all imputations about them are removed and as they are beheld by an ārya, one who has perceived emptiness directly.

   That said, the semantic range of the term translated by Kumārajīva in this way, at least in the *Upadeśa*, seems mildly plastic, so much so that one is tempted at times to translate it as "ultimate-reality aspect of dharmas" or "reality aspect of dharmas," or "the nature of dharmas in reality," or "true nature of dharmas," however, all of these other approaches verge on implying the actual existence of something substantial, some sort of little "peach-pit" of "genuine reality" at the core of any given dharma. This of course is completely off the map of acceptability in emptiness-conversant Buddhist discourse. Hence, unless forced by context to make minor variations, I am using as the preferred translation "true character of dharmas" or something very close to it.

4. The "perfection" connotation of "*pāramitā*" is explained in Chinese commentaries and in Sino-Buddhist translations of Indian shastraic works as linked to an original Sanskrit meaning of "to go across to the other shore." This is in turn associated with the Buddhist concept of the spiritual path as consisting primarily of traversing the "sea of suffering" and reaching "the other shore" metaphorically representing the cessation of suffering in nirvāṇa. In this class of secondary canonical literature, the term most often covers a range of verbal, adjectival, and nominal uses meaning "to perfect; perfected; perfection," etc.

   In Mahāyāna contexts (and virtually all of Chinese Buddhism and practice is, as with Nāgārjunian doctrine, Mahāyānistic), this concept is inextricably wedded to the aspiration to bring about universal spiritual liberation in all beings. Any actions or aspirations *not* having that goal in mind (such as the individual-liberation practices aimed exclusively at arhatship or pratyekabuddhahood) are, by the terms of this definition, *not* qualifiable as *"pāramitā."*

Monier-Williams *Sanskrit-English Dictionary* features the following primary definitions for this term: gone to the opposite shore; crossed, traversed; transcendent (as spiritual knowledge); coming or leading to the opposite shore, complete attainment, perfection; transcendental virtue.

5. These reduced-font parenthetical notes originate with the Chinese edition of the text and may or may not have first been placed with it by Kumārajīva's editors on his instruction.

6. There is a probable scribal error in the Chinese text involving the erroneous substitution of 生 for the graphically very similar 出.

7. The category titles beginning here and continuing on through the lists of "ten" are in some cases tentative translations, this because some list titles are seldom encountered and difficult to research with accuracy. Bhikkhu Bodhi was particularly helpful in catching and correcting some of my most egregious initial-draft errors.

8. According to the *Satya-siddhi-śāstra* (成實論), these are: solidity of explanation, solidity of meditative concentration, solidity of views, and solidity of liberation (T32.1646.250b-c.)

9. These "nine-fold" category titles seem obscure, perhaps due to minor textual corruptions. Although there are a number of variants offered in the different editions, they do not resolve this difficulty.

10. Substituting "ten" (十) for the apparent scribal error "great" (大).

11. Adopting here the variant "two" (二) for the second "one" (一) in this sentence of the Taisho text, this in response to force of logic and also the parallelism which should occur with the question to which this statement is offered in reply.

12. This is a reference to the 20-page section from *Exegesis* Chapter 20 which discusses the three factors involved in any act of giving (benefactor, recipient, gift). It corresponds to Taisho 147a–150a.

Part Six Variant Readings from Other Chinese Editions

[190n04] (度) - [石]
[190n05] 第二十九卷第十八 = 第二十三十八 [石], (第二十九) - [元] [明]
[190n06] 九 = 四 [宮]
[190n07] ([經]) - [宋] [宮] [石]
[190n08] ([論]) - [宋] [宮] [石]
[190n09] 實 = 是 [宋] [元] [明] [宮], (實) - [石]
[190n10] 說 = 言 [宋] [元] [明] [宮]
[190n11] 止 = 屬 [宮]
[191n01] (大智度論釋般若相義第三十)十二字 - [宮] [石], (大智度論) - [明]
[191n02] 釋 + （初品中）[宋] [元] [明]
[191n03] (第三十) - [元] [明]
[191n04] 獨 = 猶 [石]
[191n05] 秦 = 此 [明]
[191n06] (諸) - [宋] [元] [明] [宮]
[191n07] (中) - [宋] [元] [明] [宮] [石]* [*1]
[191n08] 慧 + （故）[元] [明]
[191n09] 煖 = 暖 [宋] [元] [明] [宮]
[191n10] 礙 = 閡 [石]
[191n11] 已 = 以 [石]
[191n12] (是為無學智) - [宋] [元] [明] [宮] [石]
[191n13] (諸) - [石]
[191n14] 大辟支佛亦 = 二 [石], (大辟支佛亦) - [宮], （二）+ 大 [宋] [元] [明]
[191n15] (亦) - [宋] [元] [明]
[191n16] 一 = 二 [宋] [元] [宮], (一) - [石]
[191n17] (三十) - [宮]
[191n18] 十 + （相或）[宋] [元] [明] [宮]
[191n19] 梨 = [黍-禾+利] [宋] [元] [明] [宮] [石]
[191n20] 攢 = 抨 [元] [明]*, = 鑽 [宮]*, = 杵 [石]* [*1]
[191n21] 酥 = 蘇 [石]
[191n22] 尿 = 糞 [宋] [元] [明] [宮] [石]
[191n23] (則) - [宋] [元] [明] [宮] [石]
[191n24] (若壞) - [宋] [元] [明] [宮] [石]
[191n25] 想 = 相 [宋] [宮]
[191n26] 悟 = 寤 [元] [明]
[192n01] 四 = 三 [宋] [元] [明] [宮] [石]

[192n02] 故 = 則 [元] [明]
[192n03] 身為牛 = 牛為身 [宋] [元] [明] [宮] [石]
[192n04] 嘗 = 常 [宮] [石]
[192n05] 渧 = 滴 [宋] [元] [明] [宮]
[192n06] 渧 = 滴 [明]
[192n07] 婦 = 妻 [宋] [元] [明] [宮]
[192n08] (說) - [宮] [石]
[192n09] 聞 = 問 [石]
[192n10] 柀 = 旀 [宋] [元] [明] [宮]
[192n11] 王 = 主 [宋] [元] [明] [宮]
[192n12] 是 = 先 [宮]
[192n13] (十) - [宮] [明]
[192n14] 結 = 諸 [宋] [元] [明] [宮] [石]
[192n15] (如) - [宋] [元] [明] [宮]
[192n16] (若) - [宋] [元] [明] [宮] [石]
[192n17] (何) - [宮]
[192n18] (如是等) - [宋] [元] [明] [宮] [石]
[192n19] 愛受 = 受愛 [宋] [元] [明] [宮] [石]
[193n01] (心) - [宋] [宮]
[193n02] 熏 = 重 [宮]
[193n03] 必 = 心 [宋] [元] [宮]
[193n04] （佛）+ 破 [宋] [元] [明] [宮] [石]
[193n05] 梨 = 利 [宋] [元] [明] [宮] [石]* [*1]
[193n06] 雇 = 顧 [明] [石]
[193n07] 雇 = 顧 [宋] [元] [宮]
[193n08] 各 = 名 [宋] [元] [明] [宮]
[193n09] 墮 = 墜 [宋] [元] [明] [宮]
[193n10] 自 + （相）[宋] [宮] [石]
[193n11] (真空) - [宋] [元] [明] [宮] [石]
[193n12] (與第三邪見) - [石]
[193n13] 見 + （人）[宋] [元] [明] [宮]
[194n01] 愛 = 受 [石]* [* 1]
[194n02] （名）+ 為 [宋] [元] [明] [宮] [石]
[194n03] 當 = 常 [宮]
[194n04] (見) - [石]
[194n05] 真 = 空 [宮]
[194n06] (貴) - [宋] [元] [明] [宮] [石]* [*1]

[194n07] （一）＋相 [元] [明]

[194n08] (有) - [宮]

[194n09] (法) - [宋] [元] [明] [宮] [石]

[194n10] (等) - [宋] [元] [明] [宮]

[194n11] (諸) - [宋] [元] [明] [宮] [石]

[194n12] 則＝相 [宋] [元] [明] [宮]

[195n01] (可) - [宋] [元] [明] [宮] [石]

[195n02] (相) - [宋] [元] [明] [宮]

[195n03] 何＋（謂無相）[石]

[195n04] 說＝脫 [宮]

[195n05] 慧＝盡 [宮]

[195n06] (分別) - [宋] [元] [明] [宮] [石]

[195n07] (次) - [石]

[195n08] (知) - [宮]

[195n09] (更不…也)十字 - [石]

[195n10] 布施持＝施 [宋] [元] [明] [宮], ＝施持 [石]

[195n11] (四) - [石]

[195n12] (道) - [宮] [石]

[195n13] 支＝枝 [宋] [元] [宮] [石]

[195n14] 減＝滅 [宋] [元] [明] [宮]

[195n15] (從名…九)八字 - [石]

[195n16] (色) - [宋] [元] [明] [宮]

[195n17] 九＋（也）[宋] [元] [明] [宮]

[195n18] (得盡…也)八字 - [宋] [元] [明] [宮] [石]

[195n19] (六禪三無色) - [宋] [元] [明] [宮] [石]

[195n20] 學＝覺 [石]

[195n21] 七＝六 [宮] [石]

[195n22] （十七行）＋十 [宮]

[195n23] (思惟道中) - [宮] [石]

[195n24] （思惟道）＋能 [宋] [元] [明] [宮]

[195n25] (一) - [宋] [元] [明] [宮] [石]

[195n26] (至) - [宋] [元] [明] [宮] [石]

[196n01] (故) - [宋] [元] [明] [宮]

[196n02] 義＝實義 [宋] [元] [明] [宮]

[196n03] 渡＝度 [宋] [元] [明] [宮]

[196n04] (大) - [宋] [元] [明] [宮]

[196n05] (故) - [宮]

[196n06] (欲) - [石]

[196n07] (中) - [宋] [元] [明] [宮]

[196n08] (得) - [宋] [元] [明] [宮]

[196n09] 懈＝應 [宮]

[196n10] (波羅蜜) - [宋] [元] [明] [宮] [石]

[196n11] 一＝二 [宋] [元] [明] [宮] [石]

[196n12] 破＝彼 [宋] [元] [明] [宮]

[196n13] 競＝竟 [宮]

[196n14] 者＝言 [宋]

[196n15] 法＋（忍）[宋] [元] [明] [宮] [石]

[197n01] (誦) - [宋] [宮]

[197n02] (復) - [宋] [元] [明] [宮]

[197n03] 不＝非 [宋] [元] [明] [宮]

[197n04] (波羅蜜) - [宋] [元] [明] [宮]

[197n05] (受) - [宋] [元] [明] [宮] [石]

[197n06] 度論卷＝論 [石]

ABOUT THE TRANSLATOR

Bhikshu Dharmamitra (ordination name "Heng Shou" – 釋恆授) is a Chinese-tradition translator-monk and one of the early American disciples (since 1968) of the late Weiyang Ch'an patriarch, Dharma teacher, and exegete, the Venerable Master Hsuan Hua (宣化上人). He has a total of 23 years in robes during two periods as a monastic (1969–1975; 1991 to present).

Dharmamitra's principal educational foundations as a translator lie in four years of intensive monastic training and Chinese-language study of classic Mahāyāna texts in a small-group setting under Master Hua from 1968–1972, undergraduate Chinese language study at Portland State University, a year of intensive one-on-one Classical Chinese study at the Fu Jen University Language Center near Taipei, and two years at the University of Washington's School of Asian Languages and Literature (1988–90).

Since taking robes again under Master Hua in 1991, Dharmamitra has devoted his energies primarily to study and translation of classic Mahāyāna texts with a special interest in works by Ārya Nāgārjuna and related authors. To date, he has translated a dozen important texts, most of which are slated for publication by Kalavinka Press.

Kalavinka Buddhist Classics Title List

Meditation Instruction Texts

The Essentials of Buddhist Meditation
A marvelously complete classic *śamathā-vipaśyanā* (calming-and-insight) meditation manual. By Tiantai Śramaṇa Zhiyi (538–597 CE).

The Six Gates to the Sublime
The earliest Indian Buddhist meditation method explaining the essentials of breath and calming-and-insight meditation. By Śramaṇa Zhiyi.

Bodhisattva Path Texts

Nāgārjuna on the Six Perfections
Chapters 17–30 of Ārya Nāgārjuna's *Mahāprājñāpāramitā Upadeśa.*

Marvelous Stories from the Perfection of Wisdom
100 Stories from Ārya Nāgārjuna's *Mahāprājñāpāramitā Upadeśa.*

A Strand of Dharma Jewels (Ārya Nāgārjuna's *Ratnāvalī*)
The earliest extant edition, translated by Paramārtha: *ca* 550 CE

Nāgārjuna's Guide to the Bodhisattva Path
The *Bodhisaṃbhāra Treatise* with abridged Vaśitva commentary.

The Bodhisaṃbhāra Treatise Commentary
The complete exegesis by the Indian Bhikshu Vaśitva (*ca* 300–500 CE).

Letter from a Friend - The Three Earliest Editions
The earliest extant editions of Ārya Nāgārjuna's *Suhṛlekkha*:

Translated by Tripiṭaka Master Guṇavarman   (*ca* 425 CE)
Translated by Tripiṭaka Master Saṅghavarman   (*ca* 450 CE)
Translated by Tripiṭaka Master Yijing   (*ca* 675 CE)

Resolve-for-Enlightenment Texts

On Generating the Resolve to Become a Buddha
On the Resolve to Become a Buddha by Ārya Nāgārjuna
Exhortation to Resolve on Buddhahood by Patriarch Sheng'an Shixian
Exhortation to Resolve on Buddhahood by the Tang Literatus, Peixiu

Vasubandhu's Treatise on the Bodhisattva Vow
By Vasubandhu Bodhisattva (*ca* 300 CE)

*All Kalavinka Press translations include facing-page source text.

CPSIA information can be obtained
at www.ICGtesting.com
Printed in the USA
BVHW041325211020
591323BV00014BA/1652